Critical Essays on Piero Sraffa's Legacy in Economics

This collection offers a critical assessment of the published works of Piero Sraffa, one of the leading economists of the twentieth century, and their legacy for the economics profession. The topics covered explore Sraffa's interpretation of the classical economists; his theory of value and distribution; his critique of partial and general neoclassical equilibrium theory; his focus on the problem of capital; and his critique of Hayek's monetary overinvestment theory of the business cycle. Specific issues investigated include intertemporal general equilibrium theory and the capital problem; the probability of reswitching; Ricardo, Malthus and the corn model; and the meaning and implication of the capital controversy. Among the contributors are many of the world's leading students of Sraffian economics, including Nobel Laureate Paul Samuelson, Christian Bidard, Edwin Burmeister, John Eatwell, Pierangelo Garegnani, Samuel Hollander, Heinz Kurz, Lynn Mainwaring, Neri Salvadori, Bertram Schefold and Ian Steedman.

Heinz D. Kurz is Professor of Economics at the University of Graz, Austria. He has also taught at the Universities of Bremen, Kiel and Rome and the New School University of New York. Professor Kurz is the author or editor of 15 works, including *Theory of Production: A Long-Period Analysis* (Cambridge University Press, 1995, co-authored with Neri Salvadori), *Capital, Distribution and Effective Demand* (1990), *Understanding 'Classical' Economics: Studies in Long-Period Theory* (1998, co-authored with Neri Salvadori), and co-editor of *The Elgar Companion to Classical Economics* (1998, with Neri Salvadori), and over 50 articles in refereed professional and academic journals. Professor Kurz is a managing editor of *Metroeconomica* and of the *European Journal of the History of Economic Thought* and serves on the editorial boards of several other professional journals.

T0334203

Critical Essays on Piero Sraffa's Legacy in Economics

Edited by

HEINZ D. KURZ
University of Graz, Austria

CAMBRIDGE
UNIVERSITY PRESS

CAMBRIDGE UNIVERSITY PRESS
Cambridge, New York, Melbourne, Madrid, Cape Town, Singapore, São Paulo

Cambridge University Press
The Edinburgh Building, Cambridge CB2 8RU, UK

Published in the United States of America by Cambridge University Press, New York

www.cambridge.org
Information on this title: www.cambridge.org/9780521580892

© Cambridge University Press 2000

First published 2000
This digitally printed version 2008

A catalogue record for this publication is available from the British Library

Library of Congress Cataloguing in Publication data
Critical essays on Piero Sraffa's legacy in economics / edited by
Heinz D. Kurz.
  p. cm.
  Includes index.
  ISBN 0-521-58089-7 (hardbound)
  1. Sraffa, Piero. 2. Economists – Italy. 3. Classical school of
economics. I. Kurz, Heinz-Dieter.
HB109.S73C75   2000
330.1– dc21   99-30162
                                                           CIP

ISBN 978-0-521-58089-2 hardback
ISBN 978-0-521-08164-1 paperback

Contents

v

Preface

Piero Sraffa was born on 5 August 1898. The centenary of this event was a welcome occasion to critically assess his legacy in economics. This volume contributes to this task. It contains a set of papers plus some comments written by a number of scholars who have repeatedly dealt with the different facets of the work of one of the most fascinating intellectuals of this century.

There are two ways to contribute to the history of economic thought: by writing about other economists, or by obliging others to write about oneself. On both counts Sraffa did exceptionally well, given the sheer number of pages he published. Whatever he was prepared to have put in print had a deep and lasting impact on the profession. A foremost historian of economic thought of this century, Sraffa was not only interested in the history of our subject for its own sake. Rather, he conceived of a meticulous and critical study of earlier political economists and of the interpretations of their works by later authors as an indispensable task in the development of a coherent economic analysis of modern society. He was of the opinion that in order to promote economic analysis one has to study the history of the subject as well as the history of the subject matter, that is, economic and social history.

As the twentieth century comes to a close, we can safely say that it has seen no other scholar who compares with Sraffa in terms of the challenge he put to the received interpretation of the history of economic thought. He successfully shattered the widespread opinion that history resembles a one-way avenue leading from primitive conceptualizations of the supply and demand approach to ever more sophisticated ones, merely leaving behind errors of reasoning and unnecessarily restrictive assumptions. Sraffa showed that there was an earlier theory, whose roots may in fact be traced back to the very inception of political economy in the seventeenth century, which was fundamentally different from the marginalist one. This theory had been developed by Adam Smith and then David Ricardo, but shortly afterwards it was aborted prematurely. This led naturally to the following tasks which Sraffa set himself: (i) to provide evidence that there was a distinct classical theory; (ii) to reconstruct and develop that theory and demonstrate its explanatory power; (iii) to show that the alternative marginalist theory was flawed.

Sraffa's early contributions were devoted to a critique of Marshall's partial equilibrium theory. In 1925 he published, in Italian, an influential paper on the relationships between cost and output (Sraffa, 1925), followed in 1926 by 'The laws of returns under competitive conditions' (Sraffa, 1926), which he was invited to contribute to the *Economic Journal*. The year 1932 saw his critique of Friedrich August von Hayek's *Prices and Production* (Hayek, 1931), entitled 'Dr Hayek on money and capital' (Sraffa, 1932a) and his rejoinder to Hayek's reply (Sraffa, 1932b). Some elements of the analytical structure of the classical theory of value and distribution were first clarified by Sraffa in his introduction to Volume I of *The Works and Correspondence of David Ricardo* (Ricardo, 1951–73), which he edited with the collaboration of Maurice H. Dobb (Sraffa, 1951). For this edition, Sraffa was awarded the golden medal Søderstrøm by the Swedish Royal Academy in 1961. The award is now commonly considered to be equivalent to the Nobel Prize in economics, since the latter had not then been established. A fully worked out formulation of the classical theory, covering a wide range of problems including joint production, fixed capital, scarce natural resources, such as land, and the choice of technique of cost-minimizing producers, using a general framework of the analysis, was then put forward in *Production of Commodities by Means of Commodities* (Sraffa, 1960). Apart from a few observations, criticism of the marginalist theory is only implicit in this book; others made it explicit during the capital controversies in the 1960s and 1970s.

'Sraffa finds it immoral to write more than one page per month.' This statement by Amartya Sen (1974, p. 331) must not be taken literally, as we now know *vis-à-vis* Sraffa's unpublished papers and correspondence in the Wren Library at Trinity College, Cambridge. They document in detail a lifetime's work: the problems he was concerned with, when and why, his method and style of work, the sources he used and the results he obtained. They also reveal his wider philosophical interests, intellectual fascinations and social passions. Since from an early stage Sraffa dated all his manuscripts, we know in most cases precisely when he tackled which question, formulated which hypothesis and came up with which finding. The publication of a selection from this enormous block of material, which comprises several thousand sheets and slips of paper and a number of notebooks, containing comments on the literature, sundry observations, ideas to be tried out and problems to be solved, lecture notes, elaborations of concepts, early drafts, etc., is currently being prepared and publication is planned during the next few years.

The present project grew out of discussions following the publication of the proceedings of a conference held in 1985 in Florence commemorating the 25th anniversary of the publication of *Production of Commodities by Means of Commodities* (Bharadwaj and Schefold, 1990). Some participants of the conference shared the feeling that in important respects the discussions had not led to clear-cut conclusions. Several problems had remained unsolved even after the debates. In particular, the following closely related questions were considered both important and insufficiently addressed during the discussion:

  (i) Is Sraffa's re-interpretation of the classical economists from Adam Smith to David Ricardo faithful to these authors, and do they approach the problem of value and distribution in a way that is fundamentally different from the later marginalist analysis?

 (ii) How is 'demand' conceptualized and what is its role in different approaches to the theory of value and distribution? Is it appropriate to consider Sraffa's 1960 analysis as a 'special case' of general equilibrium theory of the Arrow–Debreu variety?

(iii) What is the meaning of the controversy in the theory of capital in the 1960s and 1970s, and do the results obtained during that controversy necessitate the abandonment of the supply and demand approach to the theory of income distribution and competitive prices?

All three questions are but variants of the question of whether there is a classical alternative to neoclassical theory.

An answer to the first question is crucial to the entire discussion about Sraffa's contribution and prejudicial as to the other two questions, for if there is no such thing as a 'classical' theory, then Sraffa's construction may be said to be built on sand. This explains why in recent years so much energy has been devoted to the interpretation, and re-interpretation, of the classical authors, especially Ricardo. Indeed, Sraffa's edition of Ricardo's works and correspondence has ignited an interest in the earlier authors and has led to an unprecedented boom in scholarly contributions to the history of economic analysis. Does the evidence support Sraffa's interpretation or has he misread the sources?

According to the critics of Sraffa's 1960 book, his theory of value and distribution is but a special case of the modern version of supply and demand theory, that is, intertemporal equilibrium theory. A frequently encountered objection is that Sraffa was engaged in the futile task of determining relative prices and income distribution entirely independently of 'demand'. Others noticed, correctly, that Sraffa assumed given gross outputs of the different commodities to be produced, but could see in this only a rudimentary formulation of the 'demand side'. The question then is: What is the role of given quantities in Sraffa and how does it relate to the conventional neoclassical conceptualization of demand?

Finally, there is the problem of capital. Some neoclassical economists admitted that the criticism implicit in Sraffa's book of traditional long-period neoclassical theory is valid, and that the theory should therefore be abandoned. However, it is also claimed that the criticism does not carry over to modern intertemporal general equilibrium theory, which does away with the concept of a 'quantity of capital', conceived of as a single magnitude that can be given independently of relative prices and prior to the determination of the rate of profits (rate of interest). The capital endowment of the economy is rather given in kind, that is, in terms of a vector of quantities of different capital goods. The critics of neoclassical theory argue on the contrary that phenomena such as reswitching and reverse capital deepening can also be discerned in inter-temporal equilibrium models and are reflected in the multiplicity of equilibria, some of which are unstable. Is all neoclassical theory, old and new, afflicted with a capital theory problem?

These are the problems tackled in this book. The idea was to have papers from both advocates and critics of Sraffa on each of the three questions mentioned, and so I invited scholars who are known for their work on Sraffa to contribute to one of these. In addition, contributors could, if they wished, comment on each other's papers, and when some-one did, the author of the paper was given the opportunity to reply. These were the only rules of the game. It is hardly surprising that the outcome would not exhibit an even distribution among the different areas of controversy. It is also not surprising that some contributors would focus exclusively on a single theme, whereas others chose to write on several.

The book is composed in the following way. Part I introduces Sraffa's works and the debates they triggered. Chapter 1, by Heinz D. Kurz and Neri Salvadori, provides a brief summary account of Sraffa's life and his published contributions to economics and the implications they had. Chapter 2 sets the stage for the following debate in terms of a reprint of Paul A. Samuelson's contribution to the 1985 conference in Florence entitled 'Revisionist findings on Sraffa', comments on the paper by Lord John Eatwell, Pierangelo Garegnani and Bertram Schefold, and Samuelson's reply. Part II deals with Sraffa, the theorist and historian of economic thought. Chapter 3, written by Paul A. Samuelson, covers a wide range of aspects of Sraffa's contributions, including the problems of returns to scale and 'demand'; in addition, there is a comment by Heinz D. Kurz and Neri Salvadori and a reply by Samuelson. Chapter 4 contains a textual analysis of Sraffa's treatment of 'demand' by Neri Salvadori. In Chapter 5, Samuel Hollander deals with the corn–ratio theory of profits, placing special emphasis on Malthus's contribution; in addition, there is a comment by Pierangelo Garegnani and a reply by Hollander. Heinz D. Kurz, in Chapter 6, is concerned with a critical account of the controversy between Friedrich August von Hayek, John Maynard Keynes and Sraffa on the relationship between the monetary and the real spheres of the economy. Part III deals with the problem of capital in the traditional long-period framework. In Chapter 7, Edwin Burmeister looks back at the capital theory controversy and assesses its significance. Christian Bidard provides a measure of the error involved in P. H. Douglas's estimation of a macroeconomic production function using a Wicksellian time-phased model in Chapter 8. In Chapter 9, Lynn Mainwaring and Ian Steedman deal with the probability of reswitching and capital reversing in a two-sector model; in addition, there are comments by Neri Salvadori and by Christian Bidard and Lucette Carter. Part IV is devoted to the question of whether, and how, the capital critique applies to intertemporal equilibrium theory. In Chapter 10, Bertram Schefold deals with paradoxes of capital and counterintuitive changes of distribution in an intertemporal equilibrium framework. The author of Chapter 11 is Pierangelo Garegnani, who argues that the concept of a 'quantity of capital' and the difficulties entailed by it are not only present in long-period neoclassical theory, but also in inter-temporal general equilibrium theory.

The papers and comments collected in this volume reflect the ongoing interest in Sraffa's contributions to economics. Even his most severe critics do not deny him the merit of having stimulated many minds. Each of Sraffa's published works turned out to be a classic and can be expected to remain essential reading for the profession on a par with the writings of the great masters of our discipline.

I should like to thank all contributors for their collaboration. I am deeply in debt to those who kindly delivered their manuscripts in good time and showed so much patience; I am grateful to those who did not exceed the final deadline by too much; I am glad that the final version of one paper finally arrived. Given the long time that has elapsed since this project was started, I would understand if some of the contributors to this volume were of the opinion that my editorship left much to be desired; I hope they will accept my apologies.

Heinz D. Kurz

References

Bharadwaj, K. and Schefold, B. (eds) (1990). *Essays on Piero Sraffa: Critical Perspectives on the Revival of Classical Theory*, London: Unwin Hyman.

Hayek, F. A. (1931). *Prices and Production*, 1st edn, London: George Routledge (2nd edn London 1935).

Ricardo, D. (1951–73). *The Works and Correspondence of David Ricardo*, 11 vols, edited by P. Sraffa with the collaboration of M. H. Dobb, Cambridge: Cambridge University Press.

Sen, A. (1974). 'On Some Debates in Capital Theory', *Economica*, **41**, pp. 328–35.

Sraffa, P. (1925). 'Sulle relazioni fra costo e quantità prodotta', *Annali di Economia*, **2**, pp. 277–328. English translation by John Eatwell and Alessandro Roncaglia in L. L. Pasinetti (ed.), *Italian Economic Papers*, Vol. 3, Bologna, 1998: Il Mulino, and Oxford, 1998: Oxford University Press, pp. 323–63.

Sraffa, P. (1926). 'The Laws of Returns under Competitive Conditions', *Economic Journal*, **36**, pp. 535–50.

Sraffa, P. (1932a). 'Dr. Hayek on Money and Capital', *Economic Journal*, **42**, pp. 42–53.

Sraffa, P. (1932b). 'A Rejoinder', *Economic Journal*, **42**, pp. 249–51.

Sraffa, P. (1951). 'Introduction', in D. Ricardo (1951–73), Vol. I, pp. xiii–lxii.

Sraffa, P. (1960). *Production of Commodities by Means of Commodities. Prelude to a Critique of Economic Theory*, Cambridge: Cambridge University Press.

Grateful acknowledgement to Routledge is made for permission to reprint Chapter 2, 'Revisionist Findings on Sraffa', from *Essays in Honour of Piero Sraffa*, edited by K. Bharadwaj and B. Schefold, London, 1989, pp. 263–330.

Contributors

Professor Christian Bidard
Department of Economics
University of Paris X - Nanterre
200, Avenue de la République
F-92001 Nanterre Cedex
France

Professor Edwin Burmeister
Department of Economics
Duke University
Durham, NC 27706
USA

Professor Lucette Carter
Department of Economics
University of Paris X - Nanterre
200, Avenue de la République
F-92001 Nanterre Cedex
France

Lord (John) Eatwell
Master of Queen's College
Queen's College
Cambridge
UK

Professor Pierangelo Garegnani
Department of Economics
'Federico Caffè'
University of Rome III
Via Ostiense, 139
I-00154 Rome
Italy

Professor Samuel Hollander
LATAPSES, CNRS
University of Nice
250, rue A. Einstein
Sophia Antipolis
F-06560 Valbonne
France

Professor Heinz D. Kurz
Department of Economics
University of Graz
RESOWI 4F
A-8010 Graz
Austria

Professor Lynn Mainwaring
Department of Economics
University College of Swansea
Singleton Park, Swansea SA2 8PP
UK

Professor Neri Salvadori
Department of Economics
University of Pisa
I-56100 Pisa
Italy

Professor Paul A. Samuelson
Department of Economics
Massachusetts Institute of
Technology
Cambridge, MA 02139-4307
USA

Professor Bertram Schefold
Department of Economics
University of Frankfurt
P.O. Box 11 19 32
D-60054 Frankfurt am Main
Germany

Professor Ian Steedman
Department of Economics and
Economic History
Manchester Metropolitan
University
Mabel Tylecote Building
Cavendish Street
Manchester M15 6BG
UK

PART I

Introduction

CHAPTER 1

Piero Sraffa's contributions to economics: a brief survey

Heinz D. Kurz and Neri Salvadori

In this note a brief summary of Sraffa's contributions to economics will be given. This summary serves two purposes. It introduces the following discussion and it informs the reader about some contributions to economics by Sraffa not dealt with at all, or dealt with only in passing, in the essays contained in this book. In addition, some of the important developments triggered by his contributions will be mentioned. The overall purpose of this note is to round up the picture of Piero Sraffa's legacy in economics. It is not claimed that the account given is complete with regard to Sraffa's own works or the body of literature inspired by them. Summaries imply selection and interpretation, and consequently reflect the predilection and views of the authors. Other people may see things differently from the way we see them.[1] However, we have made an effort to present things as impartially as is possible to us.

1   Early works

Piero Sraffa was born in Turin, Italy, on 5 August 1898.[2] After graduation from the local university he went to the London School of Economics (1921–22). In England he was introduced to John Maynard Keynes who invited him to contribute an article on the Italian banking system for the *Manchester Guardian*, and a paper entitled 'The Bank Crisis in Italy' for the *Economic Journal* (Sraffa, 1922). This article, which contained an attack on the Fascists, provoked fierce reactions

---

[1] In what follows we draw partly on a book and papers written together (see, in particular, Kurz and Salvadori, 1995, 1997).
[2] On Sraffa's life and work, see Roncaglia (1978), Potier (1991) and Schefold (1996).

3

from the Mussolini government. Nevertheless, in November 1923 Sraffa was appointed to a lectureship in Political Economy and Public Finance at the University of Perugia. The preparation of his lectures stimulated him to write his first influential work in economics, 'Sulle relazioni fra costo e quantità prodotta' (1925), which contains an analysis of the foundations of decreasing, constant and increasing returns in Alfred Marshall's theory and a critical discussion of the entire partial equilibrium approach. Not least due to this article, Sraffa was appointed to a full professorship in Political Economy at the University of Cagliari, a post he held *in absentia* to the end of his life, donating his salary to the library. Francis Y. Edgeworth's high opinion of the article led to an invitation to publish a version of it in the *Economic Journal* (cf. Sraffa, 1926). This paper starts with the observation:

A striking feature of the present position of economic science is the almost unanimous agreement at which economists have arrived regarding the theory of competitive value, which is inspired by the fundamental symmetry existing between the forces of demand and those of supply, and is based upon the assumption that the essential causes determining the price of particular commodities may be simplified and grouped together so as to be represented by a pair of intersecting curves of collective demand and supply. This state of things is in such marked contrast with the controversies on the theory of value by which political economy was characterised during the past century that it might almost be thought that from these clashes of thought the spark of an ultimate truth had at length been struck. (Sraffa, 1926, p. 535)

Sraffa did not agree with this view, which was the 'mainstream' of the time, at least in England and in the English-speaking countries. He objected that in 'the tranquil view which the modern theory of value presents us there is one dark spot which disturbs the harmony of the whole'. This 'dark spot', he added, is the supply curve, based upon the combination of the laws of increasing and diminishing returns. Its foundations, he maintained, 'are actually so weak as to be unable to support the weight imposed upon them' (ibid., p. 536).

Consider the usual textbook partial equilibrium argument. A change in one market (e.g. a shift in the demand curve for wine) is taken to have first an effect on the equilibrium of that market (e.g. a change in the price and the quantity of wine produced), and then perhaps an effect on the other markets as a consequence of the change in price and quantity determined in the market where the original change took place (e.g. a shift in the demand for grapes, used to produce wine, and in the demand for beer, a wine substitute). If it can be assumed that the effects on the other markets are of a second order of magnitude with respect to the effect obtained on the equilibrium of the market in which the original change took place, and if these former effects are assumed to be so small that they can be neglected, at least at a first stage, then the supply and demand curves of a given market can be considered, in regard to small variations, as independent both of each other and of the supply and demand curves of all other commodities.

Sraffa's criticism focuses on variable returns, distinguishing between the following cases: variable returns that are (i) internal to the firm; (ii) external to the firm but internal to the industry; (iii) external to both the firm and the industry. Variable returns of type (i) are obviously incompatible with the assumption of perfect competition, whereas variable returns of type (iii) are incompatible with the method of partial equilibrium. Only variable returns of type (ii), whose empirical importance is doubtful, are shown to be compatible with Marshall's analysis of the supply curve of an industry in conditions of perfect competition.

Sraffa (1925, 1926) showed that variable returns of type (iii) are incompatible with the method of partial equilibrium in terms of the following argument: it cannot be excluded that a change in the quantity produced by a variable cost industry *at the same time* entails a change in the costs of firms in *other* industries as it entails a change in the costs of firms in the industry in which the change in the quantity produced took place. A typical example is that in which the same quality of land is used to produce two different commodities, say grapes and hops. An increase in the production of grapes, for instance, may lead to a rise in the cost function of the producers of grapes because of an increase in the rent paid for the use of the land, but this rise in rent would likewise affect the cost function of the producers of hops. The changes in costs would be of the same order of magnitude in both industries, so that it would be illegitimate to disregard the changes in the cost functions of firms outside the industry in which the quantity produced has changed (i.e. hops), while only taking into account the changes obtained in the cost functions of firms inside the industry in which the variation in quantity took place (i.e. grapes). The necessity to take other industries into account is accentuated in the case in which these industries provide means of production to the industry in which the implications of a change in quantity is studied.

When a change in the quantity produced by a variable cost industry does not entail a change in the costs of firms in other industries, the variable costs are said to be *internal to the industry*. A typical example is that in which returns are decreasing because land is in short supply and each quality of land is specific to the production of a single commodity only. If the economies or diseconomies responsible for variable costs are external to the firm and internal to the industry, variations in the quantity produced by one industry may affect the cost functions of the firms outside that industry only as a consequence of the change in the equilibrium price and quantity of the commodity produced by the industry in which the variation took place. This would be an effect of the second order of magnitude only, the presence of which, it could be contended, is perhaps compatible with using the *ceteris paribus* clause (see also Roncaglia, 1978; Panico, 1991; Samuelson, 1991; Kurz and Salvadori, 1995, chaps 1 and 13).

From this, Sraffa (1925) concluded that with regard to small variations in the quantity produced, the assumption of constant returns is the most convenient one for the analysis of the supply curve of an industry under competitive conditions. This view is repeated towards the end of the first part of the 1926 paper and interpreted as giving support to the classical doctrine: 'the old and now obsolete theory which makes it [the competitive value] dependent on the cost of production alone appears to hold its ground as the best available' (1926, p. 541). Yet this proposition could not leave Sraffa satisfied. He was confronted with two alternatives: either to abandon the assumption of perfect competition or to abandon partial equilibrium analysis. As is well known, Sraffa initially hinted at the first route, but soon embarked on the second.

In his 1926 paper the second alternative was ruled out on the grounds that an examination of 'the conditions of simultaneous equilibrium in numerous industries' is far too complex: 'the present state of our knowledge... does not permit of even much simpler schema being applied to the study of real conditions' (ibid., p. 541). There remained the first alternative, which was also motivated in terms of two related arguments. First, '[e]veryday experience... that a very large number of undertakings – and the majority of those which produce manufactured consumers' goods – work under conditions of individual diminishing costs' suggests the abandonment of the hypothesis of perfect competition (ibid., p. 543). Secondly, it is argued that the

chief obstacle against which [business men] have to contend when they want gradually to increase their production does not lie in the cost of production... but in the difficulty of selling the larger quantity of goods without reducing the price, or without having to face increased marketing expenses. This... is only an aspect of the usual descending demand curve, with the difference that instead of concerning the whole of a commodity, whatever its origin, it relates only to the goods produced by a particular firm. (ibid.)

In his 1926 paper, Sraffa therefore suggested retaining partial equilibrium analysis. This was possible, however, only at the cost of abandoning the concern with the free competition form of markets: in order to preserve the partial framework the analysis had to be limited to the study of economies internal to the firm. Sraffa's proposal was taken up by several authors and triggered a rich literature on market forms which bloomed during the 1930s (see, especially, Joan Robinson, 1933). Apart from a contribution to the 1930 *Economic Journal* symposium on increasing returns, Sraffa did not participate further in the debate on the Marshallian theory of value. Keynes, in the 'Note by the Editor' introducing the debate, called Sraffa's intervention a 'negative and destructive criticism'. This assessment is confirmed by Sraffa's concluding remark in his rejoinder to Robertson:

I am trying to find what are the assumptions implicit in Marshall's theory; if Mr Robertson regards them as extremely unreal, I sympathise with him. We seem to be agreed that the theory cannot be interpreted in a way which makes it logically self-consistent and, at the same time, reconciles it with the facts it sets out to explain. Mr Robertson's remedy is to discard mathematics, and he suggests that my remedy is to discard the facts; perhaps I ought to have explained that, in the circumstances, I think it is Marshall's theory that should be discarded. (Sraffa, 1930, p. 93)

We know that Sraffa's analytical concern following the 1926 paper was 'the process of diffusion of profits throughout the various stages of production and of the process of forming a normal level of profits throughout all the industries of a country...[a problem] beyond the scope of this article' (1926, p. 550; see also Eatwell and Panico, 1987).

2 The collaboration with Keynes and the controversy with Hayek

In the mid-1920s Sraffa was offered a lectureship in Cambridge which he assumed in October 1927, starting to lecture on advanced theory of value in the Michaelmas Term 1928–29. He was to lecture for only three years. A main reason for giving up teaching was that by that time Sraffa was convinced that Marshallian analysis could not be remedied and that an alternative analysis had to be elaborated, the beginnings of which took shape in the systems of equations of production Sraffa formulated in the late 1920s (see Kurz, 1998). In 1930 Sraffa was appointed to the position of librarian of the Marshall Library and was also placed in charge of the Cambridge programme of graduate studies in economics.

Shortly after his arrival in Cambridge, Sraffa showed Keynes the set of propositions which were to grow into *Production of Commodities by Means of Commodities*. However, his work on the manuscript was delayed both by the intense debate in Cambridge surrounding Keynes'

Treatise on Money and, later, *The General Theory*, and by Sraffa assuming, in 1930, the editorship of the Royal Economic Society edition of *The Works and Correspondence of David Ricardo*. Sraffa participated in the famous Cambridge 'Circus' and was known for his breadth of knowledge and impeccable logic. This is neatly illustrated by a short note written by Joan Robinson to Keynes in 1932:

I think that like the rest of us you have had your faith in supply curves shaken by Piero. But what he attacks are just the one-by-one supply curves that you regard as legitimate. His objections do not apply to the supply curve of output [as a whole] – but Heaven help us when he starts thinking out objections that do apply to it! (Keynes, *CW*, Vol. XIII, p. 378)

There is evidence that the fastidious Sraffa did not think highly of the way Keynes wrote his books, and especially the *General Theory*. He gradually withdrew from the Circus. His collaboration with Keynes became largely restricted to the field of the history of ideas. Thus in 1935 the two edited David Hume's *Abstract of a Treatise on Human Nature* (Hume, 1938). In their introduction they argued convincingly that the previous attribution of this essay to Adam Smith could not be sustained.

In 1931, Friedrich August von Hayek published *Prices and Production*, a book based on four lectures given at the London School of Economics (Hayek, 1931a), and the first part of his critical review in two instalments of Keynes' *Treatise on Money* in *Economica*, entitled 'Reflections on the Pure Theory of Money of Mr. J. M. Keynes' (1931b). In both contributions Hayek rejected the explanation of economic crises in terms of a deficient aggregate demand. In his book he elaborated the 'Austrian' approach to the theory of money and economic fluctuations, tracing crises back to 'misdirections of production' caused by the banking system fixing the money rate of interest below the 'equilibrium rate'. Keynes tried to answer the challenge, but like other Anglo-Saxon and American economists apparently had difficulties in understanding and countering Hayek's view because of a lack of knowledge of the main building blocks of his analysis: Paretian general equilibrium theory and Böhm–Bawerkian theory of capital and interest. Keynes invited Sraffa, who was familiar with both intellectual traditions, to accomplish what he himself had difficulties in doing, that is, ward off Hayek's attack.

In 1932 Sraffa published 'Dr. Hayek on Money and Capital' in the *Economic Journal* (Sraffa, 1932a). Hayek replied in the same year (Hayek, 1932), followed by a short rejoinder by Sraffa (1932b). Sraffa's criticism in his review article was purely internal: he scrutinized the consistency of Hayek's argument in the context of the latter's own analytical framework, and showed that Hayek had committed a number of serious blunders which deprived his analysis of all explanatory value. By assuming that money had only a single function – that of a means of exchange – and thus ignoring its role as a store of value, Hayek had been dealing with an economic system with 'emasculated' money. How could such an economy behave differently from an economy without money, that is, a barter economy? Apparently, Sraffa argued, Hayek must have introduced an element that is extraneous to the discussion which causes the difference. This element is said to become visible in Hayek's treatment of what he called the case of 'voluntary saving' on the one hand and that of 'forced saving' on the other. The first of the polar cases concerns a change in one item of the 'fundamental' data of economic equilibrium: intertemporal preferences. In Hayek's marginalist setting, an increase in 'voluntary saving' means the decision of agents to forgo present for future consumption. In an economic system with a given and constant labour supply and a given and constant technical knowledge, this involves that more 'roundabout', or 'capitalistic', processes of production will be adopted, characterized by a higher consumption output per capita. This, in turn, involves a change in the proportion of gross income spent on consumption and the proportion spent on capital goods, that is, a change in gross savings. Net savings will be positive only during the transitory phase until a new and stable equilibrium is reached.

While in Hayek's view this case is unproblematic, the other concerns interventions into the 'voluntary decisions of individuals' and thus infringes upon their freedom of action. A money rate of interest fixed below the 'equilibrium' rate by the banking system leads to an expansion of producers' or of consumers' credit. In the former case producers will find it profitable to lengthen the 'average period of production'. This is only possible, however, if labour and nonspecific factors of production are shifted from lower stages of production, that is, those that are close to the 'maturing' of the consumption goods, to higher stages, thereby imposing on agents a reduction in consumption, that is, 'forced saving'. Eventually incomes will rise and since the preferences of agents have not changed, consumption demand will go up. Prices of consumer goods will rise, indicating to producers that it is profitable to adopt less 'roundabout' processes of production. As a consequence, capital has to be reduced again – a process that 'necessarily takes the form of an economic crisis' (Hayek, 1931a, p. 53). After a costly trip and on the assumption that the banking system eventually corrects its error, the system is bound to return to its original equilibrium.

Interestingly, while in Hayek's opinion the 'artificial stimulant' of inflation in the shape of producers' credits can do no good, such a stimulant in the shape of consumers' credits is said to do harm, because it tends 'to frustrate the effect of saving' (ibid., p. 57). Accordingly, inflation through consumers' credits would effectively decrease capital and push the system to a new equilibrium with a lower consumption output per capita. Sraffa's dry comment reads: 'Thus Dr. Hayek will have it both ways' (Sraffa, 1932a, p. 48). Hayek's claim that the two cases are not analogous finally reveals the 'error or irrelevancy' which is responsible for the fact that, contrary to what one would have expected, a rise or fall in the quantity of 'emasculated' money can make a difference.

Sraffa also took issue with Hayek's claim that a difference between the actual or money rate of interest and the 'natural' or 'equilibrium' rate is a characteristic of a money economy (ibid., p. 49). He illustrated his argument in terms of an example which introduced the concept of the *own-rate of interest*, or, as he preferred to call it, the 'commodity rate of interest'. Both in the monetary and the barter economy, loans are made in terms of all commodities for which there are forward markets. Out of equilibrium these own rates will be different for at least some commodities. Hayek's opinion that in a 'disequilibrium' caused by a sudden increase in money supply (in the propensity to save) the natural rate of interest would be above (below) the money rate does not make sense, because out of equilibrium there is no such thing as *the* 'natural' rate; there will rather be a multiplicity of 'natural' rates.

Apparently, Keynes was very pleased with Sraffa's performance: it had effectively countered the assault on his intellectual project launched by Lionel Robbins and his circle at the LSE and allowed him to develop the *General Theory* undisturbed from any further interventions by the Austrian economist. In Chapter 17 of the *General Theory*, 'The Essential Properties of Interest and Money', Keynes wanted to pay tribute to Sraffa by making use of the concept of own rates of interest, arguing that the money own rate of interest is determined by liquidity preference, which, in a given time and place, is a conventional datum (cf. Keynes, *CW*, Vol. VII, pp. 222–44). As we know from his yet unpublished papers, Sraffa was not at all happy with what Keynes had done and was rather critical of his liquidity preference theory. His main objection was 'that the advantages involved in *holding* a commodity have no relation to its "own particular rate of interest"; and indeed no properties of that commodity (apart from expected price change) have any relations to the difference between its rate and other rates.' Keynes was wrong in assuming that the own rates of interest on different articles corresponded to the different advantages or disadvantages (yield, carrying cost, liquidity) associated with their possession. If no changes in price are expected, *all* commodities will have the same rate of interest.

3 The edition of Ricardo's *Works and Correspondence*

By the late 1940s, the publication of the Ricardo edition had been long delayed (see Pollit, 1990). The first volumes of the *Works and Correspondence of David Ricardo* were finally published in 1951 (Ricardo, 1951–73). This edition, for which Sraffa was awarded the golden medal Søderstrøm in 1961 by the Swedish Royal Academy, is widely acknowledged to be a scholarly masterpiece. In his 'Introduction' to Volume I, Sraffa presented an interpretation of the classical approach to the theory of value and distribution which differed markedly from the then dominant interpretation that had been put forward by Alfred Marshall. As we know from the manuscript of Sraffa's lectures on advanced value theory in the late 1920s and early 1930s and from his 1926 characterization of the classical theory of value, Sraffa had originally read Ricardo through the lens of Marshall's interpretation. (Indeed, for quite some time Marshall *was* economics for Sraffa.) A careful reading of Ricardo's writings eventually convinced him that this interpretation did not stand up to close examination.

The new interpretation centres around the concept of social *surplus*. Since in Ricardo's view the problem of income distribution 'is the principal problem in Political Economy' (*Works*, I, p. 6), Ricardo's main concern was with elaborating a coherent theory of the rate of profits, based on that concept: 'Profits come out of the surplus produce' (*Works*, II, pp. 130–31; similarly *Works*, I, p. 95). According to Sraffa, the development of Ricardo's thoughts on the matter can be divided into four steps (cf. Sraffa, 1951, pp. xxxi–xxxiii). These steps reflect Ricardo's consecutive attempts to simplify the problem of distribution.

The first step consisted of eliminating the problem of the rent of land in terms of the theory of extensive rent developed in Ricardo's *Essay on the Influence of a low Price of Corn on the Profits of Stock*, published in 1815 (see *Works*, IV). This allowed him to focus attention on marginal, that is, no-rent, land: 'By getting rid of rent, which we may do on the corn produced with the capital last employed, and on all commodities produced by labour in manufactures, the distribution between capitalist and labourer becomes a much more simple consideration' (*Works*, VIII, p. 194). The theory of extensive rent also provided the basis for a first criticism of what Ricardo called Smith's 'original error respecting value' (*Works*, VII, p. 100), that is, the latter's doctrine that 'the natural price itself varies with the natural rate of each of its component parts, of wages, profit, and rent' (Smith, *WN*, I.vii.33). As Ricardo stressed in the *Principles*, the price of 'corn is not high because a rent is paid, but a rent is paid because corn is high' (*Works*, I, p. 74).

If the high price of corn were the effect, and not the cause of rent, price would be proportionally influenced as rents were high or low, and rent would be a component part of price. But that corn which is produced [on marginal land] is the regulator of the price of corn; and rent does not and cannot enter in the least degree as a component part of its price. Adam Smith, therefore, cannot be correct. (*Works*, I, p. 77)

In Sraffa's interpretation, the second step consisted of trying to get rid of the problem of value by assuming the 'corn model': with wages as the only capital advanced at the beginning of the period of production and wages paid in terms of corn, the rate of profit obtained in corn production can be ascertained directly as a ratio of quantities of corn – that of the surplus product to the corn capital advanced – without any need to have recourse to prices. With corn entering the production of all other commodities (as the only wage good and possibly also as an input) the prices of these commodities would have to adjust such that the same competitive rate of return could be earned in their production. Sraffa stressed: 'Although this argument is never stated by Ricardo in any of his extant letters and papers, he must have formulated it either in his lost "papers on the profits of Capital" of March 1814 or in conversation [with Malthus]' (Sraffa, 1951, p. xxxi).[3]

Yet Ricardo did not, of course, dispute the correctness of Malthus's observation that there is no industry in which the composition of the product is exactly the same as that of the capital advanced. It is here that the theories of distribution based on the concept of social surplus are confronted with the problem of value. For in physical terms the general rate of profits is the ratio between the social surplus and the social capital. Since the two aggregates of heterogeneous commodities generally differ in composition, they cannot be compared unless they are made commensurable, that is, expressed as *value* magnitudes. Therefore, in a third step, in the *Principles* Ricardo presented a theory of value according to which the exchange values of commodities are regulated by the quantities of labour needed, directly and indirectly, in their production. The surplus product and the social capital, that is, the two magnitudes whose ratio gives the general rate of profits, could thus be 'measured' in terms of embodied labour. Hence, what was to become known as the 'labour theory of value' was introduced by Ricardo precisely in order to overcome the analytical difficulty encountered in his attempt to explain prof-

---

[3] Sraffa's 'corn model' interpretation gave rise to a large and still mounting literature; see the references in Kurz and Salvadori (1995, pp. 87–9); see also Hollander (1995) and De Vivo (1996).

its in terms of the surplus product left after making allowance for the cost of production, including the wages of productive workers.

However, Ricardo soon realized that the principle that the quantity of labour bestowed on the production of commodities regulates their exchangeable value cannot be sustained as a 'general rule' of value: it is 'considerably modified by the employment of machinery and other fixed and durable capital' (*Works*, I, p. 30). With different proportions of (direct) labour to means of production in different industries, and with different durabilities of these means of production, relative prices would not only depend on the quantities of total labour 'embodied' in the various commodities, but also on the level of the rate of profits, and would change with that level. This is so because with (compound) interest the weight of the profit component in prices depends on the rate of profits. Ricardo's search for a measure of value that is 'invariable' with respect to changes in distribution, that is, variations in the real wage rate and the associated contrary variations in the rate of profits, is considered by Sraffa as the final step in Ricardo's efforts to simplify the theory of distribution. The measure of value he was in search of was meant to corroborate his conviction that the laws of distribution 'are not essentially connected with the doctrine of value' (*Works*, VIII, p. 194).[4]

Sraffa deserves the credit for having rediscovered the 'classical' approach to the theory of value and distribution. After its excavation, that approach had to be elaborated and, if possible, given a logically coherent formulation, taking into consideration all the economic phenomena such as fixed capital, joint production and natural resources with which the earlier authors had grappled with only limited success.

4   Production of commodities by means of commodities

From the mid-1950s, Sraffa eventually found time to put together, revise and complete his notes on the classical approach to the theory of value and distribution. The resulting book was published in 1960 and entitled *Production of Commodities by Means of Commodities. Prelude to a Critique of Economic Theory* (Sraffa, 1960). As regards the critique implicit in the book, the main target was marginal theory:

It is...a peculiar feature of the set of propositions now published that, although they do not enter into any discussion of the marginal theory of value and distribution, they have nevertheless been designed to serve as the basis for a critique of that theory. If the foundation holds, the critique may be attempted later, either

---

[4] For a detailed discussion of Ricardo's search for an 'invariable' measure of value, and its relationship to Sraffa's 'Standard Commodity', see Kurz and Salvadori (1993).

by the writer or by someone younger and better equipped for the task. (Ibid., p. vi)

Since the publication of the book the critique has been carried out in the so-called Cambridge controversies in the theory of capital (see Harcourt, 1972; Garegnani, 1990; Kurz and Salvadori, 1995, Chap.14). Major representatives of the neoclassical school openly admitted that the criticism levelled at long-period neoclassical theory is indeed correct.[5] The question remained whether the critique (or elements of it) carries over to short-period neoclassical analysis, that is, the theories of inter-temporal and temporary equilibrium.

According to some interpreters, Sraffa's book was exclusively designed for the negative task of serving as the basis for a critique of neoclassical theory. However, this interpretation cannot be sustained. Sraffa's work was first and foremost constructive. (Sraffa's concern with the construc-tive task becomes obvious when reading his unpublished papers in the Wren Library at Trinity College, Cambridge.) He may be said to have followed Spinoza's famous dictum *determinatio est negatio*: by elaborat-ing a coherent theory of income distribution and relative prices he sought to prepare the ground for the critical task.

As Sraffa made clear in the preface, the standpoint taken in his book 'is that of the old classical economists from Adam Smith to Ricardo, [which] has been submerged and forgotten since the advent of the "mar-ginal" method' (Sraffa, 1960, p. v). The affiliation of his analysis with the theories of the old classical economists is stressed again in the following remark concerning the concept of 'price' or 'value' adopted in the book: 'Such classical terms as "necessary price", "natural price" or "price of production" would meet the case, but value and price have been preferred as being shorter and in the present context (which contains no reference to market prices) no more ambiguous' (ibid., p. 9). Finally, Appendix D to the book provides additional 'References to the Literature' concerning special ideas and concepts of classical derivation, 'the source of which may not be obvious' (ibid., p. 93). Hence his book was explicitly designed to reconstruct the classical theory of value and distribution. (For addi-tional evidence see Kurz, 1998.)

---

[5] For example, Frank H. Hahn frankly admitted that the Sraffa-based critique is correct with respect to 'many writers whom we regard as neoclassical who have either made mistakes of reasoning or based themselves on special assumptions which have themselves nothing to do with neoclassical theory' (Hahn, 1982, p. 354). In another place, Hahn admitted that he himself 'every so often slipped into the aggregate version of the neoclas-sical model' (Hahn, 1972, p. 8). He also expressed the opinion that 'Sraffa's book contains no formal propositions which I consider to be wrong although here and there it contains remarks which I consider to be false' (1982, p. 353).

Scrutiny shows that Sraffa follows the classical authors not only in terms of the method adopted and the general approach chosen, but broadly also in terms of the two-part structure of their argument. In one part he is concerned with investigating *given* 'systems of production'. The relationship between relative prices, the general rate of profits and the wage rate implicit in the given system of production, or 'technique', is analysed partly in formal terms: it is systems of equations that prove to be appropriate in this context. Subsequently, Sraffa turns to the problem of which system of production will be adopted from a set of alternative systems, that is, the choice of technique problem. Hence, what was initially taken as given is now an *unknown*. This is dealt with in Chapter XII, 'Switch in Methods of Production'. Sraffa assumes that the choice between alternative techniques 'will be exclusively grounded on cheapness' (ibid., p. 83). In other words, he is concerned with determining the *cost-minimizing* system(s) of production. In comparing different methods of production to produce the same commodity, the phenomena of *extra costs* and *extra profits* make an appearance. Although Sraffa does not provide a formalization of his argument, it is clear that in this context inequalities rather than equations would be appropriate.

Sraffa proceeds in the following way. In Chapter I he deals with an economic system actually in operation, assuming that it is capable of *self-replacement*, that is, of each commodity it produces as much (i) as is needed in order to make good the quantity used up of the commodity under consideration as a means of production across all industries of the economy, (ii) plus the quantity of it needed to provide food, shelter etc. at a given (minimum) level for those engaged in production. He then assumes that any remaining surplus product, that is, quantities of the different commodities produced in excess of the requirements of self-replacement, are made to disappear. This leaves him with a system which he calls 'Production without Surplus'. He finds out that in such a system the relative exchange values of commodities, or price ratios, 'spring directly from the methods of production and productive consumption' (ibid., p. 3). In Chapter II he brings the surplus back into the picture, assuming that this surplus will be distributed in the form of profits on capital at a uniform rate, that is, in proportion to the capital advanced in each industry. Since the means of production and means of subsistence advanced in each industry at the beginning of the (uniform) production period consist of sets of heterogeneous commodities, the magnitude of each industry's capital can only be ascertained once prices are known. However, prices cannot be determined independently of the rate of profits. Hence, Sraffa concludes, prices and the rate of profits must be determined *simultaneously*. The concept of surplus then leads to the distinction between *basic* and *non-basic products*, and to the assumption that there exists at least one basic commodity. Basic products enter directly or indirectly into the production of all commodities, whereas non-basic products do not. The main aim of Chapter III is to provide a first discussion of price movements consequent upon hypothetical changes in distribution on the assumption that the methods of production remain unchanged. Sraffa concludes 'this preliminary survey of the subject' (ibid., p. 15) by asserting that

the relative price-movements of two products come to depend, not only on the 'proportions' of labour to means of production by which they are respectively produced, but also on the 'proportions' by which those means have themselves been produced, and also on the 'proportions' by which the means of production of those means of production have been produced, and so on. The result is that the relative price of two products may move . . . in the opposite direction to what we might have expected on the basis of their respective 'proportions'; besides, the prices of their respective means of production may move in such a way as to reverse the order of the two products as to higher and lower proportions; *and further complications arise, which will be considered subsequently.* (Ibid., p. 15; emphasis added)

The complete analysis of price movements in the case of single production is provided in Chapter VI. This chapter also contains the well-known example of the 'old wine' and the 'oak chest', showing that the difference between the prices of two commodities can be positive or negative depending on income distribution. The analysis is significantly simplified by the use of the 'Standard Commodity' as numéraire. Chapters IV and V of Sraffa's book are in fact devoted to the introduction of this tool of analysis and to the study of its properties.

Part II of Sraffa's book generalizes the study in Part I, which was restricted to circulating capital only, to the case of multiple-product industries. It contains impressive counter-evidence to William Stanley Jevons's contention that the classical approach is in principle incapable of dealing with this more realistic and complex case and, as a result of this and other weaknesses, had to be abandoned and a new theoretical approach explored (see Kurz, 1986). Sraffa deserves the credit for having demonstrated that the multiple-product industries framework is suited to the analysis of a wide range of problems, including fixed capital and land.

The method of treating what remains of *fixed capital* goods at the end of the production period as part of the gross output, jointly with those products which are the primary object of the productive activity, fits easily into the classical picture and was first introduced by Robert Torrens in the course of a criticism of Ricardo's doctrine (Sraffa, 1960,

p. 94). The method allows the correct calculation of the annual charge on the fixed capital consisting of the payment of profit at the uniform rate and the depreciation that makes possible the replacement of the durable instrument of production when it is worn out. Most importantly, the method is not restricted to the simplified case of constant efficiency, but has general validity (ibid., p. 66). It is shown that the depreciation quotas, and thus the price of ageing machinery, cannot be ascertained independently of distribution, which is contrary to a widespread belief that finds expression in *ad hoc* rules such as linear depreciation, 'radio-active decay' or 'depreciation by evaporation'.

In the case of constant efficiency, the value of an item of fixed capital decreases linearly during its lifetime of n years only if $r = 0$, whereas for $r > 0$ the value follows a stepped curve which will be the more concave toward the origin the higher the rate of profits (ibid., p. 71). This variation in the time profile traced by the price of the ageing fixed capital good when the rate of profits changes is exclusively due to the necessity of maintaining the uniformity in price of all items of the commodity irrespective of the age of the fixed capital goods by means of which they are respectively produced. Obviously, the area below such a curve, defined for a particular level of r, is a measure of the aggregate value of a capital stock consisting of n pieces of the durable instrument of uniform age distribution. As Sraffa stresses, 'the interest of this type of price-variation is chiefly from the standpoint of capital theory' (ibid., p. 72), since it is made clear that the value of a given *physical* capital stock cannot be ascertained prior to the determination of r.

Unlike capital, which consists of produced means of production derived from the production process, *natural resources*, such as land, can be taken as external elements of production, measured in their own physical units. 'Being employed in production, but not themselves produced, they are the converse of commodities which, although produced, are not used in production' (ibid., p. 74), that is, the converse of non-basics that are pure consumption goods. In accordance with Ricardo's treatment of the problem under consideration, Sraffa starts from a given system of production, that is, given quantities of the commodities produced and given methods of production in use, and a given distribution of income between wages and profits. He then indicates how such a constellation can be conceived of 'as the outcome of a process of "extensive" ... [or] "intensive" diminishing returns' (ibid., p. 76). Elaborating on Sraffa's approach, several contributions were concerned with the study of changes in the relations between the distributive variables (including rents) and prices, corresponding to autonomous changes in one of the distributive variables (the rate of profits, r, or the wage rate, w) or in outputs.

Part III of Sraffa's book is devoted to a discussion of the problem of the choice of technique. There Sraffa showed that it cannot be presumed that techniques can be ordered monotonically with the rate of interest. In the Cambridge capital controversies, his findings were used in order to criticize neoclassical theory. *Reswitching* was defined as a situation in which a technique is cost-minimizing at two disconnected ranges of the rate of interest and not so in between these ranges. Samuelson emphasized that 'this phenomenon can be called "perverse" only in the sense that the conventional parables did not prepare us for it' (Samuelson, 1966, p. 578). The implication of the possibility of the reswitching of techniques is that the direction of change of the 'input proportions' cannot be related unambiguously to changes of the so-called 'factor prices'. The central element of the neoclassical explanation of distribution in terms of supply and demand is thus revealed as defective. The demonstration that a fall in the wage rate (that is, a rise in the rate of interest) may lead to the adoption of the less 'labour-intensive', that is, more 'capital-intensive', of two techniques destroyed, in the minds of the critics of neoclassical theory, its concept of substitution in production. Moreover, since a fall in the wage rate may cheapen some of the commodities, the production of which at a higher level of the wage rate was characterized by a relatively low labour intensity, the substitution among consumption goods contemplated by the traditional theory of consumer demand may result in a higher, as well as in a lower, labour intensity. It follows that the principle of substitution in consumption cannot offset the breakdown of the conventional principle of substitution in production.

We talk of 'reverse capital deepening' when the relationship between the *value* of capital (per head), expressed in terms of a given consumption unit, and the rate of interest is increasing. The negative implication of reswitching and reverse capital deepening for traditional theory can be illustrated by means of the example in Figure 1, in which the value of capital (in terms of the consumption unit) corresponding to the full employment level of labour is plotted against the rate of profits. Obviously, if with traditional analysis we would be prepared to conceive of the curve KK' as the 'demand curve' for capital, which, together with the corresponding 'supply curve' $K^*K^{*\prime}$, is taken to determine the equilibrium value of the rate of interest, r, we would have to conclude that this equilibrium, although unique, is unstable. With free competition, conceived of, as it is in neoclassical theory, as including the perfect flexibility of the distributive variables, a deviation of r from r^* would lead to the

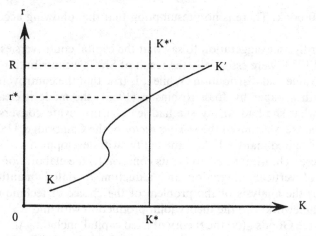

Figure 1

absurd conclusion that one of the two income categories, wages or profits, would disappear.

In the Preface to *Production of Commodities*, Sraffa stressed that he had not introduced any assumption on returns in the book since it was not concerned with *changes* either in the *scale of production* or in the *proportions* in which the 'factors of production' are employed (1960, p. v). The effects of these changes on the costs of production were central to his critique of Marshall's supply functions in the 1920s.[6] A comparison of that critique with *Production of Commodities* shows that in both the reference is essentially to the same determinants of variable returns. That is, Sraffa's analysis of the relationship between quantities produced and prices is carried out in terms of basically the same factors. Panico and Salvadori (1994) provided a detailed account of this fact (see also Kurz and Salvadori, 1995, pp. 418–21).

5   The consequences of Mr. Sraffa

As has variously been indicated, each of Sraffa's published contributions had some remarkable consequences and led to important developments in economics. In this concluding section we shall briefly sketch the impact

---

[6] In the 1925 article, it is stated that increasing returns are related to *changes in the scale of production* whereas diminishing returns are related to *changes in the proportions* in which 'factors' are employed.

of his 1960 book. There is no presumption that the following account is complete.

It is hardly an exaggeration to say that the capital controversies in the 1960s and 1970s were essentially the result of Sraffa's contribution to the theory of value and distribution. While it is true that the controversy was started with a paper by Joan Robinson (1953), she made it clear that much of what she had to say she had learned in private conversations with Sraffa. He was indeed the *spiritus rector* of the Cambridge, UK, side. His work inspired many scholars and led to swift developments in several areas of research. Major achievements concern: (i) the elaboration of the concepts of vertical integration and reduction to dated quantities of labour; (ii) the analysis of the problem of the choice of technique in a general framework; (iii) the theory joint production with and without the 'Rule of Free Goods'; (iv) the theory of fixed capital, including the case of jointly utilized machines; (v) the theory of rent and of exhaustible resources; (vi) the analysis of different forms of technical progress; (vii) the theory of foreign trade; (viii) the analysis of the gravitation of market prices to 'natural' prices. Several received doctrines were scrutinized and shown to be tenable only in special cases. These include: (i) the Marxian labour value-based approach to the theory of the rate of profits and relative prices; (ii) the traditional long-period marginal productivity theory of value and distribution; (iii) the Heckscher–Ohlin–Samuelson theory of international trade (see, in particular, Garegnani, 1960, 1970, 1990; Pasinetti, 1977, 1980; Schefold, 1971, 1989, 1997; Steedman, 1977, 1979, 1988; Quadrio-Curzio, 1967; Mainwaring, 1984; Salvadori, 1988; Salvadori and Steedman, 1990; Kurz, 1990; Eatwell, Milgate and Newman, 1990; Bharadwaj and Schefold, 1990; Caminati and Petri, 1990; Bidard, 1991; Kurz and Salvadori, 1995, 1998a, 1998b).

However, Sraffa's contributions also inspired many of those who advocated one version or another of marginalism. These scholars had to face the criticisms put forward, and in doing so they came up with new results and new interpretations of old ones. It was Paul A. Samuelson, in particular, who tirelessly took on the challenge and wrote several essays dealing with Sraffa's contributions (see, in particular, Samuelson, 1962, 1966, 1975, 1987, 1991). He also showed that certain findings were anticipated in his earlier works (see, especially, Samuelson, 1957, 1959; see also Bruno, Burmeister and Sheshinski, 1966; Burmeister, 1980; Hahn, 1982). It was particularly Samuel Hollander who questioned Sraffa's interpretation of the classical economists (see Hollander, 1973, 1979, 1995).

It is to be hoped that this volume will contribute to a clarification of at least some of the questions raised and thereby release energies to pursue promising directions of research. The time of its publication marks a watershed in the interpretation of Sraffa's contributions, because it is to be expected that within the next couple of years a selection of Sraffa's hitherto unpublished manuscripts and correspondence will come out. In the light of this material, which is both huge and very complex, some interpretations will turn out to be untenable, others will have to be modified somewhat and in some respects entirely new interpretations will have to be sought. Adapting Sen's well-known dictum, cited in the Preface, we may say that Sraffa apparently found it immoral to *publish* more than one page per month. The group of scholars who are preparing the edition of his manuscripts and correspondence would be ill-advised to follow this maxim.

References

Bharadwaj, K. and Schefold, B. (eds) (1990). *Essays on Piero Sraffa: Critical Perspectives on the Revival of Classical Theory*, London: Unwin Hyman. (Second printing London 1992: Routledge.)

Bidard, Ch. (1991). *Prix, reproduction, rareté*, Paris: Dunod.

Bruno, M., Burmeister, E. and Sheshinski, E. (1966). 'The Nature and Implications of the Reswitching of Techniques', *Quarterly Journal of Economics*, **80**, pp. 526–53.

Burmeister, E. (1980). *Capital Theory and Dynamics*, Cambridge: Cambridge University Press.

Caminati, M. and Petri, F. (eds) (1990). *Convergence to Long-Period Positions*, Special issue of *Political Economy. Studies in the Surplus Approach*, **6**.

De Vivo, G. (1996). 'Ricardo, Torrens, and Sraffa: A Summing Up', *Cambridge Journal of Economics*, **20**, 387-91.

Eatwell, J., Milgate, M. and Newman, P. (eds) (1990). *Capital Theory*, London: Macmillan.

Eatwell, J. and Panico, C. (1987). 'Sraffa, Piero', in J. Eatwell, M. Milgate and P. Newman (eds), *The New Palgrave: A Dictionary of Economics*, London: Macmillan, Vol. 4, pp. 445–52.

Garegnani, P. (1960). *Il capitale nelle teorie della distribuzione*, Milan: Giuffrè.

Garegnani, P. (1970). 'Heterogeneous Capital, the Production Function and the Theory of Distribution', *Review of Economic Studies*, **37**, pp. 407–36.

Garegnani, P. (1990). 'Quantity of Capital', in J. Eatwell, M. Milgate and P. Newman (1990), pp. 1–78.

Hahn, F. H. (1972). *The Share of Wages in the National Income: An Enquiry into the Theory of Distribution*, London: Weidenfeld and Nicolson.

Hahn, F. H. (1982). 'The Neo-Ricardians', *Cambridge Journal of Economics*, **6**, pp. 353–74.

Harcourt, G. C. (1972). *Some Cambridge Controversies in the Theory of Capital*, Cambridge: Cambridge University Press.

Hayek, F. A. (1931a). *Prices and Production*, 1st edn, London: George Routledge (2nd edn London 1935).

Hayek, F. A. (1931b). 'Reflections on the Pure Theory of Money of Mr. J. M. Keynes', *Economica*, **11**, pp. 270–95.

Hayek, F. A. (1932). 'Money and Capital: A Reply', *Economic Journal*, **42**, pp. 237–49.

Hollander, S. (1973). *The Economics of Adam Smith*, Toronto: Toronto University Press.

Hollander, S. (1979). *The Economics of David Ricardo*, Toronto: Toronto University Press.

Hollander, S. (1995). 'Sraffa's Rational Reconstruction of Ricardo: On Three Contributions to the *Cambridge Journal of Economics*', *Cambridge Journal of Economics*, **19**, pp. 483–9.

Hume, D. (1938). *An Abstract of a Treatise on Human Nature*, edited, with an introduction, by J. M. Keynes and P. Sraffa, London. The introduction is reprinted in Keynes, *CW*, XXVIII, pp. 373–90.

Keynes, J. M. (1973). *The Collected Writings of John Maynard Keynes*, edited by D. Moggridge, Vols I–XXX, London: Macmillan. (Referred to as *CW*, volume number, page number.)

Kurz, H. D. (1986). 'Classical and Early Neoclassical Economists on Joint Production', *Metroeconomica*, **38**, pp. 1–37.

Kurz, H. D. (1990). *Capital, Distribution and Effective Demand. Studies in the 'Classical' Approach to Economic Theory*, Cambridge: Polity Press.

Kurz, H. D. (1998). 'Against the Current: Sraffa's Unpublished Manuscripts and the History of Economic Thought', *European Journal of the History of Economic Thought*, **5**, pp. 437–51.

Kurz, H. D. and Salvadori, N. (1993). 'The "Standard Commodity" and Ricardo's Search for an "Invariable Measure of Value"', in M. Baranzini and G. C. Harcourt (eds), *The Dynamics of the Wealth of Nations. Growth, Distribution and Structural Change. Essays in Honour of Luigi Pasinetti*, New York: St. Martin's Press, pp. 95–123.

Kurz, H. D. and Salvadori, N. (1995). *Theory of Production. A Long-Period Analysis*, Cambridge, Melbourne and New York: Cambridge University Press.

Kurz, H. D. and Salvadori, N. (1997). 'On Critics and Protective Belts', in A. Salanti and E. Screpanti (eds), *Pluralism in Economics*, Aldershot: Edward Elgar, pp. 232–55.

Kurz, H. D. and Salvadori, N. (1998a). *Understanding 'Classical' Economics. Studies in Long-Period Theory*, London: Routledge.

Kurz, H. D. and Salvadori, N. (eds) (1998b). *The Elgar Companion to Classical Economics*, 2 vols., Aldershot: Edward Elgar.

Mainwaring, L. (1984). *Value and Distribution in Capitalist Economies. An Introduction to Sraffian Economics*, Cambridge: Cambridge University Press.

Panico, C. (1991). 'Some Notes on Marshallian Supply Functions', *Economic Journal*, **101**, pp. 557–69.

Panico, C. and Salvadori, N. (1994). 'Sraffa, Marshall and the Problem of Returns', *The European Journal of the History of Economic Thought*, **1**, pp. 323–43.

Pasinetti, L. L. (1977). *Lectures on the Theory of Production*, London: Macmillan.

Pasinetti, L. L. (ed.) (1980). *Essays on the Theory of Joint Production*, London: Macmillan.

Pollit, B. H. (1990). 'Clearing the Path for "Production of Commodities by Means of Commodities": Notes on the Collaboration of Maurice Dobb in Piero Sraffa's Edition of the "Works and Correspondence of David Ricardo"', in Bharadwaj and Schefold (1990), pp. 516–28.

Potier, J.-P. (1991). *Piero Sraffa Unorthodox Economist (1898–1983): A Biographical Essay*, London: Routledge.

Quadrio-Curzio, A. (1967). *Rendita e distribuzione in un modello economico pluri-settoriale*, Milano: Giuffrè.

Ricardo, D. (1951–73). *The Works and Correspondence of David Ricardo*, 11 vols, edited by P. Sraffa with the collaboration of M. H. Dobb, Cambridge: Cambridge University Press. (In the text quoted as *Works*.)

Robinson, J. V. (1933). *Economics of Imperfect Competition*, London: Macmillan.

Robinson, J. V. (1953). 'The Production Function and the Theory of Capital', *Review of Economic Studies*, **21**, pp. 81–106.

Roncaglia, A. (1978). *Sraffa and the Theory of Prices*, New York: John Wiley.

Salvadori, N. (1988). 'Fixed Capital within the Sraffa Framework', *Zeitschrift für Nationalökonomie*, **48**, pp. 1–17.

Salvadori, N. and Steedman, I. (eds) (1990). *Joint Production of Commodities*, Aldershot: Edward Elgar.

Samuelson, P. A. (1957). 'Wages and Interest: A Modern Dissection of Marxian Economic Models', *American Economic Review*, **47**, pp. 884–912.

Samuelson, P. A. (1959). 'A Modern Treatment of the Ricardian Economy. I. The Pricing of Goods and of Labor and Land Services. II. Capital and Interest Aspects of the Pricing Process', *Quarterly Journal of Economics*, **73**, pp. 1–35 and 217–31.

Samuelson, P. A. (1962). 'Parable and Realism in Capital Theory: The Surrogate Production Function', *Review of Economic Studies*, **29**, pp. 193–206.

Samuelson, P. A. (1966). 'A Summing Up', *Quarterly Journal of Economics*, **80**, pp. 568–83.

Samuelson, P. A. (1975). 'Trade Pattern Reversals in Time-Phased Ricardian Systems and Intertemporal Efficiency', *Journal of International Economics*, **5**, pp. 309–63.

Samuelson, P. A. (1987). 'Sraffian Economics', in J. Eatwell, M. Milgate, and P. Newman (eds), *The New Palgrave: A Dictionary of Economics*, London: Macmillan, Vol. 4, pp. 452–61.

Samuelson, P. A. (1991). 'Sraffa's Other Leg', *Economic Journal*, **101**, pp. 570–4.

Schefold, B. (1971). *Mr. Sraffa on Joint Production*, Ph.D. Thesis, University of Basle, mimeo.

Schefold, B. (1989). *Mr. Sraffa on Joint Production and Other Essays*, London: Unwin Hyman.

Schefold, B. (1996). 'Piero Sraffa 1898–1983', *Economic Journal*, **106**, pp. 1314–25.

Schefold, B. (1997). *Normal Prices, Technical Change and Accumulation*, Houndmills, Basingstoke and London: Macmillan.

Smith, A. (1976). *An Inquiry into the Nature and Causes of the Wealth of Nations*, 1st edn 1776, Vol. II of *The Glasgow Edition of the Works and Correspondence of Adam Smith*, edited by R. H. Campbell, A. S. Skinner and W. B. Todd, Oxford: Oxford University Press. (In the text quoted as *WN*.)

Sraffa, P. (1922). 'The Bank Crisis in Italy', *Economic Journal*, **32**, pp. 178–97.

Sraffa, P. (1925). 'Sulle relazioni fra costo e quantità prodotta', *Annali di Economia*, **2**, pp. 277–328. English translation by John Eatwell and Alessandro Roncaglia in L. L. Pasinetti (ed.), *Italian Economic Papers*, Vol. 3, Bologna: Il Mulino, 1998, and Oxford: Oxford University Press, 1998, pp. 323–63.

Sraffa, P. (1926). 'The Laws of Returns under Competitive Conditions', *Economic Journal*, **36**, pp. 535–50.

Sraffa, P. (1930). 'A Criticism' and 'Rejoinder', contributions to the Symposium on 'Increasing Returns and the Representative Firm', *Economic Journal*, **40**, pp. 89–93.

Sraffa, P. (1932a). 'Dr. Hayek on Money and Capital', *Economic Journal*, **42**, pp. 42–53.

Sraffa, P. (1932b). 'A Rejoinder', *Economic Journal*, **42**, pp. 249–51.

Sraffa, P. (1951). 'Introduction', in D. Ricardo (1951–73), Vol. I, pp. xiii–lxii.

Sraffa, P. (1960). *Production of Commodities by Means of Commodities. Prelude to a Critique of Economic Theory*, Cambridge: Cambridge University Press.

Steedman, I. (1977). *Marx After Sraffa*, London: N.L.B.

Steedman, I. (ed.) (1979). *Fundamental Issues in Trade Theory*, London: Macmillan.

Steedman, I. (ed.) (1988). *Sraffian Economics*, 2 vols, Aldershot: Edward Elgar.

CHAPTER 2

Revisionist findings on Sraffa

Paul A. Samuelson

Piero Sraffa was a great economist whom I remember with warm admiration. He wrote too little, which is our loss. His reputation tends to get tied up with ideological jockeyings within our profession. Perhaps this is inevitable but I regret it – for, ideology aside, mainstream economists of the mathematical or literary persuasion can benefit much from Sraffa's contributions and also from the problems that his works pose for further investigations.

By chance, the *New Palgrave* (Eatwell, Milgate and Newman, 1987) contains two articles on Sraffa, both of some length. The one by me originated accidentally: I was not the editors' natural choice for this topic, but they wanted my participation and were willing to indulge my preferences to write out some views on Wicksell and also on Sraffa. The other *Palgrave* article on Sraffa, by John Eatwell and Carlo Panico, is seen to have some overlap with mine; still readers of this valuable new reference will, I daresay, benefit from the differences in viewpoint registered by the different authors. (It should be said that, until the finished volumes appeared, I could not benefit from the thoughtful Eatwell–Panico treatment; that is perhaps all for the better since differences can be more interesting than agreements.)

Here, also by invitation of hospitable editors, are some further thoughts on Sraffa. They are neither listed in strict chronological order nor ranked by relative importance.

1   Scholar as young man

One yearns to know more of Sraffa's early Italian years. Schumpeter, in his graduate lectures at Harvard in the mid-1930s, referred to Sraffa as unfortunately spoiled by having been born too affluent. No doubt

Schumpeter was expressing regret that Sraffa did not write more, but this diagnosis as to cause for that seems quite unwarranted. (Rumour has it that Sraffa did die well off, leaving behind him gold in Swiss vaults for Trinity College. According to Kaldor's obituary piece on Sraffa for the British Academy, this legacy seems to have been the fruit of a daring coup in which Sraffa staked his all on the comeback of Japanese bonds after that country's defeat. What theory of inductive inference, I wonder, could have persuaded me to make a like investment?)

2   Writer's block

The myth of Sraffa as dilettante gained from such stories as I heard in the 1930s (perhaps from Robert Bryce, the Canadian John the Baptist who brought Keynes' message to America in 1935). Sraffa is supposed to have begged off being named director of research at Cambridge when he learned this might require his attending an occasional before-noon meeting; as assistant director he could avoid that risk, and for many years the 'graduate' curriculum at Cambridge was reported to involve attending a seminar with other non-Englishmen at which Sraffa presided while classmates presented papers in turn.

Several times I have head the following sample of Keynes' wit. When Maynard was told that a mysterious ailment of Nicky Kaldor's was diagnosed as athlete's foot, he is reported as saying: 'I don't believe it. Next you'll be telling me Piero suffers from writer's cramp.'

Sraffa's block against lecturing was even more pathetic than his writer's block. The story used to be repeated in Cambridge of a series of lectures Professor Pigou had arranged on great economists. Sraffa of course was to speak on Ricardo. But as the day approached, he could not face the ordeal, pacifying Pigou by a gift of gooseberry jam and the promised substitution of Kaldor, who cheerfully agreed to volunteer as substitute. Posterity is grateful to the incident for Kaldor's brilliant 1955 article in which Ricardo's model is artfully presented as one alternative to neoclassical Clarkianism. (Since writing these words I have read the 1984 Italian interview with Kaldor – Christina Marcuzzo, 1986 – where a definitive version of this incident is told.)

3   Thursday conversations at Trinity

One yearns to know more about Sraffa's precise influences on Wittgenstein.

4   The spectacles one peers through

Sraffa's relationship to the Communist Party and to various Marxian
factions, whatever its biographical interest and testimony for Italian intellectual history, has little bearing on his scholarly economics. Sraffa's
general interest in Marxian economics is quite another matter. He was
50 when I first knew him; and the puzzlement this sophisticated intellectual engendered in me by orally defending such a notion as Smith's
concept of *productive* labour (whereby concrete *goods* are given a primacy
over ephemeral *services*) suddenly evaporated when I came to hypothe-
size that this sophisticated mind had a penchant for Marxian notions.
This paradigmatic insight for understanding Sraffa served the observer
well.

5   Monetary insights

One should constantly nominate suspicions in economics. Marx's legacy
is valuable in this regard. But of course nomination and election are quite
distinguishable procedures in an empirical science, and in this regard the
algebraic worth of Karl's value-added is problematic.

Eatwell and Panico (1987, pp. 448–9) point out that Sraffa's early
monetary writing – his 1920 Italian thesis and 1922 work for Keynes –
sided with the angels (Cassel, Keynes and Hawtrey, as against Wicksell
and Einaudi) in opposing a return to pre-war gold parities with the
entailed deadweight losses from deflation. So far, so good. But one
hopes that the following paraphrase of Sraffa's 1920 thought is taken
out of context: '... the *normal* value of a currency is completely "conventional", i.e. it can be at *any* level that common opinion expects it to
be.' Chancellor Churchill made his 1925 boo-boo in part because the
current ephemeral belief that the pound would be restored to its 1914
value made it float *temporarily* and misleadingly near to that disastrous
level of overvaluation. Of course, Wicksell was wrong and Cassel was
right on post-war restorations of parity. *Any* absolute price level can
obtain (if the right things are done to sustain it); but Couéism is silly
monetary economics.

Also, Sraffa's nominated suspicion that class interests shape price-level
policy decisions and achieve significant alterations in income distribution
fares poorly under the test of economic history. To be sure, the indus-
trialist Hugo Stinnes was splashed in the 1920–3 inflation and Heidelberg
University was permanently penalized. But, as Schumpeter used to say,
the rooms of capitalism's hotel are fully occupied, albeit, with a *changing*
set of people. Even Keynes' eclectic view of the 1923 *Tract*, that long

waves in the price level generate systematic changes in the terms of trade between risk-taking entrepreneurs on the one hand and rentiers on the other, has had to be attenuated in this century. What is surprising is not how much *hysteresis* there is of the type Sraffa suspected, but rather how little! One capitalist gains when waves move sand to his Florida beach; another loses. But this speaks little for a Marxian model of oceanography.

6   Reproduction models of Quesnay–Marx

Sraffa's 1960 input/output economics, like that of Leontief in the 1925–39 years (and that of Adolph Löwe and Fritz Burchardt in Kiel around 1930), one had supposed was influenced by Marx's Volume II tableaux of steady and expanded reproduction. It is useful to learn from Eatwell and Panico (1987) that Marx's reproduction schemes were indeed the source of the initial notes that Sraffa showed to Keynes around 1927 and from which the 1960 Sraffa classic evolved. There seems no evidence that Sraffa knew the related 1898 works of the Russian V. K. Dmitriev; although von Bortkiewicz was Leontief's Berlin mentor, he tells me he knew Marx's work but not Dmitriev's. For the Metzler *Festschrift* (Samuelson, 1974b), eschewing the puffery in which Morishima (1973) declared Marx to be the peer of Walras as *mathematical* (!) economist, I pronounced Marx's most important *analytical* contribution to economics to be those reproduction models from Volume II, which gets least read.

Marx's admiration (merited admiration) for Quesnay stemmed from his own struggle with reproduction tableaux. Marx's successful struggle – which was purely arithmetic rather than mathematical and which avoided groping (successfully or otherwise) with the so-called 'transformation' problem – was motivated by Marx's erroneous belief that Adam Smith cheated in claiming to break down a good's price and a society's national income into the eclectic triad of wage component, land-rent component and interest (or, sans uncertainty, profit) component. Marx suspected that a *fourth* component of used-up capital goods somehow escaped appropriate inclusion: in a world where iron needs coal input and coal needs iron input – indeed where corn needs as input corn itself – Marx suspected Smith of perpetrating on his reader a value-added calculus that involved the swindle of an *infinite* regress. In tens of thousands of words and repeated MSS bequeathed to Engels, Marx grappled with this perplexity – which has naught to do with a category of income that involves 'surplus' since it arises in a zero interest, zero rent model.

Paradoxically, Marx's successful depiction of tableaux of *stationary reproduction* and (geometrically) *expanding reproduction* does vindicate

Smith's triad in precisely the manner that Dmitriev ([1898] 1974), Leontief (1941), Dorfman, Samuelson and Solow ([1958] 1987), and Sraffa (1960) were to elaborate on. An infinite time-receding matrix multiplier series converges identically to the Dmitriev–Marx simultaneous equation solution to the problem when Marx carries forward at compound interest the earlier-stage factor outlays up to the final date of the present: $\sum_0^\infty a'(1 + r)' \equiv [I - a(1 + r)]^{-1}$ in matrix terms, post-multiplied into direct primary factor requirements.[1] The following numerical example elucidates the theorem.

Consider a model with two goods: (subsistence) corn and (luxury) silk. To produce 1 of corn requires 1 acre of direct land and $\frac{1}{2}$ unit of the other good as input; to get 1 of silk requires 1 of direct labour and $\frac{1}{2}$ of the other good as input. Each labourer needs a *subsistence* wage of $\frac{1}{4}$ corn, paid at the beginning of the period, to keep the labour supply stationary. The profit rate is observed to be $33\frac{1}{3}$ per cent per period. Like workers, property owners save nothing, spending all their rent and interest incomes on silk consumption. Suppose the wage is £1 per unit and the rent is £1 per acre (both paid *pre factum*). It can be calculated that, by coincidence, both goods have a competitive price of £4 per unit. Only one steady-state reproduction tableau is consistent with our specified data of 200 workers and 150 units of land. The tableau of Marx and bourgeois economics must be as in Table 1.

Marx's calculated tableau gives the same tripartite breakdown of income and price(s) as Smith will get from (i) adding up the value-added in all the (infinite) rounds of previous stages of production, taking care (ii) to reckon the compound interest earnable on all the earlier outlays on the primary inputs from time of purchase to the present day of price reckoning. All this is a routine exercise in Dorfman–Samuelson–Solow ([1958] 1987) and Sraffa (1960) algebra: with W and R being the nominal wage and rent rates, r the profit rate, C_j's the final consumptions,

---

[1] My explorations in Marx's development do not fully concur with Garegnani's. There is no page on which Marx perceives how to solve the matrix *Mehrwert* relations $p = a_0(1 + m) + pa = (1 + m)a_0[I - a]^{-1}$. Such a mode of solving therefore cannot be a springboard to a successful solution of the Sraffa relations $P = a_0(1 + r) + Pa(1 + r) = a_0(1 + r)[I - a(1 + r)]^{-1}$. I hail Marx's numerical tableaux of Volume II, but find it odd that my matter-of-fact erase-and-replace explication of the transformation problem should be considered by Professor Garegnani as being in some sense rebutted by the Sraffa (1951) exposition of what I called in the last section Ricardo's lost-Atlantis 1815 paradigm. The 1815 fabrications are what we get by *not* making any detours or mistakes; the price ratio changes induced in the 1815 model by demand–taste changes are precisely what the *Mehrwert* model mistakenly puts at zero. It is a case of 1960 Sraffa against 1867 Marx.

Table 1. *Tableau of stationary reproduction (profit rate $= 33\frac{1}{3}\%$)*

Departments	Corn input	Silk input	Labour (wages)	Land (rent)	Profit	Gross outputs	Final outputs
Corn	£0	£300	£0	£150	£150	£600	£200
(150 units @ £4)							$= £(600 - 400)$
Silk	£400	£0	£200	£0	£200	£800	£500
(200 units @ £4)							$= £(800 - 300)$
	£400	£300	£200	£150	£350		£700

$£(200 + 150 + 350) =$ national income $= £(200 + 500)$
wages + rent + interest $= NI$ $\qquad = \Sigma P_j C_j$

and P_j's the goods' nominal prices, $\sum P_j C_j = (W[0\,1] + R[1\,0])$ $[I + a(1 + r) + a^2(1 + r)^2 + \ldots]$. Note that this contrived case of equal organic composition of capital carefully avoids any detour into distorting equalized rates of surplus values (percentage mark-ups on *wage outlay alone* to the neglect of return on raw material and/or rent outlays). No wonder Steedman regarded *Marx after Sraffa* (1977) as properly being where Smith was *before* Marx. Bortkiewicz would concur.

7   Macroeconomic skirmishing

My meandering thoughts regress from 1960 to Sraffa's 1932 polemic on Hayek's *Prices and Production* (1931). After a brief period in vogue, in accordance with Oscar Wilde's dictum that 'these days to be understood is to be found out', Hayek's book has earned its benign neglect. As both of the cited *Palgrave* articles aptly pointed out, Sraffa's 1932 article is notable for his defining the concept of an *own-rate of interest in terms of a specified good*. If 100 rice today trade for 106 rice next year, the own-rice-rate of interest is 6 per cent. If the market basket of goods in the price-level index rises in price by 2 per cent in the year and my dollar earns a nominal interest rate of 10 per cent, my real rate (own-rate in terms of the goods basket) is only 8 per cent – 10−2 per cent or, more exactly, $[(110/1.02) - 100]\% = 7.84\ldots\%$. In the literature on Irving Fisher and Keynes, the own-rate concept lives on purged of some of its *General Theory* ambiguities.

I reread the 1932 item for my *Palgrave* piece but scarcity of space accorded it only perfunctory mention. Let me report here that the allegedly pen-tied scholar, when urged by Keynes to attack Hayek, displayed a brilliant and cutting argumentative style. However, now that the heats of the arguments have cooled down after half a century, the modern reader perceives that Sraffa did not identify the rotten core of the Hayek work but engaged mostly in formalistic word-play concerning such Jesuitical concepts as neutrality of money. Had Sraffa worked the other side of the street, his subtle mind could have formulated for Hayek impeccable descriptions of processes in which, for a time, interest rates are contrived to be lower in real terms than they can remain in the longer run. What was harmful in the Hayek lectures was not their failure to achieve Wittgenstein rigour in formulating their scenarios!

I heard David Laidler in Sweden, during the 1987 meeting celebrating the fiftieth anniversary of the so-called Stockholm School, speculate on why Keynes' *General Theory* had the lasting power that *Prices and Production* and the Ohlin–Myrdal–Lindahl–Lundberg paradigms of the Stockholm School failed to attain. Having lived through those years of yore, I could have told him there was no mystery: the Swedish School messages and paradigms overlapped with, and were dominated by, the post-*General Theory investigations*. Those of them that deserved to live on did and do live on (for example, the Lundberg-like dynamizing of the 1936 statics). The Hayek effort died because, in the midst of a great depression that almost ended capitalism and led down the road to serfdom, it concentrated on parables in which a system must for methodological reasons be started out at full employment and in which the induced shortening of the period of production was non-cogently identified with the depression process then in being. As Lionel Robbins came to regret in reflecting on his misguided *The Great Depression* (1936), every policy insight of the 1931 opus was perverse: with one in four unemployed in Germany and the United States, to regard any expansion of funds for consumption as an evil sin was a programme inviting rejection by good-sense lay people and economists. (Even Hayek had second thoughts.) What died deserved to die. Still, schemata that illuminate how policies that promote over-full employment will entail predictable reactions will Phoenix-like rise from the dead in other times. Science, one hopes, can do better than reel from one non-eclectic exaggeration to another.

8   The fatal 1926 error

The two *Palgrave* articles are diametrically different in their evaluation of the 1926 article on competitive returns that brought Sraffa early fame. Both of course agree with his critique of Marshall's attempt to paper over the incompatibility of a firm's falling marginal cost with perfect competition.

Helping 1920s Cambridge catch up to 1838 Cournot was a valuable, needed, Sraffian contribution, which did stimulate Joan Robinson and Kahn to those imperfect competition advances that paralleled the contemporary American work of J. M. Clark and Chamberlin. No argument on this.

But on the other half of the 1926 classic – Sraffa's purported demonstration that the category of *constant* competitive cost constitutes the only empirical box with appreciable content – the *Palgrave* articles are 180° apart. I state (Samuelson, 1987a, pp. 458–9). 'This is plain wrong. Sraffa's 1960 book demonstrates that...[as does] Joan Robinson's famous 1941 *Economica* article on rising supply price....' As soon as two competitive goods involve different land/labour proportions, the *production possibility* frontier is curved and not straight in the fashion Sraffa needs. A *Palgrave* editor (not Eatwell) in a letter to me suggested in effect that for small (enough) movements the curved frontier would look flat. When I replied that this is an evasion of the question of whether the second derivative is itself zero (or even 'near zero'), he responded by saying that Sraffa was not a trained mathematician – which agrees with my point that Sraffa by pure rhetoric convinced himself and my generation of students of a simple error. I reproach myself that, for a dozen years, I was taken in and passed on to students defective reasoning and conclusions. When I reread the 1926 article with a magnifying glass, I perceived it to be blue smoke: Sraffa does not even purport to provide a cogent proof of anything – by suggestion, and implicit appeal to what is legitimate in (Marshallian) *partial* equilibrium methodology, the cases where alterations in composition of demand alter competitive price ratios are minimized. This is not even good Ricardo! Ricardo never expected Bordeaux wine (*vin ordinaire* or select Chateau) to have a price independent of quantity; and he expected a shift in demand toward goods of high labour intensity (soldiers' services) to raise labour's distributive shares. Eatwell and Panico (1987, p. 448) quote without blushing Sraffa's innocent proposal that, since unit costs of production are (sic) 'constant in respect to small variations in quantity produced,... the old and new obsolete theory which makes it [price, under variations in demand] dependent on the cost of production alone appears to hold its ground as the best available.' The issue is not whether small changes in an independent variable induce small changes in a dependent variable, but rather whether the instantaneous derivative of the function is negligibly small. The economics profession, while saluting Sraffa (1926) as a classic, has resolutely ignored its novel supply-curve findings.

To underline that my criticisms are not captious, and that the exceptions to Sraffa's claims cannot be discounted as belonging to some 'peculiar' concatenation of industry and firm 'externalities–internalities', I here present an impeccable Marshallian model in which (a) each of n goods is produced by transferable labour and a specialized land specific to itself, (b) every person's demand function for each of the n goods is strictly independent of every other good's price or quantity (strongly additive independent utilities), (c) for every person the marginal disutility of labour is a strict constant ('objectively' identifiable from market data). The example glaringly contradicts Sraffa's constancy of costs and obeys *all partial* equilibrium requirements (at the same time that it is a *full* general equilibrium model, a congruence Alfred Marshall never quite achieved). See Samuelson (1971b), for more on such a rigorous partial equilibrium as applied to trade theory. Moreover, in the sense of the mathematicians Smale and Thom, the example's properties are *generic* not singular, persisting when industries use the *same* inputs in varying proportions. At the same time that every firm can be regarded as a price taker, a systematic shift in the composition of demand towards some goods and away from others will systematically raise the market terms of trade of the newly preferred items. The 1926 attempt to fob off on the twentieth century a value taxonomy that was already obsolete in the early nineteenth century can hardly be termed a brilliant failure.

9   Demand effects when production is joint

Smith, Longfield, Cournot, Thünen, Mangoldt and Marshall well understood that joint production makes price ratios depend on the composition of demand (even, I may add, in a timeless technology where labour is the sole factor of production). A new taste for mutton lowers the relative price of wool, etc. In 1926 Sraffa never brought these banalities into doubt.

It is a pity therefore that Eatwell and Panico (1987, pp. 449–50) glean the impression from Part II of Sraffa (1960) that the influence of demand composition on relative prices is absent in Part II in the same way that it can be absent from Part I's model involving labour as the sole factor of production and no jointness of production. (See their exact sentence bridging pages 449 and 450 for explicit utterance of their untruth.) Although Sraffa's 1960 treatment of joint production (1) is quite fragmentary, (2) involves a number of non-optimalities and a few errors, and (3) contemplates *special equalities* cases that bias the reader towards overlooking demand influences, Sraffa, as far as I can remember, never explicitly claims the absence of demand influences.

Let me spell out a few examples that negate the Eatwell–Panico contention. To get 1 corn suppose we need either 5 of labour and 1 of land or 2 of labour and 2 of land. (The reader is licensed in all cases to add the requirement that 1 of corn also requires 1/10 of corn as seed, thereby qualifying corn as a bona fide *basic* good.) Assume the interest rate is always zero. (The reader may put in any other constant for the interest rate that is less than 900 per cent per period.) Assume 1 of cloth is producible out of 1 of labour and 1 of corn. Assume steady-state fixed supply of land; and, for the supply of labour, assume either that it also is fixed or that its supply adjusts to fulfil a subsistence real wage in terms of corn.

This is a joint-production model. Land being permanently durable, our 5 of labour and 1 of land can be thought of as producing along with 1 of corn also 1 of land itself. Etc.

Now we must ask whether the terms of trade between corn and cloth are the same when property owners want to consume those goods in 100-to-1 proportions as in 1-to-100 proportions. The answer is strongly in the negative. It is no defence of error to say that the example violates Sraffa's frequent restriction to equality between the number of goods (three for corn, cloth and land) and the number of processes used (three or two depending upon the exact composition of final demands). On some pages of Sraffa (1960, Part II), moreover, that restriction would be self-contradictory.

A less obvious, and therefore more telling example of the narrowness of Part II's treatment of joint production is the following case: 1 of labour and 1 of corn produces 3 of wool and 1 of mutton; alternatively, 1 of labour and 1 of corn can produce 1 of wool and 3 of mutton. 1 of labour and 1/10 of corn produces 1 of corn. (Remark: instead of wool and mutton, the example can be made to involve machines and raw materials.) Sraffa observes a system in being, with three goods being produced by the three feasible processes: the terms of trade twixt mutton and wool, we see from symmetry without boring calculation, is 1-to-1 when final demands for wool and mutton are in exact balance.

Now shift final demand towards a bit more of wool and a bit less of mutton. What happens to P_{wool}/P_{mutton}? Nothing. It remains at 1/1. Eatwell and Panico are apparently (in *this* case) right? No. Only along a facet of *limited* quantitative magnitude does Sraffa contrive a horizontal, so-called *classical* supply curve ss'. Let the final demand for wool move to more than three times the final demand for mutton and the system will *endogenously* cease to use the process that produces relatively much of mutton. Sraffa *endogenously* loses the quality of number of goods and number of processes he provisionally specified initially.

What causes the loss? Shifts in composition of demand, the influence Eatwell and Panico thought to deny.[2]

Can counsel for Sraffa and Eatwell and Panico not find a joint-production case in which demand shifts are powerless to alter cost ratios? Yes, I can contrive a weak jointness case in which a generalization of the no-joint-product 1949 non-substitution theorem does obtain. Let the number of goods and feasible processes by specified as equal (already an arbitrary narrowing of reality). Denote by $[a_{ij}]$ the usual *input* coefficient matrix, in this case specified to be positive and square and obeying familiar Hawkins–Simon conditions for being 'productive'. Write the von Neumann *output* coefficient matrix as $[b_{ij}]$, also square and positive in this case.

Now restrict the $[b_{ij}]$ coefficients by requiring that the off-diagonal coefficients all be 'near' to zero; restrict the diagonal terms so that they are all near to the same positive constant, which might as well be unity. In effect, I am saving the day by weakening the degree of jointness of production as near to the vanishing point as will save the face of the argument.

In this contrived case of *diagonal dominance*, the following inverse matrix exists and has all positive coefficients: $[b_{ij} - a_{ij}]^{-1} = [A_{ij}]$. Then, provided the interest rate is sufficiently near to zero, we can be sure that no shift in (positive) *final* demands can induce a shift out of Sraffa's initial regimen of real individual goods costs calculable *from technology alone*.

[2] Some continental mathematicians contemplate models in which my two processes are replaced by N processes for wool-or-mutton production: thus, add to $(3, 1)$ and $(1, 3)$ the new processes $(3/4, 25/8)$ and $(1/2, 26/8)$. Begin say with balanced final demand, so that both $(3, 1)$ and $(1, 3)$ are initially used equally. 'See,' they say, 'Sraffa has two goods (wool and mutton) and two processes used. After Samuelson alters final demand considerably toward wool, he may induce a competitive shift in the use of processes so that $(1, 3)$ and $(3/4, 25/8)$ are solely used: *still*, equality of number of goods and processes is *generically* implied; $2 = 2$. So it goes when the yen for wool goes up further. Sraffa is vindicated.' No. Only the face of the argument is saved. And saved but temporarily. Already demand shifts do *endogenously* shift terms of trade – in negation of 'classical' constancy. Furthermore, with the number of von Neumann activities specified to be finite, for large enough specified taste changes, eventually $2 = 2$ is replaced by $2 > 1$. Furthermore, suppose we choose to measure what is 'generic' by a metric that (say) asks what happens when all people choose to spend the fraction of income c on wool and $(1 - c)$ on mutton. Then the borderline point at which one of the processes begins to be substituted for another does not correspond to an interval that is of mathematical measure zero. So, after all, $2 > 1$ is *not ungeneric* looked at in this possible and relevant way!

The example is beautifully contrived to show how limited, not how universal, the costs alone approach to economics must be. (Added in light of Schefold's Comment: There are also cases where $[b - a]^{-1}$ is positive even though b is not diagonally dominant for any choice of units.)

10   The irrelevance of Sraffa's 'standard commodity'

Most sceptics of the microeconomics dominant from Smith and Walras to Debreu (1959) and von Neumann (1935–6), understandably, are not virtuosi of matrix inequalities. It is therefore a natural comfort to them to be told that Sraffa (1960) establishes the concept of a *standard* (or reference) basket of commodities. This helps legitimize Ricardo's hankerings for a labour theory of value, and illuminates Marx's parable concerning how competition exploits workers by making each of them work A hours of the day for themselves and B hours for the capitalists, with the B/A *rate of surplus value* (*Mehrwert*) somehow 'revealing' the source of profit and its laws of motion under capitalism.

Alas, this too is blue smoke. No substantive deficiency of the labour theory of value is ameliorated by the *standard* commodity concept pioneered in Sraffa (1960). Eatwell and Panico (1987, p. 450) advance no bold claim for the *standard* commodity, admitting its use is redundant once market competition has established the simultaneous equations of equilibrium, conceding that the concept may be too complex, but concluding lamely that 'It has the virtue, however, of being analytically correct'. The 'it' that is correct is not an existent 'revealer' or 'clarifier'. What is correct is only that a square, non-negative indecomposable matrix possesses a unique right-hand characteristic vector whose elements can be used as weights to form a market basket of goods, in terms of which there is defined a (*post factum*) real wage that has a linear trade-off with the profit rate over any interval of the latter where the matrix in question provides the competitively viable technology for a no-joint-product system. No word in this last sentence is omittable. And from that valid sentence no comfort for the labour theory of value can be gleaned – as I shall demonstrate.

Eatwell (1987) pens a separate *Palgrave* item on the *standard* commodity, calling it an illustrating and clarifying ancillary device, a *Hilfskonstruktion*. My exposition will explicate why I think it can as aptly be called a *roter* herring.

Now to spell out why the concept of the standard commodity is useless to ameliorate the faults of a labour theory of value or to reveal the essence of labour exploitation. The labour theory of value, let it be agreed, is faultless when profits and land scarcity are ignorable. Smith knew that and was too shrewd to try to explain labour exploitation by a model whose correctness comes only when there is no exploitation.

The faults of the labour theory of value include the following:

A. *A change in the composition of demand, towards or away from 'relatively labour–land intensive' goods, in real life alters goods' relative prices.* (Sraffa's failure to single this out for notice is inexplicable: his own 1960 Chapter 8 negates his acceptance of Ricardo's belief that the complications of land rent for relative price can be finessed by concentrating on goods produced at the external margin of no-rent land. Where that margin falls is affected *endogenously* by the composition of demand – as many of Ricardo's own paragraphs reveal.)

Even in the Santa Claus case where Sraffa can define a single standard commodity, this fault of the labour theory is *not in the least bit* touched by any use of the standard commodity, QED.

B. The 1867 labour theory of value (cum exploitative mark-ups proportional to wages) fails to analyse how the distribution of income – the relative fractional shares of wages, rents, interest – is dependent on the *composition* of demand. Even when all lands are redundant and all rents are zero, and when the profit rate and the subsistence wage vector are somehow frozen, a shift in the composition of capitalists' demands can be expected to alter the profit/wages distributive share. The *standard* commodity is powerless to paper over all these shortcomings. (One exception: in the singular case of equal organic compositions of capital, all price ratios of goods *happen* to agree with ratios of embodied labour contents; relative factor shares *happen* to be invariant to demand shifts; the rate of surplus value *happens* then to be uniform over industries as a consequence of the empirical uniformity of the profit rate; but, on this razor's edge, the transformation problem evaporates and no scientific novelty is introduced by the *Mehrwert* treatment of surplus. Remark: impeccable Sraffa–Leontief steady-state analyses with the interest rate somehow specified *also* underemphasize the role that *supply* of capital goods can play in determining factors' distributive shares.)

C. To determine which technical innovations will be competitively viable, the labour theory of value and the 1867 Marxian paradigm of equalized rates of surplus value provide incorrect policy advice and incorrect predictions. After innovation there are definable as many *different* standard commodities as there are square sub-matrices viably choosable from a rectangular matrix. Now, generally, *the system* has no standard commodity: if the concept were able to help Ricardo's defective labour theory – which it cannot do – it would be helpful only in the unrealistic case where at *all* rates the *same* indecomposable set of techniques were competitively viable. Eatwell's *Palgrave* article on the standard commodity (Eatwell,

1987) needs to be augmented by demonstration of how *limited* the economic domain is in which a *standard* commodity can be defined.

Thus joint-product systems generally do *not* possess a *standard* commodity. Neither do systems that have any viable technologies different from their golden rule zero-interest-rate technology. Nor do simple Ricardo systems that are decomposable (labour hunts deer and labour hunts beaver). If a defence of the labour theory were a valid one, how could it self-destruct when certain input coefficients change from epsilon to zero or when certain characteristic vectors become complex numbers? The *standard* commodity is thus seen to be no saviour of a defective labour theory of value. QED.

To prove my various QED's, the reader need only contemplate one example. 1/10 of wheat and 1 of labour (or it could be 1 of land) produce 1 of wheat. 1 of wheat and 1 of labour produce 1 of bread. We need no matrix algebra to identify Sraffa's *standard* commodity as a basket containing only wheat. Every defect in the labour theory of value remains and cannot be erased by any use of the standard concept. The importance of the concept is especially evident in the plausible case where the subsistence wage involves bread, which is not even in Sraffa's market basket!

For later reference, the reader may contemplate an invention that can produce 1 of bread out of 1/6 of labour, 1/2 of bread, and 1 of wheat. The labour theory of value cannot tell us, what is true, namely that only at interest rates below a critical one will this invention be a viable one. Soon I shall show that this non-esoteric situation refutes the Ricardo–Stigler contention that the defective labour theory of value is 'at least 93 per cent accurate'.

D. Present-day sophisticated defenders of Marx's paradigms of the labour theory of value *à la* equalized rates of surplus value admit that the 1867 result differs substantively from competitive reality. But they hope to make the case that, somehow, Marx's approximation yields deep *macro*economic insights and 'understanding'. A patient audit of every different such claim, I and members of my MIT seminars have found, leads only to disappointment. Here is but one sample, a famous case in the post-1867 literature.

Marx refers often to an alleged 'law of the falling rate of profit'. Abstractly put, his attempted *deduction* of this law involves the following factorization of the rate of profit

$$r = \text{total profits/total capital}$$

$$= (\text{profits/wages}) \, (\text{wages/total capital}) = A \times B$$

where total capital is the sum of wages advanced plus non-labour items of capital (called 'constant capital'). The thoughtful reader will note that, if this approach is fruitful, it certainly does not presuppose the validity of the odd 1867 hypothesis that labour-intensive industries have the same (profits/wage) ratio that other industries do. The purpose of rehashing this ancient issue here is to show how Sraffa's 1960 paradigm brings into doubt the fruitfulness of Marx's factorization.

Marx's key notion is that modern times usher in a 'rise in the organic composition of capital', which is interpretable as a decline in the second factor of wages/(wages + constant capital), B. Then, provided we can presume that the first factor of 'exploitation' – profits/wages or A – stays the same, we can deduce that the product – the rate of profit – of the two factors falls.

Let us test the cogency of the crucial *ceteris paribus* clause that Marx invokes almost without realizing what is involved. Sraffian analysis will be our measuring rod. Different cases need analysing.

(i) The class struggle raises the wage rate in a fixed-coefficient Sraffa model that lacks land and joint products. In terms of Sraffa's input/output matrix a and his row vector of direct labour requirements $a_0 = [a_{01}, \ldots, a_{0n}] = [a_{0j}]$, Marx's factorization involves a monstrously complicated and ambiguous expression. For this thought experiment, as the rate of profit falls from its Sraffian maximum to zero, the factor A does not stay constant in the fashion Marx needs but rather falls monotonically!

(ii) Suppose the interest rate r is falling because of some possible 'deepening of capital' in the Clark–Solow fashion. Should Marx be given credit for an 1867 anticipation and proof of this process and its effects on the profit rate?

Hardly. Only along the singular Cobb–Douglas razor's edge does his fixed A, falling B story apply. For the case where the elasticity of substitution is greater than unity, Marx's A rises as B falls; for the more realistic case where the elasticity of substitution is fractional, Marx's A falls.

(iii) The case of exogenous technical changes is what Marx and most of us think is the most interesting one. By 1867 unsophisticated observers formed the strong impression that innovation and scientific advance had somehow enlarged the role of non-labour inputs relative to direct labour. An enhanced organic composition of capital due to technical change seemed the natural way to describe this – a greater role for dead labour at the expense of live labour would be the Pickwickian Marxian description of this. (Paradoxically, one of Sraffa's greatest contributions was to demonstrate that it is, in general, *not* possible to associate lower interest rates with 'more roundabout', 'more mechanized', more time-consuming modes of production, a finding as fatal to neoclassical parables as to the notion of recognizable shifts in 'the organic composition of capital'.)

Students of von Neumann, Sraffa and Solow know that technical change can either *raise* competitive profits rates or raise real wage rates (or raise both). No law of the (necessarily) declining rate of profit is factually or deductively true. Even empirical presumptions have not been justified by knowledge of economic history.

The remarkable increase in the system's 'productivity' after the industrial revolution can take place with what Marx calls the organic composition of capital falling rather than rising. Sraffa has taught us to recognize 'Wicksell effects', which can be purely pecuniary effects masquerading as technical changes. Exactly the same thing can be said of 'Marx effects', $C/(C + V)$ changes that occur with the same *technical* coefficients at different profit rates.

Above all, the factorization $A \times B$ kept Marx in darkness about the Sraffa–Samuelson truth concerning a competitive economy sans land and joint products: if the profit rate falls, the real wage cannot fall and create worker immiseration; if the real wage falls for *any* reason, the competitive profit rate must rise. Similar truths concerning the real wage and the 1867 rate of surplus value *cannot* be asserted for a competitive economy.

11   Hollow victory of standard commodity for the transformation problem

Suppose by singular chance that the subsistence goods vector, which each worker's real wage must be able to buy if the labour supply is to be in stationary equilibrium, involves the various goods in exactly the same proportions as are involved in the standard commodity market basket – a monstrous assumption; and suppose that by singular chance all non-workers choose to consume goods in those same proportions. Or, alternatively, assume that by fortuitous cancellation the deviation of workers' subsistence from the standard vector happens to be just opposite in sign and of exactly the same magnitude as the deviation of the capitalists' consumption vector from the standard vector; in consequence their sum, the total consumption vector, is to be exactly proportionate to the standard commodity.

In this admittedly academic case, not expected remotely to be encountered in any real-life situation, we can draw up for Marx a tableau of steady reproduction expressed in correct prices of production terms. Presumably, he could draw up for himself an alternative tableau expressed in his 1867–85 marked-up values, obeying his usual Volume

II conditions of equalized *rates of surplus value (Mehrwert)* and *eschewing any explicit* rate(s) of profit.

To *his* values tableau, Marx could in this specially contrived case apply *his* proposed 1894 Volume III algorithm for the transformation problem. The resulting new tableau – known by us and by him generally *not* to be quite the desired correct tableau expressing the true competitive prices data – happens (in our singular case where the physical consumption vector is exactly proportional to Sraffa's existent standard commodity) to match exactly the correct Smith–Walras–Dmitriev–Bortkiewicz–Seton–Sraffa competitive prices tableau. (Newman, Meek, Burmeister and others have provided proof of this essentially matrix theorem, as described in Eatwell, 1987, pp. 478–80, and mentioned in the *Palgrave* article on the transformation problem – Hunt and Glick, 1987, p. 689 – in connection with the 1972 work of Alfredo Medio.)

This singularity-case defence of Marx is generally recognized to be a hollow defence, belonging to the category of argument: 'If my Aunt Sally had wheels she'd be a stage coach but generally, like most aunts, she's only a biped.'

Equally hollow is Marx's suggested device of concentrating on that particular good whose organic composition happens to be precisely that of the whole system. How does one recognize which of the vast array of industries is at (or really near to, and *stays* near to) the social average? And why think that *its* organic composition ratio is measured in Marxian values, c_j/v_j, rather than C_j/V_j whose capital letters denote the (as yet) unknown cum-profit *prices* magnitudes.

12   Perhaps unintended Sraffian insights concerning Ricardo and Marx: Ricardo

Most admirers of Sraffa, one discovers, believe that his 1960 classic (a) lends comfort to a Ricardian labour theory of value, and (b) provides a measure of justification for Marx's surplus value novelties of 1867. I believe that a careful reading of *Production of Commodities by Means of Commodities* and sympathetic mathematical extensions of it and of von Neumann's general equilibrium activity model leads to the reverse.

(a) Sraffian analysis confirms that Ricardo's model, shorn of all gratuitous approximations, has to be a three-component model of value: along with the well-understood labour component, there is the subtle interest-rate component and also the land-requirement component. The lost-Atlantis model of 1815

Ricardo, beloved by Kaldor, Sraffa and Garegnani (1987), bears out this contention of mine.

(b) Had the author chosen to apply himself, not only to a critique of 'the marginal theory of value and distribution', but also to a critique of Marx's paradigm of an equalized rate of surplus value by industries (*Mehrwert*), Sraffa's analysis could provide a sharp Occam's razor of demolition.

If my contentions are demonstrable, why the popular beliefs to the contrary? I abstain from attempting an explanation. However, at least two contributing factors can be identified. Piero Sraffa himself wrote in approval of aspects of Ricardo and Marx that are deemed dubious by mainstream historians of economic thought who write in the vein of what I call the Whig history of science (Samuelson, 1987b). A second factor is that Sraffa was critical of neoclassical marginalism and many of his readers were led by that to discern merit in classicism and in the Marxian alternative to mainstream economics.

This present revisionist exposition concerning Sraffa eschews all defence of neoclassicism and intends to couch its every basic argument in terms of von Neumann's discrete activities technology. In this I resemble such post-Marxians as Ian Steedman and John Roemer (and, for that matter, Joan Robinson).

Leaving to the next section what is entailed for the Marxian transformation problem by Sraffa (1960), let me here use my scarce time to explicate the failure of Stigler's defence of Ricardo's so-called *93 per cent labour theory of value*.

Stigler (1958) himself agrees with me that Ricardo knew he had to augment the labour component by an interest component to be generally accurate. (For the 1958 date, Stigler is remarkably tolerant toward Ricardo's belief that he could somehow exclude a rent component.) But he quotes Ricardo's numerical example (Ricardo, [1817–21] 1951, p. 36) of goods that differ in their time-roundaboutness, and accepts uncritically Ricardo's inference from the example that the price ratio of two goods could be affected by a feasible change in the interest rate and the wage rate that 'could not exceed 6 or 7 per cent'.

Two years later, after Stigler could have read Sraffa (1960), he could discover that we can pick for Ricardo a non-bizarre numerical example in which a change in the profit rate from 6 per cent to 6.1 per cent could easily alter P_2/P_1 from 1.0 to 10^6 or to 10^{-6}. Moreover, in Sraffa input/output matrices that look entirely plausible, as the interest drops from its von Neumann maximum to zero, a similar price ratio can oscillate by 70 per cent almost as well as by 7 per cent. Ricardo escaped noticing this because his examples are 'Austrian' rather than 'Leontief'. As soon as outputs require other goods and themselves as inputs, the inverse matrices can become very ill-conditioned indeed.

Here is a horrendous example intended to frighten innocent children. To produce coal 1 period from now takes 1 of labour. To produce 1 of rye takes 9/10 of rye and 1/100 of labour. To produce 1 of corn takes 1/10 of corn and 1 of labour. Ricardo observes a profit rate of 10 per cent per period. Now, for some reason the profit rate rises to 11.1 per cent, surely not a fantastic change. Let Ricardo and Stigler calculate how P_{rye}/P_{corn} rises from unity to 100. Shall we coin for Ricardo a belief in a 1 per cent theory of value? (And what does the other 99 per cent refer to?)

Here is the 1815 lost-Atlantis corn-to-corn model attributed to Ricardo. 1 of corn a period from now requires 1/10 of corn, N of labour, $1/N$ of land, where N can be any of 1, 2, ..., 10, 1/2, 1/4. Cloth requires 1 of labour and 1 of corn. When Garegnani (1987) and I calculate its behaviour under various assumptions about the supply of land, the subsistence wage vector, the capitalists' rates of time preference and/or saving propensities, and when we vary the compositions of capitalists' consumption demands, we see that the resulting behaviour are inconsistent with any Marxian or Ricardian labour theories of distribution. Its price ratios alter with composition of demand as in Walras and Debreu and Solow. Indeed, it behaves like 1960 Sraffa, which is my point about it *and* about Sraffa's system.

13 How Sraffian analysis debunks proposed Marxian transformation problem solutions

Trojan horses within the Marxian camp are those who get right the economics of competitive price: namely, John Roemer and Ian Steedman, along with Piero Sraffa and Ladislaus von Bortkiewicz. They not only spot what is erroneous in Marx's transformation treatment (Marx, 1894, ch. 9) but perceive that the correct prices solution is achievable only by solving the high-degree Sraffian equations (a 15th degree polynomial if the system consists of fifteen Sraffian *basic* goods, etc.). This establishes the fundamental futility theorem: first solving the 1867 values tableau problem involving an irrelevant inversion of a 15-by-15 zero-profit matrix, and then solving a 1st degree subsistence wage equation, gets you *nowhere* on your search for correct competitive profit rate and correct real-price and price-wage ratios. When I played the role of the Hans Christian Andersen child (Samuelson, 1970, 1971a) and pointed out that the Emperor wore no clothes – showing that from Dmitriev and Bortkiewicz, through Sweezy, Winternitz, Dobb, Meek, Seton, and the rest, the transformation algorithm from 'values' to 'prices' was an 'erase and replace' procedure – no perceptible dent was made on the stable of *Palgrave* writers on kindred topics.

What I call a 'detour' Garegnani (1987, p. 567) calls a 'mistake' by Marx. Garegnani believes that the mistake was a fruitful one because it led Marx (almost) to a correct Sraffian theory of competitive price. Whether this theory of genesis of progress is accepted or rejected, one erases a recognized mistake and desists from perpetuating it.

Lack of time prevents me from applying Occam's razor to various 'new solutions' to the transformation problem – such as that of Duménil, Foley and Lipietz covered in Hunt and Glick (1987, p. 690) or that of Wolff, Roberts and Callari (1982). One puts to them the question 'Cui bono?', and hopes for a better answer than a quotation from Marx of possible relevance. The search for values tableaux that agree in various scalar totals with prices of production tableaux is a sterile search, as Seton (1957) long ago made clear.

14   The non-optimality of unequalized profit rates

Although Sraffa does not investigate the problems of *intertemporal efficiency*, his specification of equalized profit rates – as against, for example, equalized 1867 *Mehrwert* rates – can be shown to be a requirement of intertemporal Pareto optimality under capitalism or socialism. If Nobel Laureate Kantorovich were alive today in the age of Gorbachev, his mathematical proofs of this post-Marxian truth would receive the attention they have always deserved. Any critique of 'marginalism' should not blind us to such truths: that would be a case of throwing out the adult along with the bathwater.

15   Autonomy of truth

The ideas of a great mind transcend their creator. I cannot honestly affirm that Piero Sraffa would happily accept my revisionist findings concerning his brain-children. But why should I sell short the subtlety and flexibility of that noble economist?

Editorial note

Professor Samuelson had been unable to attend the conference but on later request kindly submitted a paper which arrived when the manuscript of the book was going to the press. The paper therefore could not be discussed by all the participants at the conference. The two main Comments and the Reply

here offered all had to be written at short notice. The editors are grateful to
John Eatwell for agreeing to submit an additional short Comment although it
had to be submitted within less than three weeks because of difficulties in communication on the one hand, and commitments to the publisher on the other. It
is hoped that the issues will be taken up in a broader discussion in other
publications.

Comment

John Eatwell

CAMBRIDGE

Having had very little time for the preparation of this Comment, I must
confine myself to answering Professor Samuelson's specific criticisms of
the articles by Carlo Panico and me (Eatwell and Panico, 1987; Eatwell,
1987), leaving comment on his wider excursions to another occasion.[1]

I will deal first with Samuelson's reference to an 'explicit utterance
of untruth' by Eatwell and Panico concerning the effects, in joint-
production models, of changes in the composition of output. Second,
I will examine his criticism of the Eatwell and Panico discussion of
Sraffa's 1926 critique of Marshallian partial equilibrium. Third, I will
turn to Samuelson's comments on my *Palgrave* entry on the standard
commodity.

Prices and demand

Samuelson refers repeatedly to the Eatwell–Panico 'error'. The error is
our supposed contention that 'the influence of demand composition on
relative prices is absent in Part II [of Sraffa's *Production of Commodities*]
in the same way that it can be absent from Part I's model involving
labour as the sole factor of production and no jointness of production'
(p. 33).

Samuelson cites, as evidence of our error, a single sentence. If this
sentence is restored to the passage from which it has been extracted, it

---

[1] The short time-span available for this comment precluded consultation with Carlo Panico;
hence he is not responsible for my remarks.

will be seen that our argument is totally different from that which Samuelson represents it to be. To avoid ambiguity it is worth quoting our argument in full:

Considerable puzzlement was engendered by Sraffa's statement in the Preface of his book that 'The investigation is concerned exclusively with such properties of an economic system as do not depend on changes in the scale of production...' (Sraffa, 1960, p. v). The absence of any reference to demand led unsuspecting readers to equate his results with the non-substitution theorem, and hence with the assumption of constant returns to scale. However, a careful reading of Sraffa's analysis reveals that no knowledge of any relationship between *changes* in outputs and *changes* in inputs, or between price and quantity is *necessary* for the solution of equations, and hence for the determination of the rate of profit and prices (given the wage). This contrasts with neoclassical theory, in which the determination of prices is dependent upon knowledge of the functional relationships between supply and demand. *If, in Sraffa's analysis, quantities should change, then any consequential change in conditions of production will result in changes in prices.*

In Part II of his book, Sraffa extends his analysis to multi-product industries and fixed capital, and to the analysis of economies with more than one non-reproducible input. As might be expected, the analysis is considerably more complex, and in some cases the results less clearcut (the solution of the system may not, for example, be unique, and the definition of basics and non-basics is more abstract than is the case with single-product industries). Yet the basic structure of classical analysis is preserved – the prices, the rate of profit, and other distributive variables (say, land rents) are determined by the conditions of production, given the wage. (Eatwell and Panico, 1987, pp. 450–1)

The final sentence of the first paragraph (emphasized here) was apparently overlooked by Samuelson. Perhaps we should have repeated it after the second paragraph too – it is the final sentence of that paragraph that he cites but does not quote. If he had quoted it, it would be evident to the reader that nowhere in that sentence is here any reference to the 'horizontal, so-called classical supply curve' or to the 'costs-alone approach' which Samuelson attempts to foist on us.

In Sraffa's analysis, any change in the composition of output that leads to a change in the conditions of production, for whatever reason, will change relative prices. There is no 'costs-alone approach'.

Sraffa's critique of the Marshallian supply curve

Samuelson argues that Sraffa's critique of the use of diminishing returns in the construction of the partial equilibrium supply curve is flawed, and that Panico and I replicate the flaws without comment. I will not deal with Samuelson's example which, interestingly, fulfils exactly the conditions Sraffa laid down for the construction of a partial equilibrium industry supply curve.

Samuelson does not seem to have grasped that Sraffa's critique is exclusively directed at *partial equilibrium* analysis. Producing general equilibrium examples as a critique of Sraffa is an exercise in irrelevance. Moreover, Samuelson fails to take account of Sraffa's own reference to general equilibrium analysis in the 1926 paper. Panico and I make these points (1987, p. 448):

Apart from his contribution in the *Economic Journal* symposium on increasing returns, Sraffa did not participate further in the debate on the Marshallian theory of cost. The reasons are not hard to seek.

First, imperfect competition theory, instead of providing a new, more concrete approach to the analysis of value and distribution, was simply absorbed into neoclassical theory. The fact that imperfectly competitive models do not provide a foundation for a theory of value seemed to enhance the status of partial equilibrium analysis, rather than hasten its rejection; with the competitive theory of value still holding sway at the level of general equilibrium (a neat rationale is provided by Hicks, 1946, pp. 83–4). The survival of the 'U' shaped cost curve as an analytical tool, constructed from the presumption of increasing, then diminishing returns, is in no small part attributable to the longevity provided by models of the imperfectly competitive firm. Nonetheless, the appearance of the 'U' shaped curve in models of the competitive firm, more than sixty years after Sraffa clearly demonstrated the illegitimacy of the construction, is an indication of just how intellectually disreputable theoretical economics can be.

Second, Sraffa's implicit identification of classical and Marxian theory with the notion that competitive value is 'dependent on the cost of production' is clearly wrong, as examination of neoclassical models which take account of 'simultaneous equilibrium in numerous industries' readily demonstrates. Sraffa had deployed general equilibrium reasoning to demolish the theory of the competitive firm and the industry supply curve. Further criticism of neoclassical theory would require consideration of general equilibrium models of value and distribution. And a constructive rehabilitation of classical theory would require a general analysis too. It would require, that is, an analysis of 'the process of diffusion of profits throughout the various stages of production and of the process of forming a normal level of profits throughout all the industries of a country' – the problem Sraffa acknowledged was 'beyond the scope of this article'. ([1926] 1953, p. 197)

An example of dubious use of the 'U'-shaped cost curve may be found in Samuelson and Nordhaus (1985, p. 479), together with the discussion of 'long-run breakeven conditions' on p. 480. A more accurate discussion of equilibrium of the competitive firm may be found in Samuelson (1947, pp. 75–80).

The standard commodity

Samuelson criticizes my reference (Eatwell, 1987, p. 476) to the standard commodity as a *Hilfskonstruktion*, i.e. a mathematical technique that aids understanding, that clarifies. He then proceeds to 'spell out why the concept of the standard commodity is useless to ameliorate the faults of the labour theory of value or to reveal the essence of labour exploitation' (p. 36). Since neither the labour theory of value nor exploitation are mentioned in my article at all, it is difficult for me to comment on Samuelson's construction.

Whether use of the physical analogue implicit in the standard commodity clarifies the determination of the rate of profit by the simultaneous solution of n equations in a classical system is, I suppose, a matter of taste. But Samuelson's hostility toward the construction of a *Hilfskonstruktion* is a little odd, when his textbook (Samuelson and Nordhaus, 1985) is littered with simple supply and demand diagrams, which he must know are, in a general equilibrium setting, typically false representations of the characteristics of a market. Why doesn't he draw correspondences? Perhaps they would not 'clarify' the argument?

Conclusion

In his introduction, Samuelson refers to 'ideological jockeyings' within our profession.

Ideological messages are often conveyed by a careful use of language. Hence Panico and I do not simply err, we 'quote without blushing', and indulge in 'explicit utterance of untruth'.

Another powerful ideological device is to remove sentences from their context, to misrepresent arguments, or to erect straw men. Samuelson's paper provides examples of all three of these techniques.

Comment

Pierangelo Garegnani

ROME

1. Professor Samuelson's contribution to the present volume is an excellent example of the difficulty that a present-day theoretical economist has

in understanding Sraffa's theoretical enterprise. The theoretical approach of Smith and Ricardo had been so totally 'submerged' (Sraffa, 1960, p. v) – as opposed to criticized and found wanting – that its reappearance in Sraffa's terse lines of his introduction to Ricardo's *Works* (Sraffa, 1951), and in the rigorous modern presentation of *Production of Commodities* (Sraffa, 1960), was bound to raise considerable difficulties of comprehension. And the fact that the approach adopted by Sraffa had been developing for over a century before Ricardo raises, if anything, additional difficulties. The analysis reappears as a comparatively finished product while the process of its development, which is important to its understanding, has been forgotten or goes unrecognized. Ironically, the difficulties would have been less in the case of a completely new theoretical departure, the germs of which would lie in a literature generally known and understood.

Questions of deadlines will prevent me from going as much as I would like into the issues that Professor Samuelson touches with respect both to pure analysis and to interpretation of the classical economists.

1   The '1926 error'

2. In his section on 'the fatal 1926 error', Samuelson attributes to Sraffa's *Economic Journal* article of that date the idea that 'the category of *constant* competitive cost constitutes the only empirical box with appreciable content', and comments:

> This is plain wrong... as soon as two competitive goods involve different land/ labour proportions, the *production possibility* frontier is curved and not straight in the fashion Sraffa needs. (p. 32)

The idea that Samuelson attributes here to Sraffa is not however the one we find in the article of 1926. There is a subtle but all-important difference. Sraffa's argument was not that the category of constant competitive cost constitutes the only box with empirical content. It was that *among the boxes that the conditions of partial equilibrium allow us to consider*,[1] constant costs constitutes the only box with some content.

As Sraffa himself clearly states at the conclusion of his argument, in the passage quoted (only partially) in the Eatwell–Panico essay (1987, p. 448) to which Samuelson refers,

---

[1] Sraffa's expression is 'particular equilibrium'. I have here adopted the more generally accepted, if less exact, denomination of 'partial equilibrium'.

In normal cases the cost of production of commodities produced competitively – *as we are not entitled to take into consideration the causes which may make it rise or fall* – must be regarded as constant in respect of small variations in the quantity produced. (Sraffa, [1926] 1953, pp. 540–1; emphasis added)[1a]

and Sraffa leaves little doubt about the fact that decreasing returns would be the typical case in a general equilibrium context.[2]

3. Briefly, Sraffa's 1926 argument starts from the fact that

the point of view [of 'particular equilibrium'] assumes that the conditions of production and the demand for a commodity can be considered in respect to small variations as being practically independent both in regard to each other and in relation to the supply and demand of all other commodities. (Sraffa, [1926] 1953, p. 538)

Otherwise, the *ceteris paribus* assumption would be violated and, in the face of a change in supply conditions of the commodity – say, a tax or bounty – we could not assume that the demand will remain fixed or that the converse will be true in the case of a shift in the demand schedule.

Now, with respect to Marshallian decreasing returns (rising long-period costs), Sraffa's argument is that, when they do occur in a particular industry, there will generally be an effect of similar magnitude on the costs of other industries as well (Sraffa, [1926] 1953, p. 539). This leaves only two possibilities: (a) abandoning partial equilibrium when the effect of the increased output of the industry on its own costs cannot be ignored; or (b) assuming constant costs also in the industry in question, when the effect on the costs of the related industries is small enough to be compatible with partial equilibrium.

The first case, Sraffa observes, is the one where the output of the industry requires a *considerable* part of the quantity of the factor 'the total amount of which is fixed, or can be increased only at a more than proportional cost' (Sraffa, [1926] 1953, p. 539). In the language of general equilibrium, this case can be described as one where a large difference exists between the proportions in which the factors are employed in the industry expanding its output and the proportions in which the same factors are employed in the industries that will correspondingly have to

---

[1a] In this Comment the pages given with respect to Sraffa's 1926 paper refer to the original paper and not to its reprint in Stigler and Boulding (1953). H.D.K.

[2] In fact, in a letter to Keynes of 8 June 1926 (quoted in Roncaglia 1978, p. 12), Sraffa explicitly rejects the very interpretation we find in Samuelson's paper: '[my] conclusion has been misunderstood and taken to imply that in actual life constant returns prevail...of course in reality the connection between cost and quantity produced is obvious. It simply cannot be considered by means of the system of particular equilibria for single commodities in a regime of competition devised by Marshall.'

contract their output.[3] In this case the increase in costs cannot be ignored in the expanding industry, but for exactly the same reason it will not be possible to ignore it either in those other industries in which the factors are used in a proportion close to that of the expanding industry. This will contradict the *ceteris paribus* condition of partial equilibrium.

The second case is where an industry employs only a small part of the 'constant factor' or, more generally, where the proportions of factors in the expanding industry are almost the same as in the contracting industries. Here, the effect on the costs of other industries using proportions of factors close to those of the expanding industry will be small, and so will be the effect on the costs of the industry in question. Then, to the extent that the former can be ignored, as is required by partial equilibrium, it must be likewise ignored in the expanding industry, where we shall accordingly have to assume constant long-period costs (Sraffa, [1926] 1953, p. 539).

As Sraffa summed up his argument in 1925:

The substance of the argument rests on the fact that the increase in production of a commodity leads to an increase in the cost both of the commodity itself, and of the other commodities of the group. The variations are of the same order of magnitude, and therefore are to be regarded as being of *equal importance*. Either we take into account these variations for all industries of the group, and we must pas from the consideration of the particular equilibrium of a commodity to that of general equilibrium; or else those variations in all industries are ignored, and the commodity must be considered as produced under constant costs. *What is inadmissible is that the equal effects of a single cause are at the same time considered to be negligible in one case, and of fundamental importance in the other.* However, it is necessary to accept this absurdity if one wishes to give a general, and not an anomalous character, to the supply curve of a product under conditions

---

[3] Here a question arises into which it is not possible to go deeper on this occasion. It was generally accepted at the time that the Marshall *ceteris paribus* assumption implied constant quantities produced of the other commodities (e.g. Barone, 1894, reported in Sanger, 1895; also Ricci, 1933). This raises the question of where the factors required for the increased output of the industry we are studying would come from within a theory where the factors are taken to be fully employed. The reply appears to rest largely on the fact that that increase in output is assumed to be small (as stressed by Marshall and recalled by Sraffa in the passage above), so that the decreases in the output of the other industries that do in fact occur are so small (say, about $1/1000$ of the already small change in the industry concerned if there were about 1,000 industries) that they can be ignored. The condition about the specialized factor 'causing decreasing returns' can then be translated, as we saw in the text, into the now more familiar form of the *different proportions* in which the quantities of factors will generally be employed in the expanding industry when compared with the contracting industries.

of increasing costs. (Sraffa, [1925] 1964, p. 324; translated in Sraffa, [1925] 1973; emphasis added)

There remains only a third possibility with respect to decreasing returns – the one in which the industry in question employs *the whole* of a scarce factor. This, Sraffa tells us, is the only case in which we can consistently consider increasing costs in the context of partial equilibrium – a case, however, of unlikely occurrence, in as much as partial equilibrium requires the industry to be small when compared wit the whole economy (Sraffa, [1926] 1953, pp. 539–40).

Considerations similar to these (which we need not enter here) are developed by Sraffa for the case of increasing returns.

4. It is surprising therefore to read in Samuelson's paper:

Sraffa...by...*implicit* appeal to what is legitimate in...partial equilibrium methodology [minimizes] the cases where alterations in composition of demand alter competitive price ratios. (p. 32; emphasis added)

One is tempted to interpret the word *implicit* in the passage as a misprint: clearly, whatever may be 'implicit' in Sraffa's 1926 article, it is not his appeal to partial equilibrium! However, the misprint interpretation will not do, because Samuelson's argument is in effect based on ignoring that appeal. The 'fatal error of 1926' would in fact exist only if Sraffa had been dealing with the supply schedule in conditions of *general equilibrium*.

No less surprising is the argument with which Samuelson attempts then to take care of Sraffa's 'implicit' appeal to partial equilibrium:

To underline that my criticisms are not captious...I here present an impeccable Marshallian model in which (a) each of *n* goods is produced by transferable labour *and a specialized land specific to itself*...The example glaringly contradicts Sraffa's constancy of costs and obeys all *partial* equilibrium requirements (at the same time that it is a full general equilibrium model, a congruence Alfred Marshall never quite achieved). (p. 32–3; emphasis added)

Rising costs are undoubtedly compatible with partial equilibrium provided each good is produced by a 'land specific to itself', but is that not exactly what Sraffa argues in his third case above?

It is in any case clear that Marshall's partial equilibrium was never meant to deal only, or even chiefly, with cases like the one described by Samuelson (or with a similar one to which Samuelson refers in another article – 1971b, p. 12). Partial equilibrium was meant to be of *general* applicability: it had therefore to be conceived as a sufficient *approximation* to general equilibrium, and *not* as a special case of the latter. (This incidentally explains why Marshall never 'achieved' Samuelson's congruence between partial and general equilibrium; that congruence was the

opposite of what Marshall intended to achieve, as it would have made the
partial equilibrium method useless.[4,5])

5. The fact that we can today so lightly dismiss partial equilibrium in
scholarly articles (though not in elementary textbooks) is perhaps a sign
of the resigned acceptance of the inapplicability of contemporary mainstream pure theory to the concrete problems for which partial equilibrium was designed – it is a sign, that is, of the descent of pure theory
towards 'rhetoric', to use Samuelson's word. That was not yet so in 1926,
when Sraffa concluded the argument I have reported with:

If diminishing returns arising from a 'constant factor' are taken into consideration, it becomes necessary to extend the field of investigation so as to examine the
conditions of simultaneous equilibrium in numerous industries: *a well-known
conception, whose complexity, however, prevents it from bearing fruit, at least in
the present state of our knowledge, which does not permit of even much simpler
schemata being applied to the study of real conditions.* (Sraffa, [1926] 1953, p. 541;
emphasis added)

And in the 1933 *Review of Economic Studies*, Umberto Ricci, a practi-
tioner of general equilibrium who, together with Barone, had accurately
studied the mathematical relations between Marshallian partial equilibrium and Walrasian general equilibrium, would still write in an article
on 'Pareto and pure economics':

But when we have ... paid the tribute due to the authors of one of the most
outstanding creations of human thought, we are compelled to limit the field of
its application. The whole apparatus gives somewhat the impression of a magic
castle, satisfying to the imagination, but of little assistance in solving the housing
problem. In more prosaic language the theory remains abstract and without
grip ... Among the theories of equilibrium enshrined in the formidable apparatus
of the formulae of [Pareto's] *Manuel d'économie politique,* ... there is to be found
no bridge leading to nine-tenths of the problems which economists set themselves ... we can by no means afford to put aside the theory of particular equilibrium as developed by Marshall and his many followers ... Pareto himself, the
most jealous custodian of the theory of general economic equilibrium, the most

---

[4] I have recalled elsewhere (Garegnani, 1987, para. 6, p. 563) Marshall's basic methodological position according to which 'the function of analysis and deduction in economics is
not to forge a few long chains of reasoning ... but to forge rightly many short chains and
single connecting links' (Marshall, 1961, Appendix C).

[5] Indeed, Samuelson himself implies a *general* applicability of partial equilibrium when he
faces the problem of inducing laymen to accept as plausible the modern apparatus of
demand and supply. He does accept there the basis of Sraffa's argumentation: 'other
things equal ... specifically this means that as we change wheat's price, we must not at
the same time change family income, or the price of the competing product or anything
else that would tend to shift the demand schedule for wheat' (Samuelson, 1973, p. 66).

sarcastic belittler of literary economics, the less sarcastic but no less resolute adversary of the theory of particular equilibria, was compelled to forget general equilibrium when he was writing his superb chapters on applied economics. (Ricci, 1933, pp. 20–1)

Today's intertemporal general equilibrium is surely no less of a 'magic castle' than the Walrasian and Paretian general equilibria of 1933.

2   Demand and prices

6. In the article of 1926, Sraffa was in effect still moving largely within the ambit of marginal theory. The classical economists were seen through Marshallian eyes, as assuming horizontal long-period supply functions which allowed them to ignore the effects of demand on prices. This was a misleading picture of classical analysis, as we now know thanks to Sraffa himself. (By that picture, Marshall was in fact attributing to the classical economists an influence of demand on prices *through* distribution and costs, and was therefore taking for granted a demand and supply theory of distribution.)

However, the article needed a follow-up: it had left open the question as to what was to be done beyond that 'first approximation' of constant costs. And the indications given by Sraffa made it difficult to see how further progress could occur *within* the accepted stream of ideas. Thus, decreasing returns, when important enough, were thought to require turning to general equilibrium – but at the same time that conception was ruled out as being 'too complex to bear fruit'.

In fact, the solution toward which Sraffa was feeling his way lay in a direction entirely different from that of Walras and Pareto: it consisted of a re-examination of the theory of distribution, a line absent from the 1926 article.[6] This re-examination and the associated revival of the classical theory of distribution and relative prices is what emerges in (1951) and (1960).

7. It is not therefore surprising that Samuelson, who looks at *Production of Commodities* (1960) in the terms of marginal theory, should see limitations in Sraffa's treatment of the effects of demand on prices. However

---

[6] At the end of the 1926 article Sraffa writes: 'the influence [of a normal level of profits throughout all the industries] on the formation of the prices of single commodities is relatively unimportant and [its] consideration is therefore beyond the scope of this article' (Sraffa, [1926] 1953, p. 550). However, where the problem of distribution indirectly emerges, in connection with the influences of the changed outputs on the prices of factor services, the solution remains the received Marshallian one, based on the equilibrium between demand and supply of factors.

what is in fact there is just a *different* way of dealing with the interaction between prices and outputs.

What is perhaps more surprising is that Samuelson should have expected to find there the demand functions of mainstream theory. Had not the criticism of capital theory been promoted by Sraffa and, in particular, by that very book (1960)?[7] And was not that criticism aimed at the explanation of distribution in terms of demand and supply of factors – as Samuelson himself did not fail to see on some occasions?[8] On the other hand, it will be agreed that the mainstream determination of the prices of commodities by their demand and supply functions is one and the same thing as that theory of distribution. (The Samuelson whom we have just seen insisting on increasing costs for commodities – the direct expression of a demand and supply equilibrium in the market for factors – is certainly well aware of this.) It would therefore seem reasonable to expect Sraffa's criticism of the traditional concept of capital (1960) to be accompanied by some different treatment of the interaction between outputs and prices.

8. In my contribution to this volume [the reference is to Chapter 5 in Bharadwaj and Schefold (1990)], I have in fact attempted to clarify how outputs can influence prices in the context of the theories of the classical economists and Sraffa. I have there pointed out how the principal mechanisms by which outputs influence prices in marginal theory –

---

[7] The first expression of this criticism to appear in print was Joan Robinson's (1953–4); regarding the derivation of that criticism from Sraffa's work, see Robinson (1973), pp. 144–5.

[8] For example, with reference to 'reswitching' and 'reverse capital deepening', Samuelson wrote: 'Such perverse effects do have consequences...stability and uniqueness problems may be raised for a Solow–Harrod growth model' (Samuelson, 1966b, p. 578), where the model in question, taken in its basic building block affected by these 'perverse' effects, is simply the long-period equilibrium of marginal theory. I cannot enter here into the question of how this criticism also affects, besides that long-period equilibrium, the 'temporary' and 'intertemporal' equilibria of contemporary theory. (It would, however, seem intuitively clear that instabilities of the long-period equilibria will show up in the sequence of the short-period 'temporary' or 'intertemporal' equilibria.)

In this connection we may incidentally note how the situation here referred to as 'long-period equilibrium', characterized by a uniform rate of return on the supply prices of capital goods, seems to be taken by Samuelson as equivalent to a 'steady-state analysis' (e.g. p. 37), with which it has in fact little in common (on the difference between the two, and on the origin of the present-day tendential identification of the two, see Garegnani, 1976a, pp. 27, 33n). In fact Samuelson appears to view Sraffa's analysis as a steady-state analysis. However, as I have argued in my Comment on Asimakopulos in this volume [the reference is to Chapter 10 in Bharadwaj and Schefold (1990)], Sraffa's analysis cannot be qualified as relating to an economy stationary or in steady growth, any more than the analyses of Smith, Ricardo and Marx can.

changes in relative outputs giving rise to changes in factor prices and hence in commodity prices – is absent in classical theory. This is because their different theory of the distribution between wages and profits (sketched in section 2 of my paper) allowed them, and Sraffa, to take the real wage (or the rate of profits) as given when determining prices.[9]

In the classical theories, therefore, demand functions and outputs could be conceived to affect prices *only through variable returns to scale and joint production*. However, the introduction of demand functions in those theories meets, among others, the difficulty that the level of individual incomes can no longer be defined by anything like the equilibria of demand and supply for factors. Thus it is difficult to see how commodity demand functions can even be constructed at a general theoretical level.

It appears that, as a result, the outputs will have to be dealt with by the different two-stage procedure which was essentially that of the classical economists (see my paper, par. 31). We determine the effect on prices of the change in our independent variable while taking the outputs as given (p. 130) (or as the independent variable in question). Then, at a second logical stage, we can consider the effects on the outputs of the change in both the prices and the independent variable causing them (say a rise in wages). At that second stage we can also consider, where necessary, the effects of those output changes back on the prices, etc.

9. This is the procedure that is reflected in Sraffa's (1960) treatment of the outputs of the several commodities as data. Instead Samuelson reads there an 'inexplicable' failure to single out that 'a change in the composition of demand, towards or away from relatively labour – land intensive goods, in real life alters goods' relative prices', and he continues:

---

[9] We may note in this respect a passage in Samuelson, p. 33 above, where he refers to Part I of Sraffa (1960) as a 'model involving labour as the sole factor of production' and he implies that this (together with constant returns to scale) is why demand need not be introduced to determine prices there. This is surprising. Produced means of production are obviously present in Part I of Sraffa (1960), and a positive rate of profits (interest) is paid on them. It is therefore a situation that should be described as one in which there are several factors of production, that is, labour and capital, or labour and the several capital goods, or the several 'dated quantities of labour'. However, what Samuelson may mean is that, since a supply of capital goods is not introduced by Sraffa with a determining role, then it is *as if* there were only one scarce factor – labour (see, for example, Samuelson, p. 33 above). If that is what Samuelson means by his 'one-factor' passage, he is incorrect: the 'supply of capital goods' is not present in Sraffa because of the different classical theory of distribution, and not because of any 'underemphasis' of the role of such supply. And the reason why demand does not affect prices is that different theory of distribution, and not any one-factor hypothesis.

[Sraffa's] own 1960 Chapter 8 negates his acceptance of Ricardo's belief that the complications of land rent for relative price can be finessed by concentrating on goods produced at the external margin of no-rent land. Where that margin falls is affected *endogenously* by the composition of demand – as many of Ricardo's own paragraphs reveal. (p. 37)

In fact, Ricardo's idea about how to avoid the complications of land rent is irrelevant. What counts is only the possibility of taking outputs as given. When the position of the marginal land depends on distribution and relative prices, prices can be easily determined once outputs are given – just as they can under Ricardo's simplified hypothesis. What is relevant is whether, as a part of the two-stage classical analysis indicated above, outputs can be taken as given when determining prices, or have instead to be determined simultaneously with prices on the basis of the traditional demand functions.

The same considerations apply to the 'narrowness' Samuelson attributes to Sraffa's treatment of joint production (pp. 33–6). Sraffa has in fact no need for special cases where prices are independent of outputs. He can quite well take care of how prices change with outputs i.e. with the 'effectual demands' of the classical authors. Of course, joint production raises the additional problem of the equality between the number of processes and the number of commodities. This equality is the normal case, as Schefold (1985a) has argued, and would seem clear once we realize, for example, that highly substitutable commodities should be treated as a single commodity in this respect (the price of mutton in the wool–mutton case certainly has much to do with the price of beef, and therefore with its process of production).

3   Standard commodity

10. One of the surprising features of Samuelson's paper is that he seems to view the standard commodity as intended to validate the labour theory of value (p. 36) – and not in the sense that the standard commodity allows one to measure the aggregates of commodities entering the determination of the rate of profits independently of distribution, just as the labour theory of value allowed Ricardo and Marx to do. From Samuelson's argument one might gather that the intended validation is that of the principle that commodities exchange according to the quantity of labour required for their production.

Thus, for example, after showing that relative prices do depend on distribution (the rate of profits), contrary to the labour theory of value, Samuelson concludes:

even...where Sraffa can define a single standard commodity, this fault of the labour theory is *not in the least bit* touched by any use of the standard commodity. (p. 37; similar passage on pp. 38–9 and *passim*)

The obvious reaction to this statement is: how could the standard commodity touch that? Who said the contrary? (Samuelson gives no precise references. One would imagine that any such error, should anybody have made it, could be quickly disposed of by pointing out that the standard commodity can only do what numéraires can do, that is, modify the absolute expression of prices, and above all, the *shape* of key relations like the wage–profits curve (of which more presently), but certainly not alter the ratios in which commodities exchange.[10]

11. I shall therefore confine myself here to what Samuelson has to say on the standard commodity as such, leaving until later his remarks concerning the labour theory of value.

The starting point here must be that the 'standard system' is not there to validate anything in particular. It is there to render 'more transparent' what is valid independently of it, that is, the properties of the system – just what changes of the 'coordinate system' (of which the standard commodity is one particular instance) are generally intended to do in any science.[11] The standard commodity and system do in fact provide an extremely simple expression of the relationship between wages and profits, and any mathematician would be surprised indeed if that expression were not to make the study of that relationship easier and more complete – whether the measurement of wages in terms of the standard commodity were to be the ultimate one, or only an intermediate step in an analysis where wages are ultimately measured in terms of other commodities.[12]

Moreover, as I have argued (Garegnani, 1987, p. 569, and 1984, p. 312), this expression of the relationship between wages and profits can be obtained by means of the simple mental picture of a known physical net product, to be divided between wages and profits, with the rate of profits originating from the proportion that the corresponding physical share of the net products bears to the equally known physical amount of capital.

[10] For the neat criticism of a claim concerning the relations between standard commodity and labour theory of value, advanced in Burmeister (1984), and similar to that by Samuelson I mentioned in the text, see Kurz and Salvadori (1987).

[11] See, for example, Rosenbaum (1963), ch. IV, p. 89. I owe the above observation about the generality and importance in mathematics of the method of changes in the coordinates system to Professor Figá Talamanca of Rome University.

[12] For instance, I personally found it easy to demonstrate by means of the standard commodity that any rate of profits *above* the maximum, the wage and prices cannot all be positive (Garegnani, 1976b, p. 427).

As a result, the mutual dependence between the wage rate and the rate of profits *is seen at a glance*. And Samuelson is undoubtedly aware of how arriving at known conclusions by a more direct and easily comprehensible route has often been of fundamental importance in science. (Some aspects of analytical geometry reflect the need for a visual representation of mathematical relations that could conceivably be treated independently of it, but I doubt Samuelson would think that these aspects of analytical geometry are useless.)

In that same article (1984), I provided some examples of that increased transparency, and correspondingly better grip over the properties of the system. One example in point was the property stated in a non-substitution theorem by Samuelson himself (Samuelson, 1966a). According to this, in a system of single-product industries, once the rate of interest (profits) is given, the real wage also is: a theorem that would have been unnecessary if the conception of the standard system had been known and in current use.

12. We may now proceed to some of the more detailed points raised by Samuelson on the standard commodity.

A. Contrary to what Samuelson holds (pp. 36–8) there appears to be no reason at all why a standard commodity (system) should be said to exist only when the same set of methods of production, one for each commodity (the same 'technique' in the common terminology, or the same 'system of production' in Sraffa's own terminology), is in use over the entire range of possible wage and profits rates (pp. 36–8) – just as there is no reason at all why we should say that Samuelson's 'factor-price frontier' for one particular technique or system of production exists only under such conditions. These theoretical constructs are intended to exhibit some properties of the system of production to which they relate, and this both in the interval (intervals) of r where the system is the most profitable, and where it is not.[13] The latter intervals are of no less theoretical interest than the former – for example, in ascertaining why the system of production in question is dominated by a second one.[14]

B. The fact that the standard commodity does not coincide with the basket of goods that workers will buy (Samuelson, e.g., p. 38) seems to be

[13] Cf. the preceding footnote.

[14] The fact that the straightline wage–profits curve corresponding to the standard commodities of each alternative system cannot be drawn in the same diagram, whereas the wage–profit curves drawn for a wage measured in a common commodity can, seems hardly relevant. What is relevant is the usefulness of the standard commodity for the analysis *of the system it pertains to*.

of little relevance, once the use of that composite commodity is properly understood. It is not only that, owing to Sraffa's treatment of it as dependent variable, the surplus wage can be measured as an abstract value quantity and therefore also in terms of the standard commodity (Sraffa, 1960, p. 33; see also Garegnani, 1984, p. 322). It is above all that the standard commodity and system may be of use even when the wage has ultimately to be measured in a different commodity (just as the treatment of an ellipsis with its centre in the origin of the Cartesian coordinates may be useful for the analysis of an ellipsis in any position whatsoever).

C. Subsistence goods will be present in the standard commodity as soon as we consider the wage variable as consisting only of its surplus element, with workers' subsistence included in the means of production. This takes care of the necessity for an 'indecomposable' matrix of input coefficients, which Professor Samuelson sees as a limitation of the standard commodity (p. 36). In fact what is required is not properly the 'indecomposability' of the matrix, but only that such a matrix should possess an irreducible sub-matrix, corresponding to what are in economic terms a group of 'basic' products (entering, that is, directly or indirectly the production of all other commodities). Now, the treatment of subsistence goods as means of production ensures that they all become 'basic commodities', so long as labour directly or indirectly enters the production of all goods.

D. We may, however, conclude our argument on the standard commodity on a lighter tone, by noting how Samuelson ends up by apparently granting to the standard commodity more than its due. He refers (p. 40) to a single-product industries case where the actual economy coincides with Sraffa's 'standard system'. The rate of profits can there be reckoned as the ratio between the physical profits and the physical capital, both consisting of standard commodity. It can therefore be also reckoned in terms of the quantities of labour embodied in the two aggregates. This would undoubtedly validate Marx's determination of *the rate of profits* in the so-called 'transformation problem'. However, Samuelson goes further and writes:

to *his* values tableau, Marx could in this specially contrived case apply *his* proposed 1894 Volume III algorithm for the transformation problem. The resulting new tableau...happens (in our singular case...) to match exactly the correct Smith–Walras–Dmitriev–Bortkiewicz–Seton–Sraffa competitive prices tableau. (p. 41)

If Samuelson means what he appears to state in the passage, he is not correct; the prices that Marx would obtain by applying the correct rate of profits to the quantities of labour embodied in the variable and constant capitals cannot generally be the correct prices.[15]

4 The labour theory of value

13. We may now proceed to Samuelson's remarks on the labour theory of value. His present views are in all essential respects identical to those he expressed a decade and a half ago during a well-known debate in the *Journal of Economic Literature* (1971–74) on Marx's economic theory. At the close of that debate he had thrown a challenge to anybody to offer evidence that

[Marx's] novel analytical innovations concerning positive equalized rates of surplus value are other than a detour *to one who would understand 19th-century or earlier-century distribution of income* . . . If I am wrong in my answer to this question – which has been *the* number one question among pro- and anti-Marx analysts from 1867 to the present day – presentation of some new and cogent argumentation controverting my contention can dispose of it. (1974a, p. 69; emphasis added)

Elsewhere (Garegnani, 1986), I have pointed out that the basis for such a 'cogent argumentation' had in fact been advanced by Piero Sraffa in his 1951 Introduction to Ricardo's *Principles*.[16] There Sraffa (pp. xxx–xxxvii) gave textual and logical evidence to the effect that Ricardo had

---

[15] This can be immediately seen by assuming that constant capital consists of a commodity (a), say 'steel', and variable capital consists of commodity (b), say 'corn'. The relative price p_a/p_b as correctly determined by estimating the capital in price terms is

$$\frac{p_a}{p_b} = \frac{(1+r)(c_a p_a + v_a p_b)}{(1+r)(c_b p_a + v_b p_b)} = \frac{c_a p_a + v_a p_b}{c_b p_a + v_b p_b} \tag{I}$$

whereas Marx's relative price is

$$\frac{p_a'}{p_b'} = \frac{(1+r)(c_a + v_a)}{(1+r)(c_b + v_b)} = \frac{c_a + v_a}{c_b + v_b} \tag{II}$$

Relations (I) and (II) will therefore give the same result only if

$$\frac{c_a + v_a}{c_b + v_b} = \frac{c_a p_a + v_a p_b}{c_b p_a + v_b p_b}$$

i.e. (after simple transformations), only if $c_a/v_a = c_b/v_b$, that is, only with equal organic composition in the production of the two commodities, in which case of course Marx's rate of profits would have been correct even in an economy not coinciding with the standard system and there would have been no transformation problem to deal with.

[16] It is in fact to this unpublished paper (Garegnani 1986) that Samuelson appears to refer his comments on p. 44, since in Garegnani (1987) there is no reference to Samuelson's 'erase-and-replace' explanation of the transformation problem. (The paper has been published in the meantime; see Garegnani, 1991.)

arrived at the labour theory of value of the *Principles* in order to overcome a central logical error in Adam Smith's *Wealth of Nations*. The
error was that, in many parts of his great work, Adam Smith had failed
to see the constraint that binds the rates of wages, profits and rents and
prevents each such rate from varying without affecting the others.[17] If
that is so, it is of course natural to think, and is in fact borne out by
considerable evidence both textual and logical,[18] that Marx, who placed
that constraint at the centre of his theoretical work, developed Ricardo's
'law of value' for that very same basic analytical purpose (Garegnani,
1987, pp. 567–8; also 1984, pp. 305–9): hardly a 'detour' then.

14. Adam Smith's error emerges when, for example, the real wage is
determined by subsistence requirements, as described in Chapter VIII
of the *Wealth of Nations*, while the rate of profits is left to be determined
(in Chapter IX) by the 'competition' of capitals.[19] This error appears to
be the result of viewing the price of a commodity as somehow capable of
accommodating the change in one of those variables without a necessary
change in some of the others.[20]

Ricardo was able to see through those misleading appearances, at first
by means of the assumption of a corn wage underlying the principle he
used that 'it is the profits of the farmer that regulate the profits of all
other trades' (e.g. Ricardo, 1951–73, VI, p. 104, IV, p. 23) – what
Samuelson calls the '1815 lost-Atlantis model of Ricardo' (see par. 18
below). As Sraffa has argued, that principle had its rational foundation in
the assumption that wages (and therefore, for Ricardo, the entire capital
ultimately used there – see Garegnani, 1984, p. 300) consists entirely of
corn. Then:

in agriculture the same commodity, namely corn, forms both the capital (conceived as composed of the subsistence necessary for the workers) and the product;
so that the determination of profit by the difference between total product and

---

[17] 'When the stocks of many rich merchants are turned into the same trade, their mutual
competition naturally tends to lower its profits, and when there is a ... like increase of
stock in all the different trades carried on in the same society, the same competition must
produce the same effect in them all' (Smith, [1776] 1960, p. 105). The passage begins with
'the increase of stock, which raises wages, tends to lower profit', but, as the context of the
passage shows, the idea is absent that the lowering of the rate of profits is a *logical
implication* of the raising of the wage rate. See also Stigler (1952), p. 203; Hollander
(1973), p. 181.

[18] Some of this evidence is given in Garegnani (1984), p. 309.

[19] Marginalist theorists avoided the error when with Wicksteed (1894) they faced the problem of the so-called 'exhaustion of the product' once each factor is remunerated at its
marginal product.

[20] As Sraffa shows (1951, pp. xxxv–vii), Smith's position was in fact connected with his view
that a rise in wages would raise all prices.

capital advanced, and also the determination of the rate of this profit to the capital, is done directly between quantities of corn without any question of valuation...It follows that if there is to be a uniform rate of profit in all trades it is the exchangeable values of the products of *other* trades relatively to their own capitals (*i.e.* relatively to corn) that must be adjusted so as to yield the same rate of profit as has been established in the growing of corn; since in the latter no value changes can alter the ratio of product to capital, both consisting of the same commodity (Sraffa, 1951, p. xxxi)

If we simplify by assuming that capital consists entirely of wages advanced for a single year, we may see the agricultural rate of profits (and therefore the general rate of profits in the economy) as given by

$$r_A = \frac{P - N}{N} \tag{1}$$

where P is a given amount of corn output and N is the wages (also a quantity of corn) for the quantity of labour required to produce it on the least-fertile land under cultivation (that which yields no rent).[21]

It is then clear that the rate of profits is determined once the real wage (a quantity of corn) is given, since the quantity of labour required to produce the quantity P of corn being given, N will also be given. Smith's 'competition of capitals', is seen to have no influence at all on the rate of profits. Nor can the rate of profits be raised, as Malthus suggested, by an increased demand for commodities from the land-owners. The rate of profits can rise only because of either a reduction in the corn wage or an improvement in the conditions of cultivation of the least fertile land in use.

15. However, it was not long before Malthus pointed out that, once forms of capital other than corn are taken into account, the rate of profits in agriculture must depend on relative prices just as it does in the other sectors. I have dealt elsewhere (Garegnani, 1982, pp. 76–7) with Ricardo's struggle with that problem in the spring of 1815. The conclusion he reached was that exchange of commodities according to the labour required to produce them could be a reasonable assumption from which to begin. To that extent, both the social product P and the necessary consumption N could be taken as known in terms of labour embodied, and the profit rate could then be calculated according to equation (1) above.

Marx inherited this problem and its difficulties from Ricardo. Ricardo had had to assume that, when measured in terms of a commodity requiring

---

[21] The position of this land is of course given together with the output of corn for the reasons I indicated in par. 8 above.

a constant quantity of labour, the value of commodities 'in the production of which no additional quantity of labour is required' remained
constant as the wage (or the difficulty of producing the wage goods)
increased (Ricardo, 1951–73, I, e.g., pp. 100–103). He had, however,
also to admit that the resulting fall in the profit rate would affect the
relative prices of all commodities, and, therefore, also their value relative
to his standard, thus running the risk of contradicting his very premise
and of arguing in a circle.

What Marx attempted was to develop and systematize the procedure
by which Ricardo himself had been trying to overcome the difficulty –
that is, by measuring 'values' in terms of a commodity that would require
a constant quantity of labour to be produced and would be an average (a
'medium') with respect to the proportions of capital to labour it
required.[22] Measured in terms of such a commodity, the value of the
social product would not change as wages changed and would be equal
to the quantity of labour it embodies relative to that embodied in the
standard. Ricardo hoped that the change in the general rate of profits
might then be determined without reasoning in a circle, and might
accordingly be used to ascertain the associated variations in the relative
prices of the individual commodities. And this is fundamentally what
Marx attempted to do in the so-called transformation problem.

16. The labour theory of value of Ricardo and Marx appears, therefore,
to have been the analytical tool that allowed them to arrive at the
necessary link that binds, one to another, the rates of remuneration
of the productive resources (Garegnani, 1984, pp. 302–3; 1987, pp.
566–7); hardly a detour, therefore, especially '...to one who would
understand 19th-century or earlier-century distribution of income'.
(That link is in fact the same one that Samuelson was to stress, nearly
a century and a half later, in terms of the 'non-substitution theorem'
referred to above.)

Equally doubtful appears to be Samuelson's 'erase-and-replace' thesis
(p. 44) – the one, that is, that he states (1971a, p. 921) when he envisages
Marx's 'values' and his 'prices of production' as 'two alternative and
discordant systems', and proceeds then to argue that Marx's 'famous

---

[22] By the time of the third edition of the *Principles*, Ricardo had in fact come to choose as
his 'invariable measure of value' a commodity that would constitute a 'medium' such that
'those commodities on one side of this medium, would rise in comparative value with it,
with a rise in the price of labour, and a fall in the rate of profits; and those on the other
side might fall from the same cause' (Ricardo, 1951–73, VIII, p. 193).

The difficulty of course was that a 'medium' in terms of which the social product would
be invariable would not have the same physical composition as the real wage and, therefore, changes of the real wage would not be measured by it before prices are determined.

transformation problem . . . is seen to involve returning from the unnecessary detour taken in volume I's analysis of values' to what elsewhere in the same article is called 'conventional economic theory' (1971a, p. 399).[23]

Here Samuelson overlooks *two* important points. The *first* is that, far from being 'an alternative and discordant system' with respect to 'prices of production', the quantities of labour embodied were seen to be an integral part of the latter system, and as necessary in order to determine the rate of profits without which prices would have remained indeterminate – so far as Marx and Ricardo could see at the time.

The *second* strictly related point is that Samuelson fails to realize how 'the conventional economic theory' of Marx's time was certainly no more aware than Marx of the fact that the price equations were sufficient to bring out the necessary relation between the real wage and the rate of profits. To the extent that the other authors did not refer to Ricardo's and Marx's labour theory of value (or to the conclusions derived on that basis) and instead confined themselves to prices, they went back to ignoring that necessary relation. Far from providing a more correct theory to which Marx could 'return' after his 'detour' on the labour theory of value, they were in fact providing what Samuelson must admit to have been a logically inconsistent account of prices and distribution. Certainly, after Sraffa, Marx could be anywhere, except back to the point where Smith was (Samuelson, p. 27)!

In fact, as I have argued (1987, p. 567; 1984, p. 305), Marx's clarification and development of Ricardo's discussion of the average commodity was an important step forward towards a more exact solution. Marx makes it clear in the manuscripts that became Volume III of *Capital* that he recognized his own arithmetical examples to be inaccurate – in so far as the prices of production are not applied there to the commodity inputs and wages, as well as to the outputs. Thus he anticipated (though he did not himself take) the next necessary step forward, the correctly formulated system of simultaneous price equations (Garegnani, 1984, pp. 307–8).[24]

---

[23] Samuelson makes it clear that the 'conventional economic theory' to which he refers is that of Marx's times, or even of 'pre-Marxist' times (see also Samuelson, 1973, p. 66).

[24] Samuelson attributes to me the idea that '[Marx's] mistake was a fruitful one because it led Marx (almost) to a correct Sraffian theory of a competitive price'. However, what I stated was that Marx's error of including a rate of profits determined by the ratio of the social surplus value to the social capital was 'suggestive' because '[it] can be envisaged by us as the result of treating as integral parts of a single method . . . what are in fact, when consistently developed, two equivalent methods each of which is sufficient to determine that [rate of profits]' (Garegnani, 1984, pp. 308–9). What is there held to be 'suggestive' is

continued

17. Samuelson is, on the other hand, attempting to crash through a door wide open to welcome him when he tells us of a non-bizarre numerical example in which a small change in distribution causes relative prices to change, quite contrary to what would happen if commodities exchanged according to the quantities of labour embodied. Having dabbled myself with such numerical examples (Garegnani, 1970, pp. 428–35), I am of course far from surprised. In fact, I greet Samuelson's own example with great pleasure, since the 'innocent children' likely to be frightened by it ought to be those belonging to the stable of the 'MIT writers', rather than to that of the 'Palgrave writers' (Samuelson, p. 44).

The fact is that if the relative prices of commodities pertaining to each system of production did not change with distribution, and commodities exchanged in proportion to the quantities of labour required to produce them, the propositions of traditional capital theory associated with the equality between marginal product and rate of remuneration, would all hold.[25] (Indeed, Samuelson himself once argued (1962) for a 'surrogate capital' which rested entirely on the labour theory of value and felt then tempted to assert that the results could be generalized; Garegnani, 1970, pp. 414–16).

Paradoxical as it may at first seem the failure of the principle that commodities exchange according to the quantities of labour embodied is of less consequence for the theory of the classical economists and

therefore the idea of a rate of profits originating from the distribution of surplus ascertainable independently of prices, and originating the rate of profits by its uniform distribution over the corresponding capital – the idea that is the basis of the auxiliary constructions of the standard system and of the integrated wage-goods system (Garegnani, 1984, pp. 313–20; 1987, pp. 570–2).

[25] In this connection we may refer to Samuelson's argument about an incompatibility between the labour theory of value and the possibility of alternative systems of production coming successively into use as distribution changes (pp. 36–40), where Samuelson appears to refer back to his argument in 1974b, p. 292, according to which 'in a regime of values the technique that minimizes "values" at $r = 0$ will minimize them for all r's – a shortcoming of the value model'. That this is not correct is shown by Samuelson (1962), where, when a 'surrogate production function' exists, the consumption good and the capital good in use always exchange according to the quantities of labour embodied. As I have remarked elsewhere (1984, p. 306n), Samuelson fails here to separate two questions. The first is that of the relative value of commodities pertaining to the *same* system of production, in relation to which the labour theory of value has always been used. The second question is that of the costs, estimated at the prices and profits of the system in use of capital goods specific to systems of production other than that in use (see, for example, Garegnani, 1970, p. 411n). It is only if the latter costs also happened to be proportional to the quantities of labour embodied, that the relative profitability of alternative systems of production could not change as distribution changes.

Marx. In fact, the role of the labour theory of value in Ricardo and Marx was fundamentally that of providing a basis for defining an average commodity by which to bring to light the relation between wages and profits. That role is compatible, in principle, with the individual commodities not exchanging according to the quantities of labour embodied. Indeed, Marx himself would have remained quite unperturbed by Samuelson's 'horrendous' example. The ratios in exchange between the commodities as determined by Marx can *also* change quite freely with distribution.

18. Before concluding on the labour theory value, let me deal with what Samuelson calls the '1815 lost-Atlantis corn-to-corn model attributed to Ricardo' (p. 43 and *passim*). The intended implicit reference is probably to the 'lost papers on ... capital' to which Sraffa refers in (1951), pp. xxxi–ii. Unfortunately, the romantic aura Samuelson attributes to those papers is spoilt by the fact that, unlike for the Lost continent, for the Lost Papers we do have a quite down-to-earth record: Trower's letter to Ricardo of 8 March 1814, where Trower say he has seen and read *the actual thing*.

The thesis that seems to underlie Samuelson's references to the 'lost-Atlantis model', or '1815 fabrications' (p. 29, fn.), so far as I can see, finds little support in the results of the literature on the question. I believe it would be fair to say that Sraffa's textual evidence has been strengthened, if anything, in the course of that discussion.[26] But of course, if Samuelson or others have new textual or logical arguments to the contrary, they would be welcome to come forth in an open discussion on this as well as on other aspects of the interpretation of the classical economists. That discussion, I am sure, would be useful for all concerned.

5   Conclusions

19. Finally, before concluding, let me comment on some minor points in Samuelson's paper.

In connection with Sraffa's degree dissertation (which was printed for private circulation, and not 'published'), the statement by Eatwell and Panico, referred to by Samuelson, according to which 'the *normal* value of a currency is completely "conventional", i.e. it can be at *any* level that common opinion expects it to be' (Eatwell and Panico, 1987, p. 447) needs better focusing. What Sraffa holds to be completely 'arbitrary'

---

[26] In the by now abundant literature on the question, see in particular Hollander (1973); Eatwell (1975); Hollander (1975); Garegnani (1982); Langer (1982); Hollander (1983); Garegnani (1983b); de Vivo (1985); Prendergast (1986a,b); Peach (1986); Porta (1986); Groenewegen (1986b).

(rather than 'conventional') is the *legal* and not the *normal* value of the currency:

It is supposed that the currency should normally be worth the weight of gold fixed by law...but that value is completely arbitrary and...is no more normal than any other value the currency may assume. (Sraffa, 1920, p. 42; my translation)

As for the true normal value of the currency, Sraffa holds it to be that for which 'no force exists tending to make it change' (ibid.).

The dissertation is evidently the work of a brilliant undergraduate (students in Italy were and still are asked to write a dissertation for the BA degree) who, however, has not yet begun his systematic advanced studies of economics and has therefore all the caution that a serious student has in such conditions. Thus, with respect to a role of the government in the distribution of income, what we find in the dissertation is the remark that, in the processes of war inflation considered there, wages adjust more slowly than prices – and the bright student emerges in the less conventional remark that the same need not be the case in a process of deflation. There the initiative for the adjustment rests with the entrepreneurs who, contrary to the workers, whose standard of living has no absolutely rigid lower limit in the short run, do have the rigid lower limit of the expenses of production which, if not covered by the sale price, make it convenient for them to suspend production, with the result that they will generally be able to force the workers to accept a cut in their monetary remunerations (Sraffa, 1920, pp. 40–1).

20. For the reasons mentioned at the beginning of this Comment, Sraffa is a very difficult author. The difficulty is made even greater than it needs be, because Sraffa's work has in effect been so little discussed on its own terms. Professor Samuelson is therefore to be thanked for what we must hope will be the beginning of a fuller discussion – a beginning that, like all beginnings, is bound to suffer from the fact that the necessary clearing of the ground has yet to be effected.

Acknowledgements

I wish to thank Dr R. Ciccone, Professors A. Roncaglia, F. Vianello of Rome University, and Dr G. Mongiovi of the New School for Social Research in New York for helpful comments on a first draft of this paper.

Comment

Bertram Schefold

FRANKFURT AM MAIN

The participants at the conference will be very grateful to Professor Samuelson for having added a major paper to the proceedings, written in a generous spirit of appreciation for an economist of a rather different persuasion. As an editor, directly concerned by some of Samuelson's observations, I take the liberty to offer some comments in an attempt to broaden the consensus in at least some areas, given that this book is dedicated to the memory of Sraffa.

I

'Mainstream economists of the mathematical or literary persuasion can benefit much from Sraffa's contributions', states Professor Samuelson. Indeed, concepts like basics and non-basics, the maximum rate of profit or the treatment of fixed capital as a joint product are now widely used, but there is less readiness to accept Sraffa's method and only limited agreement has been obtained on the extent to which Sraffa's critique of the concept of capital applies. I should like to start my Comment by advancing the latter argument by a small step, since insight into the critique (where much remains to be developed) may help to gain acceptance for the method.

Let us first agree on properties of long-run equilibria that are accepted by economists of both classical and neoclassical origin: prices, wage rates, rents for lands of the same quality and the rate of profit are uniform. The uniformity of the rate of profit is a long-run equilibrium condition not only in classical but also in neoclassical theory. It may from the start be assumed to hold as a result of competition. The rate of profit is in general not uniform in this sense in *intertemporal general equilibrium* models, but, to the extent that they are not due to permanent scarcities, the inqualities of different own-rates of interest of different commodities even then tend to disappear as a result of a special form of a competitive process, and a unique uniform rate of profit emerges as the time horizon is shifted towards infinity (Bewley, 1982).

Differing own-rates of interest were introduced in Sraffa's critique of Hayek. I wonder whether it would not have been better if Sraffa had

69

revealed more of his critique of the Austrian theory of capital on that occasion. We do not know how far it had been developed at the time, but he wrote: 'A considerable part of the book is taken up by preliminaries about the relations between the quantity of capital and the length of the process of production and about the proportions in which the flow of money is divided between the purchase of consumer's goods and the purchase of producer's goods. Dr. Hayek as it were builds up a terrific steam-hammer in order to crack a nut – and then he does not crack it. Since we are primarily concerned in this review with the nut that is not cracked, we need not spend time criticizing the hammer' (Sraffa, 1932, p. 45). A critique of Hayek's theory of capital would *eo ipso* also have been one of any supposition of a – barring monetary disturbances, i.e. in the absence of forced saving – spontaneous tendency towards a neoclassical equilibrium at full employment. This might have allowed a more effective attack on the 'rotten core of the Hayek work' than was provided by Sraffa's early critique of the erroneous monetary theory of the cycle.

For those interested in Sraffa's later work the review is important because it helps to elucidate the problematic of the multiplicity of own-rates of interest when relative prices are changing, as in Keynes, where own-rates of interest are used to analyse the short-run equilibrium at less than full employment. I am told that Professor Samuelson, later a pioneer in turnpike theory, dedicated a maiden paper to this connection.

Sraffa interprets inqualities of own-rates of interest of commodities as expressions of differences between the market price and the cost of production (Sraffa, 1932, p. 50). In fact, he considers 'the case of a non-money economy, . . . when equilibrium is disturbed, and during the time of the transition, the "natural" rates of interest on loans in terms of the commodities the output of which is increasing [because an initial deficiency of supply is being made good] must be higher, to various extents, than the "natural" rates on the commodities the output of which is falling; and that there may be as many "natural" rates as there are commodities. It will be noticed that, under free competition, this divergence of rates is as essential to the effecting of the transition as is the divergence of prices from the costs of production; it is, in fact, another aspect of the same thing' (Sraffa, 1932, p. 50).

The formal similarity of a classical equilibrium with a uniform rate of profit and a neoclassical one where own-rates of interest are equal has led to the claim that the world of *Production of Commodities* is only a special case of the Debreu world where divergent own-rates of interest are allowed for. Sraffa is said to deal with that special case in which initial endowments happen to be such that relative prices may remain constant in the intertemporal equilibrium so that own-rates are all equal and we may speak of a uniform rate of profit (Hahn, 1982).

Against this I have argued elsewhere in this book and in Schefold (1985b) that there are profound differences relating not only to the theories about the genesis of such equilibria, but also to the state that is reached. In fact, the domain of application for such long-run equilibria is larger in the *classical* approach because of the different explanation of distribution and employment and different assumptions about effective demand. In neoclassical equilibrium, prices of goods are determined simultaneously with prices of factors, i.e. with distribution, while classical theory proceeds sequentially: prices of commodities in a classical long-period position are determined on the assumption that the real wage rate or the rate of profits is already exogenously given. Several contributions to this volume discuss alternative theories of distribution: they imply that Sraffa does not refer to a full-employment position.

As to a possible genesis of a neoclassical long-run equilibrium, the divergence of own-rates of interest in a Debreu-type intertemporal equilibrium is proof of a peculiar kind of disequilibrium. It is true that there is an equilibrium in so far as arbitrage would not be profitable: a higher own-rate of interest of a particular commodity does not indicate that one should move into the corresponding industry in order to obtain a higher rate of profit because relative prices change. Rather, it indicates a falling price and that the supply of the commodity is already being increased at a rate that is such that neither excess profits nor losses are being made. But the divergence of the own-rates of interest in the early periods of an intertemporal equilibrium reflects the slowness of the adaptation of production with given endowments – which are employed fully or receive zero prices – to demand, which is ultimately derived from demand for consumer goods. The situation implies a disequilibrium at the beginning in so far as the stocks of endowments of capital goods had once been accumulated to be utilized fully, and equilibrium in the capital goods market must mean not only that capital goods receive a positive price but also that their price corresponds to the cost of production. The prices for endowments of capital goods at the beginning of a Debreu equilibrium are just demand prices; the supply conditions as governed by earlier costs of production are, as it were, simply forgotten when time starts. Viewed as a model describing a process of adaptation, the intertemporal model is deficient in so far as it does not take deceived expectations generated by unused initial endowments into account.

If the Debreu equilibrium is thus understood to start from an initial disequilibrium situation which is, with perfect foresight, transformed into an equilibrium, the proof of the temporary nature of the divergence of own-rates of interest must be that they disappear in the long run – this is precisely what happens according to the results on turnpike properties of intertemporal general equilibria that have been assembled since Bewley's pathbreaking work of 1982. The long-run equilibrium therefore is not only a special case of an intertemporal equilibrium that happens to have endowments in 'correct' proportions, but also the centre of gravitation of an intertemporal equilibrium, if that is formulated as one with a distant time horizon (Duménil and Lévy, 1985), in the special case of permanent market-clearing, full employment and perfect foresight during the process.

Of course, in any neoclassical world with distribution governed by supply and demand for factors of production, relative prices will be constant in the long run only if the relative scarcities of primary factors have no reason to diverge as time goes on – reasons for divergence, which must be excluded, are e.g. the exhaustion of resources (Radner, 1988). Turnpike theorems with recursive utility show that preferences need, on the other hand, not be expressed in terms of discounted utility functions, where the utility function for each period would be assumed to be constant; they are explained directly as evaluations of consumption paths stretching over an infinite horizon, and they are such that the initial endowments of capital goods have no influence on the final stationary state (Epstein, 1987). It has been suggested by Garegnani (1976a) that the old neoclassical notion of long-period equilibrium was replaced, following Hicks and others, by temporal and intertemporal equilibrium concepts. Now, the old concept, in the form of a terminal stationary state with a uniform rate of return, has surfaced again.

What is really at issue is the confrontation of the classical and neoclassical theories of long-period equilibrium themselves (see Garegnani's main paper in this volume [the reference is to Chapter 5 of Bharadwaj and Schefold (1990)]); the intertemporal model provides only a special case of a process of convergence to a neoclassical long-period equilibrium, and, if endowments happen to be in 'correct' proportions from the start, there is no problem of convergence.

However, the attempts to show how the neoclassical long-period equilibrium is generated as a terminal state of an intertemporal equilibrium have the merit of clarifying conditions for the convergence, and here I come to my point: as results from Epstein (1987, p. 341), it appears to be necessary, in order to prove the convergence to the long-run equilibrium, to postulate that the economies are 'regular' in the sense of Burmeister (1980). This means, essentially, the reswitching and Wicksell effects have been ruled out by simple assumption. It indicates that the critique of capital concerns all kinds of truly long-run neoclassical equilibria, not only Clarkian parables. It had been claimed that the modern versions of intertemporal equilibrium were immune against the critique; now the task is to show how it extends to neoclassical long-period equilibria as soon as it is asked how they can be attained or be stable.

II

Among the criticisms raised by Samuelson, if not against Sraffa then against some of his followers, one looms particularly large: the neglect of the effect of changes in demand on changes of prices in a system of prices of production with a given rate of profit. Mistaken is the 'impression from Part II of Sraffa (1960) that the influence of demand composition on relative prices is absent in Part II in the same way that it can be absent from Part I's model involving labour as the sole factor of production and no jointness of production' (see p. 33 of Samuelson's paper).

I doubt that many of the relevant authors are really guilty of ignoring such essential relationships; Eatwell has clarified the point concerning his own presentation in his Comment. In order to avid unnecessary controversy, I shall simply state how I see the problem with regard to land and joint production.

It may be recalled that the conditions of production and the levels of output are regarded as given in the first ten chapters of the book; it is clear that prices of production would change even in the single-product case if returns to scale are not constant and the level of output was varied. In fact, the analysis starts with technology, outputs, employment and distribution *all* taken as determined, and changes of these data are analysed one by one. Sraffa himself never presented an analysis of the interaction of these factors, and it is doubtful whether a complete theory will ever be devised that would explain all their variations in historical conditions.

The properties of prices which may be considered if distribution changes and outputs are kept constant are few, but essential: the best-known example is the change in the value of capital as a consequence of a *hypothetical* change of the distributive variable. The capital controversy has proved that the thought experiment is relevant although one knows that an *actual* change of the distributive variable may cause switches of technique. An actual change in distribution is also likely to affect the composition of output, in particular of investment. There is therefore only limited, but relevant scope for an analysis with changes in distribution and the levels of output taken as given.

The analysis of prices is supported by *hypothetical* alterations of the quantity system (e.g. in the construction of subsystems) which could correspond to real variations of output levels only in the case of constant returns.

If *actual* outputs are assumed to change, with constant returns to scale and with the rate of profit being kept fixed, prices of production remain constant in the single-product case. In joint-production systems and/or if land is considered, such output changes usually induce changes in the method of production (entailing price changes) if they are large, but prices of production will in general stay constant if the changes considered are small. It would perhaps be more straightforward to establish this result by considering changes of given levels of *gross* output to be produced (including investment), but I shall argue in terms of *net* outputs (of consumption goods) because the corresponding model has been thoroughly analysed and is better known. I start with land.

Sraffa, following a long tradition, distinguishes two main types of rent: a familiar example of differential rent of the first kind is the Ricardian cultivation of different lands such that the price of the produce is determined on a marginal no-rent land (which pays no rent because it is not fully utilized). Differential rent of the second kind is illustrated by the use of a well-defined piece of homogeneous land, say the Principality of Monaco, which is used fully by means of two methods, say flats in old villas or in sky-scrapers, such that the combination of the more land-using (villas) and less land-using, but more cost-intensive technique (sky-scrapers) allows the satisfaction of a given demand for the produce (flats for people who want to escape the payment of taxes elsewhere). In both cases, needs and production may rise continuously, with the extension of cultivation on the no-rent land or with the displacement of the more land-using method by the less land-using one, while rents and prices rise spasmodically (as soon as new marginal lands or even less land-using, more cost-intensive techniques have to be brought in). The step function so constructed for either type of rent will be called a normal cost curve. It is clear that the level of output is among the determinants of the step reached, i.e. it codetermines the last land used (first kind of rent) or the methods to be combined (second kind), but only sufficiently large changes of that level lead, with a given spectrum of techniques, to a different step, so that prices remain unchanged with small changes. I want to avoid the possible transition to a continuous change of technique and to non-constant returns in order to focus on this conceptually simplest model.

It has been shown how rents and land may be eliminated in those cases from the system at given levels of output in order to express the prices of basics, either by considering the price at the extensive margin or by combining the two methods in the case of differential rent of the second kind linearly in such a way that rent and land disappear from the combined process ('intensive margin'). By means of this procedure, one can 'get rid of rent' in the consideration of the basic system, *but the exercise is valid only within the stated assumptions*, in particular if only hypothetical price changes are considered and output does not change at all, or little – a familiar application being the proof that taxes on rents fall wholly on landlords (as long as the reduction of the purchasing power of landlords and the increase of that of the state does not affect the methods of production of basics, e.g. through a large change in the composition of output).

In neoclassical theory, land is treated as a primary factor parallel with labour. This leaves room for a determination of rent through demand and supply on land that is cultivated fully by means of one method only, without an explanation of the rent as a differential between the cost of production of this method and some other method, on the same or on some other land. Such a treatment of land also appears in Samuelson's paper, e.g. in his Tableau (p. 33). The assumption seems to be incompatible with a post-Smithian classical theory (leaving aside the special case of monopoly rent and the dubious concept of absolute rent); it would imply that any small change of output may affect rents and prices even if there are constant returns, both for industrial processes and in the expansion of the scale of production of any given piece of land.

I can see two reasons for Samuelson's procedure. One is the repeated combination of a neoclassical approach to rent with Sraffian problems of capital theory in order to extend the critique of the neoclassical theory of capital to the neoclassical hypotheses about land and rent by Metcalfe and Steedman (1972) and other writers.

A more important reason is this. A neoclassical author might cross the normal cost curve with a demand curve falling from the left to the right so that something very similar to the cross of the supply and the demand curve would be obtained. If this intersection was found on a vertically ascending part of the normal cost curve he might say that an equilibrium had been determined such that the price was above the cost of production 'at the margin', and rent or surplus profits correspondingly higher, so that the equilibrium would not be presented by configurations of the Sraffa type. Instead, a separate determination of rent through demand would have been established, as in several of Samuelson's examples. A deeper justification could be based on the following observation: even if we take a classical view of demand, market forces must raise the price of the product, as the expansion of production stops temporarily whenever a new marginal land or a more cost-intensive technique has to be brought in *before* the switch in the methods of production can take place. Should we therefore not say that 'demand' is the true determinant of rents?

What would Sraffa have replied? Thanks to the changes of land with differential rent of the first kind and thanks to the changes of method in the case of differential rent of the second kind, a 'progressive increase of production on the land' is possible and '*output* may increase continuously although the methods of production are changed spasmodically' (Sraffa, 1960, p. 76, emphasis added). Here we have, in chapter 11 an actual change of output levels, but the rate of profit is assumed to stay constant and no theory to explain output is offered. To provide it, many elements would have to be brought in, in particular the principle of *effective* demand in a form compatible with the explanation of distribution; the determination of consumption should not contradict the critique of the neoclassical theory of distribution and employment.

Most contributions to this volume deal with particular aspects of this research programme. It is clear that the level of output affects the level of cultivation, but the influence of demand on rent could not justify the conclusion that rents ought to be explained in terms of supply of and demand for goods and factors in an interdependent full-employment equilibrium, as derived from subjective preferences. Beyond the critique of marginalism, a different theory of demand has to be provided. As is well known, the classical authors interpreted effective demand for each commodity as a specific quantity demanded at the normal prices. But what determines effective demand? In order to face the challenge, I discuss a special and simplified model that relates output to consumption on the assumption that growth rates (investment) and the rate of profit are given. It is further explained in Section III on joint production.

First, I have proposed elsewhere in this book [the reference is to Chapter 7 of Bharadwaj and Schefold (1990)] that the demand for consumption goods be dealt with in terms of given needs, as Smith, Ricardo and their followers did, and that the responsiveness of the demand for consumption goods to prices be represented in terms of changes in methods of domestic production for the fulfilment of those given needs. Consumption commodities are means of production for household processes; these are added to the system of industrial processes of production. (The responsiveness of demand to income similarly is related to migration between groups of consumers.) The irreversibility of important demand changes, the impossibility of ascertaining what demand would be at prices significantly different from actual prices, and links between socially determined consumption patterns and economic stratification may thus be taken into account. My discussion of this and of the relative merits of this and of the neoclassical approach to consumer theory cannot be repeated here.

Needs are transformed and distribution changes in the process of development so that our *ceteris paribus* assumptions yield only first approximations, but the formulation of hypotheses concerning the interaction of accumulation, the formation of needs and distribution are beyond the scope of this comment, since Samuelson also takes changes of demand and the rate of profit unexplained as given. This is in keeping with the fact that the discussion is focused on the classical theory of value, but he does not address the question of which theory of demand would be appropriate in the context he considers. Given needs imply that the concept of effective demand is simplified: the normal quantity demanded is determined independently of the price of production, except in so far as there are possibilities of substituting processes and commodities to satisfy the same need.

To the extent that needs are given, the vertical sections of the normal cost curve are then only temporarily met with in the process of accumulation, and this will happen even if the demand for some commodities is price-elastic, provided the explanation of price elasticity of my main paper is used.

The normal or long-period position is found on the horizontal steps. Classical analysis proceeds sequentially. The methods of production are slowest to change. Within that framework, needs and hence normal quantities expand gradually. This is of importance for a (stylized!) interpretation of such an equilibrium as a normal position: actual demand is likely to fluctuate at any time. If the fluctuations are small, they will not lead to a displacement of the equilibrium and a fundamental change in the prices of production. As long as we argue in terms of given needs, whose normal level is fixed or grows slowly relative to rapid fluctuations, positions on the 'steps' are – locally – stable. A major change in effective demand may upset the long-period position itself and cause a change in the course of accumulation.

Second: if demand raises the price beyond the level at which it is 'supported' by the marginal method or combination of methods, the increase is at first to be considered as one of the market price. The normal level of the price of production would then be ill-defined (unless a neoclassical demand curve were used), which is why such a constellation is usually not considered as a long-period position, and a further argument may be advanced to justify Sraffa's assumption. If the constellation is expected to persist for some time, rents are higher than what can be explained through a differential of productivity, and this provides an *incentive* to innovate and to introduce a *new* method of production that allows a profit to be made according to the normal rate of profit at the elevated level of land rent. There may even be an artificial marginal land, as actually happens in the Principality of Monaco where they are filling up the sea on the shore to push out the coast line, or there may be a compromise and the use of old villas is combined not with sky-scrapers but with the construction of intermediate houses. As a result of such an introduction of a new method, the long-period position will again be established on a new horizontal segment of the normal cost curve, eliminating the formal underdeterminacy of the Sraffa system that occurs if the market price raises rent above the normal level.

The picture of a normal cost curve monotonically rising with output does not always hold. Saucier (1981) has shown that the steps may also go down if several lands and agricultural outputs are involved (contrary to Samuelson, 1987a, p. 458).

III

Under classical assumptions, there is a (not complete!) analogy between the contention that the main forms of rent must be explained in terms of the two kinds of differential rent on the one hand and the proposition that joint-production systems will be 'square' on the other. Let us now stick to the model with given needs. In equilibrium, there cannot be more processes than there are commodities produced; otherwise we have an overdetermination of prices at a uniform rate of profit (which corresponds to the competition between different processes of production at unequal rates of profit in the real world). On the other hand, we cannot, except by a fluke, have fewer processes than there are commodities with a positive price, because needs are given in fixed proportions and, with constant returns, fewer than n processes will not be sufficient to produce n commodities in given proportions. Square systems then emerge if the rule is added that unprofitable activities are not used and overproduced goods receive zero prices (they are not called commodities).

Thus we have the *formal* argument, proposed by Steedman (1976) and rigorously proved by Schefold (1978b and 1988), using inequalities under general assumptions: a given uniform rate of profit and a, in general lower, rate of growth are imposed. (The two rates need not be close to each other, and the uniformity of the rate of growth – analytically convenient but not really classical in spirit – is not essential to the argument; the classical long-period position certainly was not meant as a stationary or steady growth equilibrium.) Then, any vector of final demand will generically result in a long-period position with the number of commodities produced being equal to that of methods used, whatever rectangular array of methods of production is given initially as a book of blueprints. The square system that thus emerges is a long-period position in which, except for flukes, local and small variations of demand are possible, which do not lead to substitutions of methods, whereas larger ones are feasible only if a new equilibrium is reached.

The *substantive* complement to this formal analysis is, on the one hand, that an *overdetermination* of prices is the rule because 'too many' processes compete. Many applications are possible, e.g. to the explanation of patterns of the price determination of obsolescent machines. The question then is which square technique dominates or is socially necessary and determines normal prices relative to which other methods show surplus profits or losses. If, on the other hand, there is an *underdetermination* of prices, the formal argument assures us that competition will eventually result in a square system. But produced goods, available in excess, that are given away free, apart from charges for handling and transportation, are not encountered often. Leaving aside costs of disposal (as considered in my main paper to this volume), the reason, explained elsewhere since Schefold (1977), is that the falling market price of a good that tends to be overproduced is a strong incentive to use that good as an input in the production of new industrial or domestic activities. In consequence, the long-run solution to underdetermination usually is not that of a bottomless fall in some market prices until we get free overproduced goods and a square solution with fewer commodities and processes but, rather, that new methods are introduced through a form of induced technical progress such that an enlarged square system is obtained and becomes the dominant technique of a new normal position.

To show that there are joint-production systems such that processes and prices do not change at all for all variations of the demand vector, Samuelson reverts to systems that I had called 'all-productive' in Schefold (1971). I should like to point out that such systems are not quite as rare as one might think because they do not presuppose diagonal dominance if there are more than two goods and processes and because it is natural to extend them to the consideration of the activity levels, given a vector of a final demand, on balanced growth paths. It can then be shown (see Schefold, 1978a) that a square Sraffa system emerging from an arbitrary technology set will in general have this property as soon as the rate of growth of the system is close to the maximum rate of growth attainable with this technology set. This means that, generically, the inverse of $\mathbf{B} - (1 + g)\mathbf{A}$ will be positive for the Sraffa system emerging from the choice of technique for rates of growth and profit both close to the maximum.

At low rates of growth and profit, all-productive systems are exceptional. But, as a result of the 'squareness' of the solutions, I have found that prices are at least *locally* invariant with respect to output changes in joint-production systems and systems with land: if the classical assumption of a given vector of needs is made, those needs may be varied, with the square solution, prices and distribution unchanged, as long as no activity level turns negative.

Finally, the question should be taken up of whether the 'square solutions' remain generic with other assumptions. In this area, much research remains to be done. Square solutions must result, if needs are different for different classes and if the solution is required to be locally stable with temporary fluctuations in demand, as I have shown in my reply to Salvadori in this volume [the reference is to Chapter 7 of Bharadwaj and Schefold (1990)]. The long-run square solutions in themselves are not generic if a neoclassical theory of demand is introduced, as stressed in Schefold (1985a) – I am indebted to Samuelson for this point, which he made on the occasion of a lecture of mine at his Institute. However, there are objections to the non-square solutions even in this case (and in the one of the *ad hoc* example presented in note 2 to Samuelson's paper[1]) if it is assumed to be in the nature of a long-period position that it must accommodate *arbitrary* small short-run changes in the outputs of all commodities. On the one hand, short-run demand changes cannot always be reduced to perturbations of preferences. On the other, there must be room to adapt quantities. Even in Marshall, cattle diseases lead to an

---

[1] According to Samuelson's assumptions, we should have one process, producing all commodities in positive amounts (r given)

$$(1 + r)(a_{11}p_1 + \ldots + a_{1n}p_n) + l_1 = b_{11}p_1 + \ldots + b_{1n}p_n$$

with $g = 0$ and demand functions proportional to income

$$c_j(ra_{11}p_1 + \ldots + ra_{1n}p_n + l_1) = (b_{1j} - a_{1j})p_j$$

where $c_j, c_1 + \ldots + c_n = 1$, indicates the share of income spent on net output of commodity j. Of these $n + 1$ equations, n are seen to be linearly independent; they determine prices in terms of the wage rate. A short-run change in demand could be accommodated only by changing all prices and has no clear effect on employment. If these unit elasticity Engel curves were to be retained, it would be better to assume long-run prices determined by a square system $[B - (1 + r)A]p = l$, long-run relative activity levels q by

$$(rqAp + ql)c_j = q(b^j - a^j)p_j; \quad j = 1, \ldots, n.$$

If L is employment (how to be derived?), the model might be closed with $ql = L$. Short-run activity levels x could deviate from q, and xl from ql. But, as stated, I should prefer to deduce Engel curves from migrations between groups of consumers with different incomes, with the needs for each group taken as given. A shift of consumers from low- to high-income groups would allow the observation *ex post* of a relationship between a rise in total income and a change in the composition of output (see also Pasinetti, 1981). The solutions would be square.

increased supply of fish in the market in the short run. With joint production, a sudden demand for mutton would have to be choked off by price rises alone if we did not have, as in Henderson ([1921, 1932] 1968, pp. 54–5), two different methods of raising sheep or if more wool results the expansion of a process – possibly a household activity – to use wool. If effective demand fluctuates, the decisive effect has to be on employment in different industries and in the aggregate; it does not operate on long-run equilibrium prices (although provisional changes in market prices may be necessary to *induce* the changes of output levels). Since it is true that the introduction of neoclassical demand theory generates the possibility of non-square long-period equilibria such that alternative square solutions would be less profitable, a dilemma arises, but it is only another indication that neoclassical demand theory is incompatible with the classical theory of prices – a point that may more forcefully be argued with regard to the theory of distribution (Garegnani, 1983a).

IV

Samuelson's observations on Sraffa's article of 1926 furnish an opportunity to return to the neoclassical interpretation of rent as a factor price. I do not think that Sraffa committed an error in his article of 1926, but he may have been misunderstood by some of his readers, and the relevance of his results may be less obvious to modern Walrasian economists than to a Cambridge Marshallian of the 1920s. First of all, the assessment should be based on Sraffa's article of 1925 (Sraffa, 1925) – which is also available in French, German and other translations (Sraffa, [1925] 1975; [1925] 1986) – since the first pages of the article of 1926 are only a summary of the earlier one. Sraffa's real dilemma was that he felt unable to accept the Walrasian approach in economics when he had found, at the end of his article of 1925, that 'These causes of variations of cost, highly important from the point of view of general economic equilibrium, must of necessity be considered to be negligible in the study of the particular equilibrium of an industry' (quoted in Roncaglia, 1978, p. 12).

The Marshallian apparatus of supply and demand curves seemed applicable only under restrictive conditions, the least implausible of which resulted in the postulate of constant costs in a competitive market. Thus Sraffa did not wish to 'fob off on the twentieth century a value taxonomy that was already obsolete in the early nineteenth century' but wanted to get rid of it altogether – a conclusion to which he came close in his earlier critique and which was openly and defiantly thrown at his opponents after softer means of conveying the message had been exhausted in the course of the debate on increasing returns (Sraffa, 1930).

As a matter of fact, Sraffa himself wrote to Keynes on 6 June 1926:

This conclusion has been misunderstood and taken to imply that in actual life constant returns prevail...in reality the connection between cost and quantity produced is obvious. It simply cannot be considered by means of the system of particular equilibria for single commodities in a regime of competition devised by Marshall. (Quoted in Roncaglia, 1978, p. 12)

For the neoclassical theory, with full employment, a first dilemma may be presented in the following terms. *Either*, a general equilibrium is assumed, the solution to which consists in one point in the space of prices and quantities if the solution is unique. Without relaxing at least one constraint, changes in costs can then only be observed if the expansion of the industry under consideration is accompanied by a contraction of other industries due to a change of preferences. This is the point of view taken in Joan Robinson's article, referred to by Samuelson. For, although she speaks of a 'supply price', her equilibrium point moves with changes of preferences. Other causes for shifts of equilibrium points giving rise to equilibrium trajectories, may be changes of technology or of endowments; for example, the changes of prices, and in particular of the wage rate, may be traced as a function of a growing labour force that is always fully employed.

Or the analysis is conducted in terms of demand and supply *curves*. We are here not interested in the demand and supply functions of individual agents or firms that express quantities offered or asked for when all prices vary parametrically, but we are interested in the meaning that can be attached to demand and supply curves in an individual market when other markets are at or near equilibrium, so that an equality of demand and supply in the particular market under consideration implies a general equilibrium. If this approach is chosen, the difficulty is that, as soon as demand and supply are not in equilibrium in the particular market, on points of the supply curve not crossed by the demand curve, there must, because of Walras's law, be at least one other market that is in disequilibrium – a difficulty encountered by Hicks in his stability analysis and dealt with by him using the assumption that the other market in disequilibrium is the money market.

Marshall's assumption, according to Sraffa, is different: he simply assumes that the market under consideration is so small, relative to all others, that a disequilibrium – provided it is not too large – implies disturbances of other markets that are sufficiently small to be ignored. Hence – a point stressed by Marshall and by Sraffa in 1925 – the demand and supply schedules can be drawn only near equilibrium.

Now it is useful to read both articles together. If an expansion of the wheat-growing industry is considered, and if land is not specific to wheat but is also used for other agricultural products, the article of 1926 states on p. 539 (as does, of course, the article of 1925) that, if there are other industries using the same type of land, rents will either not be appreciably affected by the necessary intensification of cultivation in all the industries concerned – this is the case (1) of constant costs, plausible if the other industries are many – or rents rise. In the latter case (2), the change in distribution, if it is sufficiently general, is then susceptible of shifting the demand curves (2a). The article of 1925, however, also stresses another aspect (on p. 324): the supply curves of other industries employing the factor will shift (2b), violating the *ceteris paribus* condition. Joan Robinson's account of the matter in her theory of imperfect competition fails to take the latter point into account, with the result that the argument is not very convincing, and there follows a muddled account of how demand curves might shift with supply (Robinson, 1969, pp. 117–18).

Of course, Sraffa was aware that there were cases in which the use of the Marshallian rising supply curve remained legitimate. It is ironic that the model proposed by Samuelson to provide a meaningful bit of Marshallian analysis in his paper, taken from Samuelson (1971b, p. 367), is precisely the one prescribed by Sraffa in 1925 (but also, more briefly, in 1926): 'These conditions [*ceteris paribus* conditions] reduce the domain to a minimum in which the assumption of rising costs may be applied to a supply curve. They are fulfilled only in those exceptional cases in which all of a factor is employed in the production of an individual commodity' (Sraffa, 1925, p. 323; my translation). In Samuelson's paper there are as many lands as there are commodities, and each land is specialized, each being specifically required for the production of each commodity. This corresponds to Sraffa's assumption that the total amount of a specific factor is used for the production of each commodity.

On the other hand, the example of the paper assumes that each industry uses transferable labour. It is assumed that the labour supply is completely elastic. This could be justified on the ground that the pool of labour used by the group of industries under consideration is small relative to the economy as a whole (this is the assumption proposed in Sraffa, 1925, p. 324). Or there is unemployment, or the disutility of the individual labourer does not change at all with the wage – both not very neoclassical assumptions.

Hence we are, in Samuelson's present paper, exactly where Sraffa stood in 1925. Since the supply of labour has by assumption been made irrelevant to the determination of the supply price, the latter depends only on the degree of intensification of the cultivation of the lands, each of which is specific to the product grown on it. Nobody could deny, least of all Sraffa, that rising supply curves will be so obtained, and Sraffa's error could only consist in his assertion that the situation under consideration is a more special case than that of constant costs. Of constant costs we may simply speak in those cases where a clear tendency to increasing or diminishing returns is absent. A one-to-one assignment of factors to products seems more particular. In this sense, the constant cost box is less empty. But a general theory cannot be so obtained.

In fact, lands tend to be specialized, but this is the result of an economic process that must be analysed, as can be done using Sraffa's (1960) method of counting the equations; it should not be simply presupposed. And complete specialization, as in the Sraffa (1925)–Samuelson (1989 [the reference is to Samuelson's chapter above]) case, will not result often. Thus, if we have twenty lands, the twentieth being marginal, and three products could be grown on each, there will be nineteen rents and three prices to be determined, so that, of sixty feasible processes, only twenty-two coexist in equilibrium, implying that at least eighteen and possibly nineteen, but never all twenty lands will turn out to be specialized (see Sraffa, 1960, p. 77).

V

I have trespassed already on the space rightfully allotted to me, but I want to take up the challenge of the 'red herring'. I think that a more significant meaning can be attached to the standard commodity than emerges from the paper, although it remains an auxiliary construct. To me (Schefold, 1976, pp. 221–25; Schefold 1986), Sraffa's standard commodity is interesting not so much because of the *result* (a standard such that the wage curve is linear if wages happen not to be advanced, implying the useful and well-known analogy with the corn model) but because of its *derivation*. In this derivation, the point is not to show that prices of production are equal or close to labour values – something that Sraffa does not contend – but to show how and why prices change with distribution for a given technology. To see this, I focus on Chapter III of the book, not on chapter IV.

It is clear to the informed reader that the 'Prelude to a Critique of Economic Theory' cannot be understood independently of the context, i.e. the formal propositions are developed not just in order to obtain abstract propositions but also with a view to questioning traditional economic beliefs, and the formal propositions obtained have, because of their abstract nature, a meaning only within the broader framework of traditional theory, both classical and neoclassical. Chapter III on the proportions between the input of labour to the inputs of means of production (how are they to be measured?) addresses the question of how changes in distribution affect changes in the prices of the outputs of single-product industries. Nowadays, after the introduction of matrix algebra to input–output systems, it is easy to give a formal solution to the apparent problems of circularity that arises where the tools for measuring the amount of inputs, i.e. prices for the given physical quantities, depend on the result of such measurements. The answer is to calculate prices of inputs and outputs simultaneously. But the calculation obliterates the economic processes leading to the formation of such prices and one is tempted to forget the economic tradition that might explain them.

Having considered simple conceptions of the numéraire (a numéraire commodity, then an arbitrary index) and having alluded to different theories of distribution (subsistence wage, given shares of national income) in the opening pages of his book, Sraffa allows the rate of profit to vary and shows that, if prices remain equal to labour values (they are equal if profits are zero), 'deficit' and 'surplus' industries will arise at positive rates of profit, and with a wage reduced from its maximum; therefore he considers a *dis*equilibrium and asks how it might be redressed. If labour values are $\mathbf{u}$, the input–output matrix is $\mathbf{A}$, the labour vector is $\mathbf{l}$, the vector of surpluses and deficits is $\mathbf{z}$, we have

$$\mathbf{u} - \mathbf{Au} - w\mathbf{l} - r\mathbf{Au} = \mathbf{z},$$

where w has been lowered a little from its original value of one and r has been raised a little from its original value of zero (there is as yet no wage curve showing which reduction of w would correspond to a given increase of r). Price changes on the input and the output side are found necessary to reduce each component of $\mathbf{z}$ to zero, and to 'achieve this object it is first of all the price ratio between each product and its means of production that one expects to come into play' (Sraffa, 1960, p. 14). One 'expects' something because there are differing traditions in economic theory. The answer of transforming values into prices of production only on the output side (redistribution of surplus value) is mistaken. (Marx was in fact aware that input prices also ought to have been 'transformed', but he neither had the analytical means to do it, nor did he see the implications.)

If Marx's solution does not help, one may turn to the neoclassical view, which here at first sight seems to be confirmed: high rates of return (surplus industries, with the corresponding component of $\mathbf{z}$ being positive) are associated with low capital intensities. But if the means of production of a capital-intensive industry are produced by labour-intensive industries, the value of the means of production of the capital-intensive industry may *fall* in consequence of the change in prices (when values are being transformed into prices), so that it is not always necessary for a capital-intensive industry to raise its own price. Sraffa therefore here prepares the reader for Wicksell effects, which are presented in a more striking manner in chapter VI.

Sraffa's main point is that the clue to understanding the reaction of prices to changes in distribution lies not only in the proportions of labour to the value of means of production in the industry under consideration, but also in the corresponding proportions in previous industries that produce those means of production, and further on backwards in 'logical' time. The 'invariable' standard of value is therefore one from which the cause of the price changes in consequence of changes in distribution (namely, the unequal proportions of labour to means of production in the industry itself and in the industries producing the means of production of that industry and further backwards) is *absent*. One and only one industry, the one that produces the standard commodity, has this property of (infinite!) recurrence with equal proportions if the system is regular in the sense of Schefold (1971).

The argument cannot be worked out in greater detail here (see Schefold, 1986, pp. 607–15). Note that causality in this context means that causes are defined relative to traditional explanations in economic theories. *Any* numéraire is invariable in that its price does not change by definition. Sraffa's standard commodity is claimed to be invariable in the more specific sense that the causes that theories of all schools adduce to explain price changes in consequence of changes in distribution are *not* to be found in the standard industry, so that it is appropriate to take the standard commodity as numéraire. It so happens that a linear wage curve results if the wage is not advanced, but, if the wage is advanced, the construction also holds and results in a hyperbola.

The *Hilfskonstruktion* is thus useful for criticizing Marx's attempt to transform values into prices, but it also helps to visualize how prices of production systematically deviate from labour values as the rate of profit is raised from zero to its actual value in a thought experiment. The standard commodity can be constructed only for the system in actual use; it therefore relates actual prices to what prices would be in the same system at a different rate of profit. Since part of its explanatory power is based on the possibility of reduction, it is not only useful for those systems for which a reduction is not possible, i.e. for the majority of joint-production systems (for which it does in fact often not exist). It is obvious that a different standard obtains if the system changes because of technical progress or larger alterations in the actual rate of profit or shifts in demand. I regard it mainly as a didactic concept, i.e. as an introduction to the logic of the classical theory of value and to puzzles of capital theory. Other uses of it can be made. Whether it was of actual help to Cambridge (UK) in the great debate I cannot say.

There are many other points in Samuelson's contribution that might be taken up, especially the transformation problem, but I do not want to defend the labour theory of value as a basis for an accurate modern analysis; the assessment of its historical function in the works of classical economists is a different matter. The real issue concerns the explanatory power of the classical and the neoclassical theories, each taken as a whole, of which the explanation of long-run prices is only a particular aspect. Economists working in the classical tradition should be extremely grateful to Samuelson's inquiring comment, not only because he compels them to deal with questions for which neoclassical theorists have well-practised (though not necessarily correct) answers (such as how the demand for consumer goods is to be modelled), but also because he challenges them to develop the broader perspective of the theory of accumulation. In this field the classical authors developed their splendid vision of the period between the earliest phases of the industrial revolution and the century that followed. The question is what their conceptual tools can contribute to the analysis of a modern world that, it is true, has changed a great deal but that quite obviously is not that of the Walrasian equilibrium either.

Acknowledgements

I should like to thank Krishna Bharadwaj and Piero Garegnani for helpful suggestions concerning my Comment. The responsibility for the final text is mine.

Reply

Inside every great scholar is a greater one. Albert Einstein, the stubbornest critic of quantum physics, ranked as a giant with Planck and Bohr in the creation of pre-Heisenberg-Schrödinger-Dirac quantum mechanics. Similarly Piero Sraffa, though it was no part of his intention, was led as if by an invisible hand to perfect time-phased mainstream microeconomics – not of course in the narrow corner of it where reside Clark and Wicksteed.

It is of this greater Sraffa that I sing. At the infancy of classical economics its scientists spoke prose and had equations and unknowns which were equal or unequal in number. When we count the number of Ricardo's equations and unknowns, we verify exactly what kind of demand and supply system his model is and learn that he can arrive at no determinate distribution of income that can be freed of the 'complications' of consumer tastes, demands, and time preferences. In the Pantheon along with Walras, von Neumann and Arrow-Debreu, Sraffa has earned pride of place. The critique of Marx, begun by Dmitriev and Bortkiewicz, achieves closure with benefits of Sraffian insights – as exemplified in the expositions of Seton, Steedman and Roemer. The fulfilment of Marx's tableaux of steady and expanded reproduction is achieved by the tools and techniques of Leontief, Sraffa, von Neumann and Morishima.

I welcome the uninhibited discussions of John Eatwell, Pierangelo Garegnani and Bertram Schefold. When scholars feel misunderstood, it is natural for them to wonder about motives. Time-consuming discussion is the only way to sort out the areas of disagreement and agreement. My regret is that an overcrowded research schedule and a tight publisher's deadline necessitated a brevity that makes for a tone of dogmatism and unamiability.

Alphabetical order for the authors is appropriate, with some inevitable repetitions. Because I received more than one version to react to, I cannot be sure I have responded to every important point and avoided responding to points later withdrawn.

Eatwell

(1) I had suggested that a revised edition of the *New Palgrave* rewrite the Eatwell–Panico sentence

Yet the basic structure of classical analysis is preserved [in Part II of Sraffa's book dealing with joint production and land] – the prices, the rate of profit, distributive variables (say, land rents) are determined by the conditions of production, given the wage.

Eatwell quotes the whole of his earlier paragraphs and declares I have misunderstood the intended meaning. Indeed I have, and a revised text seems to me all the more needed. The reader may judge from my account whether the misunderstanding was an 'ideological device' involving removal of 'sentences from their context', misrepresentation of 'arguments', and 'erection of straw men'. Or whether it was a genuine attempt to isolate what is valid in a 'classical' paradigm as against a post-1870 paradigm.

Can the distribution of income be analysed in some classical fashion independently of the composition of demand? Can relative prices of factors and the profit rate have their equilibrium determined by technology independently of subjectivist utility and time preferences?

The answer given by mainstream economics is No.

The erudite Jacob Viner, my mentor at the University of Chicago, counselled: 'Try to read an author for sense, not for error.' I tried. The indicated Eatwell–Panico sentence, if I extended to the word 'wage' the implicit adjective 'real', could be construed *not* to be an untruth in Part I Sraffa – this by virtue of the 1949 non-substitution theorem. In the face of this non-malicious interpretation, what was I to think of the preceding sentences, which said:

In Part II...[of] Sraffa...[with] multi-product industries and fixed capital, and...economies with more than one non-reproducible input...Yet the basic structure of classical analysis is preserved...

and then followed the sentence that I declared to be untrue as applied to Part II.

Was I wrestling with a straw dummy? If readers were to plough through my tedious correspondence files with Sraffians, they would realize how many authors believe that relative prices of joint products are, for a fixed profit rate, invariant to [sufficiently small?] changes in the composition of demand [almost always?].

Since, like Oliver Twist, I am asking for more revisions, I suggest that the two *Palgrave* authors re-examine all these mooted passages. In particular, there will be found to be no valid 'contrast[s] with neoclassical theory, in which determination of prices is dependent upon knowledge of the functional relationships between supply and demand' – in any Sraffa model involving, say, corn produced by labour and land while cloth is produced by labour and corn. When landowners change their tastes for corn and cloth, that changes relative prices and the distribution of rents and wages in Wicksell's demand/supply neoclassical fashion (which is also Smith's and Ricardo's). Etc., etc.

(2) Were generations of readers of Sraffa's 1926 classic right or wrong to believe that the category of increasing cost and rising supply price was demonstrably an empty box? I said they were misled. Eatwell argues that, in 'general equilibrium', a shift in relative demand toward one good does raise its competitive price, but argues that it is an irrelevancy to bring in general equilibrium since Sraffa's critique is exclusively directed at partial equilibrium.

I agree that it was the fuzzinesses of Marshall's partial equilibrium that Sraffa grappled with – and, I would add, that ultimately mired Sraffa down in a basic non sequitur. But, after I have solved for Marshall and Sraffa *all* the ambiguities of partial equilibrium, why does Mr Eatwell not applaud my debunking Sraffa's claim that 'the old and now obsolete theory which makes it [price] dependent on cost of production alone appears to hold its own as the best available'.

It is not the 'best available'. It was not the best in 1926 (or in 1925). My exact example, which Eatwell says 'fulfils exactly the conditions Sraffa laid down for the construction of a partial equilibrium industry supply curve', refutes Sraffa's attempt to base price on cost alone to the exclusion of *dd* demand curves. Let marginal utility of wine rise relative to that of rye, and the box of rising supply price will be seen to be non-empty – even 'approximately'.

Rereading the *Foundations* (Samuelson, 1947, pp. 75–80) passage Eatwell commends and the Samuelson and Nordhaus (1985, 479–80) passage he finds 'dubious', I find nought to react to in connection with the 1926 Sraffa article or with the expositions themselves.

(3) Eatwell is right that, if textbook writers like me use examples and diagrams that I know to be so oversimplified as to be false representations, it would be churlish to fault him for using Sraffa's *standard commodity* as a simplifying device to explicate how an input–output system with one primary factor has its real prices determined uniquely for each profit rate.

My point is missed. My point is that the *standard commodity* does *not* clarify anything. It does not illuminate 'reswitching'; Wicksell effects; the incidence on relative factor shares of accumulation, innovation, time preference, or tastes changes; the labour theory of value's domain of applicability; the chimera of 'absolute' value; ... When more than one technique is competitively viable, no *standard commodity* obtains; under various decomposabilities, none obtains. Its disappearance is no loss; and, in the one-technique, indecomposable single-products case, its appearance is no gain.

My pointing all this out is hardly odd. The reason that the concept does not fade into an appendix on *local* eigenvectors is that Piero Sraffa, late in the task of editing his magisterial Ricardo, bethought to make some sense of notions of *absolute* value: rather than dither between shortest-lived shrimp on the seashore and ancient-trees' masts, or diddle with goods of average time intensity, neo-Ricardians aspired to the objectivity of a Frobenius–Perron matrix's right-hand eigenvector as weights for a market basket. One inessential error in Marx's transformation algorithm could even be lightened when the economy is in a *standard* gross state.

Fun is fun, and heaven knows mathematical economists have their turnpikes and other pebbles on the beach. The only caution is to know the difference between a pebble and a pearl.

Garegnani

(1) I shall concentrate on those points in my critique of Sraffa's classic 1926 paper that have not already been addressed in my reply to Eatwell.

A new point here is that, in Sraffa's longer Italian version of 1925, he is said to have endorsed my position – namely that, as a matter of exact logic, the box of increasing-cost, rising supply is not empty even in an impeccable partial equilibrium model. (Wheat and wine use respective lands specialized for them.) Two people seem to deserve congratulations: Piero Sraffa and I.

How was one to know in the Viner or Schumpeter seminars of 1934–5 that the 1926 author knew better than he wrote? The many merited reprints of the 1926 classic never carried author's alterations to warn of this.

The issue has never been 'Marshall's partial-equilibrium approximations' versus 'classical economics'. It has been Menger and Jevons and Walras versus Ricardo, Mill and Cairnes. It has been Böhm-Bawerk, Wicksteed, Pareto and Wicksell against Marx and Ricardo – with Dmitriev, Bortkiewicz and Seton keeping the score.

What a cleaned-up version of Sraffa (1926) establishes is how *nearly empty* are *all* of Marshall's partial equilibrium boxes. To a logical purist of Wittgenstein and Sraffa class, the *Marshallian partial* equilibrium box of *constant* cost is even more empty than the box of *increasing* cost. I should have said that in *Palgrave* and in my revisionist paper on Sraffa. Piero Sraffa should have said that in 1925 and 1926.

Proof: When all goods use all factors in the same proportions (and a universal non-substitution theorem obtains), which is the most favourable case for 'constant costs', then can Marshall write down *rigorously* a *partial* equilibrium analysis? No. The *ceteris paribus* assumptions he needs do not obtain. QED. As we let Sraffa (1926) fade into history, we are left with no *empirical* primacy for the constant-cost approximation.

(2) Garegnani says I have read Sraffa (1960) with marginalist eyes. I say I have read it with von Neumann eyes, Leontief eyes, Debreu and Koopmans eyes, Dorfman–Samuelson–Solow eyes and Morishima eyes. Later I reread it with Garegnani, Pasinetti and Schefold eyes.

I do reread Ricardo and Smith with all those same eyes and I deny that Ricardo failed to understand how changes in demand and outputs altered factor prices and relative goods prices. The blindness, if any, is in Mr Garegnani's caricature of a classical economist and there is nothing Clarkianly neoclassical about recognition of this pre-marginalist banality. Who begrudges Mr Garegnani *his* two-stage procedures? But why bind *them* on Mr Ricardo or Mr Mill?

When Ricardo addresses a change in tastes toward labour-intensive goods during the Napoleonic War's need for standing armies, he perceives that this raises the intermediate-run real wage relative to real land rents. He perceives that, in *his* longer run, this adds to the equilibrium population. He perceives that this alters the distribution of income in all runs.

Neither in 1814–15, nor 1817 nor 1823, would Ricardo make the elementary mistake of considering the real wage–profit rate trade-off to be independent of the abundance or scarcity of land. Ricardo's glass is alternately half-empty and half-full. Sometimes his real wage rate cleaves to a specified subsistence level; sometimes it evolves downward toward that asymptote; sometimes the industrial revolution is catapulting it upward. Ricardo's long-run profit-rate plateau is even more weakly hypothesized.

My 1959 *QJE* articles on the Ricardian system showed that I have no marginalist qualms about going all the way to extreme long-run Ricardian poles, culminating in his physiocratic *Land* (not Labour) Theory of Value. But why should I or Garegnani saddle this singular case on the general reader in political economy? That seems antiquarian decadence. It is derogatory toward the classical writers and their system, and for no necessary or even useful purpose.

Garegnani's further remarks about 'squareness' of joint-product matrices and *local* price-ratio invariances are taken care of in my discussion of Bertram Schefold's Comment and can be omitted here.

(3) On the *standard commodity* there is overlap between the Eatwell and Garegnani positions. That vectoral concept, Garegnani reassures us, 'is not there to validate anything in particular...[but] to render "more transparent" what is valid independently of it...' (Garegnani, n. 15, gives as an example the use of x^* in $(1 + r^*)Ax^* = x^*$ to demonstrate that, for $r^* < r$, $P = Wa_0(1 + r)[I - A(1 + r)]^{-1}$ cannot have a positive P/W vectoral solution.)

On p. 59, Garegnani compares the piecewise (real-wage profit-rate) trade-offs over *local* intervals of $1 + r$ with piecewise different *standard commodities*. The logic of the two cases is disparate: there is one and only one trade-off locus no matter (1) how variable the techniques, (2) how decomposable or indecomposable the technologies. By contrast, *no* unique market basket defines a real wage linear in the profit rate when techniques are variable or decomposable. A locus that is piecewise linear is *not* linear, and as Garegnani well understands the linear pieces do not even belong on the *same* $W/\sum P_j x_j$ vertical axis! It is because, as my critics so well say, the construct does nothing essential for them that its non-existing cases occasion no trouble and so little notice. My Åkerman *Festschrift* positive-profit-rate non-substitution theorem, as I review its explication, does not benefit from Garegnani's proposed vectoral exposition.

I devoted most of my 1983 Alexander Ehrlich *Festschrift* tribute to discussing Marx without matrices, using a one-commodity case to demonstrate how scarcity and plentitude of capital good(s) determine the rate of profit and the real wage. It is a case so singular as to make transparent the superfluousness of the *standard commodity* concept. I therefore am not sure whom the joke can be on if Garegnani somehow infers that I have given the *standard commodity* more than its due. Zero is hardly an excessive rating.[1]

(4) Garegnani's section 4 deals with the labour theory of value. Once again he claims that a corn-only model that Ricardo used in 1814–15 discussions with Trower and Malthus does cogently vindicate the labour theory of value. In this connection Garegnani appeals to Sraffa's 1951 *Introduction* to Ricardo's *Principles* for an alleged cogent demonstration that Ricardo had detected and overcome a basic Smith flaw and had done so by arriving at the labour theory of value. And, he proclaims, Ricardo's Herculean task was creatively buttressed by Marx's 1867–1885–1894 paradigms of equalized *rate of surplus value* and Marx's successful *Weltanschauung* concerning the 'transformation' problem.

I shall rebut by showing that a corn-only model violates any labour theory of value as fundamentally as the general *n*-good case does. I shall show that Smith's lowering of the profit rate as a result of more capitals competing with each other is transparently vindicated as a

---

[1] I quite agree with Garegnani that a square $[a_{ij}]$ that is *de*composable may have associated with it a subsistence wage vector, $0 \leq [m_i] \neq 0$, such that its associated 1957 Seton matrix, $[s_{ij}] = [a_{ij} + m_i a_{0j}]$ is *in*decomposable and possessive of a unique (normalized) column eigenvector. Such a Seton *standard commodity* is not Sraffa's 1960 *standard commodity*. Sraffa tried to build on the rock of technology. The Ricardo circle knew well that any subsistence wage vector adjusted endogenously to land/labour scarcities: in densely settled Ireland, the potato superseded meat and grain; Ricardo and Mill, along with the later Marx, reduced their *subsistence* model of wage supply to a virtual convention once they divorced subsistence from a hard physiological basis and could make it fit *ex post* any and all observations. Once we augment the direct labour vector $[a_{0j}]$ by a direct land vector $[a_{-1j}]$, the Seton $[s_{ij}]$ matrix and standard commodity lose their autonomous dependence on the (a_0, m, a) coefficients.

logical and empirical possibility against Ricardo's Smithian strictures precisely in the corn-only case! Garegnani's attempt to defend Marx's detours in the transformation problem will be seen to lack cogency.

Samuel Hollander and Garegnani dispute textual matters. Was there an 1814–15 lost-Atlantis model for Trower, Malthus and Ricardo to debate about? Personally, I'd be overjoyed if a manuscript find in some English country home completely vindicated Garegnani. I shall fabricate the find.

Corn and labour and land inputs can produce corn output after one period. (Cloth is similarly producible but by labour and corn as inputs.) With corn Sraffa's only *basic*, if there is to be a steady state, the profit rate that prevails in autonomous agricultural production must be matched by the profit rate elsewhere.

Our 1815 find has Ricardian arithmetic. 1 of corn can be produced on 10 acres with 1 of labour and 1/10 of corn inputs. Or, if we halve the acres, we can double the non-land inputs – and so forth in the continuous land–non-land mode of the classicals. Also, to give Smith his fair chance, the example permits the following alternative techniques to the (1 labour, 1/10 corn) technique: $(\frac{1}{2}, \frac{1}{4})$, $(2, 1/20)$.

Now we calculate how Ricardo's labour theory of value is neither 100 per cent right, nor 93 per cent right *à la* Stigler. It is simply a wrong one-parameter theory of value when every schoolboy – whether named Adam, David, Léon, Karl or Pierangelo – knows that only a three-parameter theory of value that gives proper scope to rent, wages and interest can properly describe (a) the distribution of income, (b) the interest rate, and (c) the $P_{\text{cloth}}/P_{\text{food}}$ and $(P_{\text{cloth}}/W, P_{\text{food}}/W)$ ratios. All this holds in every run. Before population changes, a new accumulation of corn seed will so compete down the P_{corn}/W ratio as to lower the switching-point profit rate *à la* Sraffa. Despite Smith's archaic language – 'more competition of capital' to describe a rise in the competitive supply of corn seed (within the same regimen of non-monopolistic competition) – Smith is right on target. (We are fortunate that Ricardo was such a fuzzy thinker since we owe his valuable *Principles* to his captious critiques of Smith!) Why did Editor Sraffa not stress that Ricardo understood the necessity for a three-parameter theory of value – at least did so more than 7 per cent of his time?

The reader may investigate how a fall or rise in the corn subsistence wage will alter the long-run interest rate, the population, and the goods' terms of trade. Or, how a change in landlords' tastes toward cloth will alter, by supply and demand, short-run $P_{\text{cloth}}/P_{\text{corn}}$, until population moves to restore the P_{corn}/W ratio. When cloth becomes part of the subsistence ration, profit in agriculture no longer unilaterally sets the profit rate. Etc., etc.

Now what besides rhetoric are we offered in the way of insight into our 1815 model by its 1867 *Mehrwert* model? In neither short nor long versions of Marx's transformation problem can I find a cogent core. The 1815 model presents him with his opportunity. I can report to the reader that I put it through the 1867, 1885 and 1894 Marx paces and they failed perfectly to provide a single valid insight. (I wrote down volume II *Mehrwert* tableaux above, below and at switchpoints. Always irrelevancies.) The reader should judge whether Ian Steedman's *Marx after Sraffa* needs any revisions in the light of the Garegnani contentions.

Let me add that I have gone back to reread exactly what Piero Sraffa wrote in 1951 and 1960 and find no words that purport to reduce a three-parameter theory of value down to a one-parameter theory of value (save possibly for the passage in his *Introduction* where he without comment refers to Ricardo's (mistaken) attempt to get rid of the complication of land for exchange theory by considering goods as produced (endogenously?) on marginal zero-rent land.)

(5) Mr Garegnani has served us all well in describing more fully Sraffa's Italian undergraduate thesis.

I completely agree that the merits of a scientist's assertions are independent of the political party he votes for or the Church he attends. When a great scholar has passed into history, those of us who knew him and his works form part of the enterprise that constitutes his scientific biography. If Isaac Newton gave me as a reference for a job at the Mint, I would not deem it necessary to mention his penchant for alchemy; but, if that penchant had aught to suggest for his theory of optics, his scientific biographers will want to weigh contemporaries' impressions of the matter.[2]

---

[2] One of Keynes' biographers, feeling a need to justify his own voyeurism, quoted Schumpeter's disparagement of Keynes as a policy adviser influenced by his childless status. This early instance of Bloomsbury-bashing no doubt plays into the prejudices of conservative anti-Keynesians. But, if it were the case that Schumpeter's arrow hit its target, we could not rule it out of civilized court. Actually, though, as I had to argue at Harvard's 350th gathering, Schumpeter was wrong on this Keynes issue. The man who wrote (in quite another 1923 connection), 'In the long run we are all dead', was a sentimental English patriot in the Edmund Burke style, a loyal son of Eton and King's and of the intellectual middle class, with a concern for posterity that Joseph Schumpeter and I could well envy. Sociobiologists like Hamilton and Wilson know that even Popes have nephews and I am not engaging in *double entendre*.

Schefold

From no one have I learned more than from Bertram Schefold. At bottom we are in agreement, not disagreement.

(1) Schefold's first comment deals at some length with the undisputed difference between *steady-state* regimens and *transient* regimens when relative prices foreseeably are altered by evolving scarcities of produced-goods endowments (possibly on a rendezvous course with an asymptotic steady state). Mainstream theorists, more lacking in interest in Sraffian matters than I, would recognize all this as part of mainstream economics: Schumpeter, Fisher, Ramsey, von Neumann, Samuelson, Malinvaud, Koopmans, Hicks, Morishima, McKenzie, etc. Dozens of the chapters in *Collected Scientific Papers of Paul A. Samuelson* (1966c, 1966d, 1972, 1978b, 1986) deal with precisely such *transient* and *steady-state* contrasts. I hail Sraffa (1932) for early stimulus, which enabled a maiden paper of mine to identify and correct a *General Theory* blemish on own interest rates by showing that the same no-excess profits are earned on all goods when relative prices are foreseeably changing – and this *independently* of the numéraire-good used and the choice among heterogeneous own-rates of interest. Heady stuff for a 21-year-old fledgling to correct a Keynes!

Nothing in Schefold's wording should deter his readers from realizing how sharp was my revisionist scalpel and how deep into neo-Ricardian arteries it cut. My censure of the labour theory of value (of Ricardo's editor; of the Garegnani belief that the lost 1815 corn-only model of Ricardo somehow saves the face of the labour theory and defends Marxian uniform-rate-of-*Mehrwert* analysis as a non-detour; and of what I had regarded as the Eatwell–Panico belief that Sraffian joint production leaves relative prices invariant under taste and demand changes) – all these critiques were directed to Schefold's present case of *permanent* rather than transient scarcities.

(2) In a long section, Schefold deals with joint products and with land as a primary factor along with labour. Here is one such permanent scarcities case. Claret is produced by labour largely on cool vineyard lands; vodka by labour largely on potato-bearing plains. Then 1926 Sraffa or 1989 Sraffians will err if they think a shift in tastes from wine to spirits will involve unchanged terms of trade between them in the *longest* run.

Every point in my revisionist critique can be purged of *all* neoclassical elements. Discrete activity analysis *à la* von Neumann and not Clark or Cobb–Douglas marginal products can push my scalpel inward. My contentions do not need to rely on indifference-contour utilitarianism; but like Adam, David and Stuart I would not want to deny that, when goods get dearer, people alter their consumption of them.

Even when the same *permanently* scarce lands can produce all the different goods, Ricardo, his editor and approving reviewers of the editor such as Stigler are simply dead-wrong to think that the complication of Smithian rent can be removed as a deviation from the labour theory of value by utilizing the *no-rent margin* for goods' relative cost comparisons. As Thünen, Wicksell, Frisch, Robbins and I have many times demonstrated, where the 'margin' (extensive or intensive) falls is an *endogenous* unknown dependent on the composition of demand and tastes. Ricardo himself occasionally lapses into good sense on the point: when land comes to be occupied by greater population, corn price rises relative to hair cuts; a permanent state of warfare, with its relative intensification of derived demand for labour-intensive soldiering, raises the population density of a region as the fruits of rent are given over to sustaining more people to be cannon fodder; in any time-run when labour and land are relatively fixed, their factorial terms of trade and shares are demand dependent.

My 1815 example of Garegnani type has already shown that a three-parameter theory of value is irreducibly needed. None of the above facts is possible under a true labour theory of value. Nor are they only 7 per cent possible under realistic conditions, as Ricardo lamely claimed with the support of one arbitrary numerical example that went down better with Stigler's (1958) computer than it did with mine.[3]

(3) Schefold is no dogmatist, and not even much interested in antiquarianism. He has a mathematical point to make in connection with joint products and land-and-labour scenarios. He admits that large enough changes in needs (or in tastes) can invalidate the non-substitution

---

[3] Schefold asserts that Saucier (1981) has shown that something I said in 1987 *Palgrave* was wrong. I deny error. The mathematics of maximization endorses what I wrote. The own competitive supply response to a single change in output price can never reverse sign. Not only is this spelled out in the 1983 enlarged edition of *Foundations*, but before the birth of Dantzig's linear programming I had proved in Samuelson (1946) from the logic of maximizing that Giffen sign reversals could not occur in a linear programming problem even more general than Stigler's least-cost diet problem. My *QJE* 1959 Ricardo Appendix, written in ignorance of Frisch's exploration of the 1930s, showed precisely how many qualities of land affect Ricardo's rents. Whatever Saucier validly established, it was not error in my 1987 sentences. The general supply inequality,

$$0 \leqq (\Delta p_1)(\Delta q_1) + (\Delta p_2)(\Delta q_2) + \ldots$$

is valid and entails, when all Δp_j vanish except for a rise in p_1, that q_1 cannot fall even when (in Schefold's words) 'several lands and agricultural products are involved'.

theorems that make equilibrium price ratios independent of the composition of demand. *Globally*, Schefold subscribes to a three-parameter theory of value. But, *locally*, he insists that *ss* supply curves can be regarded generally as flatly horizontal.

Speaking loosely, we can say that shifts in *dd* curves can cause intersections with *ss* curves to occur at different P_i (or P_i/P_j) levels – as the Mill–Ricardo trade theory and the Jevons–Walras paradigm stressed. But, Schefold insists, almost all vertical *dd* curves find their equilibrium intersections on the flats of the *ss* steps and not on the risers. *Locally* [my words, not his], the labour-only invariances do hold.

To a mathematician, the issue involves 'squareness of the effective submatrix', whether it is generally true that the number of goods and processes (counting land as a joint product) endogenously turn out to be equal. Such a contention is almost correct. If it were completely correct, that would not suffice to save the labour theory of value; but it would be an interesting fact.

First, I stress fundamentals. It was a well-known Frank Graham fallacy in the second quarter of this century that *n*-good and two-country comparative advantage models – or *n*-good and *m*-country models – had no need (*No* need? Virtually no need...) for demand functions to determine equilibrium terms of trade. The same linear programming calculus of rank of submatrixes of rectangular matrixes was involved. In the end, Graham was seen to be quibbling. The reader can predict that, in the end, just before everyone admits that land rents do affect relative prices, it will be argued that 'At least in proper post-Smith models, such and such holds...'.

Thirty years ago in the *QJE* I worked out the linear programming of discrete Ricardian models with differing land qualities. Even in the timeless case or the zero-profit-rate case, the constancy of relative prices entailed by the labour theory of value or the land theory of value was denied. Dantzig's fundamental theorem of linear programming – that extrema can always occur on vertex points – was utilized

Digression on 'squareness'

We are all in Bertram Schefold's debt since he has been early and preeminent in working out Sraffian joint-production relations. Still that literature has a long way to go to catch up with the general von Neumann–Koopmans inequality–equality analysis of the following type:

$$[P_1 \ldots P_n] \begin{bmatrix} b_{11} & \cdots & b_{1m} \\ \vdots & & \vdots \\ b_{n1} & \cdots & b_{nm} \end{bmatrix} \leqq W[a_{01} \ldots a_{0m}] (1+r)$$

$$+ [P_1 \ldots P_n] \begin{bmatrix} a_{11} & \cdots & a_{1m} \\ \vdots & & \vdots \\ a_{n1} & \cdots & a_{nm} \end{bmatrix} (1+r)$$

$$W, \ P_j \geqq 0, \ b_{ij} \geqq 0, \ a_{ij} \geqq 0, \ 1+r > 0, \ m \lessgtr n \tag{1a}$$

$$[b_{ij} - a_{ij}] \begin{bmatrix} x_1 \\ \vdots \\ x_m \end{bmatrix} = \begin{bmatrix} C_1 \\ \vdots \\ C_n \end{bmatrix} \geqq 0, \quad [a_{0j}] \begin{bmatrix} x_1 \\ \vdots \\ x_m \end{bmatrix} = L > 0$$

$$[P_j] [C_i] = WL + r[P_j] [b_{ij} - a_{aj}] [x_i] > 0$$

$$C_i \geqq 0, \ r \geqq 0, \ x_i \geqq 0. \tag{1b}$$

Even when generalized Hawkins–Simon conditions are assumed for the (b, a) matrices, we are infinitely far from a determinate unique solution for our steady-state system. Schefold proposes his own version of a theory of consumer 'needs'. Whether a quorum of modern economists will find it of interest and worth does not have to be pronounced on here: it consists of specifying that the (C_i/C_1) ratios be *exogenously* specified at any and all possible non-negative levels; as we shall see, it is a non-generic specification in the sense that it is embeddable in a more general manifold in such a way that (some of) its qualitative properties are lost by an epsilon-small deviation from its Schefold stipulation.

The purpose of all this was to try to show that, *almost always*, the competitive solutions to (1) will involve 'square' Sraffian production: thus, even when $m \gg n$, $m - n$ of the x intensity levels will be competitively non-viable and the number of x-activities used positively will equal the number of goods produced positively.

Specify six b_{ij}'s, six a_{ij}'s, three a_{0j}'s, one Schefold's needs variable $C_2/(C_1 + C_2)$ or c, and one r, all of which can generically be supposed to be positive. The remaining dozen variables can be specified to obey *any* positive joint-probability density function:

$$(b_{11}, \ b_{12}, \ b_{13}, \ b_{21}, \ b_{22}, \ b_{23}, \ a_{11} \ldots a_{23}, a_{01}, \ a_{02}, \ a_{03}, \ c, \ r)$$

Schefold's c can take on any value in the $[0, 1]$ interval and r any value in a neighbourhood of zero.

I now enumerate the possible results.

First, part of the 17-variable space will not permit of any steady state with positive net consumptions. Never mind: redefine the measure so that the feasible points in the Hawkin–Simon region add up in probability to unity with r permitted to be positive in some interval above zero.

Second, part of the space falls into that 'special domain' where, at $r = 0$ and its neighbourhood, one of the three processes is competitively dominated: say, x_3 is the zero one. In the following special domain, Schefold and I are quite agreed that the non-substitution theorem of Sraffa's Part I is in effect satisfied and the C_2/C_1 ratio does *not* affect the P_2/P_1 equilibrium at each specified r. This special domain is where

$$\begin{bmatrix} (b_{11} - a_{11}) & (b_{12} - a_{12}) \\ (b_{21} - a_{21}) & (b_{22} - a_{22}) \end{bmatrix}^{-1} = \begin{bmatrix} J_{11} & J_{12} \\ J_{21} & J_{22} \end{bmatrix} > 0 \tag{2}$$

Incidentally, Schefold believes I underestimate the 'probability' contained in this special domain: I don't know how to decide whether he should be agreed with in this (in the case of either $n = 2$, or $n > 2$ where 'diagonal dominance' becomes a more intricate concept).

Third, since the above special domain has only fractional probability, we face positive probability for the traditional cases of joint production described by Smith, Longfield, Mangoldt, Marshall, Hubert Henderson and a horde of pre-Sraffa writers. It is sufficient to contemplate the hoary wool–mutton example, or the taxicab-worked-hard-or-easy-when-new example, to demonstrate the following:

There is positive-probability measure, not zero-probability measure, that competitive production is *not* 'square' in the Schefold universe. Square production is *not* 'almost always' true.

I have published examples like the following: 1 labour produces 1 red sheep that contains 3 of wool and 3 of mutton. Or: 1 labour produces 1 blue sheep with 4 of wool and 1 of mutton. Or: 1 labour produces 1 green sheep with 1 of wool and 4 of mutton.

When people want wool and mutton in exactly equal Schefold proportions, a singular case that almost never happens, only red sheep are produced. This deviation from squareness is trivially rare and I forbear to count it against Mr Schefold.

Now consider the positive measure in which people 'need' a bit more of wool than of mutton. Mr Schefold gets his squareness. Red and blue sheep are both produced and only them. *Local* swings in his C_2/C_1 ratio leave P_2/P_1 invariant at $1/2$. The blade of vertical dd demand is weak relative to the ss supply blade (on the flat step).

Schefold well understands that a shift of *his* demand to wool being newly needed in fractional amount compared to mutton again produces squareness at first: only red and green sheep are produced; and, so to speak in neoclassical fashion, the newly prized wool has its relative price coaxed up from $1/2$ to 2 (the increasing-cost case!).

So far squareness? Yes. But further shifts in the Schefold needs parameter c, below $1/3$ or above 3, loses squareness with positive measure.

For C_2/C_1 above 3 only green sheep are competitively producible and we have lost squareness. With similar positive probability C_2/C_1 will be below $1/3$, only blue sheep will be producible, and squareness will be lost. With these same probabilities one of the goods will have zero price – or, if disposal costs are unavoidable, even a negative price.[4]

Indeed, if red sheep had their productivities grow from (3 wool, 3 mutton) to above $(4, 4)$, for *almost all* Schefold's C_2/C_1 ratios, squareness and all-positive prices would be lost.

Economic squareness's universality is even more limited by the consideration that extreme price changes realistically modify even the neediest of needs. Schefold sees the point, even in exaggerated form, when it is a question of technology and innovation. For him, Necessity is indeed the mother of invention, and Nature indeed abhors the vacuum of a redundant harvest and a free good. But, beyond the thin line of his needs psychology, diplomatic recognition is withheld.

Schefold and I agree that, when C_j demanded is affectable by price, the probability measure of non-square equilibria is definitely positive even when all P's are stipulated to be positive. By stipulating *vertical dd* demand curves, almost all his intersections with the ascending ss stairs are on the flat of steps and not on the risers. The Schefold construction is not *generic*, but rather infinitely unrobust. When he lets his dd's be tilted ever so little from the vertical – and whose theory is so exact as to permit no perturbation at all? – Schefold will encounter positive measure of non-squareness cum positive prices and intersections of dd on ss risers.

Does much of this smack to the reader of Middle Age casuistry concerning how many angels can dance on the end of a pin? If so, join with

---

[4] *Editorial note*: After some hesitation, I use my discretion as an editor to clear up a possible misunderstanding. According to the example, we either have an additional disposal process or only one process and one good with a positive price so that the system that actually emerges *is* square according to *my* definition. I have consistently proposed that only goods with non-zero prices and processes with non-zero activity levels should be counted (p. 196, p. 309); my zero-probability theorem rests on this assumption. (BS)

my complaints and address them to the appropriate post-Sraffian authorities.

In any case the *global* truth that subjectivist demand alters Part II price ratios save in the special domain described above can no longer be in dispute and is independent of the angels-on-pins squareness calculi. Should one laugh or cry when a commentator admits that *local* invariance is compatible with global lack of invariance but excuses not using the local/global distinction because it has become 'controversial in the Sraffian literature'?

Approximation theory can save no argument or the face of any arguer. Consider a Clark–Solow paradigm in which joint production never involves as many techniques as there are goods, in which positive prices are determinable but only by demands–needs considerations, and in which everyone agrees that land invalidates the labour theory of value and *all* nonsubstitution theorems. Piero Sraffa would turn over in his grave to contemplate such a marginalist's orgy. Nonetheless, Mr Schefold and Mr Garegnani will agree with me that it is a trivial theorem (of approximating an arc by broken line segments) that permits us to specify Sraffa-discrete models that come as closely as we like to having *all* the qualitative and quantitative properties of the Clark–Solow heresy! (As tit for tat, Clark–Solow models come as close as we like to having double-reswitching, 'perverse Wicksell' effects, and plateaus of consumption that both rise and fall with the interest rate. Philip Wicksteed and Bates Clark had a lot to learn from Piero and Joan!)

(4) The reader's patience and my time are by now exhausted. Concerning Schefold's final effort to find a useful role for the *standard commodity*, let me be over-brief. In the single-products case with a single set of $[a_{ij}, a_{0j}]$ coefficients, P_i/P_j ratios are known to be able to vary with $1 + r$ like the ratio of an n'th degree numerator to an n'th degree denominator. Many ups and downs are, in general, possible when n exceeds 2. If the reader learns something further from the *standard commodity* construct that is deemed interesting, I applaud from a distance.

However, as soon as we admit the realism of *alternative* viable techniques at different profits rates, *all is lost*. Literally any (and *all!*) qualitative patterns for P_i/P_j can occur and none of the multiplicity of local-piecewise straightline-segment loci puts limits on what can qualitatively obtain.

There is a paradoxical turnaround. I used to have to counsel my neoclassical friends to give up the oversimplification that Garegnani, Pasinetti and Morishima showed them does not exist. Now I must nag my Sraffian friends to give up untenable *standard commodity* oversimplifications.

References

Barone, E. (1894). 'Sulla "Consumers Rent" ', *Giornale degli Economisti.*

Bewley, T. (1982). 'An Integration of Equilibrium Theory and Turnpike Theory', *Journal of Mathematical Economics*, **10**(2/3), pp. 233–67.

Bharadwaj, K. and Schefold, B. (eds) (1990). *Essays on Piero Sraffa: Critical Perspectives on the Revival of Classical Theory*, London: Unwin Hyman. Second printing London 1992: Routledge.

Burmeister, E. (1980). *Capital Theory and Dynamics*, New York: Cambridge University Press.

Burmeister, E. (1984). 'Sraffa, Labor Theories of Value, and the Economics of Real Wage Rate Determination', *Journal of Political Economy*, **92**(3), pp. 508–26.

Debreu, G. (1959). *The Theory of Value*, New York: John Wiley.

de Vivo, G. (1985). 'R. Torrens and Ricardo's "corn ratio" theory of profits', *Cambridge Journal of Economics*, **9**(1), pp. 89–92.

Dmitriev, V. K. ([1898] 1974). 'First Essay: The Theory of Value of D. Ricardo – an Attempt at a Rigorous Analysis', in V. K. Dmitriev, *Economic Essays on Value, Competition and Utility*, Cambridge: Cambridge University Press, pp. 37–95.

Dorfman, R., Samuelson, P. A. and Solow, R. M. ([1958] 1987). *Linear Programming and Economic Analysis*, New York: Dover.

Duménil, G. and Lévy, D. (1985). 'The Classicals and the Neoclassicals: A Rejoinder to Frank Hahn', *Cambridge Journal of Economics*, **9**(4), pp. 327–45.

Eatwell, J. (1975). 'The Interpretation of Ricardo's Essay on Profits', *Economica*, **42**, May.

Eatwell, J. (1987). 'Standard Commodity', in J. Eatwell, M. Milgate and P. Newman (eds), Vol. 4, pp. 476–8.

Eatwell, J. and Panico, C. (1987). 'Sraffa, Piero (1898–1983)', in J. Eatwell, M. Milgate and P. Newman (eds), Vol. 4, pp. 445–52.

Eatwell, J., Milgate, M. and Newman, P. (eds) (1987). *The New Palgrave. A Dictionary of Economics*, Vols 1–4, London: Macmillan.

Epstein, L. G. (1987) 'The Global Stability of Efficient Intertemporal Allocations', *Econometrica*, **55**(2), pp. 329–55.

Garegnani, P. (1970). 'Heterogenous Capital, the Production Function and the Theory of Distribution', *Review of Economic Studies*, **37**(3), pp. 407–36; reprinted in E. K. Hunt and J. G. Schwartz (eds), (1972), pp. 254–91.

Garegnani, P. (1976a). 'On a Change in the Notion of Equilibrium in Recent Work on Value and Distribution', in M. Brown, K. Sato and P. Zarembka (eds), pp. 25–45.

Garegnani, P. (1976b). 'The Neoclassical Production Function: Comment', *American Economic Review*, **66**(3), pp. 424–7.

Garegnani, P. (1982). 'On Hollander's Interpretation of Ricardo's Early Theory of Profits', *Cambridge Journal of Economics*, **6**(1), pp. 65–77.

Garegnani, P. (1983a). 'The Classical Theory of Wages and the Role of Demand Schedules in the Determination of Relative Prices', *American Economic Review, Papers and Proceedings*, **73**(2), pp. 309–13.

Garegnani, P. (1983b). 'Ricardo's Early Theory of Profit and its "Rational Foundation": A Reply to Professor Hollander', *Cambridge Journal of Economics*, **7**(2), pp. 175–8.
Garegnani, P. (1984). 'Value and Distribution in the Classical Economists and Marx', *Oxford Economic Papers*, **36**(2), pp. 291–325.
Garegnani, P. (1986). 'The Labour Theory of Value: Detour or Analytical Advance?' Paper Presented at the Conference of History of Economics, 1986, mimeo; also deposited at the Marshall Library, Cambridge University, UK.
Garegnani, P. (1987). 'Surplus Approach to Value and Distribution', in J. Eatwell, M. Milgate and P. Newman (eds), Vol. 4, pp. 560–74.
Garegnani, P. (1991). 'Some Notes for an Analysis of Accumulation', in E. J. Nell *et al.* (eds), *Beyond the Steady State*, London: Macmillan.
Groenewegen, P. D. (1986). 'Professor Porta on the Significance of Understanding Sraffa's Standard Commodity and the Marxian Theory of Surplus: A Comment', *History of Political Economy*, **18**(3), pp. 455–62.
Hahn, F. H. (1982). 'The Neo-Ricardians', *Cambridge Journal of Economics*, **6**(4), pp. 353–74.
Hayek, F. A. v. (1931). *Prices and Production*, London: Routledge & Kegan.
Henderson, H. ([1921, 1932] 1968). *Supply and Demand*, Cambridge: Cambridge University Press.
Hicks, J. R. ([1939] 1946). *Value and Capital*, 2nd edn, London: Oxford University Press.
Hollander, S. (1973). 'Ricardo's Analysis of the Profit Rate, 1813–15', *Economica*, **40**, August, pp. 260–82.
Hollander, S. (1975). 'Ricardo and the Corn Profit Model: Reply to Eatwell', *Economica*, **42**, May, pp. 188–202.
Hollander, S. (1983). 'Professor Garegnani's Defence of Sraffa on the Material Rate of Profit', *Cambridge Journal of Economics*, **7**(2), pp. 167–74.
Hunt, E. K. and Glick, M. (1987). 'Transformation Problem', in J. Eatwell, M. Milgate and P. Newman (eds), Vol. 4, pp. 688–91.
Kurz, H. D. and Salvadori, N. (1987). 'Burmeister on Sraffa and the Labor Theory of Value: A Comment', *Journal of Political Economy*, **95**(4), pp. 870–81.
Langer, (1982). 'Further Evidence for Sraffa's Interpretation of Ricardo's Early Theory of Profits', *Cambridge Journal of Economics*, **6**(4), December, pp. 397–400.
Leontief, W. W. (1941). *The Structure of American Economy, 1919–1929*, Cambridge, MA: Harvard University Press.
Marcuzzo, M. C. (1986). 'Introduction', in N. Kaldor (1986), *Ricordi di un economista*, Italy: Garzanti.
Marshall, A. ([1920] 1961). *Principles of Economics*, 9th enlarged edition by C. W. Guillebaud, London: Macmillan.
Marx, K. (1894). *Das Kapital*, Vol. 3, F. Engels (ed.), 1st edn, Hamburg: O. Meissner.
Medio, A. (1972). 'Profits and Surplus Value: Appearance and Reality in Capitalist Production', in E. K. Hunt and J. G. Schwartz (eds), *A Critique of Economic Theory*, London: Penguin Books, pp. 312–46.
Metcalfe, J. S. and Steedman, I. (1972). 'Reswitching and Primary Input Use', *Economic Journal*, **82**, March, pp. 140–57.

Morishima, M. (1973). *Marx's Economics: A Dual Theory of Growth*, Cambridge: Cambridge University Press.

Neumann, J. v. (1935/6). 'Über ein ökonomisches Gleichungssystem und eine Verallgemeinerung des Brouwerschen Fixpunktsatzes', in K. Menger (ed.) (1937), *Ergebnisse eines mathematischen Kolloquiums*, Leipzig: Deuticke, pp. 73–83.

Pasinetti, L. L. (1981). *Structural Change and Economic Growth – A Theoretical Essay on the Dynamics of the Wealth of Nations*, Cambridge: Cambridge University Press.

Peach, T. (1986). 'Ricardo's Early Treatment of Profitability: Reply to Hollander and Prendergast', *Economic Journal*, **96**, December.

Porta, P. (1986). 'Understanding the Significance of Piero Sraffa's Standard Commodity: A Note on the Marxian Notion of Surplus Value', *History of Political Economy*, Fall, pp. 443–54.

Prendergast, R. (1986a). 'Comment on Peach', *Economic Journal*, **96**, December, pp. 1098–1104.

Prendergast, R. (1986b). 'Malthus' Discussion of the Corn Ratio Theory of Profits', *Cambridge Journal of Economics*, **10**(1), pp. 187–9.

Radner, R. (1988), 'Intertemporal General Equilibrium', IEA Conference 'Value and Distribution', mimeo, Bologna.

Ricardo, D. ([1817–21] 1951). *On the Principles of Political Economy and Taxation*; reprinted in D. Ricardo (1951–73), Vol. 1.

Ricardo, D. (1951–73). *The Works and Correspondence of David Ricardo*, edited by P. Sraffa with the collaboration of M. H. Dobb, Vols. 1–11, Cambridge: Cambridge University Press.

Ricci, U. (1933). 'Pareto and Pure Economics', *Review of Economic Studies*, **1**.

Robbins, L. (1936). *The Great Depression*, London: Macmillan.

Robinson, J. V. (1941). 'Rising Supply Price', *Economica*, New Series, **8**(2), pp. 1–8.

Robinson, J. V. (1953–4). 'Production Function and the Theory of Capital', *Review of Economic Studies*, **21**(2), pp. 81–106.

Robinson, J. V. (1969). *The Economics of Imperfect Competition*, 2nd edn, London: Macmillan.

Robinson, J. V. (1973). *Collected Economic Papers*, Vol. 4, Oxford: Blackwell.

Roncaglia, A. (1978). *Sraffa and the Theory of Prices*, Chichester, New York: John Wiley.

Rosenbaum, R. (1963). *Introduction to Projective Geometry and Mathematical Analysis*, London: Wesley.

Samuelson, P. A. (1946–47). 'Comparative Statics and Logic of Economic Maximizing', *Review of Economic Studies*, **14**, pp. 41–3, reprinted in (1966c), pp. 54–6.

Samuelson, P. A. (1947). *Foundations of Economic Analysis*, Cambridge, MA: Harvard University Press.

Samuelson, P. A. (1959). 'A Modern Treatment of Ricardian Economy', *Quarterly Journal of Economics*, **76**, February, pp. 1–35, and May, pp. 217–31.

Samuelson, P. A. (1962). 'Parable and Realism in Capital Theory: The Surrogate Production Function', *Review of Economic Studies*, **29**, pp. 193–206.

Samuelson, P. A. (1966a). 'A New Theorem on Nonsubstitution', in (1966c) edited by J. E. Stiglitz, *The Collected Scientific Papers of Paul A. Samuelson*, Vol. 1, Cambridge, MA: MIT Press, pp. 520–36.

Samuelson, P. A. (1966b). 'A Summing Up', *Quarterly Journal of Economics*, **81**, November, pp. 568–83.

Samuelson, P. A. (1966c, 1966d, 1972, 1978b, 1986). *Collected Scientific Papers of Paul A. Samuelson*, Vols. I–V, Cambridge, MA: MIT Press.

Samuelson, P. A. (1970). 'The "Transformation" from Marxian "Value" to "Competitive" Prices: A Process of Replacement and Rejection', *Proceedings of the National Academy of Sciences*, Vol. 67 (September), pp. 423–5; reprinted in (1972), pp. 268–75.

Samuelson, P. A. (1971a). 'Understanding the Marxian Notion of Exploitation: A Summary of the So-Called Transformation Problem Between Marxian Values and Competitive Prices', *Journal of Economic Literature*, **9**(2), pp. 399–431; reprinted in (1972), pp. 276–308.

Samuelson, P. A. (1971b). 'An Exact Hume–Ricardo–Marshall model of International Trade', *Journal of International Economics*, **1**(1), February, pp. 1–18; reprinted in (1972), pp. 356–73.

Samuelson, P. A. (1973). 'Reply on Marxian Matters', *Journal of Economic Literature*, **11**(1), pp. 64–8.

Samuelson, P. A. (1974a). 'Insight and Detour in the Theory of Exploitation', *Journal of Economic Literature*, **12**(1), pp. 62–70.

Samuelson, P. A. (1974b). 'Marx as Mathematical Economist: Steady-State and Exponential Growth Equilibrium', in G. Horowich and P. A. Samuelson (eds), *Trade, Stability and Macroeconomics: Essays in Honor of Lloyd A. Metzler*, New York: Academic Press, pp. 269–307.

Samuelson, P. A. (1978). 'The Canonical Classical Model of Political Economy', *Journal of Economic Literature*, **16**, December, pp. 1415–34.

Samuelson, P. A. (1987a). 'Sraffian Economics', in J. Eatwell, M. Milgate and P. Newman (eds), Vol. 4, pp. 452–61.

Samuelson, P. A. (1987b). 'Out of the Closet: A Program for the Whig History of Economic Science', Keynote Address at History of Economics Society Boston Meeting; 20 June, Published in *H. E. S. Bulletin*, **9**(1), 1987.

Samuelson, P. A. and Nordhaus, W. D. (1985). *Economics*, New York: McGraw-Hill.

Sanger, C. P. (1895). 'Recent Contributions to Mathematical Economics', *Economic Journal*, **5**, March, pp. 113–28.

Saucier, P. (1981). 'Le choix de techniques en situation de limitations de ressources', Doctoral Thesis, University of Paris II.

Schefold, B. (1971). *Piero Sraffas Theorie der Kuppelproduktion, des Kapitals und der Rente*, dissertation (English title: *Mr Sraffa on Joint Production*), Basle: private print, 2nd edn in Schefold (1989).

Schefold, B. (1976). 'Nachworte', in P. Sraffa (ed.), *Warenproduktion mittels Waren*, Frankfurt/M.: Suhrkamp, pp. 129–226.

Schefold, B. (1977). 'Energy and Economic Theory', *Zeitschrift für Wirtschafts- und Sozialwissenschaften*, **97**, pp. 227–49.

Schefold, B. (1978a). 'Multiple Product Techniques with Properties of Single Product Systems', *Zeitschrift für Nationalökonomie*, **38**(1–2), pp. 29–53.

Schefold, B. (1978b). 'On Counting Equations', *Zeitschrift für Nationalökonomie*, **38**(3–4), pp. 253–85.

Schefold, B. (1985a). 'Sraffa and Applied Economics: Joint Production', *Political Economy*, **1**(1), pp. 17–40.

Schefold, B. (1985b). 'On Changes in the Composition of Output', in *Political Economy – The Surplus Approach*, 1(2), pp. 105–42.
Schefold, B. (1986). 'The Standard Commodity as a Tool of Economic Analysis: A Comment on Flaschel', *Journal of Institutional and Theoretical Economics – Zeitschrift für die gesamte Staatswissenschaft*, 142, pp. 603–22.
Schefold, B. (1988). 'The Dominant Technique in Joint Production Systems', *Cambridge Journal of Economics*, 12(1), pp. 97–123.
Seton, F. (1957). 'The Transformation Problem', *Review of Economic Studies*, 24(3), pp. 149–60.
Smith, A. ([1776] 1960). *The Wealth of Nations*, 2 vols, London: Dent and Sons.
Sraffa, P. (1920). *L'inflazione monetaria in Italia durante e dopo la guerra*, Milan.
Sraffa, P. (1925). 'Sulle relazioni fra costo e quantità prodotta', *Annali di Economia*, 2(1), pp. 277–328.
Sraffa, P. ([1925] 1964). 'Sulle relazioni fra costo e quantità prodotta', *La Revista Trimestrale*, March, pp. 177–213.
Sraffa, P. ([1925] 1973). Translation of 'Sulle relazioni fra costo e quantità prodotta' by J. Eatwell and A. Roncaglia, mimeo.
Sraffa, P. ([1925] 1975). 'Sur les relations entre coût et quantité produite', in P. Sraffa (1975), *Ecrits d'économie politique*, Paris: Economica, pp. 1–49.
Sraffa, P. ([1925] 1986). 'Über die Beziehungen zwischen Kosten und produzierter Menge', in B. Schefold (ed.), (1986), *Ökonomische Klassik im Umbruch – Theoretische Aufsätze von David Ricardo, Alfred Marshall, Vladimir K. Dmitriev und Piero Sraffa*, Frankfurt/M.: Suhrkamp, pp. 137–93.
Sraffa, P. (1926). 'The Laws of Returns under Competitive Conditions', *Economic Journal*, 36, December, pp. 535–50.
Sraffa, P. ([1926] 1953). 'The Laws of Returns under Competitive Conditions', in G. J. Stigler and K. E. Boulding (eds), *Readings in Price Theory*, London: Allen & Unwin.
Sraffa, P. (1930). ' "A Critique" and "A Rejoinder" in "Increasing Returns and the Representaive Firm" ': A Symposium', *Economic Journal*, 40(21), pp. 89–92, 93.
Sraffa, P. (1932). 'Dr Hayek on Money and Capital', *Economic Journal*, 42(1), pp. 42–53.
Sraffa, P. (1951). 'Introduction', in D. Ricardo (1951–73), Vol. 1, pp. xiii–lxii.
Sraffa, P. (1960). *Production of Commodities by Means of Commodities. Prelude to a Critique of Economic Theory*, Cambridge: Cambridge University Press.
Steedman, I. (1976). 'Positive Profits with Negative Surplus Value: A Reply', *Economic Journal*, 86, December, pp. 873–6.
Steedman, I. (1977). *Marx after Sraffa*, London: New Left Books; reprinted London: Verso, 1981.
Stigler, G. J. (1952). 'The Ricardian Theory of Value and Distribution', *Journal of Political Economy*, 60, June.
Stigler, G. J. (1958). 'Ricardo and the 93% Labor Theory of Value', *American Economic Review*, 48(3), pp. 357–68.
Stigler, G. J. and Boulding, K. E. (eds) (1953). *Readings in Price Theory*, London: Allen & Unwin.
Wicksteed, P. H. ([1894] 1932). *Co-ordination of the Laws of Distribution*, London: London School Reprint, No. 12.

Wolff, R. D., Roberts, B. and Callari, A. (1982) 'Marx's (not Ricardo's) Transformation Problem: A Radical Reconceptualization', *History of Political Economy*, 14(4), pp. 564–82.

PART II

Returns to scale, demand, money and interest, and the classical tradition

CHAPTER 3

Sraffa's hits and misses

Paul A. Samuelson

Pressure of other research at first prevented me from responding favourably to the Editor's request for a new paper on Sraffian economics. However, I was glad to have my 1990 revisionist paper included in this colloquium, and did welcome the suggestion that a new Addendum be included. If a scholar in his ninth decade is to record his considered opinions on an important topic, it had better be a matter not of *when* but of *now*. So, reconsidering, I do offer here some further informal analyses.

Dr. Samuel Johnson said that being hung in the morning greatly clarifies the mind. Nonsense. It is more likely to paralyze coherent thought. True though that as the days grow shorter, one does dispense with nice diplomacies and ancient jockeyings for victories. Knut Wicksell (1919) at long last wrote out exactly what he faulted and admired in Gustav Cassel's work. To exaggerate a bit, it was a case of then or never, and on a take it or leave it basis posterity is the richer for this.

1 The one basic novelty

What did I learn from Piero Sraffa's 1960 classic? One thing. An important thing.

Here, too briefly, is that one special thing I learned from Piero Sraffa. In much of this section I quote from my paper in honour of Pierangelo Garegnani (see Samuelson, 1999).

A. Long before 1960 one understood that, in general, no scalar magnitude can denote what is the 'accumulation of capital' when a society abstains from present consumption to effectuate a permanent rise in potential future consumption. The capital/output ratio, as Joan Robinson (1956) demonstrated, is a treacherous guide because of

111

'Wicksell' and other effects. No reliable independent meaning can be given to 'more or less roundaboutness', or to 'degree of mechanization' and other measures of capital 'intensity'.

B. Even when capital is intrinsically vectoral rather than scalar, its real return, as measured by its *steady-state* or stationary-state rate of *interest : profit*, is indeed a *scalar* parameter in equilibrium. For each rate of interest, r, there is a determinate maximal level of sustainable '*consumption*', c, vectoral (or as a *scalar* once the market-basket composition of consumptions is specified).

C. Around 1960, one could therefore still describe the following process of capital accumulation: when society is not already at a golden-rule state of technology, by sacrificing some vectoral amounts of current consumption over a finite time period, it can achieve a permanently higher time path of (vectoral) consumption forever. In a convex technology (of Sraffa or von Neumann type, or of Clark–Walras neoclassical type), an *intertemporal law of diminishing real returns* invariably obtains for the vectors involved. None of that is vitiated by possible 'reswitching', Wicksell effects, joint products or anything else.

D. Although any close reader of Irving Fisher's 1907 *The Rate of Interest* should have known better, I hoped around 1960 to be able to summarize the essence of C above by asserting that, as r rises above the golden-rule rate (of, say, zero), c of consumption must if anything fall in the entailed stationary state equilibrium. If we can write c as a function of r, $c = f(r)$, then

$$\text{Max } c = \text{Max}_r f(r) = f(0), \qquad f'(r) \leq \text{ near } r = 0$$

There is no error in the above *local* relation. Where my thinking went wrong was in believing that $f'(r)$ and $(\Delta c)\,(\Delta r)$ had to be (if not zero) negative.

Although I may never have put such a false conjecture into explicit print, it was from brooding over Sraffa that I learned the truth, that

$f(r)$ can rise – but not to above $f(0)$ – for ranges of r a finite distance above the golden-rule r^*.

It may be added that Liviatan–Samuelson (1969) had, by another route, fabricated a one-capital-good joint-product model for which $f(r)$ is a single-valued, falling for r near 0 but recovering part way for an intermediate interval of r, and then falling indefinitely. It is evident that convexity of technology does not imply convexity of steady-state $[f(r),\ w(r)]$ loci.

When I chanced to write the above to a French savant, he objected: 'But that is nowhere in Sraffa! Never did he speak of golden ages. And too rarely did Sraffa leave the realm of price dualities in an input–output model to elaborate on its quantity dualities.'

I replied: 'Each of your words is true. But you are too young to recognize the innuendo of the author. Long before Joan Robinson (1956, pp. 109–10 on the Ruth Cohen phenomenon), Piero had proved to himself that there can (in general) exist no objective way to decide that Technique A, in comparison with Technique B, is more "capital-intensive", "roundabout" or "durable". The critique of Eugen von Böhm-Bawerk by Irving Fisher (1907, pp. 351–55) might earlier have convinced me of this, but I was playing tennis the mornings that Jacob Viner and Joseph Schumpeter lectured on those subjects.' To the trained ear, the 1960 Sraffa book whispers the relevant hints.

'What, only one thing learned from a classic? You must be pretty dumb', readers may aver.

No. There were indeed many theorems and lemmas to be learned from *Production of Commodities by Means of Commodities*, but for the savvy youngsters in the Leontief Circle, the important ones were pretty much old hat before Sraffa. At the Corfu International Economics Association meeting in September 1958, Piero told me: 'Now that I've finished the Ricardo editing, I've taken up my old notes on capital matters. You know, I find nothing has changed. Soon I'll bring out a book on the subject.' A book from Sraffa! I was enchanted, but I said to myself that the post-von Neumann explosion of game and programming theory had evidently not reached the inner walls of Trinity College!

Later, in the spring of 1960, I received the page proofs of the 1960 book from the Cambridge University Press. To their question, 'Shall we bring out a separate American publication?', I replied in enthusiastic affirmation. I recalled G. H. Hardy's romantic 1915 recognition of the genius of Ramanujan from an unsolicited letter from a poor clerk in a poor region of a poor colony. As Hardy (1940) proudly boasted, the dozen-odd infinite-series expansions in that letter he could recognize were riches of genius. Having this in mind, I wondered to myself: 'What if I got this in the mail, not from Cambridge, but from an anonymous graduate student at East Arizona Tech? Would I have the acumen to recognize its quality?'

One tells anecdotes in order to make a scientific point. The Sraffa work is *outside* normal cumulative science in the sense of Thomas Kuhn's 1962 *Structure of Scientific Revolution*. It is a work in mathematical economics by an amateur, an autodidact. It has the properties of such. The book has more in it than the author knows. It is not the better for its imperfections. (As Hardy came to admit, Ramanujan could have been even more incredibly original if he had been well grounded in rules of proof and in frontier mathematical knowledge.) However, we can be gratified that Sraffa was not inhibited from publishing his innovations by any conscious feeling of ignorance concerning the Frobenius–Minkowski theory of non-negative real matrices, and he did benefit from Cambridge world-class mathematicians.

Let me be concrete. Chapter 1 begins with a subsistence economy where produced inputs suffice barely to produce themselves. In 1960, a Ph.D. candidate at Stanford, Rochester, MIT, Harvard or Berkeley would be obliged to cite John von Neumann (1937, 1945), Wassily Leontief (1941, 1953), of course, and most important of all the Hawkins and Simon (1949) conditions that precisely identify when an input–output system is *net productive* or is on the borderline of subsistence (see Technical Note 1).

Pendantry. Pedantry. Pedantry. No. The inefficient bifurcation of the literature into two streams has not generated Kuhnian breakthroughs of supernormal science. The whole is less than the sum of its dishevelled parts.[1]

After Joan and Piero had shown that feasible per capita stationary consumption can be cut rather than raised by a drop in interest rates, I had to learn for myself that a J. B. Clark system with genuine smooth marginal productivities can be as capable of *per capita consumptions that sometimes rise when the profit rate rises* as discrete-technology von Neumann–Sraffa systems can. Marginalist models can come as close as you like to reswitching, and in any case reswitching is a red herring, being a sufficient but not a necessary condition for the phenomenon that matters. Thus Böhm-Bawerk (1889) *cum* marginal products can encounter (normal!) cases where lowering the interest rate kills off some stationary-state consumption and production! Post-1960 researches, mainstream and heterodox, add to our knowledge of conditions sufficient to banish reversals in the (profit rate, per capita consumption) relation, and of conditions necessary or sufficient to produce reversals.

Warning: this which Sraffa taught me has essentially nought to do with production of commodities by means of themselves as commodities. Nought to do with existence of Sraffa's basics – where coal needs iron,

---

[1] I have mentioned in print that neither Wassily Leontief nor Piero Sraffa has seemed ever to cite the other's work in print. That makes things even? No, it is two warts on the face of science.

iron needs coal, and *all* goods need one and both of these two.[2] My Footnote 2 on Böhm-Bawerk's triangular system *sans* basics makes this independence clear. *A fortiori*, all this has nought to do with successful or unsuccessful critiques of marginalism.

The Böhm-Bawerk example, and *every* behaviour of neoclassicism, can essentially be reproduced up to the thousandth decimal place of accuracy by strict examples of discrete technology à la von Neumann–Sraffa and also, as we shall see, vice versa: strict neoclassical systems of infinite alternative techniques can come as close as we like to *any and all* behaviours of Sraffian finite paradigms. This I did not have to learn from 1960 Sraffa, which indeed obscured the matter. Study of Walras's second edition of *Eléments* (1889), in comparison with his 1896 third edition's marginal products, made that obvious to anyone who realized that smooth curves can always be arbitrarily closely approximated by straight-line chords and vice versa (see Technical Note 2).

2 The doomed critique of marginalism: constant returns?

An honest audit of a purported scientific revolution must record, along with its hits, its misses. What did it fall short of perceiving? Which elements of empirical fact and of normative truth about Pareto optimality did it tend to obscure rather than illuminate?

When giving guest lectures to students during the rebellious late 1960s and early 1970s, I learned that what they considered important in Sraffian economics was his promised future critique of marginalism. After a third

---

[2] Consider Böhm–Bawerk's Austrian case, where $Q_t = F[L_{t-1}, L_{t-2}, L_{t-3}]$ and where the partial derivatives of marginal products, $\partial F/\partial L_{t-j}$ and $\partial^2 F/\partial L_{t-1}\partial L_{t-j}$ nicely exist to provide us with the kind of neoclassical distribution theory that a Garegnani (1960) or post-1960 Pasinetti would find displeasing. For this paradigm, the stationary-state per capita consumption is the following function of the equilibrium interest rate of $1 + r^*$:

$$c[1 + r^*] = Q^*/\Sigma_1^3 L_j^* = F[L_1^*, L_2^*, L_3^*]/\Sigma_1^3 L_j^*$$

where

$$\frac{\partial F[L_1^*, L_2^*, L_3^*]/\partial L_2}{\partial F[L_1^*, L_2^*, L_3^*]/\partial L_1} = 1 + r^* = \frac{\partial F[L_1^*, L_2^*, L_3^*]/\partial L_3}{\partial F[L_1^*, L_2^*, L_3^*]/\partial L_2}$$

The Jacobian matrix of this system permits $c'[1 + r^*]$ to change from its negative sign near $r^* = 0$ to a positive sign even when F has every neoclassical property of being first-degree homogeneous and strongly quasi-concave! Sraffa and Joan Robinson taught us more than they dreamed of in their philosophy. See Samuelson (1966, 1994) for more on this. Note that when F has only the two arguments $[L_{t-1}, L_{t-2}]$, $c'[1 + r]$ cannot be positive and the simplest mainstream parable remains valid.

of a century of exploration and reflection on that issue, I have considered opinions that ought to be put in the amber of published discussion. They may be the most important part of my present recorded reflections.

Sraffa's book, he tells us (1960, pp. iii, v–vi), is a 'Prelude to a critique of economic theory'. More specifically, a critique of *marginalism* (call it neoclassicism, if you wish) is to be the next step. 'If the (1960) foundations hold, the critique may be attempted later, either by the writer or someone younger and better fitted for the task.' Extrapolating Piero's speed of composition, we cannot be surprised that he never provided such a critique. I once nursed the hope that among his papers at Trinity, or in Italy, treasures would turn up. That happy eventuality I must now doubt on the basis of all we know about the scholar, but personality traits aside, the Bayesian probabilities of cogent Sraffian fragments on marginalism seem low based on the disappointing *quality* of the few remarks the 1960 author does provide us. The reference to Philip Wicksteed (1914, pp. 18–20; 1933, pp. 790–96) seems a confused citing of a confused and confusing text. Wicksteed for once makes mountains out of trivial hills, and he does not succeed in climbing up and down those mole hillocks.[3]

Sraffa is correct that, in steady states of equilibrium where only one set of input proportions are maintained, any marginal products that exist cannot be *identified*. That tells nothing about when they do and do not exist, and therefore *that* cannot be an analysis *cogently* 'designed to serve as the basis for a critique of that theory' ('the marginal theory of value and distribution', 1960, p. vi). Fortunately, the 1960 book is better than its 78 pages of Parts I and II alone (with their postponing consideration of alternative feasible techniques).

In cautioning (p. v) against readers 'mistaking spurious "margins" for the genuine article', the author seems to overlook that much of his first 78 pages themselves do involve shifts in the 'scale of an industry' – as, for example, in working with specified *standard* market baskets of productions, or in supposing that demand and taste shifts do not alter real prices in a no-joint-product world, and as, for example, in Chapter I's crucial sole footnote.

---

[3] When corn is produced by a first-degree-homogeneous function of homogeneous labour and homogeneous land, there are no terminological perplexities. When heterogeneous lands and homogeneous labour are alternative ways to produce homogeneous corn, there are no terminological or logical perplexities – as the 1960 Chapter IX on Land could have clarified if only its few pages had used the space devoted to the topic of the standard system in favour of the programming inequalities–equalities of competitive arbitrage. See, for example, a modern treatment of the Ricardian economy in Samuelson (1959, Appendix, particularly pp. 28–35).

This brings me to the state of ambiguity, scandalous after a third of a century, on the question of whether input–output analysis can be content with a position of agnosticism on the question of an axiom of 'constant returns to scale'. As I hope to demonstrate mathematically, the author wants to play in a poker game where he has not put up the ante. No one need play in a specified game, but if you do play, you must not tolerate self-contradictory rules. A single contradiction in a logical system of axioms makes nothing provable in it (because *any*thing and its negation are implied theorems in it).

My purpose is not to conduct a one-sided debate with a dead scholar. My plaintiff brief, which must stand on its merits not on anyone's ideology, is against a generation of Sraffian writers who are very much alive and have not done their duty in proving that they are entitled to have their cake and eat it too. Constancy of returns to scale (or non-constancy) is crucial for its own sake. It is not crucial at all for a cogent rejection of neoclassical marginalism in favour of some claimed alternative classical paradigm (of distribution, pricing and dynamic growth). Thus, if increasing returns to scale obtains in the real world, so as to entail Chamberlin's (1933) imperfect competition, post-Kaldorian and 1867–1894 Marxian paradigms are as much impacted as are Clark–Solow models.

We can begin with page 1 of the book, then follow up with Chapter II and with Chapter IX on land, and end with the final seven pages that constitute the novelty in the work's contribution.

Wheat and iron outputs (p. 3) are each producible out of themselves as inputs, à la von Neumann (1937, 1945). By definition of this as being a Sraffian subsistence economy, these commodities can just barely reproduce themselves in the stationary state. From out of the blue, Sraffa gives the reader a single-instant picture, describable in the following modern production–function language:

$$\text{Wheat output at } t + 1 = f^1 \text{ [wheat input at } t, \text{ iron input at } t]$$

$$\text{Iron output}^{t+1} = f^2 \text{ [wheat-for-iron}^t, \text{ iron-for-iron}^t] \quad (1)$$

Here $f^1[\ ]$ and $f^2[\ ]$ are Sraffa's production functions. His snapshot reveals the following arithmetical numbers:

$$Q_1^{t+1} = f^1[Q_{11}^t, Q_{21}^t] = f^1[280 \text{ qr. wheat, 12 t. iron}]$$

$$= 400 \text{ qr. wheat}$$

$$Q_2^{t+1} = f^2[Q_{12}^t, Q_{22}^t] = f^2 [120 \text{ qr. wheat, 8 t. iron}]$$

$$= 20 \text{ t. iron} \quad (2)$$

Note that each period's outputs are specified to provide just enough inputs as are needed to reproduce the equilibrium indefinitely:

$$Q_1^{t+1} = Q_{11}^t + Q_{12}^t = 280\,\text{qr.} + 120\ \text{qr.} = 400\ \text{qr. wheat}$$

$$Q_2^{t+1} = Q_{21}^t + Q_{22}^t = 12\,\text{t.} + 8\,\text{t.} = 20\,\text{t. iron} \tag{3}$$

Theorem: *If(!), and only if(!), production obeys the law of* constant returns to scale, *we can write the* $f^j[Q_{1j}, Q_{2j}]$ *functions more specifically in the following* anti-neoclassical fashion:

$$Q_1^{t+1} = 400\ \text{Min}\ [Q_{11}^t/280,\ \ Q_{21}^t/12]$$

$$= \text{Min}\ [Q_{11}^t/(280/400),\ \ Q_{21}^t/(12/400)]$$

$$\equiv \text{Min}\ [Q_{11}^t/a_{11}, Q_{21}^t/a_{21}]$$

$$Q_2^{t+1} = 20\ \text{Min}\ [Q_{12}^t/120,\ \ Q_{22}^t/8]$$

$$= \text{Min}\ [Q_{12}^t/(120/20),\ \ Q_{22}^t/(8/20)]$$

$$\equiv \text{Min}\ [Q_{12}^t/a_{12}, Q_{22}^t/a_{22}]$$

$$0 \le \begin{bmatrix} a_{11} & a_{12} \\ a_{21} & a_{22} \end{bmatrix} = \begin{bmatrix} 280/400 & 120/20 \\ 12/400 & 8/20 \end{bmatrix} = \begin{bmatrix} 0.7 & 6 \\ 0.03 & 0.4 \end{bmatrix} \tag{4}$$

By convention, if an input–output technical coefficient a_{ij} is zero, we agree to omit its Q_{ij}^t from the $\text{Min}\,[\ldots, Q_{ij}^t/a_{ij}, \ldots]$ expression. Also, no a_{ij} can be negative under free disposability conditions.

Sraffa never writes down the above production functions but, as will be demonstrated, if they are denied the vast corpus of post-Sraffian literature collapses like a soufflé.

Under the same 'If, and only if' proviso stated above, the actual production functions of the system photographed at one instant could just as well be Cobb–Douglas neoclassical rather than the above Walras *Eléments* (pre-third edition) version written here in Equation (4). Once you tell me they are to be Cobb–Douglas, they definitely are thereby 'identified' as having to be the following neoclassical production functions:

$$Q_1^{t+1} = 400 \, (Q_{11}^t/280)^{0.7}(Q_{21}^t/12)^{0.3},$$

$$Q_2^{t+1} = 20 \, (Q_{12}^t/120)^{0.6}(Q_{22}^t/8)^{0.4} \tag{5}$$

Why (0.7 and 0.3) and (0.6 and 0.4)? There is no black magic involved, merely recognition that the relative shares of wheat in the unit costs of Equation (4)'s two goods can be shown to be 0.7 and 0.6, respectively. Remark: other Cobb–Douglas choices could have produced the snapshot, but obviously Sraffa wants his data to represent the *best* that the system can do and still be barely reproductive, which narrows the choice down to Equation (5).

We are beginning to see that the author was misguided to believe that his expositional departures from the literature [from, I suppose, Vladimir Dmitriev (1898), Ladislaus von Bortkiewicz (1907a), Leontief (1928, 1941, 1953), Tjalling Koopmans *et al.* (1951), Robert Solow (1952), Dorfman, Samuelson and Solow (1958), Michio Morishima (1959), Paul A. Samuelson (1959),...] were *well* 'designed to serve as the basis for a critique of that [marginalist version of value and distribution] theory' (p. vi). Only in his last chapter does he begin to analyse how to handle alternative techniques if they exist – as they realistically will.

The arithmetic example on the first page is useful to understand this. The 2-good subsistence system there, Equations (1) here, is declared to define a unique set of relative prices, (P_2/P_1) when $n = 2$ or in general $(P_2/P_1, \ldots, P_n/P_1)$, 'which if adopted by the market restores the original distribution' (p. 1), '... which ensures replacement all round' (p. 2),... 'which if adopted restores the original position...' (p. 2). What is this language about the market choosing to adopt this or that definition of price? The market has no mind of its own. Only under strict specifications will Darwinian competition *enforce* certain price–cost inequalities–equalities – as Sraffa would learn if he tried to exercise his imagined freedom to assume *increasing* returns to scale of (say) second-degree-homogeneity type. Thus, let a Sraffian try rewriting Equation (4) as

$$Q_j^{t+1} = \left\{ \text{Min} \, [Q_{1j}^t/a_{1j}, \ldots, Q_{nj}^t/a_{nj}] \right\}^2 \bar{Q}_j, \qquad j = 1, \ldots, n \tag{6}$$

or try rewriting Equation (6) with the exponent 2 changed to 9/10, as with *diminishing* returns to scale, or let each *j*th commodity have a different exponent: some above 1, some below 1, some at 1. A true agnostic will let the exponent differ according to scale for each commodity, but the author's coyness about commitment makes him no source to go to for factual knowledge about any of this.[4]

Does it matter? Of course it does as soon as the author hazards assertions about how the prices of standard or of other market-baskets of goods will vary with the profit rate.

If all this sounds complicated, it is. That is why I devoted most of an MIT semester in the early 1960s to exploring whether useful sense can come from *explicitly denying* constant returns to scale. When I had exhausted all efforts, we were left with an empty set of results. To my knowledge no Sraffian hitherto, or since, has had better luck. How many thirds of centuries must go by with the matter being treated as if unresolved?

Now suppress all t superscripts which become, in stationary states, for $i, j = 1, \ldots, n,$

$$Q_j^{t+1} \equiv Q_j^t \equiv Q_j, \qquad Q_{ij}^t \equiv Q_{ij}, \qquad a_{ij} \equiv Q_{ij}/Q_j \qquad (7)$$

---

[4] Paolo Varri (1987, p. 380), in a *Palgrave* piece on Fixed Capital, illustrates the uneasiness and mysticism about Sraffian prices as a new kind of prices, saying:

> The meaning of these prices has nothing to do with marginal or neoclassical theory. They represent a more fundamental [sic] concept: the exchange rates which ensure the reproduction of the economic system.

This seems like science fiction. It is the production equalities of $280 + 120 = 400$ and $12 + 8 = 20$ that 'ensure' the reproduction of the stationary state – provided the 400 and 20 harvests are properly allocated between industries. The book's author dictates that, and without indicating what algorithm of tâtonnement is to bring it about (i.e. to convert transitory Equation (8) here to Equation (1) of Sraffa). If entry is free, knowledge is ubiquitous, and inputs are dispersely owned – and if technology is minutely divisible among sub-firms of any size, so that people will stay being 'price takers' in self-sustainable auction markets – then market-clearing competitive markets can be the mechanisms for providing society's appropriate stage directions of behaviour. However, if returns are increasing so that collusion of owners is entailed, price takers become price namers and Sraffa's asserted terms of trade, '10 qr. of wheat for 1 t. of iron' (p. 1) is not at all realized. The defining matrix relation of $P = Pa$, when $[a_{ij}] = [Q_{ij}/\sum_i Q_{ij}] > 0$ and when $\det[I - a] = 0$, can be asserted by Humpty Dumptyism, but we are interested in such Ps only to the extent that they bear a relation to some real economic drama? This, we see again and again, comes when and only when the axiom of constant returns to scale obtains. Incidentally, the 'negative prices' that raise controversies in Sraffians' dialogues on joint production arise as artifacts only when Sraffa's special equalities are respected instead of the proper duality equalities–inequalities of market-clearing behaviour. If axioms of *free disposability* and *divisibility* of goods obtain, then all competitive prices that arise will be non-negative. The defects in Sraffa's Part II on joint products are touched upon by Samuelson (1990) and will not be further treated here. They are easily handled by von Neumann inequality dualities and ought to become standard in the post-Sraffian literature.

This suggests that our relative prices be time-invariant too. Sraffa is shy, or coy, about saying that his prices are to be competitive market prices, never greater than the respective goods' minimized unit costs. (In Robinson's East Anglia, for a time, *simultaneous equations* were considered viciously circular if P_j's unit cost depended upon P_i (and possibly P_j) that was considered somehow unkosher.) Thus, Marx (III, 1894) preferred the term 'prices of production' to '(minimized) unit costs of production', and Sraffa eschews going beyond speaking of his basics' prices as those that enable advances to buy inputs while being able to earn the system's (specified) rate of profit and still have receipts sufficient to compensate for the advances *ad perpetuum*.

There is in any case no way of avoiding simultaneous equations, which Sraffa recognizes. As we shall see, his prices are in every case precisely those of perfect-competition's arbitrage: its inequalities, equalities and dualities. All this applies equally to his defined basics and non-basics, and my conscience as a teacher bothers me that our seminars have to waste so much student time on that not very important distinction. If the sterile quest for the chimera of Ricardo's absolute measure of value had been abandoned stillborn, the Sraffian literature would gain in relevance and appeal. Later I say more on this.

Even in the subsistence economy, incapable of sustaining a positive interest rate, suppose Sraffa's snapshot had been the following instead of my Equation (1) above:

$$350 \text{ wheat} + 15 \text{ iron} \rightarrow 500 \text{ wheat}$$

$$90 \text{ wheat} + \quad 6 \text{ iron} \rightarrow \quad 15 \text{ iron} \tag{8}$$

It was then *not* in *its* stationary state. Not to worry. The author says (p. 5, n. 1): '...every system of the type under consideration [i.e., just barely productive] is capable of being brought to such a state merely by changing the proportions in which the individual equations enter it.' Oops! Only in constant returns to scale technologies do proportions matter and *alone* matter! Otherwise scale and proportions interact to deny the quoted claim. To see this let the snapshot data of Equation (8) come from Equation (6)'s allegedly admissible Sraffian form. Then Sraffa can never succeed in arriving at his Equation (1) by specifying appropriate relative inputs into Equation (6)'s proposed form for Equation (8). QED.

We can gain further insights from this devastating rebuttal. Suppose that half the inputs in Sraffa's example of Equation (1) become specified *not* to be needed any more. Then each and every output could be twice the sum of itself used as inputs, and thus the system could grow exponentially, doubling every period in accordance with what Sraffa (p. 6) asserts would be its 100 percent profit rate per period. Who can believe *that* if constant returns to scale is in any way *denied*? Von Neumann knew better.

Suppose the folk on Sraffa's Island X acquire the technical knowledge to be observed on two other subsistence islands:

Island Y

$$140 \text{ wheat} + 6 \text{ iron} \rightarrow 200 \text{ wheat}$$

$$60 \text{ wheat} + 4 \text{ iron} \rightarrow \quad 10 \text{ iron}$$

Island Z

$$200 \text{ wheat} + 16 \text{ iron} \rightarrow 400 \text{ wheat}$$

$$200 \text{ wheat} + \quad 4 \text{ iron} \rightarrow \quad 20 \text{ iron}$$

For anyone not in a Pickwickian mood of nihilism concerning any and all returns to scale, Island Y will be of no *new* interest. It looks to be the same technology as Sraffa's, happening to be sampled at half his scale. Would it be useful for a Sraffian to disagree with this interpretation?

Now turn to Z. It gives us *new* technical options: along with Island X's $(a_{11} \ a_{21})$ of Equation (4), we also have $(a'_{11} \ a'_{21}) = (200/400 \ 16/400)$ and also, along with old $(a_{12} \ a_{22})$, we have $(a'_{12} \ a'_{22}) = (200/20 \ 4/20)$. Peeking into all the chapters of the book, we realize that our own island is no longer a subsistence economy. At the zero interest presupposed in the old subsistence state, Darwinian competition will lead us as if by an invisible hand to produce wheat with Island Z's technique and iron with *our* technique. The same efficiency now goes for autarkic Island Z. When our subsistence state betters itself, it becomes a net production (or surplus) state. It can grow for ever at some positive exponential rate $1 + g^* > 1$ (in this example, $g^* = 2\frac{1}{3}$ per period). We can pay any positive profit rate less than g^* and can still afford to pay needed primary labour and primary land positive wages and rental rates.

Do you believe that? It is nonsense to do so if production functions are homogeneous of degree 2 or of degree 1/2! All of Part III's nice rules about switchpoints are inapplicable nonsense under the same licentiousness. Taking a linear blend at critical *switch* interest rates $\bar{r}$, where two alternative techniques are indifferent, is quite unwarranted (unfeasible!) if returns to scale are variable.

The young Sraffa's original instinct in the 1920s to presume (with Keynes) constant returns to scale was thus not gratuitous. I suspect he abandoned it for two or more reasons. (1) The unimportant conjecture is that Sraffa, at times in 1925 and after, may have used *constant returns* as a loose equivalent to *constant cost*, and used *decreasing returns* as loosely *increasing cost and supply*. In any case, after the heat of debate, his 1926 brief for constant cost may well have lost self-esteem. (It should have, in my reiterated view.) (2) More importantly, he never worked through the literal consequences for his 1960 book of departures from the returns conditions that market-clearing competition depends upon.

I should add at this point that my (unreported) attempts to make a defence for Sraffa's agnosticism by regarding his prices as planner's prices in an efficient non-market society all failed. The marginalist shadow prices of such a scenario lack the *average*-price properties that are intrinsic to Sraffa's equations in the book, except of course under special explicit constant-returns axioms.[5]

In sum, if a Sraffian denies constant returns to scale, the one-hundred-page 1960 classic evaporates into a few paragraphs of vapid chit-chat.

3   Mathematical heart of Sraffa

Now combine Chapter II with Chapter XI and Part III. Here is how a 3-good, 2-primary-factor Sraffa paradigm will look when (for simplicity) each good can be produced with two alternative techniques and without joint intrinsic products or durable machines. I write $(a'_{Lj}\, a'_{Tj};\, a'_{1j}\, a'_{2j}\, a'_{3j})$ and $(a''_{Lj}\, a''_{Tj};\, a''_{1j}\, a''_{2j}\, a''_{3j})$, where a_{Lj} stands for direct primary labour requirements and a_{Tj} stands for direct primary land requirements. Labour and land are each homogeneous with stipulated total supplies. Stationary states obtain

$$L'_1 + L''_1 + L'_2 + L''_2 + L'_3 + L''_3 \leq \bar{L} > 0, \qquad L_j \text{ non-negative}$$

$$T'_1 + T''_1 + T'_2 + T''_2 + T'_3 + T''_3 \leq \bar{T} > 0, \qquad T_j \text{ non-negative}$$

For $j = 1, 2, 3,$ $\qquad\qquad\qquad\qquad\qquad\qquad\qquad\qquad$ (9)

$$Q_j = \text{Min}\ [L'_j/a'_{Lj},\, T'_j/a'_{Tj},\, Q'_{1j}/a'_{1j},\, Q'_{2j}/a'_{2j},\, Q'_{3j}/a'_{3j}]$$
$$\quad + \text{Min}\ [L''_j/a''_{Lj},\, T''_j/a''_{Tj},\, Q''_{1j}/a''_{1j},\, Q''_{2j}/a''_{2j},\, Q''_{3j}/a''_{3j}]$$

$$= \sum_{k=1}^{3} Q'_{jk} + \sum_{k=1}^{3} Q''_{jk} + C_j, \qquad 0 \leq C_j = \text{consumption of } j$$

$$\text{(10)}$$

---

[5] Neo-Ricardian Sraffian models of Smith and Ricardo make no sense if the constant returns to scale that they presumed under competition gets explicitly denied. The classicists did not realize they 'spoke prose', but that prose had to be for the most part first-degree homogeneous.

Write the nominal wage rate as W, the nominal rent per acre (each paid at the *beginning* of the period) as R and the interest rate as r. Then real steady-state prices and distribution involve

$$\text{Min}\left[(Wa'_{Lj} + Ra'_{Tj})\,(1+r) + \sum_{i=1}^{3} P_i a'_{ij}(1+r) \right.$$

$$\left. (Wa''_{Lj} + Ra''_{Tj})\,(1+r) + \sum_{i=1}^{3} P_i a''_{ij}(1+r) \right]$$

$$= P_j, \qquad j = 1, 2, 3$$

$$= Wa^*_{Lj}\{R/W,\ 1+r\} + Ra_{Tj}a^*_{Tj}\{R/W, 1+r\}$$

$$[I - a^*\{R/W, 1+r\}\,(1+r)]^{-1}$$

$$= WA^*_{Lj}\{R/W, 1+r\} + RA^*_{Tj}\{R/W, 1+r\} \qquad (11)$$

where the starred a's are competition's chosen least-cost methods, and the starred A's are total (dated!) labour and land requirements. (The choice is from the 2^3 matrices that can be formed by *independently* using for each good either its ( )$'$ or ( )$''$ technique.)

None of this Sraffa–Leontief wisdom applies if returns are essentially non-constant to scale. Unlike Sraffa, von Neumann knew that his growth model had to obey constant returns to scale.

In the smooth neoclassical case, the $(a_{Lj} \ldots a_{3j})'$ and $(a_{Lj} \ldots a_{3j})''$ vectors are replaced by an infinite variety of alternative $(a_{Lj} \ldots a_{3j})$ coefficients connected by each good's relation(s):

$$1 = F^j[a_{Lj}, a_{Tj}, a_{1j}, a_{2j}, a_{3j}], \qquad j = 1, 2, 3 \qquad (12)$$

where each $F^j[\ ]$ is a concave, smooth, first-degree-homogeneous production function. Always, at each $(R/W, 1+r)$, an optimal $[a^*_{Lj}\{R/W, 1+r\}\, a^*_{Tj}\{R/W, 1+r\}\, a^*_{ij}\{R/W, 1+r\}]$ set of coefficients will be ground out by Darwinian competition.

As we go from ( )$'$ and ( )$''$ choices to a rich variety of techniques, we can approach qualitatively and quantitatively step-function approximations to smooth curves of market-clearing supply and demand (again, see Technical Note 2).

Always, in these single-product Clarkian or Sraffian technologies, a well-behaved *factor–price frontier* obtains for each good:

$$1 + r = \Phi^j(R/P_j/W/P_j), \qquad j = 1, 2, 3 \qquad (13)$$

where $-\Phi^j(\ )$ is a quasi-concave function that is monotone-increasing. Reswitching or the mentioned permitted reversals in the $(1 + r,$ consumption menu) relationships do not affect the good behaviour of Equation (13)'s factor–price frontiers, whether technologies are discrete and finite à la von Neumann–Sraffa or uncountably infinite as with Clark–Solow–Meade.

I have written out explicitly some things Sraffa did not write out in his book. This way we can see precisely what Ricardo's (1) labour-cum-land, (2) time-phased technologies and (3) subsistence-wage paradigm look like through correct 1960 Sraffian spectacles. Call it a neo-neo-Ricardian theory, but recognize that it is quite different from what those who call themselves neo-Ricardians usually talk about when they compare modern and old-time paradigms.

Equations (9), (10) and (13), which eschew smooth Clarkian production functions, have exactly the essential properties of a Haberler–Heckscher–Ohlin–Fisher *post*-1870 paradigm.

1. Far from giving comfort to a *labour theory of value* as an approximation to reality, the model teaches us that Ricardo's complications to the labour theory of value from problems of time can be much more than the Ricardo–Stigler seven percent (see Stigler, 1958). With outputs as inputs, the aberration can easily be 70 or 99 percent.

2. Ricardo could not avoid perceiving the 'time' complication, but neither he nor his editor took proper note of the *irreducible negation of the labour-only dogma that is introduced by land*. When goods differ in their land/labour intensities (for positive-rent and endogenous zero-rent lands!), changes in tastes for corn and cloth completely destroy the hope of relating relative prices to an invariant ratio of respective embodied-dated-labour contents of the goods. Where the external margin for land falls, and how big or small Ricardo's marginal-labour cost will be, these become *endogenous* not exogenous variables – thereby emasculating all meaningful content of a labour theory of value formulation.

The Sraffian model of my Equations (9), (10) and (13) clinches the point.

3. When the real world offers *alternative* techniques,

$$(a'_{jL}, a'_{jT}, \ldots, a'_{ij}, \ldots), \qquad (a''_{jL}, a''_{jT}, \ldots, a''_{ij}, \ldots),$$

$$(a'''_{jL}, a'''_{jT}, \ldots, a'''_{ij}, \ldots), \ldots,$$

then what are smooth demand and supply curves in smooth neoclassical technologies become step-function loci in Sraffa land. In a Gerald Shove (1930) jigsaw puzzle world, where catalogues offer a variety of alternative items and where suppliers are prepared to insert inbetween variants whenever demand warrants, the lengths of the steps and of their risers shrink in importance and the von Neumann *inequality bounds* become tighter and tighter around the system's equilibrium variables.

Query. If Pero could be brought to life, or if followers would volunteer to field questions on his behalf, what would be the answer to the following questions?

Are there not observable 'margins' (observable equalities or bounds) here? Are such margins '*spurious* margins' or the 'genuine article'?

My answer to these questions is manifest. Under the conditions specified (and with no pretence toward *aggregation* of *scalar* capital), Wicksteed and I would understand this model to have the general qualitative properties of Walras (1896), multi-commodity J. B. Clark (1899), Wicksteed (1894) and Arrow-Debreu (1954). Wouldn't it be nice if Sraffa had left us in an old trunk an outline of precisely these truths? (Of course I wryly jest.)

Figure 1 illustrates neoclassical versions of neo-neo-Ricardianism, and various Sraffian approximations to them. In Figure 1(a), AA' is the neoclassical production-possibility frontier in the short run when supplies of labour, land and capital are fixed. Figure 1(b) shows the three factor prices (W/P_{corn}, R/P_{corn}, $1 + r$) depicted by their respective distances from the sides of the equilateral triangle and standardized so that their sum is unity. (The top point betokens high profits; the right-hand point means a high corn wage; the left-hand point means high rent.) The locus aa' traces out induced changes in distribution as consumer tastes change from much cloth at a to much corn at a'.

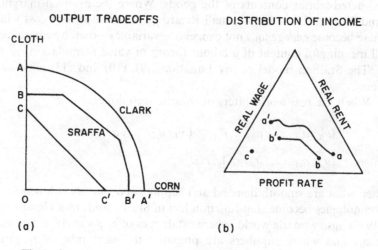

Figure 1

In Figure 1(a), BB' is the Sraffian counterpart to AA'; in Figure 1(b), bb' is the Sraffian counterpart to aa'. (Explanation: corn happens here to be relatively land-intensive and with a relatively high wage/profit ratio; cloth is the reverse.) The reader can construct a pair of new diagrams to handle the longer run where (say) population size adjusts to a subsistence corn real wage and accumulation acts to preserve a fixed $1 + \bar{r}$. (Remarks: in the 1960 Parts I and II limiting case of a *single technique*, factor returns are indeterminate when their totals are in fortuitous balance; for factor supplies generically in *any* proportions, one of Part I's factor share will be *zero or all* under ruthless short-run competition. CC in Figure 1(a) is included to portray the Santa Claus case where all goods happen to require all factors in the same proportion. Only the face of the labour theory of value is then saved by the implied invariance in the P_{cloth}/P_{corn} ratio since, as shown in point c in Figure 1(b), virtually 90 percent of the national income can go to land rent rather than to wages! CC' can be either Sraffian or Clarkian.)

4   The futility of Sraffa's standard commodity

My 1990 revisionist paper on Sraffa devoted paragraphs 10–11 to demonstrating the irrelevance and lack of usefulness of his standard commodity. No need to repeat here the argument that it cannot help defend Ricardo's attempted labour theory of value or Marx's formulation of the transformation problem. Here I ought to move on to show why Sraffa's standard does not cogently interpret and effectively help out any Ricardian's (misguided) hankering for an absolute or invariable measure of 'value'. In the 1993 Luigi Pasinetti *Festschrift*, Heinz Kurz and Neri Salvadori have provided a truly valuable survey of Ricardo's wanderings and Sraffa's proposed innovation. Analysts today and antiquarians in the next century will benefit from their efforts. They confirm my view that Ricardo's itch for absolutes was psychosomatic, and that the Sraffian construct does not succeed in scratching *it*.

Begin in 1810, when Ricardo was a rich broker beginning to study economics and when the Napoleonic Wars' expansion of the currency was having the usual inflationary effects on prices (including the prices in paper currency of precious metals such as gold and silver). Practical people sensibly tried to estimate how much prices rose for particular goods and for collections of goods. (Half a century before Jevons, primitive index numbers of prices were glimpsed.) Instead of welcoming this attempt to separate 'real' changes from 'non-real', what Keynes called the subtlest mind that ever came to economics said in effect at the time of the *Bullion* controversy (I paraphrase Kurz and Salvadori, 1993, p. 96):

No. Rather than measure average price changes, one will better separate the real and the unreal by measuring how price(s) change relative to some [single?] reference commodity whose purchasing power is constant or changes little in the short run. Experience has indeed taught '...that the *value* of gold or silver...for short spaces of time their value is tolerably fixed' [High Price of Bullion, *Works*, III, p. 64n., Ricardo's emphasis]. Therefore, compare individual or means of price changes relative to an ounce of such gold stuff [my wording].

Ricardo's goal is the *intertemporal and interspatial comparison* of price vectors, which tries to separate out *real* and *un*real changes. In *balanced* inflations, for example, the vector (P_j/P_{gold}) (or P_j in ounces of gold) might be virtually constant. By contrast $(P_j/P_{\text{strawberries}})$ will be contaminated by seasonal shifts in tastes and weather. Since Ricardo was building up toward an exaggerated confidence in the labour theory of value, one wonders why his 1810 proposal is to be preferred to concentration on the (P_j/wage) vector itself – or, we might add, the $(P_j/[\frac{1}{2}W + \frac{1}{2}\text{rent}])$ vector?

Seventy-five years ago the American philosopher John Dewey was asked what he thought of IQ measurements. Flippantly he replied: 'It's like trying to decide which of two people is heavier by looking in a pasture of heterogeneous rocks for the items you think most nearly match the individuals. And then *guessing* the weight of those rocks!'

Anyone who swallows a commodity theory of money must have peculiar ignorance about the technology of gold mining to expect particularly low standard deviations and zero mean-trend values in short-run (P_{gold}/W) time series of costs (quantity theorists do less badly), but at least Ricardo in 1810 is operating in the real world of economic history and policy debate. By 1817–21 Ricardo (1951–73) has turned theological and terminological. Now a good's 'value' is ever its labour content or purchasing power over labour. The vector $(P_j/W, P_{\text{gold}}/W)$, or for that matter $(P_j/W, P_j/\text{rent})$, could be better examined item by item, or by market basket, to see how real inventions, real changes in consumers' tastes, real changes in population and required subsistence-wage rates, and real changes in interest rates will affect ratios of elements in such vectors. My Sraffian-like equations presented here are useful to do precisely that and, except for the complication that iron may need coal and coal need iron, Ricardo displayed full powers to handle such equations. The effects of a wartime issue of currency could be contrasted with the comparative statics of these equations.

Why the itch for an absolute or invariable measure of VALUE? Kurz and Salvadori mention the 'time-honoured problem of distinguishing between "value" and "riches"' of Sir William Petty (1690), Adam Smith (1776) and other pre-1821 writers. *That* covers a can of disparate worms. Thus, Smith worried that our welfare would be much more hurt if all the water or air were taken from us than if all the diamonds or silks were, while at the same time each unit and all the air and water do command much less in the marketplace than do diamonds and silks. After 1870, the distinction between marginal and total utility properly explicates the puzzle. Despite the puffery for David Ricardo by Alfred Marshall (1890; 1961, p. 814), David cuts no heroic figure in *this* resolution. What counts here is that *theological and terminological insistence on absolute and invariable measures impede rather than induce clear thinking of these 'real' matters.* (In chasing down citations to Ricardo's *Principles*, I was struck anew with how muddled are some of Ricardo's wordings and joustings with J. B. Say. Editor Sraffa chastely desists from all normative comments.)

On reflection, Ricardo came to realize that exogenous *and endogenous* changes in any economic system must necessarily and always be capable of changing any and every commodity's $(P_j/W, P_j/R, P_j/P_i, P_j/P_{\text{gold}})$ ratios. Instead of this causing him to drop the search for the Dewey-rock unicorn, he narrows his focus to *one* kind of endogenous change: a drop in the interest rate (somehow occasioned) and a rise in the return of the primary factor(s) in terms of labour alone. (One would have thought it better for him to have contemplated *all* changes in the vector of real $(W/R, r, L/T$, tastes) and worked out their effects on $(P_j/P_i, P_j/W, P_j/R)$. The hole in the doughnut of Ricardo's labour theory of value haunts his guilty conscience.)

Now Ricardo looks for a rock, for a good, whose P_j/W is raised by a rise in the $1 + r$ interest rate that is intermediately normal between that of 100-year trees and one-minute shrimp gathered on the seashore. Why that 'mean' is golden or useful as a comparison rock for measuring absolute or invariable 'value' is simply and gratuitously taken for granted.

One who devotes decades to editing Ricardo is prone to take his every preoccupation seriously. Sraffa comes to notice that a set of basics, in a no-joint-product, labour-the-only-primary-factor, SINGLE TECHNIQUE scenario possesses a unique vectoral market-basket of goods which has *its* real wage (paid at end of the period) drop *linearly* as the profit rate rises from *zero* to its technological *maximum*. (Frobenius theorem: every non-negative $[a_{ij}]$ matrix that is *indecomposable* has a right-hand characteristic vector $[Q_i]$ that is positive and unique but for scale, so that $a(1 + r_{max})\bar{Q} = \bar{Q}$. *Ergo,* $W(1 + r)/\Sigma_1^n P_j \bar{Q}_j = \alpha[1 - (r/r_{max})].)$ [6]

One notices that whenever the basic goods differ in their direct and indirect labour intensities, some of them have real wage rates (have loci of $W(1 + r)/P_j$) that are pushed downward by a specified $(1 + r)$ rise in degree that locally *exceeds* the fall of Sraffa's STANDARD vector real wage; and necessarily some other basic must have its $W(1 + r)/P_k$ fall curvilinearly *slower* than the STANDARD's.

This Sraffian offering to Ricardo: what does it accomplish? How does it compare with, say, a market basket of goods constructed along Etienne Laspeyres, Hermann Paasche, or Fisher ideal index lines? How inferior is looking at it to studying the observable change in $(1 + r)$ [wages' fractional share] induced by all degrees of permissible $(1 + r)$ rise?

---

[6] Here is one way, an alternative to the 1960 way, to bring out the economic meaning of the standard vector. An indecomposable, net-productive, single technique can grow at a maximal rate, $1 + r^*$, if all is ploughed back as inputs, and the *positive* vector of productions (*and* of net ploughbacks) are in the proportions of the right-hand characteristic vector $\bar{Q}$. This is a special case of von Neumann's balanced-growth vector when several techniques are feasible.

For this standard vector, a non-spurious marginal productivity interpretation of $1 + r^*$ holds. The vector of inputs $\bar{Q}$ at t will *produce* at $t + 1$ (incrementally, totally and on average) exactly $(1 + r^*)$ times itself, r^* being the scalar intensity of the vectoral augmentation. Here is the story, followed by the scalar (non-vectoral) 'neoclassical' story:

$$[(1 + \epsilon)Q^t - Q^t]/\epsilon = r^*\bar{Q} \text{ for } 0 < \epsilon \text{ and as } \epsilon \to 0 \tag{6.1}$$

$$K^{t+1} = (1 + r^*)K^t \text{ for my bank account} \tag{6.2}$$

where

$$\partial K^{t+1}/\partial K^t = 1 + r^* \tag{6.3}$$

For a Clark–Ramsey–Solow neoclassical story, let

$$K^{t+1} + C^{t+1} = \alpha(L^t K^t)^{1/2} \tag{6.4a}$$

$$L^{t+1} = (1 + g^*)L^t = 2L^t \tag{6.4b}$$

$$C^t \equiv 0 \tag{6.4c}$$

If and only if $\alpha = 2$ will r^t be constant through time at $r^* = 1$, and $1 + r^*$ will then satisfy the scalar marginal-productivity determination

$$\partial K^{t+1}/\partial K^t = \tfrac{1}{2}\alpha(L^t/K^t)^{1/2}$$

$$= \tfrac{1}{2}\alpha(1)^{1/2} = 4/2 = (1 + 1) = 1 + r^* \tag{6.5}$$

Any fixed proportions for the (K_t/L_t) ratio other than unity will fail to achieve (maximal) feasible balanced exponential growth.

continued

When does the Sraffian construct *not* exist? When is it not even an *internal mean* of *all* $[W(1 + r)/P_j]$ items? How does the real-world existence of land and other non-producible natural resources affect Sraffa's brainchild? How is the concept impacted by real-world jointness of production?

All of these questions have been discussed somewhere in the literature, some of them by me and generations of MIT students. Kurz and Salvadori, as befits a sympathetic account, provide a useful survey of most of these issues. Here are some abbreviated comments.

1. In real life, when Leontief's students study census data on two-digit and three-digit classification of industries, they can 'identify' indecomposable $[a_{ij}]$ matrices *only after aggregating* sectors. Such aggregation can introduce *spurious* indecomposability when no one of the 50,000 commodities can be found with the property of being needed by *every* industry.

In other words, outside of the mathematical economics seminar room where we use indecomposable matrices as simplifying expositional devices for stating Frobenius–Perron matrix theorem, BASICS probably do not exist. (I do not insist on this, but it is noteworthy that *no* system of basics could ever have got started *after* the Big Bang. Realistically, innovators would have to have fabricated by *decomposable* labour-intensive activity the first inventories of basics that could thereafter be competitively viable to reproduce themselves.) I believe in a plethora of independent *sub*-systems that are indecomposable. This denies BASICS.

If exogenously supplied labour is a needed primary factor along with the $(\bar{Q}_{ij})$ and if workers are the only units that redundantly 'consume', then consuming their positive income share will slow down the growth process. If and only if they oddly choose to consume in $[C_j]$ proportions proportional to the technical $\bar{Q}$ vector will there be self-sustaining *exponential* (balanced) growth at $(1 + \sigma r^*)$, where $\sigma r^* < r^*$ is the ruling interest rate and σ is non-consuming rentiers' fractional share of national income.

Duality theory enables us to define $[a_{ij}]$'s existent left-hand eigenvector, $\bar{P}a = \bar{P}/(1 + r^*) > 0$.

Clearly, $\bar{P}a\bar{Q} = \overline{PQ}/(1 + r^*)$,   gross aggregate cost

$$\overline{PC} = \bar{P}[I - a]\bar{Q} = r^*\bar{P}Q, \quad \text{national income}$$

$$= \text{profit share} + 0 \text{ wage share}, \quad \text{when } W/\bar{P}_j \equiv 0 \tag{6.6}$$

Note that all of this has taken no notice of competitive prices. All of it is subject to the same limitations arising from (i) non-indecomposability, (ii) land as a primary factor limiting labour's productivity, (iii) alternative techniques somewhere viable – as belaboured above.

Marxians handicapped themselves when concentrating on zero or near-zero r evaluations. Sraffians will handicap themselves when concentrating on zero or near-zero wage configurations, which is part of what concentrating on standard commodities involves.

2. Related to the above point, but distinct from it, is the observation that a set of basics which exists could well be of minor fractional importance in the national income. Basics sound basic; non-basics sound like frills and luxuries. There is no warrant for this. Once we go beyond believing that water, earth and fire constitute the raw ingredients of everything, we contemplate cases like the following extreme: sugar needs a pinch of itself along with primary labour and land as inputs. Every other good needs a pinch of sugar among its inputs. The set of basics is then not empty: it consists of the one good sugar and, for dramatic exposition, suppose that expenditure on sugar never reaches one-thousandth of the national income.

$W(1 + r)/P_{sugar}$ does fall *linearly* as the profit rate goes from zero to its maximum of $1 + r^* = 1/a_{sugar,sugar}$. So? Little comfort for Ricardo's gratuitous itch here.

Therefore, let us add salt to the basics. Sugar and all goods now also need a pinch of salt as input. Now sugar and salt are basics, and let their total in the national income never exceed say one-seven-hundredth. Now a Sraffa basket of, say, 1 sugar and 0.01 salt defines a real wage that falls linearly – while one of the pair $[W(1 + r)/P_{sugar}, W(1 + r)/P_{salt}]$ has a concave profile and the other has a convex profile, thereby bracketing Sraffa's straight line.

Cui bono for Ricardo's purpose or anyone's purpose? It could well be that *every* other good has a $[W(1 + r)/P_j]$ profile that *lies outside* either and both of the basics' profile(s).

At the least, some Laspeyres or Divisia index of goods can provide a better reference mean than the new Sraffa tool.

3. Dramatic cases alert one to the generic possibilities. Suppose all goods, $j = 1, \ldots, n$, are always consumed in such a way that invariant proportions of individual's income and of NI are $(k_1 \ldots k_n)$ constants. Suppose the first s goods are basics. Their $\sum_1^s k_s$ can be a large or small fraction of unity. Moreover, Sraffa's linear $[W(1 + r)/P_{standard}]$ could well have little resemblance to the behaviour of $[W(1 + r)/\sum_1^n P_j k_j]$ or $[W(1 + r)/\sum_1^n P_j C_j]$ that statistician Simon Kuznets would record.

If compelled to address Ricardo's psychosomatic itch, I would seriously propose the plain-person's Kuznets calculation of how $W(1 + r)/\sum_1^n P_j C_j$ deterministically drops as r rises from zero to Sraffa's r_{max}. (C_j is the net consumption of good j in our stationary state.) Even where every commodity is a basic, it will generally *not* be true that raising r to halfway on its admissible range will result in exactly or approximately a 50% drop in measured real post-factum wages. (Why should *that* be true, and why care when it generally is not?) One can still harmlessly babble: interest-rate increases lower real wage reckoned in long-lived trees more than they lower real wage in haircuts or shrimp-gathering, and sophisticates can still warn that goods A and B cannot always be reliably ranked in terms of 'time intensity'.[7]

Not only does the Sraffa construct deviate from the mean–aggregate ratio, I would not be surprised if Monte Carlo experimentations with randomly sampled a_{ij} and a_{Lj} coefficients revealed a definite bias in the standard vector. To test this, play with my sugar and salt world, where only sugar is the basic and where most other goods are produced primarily by labour and a pinch of salt. When $W(1 + r)/P_{sugar}$ falls *linearly*, then precisely because P_{pepper} has *in it* the interest-bearing P_{sugar} component, W/P_{pepper} may tend to drop faster at first than W/P_{sugar}. Concretely,

---

[7] Kurz and Salvadori (1993, p. 120, n. 11) point out what they identify as an obvious error in Mark Blaug (1987). Then, in a left-handed compliment, they gratuitously absolve Samuelson from having made that error. (When the small-town editor was reproached for reporting 'John Smith was drunk last week', he changed the headline to 'Smith was sober last week'.) I come into their 1993 Footnote 11 for asserting in *Palgrave* (1987, p. 456) that 'Sraffa...thought that [$W/P_{standard}$ linearly declines with r] somehow provided Ricardo with a defence for his labour theory of value.' For this, the authors say:

> [1] There is no evidence whatsoever in support of this interpretation. [2] Sraffa...emphasized that the Standard commodity is 'a purely auxiliary construction'...and [3] cannot alter its [the system's] mathematical properties. (1993, p. 120; my numberings)

Before I agreed to reformulate what I now guess was in Sraffa's mind during 1927–1960, and appraise how close post-1960 writers are to *his* understandings, it must be noted that what I have numbered [2] and [3] is not cogent rebuttal to my alleged error of [1]. If I erred in attributing to Sraffa interest in defending what I regard to be erroneous Ricardo infatuation with the labour theory of value, it was in no degree because I believed Sraffa to make the Blaug error. Why drag that into appraising *my* critique?

I indict Ricardo (and Sraffa) for not explicitly following Smith in formulating a *tripartite* model of relative prices, real prices and distributive shares based on the *three*some of labour, land and time-phased produced inputs. (Ricardo wrongly missed out in understanding the complications engendered by land(s); for all his complaining about Smith, Ricardo did recognize that his own 'values' paradigm entailed time-phasing deviations, but through some 8 years of dithering he persuaded himself that the deviations were quantitatively minor – viz. the Ricardo–Stigler 93% labour theory of value. See Coleman (1990) for argumentation that 93% could well be 3%.) Ricardo's preoccupations with absolute and invariable measures of value are part of the indictment that post-Smithians like me cogently include in our brief. I agree with Kurz–Salvadori that Sraffa's pages on the STANDARD commodity provide no shred of cogent defence for the defendant(s) indicted. (*That* was my *Palgrave* point, and I need not have complicated it by pronouncing on what Sraffa *thought* his standard commodity had to do with this.) I hope they agree with me that some representative Sraffians have taken a less unsympathetic attitude on *this* matter.

continued

when expenditures on the goods consumed are in proportions invariant to $1 + r$, I would want to explore whether a rise of r halfway to r_{max} will cause Kuznets to observe *more* than a 50% drop in empirical wage share; Sraffa's benchmark in such cases would give a biased upward wage share. Eager readers might work out 'random' choices of coefficients and check whether a systematic bias does exist. Even if the characteristic vector is found to err as much in one direction as the other, why should Ricardo tolerate the gratuitous variance from the Kuznets data which comes from Sraffa's proposal?

Indecomposability and basicness is not a metric character of quantitative relevance. It depends qualitatively on a shibboleth: drop that pinch-of-salt requirement and you have not perceptibly changed anything in the real economic world, but you have perpetrated a tempest in Sraffa's teacup, wiping out half of all his basics!

Before leaving this point, I should take up von Neumann's case of cancerous exponential growth *sans* limiting land supply. For it, sugar and any other basic can grow most rapidly in the proportions of Sraffa's STANDARD. (Non-basics grow in entailed proportions, including possibly their coming to have *infinite* or *zero* relative price!) The standard vector to me is more importantly the von Neumann vector than the Sraffa vector. With multiple independent sub-basics, no standard exists!

4. To cut short a possibly boring topic, consider how to illuminate idle questions like the following: How many inflection points can $(1 + r)W/P_n$ have when the number of goods is given as $n = 3, 4, \ldots$? How many double-switching points can the eight-technique model of Equation (10) possibly have? Etc. These are all part of the P_i/P_j dependences upon $1 + r$. The theory of equations, Sturm's tests and more complicated

---

On what is a different issue, as I write now in 1993, I would not be surprised or distressed if some back of Sraffa's envelope turned up in the future that was found to say:

My studies have convinced me that the single-technique, labour-only model with an indecomposable core, and which defines a unique standard vector, speaks not at all to the empirical and theoretical usefulness of that standard concept or to the merits and demerits of Ricardo's preoccupation with *labour values*.

Piero's was a subtle mind, which had thought long and hard on these (mathematical!) relationships. His pen writes as if a lawyer were at hand to ensure that no vulnerable sentence appears. I honour him for that, and with my own students felt obligated to point out the subtlety of the text that in one place uses indefinite articles such as 'a' and in another uses definite articles such as 'the', or 'the unique'. What all of Sraffa's readers can agree on is that in the 1960 classic there are no passages like the above back-of-the-envelope fragment or its negation. (So to speak, nowhere does he say, 'I have stopped beating my horse'.)

extensions to ratios of polynomials would be what we must study if these questions were not too frivolous for us to try to answer. If Sraffa's construction were a useful auxiliary for that purpose, it might deserve a modest paragraph in the comprehensive treatises, but is it? Toward what is it an 'auxiliary'?

5. Up until now I have played along with the supposition of but one single $[a_{Lj} \, a_{1j} \ldots]$ technique. As in Part III (1960), let there now be more than one competitively viable technique. Ricardo has now lost the linear reference proffered to him. (Who steals my purse steals trash.) Now, for $0 \le r \le r_{\text{switch}}$, one STANDARD market basket serves; for some other r, it is irrelevant. The King is dead, long live the King, a drama replayable a few or a hundred times as selfish competitors are induced by changes in interest rates to switch their orders from machine-tool catalogues.

It is fortunate that there was no previous usefulness in the standard concept, since that would be lost in any scenario which was at all realistic.

6. Staying with no jointly produced goods, how does the realistic intrusion of Ricardian land affect the Sraffa offering? On the extreme supposition that one technique $(a_{Lj} \, a_{Tj} \ldots a_{ij} \ldots)$ obtains always, and that from somewhere the wage/rent ratio is held invariant while $1 + r$ rises from unity to its maximum, the device works as well (or as badly) as in the labour-only case, but when W/R varies generically *and systemically with* $1 + r$, all is lost.

Ricardo and I have to realize that optimal proportions of land to labour are affected by changes in the interest rate. When vectors of capitals $(Q_{1j} \ldots Q_{nj})$ differ at different $1 + r$ levels, depending on whether one of them is 'more complementary' to land than labour – as is expressible in non-classical Sraffian discrete technologies – there are no *linear* paths in the $(W/P_j, R/P_j, 1 + r)$ loci described in Equation (13) here.

Distribution is complicated in Ricardo's world of labour, land and time-phasing. Had Sraffa developed his critique of marginalism further, he might have come to see how preliminary his Prelude still was.

7. To conserve space, I conclude with a few words on joint products and Sraffa's standard concept applied to them. Preoccupation with it entails preoccupation with the unrewarding definitional complexities of *indecomposability* for such systems. These conquered, we need to flesh out the treatment of inequalities and dualities that Sraffa's Part II never properly addressed.

Let all this be properly done. We are then left with the anticlimax that, for admissible non-negative *rectangular* matrixes $[b_{ij}]$ and $[a_{ij}]$, and admissible von Neumann $[b_{ij} - a_{ij}]$ matrixes, there may exist only in the complex number system $\alpha + \beta\sqrt{-1}$, characteristic vectors. No one seriously wants to make STANDARD market baskets of say two Basics, with weights of $(0.1 + 0.9\sqrt{-1})$ and $(0.9 + 0.1\sqrt{-1})$. As Carlo Manara (1980, pp. 9–11) has shown, there may exist *no* real characteristic vectors to serve as a standard commodity for admissible *single*-technique joint-product systems.

A catastrophe? No, no catastrophe. There was little of value (to me, to Ricardo, to Sraffa) to be lost and no tragedy in the Manara finding that some *b–a* matrixes lack *real*-number characteristic Sraffian vectors.

My 1990 paper, preliminary to this one, makes it unnecessary to elaborate here on the fact that, even when there exist as many usable activities as there are goods, so the locally relevant sub-system is 'square', it will still be generically true – almost generically so – that competition chooses *endogenously* to go from one square principal-minor to *another* square principal-minor as the result of changes in tastes alone. Constant costs and invariant price ratios (which are not even mandatory when production is not joint but primary factors are more than one) will obtain only in severely limited cases of joint production and when labour is the only primary factor.

5   How limitations of land and capitals get underplayed

Steady states of equilibrium are subsets of the dynamic paths that economic systems can and do follow. These steady states are, in the nomenclature of politics, minority states rare in comparison with the totality of states. The exceptions to this truth occur in the special circumstances of heavily dampened systems that *rapidly converge* to their asymptotes, and which are only rarely perturbed by further exogenous shocks. Keynes recognized this when he said, 'In the long run we are all dead.' He did not mean by this, be cavalier in taking account of the future in comparison with the present. Instead he was reminding us that each future grows out of present presents.

The banalities of the previous paragraph must be reasserted to make the point that the post-1959 Sraffian literature lamentably has shifted undue attention to long-run equilibrium relations. When a Dobb thinks about China or Russia, he ought (like Kuznets) to concentrate on the primitive vectors of capital goods that these societies possess. They should analyse what sacrifices of current consumption may be required if capital vectors are to be built up. They cannot expect different goods to have common own-rates of interest along the transient paths of competitive arbitrage. Piero Sraffa (1932), when criticizing Friedrich Hayek's 1931 *Prices and Production*, insisted on all this in an innovative way. Joan Robinson, to her dying day, expressed scepticisms concerning the usefulness in the real world of exponential paths of equilibrium. However, when you examine the 1960 Sraffa book, you are hard put to find a single passage grappling with dynamic trajectories of induced $P_i(t)/P_j(t)$ changes. If, as I did cursorily for the present effort, you sample a score of post-Sraffian writings in *Palgrave* or elsewhere, you will verify that the 1960 preoccupation prevails.

Why does that matter? It matters because the scarcity of capitals is hidden from view through steady-state spectacles. When Nicholas Georgescu-Roegen (1951) and Samuelson (1951) prattle about non-substitution theorems in Leontief systems, we do not dramatize for readers how a shift of tastes from ballet to bourbon will (at each somehow prescribed interest rate) require a vast reduction of some elements of society's capital VECTOR and a vast increase in some other elements – with no Clarkian neutrality of *net* effect being conceptually definable. Students from a Marxian tradition of *Mehrwert* are not bothered by this: they have been taught that constant capital or 'dead labour' is sterile anyway in comparison with vital direct (or 'live') labour. Any planned utopia that fails to emancipate itself from these notions fatally handicaps its own efficiency and progress.[8]

---

[8] Samuelson (1975) has demonstrated the 'intertemporal Pareto-optimality' of competitive arbitrage pricings, *statically* and *dynamically*. Also, Samuelson (1994), in a discussion of new elegant German reproductions of Böhm-Bawerk's 1889 *Positive Theory of Capital* and Irving Fisher's 1907 *Rate of Interest*, calls attention to the Bernard Shaw, V. I. Lenin and Joan Robinson view that once capitals have been accumulated, their returns are rents like Henry George land rents and are therefore available for confiscation by an egalitarian society. I am not a besotted admirer of Friedrich Hayek's *laissez-faire* views, but I do salute his deep 1945 refutation of this naive viewpoint as applied to real life, where knowledge is seriously incomplete in the marketplace.

An important Sraffian 'hit' is that, as Ian Steedman's *Marx After Sraffa* (1977) points out, his 1960 classic is the Trojan Horse in the Marxian seminars on the so-called 'transformation problem'. See Marx (1895), Dmitriev (1898), von Bortkiewicz (1907a), Seton (1957) and Samuelson (1971). Sraffa, the friend of the Italian Marxian communist Gramsci, quietly debunks Marx's paradigm of *Mehrwert*, in which only direct-wage outlays earn an exploitative mark-up. For Sraffa's cost-of-production relationships, constant capital is not dead labour product that needs receive a positive interest yield as surplus. 1960 Sraffa jettisons the *labour theory of value* and replaces it by the 'dated-labour theory': if his chapter on land had been properly made explicit, Sraffa's would have been a land–labour–interest (or time-phased) theory of value, with what Marshall would call 'normal prices' rather than with classical natural price constancies.

6   Conclusion

I have concentrated here more on Sraffa's misses than on his hits. Good wine needs no bush. Like Wicksell on Cassel, I want to nominate for the record some nagging doubts. Peer groups can in the end elect or reject nominated viewpoints, and although I love Wicksell and have some contempt for Cassel's scholarly manners, I judge some of Wicksell's 1919 criticisms to have been wrong. Examples: Cassel is not in error to believe that *numerical* utility is not needed for (or identifiable from) non-stochastic demand data; again, Cassel's early 1918 version of the Harrod–Domar multiplier–accelerator exponential process is valuable despite Wicksell's exaggeration of the importance for early twentieth century Sweden of diminishing returns due to land scarcity. (My own insistence on 'land' in Equations (9)–(13) is motivated by more than land's deserved importance in GNP. Ricardo without land is Hamlet without the Prince. Besides, lands stand for and dramatize the *realistic* lack of homogeneity of the important *primary* factors in the real world: women vs. men; high IQ DNA vs. low; prime vineyard lands vs. scrub pastures. Smith's one-third for labour, one-third for rent, one-third for interest and profit seems better factually than zero for natural resources, 75 percent for wages (heterogeneous workers' rents) and 25 percent for profits.)

Wicksell's misses do not impair the worth of his hits. I hope the same can be said of my effort, whose fruits need to be tested and weighed. Actually, my half a dozen articles purporting to question some Sraffian doctrines have not, to my eye, made palpable dents in the beliefs of contemporary Sraffians. By contrast, and this is only proper and to be expected, my few stumbles in this rough terrain have not gone unnoticed.

As I read the 1960–1993 literature, I sense that mathematical Marxianism of the Paul Sweezy (1942) type has paradoxically been undermined by Sraffa's prices-of-production alternative paradigm to equalized *Mehrwert*. I have in mind such Trojan horses (not pejorative appellations) as Ian Steedman, *Marx After Sraffa* (1977) and John Roemer (1977).

Not less paradoxical is my finding that Editor Sraffa's compilation of David Ricardo's *Works* has resulted in modern microscopes being put on them to reveal a rich pasture of warts rather than beauty marks. When I began to study economics some six decades ago, none of us read Ricardo but we took for granted that there were subtle treasures therein. Our teachers had lost interest and involvement, but their teachers, our grandparents, had argued endlessly about whether Ricardo did or did not believe in a labour theory of value. (When I put that question to Piero Sraffa in 1948 on the Cambridge Backs, he shrugged his shoulders and replied Delphically: 'He did and he didn't.' I understood and I didn't.)[9]

Of the many post-1960 doubts aired here, a brief summing up would run as follows.

1. Without constant returns to scale, the Leontief–Sraffa matrix apparatus is virtually without economic content and interest. If the axiom is violated at the industry level, price-and-unit-cost correspondences must be replaced by Chamberlin–Cournot monopolistic–competition alternatives. *External*-economy increasing returns won't refute my point.

2. The existence or non-existence of basics is of limited empirical and theoretical importance even in the absence of joint products and non-labour primary factors. When basics do exist and constitute a small fraction of the GNP, constructions based on them are of fractional interest. Whatever their weight in the total, as soon as more than one viable technique exists, there is a plethora of standards. In the most favourable case for Sraffa, the 'auxiliary' knowledge about $(\partial/\partial r)[P_1/W \ldots P_n/W]$ contributed by this 'auxiliary' concept of Sraffa is, to my mind, virtually zero. Ricardo's pathetic hankering for an absolute or invariable measure of value (or price or ...) remains as pathetic after 1960 as before, and it was a pathetic fault in Piero Sraffa as editor not to point this out cogently.

3. No single homogeneous primary factor of production obtains in real life. When we add land(s) (or multiple grades of labour) to a Sraffa–Leontief system, price ratios and the profit rate (W/R, P_j/P_1, P_j/W, $1 + r$) are competitive *endogenous* unknowns subject to supply and demand in

---

[9] It is part of the intellectual history of our times that Piero Sraffa helped propel Ludwig Wittgenstein from his *Tractatus* phase to his ultimate phase by introducing into their railway station discussion on the language game, 'Then what do you make of this [Sicilian hand gesture]?'. The late Alexander Gerschenkron, Harvard's erudite economic historian, mentioned to me that there is a similar colloquy in Thomas Mann's 1924 *Magic Mountain*. 'Could Sraffa have been remembering, consciously or unconsciously, that passage?' Gerschenkron asked. 'Why not write to him at Trinity,' I suggested. Gerschenkron hesitated to do that but, on my urging, wrote to Maurice Dobb to put to Sraffa the question if he thought that acceptable. Gerschenkron reported: 'Dobb replied that Piero confirmed he had never read *Magic Mountain*'. Another time, I was puzzled about whether Sraffa meant by his words 'constant returns' (1) constant returns to scale, or (2) 'constant costs' as the special case of (1) where factor proportions happen to be uniform? I was hesitant to press him in correspondence, so I enlisted Joan Robinson to ask him. She reported that Piero asked what else could he have meant than 'constant returns *to scale*?'.

multiple markets – markets which clear in every run in time with equilibria that depend on tastes, endowments and relevant factor-supply relationships. Qualitatively, the resulting inequalities of comparative statics – $(\Delta P_i)(\Delta Q_i) \geq 0$ and all that – are precisely the same whether the discrete-technology system has many or few alternative techniques and/or has much or little variability in proportions. *All* the qualitative intertemporal properties of a Sraffa–von Neumann discrete technology can be mimicked in a smoothly differentiable technology, and vice versa. (In both paradigms, a bunching of techniques *near* each other will create the same sensitivity of factor shares in GNP to minute changes in input endowments, etc.) See Samuelson (1949, 1987, 1991a, 1991b).

4. I strongly believe, on the evidence, that Smith, Ricardo and J. S. Mill used essentially *the same logical paradigm* as did Walras and Arrow and Debreu. (Edward Chamberlin is another matter, as is Ralph Gomory's (1958) integer programming.) Until missing papers surface in the Sraffa files with *new* devastating critiques of 'marginalism', or until living Sraffians produce such new critiques not yet to be found in the literature, there will seem no need to qualify the first two sentences of this paragraph.

Years ago in a Presidential AEA address I scolded the public for taking John Kenneth Galbraith too seriously, and scolded us professionals for not taking him seriously enough. Maybe I was at least half right.

Today, if I need to scold Sraffians for taking *Production of Commodities by Means of Commodities* too seriously, I must scold mainstream economists for not taking it seriously enough.

It is a beautiful work for all its idiosyncrasies. Piero Sraffa was a marvellous personality and personage. Joan Robinson (1933), Roy Harrod, Michal Kalecki (1971) and Nicholas Kaldor (1937, 1960a, 1960b) – individually and collectively – added to our understanding of mainstream economics and its limitations and to our understanding of the world. My Nobel medallion would have a greater lustre to my eye if *their* just rewards had been justly recognized.

Technical notes

1. Hawkins–Simon and Sraffa's subsistence technologies. The traditional subsistence economy of Malthus and Darwin, applicable to men, rabbits and sagebrush, contemplates stationary states with a population density relative to fixed land at a critical ratio where output per capita is just adequate to keep populations from either declining or increasing. Sraffa's Chapter I has its own, related but distinguishable, definition.

For Sraffa a technology is a (barely) subsistence one, where by definition the stationary levels of total outputs, $(\bar{Q}_i)$, are just adequate to provide the (Q_{ij}) inputs of themselves needed for their total production and reproduction. He begins with *all* produced inputs strictly positive – as in (p. 3)'s

200 qr. wheat and 12 t. iron *produces* 400 qr. wheat

120 qr. wheat and 8 t. iron *produces* 20 t. iron

or

$$Q_{11} \text{ and } Q_{21} \rightarrow Q_{11} + Q_{12} = \bar{Q}_1, \quad Q_{21} \text{ and } Q_{22} \rightarrow Q_{21} + Q_{22} = \bar{Q}_2$$
(1.1)

Notationally, I write total outputs as $(Q_1 \, Q_2 \ldots)$, inputs of goods $(1, \ldots, n)$ needed to produce Q_j of good j as $(Q_{1j} \ldots Q_{nj})$, and the technical a_{ij} coefficients giving the needed inputs normalized to produce *one* of good j as $(a_{11} = Q_{11}/Q_1,$ $a_{12} = Q_{12}/Q_2, \ldots, a_{ij} = Q_{ij}/Q_j, \ldots)$. Sraffa's adequate but self-handicapping notation translates as $(Q_1 \, Q_2 \ldots) = (A \, B \ldots)$; $(Q_{11}, Q_{21}, Q_{12}, Q_{22}, \ldots) =$ $(A_a, B_a, A_b, B_b \ldots)$. Also $(a_{11}, a_{21}, a_{12}, a_{22}, \ldots) = (A_a/A, B_a/A, A_b/B, B_b/B, \ldots)$, etc.

Equation (1.1) is *one snapshot* of the technology. That same technology, Sraffa presumes (p. 5, n.1), would be capable of showing a *second snapshot* such as

100 wheat and 6 iron *produces* 200 wheat

120 wheat and 8 iron *produces* 20 iron (1.2)

In his words (p. 5, n.1): '... every system of the type under consideration [such as Equation (1.2)] is capable of being brought to such a [self-replacing] state [proportional to Equation (1.1)] merely by changing the proportions in which the individual equations enter it.' Thus, by his third page, the author has answered in the affirmative his own question: Am I *necessarily* assuming *constant returns to scale*? Yes, his own logic tells us, for the quoted sentence is the necessary and sufficient condition for one to convert any single snapshot, of the type

$$\bar{Q}_1/400 = \text{Min} \, [Q_{11}/200, Q_{21}/12], \quad \bar{Q}_2/20 = \text{Min} \, [Q_{12}/120, Q_{22}]$$
(1.3)

regarded as valid for the one special case of $(Q_{11}, Q_{21}, Q_{12}, Q_{22};$ $Q_1, Q_2) = (200, 12, 20, 120; \, 400, 20)$, to be *necessarily valid* for *any* positive Q_{ij}. If this first-degree-homogeneous formulation of Equation (1.3) were not valid – and, say a two-degree-homogeneous, or a 1/3-degree-homogeneous, or a varying-degree-homogeneous function were assumed valid – then it would be inadmissible for Sraffa to be able to convert Equation (1.2) into Equation (1.1) or its scale equivalent. QED.

Chapter I's definitional condition for Sraffian subsistence, written as

$$Q_{i1} + \ldots + Q_{in} + 0 = \bar{Q}_i > 0 \qquad i = 1, \ldots, n$$
(1.4)

is equivalent in matrix terms to saying that $(\bar{Q}_i)$ is *a positive characteristic right-hand column vector* of the $a = [a_{ij}] = [Q_{ij}/\sum_k Q_{ik}]$ matrix

$$
\begin{bmatrix} a_{11} & \cdots & a_{1n} \\ \vdots & & \vdots \\ a_{n1} & \cdots & a_{nn} \end{bmatrix} \begin{bmatrix} \bar{Q}_1 \\ \vdots \\ \bar{Q}_n \end{bmatrix} = (1) \begin{bmatrix} \bar{Q}_1 \\ \vdots \\ \bar{Q}_n \end{bmatrix}, \qquad aQ = Q \tag{1.5a}
$$

$$
[I - a][\bar{Q}] = \begin{bmatrix} 1 - a_{11} & \cdots & -a_{1n} \\ \vdots & & \vdots \\ -a_{n1} & \cdots & 1 - a_{nn} \end{bmatrix} \begin{bmatrix} \bar{Q}_1 \\ \vdots \\ \bar{Q}_n \end{bmatrix} = 0 \tag{1.5b}
$$

If Equation (1.5b) is to have a non-zero vector solution for $(\bar{Q}_i)$, we know $I - a$ must be singular with a zero determinant:

$$
\det[I - a] = \begin{vmatrix} 1 - a_{11} & \cdots & -a_{1n} \\ \vdots & & \vdots \\ -a_{n1} & \cdots & 1 - a_{nn} \end{vmatrix} = 0 \tag{1.5c}
$$

Actually, unknown to Sraffa publishing in 1960, David Hawkins and Herbert Simon (1949) gave a classic proof for a technology to be *net-productive* or to be *barely* so. See Robert Dorfman, Paul Samuelson and Robert Solow (1958, pp. 253–64) for a discussion of many equivalent Hawkins–Simon conditions: necessary conditions, sufficient conditions, necessary-and-sufficient conditions.

For brevity, I note that if $[Q_{ij}]$ and $[a_{ij}]$ are all positive, then Equation (1.5c) is assuredly both necessary *and* sufficient. In Sraffa's terms, *all* goods are then basics (*each* needed directly or indirectly to produce *every* good; in this overstrong case of positivity, *directly*).

Sraffa (pp. 4–5) notes that some Q_{ij}'s can be zero rather than positive. Page 8 says, correctly says, that a subsistence a cannot be of the form that includes a non-basic along with basics, but little definite is given about what a_{ij}'s can be zero for Sraffa. It is understandable that Sraffa in his sixth decade would not know of Hawkins–Simon (1949) and Dorfman–Samuelson–Solow (1958), but in view of Kaldor, David Champernowne (1945) and the Cambridge discussions of John von Neumann (1937, 1945), it was self-indulgent of him not to relate his subsistence technology to the von Neumann closed growth model capable only of zero growth and a zero interest rate. On the issue of a's being indecomposable, so that all the goods are to be basics in the Sraffa zoo, von Neumann's over-strong condition for irreducibility boils down in Chapter I's no-jointness-of-production case to the following anticlimax: *Any* diagonal Q_{ii} or a_{ii} may be zero, but *all* off-diagonal a_{ij}'s or Q_{ij}'s must be positive. Even for Sraffa, this would be gratuitously over-strong. (Von Neumann was not nodding but he was in an over-hurry.)

Actually, any of the following sign patterns for a are legitimate subsistence economies, satisfying the spirit of Equations (1.4) and (1.5), but only a subset of them satisfy Sraffa's gratuitously special requirement (1960, p. 8) that only systems possessing basics are to be discussed in his book.

$$[1], \quad \begin{bmatrix} + & + \\ + & + \end{bmatrix}, \quad \begin{bmatrix} + & + & + \\ + & + & + \\ + & + & + \end{bmatrix} \tag{1.6a}$$

$$\begin{bmatrix} 0 & \frac{1}{2} \\ 2 & 0 \end{bmatrix}, \quad a_{12}a_{21} = 1; \quad \begin{bmatrix} + & + \\ + & 0 \end{bmatrix}, \quad a_{12}a_{21} = 1 - a_{11} \tag{1.6b}$$

$$\begin{bmatrix} 0 & \frac{1}{2} & 0 \\ 2 & 0 & 0 \\ 0 & 0 & 1 \end{bmatrix}; \quad \begin{bmatrix} + & + & 0 \\ + & + & 0 \\ 0 & 0 & 1 \end{bmatrix}, \quad \begin{vmatrix} 1 - a_{11} & -a_{12} \\ -a_{21} & 1 - a_{22} \end{vmatrix} = 0 \le 1 - a_{ii} \tag{1.6c}$$

$$\begin{bmatrix} 0.9 & 0 \\ 0 & 1 \end{bmatrix} \tag{1.6d}$$

Why does it matter that the real world can often have *no* set of basics? Why not humour Piero Sraffa's idiosyncratic refusal to contemplate technologies, like those in Equation (1.6c)? It matters because the general is always to be preferred to the (gratuitously) special. It matters because so much of the 1960 book, which is in any case less than 100 pages, is literally wasted on verbiage concerning basics. (For example, the palaver about standard commodities.) Remove the pages dealing with an irrelevancy and you have a very small book indeed, one with gaping vacuums that (to mix a metaphor) now stand out. The five-page Chapter XI on land is a glaring example. Any work calling for a repudiation of mainstream paradigms in favour of a return to pre-1870 classicism should have a long and deep chapter on land. Instead we have a trivial preoccupation with how to fit land into the mould of joint production, and how to define for such models the definition of basics. What we lack are recognitions of how a 2-primary-factor-cum-time-phasing paradigm vitiates Ricardian labour-theory-of-value approximations, and how joint production paradigms necessitate going beyond Sraffian equalities (with their bizarre negative prices in a universe of free disposability!) in favour of Dantzig–von Neumann inequalities–equalities.

I return now to point out that in subsistence economies of the Equation (1.6c) type, which possess no non-empty set of basics, Sraffa's Chapter I artifact of 'exchange-values' (that 'restore[s] the original distribution of the products' and makes the process repeatable) simply does not *uniquely* exist. Where 1 of wheat by itself produces 1 of wheat, and 1 of iron by itself produces 1 of iron, Sraffa's p_2/p_1

is *any* positive number, and the same holds for vectors of prices in multi-good subsistence systems that split into independent parts.[10] That such indeterminacy does not matter reveals that unique determinancy (when it obtains) does not really matter after all!

The Hawkins–Simon analysis can assure Sraffa of the following:

If and only if all goods in the subsistence economy are basics, so that

$$I + a + a^2 + \ldots + a^{n-1} > 0 \tag{1.7a}$$

and a is assuredly indecomposable, a will possess both a right-hand characteristic column vector $\bar{Q}$ and a left-hand characteristic row vector $\bar{P}$, which are both positive and unique save for arbitrary scale

$$0 < \bar{Q} = a\bar{Q}, \qquad 0 < \bar{P} = \bar{P}a \tag{1.7b}$$

P/P_1 and Q/Q_1 unique vectors; also, every $(n-1)^2$ minor of $I - a$ is positive and $I - a$ is of rank $n - 1$.

However, when a subsistence a has no basics, as in Equation (1.6c), the correct necessary and sufficient Hawkins–Simon conditions for a to be a barely subsistence technology is that

$$\det[I - a] = 0 \tag{1.8a}$$

$$\text{Every principal minor of } [I - a] \text{ to be non-negative} \tag{1.8b}$$

My example in Equation (1.6d) illustrates the inadequacy of Sraffa's 'equalities approach' in comparison with the more general von Neumann (1945) equalities–inequalities approach. Suppose a technology can produce autonomous exponential growth of wheat but only steady-state reproduction of iron. Then modern students of non-linear programming, as in Tjalling Koopmans (1951), will consider this to be a subsistence economy. (A chain is only as strong as its weakest link. The most slowly growing autonomous sub-economy determines the maximum growth rate of the system, which is zero in this case. Von Neumann's minimum interest rate is here zero, and the steady-state price(s) of the redundantly growing sub-sector(s) is zero in virtue of those goods' redundancy.) Hawkins–Simon's Equation (1.8) still applies.

[10] The lack of uniqueness of Sraffa's (P_j/P_1) characteristic vector in Chapter I when (1.6c) occurs and no basics exist is a bit reminiscent of the Kurz and Salvadori (1991 [1992a], 1995, pp. 155–6) *curiosum*, in which alternative choices of techniques exist in a subsistence economy of the type that can lead to some indeterminacy of (P_j/P_1) prices. It is to be noted, though, that (1.6c) here involves solely one (a_{ij}) matrix. My same indeterminacy would also hold for the (1.6c) pattern applied to a net productive case like $a_{11} = 1/2 = a_{22} = 1/2$, $a_{12} = 0 = a_{21}$. At $1 + r^* = 2$, no primary factor could be paid a positive return, and the P_2/P_1 ratio would be indeterminate. For $1 < 1 + r < 2$, the wage and rent rates could both be positive and P_2/P_1 could be determined from (wage/rent, r) parameters alone. As $r \to 1$, P_2/P_1 would approach a determinate limit, but that is only one point on the continuum of P_2/P_1's that are admissible at $r^* = 1$ (when needed, labour and land stay conveniently available at zero factor prices).

I conclude this discussion of Chapter I subsistence with the generalized Hawkins–Simon analysis of technologies that are net productive, or in Sraffian language are 'surplus' technologies. In Chapter II (1960, p. 7), Sraffa increases his subsistence example's wheat harvest by seven-sixteenths, or 43.75 percent. Now that some a_{ij} is reduced, what was barely self-reproducing becomes capable of positive exponential growth. He does tell us that his new steady-state prices are

$$P_2/P_1 = 15\text{qr. wheat per ton of iron} \qquad (1.9a)$$

$$\text{Profit or interest rate} = 25\% \text{ per period} \qquad (1.9b)$$

Page 6 defines his post-subsistence prices as the following positive left-hand characteristic row vector of the new a, and $1 +$ the profit rate as a's real-and-positive *eigenvalue*:

$$\bar{P}a = (1 + \bar{r})^{-1}\bar{P} > 0, \qquad \bar{r} > 0 \qquad (1.10a)$$

When Sraffa's a is stipulated to be indecomposable, $\bar{P}/\bar{P}_1$ is unique and positive and so is $\bar{r}$. In the usual Marxian *Weltanschauung*, Q_{ij} capital (so-called 'constant capital') is sterile. A self-critical Marxian will notice that the $\bar{r}$ eigenvector of Sraffa (1960, p. 6), of Equation (1.10a), and of von Neumann generally is a pure-productivity rate of profit – as Nicholas Kaldor (1937) discussed in his polemic with Frank Knight.

Although Sraffa does not mention it, the system could grow at any uniform exponential rate of less than exactly 25 percent per period (and at the same time choose to be consuming one or another exponentially growing vector of basics). Sraffa, a critic of Walrasian competitive pricing, paradoxically neglects the new $\bar{Q}$ vector of uniform maximal growth to concentrate on the new $\bar{P}$ vector of better-than-subsistence a.

It follows that the positive vector mode of maximal growth, $\bar{Q}$, is the uniquely positive column eigenvector, and the growth rate equals Sraffa's same $\bar{r}$:

$$a\bar{Q} = (1 + \bar{r})^{-1}\bar{Q} > 0, \qquad \bar{Q}/\bar{Q}_1 \text{ unique} \qquad (1.10b)$$

Now, however, the net productive a can have its basics supplemented by so-called luxuries (or, better, non-basics, since the oxygen needed for life itself could be a non-basic that is hardly a mere luxury). Now Sraffa's typical case can be written to involve m basics and $n - m$ non-basics, as in the block matrix.

$$0 \le a = \begin{bmatrix} a' & a'' \\ 0 & a''' \end{bmatrix} \qquad (1.11a)$$

a' m-by-m, $m < n$; a'' m-by-$(n - m)$ and not all 0's; a''' $(n - m)$-by-$(n - m)$

$$I_m + (a') + (a')^2 + \ldots + (a')^{m-1} > 0 \qquad (1.11b)$$

Every principal minor of a''' to be *positive* \qquad (1.11c)

If $[I - a''']$ has a real characteristic $\bar{r}''' <$ than the $\bar{r}'$ of a',

straightforward complications arise \qquad (1.11d)

2. The truly classical 'subsistence' state. When Sraffa's original 'subsistence' economy reports that wheat and iron alone produce wheat and iron each, and in amounts of total outputs that respectively just equal total inputs, no explicit mention is at first made of labour as a cooperating input. However, by Chapter II, it is made clear that needed labour is getting its subsistence wage of wheat (and possibly of iron) in the background. Thus, when 280 of wheat is needed to produce 400 of wheat, that 280 might already include (say) 100 of wheat for (say) 100 workers' needed subsistence – along with the residual 180 of wheat needed as seed input. Notationally, call $a_{\text{wheat,wheat}}$ or a_{11} the technical input of wheat needed for one unit of wheat production: in the example, $a_{11} = 180/400 = 0.45$. Add to a_{11} what Francis Seton (1957) aptly calls the 'feeding coefficient' of $100/400 = 0.25$; then that gives Sraffa's reported $a_{11} = f_{11} = 0.45 + 0.25 = 0.70 = 280/400$.

There is no room in that exposition of Sraffa for the positive land rent and (possible) positive interest rate that characterizes the conventional Malthus–Darwin subsistence stationary state. As in many a Marx tableau of reproduction, Sraffa here ignores land as a constraining input – until the brief Chapter XI where land is given a walk-on part in the second act of joint products – instead of being treated as a primary input like labour. Along with the a_{ij} and f_{ij} technical coefficients, in a single-product scenario, one specifies needed-land coefficients $(a_{\text{land},1}, a_{\text{land},2}, \ldots)$.

Taken literally, Sraffa's ecological scenario is a special and odd one. We can envisage three independent planets. On A, the only technique can keep no positive stationary state alive. Any initial endowments of wheat and iron will erode away, because their use as technical and feeding inputs yield less output than themselves. On Planet B, with Goldilocks' just-right, not-too-hot-not-too-cold technology, one reportable scale of stationary state can occur: for any jury who concludes that constant returns to scale is the only interesting case that obtains, Planet B can be magnified a trillion-fold in scale or can be shrunk down a trillion-fold. For Planet C (which is *net* productive à la Hawkins and Simon (1949)), exponential self-growth is suggested to be possible *ad infinitum* and/or positive net consumption can be pulled out forever from the initially endowed system.

Classical economics if anything overstressed constraining land. Where post-Newton man is concerned, the same is true of Darwinian paradigms – as in the *logistic* model of Verhulst (1838), Lotka (1925) and Pearl (1925), where environmental scarcity is what determines the evolutionary equilibrium capacity. It would be fortuitous if land-augmenting technical change permitted realistic ignoring forever of natural-resource constraints. That the Second Law of Thermodynamics grinds exceedingly fine would be apparent were it not for post-Newtonian scientific breakthroughs that play no role in static microeconomic models.

To use later terminology, Sraffa is in a Roy Harrod (1939, 1948) world where limited environmental resources do not constrain. To realize the more common 1750–1870 *Weltanschauung*, all three planets are on the technological menu, and endogenously, the subsistence-state equilibrium is found at population densities that select from the broad menu a Planet C item. If only the Planet A choice is realistic, we have deserted islands. If only Planet B is realistic, a non-generic razor's edge case of probability zero, except under egalitarian socialism, no positive population is viable. With a continuum of Planet C-feasibilities, involving $[a_{ij} + f_{ij}]$ coefficients which are at least lower than Sraffa's

$$\begin{bmatrix} 280/400 & 12/400 \\ 120/20 & 8/20 \end{bmatrix}$$

coefficients, a non-property-owning working class can reproduce itself inside of C only at one bare-subsistence wage-consumption level and at a scale that will depend on the taste allocations of the property owners. (If they change to consume more iron, whilst workers subsist only on wheat, the equilibrium of the population will become higher than when property rentiers demand much wheat.)

I think it a pity that the 1960 classic did not give the reader a few pages on this core of *classical* economics. To do so would not have weakened any valid future critique of 'marginalism'. Among early writers Cantillon (1755), Quesnay (1758), Thünen (1826–1850) and Marx (*Capital*, Vol. II, 1885) gave some signs of sensing the circular interdependence problem entailed when iron as output needs, directly or indirectly, some of the iron itself, but no one seems to have pointed rigorously to the analytic solution until Dmitriev (1898, 1904). Bortkiewicz (1907b) reported on Dmitriev's brilliant work, but neither Leontief nor Sraffa seem to have known of it until after 1940. (I owe to Heinz Kurz's researches on the Sraffa papers the suggestion that only in the 1940s did Sraffa become aware of the writings of Bortkiewicz, Dmitriev and von Neumann. One who can be nameless here suggested to me that Leontief, as a student of Bortkiewicz, must have known of, and been able to read, the Dmitriev Russian-language breakthrough on this point. To check up on this, I quizzed my old master when he was in relaxed mood and learned that indeed, while he knew Marx, he did not know the Dmitriev item in his days at St. Petersburg, Berlin and Kiel.)

References

Arrow, K. and Debreu, G. (1954). 'Existence of an Equilibrium for a Competitive Economy', *Econometrica*, **22**, pp. 265–90.

Blaug, M. (1987). 'Classical Economics', in J. L. Eatwell, M. Milgate and P. Newman (eds), *The New Palgrave. A Dictionary of Economics*, Vol. 1, London: Macmillan, pp. 434–45.

Böhm-Bawerk, E. von (1889, 1959). *Kapital und Kapitalzins*, Vol. II. Positive Theorie des Kapitals, Innsbruck: Wagner. Translated into English in 1959 by G. D. Huncke and H. F. Sennholz as *Capital and Interest*, Vol. II. Positive Theory of Capital. South Holland, IL: Libertarian Press.

Bortkiewicz, L. von (1907a). 'Wertrechnung und Preisrechnung im Marxschen System', *Archiv für Sozialwissenschaft und Sozialpolitik*, **25**. Translated into English in 1952 as 'Value and Price in the Marxian System', *International Economic Papers*, **2**, pp. 5–61.

148   P. A. Samuelson

Bortkiewicz, L. von (1907b). 'Zur Berichtigung der grundlegenden theoretischen Konstruktion von Marx im 3. Band des "Kapital"', *Jahrbücher für Nationalökonomie Statistik,* **34,** 319–35. Translated into English in P. M. Sweezy (ed.), *Karl Marx and the Close of his System,* New York: Kelley, pp. 199–221.

Cantillon, R. (1755). *Essai sur la Nature du Commerce en Général.* First published in English for the Royal Economic Society, London: Macmillan, 1931. Reissued, London: Frank Cass, 1959.

Cassel, G. (1918). *Theoretische Sozialökonomie,* Leipzig: C. W. Winter.

Chamberlin, E. H. (1933, 1962). *The Theory of Monopolistic Competition,* Cambridge, MA: Harvard University Press.

Champernowne, D. G. (1945). 'A Note on John von Neumann's Article on "A Model of Economic Equilibrium",' *Review of Economic Studies,* **13,** pp. 10–18.

Clark, J. B. (1899). *The Distribution of Wealth,* New York: Macmillan.

Coleman, W. (1990). 'The Defect in Ricardo's Argument for the 93 per cent Labour Theory of Value', *Australian Economic Papers,* June, pp. 101–6.

Dmitriev, V. (1898, 1904). *Ekonomischeskie Ocherki.* Translated into English in 1974 as D. M. Nuti (ed.), *V. K. Dmitriev Economic Essays on Value, Competition and Utility,* Cambridge: Cambridge University Press.

Dorfman, R., Samuelson, P. A. and Solow, R. M. (1958). *Linear Programming and Economic Analysis,* New York: McGraw Hill.

Fisher, I. (1907). *The Rate of Interest, its Nature, Determination and Relation to Economic Phenomena,* New York: Macmillan.

Garegnani, P. (1960). *Il capitale nelle teorie della distribuzione,* Milano: Giuffrè.

Georgescu-Roegen, N. (1951). 'Some Properties of a Generalized Leontief Model', in T. C. Koopmans *et al.* (eds) *Activity Analysis of Production and Allocation,* New York: John Wiley.

Gomory, R. (1958). 'Outline of an Algorithm for Integer Solutions to Linear Programs', *Bulletin of the American Mathematical Society,* **64.**

Hardy, G. H. (1940). *Ramanujan: Twelve Lectures on Subjects Suggested by His Life and Work,* Cambridge: Cambridge University Press.

Harrod, R. (1939). 'An Essay in Dynamic Theory', *Economic Journal,* **49,** pp. 14–33.

Harrod, R. (1948). *Towards a Dynamic Economics: Some Recent Developments of Economic Theory and Their Application to Policy,* London and New York: Macmillan.

Hawkins, D. and Simon, H. (1949). 'Note: Some Conditions of Macroeconomic Stability', *Econometrica,* **17,** pp. 145–48.

Hayek, F. (1931). *Prices and Production,* London: Routledge.

Hayek, F. (1945). 'The Use of Knowledge in Society', *American Economic Review,* **35,** pp. 519–30.

Kaldor, N. (1937). 'Annual Survey of Economic Theory: The Recent Controversy on the Theory of Capital', *Econometrica,* **5,** pp. 201–33.

Kaldor, N. (1960a). *Essays on Value and Distribution,* Glencoe, IL: The Free Press.

Kaldor, N. (1960b). *Essays on Economic Stability and Growth,* Glencoe, IL: The Free Press.

Kalecki, M. (1971). *Selected Essays on the Dynamics of the Capitalist Economy 1933–1970,* Cambridge: Cambridge University Press.

Koopmans, T. *et al.* (eds) (1951). *Activity Analysis of Production and Allocation Proceedings of a Conference*. Cowles Commission for Research in Economics Monograph No. 13, New York: John Wiley; London: Chapman & Hall.

Kuhn, T. (1962). *Structure of Scientific Revolution*, Chicago and London: University of Chicago Press.

Kurz, H. and Salvadori, N. (1991). 'The Non-Substitution Theorem Revisited,' *Working Papers in Political Economy*, 26. New York: New School for Social Research, Graduate Faculty. Revised version entitled 'The Non-Substitution theorem: Making Good a Lacuna', published in *Journal of Economics*, 1994, 59(1), pp. 97–103.

Kurz, H. and Salvadori, N. (1992a). *Theory of Production. I*, Milan: Istituto di Ricerca sulla Dinamica dei Sistemi Economici.

Kurz, H. and Salvadori, N. (1992b). *Theory of Production. II*, Milan: Istituto di Ricerca sulla Dinamica dei Sistemi Economici. Published in English (with Vol. I) 1995 as *Theory of Production. A Long-Period Analysis*, Cambridge: Cambridge University Press.

Kurz, H. and Salvadori, N. (1993). 'The "Standard Commodity" and Ricardo's Search for an "Invariable Measure of Value"', in M. Baranzini and G. C. Harcourt (eds), *The Dynamics of the Wealth of Nations. Growth, Distribution and Structural Change. Essays in Honour of Luigi Pasinetti*, New York: St Martin's Press.

Leontief, W. (1928). 'Die Wirtschaft als Kreislauf' ('The Economy as a Circular Flow'), *Archiv für Sozialwissenschaft und Sozialpolitik*, 60, pp. 577–623.

Leontief, W. (1941). *The Structure of American Economy, 1919–1929*, Cambridge, MA: Harvard University Press.

Leontief, W. (1953). *Studies in the Structure of the American Economy*, New York: Oxford University Press.

Liviatan, N. and Samuelson, P. A. (1969). 'Notes on Turnpikes: Stable and Unstable', *Journal of Economic Theory*, 1, December, 454–75.

Lotka, A. J. (1925). *Elements of Mathematical Biology*, Baltimore: Williams and Wilkins; New York: Dover, 1956.

Manara, C. F. (1980). 'Sraffa's Model for the Joint Production of Commodities by Means of Commodities', in L. L. Pasinetti (ed.), *Essays on the Theory of Joint Production*, New York: Columbia University Press, particularly pp. 9–11.

Mann, T. (1924). *The Magic Mountain*, Berlin: S. Fischer.

Marshall, A. (1890–1921, 1961). *Principles of Economics*, 9th (variorum) edn, in C. W. Guillebaud (ed.), Appendix I, pp. 813–21, particularly p. 814, London: Macmillan.

Marx, K. (1867, 1885, 1894). *Das Kapital*. Vols. I–III, Hamburg: Verlag von Otto Meissner.

Morishima, M. (1959). 'Some Properties of a Dynamic Leontief System with a Spectrum of Techniques', *Econometrica*, 27, pp. 626–37.

Pasinetti, L. L. (1960). 'A Mathematical Formulation of the Ricardian System, *Review of Economic Studies*, 27, pp. 78–98.

Pasinetti, L. L. (1962). 'Rate of Profit and Income Distribution in Relation to the Rate of Economic Growth', *Review of Economic Studies*, 29, pp. 267–79. Reproduced as Chap. 5 in L. L. Pasinetti, *Growth and Income Distribution*, Cambridge: Cambridge University Press.

Pearl, R. (1925). *The Biology of Population Growth*, New York: Alfred A. Knopf.

Petty, Sir W. (1690). *Political Arithmetick*. Reprinted in C. Hull (ed.), *Economic Writings*, 1899. Reprinted, New York: A. M. Kelley, 1964.

Quesnay, F. (1758). *Tableau Economique*. 1st edn, Paris; 2nd edn, 1759; 3rd edn, 1759. Republished and translated in M. Kuczynski and R. L. Meek (eds), 1972. *Quesnay's Tableau Economique*, London: Macmillan.

Ricardo, D. (1951–73). *The Works and Correspondence of David Ricardo*, ed. P. Sraffa with the collaboration of M. H. Dobb, Vols I–XI, Cambridge: Cambridge University Press.

Robinson, J. (1933). *The Economics of Imperfect Competition*, London: Macmillan, see especially pp. 116–17.

Robinson, J. (1956). *The Accumulation of Capital*, Homewood, IL: Richard D. Irwin.

Roemer, J. (1977). 'Technical Change and the Tendency of the Rate of Profits to Fall', *Journal of Economic Theory*, 16(2), pp.403–24.

Samuelson, P. A. (1949). *Market Mechanisms and Maximization*. Part I. *The Theory of Comparative Advantage*; Part II. *The Cheapest-Adequate-Diet Problem*; Part III. *Dynamics and Linear Programming*. Published by the RAND Corporation, Parts I and II, 28 March 1949, Part III, 29 June 1949. See especially Part III. Reproduced as Chap. 33 in *The Collected Scientific Papers of Paul A. Samuelson*, Vol. 1, Cambridge, MA: MIT Press, 1966.

Samuelson, P. A. (1951) 'Abstract of a Theorem Concerning Substitutability in Open Leontief Models', Chap. VII in T. C. Koopmans et al. (eds), *Cowles Commission for Research in Economics, Activity Analysis of Production and Allocation*, New York: John Wiley. Reproduced as Chap. 36 in *The Collected Scientific Papers of Paul A. Samuelson*, Vol. 1, 1966, Cambridge, MA: MIT Press.

Samuelson, P. A. (1959) 'A Modern Treatment of the Ricardian Economy. I. The Pricing of Goods and of Labour and Land Services. II. Capital and Interest of the Pricing Process', *Quarterly Journal of Economics*, 73 (February–May), pp. 1–135; 217–31. Reproduced as Chap. 31 in *The Collected Scientific Papers of Paul A. Samuelson*, Vol. 1, Cambridge, MA: MIT Press, 1966.

Samuelson, P. A. (1966). '[Paradoxes in Capital Theory] A Summing Up', *Quarterly Journal of Economics*, 80 (November), pp. 568–83. Reproduced as Chap. 148 in *The Collected Scientific Papers of Paul A. Samuelson*, Vol. 3, Cambridge, MA: MIT Press, 1972.

Samuelson, P. A. (1971). 'Understanding the Marxian Notion of Exploitation: A Summary of the So-called Transformation Problem Between Marxian Values and Competitive Prices', *Journal of Economic Literature*, 11, 399–431. Reproduced as Chap. 153 in *The Collected Scientific Papers of Paul A. Samuelson*, Vol. 3, Cambridge, MA: MIT Press, 1972.

Samuelson, P. A. (1975). 'Trade Pattern Reversals in Time-Phased Ricardian Systems and Intertemporal Efficiency', *Journal of International Economics*, 5(4), pp. 306–363. Reproduced as Chap. 251 in *The Collected Scientific Papers of Paul A. Samuelson*, Vol. 4, Cambridge, MA: MIT Press, 1977.

Samuelson, P. A. (1987). 'Sraffian Economics', in J. Eatwell, M. Milgate and P. Newman (eds.), *The New Palgrave. A Dictionary of Economics*, Vol. 4, London: Macmillan, pp. 452–61.

Samuelson, P. A. (1990). 'Revisionist Findings on Sraffa', in K. Bharadwaj and B. Schefold (eds), *Essays on Piero Sraffa. Critical Perspectives on the Revival of Classical Theory*, London: Unwin Hyman.

Samuelson, P. A. (1991a). 'Conversations with my History-of-Economics critics', in G. K. Shaw (eds.), *Economics, Culture and Education Essays in Honour of Mark Blaug*. Cheltenham: Edward Elgar.

Samuelson, P. A. (1991b). 'A Sweeping New Non-Substitution Theorem: Kaldor's Discovery of the von Neumann Input–Output Model', in E. J. Nell and W. Semmler (eds), *Nicholas Kaldor and Mainstream Economics, Confrontation or Convergence?* London: Macmillan.

Samuelson, P. A. (1994). 'Two Classics: Böhm-Bawerk's *Positive Theory* and Fisher's *Rate of Interest* Through Modern Prisms', in B. Schefold *et al.* (eds), *Klassiker der Nationalökonomie Irving Fisher, The Rate of Interest*, Dusseldorf: Verlag Wirtschaft und Finanzen.

Samuelson, P. A. (1999). 'The Special Thing I Learned from Sraffa', Chap. 2 in G. Mongiovi and F. Petri (eds), *Value, Distribution and Capital: Essays in Honour of Pierangelo Garegnani*, London and New York: Routledge.

Seton, F. (1957). 'The "transformation problem"', *Review of Economic Studies*, **24**, pp. 149–60.

Shove, G. (1930). 'The Representative Firm and Increasing Returns', *Economic Journal*, **40**, pp. 113–24.

Smith, A. (1776, 1937). *An Inquiry into the Nature and Causes of The Wealth of Nations*, Cannan edn, New York: Modern Library.

Solow, R. M. (1952). 'On the Structure of Linear Models', *Econometrica*, **20**(1), pp. 29–46.

Sraffa, P. (1926). 'The Laws of Returns under Competitive Conditions', *Economic Journal*, **36**, pp. 535–50.

Sraffa, P. (1932). 'Dr. Hayek on Money and Capital', *Economic Journal*, **42** (March), pp. 42–53.

Sraffa, P. (1960). *Production of Commodities by Means of Commodities. Prelude to a Critique of Economic Theory*, Cambridge: Cambridge University Press.

Steedman, I. (1977). *Marx After Sraffa*, London: New Left Books.

Stigler, G. J. (1958). 'Ricardo and the 93% Labor Theory of Value', *American Economic Review Supplement*, **46**, pp. 357–67.

Sweezy, P. (ed.) (1942). *The Theory of Capitalist Development: Principles of Marxian Political Economy*, New York: Monthly Review Press.

Thünen, J. H. von (1826–50). *Der isolirte Staat in Beziehung auf Landwirtschaft und Nationalökonomie*, Hamburg: Perthes; Rostock: Leopold.

Varri, P. (1987). 'Fixed Capital', in J. Eatwell, M. Milgate and P. Newman (eds), *The New Palgrave. A Dictionary of Economics*, Vol. 2, London: Macmillan Press.

Verhulst, P. F. (1838). 'Notice de la loi que la population suit dans son accroissement', *Correspondence Mathématique et Physique Publiée par A. Quételet*, Brussels, **10**, pp. 113–21.

von Neumann, J. (1937, 1945). 'Über ein ökonomisches Gleichungssystem und eine Verallgemeinerung des Brouwerschen Fixpunktsatzes', *Ergebnisse eines mathematischen Kolloquiums 8*, ed. Karl Menger. Translated into

English in 1945 as 'A Model of General Economic Equilibrium', *Review of Economic Studies*, **13**, pp. 1–9.

Walras, L. (1889, 1896). *Eléments d'économie politique pure*, 2nd and 3rd edns. Lausanne: F. Rouge; Paris: Guillaumin; Leipzig: Duncker & Humblot. Translated into English 1954 as *Elements of Pure Economics or The Theory of Social Wealth*, Homewood, IL: Richard D. Irwin.

Wicksell, K. (1919). 'Professor Cassel's System of Economics'. English translation from *Ekonomisk Tidskrift*, No. 21, appearing 1934 in L. Robbins (ed.), *Lectures on Political Economy* by Knut Wicksell, Vol. I, Appendix I, London: Routledge & Kegan Paul.

Wicksteed, P. (1894). *An Essay on the Co-ordination of the Laws of Distribution*, London: Macmillan.

Wicksteed, P. (1914, 1933). 'The Scope and Method of Political Economy in the Light of the "Marginal" Theory of Value and Distribution', *Economic Journal*, **24**, (March). Reprinted in 1933 in L. Robbins (ed.), *The Common Sense of Political Economy*, London: George Routledge.

Comment

Heinz D. Kurz and Neri Salvadori

In his paper, Paul A. Samuelson focuses attention especially on the following problems: (i) can Sraffa (1960) do without constant returns to scale; (ii) what is the use of the Standard system and Standard commodity; (iii) is there a 'classical' alternative to the 'marginalist' or 'neoclassical' approach to the theory of value and distribution? In passing he also comments on a couple of other issues including (iv) the importance or otherwise of the distinction between basic and non-basic commodities, (v) Sraffa's treatment of joint production, and (vi) the question of simultaneous equations. In what follows we shall point out in which respects and why our reading of Sraffa and some other authors differs from that of Samuelson. We try to be as brief as possible. The interested reader may want to consult Kurz and Salvadori (1995) for a more detailed exposition of the arguments sketched.

The authors should like to thank Bertram Schefold for valuable comments on an earlier draft of this comment. Neri Salvadori thanks the MURST and the CNR for financial support.

(i)　　Returns to scale

Samuelson introduces the part of his paper entitled 'The Doomed Critique of Marginalism: Constant Returns?' with the assessment that it may be 'the most important part of my present recorded reflections' (p. 116), and concludes it with the statement: 'In sum, if a Sraffian denies constant returns to scale, the one-hundred-page 1960 classic evaporates into a few paragraphs of vapid chit-chat' (p. 123). Samuelson attempts to 'demonstrate mathematically' that Sraffa has to assume constant returns to scale and attacks 'a generation of Sraffian writers who are very much alive and have not done their duty in proving that they are entitled to have their cake and eat it' (p. 117).

As it well known, in his criticism in the 1920s of the Marshallian analysis of variable-cost industries within the framework of partial competitive equilibrium (cf. Sraffa, 1925, 1926), Sraffa argued that the Marshallian analysis has to assume that variable costs are due to economies of scale and are *internal to the industry and external to the firm*. The former condition is a requirement of partial analysis, the latter of the assumption of free competition. In the 1926 paper, Sraffa suggested retaining partial equilibrium analysis. This was possible at the cost of abandoning the concern with the free competition form of markets: in order to be able to preserve the partial framework, the analysis had to be limited to the study of economies internal to the firm. Yet this is not the only possible way of coping with the critique of the Marshallian analysis. There is an alternative route that could be followed, which consists of retaining the concern with the free competition form of markets but abandoning partial analysis. This involves assuming that variable returns are a consequence of economies *external to the firm*. This is the route followed by Sraffa (1960).[1]

Assume single production and let **q** be the *n*-vector of quantities of commodities produced in the different industries. For a given **q** the processes available to firms are given irrespective of the question of returns with respect to industries, returns within firms being constant.[2] The choice of technique can be carried out so that a unique price vector **p** and a unique wage rate *w* (in terms of some numéraire) can be determined for each given level of the rate of profit *r*. Since this operation can be

---

[1] According to another interpretation, Sraffa's approach can also be considered to cover the case of contestable markets. It is argued that in this case the issue of whether variable returns are connected with internal or external economies does not arise.

[2] Therefore, we do not agree with Samuelson, who contends that 'If the Axiom [of constant returns to scale] is violated at the industry level, price-and-unit-cost correspondences must be replaced by Chamberlin–Cournot monopolistic-competitition alternatives' (p. 139).

performed for any (feasible) vector $\mathbf{q}$, the analysis will determine a function[3]

$$(\mathbf{p}, w) = F(\mathbf{q}, r)$$

where a vector of gross outputs $\mathbf{q}$ is feasible if there are techniques available that allow its production.

Clearly, the above function (or correspondence) depends on the kind of returns prevailing in the economy. Thus, with constant returns to scale throughout, the function is a constant function with respect to $\mathbf{q}$. If returns are decreasing because certain qualities of land are in short supply and the technology is such that only extensive rent arises, then $\mathbf{p}$ is an increasing step-function with respect to $\mathbf{q}$, provided that labour is used as the numéraire, that is, $w = 1$. In the general case, the above correspondence has not yet been fully explored, but it is known that if intensive diminishing returns are allowed for, then prices can locally go up or down with respect to changes in $\mathbf{q}$. Hence, we cannot agree with Samuelson's claim that if constant returns to scale are not explicitly assumed in Sraffa's analysis, we are left with an 'empty set of results' (p. 120).

To conclude this section, we wonder what is the factual basis of Samuelson's 'suspicion' that Sraffa may have abandoned the assumption of constant returns to scale because 'he never worked through the literal consequences for his 1960 book of departures from the returns conditions that market-clearing competition depends upon' (p. 123). At any rate, we are not aware of any evidence from Sraffa's own writings that could lend support to this view.

(ii)   Standard system

In the part entitled 'The Futility of Sraffa's Standard Commodity', Samuelson reiterates his 1990 view as to 'the irrelevance and lack of usefulness' of Sraffa's respective concept. To this he adds:

No need to repeat here the argument that it cannot help defend Ricardo's attempted labour theory of value or Marx's formulation of the transformation problem. Here I ought to move on to show why Sraffa's standard does not cogently interpret and effectively help out any Ricardian's (misguided) hankering for an absolute or invariable measure of "value". (p. 127)

---

[3] This is so only if all commodities are produced. If only some commodities are produced that relationship between $(\mathbf{p}, w)$ and $(\mathbf{q}, r)$ is a correspondence (cf. Kurz and Salvadori, 1995, Section 3 of Chapter 5).

We do agree with each of these statements. At the same time we insist that none of them contains anything that could be seen as a criticism of Sraffa for the simple reason that Sraffa nowhere used the Standard commodity in order to accomplish what (according to Samuelson and other interpreters) cannot be accomplished. While some interpreters of Sraffa may be criticized for having attributed to the Standard commodity properties which it does not possess and for which it was not designed, this criticism cannot be levelled at Sraffa. Having said this, we do not agree with Samuelson that the Standard commodity is irrelevant and useless. We also do not agree that Ricardo's search for an invariable measure of value is 'theological' (p. 128), 'psychosomatic' (p. 127) and 'pathetic' (p. 139).

As regards Ricardo, the search for an invariable measure of value is but an expression of Ricardo's awareness of the difficulties of the theory of value, a major difficulty being due to compound interest. In Ricardo, the concept of an 'invariable' measure of value was meant to single out the determinants of value, that is, those factors which, if changed, would affect the prices of commodities with the exception of the price of the standard of value. Hence, already at Ricardo's hands the search for an invariable measure of value was at least partly an analytical tool designed to render the theory of value and distribution precise and simple. While Ricardo's search for such a measure indeed turned out to be a search for a will-o'-the-wisp, given the properties he required the measure to possess, this does not mean that his efforts were totally futile. In the course of his investigation, and despite his fruitless wanderings, he was able to illuminate the intricacies involved and render more precise than presumably any author before him the factors affecting relative prices.

As regards the Standard commodity, we have argued elsewhere that 'Sraffa, for perfectly good reasons it seems, saw only a single analytical purpose of the Standard commodity, i.e. to simplify the analysis of the effects of changes in the division of the product between profits and wages on prices' (Kurz and Salvadori, 1993, p. 118). In this view the Standard commodity is an *analytical tool* useful in the study of the dependence of relative prices on income distribution. We added:

It deserves mention that these results [i.e., those obtained by Sraffa in regard to single-product systems] can also be obtained by using the Perron–Frobenius Theorem. In fact, Sraffa's demonstration of the existence and uniqueness of the Standard commodity can be considered a (not fully complete) proof of this theorem. Yet Sraffa does even better, simultaneously providing an economic rationale of the analytical tools he uses. (ibid., p. 111)

Hence, in our view the Standard commodity is relevant and useful, but not indispensable. In one place Samuelson appears to come close to this interpretation: he stresses that 'we can be gratified that Sraffa was not inhibited from publishing his innovations by any conscious feeling of ignorance concerning the Frobenius–Minkowski theory of non-negative real matrices' (p. 114; see also p. 129). It was indeed precisely the elaboration of the ingenious concept of the Standard commodity which enabled Sraffa to accomplish a task which otherwise would have required a knowledge of the relevant parts of linear algebra. Sraffa himself forged the tools of his analysis. In addition, it should be noted that he was very clear about the limited scope of the tool under discussion: 'The Standard system is a purely auxiliary construction. It should therefore be possible to present the essential elements of the mechanism under consideration without having recourse to it' (Sraffa, 1960, p. 31). The mechanism referred to is the adjustment of relative prices consequent upon a change in distribution. This should suffice to answer Samuelson's question: 'Toward what is it an "auxiliary"?' Moreover, it should be clear that in contradistinction to his claim the Standard system does not 'involve shifts in the "scale of an industry"' (p. 116) in any real sense: its construction is a pure thought experiment preserving the technical characteristics of production (per unit of output) of the actual system under consideration.

Samuelson expresses the view that our criticism of his statement 'Sraffa, for reasons not easy to understand, thought that $[w = 1 - (r/R)]$'s truth somehow provided Ricardo with a defence for his labour theory of value' (Kurz and Salvadori, 1993, p. 120) is somewhat mistaken. He clarifies that he 'in no degree' intended to attribute to Sraffa a view similar to the one expressed by Blaug that prices can be made independent of distribution by an appropriate choice of the numéraire. To this he adds: 'I indict Ricardo (and Sraffa) for not explicitly following Smith in formulating a *tripartite* model of relative prices, real prices, and distributive shares based on the *three*some of labour, land, and time-phased produced inputs.' In brackets follows the adjunct: '*That* was my ... point, and I need not have complicated it by pronouncing on what Sraffa thought his Standard commodity had to do with it.' He concludes: 'I hope they agree with me that some representative Sraffians have taken a less unsympathetic attitude on *this* matter' (pp. 133–4, fn. 7). In this latter regard we do indeed agree with him. It is not clear to us what Samuelson means when indicting Ricardo and Sraffa, because these authors corrected logical flaws and deficiencies in Smith's analysis of value and distribution.

(iii) On alternative approaches to the theory of value and distribution

Samuelson confirms that Sraffa's work 'is *outside* normal cumulative science in the sense of Thomas Kuhn's 1962 *Structure of Scientific Revolution*' (p. 113; Samuelson's emphasis). At the same time he deplores what he calls an 'inefficient bifurcation of the literature into two streams;' (p. 114). In his view there is no 'alternative classical paradigm' to 'neoclassical marginalism' (p. 117). Sraffa's analysis is rather envisaged as exhibiting 'the general qualitative properties of Walras (1896), multi-commodity J. B. Clark (1899), Wicksteed (1894) and Arrow–Debreu (1954)' (p. 126). Samuelson stresses: 'I strongly believe, on the evidence, that Smith, Ricardo, and J. S. Mill used essentially the *same logical paradigm* as did Walras and Arrow–Debreu' (p. 140). He attempts to demonstrate the alleged family resemblance of the different theories in terms of production possibility and factor price frontiers.

On this we agree and we do not. We fully share Samuelson's view that '[t]he time-phased input–output system has many of the regularities enjoyed by a maximum system, provided that the competitive solutions are correctly treated.... Whether one is neoclassical or not, or Marxian or not, the logic of such systems fits well into the Weltanschauung that permeates this book [i.e., the *Foundations of Economic Analysis*]' (Samuelson, 1983, p. 584). Therefore, we agree if Samuelson wants to say that *any* long-period theory of prices must satisfy Sraffa's equations of production (cf. Kurz and Salvadori, 1995, pp. 22–33). However, we do not agree if he wants to say that the different theories referred to all belong to the demand and supply 'paradigm'.

Scrutiny shows that the contributions to the theory of value and distribution of 'classical' derivation share a common feature, the many differences between different authors notwithstanding: in investigating the relationship between the system of relative prices and income distribution they start from the same set of *data* or rather *independent variables*. These independent variables concern the 'system of production' in use, characterized, as it is, by:

(i)   the set of technical alternatives from which cost-minimizing producers can choose;

(ii) the size and composition of the social product;

(iii) the ruling wage rate(s) (or, alternatively, the rate of profits);

(iv) the quantities of different natural resources, in particular land, available.

The treatment of wages as an independent variable and of other distributive variables, especially profits, as dependent residuals exhibits a fundamental *asymmetry* in the classical approach to the theory of value and distribution.

In correspondence with the underlying *long-period* competitive position of the economy, the capital stock is assumed to be fully adjusted to these data, in particular to the levels of output. Hence the 'normal' desired pattern of utilization of plant and equipment would be realized and a uniform rate of return on its supply price obtained. It turns out that these data are sufficient to determine the unknowns or dependent variables, that is, the rate of profits (or, alternatively, the wage rate(s)) and relative prices. No additional data are needed to determine these unknowns. Thus the classical authors separated the determination of profits and prices from that of quantities, taken as *given* in (i) and (ii) above. The latter were considered as determined in another part of the theory, that is, the analysis of accumulation and economic and social development.

In contradistinction, the data or independent variables from which marginalist or 'neoclassical' theory typically begins its reasoning are the following. It takes as given:

   (i)   the set of technical alternatives from which cost-minimizing producers can choose;
  (ii) the initial endowments of the economy including labour, land(s) and capital and the distribution of property rights among individual agents;
 (iii) the preferences of consumers.

As regards the specification of 'initial endowments', we have to distinguish between the 'original' factors of production, such as different kinds of labour and different kinds of land, and a factor called 'capital'. While the former are generally given in kind and measured in terms of the respective factor's own natural unit, there are two different treatments of the economy's 'endowment' with 'capital'. First, there is the treatment of 'capital' as a single item; second, there is the treatment of 'capital' as a given set of physical stocks of capital goods. Major representatives of the first alternative include Jevons, Böhm-Bawerk, Marshall and Wicksell, whereas Walras and Arrow–Debreu adopted the second alternative. While the first alternative preserved the classical economists' concern with the *long-period* equilibria of the economic system, characterized by a *uniform* rate of profits and uniform rates of remuneration for all primary factors of production, the second alternative, in order to avoid the difficulties encountered with Walras' capitalization equations, deliberately did away with this concern: starting from a vector of concrete capital goods in given supply implied that only *short-period* equilibria could be studied.

Sraffa's approach shares all the characteristic features of the 'classical' approach. In particular, he does *not* start from given endowments of capital goods. Therefore, all attempts to interpret Sraffa's analysis as a 'special case' of neoclassical analysis appear to be mistaken. (For a more detailed exposition of this argument, see Kurz and Salvadori, 1995, pp. 451–5.) We wonder in particular what is the 'Sraffian counterpart' of the 'neoclassical production-possibility frontier in the *short run* when supplies of labour, land, and *capitals* are fixed' (p. 126; emphases added).

Finally, it ought to be recalled that Sraffa effectively demolished traditional neoclassical analysis, which starts from the assumption of a given 'quantity of capital'. As he pointed out, reswitching and capital reversing 'cannot be reconciled with *any* notion of capital as a measurable quantity independent of distribution and prices' (Sraffa, 1960, p. 38; Sraffa's emphasis). Samuelson himself has repeatedly paid tribute to Sraffa for this; see, in particular, Samuelson's 'A Summing Up' of the 1966 symposium on capital theory organized by the *Quarterly Journal of Economics* (Samuelson, 1966).[4]

(iv) Basics and non-basics

In Samuelson's view, the distinction between basic and non-basic commodities is 'not very important' (p. 121). At first sight this judgement is difficult to appreciate because basic commodities exhibit various properties which non-basics do not. Yet what Samuelson really maintains is that 'outside of the mathematical economics seminar room where we use indecomposable matrices as simplifying expositional devices for stating Frobenius–Perron matrix theorems, BASICS probably do not exist' (p. 131). A few lines further down he conjectures that 'a set of Basics which exists could well be of minor fractional importance in the National Income. Basics sound basic; Non-Basics sound like frills and luxuries. There is no warrant for this' (p. 132). Hence, in his opinion it is doubtful that there are basics in the real economy, and if there are, that they are important.

---

[4] It is unclear to us why Samuelson calls reswitching 'a red herring' on the ground that it is 'a sufficient but not necessary condition for the phenomenon that matters' (p. 114).

Whatever the names given to different kinds of commodities, what matters are the different roles performed by them in production and consumption. Sraffa focuses attention exclusively on production. His distinction between basics and non-basics is *purely* technological, that is, whether or not a commodity enters (as a means of production) directly or indirectly into the production of all commodities. Therefore, the distinction says nothing about the importance of a commodity in consumption. A non-basic may very well be an essential (even indispensable) consumption good. Sraffa makes a single assumption, namely that there is at least one basic (Sraffa, 1960, p. 8), that is, at least one basic in altogether k commodities, however large k is! This assumption does not seem to be excessively strong. It is equivalent to the assumption that no commodity can be produced without a material input, and that the economy cannot be divided in parts which are totally separated from each other (as in Samuelson's examples (1.6c) and (1.6d), p. 143) in the sense that they produce totally different commodities, and each part trades with the others just for the purpose of consumption since there is no other need to trade. On the other hand, such a weak assumption allows for a rich harvest of results. For instance, it implies that there is a maximum rate of profits, that there is a (composite) commodity which, if used as numéraire, implies that the wage rate as a function of the profit rate is a straight line, and a number of other properties. Hence, we cannot agree with Samuelson that 'Existence or non-existence of Basics is of limited empirical and theoretical importance.... When Basics do exist and constitute a small fraction of the GNP, constructions based on them are of fractional interest' (p. 139).[5]

(v)   Joint production

Samuelson argues that

the 'negative prices' that raise controversies in Sraffians' dialogues on joint production arise as artifacts only when Sraffa's special equalities are respected instead of the proper duality equalities–inequalities of market behaviour. If axioms of *free disposability* and *divisibility* of goods obtain, then all competitive prices that arise will be non-negative. (p. 120, fn. 4)

---

[5]We obviously agree with him that 'Realistically, innovators would have to have fabricated by *decomposable* labour-intensive activity the first inventories of Basics that could thereafter be competitively viable to reproduce themselves' (p. 131). We are sure that he will also agree with us that no process used for the production of a prototype is a process used in the long run.

In addition, in his 'Technical Note 1' he maintains that 'joint production paradigms necessitate going beyond Sraffian equalities (with their bizarre negative prices in a universe of free disposability!) in favour of Dantzig–von Neumann inequalities–equalities' (p. 143).

While we do agree that Sraffa's approach to joint production is not fully satisfactory, we think that Samuelson's assessment of it is difficult to sustain. Sraffa's assumption that the number of independent processes in the system is equal to the number of commodities produced cannot be sustained in general. His justification of this assumption in terms of the 'requirements for use' (Sraffa, 1960, p. 43, fn. 2) is valid only in some circumstances. This does not mean, however, that his analysis of joint production is without value.

The starting point of Sraffa's respective argument is the observation that while with single production no price can become negative as a result of the variation of the wage rate between zero and its maximum value, given the ('square') system of production, with joint production this is no longer true. He comments on this:

This conclusion is not in itself very startling. All that it implies is that, although in actual fact all prices were positive, a change in the wage might create a situation the logic of which required some of the prices to turn negative: and this being unacceptable, those among the methods of production that gave rise to such a result would be discarded to make room for others which in the new situation were consistent with positive prices. (ibid., p. 59)

Hence, Sraffa is aware of the fact that the positivity of prices cannot be guaranteed if there is no choice of technique. As to the substance of Sraffa's suggested way out of the impasse arising from the negativity of the price of a joint product, it is tantamount to the *ad hoc* assumption that there is always one or several processes of production such that the phenomenon of negative price disappears. Sraffa in fact adopts this assumption rather than von Neumann's assumption of free disposal. Clearly, the former assumption is no more *ad hoc* than the latter, which is equivalent to the assumption that for each process producing a given product there is another process which is exactly identical to the first one except that the product under consideration is *not* produced (cf. Kurz and Salvadori, 1995, p. 228). Therefore, it is not clear what Samuelson means when he speaks of 'bizarre negative prices in a universe of free disposability'. In Sraffa there are *neither* negative prices *nor* is there free disposal.

In the 'real world' disposal is never really free, nor can it always be counted upon that the set of alternatives from which cost-minimizing producers can choose is such that none of the joint products will ever be overproduced, that is, 'requirements for use' will be exactly matched. Hence, both the von Neumann and the Sraffa approach to joint production involve strong abstractions. An alternative would be to allow for *costly* disposal (see, for example, Kurz and Salvadori, ibid., pp. 202–3). There is nothing wrong or bizarre with a *negative* price, because the price of a product which *must* be disposed of in a costly way must be negative if nobody is interested in taking it for free.

(vi)   On simultaneous equations

Finally, we should like to remark on the simultaneous equations approach in the theory of value and distribution. In one place Samuelson maintains that 'Sraffa is shy, or coy, about saying that his prices are to be competitive-market prices, never greater than the respective goods' minimized unit costs.' In brackets he adds: 'In Robinson's East Anglia for a time *simultaneous equations* were considered viciously circular' (p. 121). To avoid possible misunderstandings the following points should be stressed. (i) Sraffa emphasizes that under competitive conditions the choice of technique 'will be exclusively grounded on cheapness' (Sraffa, 1960, p. 83). (ii) The idea that simultaneous equations are 'viciously circular' was widespread in economics (and still is in some circles): Böhm–Bawerk, for example, chastised simultaneous equations as 'a mortal sin against all scientific logic'. (iii) Sraffa is explicitly opposed to this view: he decides to avoid the use of the term 'costs of production', as well as that of 'capital', precisely because these terms could wrongly give the impression that the problem of simultaneous determination could be circumnavigated. These terms, he points out, 'have come to be inseparably linked with the supposition that they stand for quantities that can be measured independently of, and prior to, the determination of the prices of the products. . . . Since to achieve freedom from such presuppositions has been one of the aims of this work, avoidance of the terms seemed the only way of not prejudicing the issue' (ibid., p. 9).

References

Kurz, H. D. and Salvadori, N. (1993). 'The "Standard Commodity" and Ricardo's Search for an "Invariable Measure of Value"', in M. Baranzini and G. C. Harcourt (eds), *The Dynamics of the Wealth of Nations. Growth, Distribution and Structural Change. Essays in Honour of Luigi Pasinetti*, New York: St. Martin's Press, pp. 95–123.

Kurz, H. D. and Salvadori, N. (1995). *Theory of Production. A Long-Period Analysis*, Cambridge: Cambridge University Press.

Samuelson, P. A. (1966). 'A Summing Up', *Quarterly Journal of Economics*, **80**, pp. 568–83.

Samuelson, P. A. (1983). *Foundations of Economic Analysis*, enlarged edition, Cambridge, MA: Harvard University Press.

Sraffa, P. (1925). 'Sulle relazioni fra costo e quantità prodotta', *Annali di Economia*, **2**, pp. 277–328. English translation by John Eatwell and Alessandro Roncaglia in L. L. Pasinetti (ed.), *Italian Economic Papers*, Vol. 3, Bologna, 1998: Il Mulino, and Oxford, 1998: Oxford University Press, pp. 323–63.

Sraffa, P. (1926). 'The Laws of Returns under Competitive Conditions', *Economic Journal*, **36**, pp. 535–50.

Sraffa, P. (1960). *Production of Commodities by Means of Commodities. Prelude to a Critique of Economic Theory*, Cambridge: Cambridge University Press.

Reactions to Kurz–Salvadori's Comments

Paul A. Samuelson

I am blessed by the thoughtful and deep and candid comments on my *Sraffa's Hits and Misses* by Professors Heinz Kurz and Neri Salvadori. Using their numbering system, (i) to (vi), I try to react constructively and advance the good cause of judging the 1960 Sraffa classic. Readers are in their debt when they force me to explicate more fully my contentions.

Non-constant returns?

(i) The Kurz–Salvadori 'Comments' fails to understand my contentions about non-constant returns to scale and, in my scoring, its final sentence's rejection of my 'untruth' is not cogently demonstrated. So let me help clear up the matter.

In response to a warning from Keynes, Sraffa, in 1960, makes clear: I do not necessarily assume *constant* returns *to scale*. Take him at his word: 'Therefore, we may apply your 1960 paradigm to the following clear departure from constant returns to scale and give it enough rope to hang itself.'

Wheat, q_1, is produced by labour and iron at strong *increasing* returns to scale; iron, q_2, is produced by labour and wheat at strong *decreasing* returns to scale. Concretely,

$q_1(t + 1) =$ wheat output

$\qquad =$ wheat consumption + wheat input

$\qquad = c_1(t + 1) + q_{12}(t + 1)$

$\qquad = 8 \, (\text{Min } [L_1(t)/2, \; q_{21}(t)/1])^4$ \hfill (1a)

$q_2(t + 1) =$ iron consumption + iron input

$\qquad = c_2(t + 1) + q_{21}(t + 1)$

$\qquad = 3 \, (\text{Min } [L_2(t)/1, \; q_{21}(t)/1]^{1/2}$ \hfill (1b)

Wheat's production function (of discrete Sraffian type!) is homogeneous of degree *four* for scale changes – increasing returns with a vengeance. Iron's is homogeneous of degree *one-half*, i.e. viciously decreasing returns to scale.

Specifying a Sraffian numerical example, like that of (1960, Chap. 2), I specify $q_{12} = q_{21} = 1$ and $q_{11} = q_{22} = 0$ in the stationary state. Relations in Equation (1) then presuppose total labour of 3, $L_1 + L_2 = 2 + 1$. The system is 'productive': positive net consumptions of wheat and iron will be $(c_1 \, c_2) = (1 \; 2)$, and gross outputs will be $(q_1 \, q_2) = (8 \; 3) = (7 + 1 \; 2 + 1)$.

Now dare to do something absurd. Calculate for Sraffians the technical coefficients that emerge from naive (input ÷ output) ratios:

$$a_{11} = q_{11}/q_1 = 0, \qquad a_{22} = q_{22}/q_2 = 0$$

$$a_{12} = q_{12}/q_1 = 1/8, \qquad a_{21} = q_{21}/q_2 = 1/3$$

$$b_1 = L_1/q_1 = 2/8 = 1/4, \qquad b_2 = L_2/q_2 = 1/3 \hfill (2)$$

What is the Sraffa-defined price ratio, P_2/P_1? If the profit rate is specified to be zero, $\bar{r} = 0$, the computer grinds out

$$P_2/P_1 = \frac{10/23}{7/23} = 10/7 \hfill (3)$$

Later, Equation (4a) will verify this. As computer hacks say, GIGO: garbage in, garbage out.

Can we squander a moment to compute Sraffa's standard commodity? Why not? It is a market basket of $\sqrt{8/3}$ units of wheat to each one unit of iron (with whatever meaning that can have in this specified returns scenario).

Playing pretend games, suppose consumers can [sic] buy goods at Sraffian real prices: $(P_1/W \ P_2/W) = (7/23 \ 10/23)$. Let workers first always spend their incomes in proportions 49/69 on wheat and 20/69 on iron – which is compatible with the pretend game that Sraffa's alleged prices in Equation (3) could be actual prices in (A) a perfect planned state, or in (B) a laissez-faire push–shove equilibrium, *cum* or *sans* 'external (algebraic) economies'. Be wary of calling (B) auction-market competition among replicable free entrants and give up Marshall–Pigou or Walras–Arrow–Debreu (*dd ss*) diagrams for it.

Let the reader now contemplate a change of tastes by workers to a regimen where 50% of income always goes to wheat and 50% to iron. The price ratio would have stayed at 10/7 if returns to scale had been constant! Only the $(L_1/L_2 \ q_{12}/q_{21})$ would then adjust. We know this from the 1949 non-substitution theorem of the Leontief literature, which Sraffians inherited in 1960. If this were called to Piero's attention, I do not think he would be surprised, but of course *none* of this applies under present specified returns when the c_2/c_1 ratio changes from the old feasible level to a new level. In neither regimen can more c_2 be got by the sacrifice of c_1 in the ratio indicated by 1960 Sraffian price ratios! We stagger from one irrelevancy to another!

Worse is to come. Specify a change from $(q_{12} \ q_{21}) = (1 \ 1)$ to $(4 \ 1)$, which is perfectly admissible. We get a new set of feasible Sraffian pseudo-numbers. New $(q_1 \ q_2 \ c_1 \ c_2 \ L_1 \ L_2 \ a_{12} \ a_{21} \ b_1 \ b_2 \ P_2/P_1$, standard commodity weights)! They will be contradictory to the old set in all possible ratios $(L_1/q_{21} \ldots P_2/P_1)$.

Here are the old and new numbers. Readers who cannot deduce them all from Equation (1) and the boldfaced numbers below have not understood the present exposition of Sraffian arithmetic and its pretended extensions. Be reminded that there has been no innovative change in *any* technological opportunity.

	q_{12}	q_{21}	L_1	L_2	q_1	q_2	c_1	c_2	a_{12}	a_{21}	b_1	b_2	P_2/P_1
Old	**1**	**1**	2	2	8	3	7	2	1/3	1/8	2/8	1/3	10/7
New	**4**	**1**	2	4	8	6	4	5	4/6	1/8	2/8	4/16	9/4

As a helpful hint, here it is calculated out:

$$\text{Old } [P_j/W] = [2/8 \quad 1/3] \begin{bmatrix} 1-0 & -\frac{1}{3} \\ -\frac{1}{8} & 1-0 \end{bmatrix}^{-1}$$

$$= [2/8 \quad 1/3] \begin{bmatrix} \frac{24}{23} & \frac{8}{23} \\ \frac{3}{23} & \frac{24}{23} \end{bmatrix}$$

$$= \left[\frac{6}{23} + \frac{1}{23} \quad \frac{2}{23} + \frac{8}{23} \right]$$

$$= [7/23 \quad 10/23], \qquad P_2/P_1 = 10/7 \qquad (4a)$$

$$\text{New } [P_j/W] = [2/8 \quad 4/6] \begin{bmatrix} 1-0 & -\frac{4}{6} \\ -\frac{1}{8} & 1-0 \end{bmatrix}^{-1}$$

$$= [2/8 \quad 4/6] \begin{bmatrix} \frac{24}{23} & \frac{8}{23} \\ \frac{3}{23} & \frac{24}{23} \end{bmatrix}$$

$$= \left[\frac{6}{23} + \frac{2}{23} \quad \frac{2}{23} + \frac{16}{23} \right]$$

$$= [8/23 \quad 18/23], \qquad P_2/P_1 = 18/8 = 9/4 \qquad (4b)$$

Suppose in addition we also specify a range of positive profit rates $\bar{r}$. Now the limits on that range alter wildly with the initial specifications of $(q_{12} \ q_{21})$, and now none of the infinity of market-basket weights of the infinity of definable pseudo-standards can support *exact exponential growth*. For these returns there exists an infinity of growth paths that exceed *any* positive exponential rate.

Indeed, shrinking the original $(q_{12} \ q_{21})$ from (1 1) to, say, (1/100 1/100) will give a non-surplus and non-subsistence economy, and why not, when 'scale now matters'. The present system, it should be noted, could never start small and accumulate into a viable system that is 'productive'. Like a small pile of uranium$_{235}$ yearning to go bing–bang, it can never by itself attain the critical mass to go active. (If labour alone can produce any specified q vector – albeit inefficiently – this paragraph loses its force.)

I could go on and on. And on.

The mortal error is to think that any of Sraffa's Part III criteria for going through a switchpoint from one best technique to another (appropriate, say, to a higher $\bar{r}$ rate) still possess applicability and relevance.

We are now in the province of parametric non-convex programming. Answers are hard and complex, but they are definite. Sraffa, at various intervals over 35 years, tried to navigate in the serene waters of linear technologies. With the help of Besicovitch and with admirable self-persistence, he almost reinvented some well-known wheels. However, in the rough waters of integer programming and non-convex parametric programming there is no evidence that he knew how to modify his 1960 procedures. The deficiencies are not merely mathematical; the basic economics is at fault when the valid preconceptions of one Santa Claus world are thoughtlessly hijacked into another more complex world.

Also, why should one want (gratuitously) to make extrapolations that are erroneous? I suspect ideology played a role. I do not mean Left versus Right ideology. I mean that Sraffa always seemed alienated from the twentieth-century trends of mainstream economics. That could explain his apparent vast ignorance of the *detailed* content of so many 1920–1960 authors. Leaving mathematical esoterica aside, it would seem to be a wilful ignorance. (There is evidence that out of reticence he never fully revealed to his Cambridge mathematician friends exactly what his needs and goals were – a self-imposed inefficiency.) Fair enough. Each to his own tastes and idiosyncrasies, but if you want to enter into the courtroom of a fundamental critique of marginalism and much else, you are ill-advised to tie one hand behind yourself. Trite counsel, but repeatedly in life I have had to remind myself of it.

1926 déjà vu all over again

(i) (continued) My point about constant returns is quite independent of the Kurz–Salvadori resurrection of ancient controversies about Sraffa's 1926 classic article. Part of that article gave a worthwhile reminder that falling marginal costs to a firm must destroy the firm's *competitive* equilibrium. Bring on Chamberlin (1933, 1962) and Robinson (1956) and reread 1838 Cournot! Another part was for at least 15 years widely interpreted to allege that: along with falling ss supply curves being ruled out in the absence of externalities, Marshall's *rising ss* curves were suspect in the *partial equilibrium* model (that was so over-touted in 1890–1925), and at best rising ss would have to be a rare curiosum. By exhaustion, Marshallian competition must therefore boil down primarily only to horizontal ss curves, and so the 1817–1848 classical model of (allegedly) constant natural prices was alleged to be not so bad (even in 1926!) after all.

To believe in such an interpretation is to believe in balderdash. Generically, that is singular coincidences aside, simple competitive models of 1750, 1817, 1920 or 1997 can expect a shift of tastes from wheat to rye to *raise* P_r/P_w. (If the process induces a change in the interest rate, the reader can make the qualification indicated.) Also, wherever the gratuitous specifications apply that Marshall needed to make *his partial* equilibrium geometry *rigorously* applicable, Sraffa ought to have deduced that: rising *ss* curves are the generic rule, gently rising or steeply rising. If *partial* equilibrium had cogently denied *this*, that would have been a mortal flaw for partial equilibrium modelling. That it does not deny this can be rigorously proved by one of an infinity of counter examples. Example: wheat and rye use transferable homogeneous labour indifferently between them; in addition wheat needs available Land A, good for wheat production only, while rye needs available Land B, good for rye only. To validate the representative-agent scenario, let all have *equal* ownership of Land A and Land B, and all render equal amounts of the transferable labour. Finally, let each have the same utility–disutility function with *independent* marginal utilities of wheat and rye (declining of course), and let all have marginal disutility of labour that is the same strict constant. (See Samuelson, 1971, Section 5, for proof of these contentions about *exact partial* equilibrium models.)

The example's result is rising *ss* curves for all goods, intersecting in a Marshallian cross with the goods' declining *dd* curves. QED. Any shift in tastes from one good to another raises the relative price of that one good. QED. What was half the fuss about in 1926? Often when I beat down resistance to this line of argument, at the end of the day I would be told: 'Well yes. And somewhere in the Italian 1925 version or the England 1926 version there are Sraffian words that do say this.' If so, Amen.

If the above were all wrong it would not matter for my present argument about non-constant returns to scale. If, for whatever reason of externalities or internalities, constant scale returns do obtain, then 1960 Sraffa–Leontief arithmetic makes some sense; if not, not.

I should add that when a 1960 book can discuss price equilibrium without having to mention firms in the industry, that is a mathematical tip-off that systematic non-constant returns to scale cannot be operative – as was known to Edgeworth, Pareto, Wicksell, Hicks and other giants.

Readers can test the robustness of my present analysis by making *all* goods have increasing returns to scale like wheat here, or making all have decreasing returns like iron here. Most interesting is to have firms enjoy increasing scale returns when they are at low scales, which then turn into decreasing scale returns at intermediate critical absolute scales. Then, when demand for the industry is 'sufficiently large' to permit *replication* of *many* medium-size firms, this will entail a '*quantum*'-economics industry behaviour that closely approximates the constant returns to scale for the industry that the 1960 Sraffa arithmetic needs for meaningful validity. For 'quantum' matters, see M. F. W. Joseph (1933), P. A. Samuelson

(1967, 1973a,b). All this is 'marginalism' at its best, a critical 'critique' of the subject that should test constructively and without affect.

The Standard system's uselessness

(ii) Kurz–Salvadori reiterate the oft-read Sraffian view that, although the Standard commodity is not needed to describe and analyse effects on relative prices of changing interest rates, it has a use in that project. Having taught input/output economics to hundreds of students, I find that contrary to my experience. It is the false claims for the Standard commodity – agreed to be false by both me and Kurz–Salvadori – that first entice the students. Then, when they see how realistic induced switchings of techniques empirically do occur, they are disillusioned with it; as they are when they learn that the concept need not exist in the real number system under feasible joint product cases – and with no adverse consequences for a comprehensive understanding of income distribution, and as they are when non-labour primary factors arise in the real world, along with heterogeneities in labour itself, and as they are when non-indecomposable systems occur, and as they are..., and....

Suppose by happy coincidence the observed actual system involved productions in the exact proportions of its von Neumann balanced growth vector. Then it is the Standard commodity that is actually being produced. Then, when the interest rate is half-way between zero and its maximum possible, labour (paid *post factum*!) does get one-half of that income exactly and capital gets one-half. What a Santa Claus theory of serendipitous distribution! However, whenever this coincidence does *not* occur, actual distribution is a more complicated high-degree-polynomial expression. I deserved no criticism for speaking of shifts in the 'scale' of an industry in going through the 'thought experiment' of looking away from *actual* distribution reality to the 'auxiliary' case of the Standard commodity, and as the previous sections of this reply demonstrated, such scale changes would be fatal to the 1960 arithmetic if constant returns to scale did *not* obtain. Of course, thought experiments can be unconstrained; they can be twice irrelevant if you want to make them so.

Classical economics as merely a supply-and-demand paradigm

(iii) Kurz–Salvadori correctly point out some important differences in the posited behaviour equations of 1750–1850 classical writers as against modern 1870– mainstream economists who are labelled neoclassicists. They should know from my writings that I affirm this rather than deny it. Thus, classicals posit a subsistence-wage determination of endogenous population, while economic demographers today entertain different hypotheses. Also, post-1870 economists offer a theory to explain the consumption demand by income receivers, whereas the classicals often ignored that issue.

None of the above touches my contention, which I know that a Luigi Pasinetti would strongly disagree with, that both classicals and moderns share the same basic paradigm that processes of supply and demand determine the competitive equilibria – long run and short run – which obtain in both their respective systems. *That* common paradigm is shared by neoclassicists like Cassel and Clark, one of whom rejects marginal utilities and marginal productivities and one of whom does not. If by your definition a 'neoclassicist' is one who (a) believes in smooth marginal productivities for produced and primary factors, and/or (b) believes in a *scalar* aggregate of capital, and/or (c) at least one of (a) and (b), then yes there is a difference in Kuhnian paradigms between the neoclassicist Frank Ramsey and the classicist David Ricardo, but what I contend is that both Ramsey and Ricardo rely on the same supply-and-demand mechanisms. (Of course I am aware of Ricardo's words claiming that he goes deeper than supply and demand.)

I tried to say, and I here reaffirm and explicate this, that a discrete-technology scenario of Sraffa or Leontief, when it has many alternative feasible techniques, can come as close as you like to a Clarkian smooth marginal-products scenario with vectoral produced inputs – as close in *all* its *qualitative* essentials of comparative statics and dynamics. Conversely, there exist smooth Clarkian technologies with *no* 'spurious margins' that can come as close as you like to any Sraffa scenario (including a 1-technique scenario) or to *any* 1817 scenario. Therefore, in a deeper sense the neo- and the classical paradigms are species of the same genus. A return by a modern Sraffian to a 'classical paradigm', if it should yield wonderful new insights, will not do so essentially because it rejects the *tools* of the modern mainstream tradition.

Every time I say something deservedly complimenting to Sraffa, that is construed to be a recantation of the methodology of mainstream economics. Properly speaking, it is rather a statement about one new thing that I have learned about the world from the genius of Piero Sraffa – about the neoclassical *and* the non-neoclassical world.

When Kurz and Salvadori say that 'Sraffa effectively demolished neo-classical economics', that is bombast. What he precisely demolished, and cogently demolished, is the erroneous notion that a lower interest rate must, if anything, raise society's producible standard of living. That erroneous notion is *not* erroneous in a Sraffa model with a single produced input; and it is not erroneous in a Clark marginal-product model with a single produced input. However, in both models, when there is more than one capital good, it can well happen – and *equally* happen! – that society's consumption plateau is higher at a higher interest rate than at a lower one. Let us render unto Caesar exactly what is Caesar's.

Classicals and post-classicals both struggled with short- and long-run distribution problems

(iii) (continued) I understood Kurz and Salvadori to hold something like the following view:

Neoclassicism (or for that matter Arrow–Debreu modern mainstream economists) tends to specify as endowments vectors of produced inputs, vectors of natural resources and homogeneous labour-supply scalars (or vectors of heterogeneous labourers), and then from these data and data on technological knowledge, they try, by supply and demand analysis, to deduce the resulting *distribution* of factors' incomes and the real relative prices of all goods and services.

What separates classical economics from these post-1870 scholars is, in their view, that before 1870 writers (a) did specify fixed vectors of 'primary land', but (b) concentrated on steady states (or stationary ones) in which exogenously specifiable real wage levels and interest-rate levels entailed the resulting endogenous permissible equilibrium quantities of outputs, real factor prices and factor requirements by industries and final distributive shares among input owners (labourers, landowners, capitalistic owners of produced inputs). When technology changed, before-and-after pictures of equilibrium each had to be constructed and reconstructed with no truly classical theory of transitional paths.

My 'scrutiny' of the literature denies this dichotomy. Yes, pre-1850 writers did concentrate much on a quasi-exogenous subsistence real wage level, asymptotically equilibrated by induced rises and falls in population numbers. Yes, Ricardo and Mill and others did have a (feebler) parallel subsistence-interest notion – never adequately spelled out and rationalized – of an effective exogenously knowable level of interest rate, above which 'accumulation' would be induced and below which 'decumulation' would be induced. However, all of them – Turgot, Smith, Malthus, Ricardo, Longfield, Mill and Mill, Senior and Marx – do deal repeatedly and at length with non-stationary processes that methodologically fall under the post-1870 rubric I have allocated to Kurz and Salvadori.

When a Pasinetti advises, back to the classical paradigm, on to a future non-neoclassical paradigm, I do not understand him to be saying: deduce steady states of population from physiological–conventional wage levels that turn human fecundity on and off; deduce long-run interest rates from Senior–Schumpeter palaver about time preference.

Where does 1960 Sraffa fit in? His pages tell us nought about whether the interest rate will be zero or be at its maximal technological level. They say nothing about how a model with fixed homogeneous labour and land supply will have its wages/rent ratio determined, and nought about how technical change is likely to alter (wages/interest rent/interest) shares.

Why 'basics' are not basic

(iv) Generality and completeness are virtues. A non-negative matrix can be *indecomposable* or not. It can have one (principal) submatrix that is indecomposable (or *more* than one, or *none*). A simple boiler plate provides all the needed qualifications for *all* cases. Each morning in class it would be tedious to run through all the qualifications. Therefore, on lazy days at MIT I might stipulate: today we will assume that *all* goods form an indecomposable input/output $[a_{ij}]$ that is positive; all are basics. Or, today we will assume that **a** has one indecomposable subset only, and all goods outside it are positively linked with it. (That is Sraffa's convention, which Kurz–Salvadori cheer-lead for.)

To insist on *it* is bad economics. It requires that the greatest editor of classical texts must ostracize the personal services so beloved by Malthus and Ricardo. (I am not allowed to use a masseur; a barber who cuts my hair with produced scissors is *de rigueur*. What scholasticism.) The bread that is produced by labour out of the wild wheat picked off land by labour – the well-known 'Austrian' example that 1817 Ricardo and 1867 Marx could handle well, and which should have shown Marx how *sterile* and gratuitous was his *Mehrwert* innovation – is ruled out of bounds. Why this theology? No important economic theorem depends on it. No Sraffa system could ever have got started if historically there had not existed a technology that violated its dogma. Nor is it true that bread now splits off independently from all the other goods. (Nor would that be a repugnant result were it true.) Bread is still affected by iron through their common dependence upon land and labour and through their competition for the consumers' dollars.

I have no interest in fighting one theology with another. My deeper criticism is to repeat that Sraffa, with only 100 1960 pages, wasted so many of his precious words on unimportant basic vs. non-basic puzzlings. Consider again as a case in point the bare five pages allocated to *land*. Instead of treating primary land in the way that Chapters II–IX had previously treated primary labour, the author chooses to classify land as a non-basic joint product, and spends our time and impatience on puzzling of how land fits into standard commodity palaver. I am a hungry Oliver Twist who complains about being given too little. (Would that Chapter XI had shown how to handle scarce homogeneous land and homogeneous labour in a 1-technique world, where no theory of distributive sharings and real prices, W/rent and (P_j/W), yields to Sraffian equalities, or had handled the easier case of a specific corn land and a specific rye land, where a classical subsistence-wage model of population size makes everything determinate at each interest rate after landowners' spending tastes are specified – and where their tastes determine whether rye-land rent rate is or is not zero. That might have caused the 1960 author to reword his 1926 downplaying of the rising supply price of P_{rye}/P_{wheat} when tastes shift toward rye, and it might have driven home how similar to post-1870 economics were the 1917 scenarios, especially when many techniques realistically displace a 1-technique specification.)

Let me borrow a fraction of the five 1960 pages on land to handle a scenario where wheat and iron each need as inputs *homogeneous* (transferable!) land and labour, along with some of the other goods as input: 1 wheat needs 2 land, 1 labour and $\frac{1}{2}$ iron; 1 iron needs 3 land, 1 labour and $\frac{1}{2}$ wheat. Set interest at zero: $1 + r = 1$. Then, as in the methodology of Chapter 2,

$$P_1 = W + 2R + \tfrac{1}{2}P_2, \qquad P_2 = W + 3R + \tfrac{1}{2}P_1,$$

$$R = \text{rent rate} = \tfrac{6}{3}W + \tfrac{14}{3}R, \qquad P_2 = \tfrac{6}{3}W + \tfrac{16}{3}R,$$

$$1 \le P_2/P_1 \ge 16/14$$

If there is one technique only, as in *all* of Part I, Sraffa knows he cannot find determinate real prices: $(P_2/P_1)^*$, $(P_1/W)^*$, $(P_2/W)^*$, $(R/W)^*$. As his friend Wittgenstein said: Whereof we cannot speak we must be silent.

Wrongful neglect of inequalities

(v) A besotted lover sees a black wart as a beauty mark on the face of the beloved. Kurz–Salvadori, instead of borrowing from Samuel Johnson's compliment to walking dogs and preaching women – 'It is not done well but it is remarkable that it is done at all' – pass up the opportunity to agree with the following paragraph.

Piero Sraffa was a self-taught mathematical economist who apparently never heard of the duality theorems of equalities–inequalities common to game theory, linear programming and (on careful reading of Fisher, Wicksell, Zeuthen, Neisser, Hicks, Schlesinger, Wald, von Neumann:

1890–1950) to the excellent economic literature on how slack redundancy makes a variable's price go and stay at zero, thereby avoiding negative prices under free disposability assumptions. (If disposability is *not* a free option, prices *should* go negative, which is a theorem in that mathematical literature.) Therefore, with charity and admiration we should commend Sraffa for exploring an imperfect solution, and with candour point out that it is inferior and point out where it is inferior. Sraffa's defended solution is to assume that, when a shift in exogenous data would make a 'square' technique entail negative prices, posit that there will be a convenient alternative viable square technique that still produces positive prices. Dr Pangloss would like this Sraffa wish list.

Instead of joining me in this amiable summing up, Kurz–Salvadori argue that all ad hoc assumptions are equally arbitrary. On the one hand, von Neumann antes up the *ad hoc* assumption of free disposability; on the other, Sraffa antes up the *ad hoc* assumption of there always existing a technical option that avoids negative prices. The dishonours are even. I know of no experts who would agree to that verdict after being given the problem with all proper names removed, and I tried a few.

Besides, if one accepts the Sraffians' view that only a *finite* number of technical options ever exist at each date, then the Kurz–Salvadori defence of Sraffa (which he himself never pressed) fails, and fails generically. Here is an example in the widely known Stigler–Cornfield 'least cost adequate diet' instance of jointness. 'You must daily get *at least* 10 calorie units *and* 10 vitamin units. Three goods are known to provide respectively the following number-per-unit of (calories vitamins) equal for the goods $(X_1 \ X_2 \ X_3)$ respectively to (3 2), (2 3), (4 1). If the goods all have equal unit prices, say \$1 each, what is the cheapest diet to buy?' (Stigler, primarily a literary economist, published on this in 1945 before George Dantzig (1951) had published in the *economic* literature the definitive mathematical theory of linear programming.)

Readers can verify, by trial and error or the *simplex* algorithm, that $(x_1^* \ x_2^* \ x_3^*) = (2 \ 2 \ 0)$ defines the cheapest diet. Yes, the relevant matrix is 'square' in the sense that no more than two goods need be bought to provide two nutrients. Modify the problem by raising the calorie requirement a little (but not too much) and indeed a new 'square' solution with sign $(x_1^* \ x_2^* \ x_3^*) = (+ \ 0 \ +)$ will emerge. However, proceed to modify the problem a lot, so that say at least 100 calorie units are now needed, while the minimal vitamins needed stay at 10. Sraffa's proposed dodge – which did work at first to avoid negative numbers by staying with a new 'square' matrix when the calorie requirement was raised by *not too much* – now does definitely fail. Only one of the possible goods can be optimally bought when the calorie/vitamin specification is made large enough, and Sraffian equalities are then definitely made inapplicable. Only X_1 can now be bought, making vitamins redundant with a zero imputation value. Even if out of pity we let Kurz–Salvadori have a fourth good or a 999th good, there will always be a calorie requirement that will mandate non-squareness of the relevant matrix. QED. For my money, von Neumann dominates over the surrogate for Sraffa proposed by his zealous followers. (The correct Dantzig theorem is that the number of goods positively bought need never *exceed* the least of [number of nutrients, number of goods]: it can, though, have to fall short of both of the pair in brackets.)

'Prices of production' vs. 'cost of production'

(vi) Kurz and Salvadori agree with me: Yes, Sraffa's 'prices of production' are precisely 'competitive costs of production', and Sraffa explicitly recognizes that. Yes, Sraffa recognizes that the minimized costs of production must involve simultaneous equations, and the logical fact that they can always be mathematically solved self-demonstrates that the circle involved is a virtuous not a vicious one. Yes, Kurz–Salvadori and Sraffa recognize that many scholars – I offer Joan Robinson as one and Marx as another; Kurz–Salvadori offer Böhm–Bawerk for a third – wrongly regard simultaneous equations as a swindle. I do not know on what evidence Kurz–Salvadori attribute to Sraffa the view that some of these opponents believe simultaneous equations can be 'circumnavigated'; my experience is that such (mistaken) sceptics generally believe that those paradigms involving circular interdependences are unsolvable and are a blemish on their opponents' economics of various subcenturies.

With all this agreement, why was my mild remark about the non-optimality of Sraffa's choice of the nomenclature 'prices of production' not applauded? Sraffa's own defence (1960, p. 8) is to liken this decision to his decision not to use in the book the 'term "capital" in its quantitative [i.e., *scalar*] connotations'. I applaud *this* latter choice by Sraffa. Models with but *one* scalar produced good have different and special properties as compared to those with vectors of heterogeneous produced goods, and Sraffa's work I deem a classic, not because it reinvents some wheels of Frobenius–Leontief matrixes, but because it demonstrates even better than Joan Robinson's 1956 explorations how basic are these scalar-versus-vector differences. I must also reaffirm what both Joan and Piero denied in separate conversations with me: those vital differences between scalar and vectoral produced-input technologies are *not* differences between smooth Clark–Samuelson marginal productivity models and von Neumann–Leontief–Sraffa discrete-techniques models. The differences are *common* to *both* techniques!

Why link 'cost of production' nomenclature to '[scalar or aggregate] CAPITAL' nomenclature? Where arises the nice abstention from prejudicing some cost issue by avoiding a still-suspect term? Surprisingly, Sraffa asserts (1960, p. 8) that cost of production has come 'to be inseparably linked with the supposition that [it stands] for quantities that can be measured independently of, and prior to, the determination of the prices of the products. (Witness the real costs of Marshall...).' I find this odd. Marshall was above all an eclectic simultaneous equation methodologist, in contrast to unidirectional writers like Böhm and Mill.

I would turn the nomenclature choice upside down. It was Marx who was the erroneous critic of Smith's resolution of steady-state long-run price into the sum of value-added wage–interest–rent components, and it was Marx who therefore used those words 'prices of production'. (As Dmitriev was the first to elucidate in 1898, Marx's gripe that Smith sends us from pillar to post in an infinite regress [actually *convergent* infinite sums!] is in fact answered by Marx's own tableau of simple reproduction when *its* simultaneous equations are properly formulated. No fool ever accused Sraffa of not knowing Marx's writing.)

When Sraffa rightly says competition select a cheapest technique, in terms of what is 'cheapness' measured? For his model it is cheaper *cost of production* (!) and nothing else that rules – cheaper total cost of all needed inputs, each input price being evaluated at the real price vector that is minimal. (For the correct theories of pure *exchange* by Jevons (1871) and Edgeworth (1881) another cheapness is guiding.) Sraffa's explication of a switch point on page 83, which Kurz–Salvadori cite, makes needless heavy weather over basic–non-basic babble. One rule only applies in competition and the scale returns it presupposes.

Synthesis

Finally, I can react to points that pertain to all of the Kurz–Salvadori (i)–(vi) comments and to their first two footnotes.

Their Footnote 2 presumably agrees that *increasing* scale returns do put us into Chamberlin–Robinson imperfect competition, but I believe they want to dissent where *decreasing* scale returns obtain for firms. No disagreement from me. Here is the needed special re-analysis for *decreasing* returns to scale. I deny that firm production functions could ever in the real world systematically and uniformly be everywhere homogeneous-of-positive-*fraction* degree. How can Dr. Samuelson tell the real world how to behave? I do not have to tell the world that: 'Industry output in *infinite* amount cannot be producible by a *finite* vector of inputs'; the same world that knows perpetual motion machines are impossible itself knows that unit costs at the industry level cannot be brought down indefinitely close to zero by spontaneous replication of infinitely many firms each producing infinitesimal amounts of output. That is not Xeno's paradox, it is Xeno's nonsense, as Wicksell insisted. Therefore, what decreasing scale returns could there be to have to worry about? (It is irrelevant to confuse decreasing *scale* returns and good old *diminishing returns* to a subset of factors, say labour, while another subset, say land, is being held constant.) The experienced reader will recall that such a confusion has occurred in connection with discussions of 1926 Sraffa. Even Kurz-Salvadori's *Comment*, purporting to controvert any claim about an 'empty set of results', adduces as non-empty *positive* result a case where 'certain qualities of land are in short supply' and in consequence a rise in taste for burgundy will raise its price. I say 'Bravo' to late recruits to the regular pre-1926 army, but diminishing returns to variable labour applied to limited land is completely in accord with standard constant returns to scale! Sraffa himself, in his rare texts and in 1948–1958 conversations with me, repeatedly used nomenclature that similarly confused the reader by virtue of not explicitly distinguishing scale returns from proportion-of-factors returns and, as has been shown again and again, the *partial* equilibrium tools of Marshall are *not* self-contradictory in such cases. If Kurz–Salvadori will re-read Allyn Young (1913), Robertson (1924) and Knight (1924), they will understand that induced external-to-the-firm diseconomies – such as rising land rents and falling wage rate/price$_q$ as industry output expands – are precisely what Walras mainstream economics is all about. Marshall and Pigou nodded when they confused 'smoke nuisance', a *technological* externality which might need to be corrected by penalty taxes, with induced rises in relative factor prices as industries expand (a *pecuniary* externality). My point was never that competitive analysis is empty of results when multiple primary factors occur; it is that the 1960 Chapter II and Chapter XII matrix arithmetic was not augmented so as to handle it. When we augment Sraffian arithmetic to handle properly the more general scenarios, all is well – *except* when, in the augmented space of [male labour, female labour, high-quality pasture land, low-quality pasture land, vineyard land], constant returns to scale is systematically denied; then that augmented matrix arithmetic will not apply. In short, Sraffa should have replied to Keynes: 'I suspect that, after I think it through, I will want to restrict my competitive analysis to constant returns to scale models where total revenues must be exhausted by total costs [inclusive of equalized profit rates]'.

In certain absolute scale ranges, I gladly admit, decreasing returns to *scale* could obtain, but below certain critical scale levels, *increasing* scale returns must assuredly obtain in the lumpy world of Democritus–Planck–Einstein–Bohr. As in the Joseph–Samuelson quantum economics world already referred to, the industry oscillates in a damped way toward constant returns to *its* scale as demand permits replication of $1, 2, \ldots, 10, \ldots$ 99 viable firms (each with U-shaped long-run unit cost schedules). 1960 Sraffa arithmetic then handles tolerably well the N-large case where constant returns to scale tolerably holds for the industry. If not, not. Paging Chamberlin–Robinson. (A *curiosum*: Let returns to scale decrease like $q = f(L)$ – with $f'(L) > 0 > f''(L), f(0) = 0 < f'(0) < \infty$, with L being the only input. Then by replicating enough 'infinitesimal firms', the industry approaches as closely as we wish to a first-degree homogeneous $F(L) = f(1)L$ and, as I insist while Sraffa reserved disagreement, the 1960 arithmetic then and only then possesses relevance. Again, if not, not. The ball again is in the Sraffians' court.)

The theory of 'contestable markets', dreamt up originally by consultants to firms indicted for anti-trust violations, lacks credibility when systematic deviations from free-entry replicability of existing firm(s) by potential new entrants do obtain. But suppose this were not so: let a large monopolist, fearing potential new entrants, price his q down to (falling) average cost and tolerate $P <$ marginal revenue. Now test the truth of Sraffa's 1960 theorem that this product's relative price is unaffected by a change in consumers' tastes. Although Sraffian matrixes proclaim precisely that, what reader believes in *that* truth now?

The upshot of economic theory and of economic history, I believe, is common to classical and 1870–1970 writers, as well as post-1970 mainstream scholars. It holds that post-Newton technological change, plus accumulation of copious vector elements of produced inputs, is what creates the rising affluence of populations The differential sharings of that affluence, among people who differentially own amounts of the heterogeneous productive inputs, is influenced by changes in the relative total supplies of factors of production: The Netherlands, as Smith claimed, had greater prosperity and lower interest rates than (say) Portugal because the Dutch had sacrificed some past current consumptions in order to accelerate accumulation (of *vectoral* capitals). Yes, I know about the possibilities of reswitching and about the difficulties of the Hahn problem – the puzzle of how, in an uncertain world with incomplete Arrow markets, somehow an approximation to intertemporal Pareto-optimality seems to characterize the micro-allocations of macro-accumulations. That super-sophistication must not divert me from what is all-important.

A generation of post-Sraffians have had their attention turned away from these important classical and post-1870 matters by a preoccupation with long-run steady-state models based upon nihilistic specifications tolerating any and all profit rates and exogenous (!) subsistence wage rates. Such steady states are the coward's way out, unless they are cogently deduced as asymptotic limits of non-stationary real-price and real-output proportionalities, asymptotic limits that are constantly changing in a Schumpeterian world. I mourn a lost generation whose counsel and empirical research are sorely needed.

References

Chamberlin, E. H. (1933, 1962). *The Theory of Monopolistic Competition*, Cambridge, MA: Harvard University Press.

Cournot, A. A. (1838). *Researches into the Mathematical Principles of the Theory of Wealth*. Translated 1929, N. T. Bacon, New York: Macmillan.

Dantzig, G. (1951). 'The Programming of Interdependent Activities: Mathematical Model', in T. C. Koopmans et al. (eds), *Activity Analysis of Production and Allocation*, New York: John Wiley.

Dmitriev, V. K. (1898). *Ekonomicheskie Ocherki*, Vyp. I. 'Teoriya tsênnosti D. Ricardo (opt' tochnago analyza)' [*Economic Essays*, Issue I, 'The Theory of Value of D. Ricardo, an Attempt at a Rigorous Analysis]'. Moscow. Translated into English in 1974 as D. M. Nuti (ed.), *V. K. Dmitriev Economic Essays on Value, Competition and Utility*, Cambridge: Cambridge University Press.

Edgeworth, F. Y. (1881). *Mathematical Psychics*, London: C. Kegan Paul.

Jevons, W. S. (1871). *The Theory of Political Economy*, London: Macmillan.

Joseph, M. F. W. (1933). 'A Discontinuous Cost Curve and the Tendency to Increasing Returns', *Economic Journal*, **43**, pp. 390–98.

Knight, F. (1924). 'Some fallacies in the interpretation of social cost', *Quarterly Journal of Economics*, **37**, pp. 579–624.

Marshall, A. (1890–1921, 1961). *Principles of Economics*, 9th (variorum) edn, C. W. Guillebaud (ed.), London: Macmillan.

Robertson, D. H. (1924). 'Those Empty Boxes', *Economic Journal*, **34**, pp. 16–31.

Robinson, J. (1956). *The Accumulation of Capital*, Homewood, IL: Richard D. Irwin.

Samuelson, P. A. (1967). 'The Monopolistic Competition Revolution', in R. E. Kuenne (ed.), *Monopolistic Competition Theory: Studies in Impact. Essays in Honor of Edward H. Chamberlin*, New York: John Wiley. Reproduced as Chap. 131 in *The Collected Scientific Papers of Paul A. Samuelson*, Vol. 3, Cambridge, MA: MIT Press, 1972.

Samuelson, P. A. (1971). 'An Exact Hume–Ricardo–Marshall Model of International Trade', *Journal of International Economics*, **1**, pp. 1–18, and particularly Sect. 5. Reproduced as Chap. 162 in *The Collected Scientific Papers of Paul A. Samuelson*, Vol. 3, Cambridge, MA: MIT Press, 1972.

Samuelson, P. A. (1973a). 'A Quantum Theory Model of Economics: Is the Coordinating Entrepreneur Just Worth His Profit?', in J. Bhagwati and R. S. Eckaus (eds), *Development and Planning. Essays in Honour of Paul Rosenstein-Rodan*, London: John Allen and Unwin, pp. 329–35. Reproduced as Chap. 214 in *The Collected Scientific Papers of Paul A. Samuelson*, Vol. 4, Cambridge, MA: MIT Press, 1977.

Samuelson, P. A. (1973b). *Economics*, 9th edn, New York: McGraw-Hill, see especially p. 479.

Sraffa, P. (1926). 'The Laws of Returns under Competitive Conditions', *Economic Journal*, **36**, pp. 535–50.

Sraffa, P. (1960). *Production of Commodities by Means of Commodities*, Cambridge: Cambridge University Press.

Stigler, G. (1945). 'The Cost of Subsistence', *Journal of Farm Economics*, **27**, pp. 303–14.

Young, A. A. (1913). 'Pigou's Wealth and Welfare', *Quarterly Journal of Economics*, **27**, pp. 672–86.

CHAPTER 4

Sraffa on demand: a textual analysis

Neri Salvadori

..., I have taken the course to express myself in terms of Number, Weight or Measure, to use only Arguments of Sense and to consider only such causes as have Visible Foundations in Nature: leaving those that depend upon the mutable Minds, Opinions and Appetites, Passions of particular Men to the consideration of others. (from the Preface to *Political Arithmetik* by William Petty)

1   Introduction

This chapter provides a textual analysis of the relevant works by Sraffa (1925, 1926, 1960) on demand. A letter to Asimakopulos dated 11 July 1971 and partially published by him (see Asimakopulos, 1990) will also be analysed. In Sraffa's writings it is not difficult to find passages that refer to the 'theory of competitive value' which 'is inspired by the fundamental symmetry existing between the forces of demand and those of supply' (Sraffa, 1926, p. 535):

Anyone accustomed to think in terms of the equilibrium of demand and supply may be inclined .... (Sraffa, 1960, p. v)

However, anyone who wants to find in those writings a quotation against the concept of 'demand' or even the concept of 'demand function' will be

I should like to thank, without implicating, Geoff Harcourt, Heinz Kurz, Gary Mongiovi, Mario Morroni, Carlo Panico, Alessandro Roncaglia, Andrea Salanti, Bertram Schefold and Ian Steedman for helpful discussions and/or comments on previous versions of this paper. I also thank participants at a seminar at the Universities of Paris-X-Nanterre and Padua and participants at a session in memory of Krishna Bharadwaj at the 20th Annual Conference of the History of Economics Society (Philadelphia, June 1993), where previous versions of this paper have been delivered. Financial supports from MURST and CNR are also gratefully acknowledged.

disappointed. I will argue that Sraffa was not of the opinion that demand does not matter but, on the contrary, that demand based on preferences (utility) is not a solid base on which to erect a theory of value and distribution. His aversion to arguing in terms of 'mutable Minds, Opinions and Appetites, Passions of particular Men' in economic analysis was not new, and can indeed be traced back to Petty (cf. the motto of this paper).[1]

Section 2 investigates some passages in the published papers written by Sraffa in the 1920s in which demand plays a role. Section 3 is divided into four subsections; each subsection investigates a particular section in Sraffa's book in which demand is involved. Section 4 is devoted to analysing the above-mentioned letter by Sraffa to Asimakopulos, and Section 5 contains some conclusions.

2   The early papers

The Italian antecedent (Sraffa, 1925) to the better known paper of 1926 in the *Economic Journal* contains not only the critique of Marshallian partial analysis that constitutes the first part of the English article, but also three long sections on the foundations of decreasing, increasing and constant returns. In the analysis of decreasing returns we find several references to demand. In this section, it is argued that decreasing returns do not find their foundation in improbable 'technical conditions', but 'must of necessity occur because it will be the producer himself who, for his own benefit, will arrange the doses of the factors and the methods of use in a decreasing order, going from the most favourable ones to the most ineffective' (Sraffa, 1925, p. 288 [p. 332]). Then Sraffa adds the following statement.

The same argument may be repeated for the case of diminishing utility (and therefore for the demand curves derived from it) which is a special case of diminishing productivity, when we consider utility as product, the commodities consumed as the variable factor of production, and the 'sensitive organism' as the constant factor. It is not any allegedly psycho-physical law which endows diminishing utility with generality, but the possibility of using different doses of a

[1] Krishna Bharadwaj (1978, p. 30) drew my attention to that passage in Petty. Her comment on the passage is also interesting: 'The supply-and-demand-based equilibrium theories of value shifted the basis of determination of value from such exclusively objective consideration to those involving utility as well as "Minds, Opinions and Appetites, Passions of particular Men"'.

commodity to satisfy different needs and the desire to utilise the first doses to satisfy the most urgent needs. (Sraffa, 1925, p. 295 [p. 338])[2]

Utility, decreasing marginal utility, and the demand function based upon these concepts are not rejected, but only differently interpreted. They are related to a sort of 'theory of needs'. However, these references to demand in the Italian antecedent of the *Economic Journal* article (Sraffa, 1926) are perhaps not startling, since in the second part of the latter paper each firm is supposed to be faced with its own *demand* curve. It is interesting, however, to read again the arguments which according to Sraffa support the idea that each firm operates in a particular market.

The causes of the preference shown by any group of buyers for a particular firm are of the most diverse nature, and may range from long custom, personal acquaintance, confidence in the quality of the product, proximity, knowledge of particular requirements and the possibility of obtaining credit, to the reputation of a trade-mark, or sign, or a name with high traditions, or to such special features of modelling or design in the product as – without constituting it a distinct commodity intended for the satisfaction of particular needs – have for their principal purpose that of distinguishing it from the products of other firms. What these and many other possible reasons for preference have in common is that they are expressed in a willingness (which may frequently be dictated by necessity) on the part of the group of buyers who constitute a firm's clientele to pay, if necessary, something extra in order to obtain the goods from a particular firm rather than from any other. (Sraffa, 1926, pp. 544–5)

Preferences are generally assumed as given. This is so also in this paper by Sraffa. However, preferences are not considered as attributes of the mind, given once and forever. On the contrary, they appear as easily changing and strongly connected with what firms either produce now or have produced in the past, or both; marketing policies are also considered. Demand function does not appear as an outcome of the analysis of the *isolated* consumer and his or her preferences. On the contrary, consumption appears as not separated from production and, in some sense, as derived from it. This point of view may appear as related to the special issue dealt with ('the preference shown by any group of buyers for a particular firm'), but it is certainly quite different from the Neo-Classical one and is very similar to that of the Classicals and Marx:

---

[2] In Sraffa's library at the Wren Library (Trinity College, Cambridge, UK) there are two offprints of this paper by Sraffa (1925) and both copies are annotated by him (see items 7575 and 7576). These annotations include references to be added to or corrected on the original paper and some remarks, mainly self-critical. One of the (self-critical) remarks is dated 3 March 1931; the others have no date reference. However, there is no remark on the quoted paragraph.

Hunger is hunger; but the hunger that is satisfied by the cooked meat eaten with knife and fork differs from hunger that devours raw meat with the help of hands, nails and teeth. Production thus produces not only the object of consumption but also the mode of consumption not only objectively but also subjectively. Production therefore creates the consumer. (Marx, *Grundrisse: Introduction to the Critique of Political Economy*, quoted by Bharadwaj, 1978, p. 61)[3]

In this section we have shown that in the 1920s Sraffa was quite inclined to consider demand, even if it appeared to him as not independent from production and related to a 'theory of needs'. Someone might conjecture that this interest in demand is just a 'slip' of the 'young' Sraffa, whereas the 'mature' Sraffa is different. Let us then consider his book.

3   Production of commodities by means of commodities[4]

In this section, a textual analysis of Sections 7, 44, 50 and 88 of *Production of Commodities* is provided. It is shown that in these sections demand is involved. It is explicitly mentioned in Section 7, whereas the concept of 'requirements for use', which appears to be very similar to it, is mentioned in Section 50. In Section 44 it is remarked that changes in prices and distribution may affect workers' expenses (if they receive a part of the surplus), whereas some changes in produced quantities are considered in Section 88. In *Production of Commodities* there are other passages in which 'demand' is referred to.[5] These sections have been chosen because Section 7 is the only place in the whole main text of the book where the words 'demand' and 'supply' are used (outside of the main text the only reference to 'demand and supply' is that in the Preface quoted above, p. v), whereas an analysis of the other sections

---

[3] Bharadwaj's comment on this passage by Marx is also interesting: 'Further, production, by making products available, creates the need for them. The need which the consumer feels for the object is induced by its perception.'

[4] This section is partially borrowed from Salvadori (1995).

[5] Section 93, for instance, considers two single-product methods producing two commodities that are regarded as identical 'for all possible *basic* uses' even if 'there are other, *non-basic* uses, some of which require the one, and some the other of the two products'. The aim of Sraffa is to analyse a situation in which '*the special non-basic uses will ensure that both methods are always employed to some extent*' (emphasis added), whereas 'for all basic uses the choice between the two methods will be exclusively grounded on cheapness'. Accordingly, a commodity is produced only if there is a *use*, and therefore a *demand*, for it. In particular, non-basic commodities, which by definition do not have the property of entering directly or indirectly into the production of all commodities, will be produced only either if they are *consumed* or if they enter, directly or indirectly, into the production of other non-basic commodities that are *consumed*.

mentioned above is enough to establish that Sraffa's contribution cannot be properly interpreted as maintaining that 'demand' does not matter.

3.1 Section 7

Section 7 of *Production of Commodities* is a 'Terminological note' (see Table of Contents). In this 'note', Sraffa justifies the use of the expressions 'prices' or 'values' for the 'ratios which satisfy the conditions of production' rather than the expression 'costs of production'. He maintains that the latter would be appropriate for a *non-basic* but not for a *basic* commodity. This is so because the exchange ratio of a basic commodity 'depends as much on the *use* that is made of it in the production of other basic commodities as on the extent to which those commodities enter its own production.' Then Sraffa adds the following parenthetical remark:

(One might be tempted, but it would be misleading, to say that 'it depends as much on the Demand side as on the Supply side'.)

The words 'demand' and 'supply' are used here just to assert that their use is misleading. It is also easily seen that in this context a reference to 'demand' when mentioning the fact that basic commodities are utilized directly or indirectly in the (re)production of all commodities would effectively be misleading. Then why is 'demand' mentioned here? It seems that the author added this parenthetical sentence to qualify his refusal of the one-way avenue from *costs* to prices as being totally different from that traced back to Walras and Marshall.[6] Whereas Walras and Marshall negated the Classicals' one-way avenue from costs to prices because they emphasized the role of demand, Sraffa negated it because costs are dependent on the prices of the commodities entering into production. The parenthetical sentence mentioned by Sraffa reminds us of this distinction.

[6] Walras, in Lecture XXXVIII of *Eléments d'économie politique pure*, starts from Ricardo's distinction between reproducible and non-reproducible commodities – the prices of the former being determined by costs of production only and the prices of the latter also being determined by demand – to argue that all commodities are, at least partially, non-reproducible and therefore demand-determined. Marshall, in Appendix I of *Principles of Economics*, tried to argue that Ricardo should have passed the action of demand in governing value 'lightly' because he should have regarded its action as less obscure than that of cost of production. I am indebted to Mario Morroni for this remark.

3.2   Section 44

In Section 44 the practice, common to the classical economists and Marx, of treating the wage rather than the rate of profits as the 'given' distribution variable is reversed. Sraffa remarks that since wages, besides the ever-present element of subsistence, may include a share of the surplus, the *real* wage rate cannot be regarded as 'consisting of specified necessaries determined by physiological or social conditions *which are independent of prices or the rate of profits*' (emphases added). That is, if workers obtain a part of the surplus, then it cannot be excluded that they consume other commodities besides those which are determined by physiological or social conditions; moreover, it cannot be excluded that workers' consumption choice depends on *relative prices and income distribution*. Hence, Sraffa argues, *if* the wage rate were still to be given from outside the system of production, it would have to be 'in terms of a more or less abstract standard, and [would] not acquire a definite meaning until the prices of commodities are determined'.

The fact that workers' demand cannot be defined on the basis of physiological or social conditions does not imply, according to Sraffa, the necessity of an analysis of the determinants of it. In the traditional Classical analysis, the role of workers' consumption is that of determining the real wage (i.e. one of the distributive variables) from outside the relations among prices that must hold if commodities are to be *reproduced*. This role can be played, Sraffa argues, by the rate of profits which, 'as a ratio', is a pure number 'and can well be "given" before the prices are fixed'. It is remarkable that an important aspect of the analysis emerges as a consequence of a difficulty of the *observer*, rather than as an *observed aspect* of reality.

3.3   Section 50

In a footnote to Section 50 'demand' is not mentioned by name, but a concept that seems very similar to it is used to justify an assumption in the text. Section 50 is the very first section of Part II, and introduces the existence of a process producing two commodities instead of just one. It seems that there 'would be more prices to be ascertained than there are processes, and therefore equations, to determine them'. 'In these circumstances', Sraffa continues, 'there will be room "either" for a second, parallel process which will produce the two commodities by a different method and [...] in different proportions', or for the production of 'a third commodity by two distinct processes' which use the two jointly produced commodities 'as means of production in different proportions'.

A footnote appended just after the former alternative has been introduced reads:

Incidentally, considering that the proportions in which the two commodities are produced by any one method will in general be different from those in which they are *required for use*, the existence of two methods of producing them in different proportions will be necessary for obtaining the required proportion of the two products through an appropriate combination of the two methods. (Emphasis added)

The same argument can also be applied to the latter alternative: the appropriate combination of the two methods producing the third commodity is 'necessary' to obtain the proportions in which commodities are 'required for use'. The section is concluded by the assumption that 'the number of processes should be equal to the number of commodities'.

This section raises a number of questions. First, are the two ways mentioned to escape the difficulty that the number of equations can be smaller than the number of prices to be ascertained the only available ways? As a consequence, is the existence of a number of processes equal to the number of commodities actually *necessary*, flukes apart, to guarantee that commodities are produced in the proportions in which they are 'required for use'? Second, is the existence of a number of processes equal to the number of commodities *sufficient* to guarantee that commodities are produced in the proportions in which they are 'required for use'? Third, why is a concept such as 'requirements for use', which appears to be so important, introduced in this way, and why is the more common notion of 'demand' not used?

Let us consider the second point first, not least because the answer is found in *Production of Commodities* itself:

Take [...] the case of two products jointly produced by each of two different methods. The possibility of varying the extent to which one or the other method is employed ensures a certain range of variation in the proportions in which the two goods may be produced in the aggregate. But this range finds its limits in the proportions in which the two goods are produced by each of the two methods, so that the limits are reached as soon as one or the other method is exclusively employed. (Sraffa, 1960, p. 47, Section 53)[7]

Hence Sraffa was well aware of the above-mentioned difficulty. The assumption of a number of processes equal to the number of commod-

---

[7] Section 53, the first section of Chapter VIII, is devoted to argue that if some commodities are produced jointly, then some of the multipliers that transform the actual system in the standard system may be negative. In this regard, the variation of 'the extent to which one or the other method is employed' is obviously a *virtual* variation and not an *actual* one.

ities is not *sufficient*: some further assumption is required.[8] We may ask why this further assumption is not stated, and if it is stated later, why the reader is not told? A possible answer is that such an assumption has *already* been provided. In the Preface to the book the reader is, in fact, informed that

[n]o changes in output and (at any rate in Parts I and II) no changes in the proportions in which different means of production are used by an industry are considered [...]. The investigation is concerned exclusively with such properties of an economic system as do not depend on changes in the scale of production or in the proportions of 'factors'. (Sraffa, 1960, p. v)

That is, the gross output quantities are given. This is an assumption imposed since the beginning. This reference can perhaps also help in answering the third question. The 'requirements for use' are *not* really first introduced in the footnote mentioned. They are just the gross output quantities that are supposed to be given.[9] Moreover, the term 'demand' would be inappropriate since the reader could associate with that term the idea that these gross output quantities *depend* on prices and incomes, which is not the case since they are taken to be *given*.

In order to answer the first question, let us consider the following example. In a two-commodity world there exists one (and only one) process. This process is specified as in Table 1. The growth rate is equal to zero, the rate of profits to 1; capitalists are assumed to spend their entire income on silk only and workers on corn only.

---

[8] Section 96 seems to contradict the above interpretation. This section is the very last section of the book and is the only one that deals with choice of technique in joint production. Here we read that 'with $k + 1$ methods (or processes) we can form k different systems of k processes, all of the systems including the new method and each of them omitting in turn one of the k old methods.' There is no reference to 'requirements for use', just a number of processes equal to the number of commodities! The sentence is clearly lacking something since a single product system (or technique) is, of course, a special joint product technique, and in the case of single production with $k + 1$ processes producing k commodities only one alternative technique is supposed to be formed, i.e. that one including the new method and not including the old method producing the commodity produced by the new method. The most obvious interpretation is that we need to add some reference to 'requirements for use' (see Salvadori, 1979, 1985; these papers, however, give to 'requirements for use' a different interpretation than that used here).

[9] In single production the gross output of industry, i, is also the gross output of commodity, i, available in the economy. Sraffa refers to both these quantities as the 'quantity annually produced' (cf. Section 3, p. 4, for instance). In joint production, the above identity is no longer valid. Sraffa refers to the gross outputs of process j ($A_{(j)}, B_{(j)}, \ldots, K_{(j)}$) as 'the products' of process j (cf. Section 51, p. 45). It is argued here that he refers to the gross outputs available in the economy as the 'requirements for use'.

Table 1

Inputs				Outputs	
Corn	Silk	Labour		Corn	Silk
1	1	1	$\rightarrow$	3	3

Long-period prices need to satisfy the following equations:

$$2(p_c + p_s) + w = (3(p_c + p_s) \tag{1a}$$

$$2p_c = w \tag{1b}$$

$$2p_s = p_c + p_s \tag{1c}$$

$$p_c + p_s = 1 \tag{1d}$$

Equation (1a) says that prices allow reproduction with a rate of profits equal to 1 and a wage rate equal to w (to be determined). Equations (1b) and (1c) state that prices allow the allocation of commodities as required by consumers. Equation (1d) fixes the numéraire. Equations (1a)–(1c) are not linearly independent, and the following solutions to Equations (1) are immediately obtained:

$$w = 2p_c = 2p_s = 1$$

This example suggests that there is another way to escape the difficulty that the number of equations can be smaller than the number of prices to be ascertained. There is not only the possibility of commodities being produced by another method in different proportions, or the possibility of commodities being utilized in the production of a third commodity in different proportions in two different methods, there is also the possibility that commodities are *consumed* in different proportions as distribution and prices change.[10]

If these are the only three possibilities, it can perhaps be claimed that the assumption of given gross output quantities eliminates the third possibility so that only the first two need actually be considered, as Sraffa did. However, this argument does not seem to be either sustainable or contestable without knowing the meaning of the assumption of given quantities. In fact, in the above example, *it is not a fluke* that commodities are produced by the only existing process *in the same proportions* in which

---

[10] In the above example, the consumption of commodity 1 per unit of labour is w/p_c and the consumption of commodity 2 per unit of labour is $(p_c + p_s)/p_s$.

they are 'required for use'. As a matter of fact, the proportions in which commodities are required for use are *adapted* to the proportions in which they are (re)produced. The assumption of given gross outputs cannot, of course, replace a theory of demand.[11]

3.4   Section 88

In Parts I and II of *Production of Commodities*, Sraffa is very accurate in considering produced quantities and operated processes as given. This is particularly clear in Chapter XI, which is devoted to 'Land' and diminishing returns. The exposition of extensive rent (Section 86), of intensive rent (Section 87) and of the problem of multiplicity of agricultural products (Section 89) is, in some sense, complicated by the fact that produced quantities and operated processes are to be considered as given. The results presented may run the risk of not being recognized as the outcome of a process of diminishing returns. In Section 88, it is remarked that the results presented in Sections 86 and 87 (and 89) are the outcome of a process of diminishing returns, and the connection existing 'between the employment of two methods of producing corn on land of a single quality and a process of "intensive" diminishing returns' is fully explained. This connection is considered 'less obvious' than the connection between the employment of n methods of producing corn on n different qualities of land and a process of ' "extensive" diminishing

[11] The (ab)use of the assumption of given gross products as a replacement for a theory of demand can be found in the literature. See, for instance, the following statement:

> ...I am certainly not in agreement with [Bidard] when he says: 'In general joint production, Sraffa's squareness axiom is hopeless'. Such a statement can only be based on assumptions about *demand* which differ from Sraffa's. If the *requirements for use are given*, for instance as gross outputs, the system will generally be square. Bidard may choose different assumptions about *demand* and about the existence of a relationship which would be stable in the long run and regulate the reaction of consumers and investors to changes in prices and incomes. If, on his assumptions, Sraffa systems are not generically square, the relative merits of the assumptions should be discussed. (Schefold, 1990b, p. 143, emphasis added.)

Some authors appear to be of the opinion that given gross outputs may be considered as reflecting the results of a theory of demand expounded in another part of the analytical scheme (see footnote 13, below). This procedure is in itself suitable, but anyone who uses it must pay attention to not assuming (implicitly) that in the neighbourhood of the solution the demanded quantities are unchanged; the suitable procedure is (implicitly) transformed in the unconvincing assumption that to all consumers all commodities are perfect complements.

returns', which is considered to be 'readily recognized'. The above-mentioned connection is reported in the following two paragraphs.

From this standpoint the existence side by side of two methods can be regarded as a phase in the course of a progressive increase of production on the land. The increase takes place through the gradual extension of the method that produces more corn at a higher unit cost, at the expense of the method that produces less. As soon as the former method has extended to the whole area, the rent rises to the point where a third method which produces still more corn at a still higher cost can be introduced to take the place of the method that has just been superseded. Thus the stage is set for a new phase of increase of production through the gradual extension of the third method at the expense of the intermediate one. In this way the output may increase continuously, although the methods of production are changed spasmodically.

While the scarcity of land thus provides the background from which rent arises, the only evidence of this scarcity to be found in the process of production is the duality of methods: if there were no scarcity, only one method, the cheapest, would be used on the land and there could be no rent. (p. 76)

These are the only paragraphs of *Production of Commodities* where Sraffa is actually not considering gross output quantities as given. Changes in quantities, however, are not necessary for the argument; they are introduced only for 'didactic' reasons in order to let the reader recognize a connection between the *given* situation and a *process*. However, at the same time, the reader cannot avoid recognizing that:

(i)   the process described is relating changes in the quantity of a single output to changes in the methods of production of that output;

(ii) the changes in methods of production mentioned in (i) impose a change in prices[12] and eventually a change in other methods of production;

(iii) when the increase in the production of the land takes place, all processes are assumed to be unchanged, i.e. returns to scale would be constant if there were no scarcity;

(iv) in the process described, the quantities of all other commodities produced using the 'land of single quality' are assumed to be unchanged.

---

[12] In a footnote appended to the word 'superseded' in the paragraph first quoted Sraffa adds 'The change in methods of production, if it concerns a basic product, involves of course a change of the Standard system', which is an implicit reference to a change in *all* prices.

Point (iii) above implies that the process of diminishing returns described in Section 88 is exactly the same as that presented in Sraffa's paper of 1925 and mentioned briefly in the previous section:

Diminishing returns must of necessity occur because it will be the producer himself who, for his own benefit, will arrange the doses of the factors and the methods of use in a decreasing order, going from the most favourable ones to the most ineffective, and he will start production with the best combinations, resorting little by little, as these are exhausted, to the worst ones. (Sraffa, 1925, p. 288 [p. 332])

Moreover, both the 1925 analysis and the analysis of Section 88 in the 1960 book build up a relation between quantities on one side and prices on the other. The analysis of 1925 is a partial equilibrium analysis and therefore deals with only two variables, i.e. the produced quantity of one commodity and the price of that same commodity. Conversely, the analysis of 1960 takes into account changes in at least one produced quantity and changes in all prices.

Point (iv) above enables the reader to see a relationship between gross output quantities and prices (for a given rate of profits) which is very similar to a sort of generalized Marshallian supply curve. Such a relationship does not incur the difficulties shown in the 1920s by Sraffa himself for the usual Marshallian supply curve, since the prices of *all* commodities depend on the gross output quantities of *all* commodities, but if price vectors are mapped by gross output quantity vectors, something else seems to be required to close the analysis (if the analysis is to be closed).[13]

In this section we have seen that in the Preface to *Production of Commodities* we are informed that all the results contained in that book refer to a given vector of gross output quantities. This fact is echoed in Section 50, where it is utilized to justify the statement that the number of processes is equal to the number of commodities involved. If this given vector of gross output quantities changes, then prices may change, and indeed they do if some natural resources that are in short supply are used

---

[13] An alternative found in the literature (Roncaglia, 1978, p. 123) is exactly that we do not need to close the analysis:

... given a specific problem (the *direct* influence of income distribution on relative prices) Sraffa considers only those elements necessary to its solution. He constructs a theory that definitively solves that problem, but which does not pretend to exhaust the entire field of economic research. Indeed, the very manner in which the limits of the theory are set out highlights the fact that other problems exist outside its competence, e.g. the determination of the distribution of income, the levels of output, the ruling technology.

Other interpretations centred on the separation of different issues can be found in Eatwell (1977) and in Schefold (1990a).

in production. This is one of the outcomes of Section 88. There is enough evidence to assert that whatever concurs in determining the gross output quantities plays an important role in determining prices. The amounts of commodities that are demanded by consumers are certainly among these determinants, and from Section 44 we understand that these amounts may depend on prices and distribution (further evidence is provided in the footnotes[14,15]). This does not mean that there is a simple way to relate demand and prices. By paraphrasing the record of the proceedings of the 1960 Corfu conference on capital theory, one could say: '*Mr. Sraffa*, while he would not suggest that if one dropped marginal utility theory demand had no effect on prices, did believe that such effects might be unpredictable. It was not that other theories said there was no effect, but merely that there was no simple effect'.[16]

---

[14] In a personal letter to me, Geoff Harcourt has remarked that 'Sraffa...read...several times' the review article of *Production of Commodities* by Harcourt and Massaro (1964) as they wrote it and 'made *lots* of comments', but he 'did not query' the point in which Harcourt and Massaro (1964, p. 454) assert that 'the elements of the actual economic system which Sraffa has included in his analysis are more important (as far as price-formation is concerned) than those left out, in particular, demand...'.

[15] Gary Mongiovi (1996) has quoted a letter to Keynes written by Sraffa in 1941, when the main propositions of what was to become *Production of Commodities* had already been formulated. Sraffa was acting as a referee for the *Economic Journal* on a paper by Ferdynand Zweig dealing with Pigou's use of external economies. Sraffa remarked that:

> ...the problem in which Marshall and countless generations were passionately interested, and in the solution of which he used ext. econs., *is now as dead as mutton: that is the problem whether demand or supply or both determine values* (Sraffa to Keynes, 15 September 1941; Mongiovi's emphasis).

The comment by Mongiovi is also interesting:

> ...the remark evidently expresses the plain and simple truth that, in condition of nonconstant returns, price cannot be determined without reference to outputs.... The question is not whether 'demand' matters, but how its influence ought to be modeled, and in particular whether it ought to be modeled in terms of price-elastic demand functions;...

[16] The original record reads: '*Mr. Sraffa*, while he would not suggest that if one dropped marginal productivity theory innovation had no effect on distributive shares, did believe that such effects might be unpredictable. It was not that other theories said there was no effect, but merely that there was now no simple effect' (Lutz and Hague, 1961, p. 325). The idea of this paraphrase came to me when I was reading a manuscript version of Mongiovi (1996), where this passage is also quoted.

4   A letter to Asimakopulos

Asimakopulos (1990) contributed a paper to a conference held in Florence in August 1985 to celebrate the 25th anniversary of the publication of Sraffa's book. In a footnote in this paper, Asimakopulos inserted the following passage from a letter by Sraffa to him dated 11 July 1971[17]:

> You say 'I don't see how demand can be said to have no influence on [...] prices, unless constant returns [...].' I take it that the drama is enacted on Marshall's stage where the claimants for influence are utility and cost of production. Now utility has made little progress (since the 1870ies) towards acquiring a tangible existence and survives in textbooks at the purely subjective level. On the other hand, cost of production has successfully survived Marshall's attempt to reduce it to an equally evanescent nature under the name of 'disutility', and is still kicking in the form of hours of labour, tons of raw materials, etc. This rather than the relative slope of the two curves, is why it seems to me that the 'influence' of the two things on price is not comparable. (Sraffa, letter to A. Asimakopulos, dated 11 July 1971, quoted by Asimakopulos, 1990, p. 342)

The question asked by Asimakopulos is 'how demand can be said to have no influence on [...] prices' if returns are not assumed to be constant. Sraffa first 'localizes' the problem: 'I take it that the drama is enacted on Marshall's stage where the claimants for influence are utility and cost of production.' In this way, 'demand' is replaced by 'utility'. Second, it is argued that utility, in contrast to 'hours of labour, tons of raw materials' has an 'evanescent nature'. Third, the conclusion is close at hand: 'the "influence" of the two *things* on price is not comparable'. (The two 'things' seem to be utility and cost of production rather than demand and supply.) If Sraffa's statement is read in this way, then Asimakopulos's question has been at least partially evaded since he seemed interested in 'demand' and not in 'utility'. However, there is another way to read the statement.

The fact that 'the "influence" of the two things on price is not comparable' does not depend on the *observed object*, i.e. 'the relative slope of the two curves', as Asimakopulos's question suggested. On the contrary, it depends on the *observer*, who has only a theory based on evanescent (and, we can add, unobservable and perhaps volatile) magnitudes to deal with demand, whereas production inputs, e.g. 'hours of labour, tons of raw materials' have a tangible and observable nature. It is a problem of strategy of research: demand is certainly extremely important in determining prices, but the observer has serious doubts on the ability of the available tools (utility) to capture it and its effects on prices. Therefore he

---

[17] Marika Asimakopulos kindly sent me a photocopy of the whole letter.

concentrates his attention on what can be captured and comprehended, i.e. the relationship between prices, income distribution and conditions of (re)production. This interpretation is confirmed by the way in which Sraffa, in Section 44, reverses the practice of treating the wage rate rather than the rate of profits as the 'given' distribution variable. Once again it is the *observer* who has to consider a distributive variable as determined from outside of the equations of prices and chooses to take the rate of profits, his unique justification being that he can do so since the rate of profits is a pure number and therefore nothing else is required.

The observer and the observed object are two faces of the same coin: there is no observed object without an observer and no observer without an observed object. In order to grasp (a finite number of elements of) the observed object, the observer needs some assumptions. These assumptions may depend on the observer himself. This fact has always been very clear to Sraffa. See, for instance, the following quite well-known passages from the papers of the 1920s:

[I]t remains to be seen if... the absence of a classification of industries according to the criterion of the variability of cost is really due to the lack of data currently available and to the inability of scholars, or if, rather, the failing cannot be found in the very nature of the criterion according to which the classification should be conducted. In particular, it remains to be seen whether the *fundamentum divisionis* is formed by *objective circumstances inherent in the various industries*, or, instead is *dependent on the point of view of the person acting as observer*; or, to put it in another way, whether the increasing and decreasing costs are nothing other than different aspects of one and the same thing that can occur at the same time, for the same industry, so that an industry can be classified arbitrarily in one or the other category *according to the definition of 'industry' that is considered preferable for each particular problem*, and according to whether long or short periods are considered. (Sraffa, 1925, p. 278 [p. 324]; all italics but the first one are added)

[T]he wider the definition which we assume for 'an industry' – that is, the more nearly it includes all the undertakings which employ a given *factor* of production, as, for example, agriculture or the iron industry – the more probable will it be that the forces which make for diminishing returns will play an important part in it; the more restrictive this definition – the more nearly it includes, therefore, only those undertakings which produce a given type of consumable *commodity*, as, for example, fruit or nails – the greater will be the probability that the forces which make for increasing returns will predominate in it. In its effects this difficulty is parallel to that which, as is well known, arises from the consideration of the element of time, whereby the shorter the period of time allowed for the adjustments, the greater is the likelihood of decreasing returns, while the longer that period is, the greater is the probability of increasing returns. (Sraffa, 1926, p. 538)

5   Concluding remarks

It is the observer who chooses the assumptions that are needed to grasp the observed object, and he chooses them not only in relation to the properties of the observed object itself, but also in relation to his own attitudes. The demand has an important role in *Production of Commodities by Means of Commodities*, even if Sraffa, for his own research strategy, is (almost) silent on it. Of course a different observer can have different attitudes, or further research can suggest that it is necessary to abandon some assumptions that might have been useful to carry research to a certain point; a different research strategy may then be more useful. Obviously, this does not necessarily mean that demand is introduced as an outcome of the analysis of the isolated consumer. On the contrary, it is possible to catch the suggestion of the young Sraffa and, consequently, to investigate the relations between production and consumption and to analyse the 'needs' that consumption is asked to satisfy.[18]

6   Epilogue

This paper was written in 1994, before I had the opportunity to see the unpublished papers by Piero Sraffa in the Wren Library, Trinity College, Cambridge (UK). Since then I have been able to read a part of the manuscripts. I decided not to change the present paper, mainly for two reasons. First, I did not see all the material. Second, what I saw did not, in any obvious way, contradict what I had written. I even came across some material which can be considered as confirming the point of view expressed above. The material referred to is to be found in folders C32 and D3/12/7.[19]

References

Asimakopulos, A. (1990) 'Keynes and Sraffa: Visions and Perspectives', in K. Bharadwaj and B. Schefold (eds), *Essays on Piero Sraffa. Critical Perspectives on the Revival of Classical Theory*, London: Unwin Hyman, pp. 331–45. Reprinted in Asimakopulos A., *Investment, Employment and Income Distribution*, Cambridge: Polity Press.

[18] This also seems to be suggested by the second Dutt lecture by Krishna Bharadwaj (1978, pp. 60–67), by Pasinetti (1981) and by a paper by Schefold (1990a).

[19] Folder D3/5 contains another offprint of Sraffa (1925). In this offprint there is a correction to the passage quoted here to which the above footnote 2 refers: the expression 'sensitive organism' is substituted by the word 'consumer'. This correction certainly does not weaken the interpretation proposed in this chapter.

Bharadwaj, K. (1978). *Classical Political Economy and Rise to Dominance of Supply and Demand Theories*, New Delhi: Orient Longman.

Eatwell, J. (1977). 'The Irrelevance of Returns to Scale in Sraffa's Analysis', *Journal of Economic Literature*, **15**, pp. 61–8.

Harcourt, G. C. and Massaro, V. G. (1964). 'Mr. Sraffa's Production of Commodities', *Economic Record*, **40**, pp. 442–54.

Lutz, F. A. and Hague, D. C. (eds) (1961). *The Theory of Capital*, London: Macmillan.

Mongiovi, G. (1996). 'Sraffa's Critique of Marshall: A Reassessment', *Cambridge Journal of Economics*, **20**, pp. 207–24.

Pasinetti, L. L. (1981). *Structural Change and Economic Growth: A Theoretical Essay on the Dynamics of the Wealth of Nations*, Cambridge: CUP.

Roncaglia, A. (1978). *Sraffa and the Theory of Prices*, New York: John Wiley (the first Italian edition was published in 1975).

Salvadori, N. (1979). Mutamento dei metodi di produzione e produzione congiunta, Università degli Studi di Siena, Istituto di Economia, Quaderni dell'Istituto di Economia, N. 6, Siena.

Salvadori, N. (1985). 'Switching in Methods of Production and Joint Production', *The Manchester School*, **53**, pp. 156–78.

Salvadori, N. (1995). '"Demand" in *Production of Commodities by Means of Commodities*', in G. C. Harcourt, A. Roncaglia and R. Rowley (eds), *Income and Employment in Theory and Practice*, London: Macmillan, pp. 154–66.

Schefold, B. (1990a). 'On Changes in the Composition of Output', in K. Bharadwaj and B. Schefold (eds), *Essays on Piero Sraffa. Critical Perspectives on the Revival of Classical Theory*, London: Unwin Hyman, pp. 178–203.

Schefold, B. (1990b). 'Joint Production, Intertemporal Preferences and Long Period Equilibrium. A Comment on Bidard', *Political Economy*, **6**, pp. 139–63.

Sraffa, P. (1925). 'Sulle relazioni fra costo e quantita prodotta'. *Annali di Economia*, **2**, 277–328. In the text the page numbers in square brackets refer to the translation by John Eatwell and Alessandro Roncaglia published in L. L. Pasinetti (ed.), *Italian Economic Papers*, vol. 3, Bologna, 1998: Il Mulino, and Oxford, 1998: Oxford University Press, pp. 323–63.

Sraffa, P. (1926). 'The Laws of Returns under Competitive Conditions', *Economic Journal*, **36**, pp. 535–50.

Sraffa, P. (1960). *Production of Commodities by Means of Commodities*, Cambridge: Cambridge University Press.

CHAPTER 5

Malthus and the corn–profit model

Samuel Hollander

1   Introduction

This chapter provides textual evidence indicating that Sraffa's famous corn–profit interpretation of the early Ricardo (Sraffa, 1951, p. xxxi; 1960, p. 93)[1] applies in fact to T. R. Malthus. Faccarello has observed: 'If indeed such a corn–profit model was really formulated, it took shape, for a brief period of time, in Malthus's fancy' (1982, p. 134), an allusion to the possible attribution *to Ricardo* by Malthus of such a model in the early correspondence. I shall demonstrate, rather, a positive adherence by Malthus – the 'mature' Malthus of the *Principles* and thereafter – to the priority of distribution over pricing, with the profit rate determined in the wage–goods (corn) sector as a ratio of physically homogenous output and input to which profit rates in other industries adjust by way of their terms of trade with corn.[2] Various criticisms of this interpretation will be considered.

The sense of Malthus's adherence to a corn–profit model must be well understood. Malthus was aware that the profit rate is conventionally defined as ratio of *values*, and indeed in his chapter 'Of the Profits of Capital' in the *Principles of Political Economy* he identifies the profit rate with 'the proportion which the difference between the value of the

My thanks to Tom Kompas, Ian Steedman and Brenda Spotton for their comments
[1] This I have questioned elsewhere (e.g., Hollander, 1979, pp. 162–3, 183–4, 685–6).
[2] I reached this conclusion over a decade ago basing myself on the *Measure of Value* (Malthus, 1823) and related correspondence: 'The determining role of agricultural profits and the solution to distribution prior to prices are Malthusian conceptions' (Hollander, 1979, p. 722). The evidence given below also draws from the *Principles of Political Economy* (Malthus, 1820, 1836).

advance and the value of the commodity produced bears to the value of the advances' (1820, p. 294; cf. a similar formulation in 1836, p. 263, discussed in Section 4). However, although the general expression for the profit rate involves value terms, the *agricultural* profit rate is expressed in physical terms and the rate thus determined is carried over to manufacturing. Secondly, Malthus spelled out the assumptions required to permit proceeding in physical terms in agriculture, and cautioned that in application the procedure might break down even should both input and output be composed of the same physical substance. The evidence points (a) to an *analytical* corn–profit model consciously spelled out – we are not engaged here with 'rational reconstruction' – and (b) to limitations in application reflecting seasonal corn-price fluctuations in uncharacteristic institutional contexts.

2 The agricultural profit rate

Assuming expansion of capital and population under conditions of diminishing agricultural returns but at *constant* per capita corn wages, we have a steady decline in the rate of profits:

If the first cause operated singly, *and the wages of the individual labourer were always the same*, then supposing that the skill in agriculture were to remain unchanged, and that there were no means of obtaining corn from foreign countries, the rate of profits must regularly and without any interruption fall, as the society advanced, and as it became necessary to resort to inferior machines which required more labour to put in action (Malthus, 1820, p. 295; emphasis added).

If then we suppose the first cause to operate singly, *and the corn wages of the individual labourer to be always the same*, the whole skill in agriculture remained unchanged, and there were no taxes nor any means of obtaining corn from foreign countries, the rate of profits must regularly fall, as the society advanced, and as it became necessary to resort to inferior machines which required more labour to put in action (Malthus, 1836, p. 271; emphasis added).

There is a complication. Malthus allows for rent even on marginal land should it be necessary to compensate landowners for withdrawing such land from its 'uncultivated state' (1820, p. 296n). (The note is absent in 1836 but the 'almost entirely' of the text which follows presumably refers to this qualification.) However, possibly on quantitative grounds, this was not seen to present a serious complication[3] and Malthus proceeds:

---

[3]The complexity is played down for agricultural *expansion*; contraction is another matter (1820, pp. 183f; 1836, pp. 177f). To this extent there is an apparent asymmetry to the model.

After this payment was made, the remainder of the produce would be divided chiefly [1836: almost entirely] between the capitalist and the labourers, and it is evident that if the number of labourers necessary to obtain a given produce were continually increasing, *and the [1836: corn] wages of each labourer remained the same*, the portion destined to the payment of labour would be continually encroaching upon the portion destined to the payment of profits; and the rate of profits would of course continue regularly diminishing till, from the want of power or will to save, the progress of accumulation had ceased (Malthus 1820, p. 296; 1836, p. 272; emphasis added).

In this case 'the profits of agriculture would be in proportion to the fertility of the land taken into cultivation, or *to the amount of the produce obtained by a given quantity of labour'* (emphasis added), with such labour assumed to receive a given corn wage – the value dimension is absent. Furthermore, 'as profits in the same country tend to an equality, the general rate of profits would follow the same course', or as he later phrased it: '...the increased difficulty of procuring food from the soil' will lower the rate of profits on the land, and 'from the land this fall will extend to all other departments of industry' (1820, p. 335; 1836, p. 297). The precise process by which the general profit rate comes into line with the agricultural profit rate will be elaborated in Section 3.

Although the *general* expression for the profit rate involves value terms, the foregoing elaboration and conclusion regarding the determination of the *agricultural* profit rate is expressed in physical units – 'the amount of the produce obtained by a given quantity of labour', with labour paid a constant corn wage. A deliberate assumption is then introduced in a note to justify the more precise expression of the profit rate in terms of 'the excess of the *quantity* produced, above the advances necessary to produce it', namely the assumption of 'an equal demand for all the parts of the same produce':

It is necessary to qualify the position in this way, because, with regard to the main products of agriculture, it might easily happen that all the parts were not of the same value. If a farmer cultivated his lands by means of domestics living in his house whom he found in food and clothing, his advances might always be nearly the same in quantity and of the same high value in use; but in the case of a glut from the shutting up of an accustomed market, or a season of unusual abundance, a part of the crop might be of no value either in use or exchange, and his profits could by no means be determined, by the excess of the *quantity*, produced, above the advances necessary to produce it [1836: as before shewn, p. 264] (Malthus 1820, p. 296n; 1836, p. 272n).[4]

---

[4] For the material alluded to (1836, p. 264), see below, Section 4.

As we shall see, the manufacturing sector is treated differently; there the downward pressure of supply on price is essential to the argument.[5]

The constancy of the corn wage in the course of growth is an expository preliminary which had to be abandoned not only as 'contrary to the actual state of things', but as entailing a 'contradiction' (1820, p. 297; 1836, p. 272). The argument turns on the point that an initial real wage *at 'subsistence'* rules out population growth and agricultural expansion, whereas an initial wage *above subsistence* which remains unchanged at that level implies (given the function relating population growth to the real wage) an impossibility, namely, constant population growth despite the zero net capital accumulation characterizing the ultimate stationary state (1820, p. 297; 1836, pp. 272–3). In the full account – which is surely one of the best in the literature – it is explained that the incidence of diminishing returns cannot fall solely on labour. For the fall in the real (corn) wage, because of its impact on the population growth rate, is constrained relative to that of the marginal product; accordingly, the effect of increasing land scarcity is to depress *both* the real (corn) wage and the profit rate to their respective minima, at which stage further expansion ceases (1820, pp. 298–9; 1836, pp. 273–4). The concluding passage must suffice: 'Such would be the necessary course of profits and wages in the progressive accumulation of capital, as applied to the progressive cultivation of new and less fertile land, or the further improvement of what had before been cultivated; and on the supposition here made, the rate both of profits and of real [1836: corn] wages would be highest at first, and would regularly and gradually diminish together, till they both came to a stand at the same period, and the demand for an increase of produce ceased to be effective.' At the close of his final section in the Profits chapter ('Remarks on Mr. Ricardo's Theory of Profits'), we are cautioned that there was no *a priori* way of specifying precisely the distribution of the incidence of diminishing returns; all depended on 'the principles of demand and supply and competition' (1820, p. 336; 1836, p. 298).

It should be remarked that the logic of Sraffa's 'rational reconstruction' does not require a constant corn wage, although obviously the location on the downward corn-wage path must at any time be known if one is to specify the profit rate and prices. It does, however, require a basket comprised solely of corn, or else variations in the corn price of

---

[5] Although in dealing with labour demand in the chapter on Wages a primary concern is to ensure that expansion of physical corn output does not depress its value – for which reason the revised edition specifies not physical necessaries but the *value* of those necessaries as constituting labour demand – the problem is now set aside without ado insofar as concerns agriculture.

manufactures play back on the denominator in the expression for the profit rate. Now although Malthus frequently assumed a mixed wage basket, he is silent on this matter when it comes to the *formal* assumptions made to legitimize a corn calculation (p. 200 above and Section 4), asserting in the second edition that 'Corn, on account of its being the main support of the labourer, is the only object in the production of which a comparison may be instituted between the quantity advanced and the quantity produced' (1836, p. 265).

3   Transmission to the general profit rate

We take up next the transmission from the agricultural to the general profit rate. The 1820 account involves the impact on manufacturing profits exerted by deteriorating terms of trade between manufacturing, and corn and labour: 'In the cultivation of land, the immediate and main cause of the necessary diminution of profits appeared to be the increased quantity of labour necessary to obtain the same produce. In manufactures and commerce, it is the fall in the exchangeable value of the products of industry in these departments, *compared with corn and labour*' (1820, p. 300; emphasis added). An elaboration allows for real-cost variations (even increases) in the manufacturing sector, but asserts that since the rates of exchange relative to corn (and labour) decline, the manufacturing profit rate is necessarily depressed:

The cost of producing corn and labour continually increases from inevitable physical causes, while the cost of producing manufactures and articles of commerce sometimes diminishes, sometimes remains stationary, and at all events increases much slower than the cost of producing corn and labour. Upon every principle therefore of demand and supply, the exchangeable value of these latter objects must fall, compared with the value of labour. But if the exchangeable value of labour continues to rise, while the exchangeable value of manufactures either falls, remains the same, or rises in a much less degree, profits must continue to fall;... (ibid., p. 300)

The reference to 'corn and labour' might be read as a *dual* input into manufacturing, labour not further decomposed, but there is every indication that labour itself is reduced to corn, for the increasing 'cost of producing corn and labour' implies a higher cost of 'producing labour' *via* the corn wage, the rise in the 'exchangeable value of labour' entailing the impact of higher real corn costs. We can therefore restate the proposition in terms of a fall in manufacturing profits with a fall in the ratio of manufacturing to corn prices, corn comprising the 'advances' to labour and entering into manufacturing costs via the labour input. If, however, the corn wage is falling, there is the complexity that the cost of producing labour rises *less* than the cost of producing corn. This complexity is not attended to.

The 1836 version reiterates the main point at stake. There are *two* sets of forces at play in profit-rate determination: 'In the cultivation of land, the cause of the *necessary* diminution of profits is the diminution in the quantity of produce obtained by the same quantity of labour' – a purely physical matter; '[in] manufactures and commerce, it is the fall in the exchangeable value of the same amount of produce' – a matter involving terms of trade (1836, p. 275). A further elaboration spells out more fully than in 1820 that the fall in manufacturing prices occurs by way of output expansion in response to profit-rate differentials created by the initial fall in agricultural returns:

The labour required to produce corn, has a constant tendency to increase from inevitable physical causes, while the labour required to produce manufactures and articles of commerce sometimes greatly diminishes, sometimes remains stationary, and at all events increases much slower than the labour required to produce corn. When, therefore, profits fall in agriculture it becomes obviously more advantageous to employ capital in manufactures and commerce than on the land; and capital will in consequence be so employed till a fall has taken place in manufactures and commercial products from their comparative abundance (Malthus, 1836, p. 275).

Here the Smithian notion of 'competition of capitals' applied specifically to manufactures is brought into play. An actual transfer of activity from agriculture to manufactures would imply contraction of the margin of cultivation; since nothing is said of this, Malthus presumably intended that *new* capital investments would flow predominantly to manufactures, eradicating differentials.[6] In this regard Malthus deviates from the pure corn–profit model which says nothing of output variation in the achievement of profit-rate equality.

---

[6] The final stage of the argument is rendered unnecessarily complex by the labour-commanded index: 'But it has been shown [Chapter 2, Section 6] that the value of the same quantity of labour will always remain the same' – i.e., that the *labour commanded* by the wage basket is constant – 'and it is evident that if the products fall in value [labour commanded], while the quantity of the labour or the value of the capital required to produce them remain the same, profits must fall,' a fall that 'must necessarily go on, till profits in manufacturing and commerce have been reduced nearly to a level with those in agriculture.' Now if (as seems to be the case) 'the value of the capital...' refers to the labour commanded by corn advances, we end up with the same proposition as in 1820 – mediated explicitly by the competition-of-capitals theorem – that the profit rate in manufactures is depressed by a fall in the terms of trade between manufactures and corn.

Despite all this, the general profit rate was only 'limited', not *governed*, by agricultural productivity conditions, the latter imposing a maximum which the general profit rate can never exceed (1820, p. 300; 1836, p. 275). The 'limiting' principle of profit-rate determination is discussed further in the final section of the chapter devoted to Ricardo's theory of profits. We shall focus on the interconnection between sectors to be found at the beginning and at the close of that section.

The opening exposition reiterates that the profit-rate trend is governed by diminishing returns: 'This continued accumulation of capital and increasing difficulty of procuring subsistence would unquestionably lower profits' (1820, p. 328; 1836, p. 293). The lower profit rate is now said to determine the new set of equilibrium or cost prices in manufacturing (taking account of differential factor proportions) in that profits enter into manufacturing costs. In this account the corn price alone rises – falling agricultural productivity outweighing the lower profit rate – *the money wage remaining unchanged*; in fact, the money measure[7] is selected to that end in order to undermine (so Malthus believed) Ricardo's account:

All commodities, in the production of which the same quantity of labour continued to be employed, but with the assistance of capitals of various kinds and amount, would fall in price, and just in proportion to the degree in which the price of the commodity had before been affected by profits; and with regard to corn, in the production of which more labour would be necessary, this article would rise in money price, notwithstanding the capital used to produce it [1836: 'notwithstanding...it' omitted], just to that point which would so reduce corn wages as to render the population stationary [1836: as to retard the progress of population in proportion to the diminution of effectual demand]; and thus all the effects upon profits, attributed by Mr. Ricardo to a rise of money wages, would take place while money wages and the value of money remained precisely the same. This supposition serves further to shew how very erroneous it must be to consider the fall of profits as synonymous with a rise of money wages, or to make the money price of labour the great regulator of the rate of profits [1836: sentence omitted]. It is obvious that, in this case, profits can only be regulated by the principle of competition, or of demand and supply, which would determine the degree in which the prices of commodities would fall; and their prices, compared with the uniform price of labour, would mainly regulate [1836: would regulate] the rate of profits (Malthus, 1820, p. 328; 1836, pp. 293–4).

That profits are 'regulated by the principle of competition, or of demand and supply', might suggest that it is the decline in manufacturing prices

---

[7] Money is assumed 'to be procured by a uniform quantity of unassisted labour without any advances in the shape of capital beyond the necessaries of a single day' (1820, p. 327; 1836, p. 293).

(in the face of a constant money wage) that actually governs the fall in the profit rate. But this is not the case. The secular fall in the profit rate is due to land scarcity, given which fall (and given the money wage), a set of equilibrium cost prices is generated throughout manufacturing incorporating that lower profit rate. It might, however, be fair to suppose that by *regulation* in this passage Malthus intended 'brought into line with' the agricultural profit rate, a process requiring an increased supply of manufactures as in the original account. The rendition reinforces, but adds little to, what was said before.

The final restatement again accords the agricultural profit rate the determining role – as a 'limiting principle' – governing the profit rate in other sectors:

At all times indeed, and on every supposition, the great limiting principle which depends upon the increasing difficulty of procuring food from the soil, or on the still more general cause, a limitation of the population, in whatever way it may be occasioned, is ready to act; [1836: But in reference to the great limiting principle, which in his [Ricardo's] system is the only one which regulates profits, namely the increasing difficulty of procuring food from the soil, it merely in fact determines the *range* of possible profits; how high they may by possibility rise, and how low they may by possibility fall. It is indeed always ready to act;] and, if not overcome by countervailing facilities, will necessarily lower the rate of profits on the land, and from the land this fall will extend [1836: from which it will extend] to all other departments of industry (Malthus, 1820, pp. 334–5; 1836, pp. 296–7).

Malthus here adds: 'But even this great principle operates [1836: But even then it always operates] according to the law of demand and supply and competition'. This might refer to the precise process by which manufacturing profit rates are brought into line with the lower agricultural profit rate described in the original statement, but we have also seen that the same insistence on market process is encountered in the discussion of the incidence of diminishing returns, and that is the likely intent (Section 2 above).

Now the text proceeds to restate the decline in the agricultural rate itself *in price terms*, and diverging from the original account which ran wholly in physical terms.[8] But the conclusion is back in line, again with emphasis on the priority of the agricultural profit rate as a *limiting*

---

[8] The argument is that to avoid a decline in the agricultural profit rate would require corn-price increases which fully compensate for the deterioration in real-cost conditions, increases which are precluded (1820, p. 335; 1836, p. 297). Nonetheless, the constraints are said to reflect 'the intrinsic nature of necessaries, and of the soil from which they are procured'. (An elaboration restates the process as involving an increase in labour embodied in corn relative to labour commanded.)

determinant of the generate rate, allowing scope for the operation of other forces – excess supply is specified in the 1836 version – keeping the general return below its potential:

The boundary to the further value of and demand [1836: effectual demand] for corn, lies clear and distinct before us. Putting importation out of the question, it is precisely when the produce of the last land taken into cultivation will but just replace the capital and support the population employed in cultivating it. Profits must then be at their lowest theoretical limit. In their progress towards this point, the continued accumulation of capital will always have a *tendency* to lower them; and at no one period can they ever be higher than the state of the land, under all circumstances will admit.

They may be lower, however, as was before stated, in any degree [1836: They may be much lower, however, as was before stated], from an abundant supply of capital compared with the demand for produce [1836... produce while the soil is still rich]; and practically they are very rarely so high as the actual state of the land combined with the smallest possible quantity of food awarded to the labour would admit of [1836: and very rarely so low as not to allow the means of further accumulation] (Malthus, 1820, pp. 335–6; 1836, p. 297).

It is not absolutely clear from this statement whether or not the impact on the profit rate of excess supply is limited to manufactures. It seems to be, but the question arises of how the agricultural rate then comes into line, a matter left in abeyance.

In his section on 'Profits as Affected by the Causes Practically in Operation' (Section III in 1820; Section IV in 1836), Malthus summarized his general position in a passage omitted in 1836 that is of considerable historiographical importance. This passage asserts: (1) that received (i.e. non-Ricardian) doctrine related the profit rate 'principally' to 'competition of capital'; (2) that diminishing returns acted *directly to depress the agricultural profit rate*, which decline then extends to the non-agricultural sectors; (3) that this latter conception had been implicitly recognized in the *Essay on Population* and in *Rent* (Malthus, 1815); (4) that in practice, having in mind both the '*extremely slow*' pressure of land scarcity and the counteracting forces at play, and taking any considerable time span (any 'period of some length'), 'competition of capital' comes into its own:

The reader will be aware that the reason why, in treating of profits, I dwell so much on agricultural profits is, that the whole stress of the question rests upon this point. The argument against the usual view which has been taken of profits, as depending principally upon the competition of capital, is founded upon the physical necessity of a fall of profits in agriculture, arising from the increasing quantity of labour required to procure the same food; and it is certain that if the profits on land permanently fall from this or any other cause, profits in manufactures and commerce must fall too, as it is an acknowledged truth that in an improved and civilized country, the profits of stock, with few and temporary exceptions which may be easily accounted for, must be nearly on a level in all the different branches of industry to which capital is applied.

Now I am fully disposed to allow the truth of this argument, as applied to agricultural profits, and also its natural consequences on all profits. This truth is indeed necessarily involved both in the *Principles of Population* and in the theory of rent which I published separately in 1815. But I wish to shew, theoretically as well as practically, that powerful and certain as this cause is, in its final operation, so much so as to overwhelm every other; yet in the actual state of the world, its natural progress is not only extremely slow, but is so frequently counteracted and overcome by other causes as to leave very great play to the principle of the competition of capital; so that at any one period of some length in the last or following hundred years, it might most safely be asserted that profits had depended or would depend very much upon the causes which had occasioned a comparatively scanty or abundant supply of capital than upon the natural fertility of the land last taken into cultivation (Malthus, 1820, pp. 316–7).

As mentioned, this passage is absent in 1836, except for a brief summary statement which focuses on the 'physical' dimension in agriculture: 'It appears then, that practically, and in the actual state of things, the physical necessity of a fall of profits in agriculture arising from the increasing quantity of labour required to produce the same quantity of food, may be so counteracted and overcome, for a considerable time by other causes, as to leave very great play to the influence of the competitions of capital' (1836, p. 284). The more extensive formulation of 1820 is, however, reiterated in substance at the close of the section under discussion in the 1820 version, and that later reformulation *does* appear in 1836 (1820, pp. 325–6; 1836, pp. 288–9).

Malthus neglects to specify whether increasing competition of capitals applies solely to manufactures, although that certainly seems to be his position, and it probably reflects the notion that in agriculture, and specifically the production of 'strict necessaries', expanded food supply creates its own demand by generating population increase, a notion already found in the 1815 pamphlet on rent. There we encounter a remarkable constraint on the applicability of regular demand–supply analysis, involving a contrast between the demand for 'strict necessaries' and the demand for other goods. Only in the general category is there meaning to demand independent of or external to supply, and here only the scarcity property applies such that reduced supply generates higher prices; in agriculture '[t]he cause of the higher price of the necessaries of life above the cost of production, is to be found in their abundance, rather than their scarcity' (1986, Vol. 7, p. 121). The purported contrast – vehemently denied by Ricardo on the grounds that relative scarcity is the general rule applicable to all cases (1951, Vol. I, pp. 405–6) – is elaborated as follows:

There is a radical difference in the cause of a demand for those objects which are strictly necessary to the support of human life, and a demand for all other commodities. In all other commodities the demand is exterior to, and independent of, the production itself; and in the case of a monopoly, whether natural or artificial, the excess of price is in proportion to the smallness of the supply compared with the demand, while this demand is comparatively unlimited. In the case of strict necessaries, the existence and increase of the demand, or of the number of demanders, must depend upon the existence and increase of these necessaries themselves; and the excess of their price above the cost of their production must depend upon, and is permanently limited by, *the excess of their quantity above the quantity necessary to maintain the labour required to produce them*; without which excess of quantity no demand could have existed, according to the laws of nature, for more than was necessary to support the producers (Malthus, 1986, Vol. 7, p. 121, emphasis added).

On this view, supply *precedes* population growth; Malthus in effect (at least in the analysis of secular trends) applies Say's law to food in a strong form – supply creates its own demand, and without lag. It will be noted, incidentally, that a corn ratio emerges quite distinctly in this passage (italicized phrase). The same theme is elaborated in the *Principles*: 'In the production of the necessaries of life' (in contrast to the case of scarce wines), 'the demand is dependent upon the product itself, and the effects are, in consequence, widely different. In this case, it is physically impossible that [1836: beyond a certain narrow limit] the number of demanders should increase, while the quantity of produce diminishes, as the demanders [1820: can] only exist by means of this produce' (1986 [1815], Vol. 7, pp. 121–2; 1820, pp. 146–7; 1836, pp. 145–6).[9]

4   An elaboration of the evidence

A passage in the Wages chapter points out that the specific concern there had been 'real' (commodity) and 'nominal' (money) wages, not *Ricardian wages* which pertained to profit-rate determination. 'Ricardian wages' are understood in 1820 as labour embodied in the wage basket, and in 1836 as *proportionate* wages (1820, pp. 291–2; 1836, pp. 260–1). The 1820 version does not indicate acceptance by Malthus of the Ricardo theorem expressed in terms of labour embodied in wages, whereas the 1836 version does accept the theorem expressed in terms of proportions[10] (with

[9] For statements by Adam Smith to the same effect, see 1937 [1776], pp. 146, 173–4. James Mill, in his early Smithian phase, rehearses the same case (Mill, 1966 [1804], pp. 23–4).

[10] For Ricardo, who uses a labour-embodied measure, the two are identical.

the gloss that '*proportionate wages* determine, or rather *are determined by, the rate of profits . . .* '). However, it is doubtful whether the reformulation (we set aside for now the gloss) indicates a significant change in perspective,[11] for elsewhere the analysis of the downward trend path of the wage and profit rates proceeds in both versions in terms of proportions: 'If poorer land which required more labour were successively taken into cultivation, it would not be possible for the corn wages of each individual labourer to be diminished in proportion to the diminished product; a greater proportion [1836: *proportion*] of the whole would necessarily go to labour [1836: to pay the wages of labour]; and the rate of profits would continue regularly falling till the accumulation of capital had ceased' (1820, p. 299; 1836, p. 274). Nonetheless, there is a new *enthusiasm* for the proportionality theorem in a section added in the second edition at the beginning of the Profits chapter.

The insertion, which carefully spells out the inverse profit–wage theorem in proportionate terms and defends it against possible criticism of its cavalier treatment of the capital component, sets out by defining the profit rate as a value rather than physical ratio following convention, but also on the grounds that output and input are comprised of *different* commodities:

Profits, as we all know, are practically estimated by the money prices of the products compared with the money prices of the advances; and as money for the short periods during which mercantile transactions last, is universally considered as measuring value and not quantity, it follows, that profits, as it has been stated, are always practically estimated by the values of the products compared with the values of the advances, and not by their relative quantities. It would be impossible indeed to compare them as to quantity, because the advances necessary to produce commodities, are never all of the same kind as the commodities produced; and when they are not the same, their *quantities* do not admit of a comparison. We cannot compare shoes or cloth with corn or labour in regard to quantity.

It is of so much importance to be fully aware of the necessity of estimating both the advances and the returns of the capitals in *value* and not in *quantity*, that it may be worthwhile to illustrate the difference in the results of the two modes of proceeding (Malthus, 1836, p. 263).

It is striking to find Malthus asserting both that advances and output are *never* all of the same kinds, and *when* this is so – one would expect him to write '*since* this is so' – value calculations are required, but the fact is that he does allow an exception, as I shall now show.

It is conceded that corn most closely satisfies the condition that input and output are comprised of the same commodity – 'there is not one

---

[11] On the direction of causality, see footnote 14 and Section 6 below.

[industry] in which so great a part of the advances is identical with the produce as in the cultivation of corn.' Even here calculation in terms of corn ratios misleads: 'Profits, as I have before stated, are always practically estimated by value, not quantity; and the real question is about the *price* of the produce compared with the price of the advances, *and not the excess of the returns in wheat above the advances in wheat*' (p. 264; emphasis added). In the example provided it is presumed that the initial outlay is in money terms which, given the initial corn price, represents a certain corn outlay;[12] but the profit ratio – a ratio of values – will vary with the corn price, a poor harvest raising the price permitting the profit rate to remain unchanged despite a fall in corn output and conversely in the case of a good harvest: 'if the profits of the cultivator were estimated by quantity they might vary between nothing and 45 per cent at the very time when estimated by price or value, as they always are practically, the cultivator was in each year making a regular profit of 20 per cent' (pp. 264–5). Malthus reiterates that despite the near homogeneity between the physical items constituting input and output in the case of corn, the profit rate entails value not physical ratios: 'Corn, on account of its being the main support of the labourer, is the *only object in the production of which a comparison may be instituted between the quantity advanced and the quantity produced; yet even here we have found that the cause which determines profits is their relative values, and not their relative quantities*' (pp. 265–6; emphasis added).

This seems to clash with the formulations according a determining role to the agricultural profit rate (at least in the 'limiting' case) perceived in terms of physical corn ratios, with the manufacturing rates coming into line by way of a rise in the *relative* corn price. However, it must be noted that the objection to the corn–profit notion turns specifically on changes in the corn price between periods (t) and ($t + 1$) due to harvest fluctuations, an irrelevant matter in dealing with secular trends, and of a different order to the objection that input in agriculture is not entirely constituted of corn.[13] There is no doubt that agriculture and manufactures are treated differently, for Malthus precludes any conceivable

---

[12] 'The farmer practically pays his labourers in money. Let us suppose that this money, with the other money outgoings amounts to L200, that in the year in which the advance is made it will purchase 100 quarters of wheat, the price of wheat being L2 a quarter, and that the rate of profits is 20 per cent, in which case the return must be 120 quarters, or 20 per cent in quantity' (pp. 263–4).

[13] Skourtos (1991) has pointed out that Sismondi, in 1827, as well as Malthus, took a similar position, i.e. he adopted the homogeneity postulate relating to agricultural input and output, but raises the problem that the market values of corn input and of corn output may deviate.

possibility of proceeding in terms of physical ratios *only in the latter sectors*: 'In manufacturing and mercantile employments, there is no approach towards a possibility of comparing the advances with the products in regard to quantity' (p. 266), whereas, as noted above, corn was 'the only object in the production of which a comparison may be instituted between the quantity advanced and the quantity produced', and we have in fact encountered the specific assumption introduced to *avoid* the complexity created by price fluctuations (1820, p. 296n; 1836, p. 272n; Section 2 above).[14]

The problem created for a physical estimate of the profit rate as well as the assumption required to avoid it are reiterated in a later chapter ('Of the Progress of Wealth'), although in the first edition only. Here the matter seems to extend beyond seasonal fluctuations and the like to a potential *secular* constraint involving 'population... checked merely by want of demand' (1820, p. 366) – alluding to excessive saving. However, even in this context reference is made to the earlier note:

Under such circumstances corn might be produced, which would lose the character and quality of wealth; and, as I before observed in a note, all the parts of the same produce, would not be of the same value. The actual labourers employed might be tolerably well fed, as is frequently the case, practically, in those countries where the labourers are fed by the farmers, but there would be little work or food for their

---

[14] The retention of the proportionality theorem cannot disguise fundamental differences with Ricardo, since Malthus adhered to the Smithian notion of a falling profit rate in consequence of increased 'competition of capitals'. (The priority accorded the agricultural profit rate relates solely to the 'limiting' case, allowing scope for the operation of competition of capitals in reducing general profits below the limit.)

In his critique of Ricardo in the revised edition (1836, pp. 295–6), he supposes capital accumulation 'increasing faster than the effectual demand for the produce at its former price', which 'abundance of supply' would depress values and disturb the wages and profit rates. These distributional movements are expressed in proportionate terms:

...a different division of the produce would take place between the labourers and the capitalists; a smaller proportion of it would go to pay profits, and a larger proportion to pay wages. Profits therefore would fall, and the money wages of labour would rise... It has been assumed that the supply is comparatively more abundant than before, on account of the increase of capital, although the productiveness of labour has remained the same. This must necessarily occasion a fall of profits, and this fall will be permanent if the same competition of capital continues. But if the *rate of profits* has fallen the elementary costs of production have fallen. In this case, the conditions of the supply of a certain quantity of gold are the advance of the same quantity of labour, with the same value of other capital, as before *and a less* remuneration for profits. Consequently the elementary cost of gold to the purchaser is less than before.

The rise in labour's proportionate share in output is the *passive reflection* of the fall in the share going to capital with increased competition of capitals – capital increasing 'faster than effectual demand', a perspective anathema to Ricardo.

grown-up sons; and from varying markets and varying crops, the profits of the farmer might be the lowest at the very time when, according to the division of the produce, it ought to be the highest, that is, when there was the greatest proportionate excess of produce above what was paid to the labourer. The wages of the labourer cannot sink below a certain point, but a part of the produce, from excess to supply, may for a time be absolutely useless, and permanently it may so fall from competition as to yield only the lowest profits (Malthus, 1820, pp. 367–8).

This secular problem arises only by extension of the excess-supply phenomenon from manufactures to agriculture, which is wholly uncharacteristic. That something of a special case is intended is suggested by an illustration attached to the comment regarding 'tolerably well paid' workers:

In Norway and Sweden, particularly the former, where the agricultural labourer either lives in the farmer's family or has a portion of land assigned to him in lieu of wages, he is in general pretty well fed, although there is but little demand for labour, and considerable competition for such employment. *In countries so circumstanced* (and there are many such all over the world) it is perfectly futile to attempt to estimate profits by the excess of the produce above what is consumed in obtaining it, when for this excess there may be often little or no market. All evidently depends upon the exchangeable value of the disposable produce (Malthus, 1820, p. 368n; emphasis added).[15]

My conclusion remains that the Sraffian corn–profit model was consciously adopted by Malthus who, however, was cautious when it came to application. The absence of the foregoing passages from the revised version may indicate a lessening of his concerns.

5   Evidence from 'The Measure of Value' (1823)

There is evidence of a strengthened adherence to the Ricardian proportionality theorem in the revised edition of the *Principles* which is amply

[15] It is not clear that Malthus was certain of his position, since he proceeds in the 1820 text to give a further justification of his position, which allows that farmers *might* obtain 'a fair profit', but only on 'the small stock' still invested in agriculture, which calculated on the total capital implies a low profit rate:

I would observe further, that if in consequence of a diminished demand for corn, the cultivators were to withdraw their capitals so as better to proportion their supplies to the quantity that could be properly paid for; yet if they could not employ the capital they had withdrawn in any other way, which, according to the preceding supposition, they could not, it is certain that, although they might for a time make fair profits of the small stock which they still continued to employ in agriculture, the consequences to them as cultivators would be, to all intents and purposes, the same as if a general fall had taken place on all their capital (pp. 368–9).

confirmed in the *Measure of Value* (Malthus, 1823).[16] In fact, the formulations of that pamphlet frequently duplicate the revisions, providing
us with their approximate dating.

It is, in principle, immaterial whether labour embodied or labour
commanded is adopted as a proportions-measuring device. In effect,
Ricardo defined the value of the output of a man-hour as unity, so
that the labour embodied in the wage per man-hour emerges as a fraction of unity, the residual constituting profits, whereas Malthus defined
the value of the wage per man-hour as unity, the labour required to
produce that wage emerging as a fraction of unity and the residual
constituting profits. The inverse wage–profit relation as a theorem
regarding proportions and all of Ricardo's substantive applications
emerge using Malthus's device and *vice versa*. Malthus, however,
believed that his labour-commanded measure permitted him to derive
the inverse wage–profit relation *because* that measure reflected constancy of the value of labour. We must explore why he was so insistent,
maintaining indeed that 'there was scarcely any of the science in which
[his standard measure of value] will not tend to simplify and facilitate
our inquiries' (p. 54).[17]

As for the theory of profits, Malthus reverts to his purported major
difference with Ricardo:

On the subject of profits, [his own correct measure] would shew, that they are
determined, not by the varying value of a given quantity of labour compared with
the constant value of the commodities which it produces, but, as is more con-
formable to our experience, by the variable value of the commodities produced by
a given quantity of labour, compared with the constant value of such labour; and
that profits never, on any occasion, rise or fall, unless the value of the produce of

---

[16] Malthus's acceptance of the substance of Ricardo's inverse wage–profit relation as a
theorem regarding proportionate shares also emerges in his *Quarterly Review* article
for 1824 treating McCulloch's *Encyclopaedia Britannica* contribution of the previous
year.

[17] He admitted that he was adding little to the conclusions already reached in the *Principles*
of 1820. The conclusions based on the constant value of labour, he wrote,

are almost exactly the same as the conclusions of that work. And the reason is, that at
that time I did not think that the labour which a commodity would command could,
with propriety, be considered as a *standard* measure of value, yet I thought it the
nearest approximation to a standard of any one object known, and consequently
applied it, on almost all occasions, to correct the errors arising from the application
of more variable measures. The conclusions, therefore, of my former and present
reasoning were likely to be nearly the same, although the premise might now admit of
further correction and illustration, and the conclusions might be pronounced with
greater precision and certainty (p. 61).

a given quantity of labour rises or falls, either from the temporary or ordinary state of the demand and supply (Malthus, 1823, pp. 55–6).[18]

This proposition is misleading.[19] It introduces 'the state of demand and supply' as if its relevance had been *demonstrated*, whereas all he had shown in his table was a varying value of the produce in terms of its command over labour given agricultural productivity and the corn wage.

What was Malthus attempting to do by this new formulation, always bearing in mind his agreement that profits are a matter of proportionate shares? He was evidently opening the door for the (Smithian) doctrine of the possibility of excess *general* commodity supply reducing revenues relative to costs, implying that no one who used Ricardo's measure of proportionate shares could allow for excess aggregate supply.[20] In point

[18]   See also the 1836 version of the *Principles* based on his own theory of value in his Chapter 2 – whereby (1) cost prices incorporate an allowance for profits and thus vary with the profit rate, and (2) the value of the (variable) commodity wage is *constant*:

> it has been shewn, in the 4th section of the 2nd chapter, that commodities which have cost in their production the same quantity of labour, or the same value of capital, are subject to great variations of value, owing to the varying rate and varying quantity of profits which must be added to the quantity of accumulated and immediate labour employed upon them, in order to make up their value.
>
> And it has further been shewn in the 6th section of the same chapter that, however variable may be the *quantity* or proportion of produce awarded to each labourer, the value of that quantity or proportion will always be the same.
>
> It is clear then that profits must be regulated upon a principle essentially different from that stated by Mr. Ricardo, and that instead of being determined by the varying value of a certain quantity of labour employed, compared with the given value of the commodity produced, they will be determined by the *varying* value of the commodity produced compared with the *given* value of the certain quantity of labour employed (1836, pp. 292–3).

A similar contrast between his own and the Ricardian perspective is given in the *Quarterly Review of* January 1824 (XXX, no. LX, p. 332).

[19]   Malthus is here comparing columns 9 and 7 of his table (1823, p. 38) rather than columns 7 and 5. The proportionate shares are less obvious, but nothing of substance is changed – it is the same whether we take '10 units' (7) as our base and (a) work 'backwards' to a quantity of labour embodied *in the wage* of 8 units (5) calculating a profit rate of $(10 - 8)/8 = 25\%$, or (b) work 'forward' to a quantity of labour commanded by the product calculating a profit rate of $(12.5 - 10)/10 = 25\%$.

[20]   This, in fact, also emerges earlier in a criticism of Torrens' 'capital' theory of value: 'Colonel Torrens, by representing capital under the form of certain quantities of cloth and corn, instead of value in labour, has precluded himself from the possibility of giving a just view either of value, profits, or effectual demand. An increase of cloth and corn from the same quantity of labour is of no avail whatever in increasing value, profits, or effectual demand, if this increased produce will not command so much labour as before, an event which is continually occurring, from deficiency of demand' (p. 18n).

of fact, Ricardo rejected the phenomenon on the wholly independent grounds of Say's Law.[21] Nothing in the *Measure of Value* – neither the table nor the discussion surrounding it – demonstrates the dependency of the profit rate on aggregate 'demand–supply'. On the contrary, the argument points to the central role played in profit-rate determination by the *corn wage* – which amounts on the 'backward looking' scheme to the *labour embodied in the corn wage* (as with Ricardo), and on the 'forward looking' scheme to a complex of the corn wage and the (physical) output of the labour for which the corn wage is paid (footnote 19 above). Deficiency of aggregate demand is a matter of supplementary doctrine, the validity of which is simply asserted in the *Measure of Value*.

Setting aside Malthus's rejection of Say's law, we must consider whether a theory of value is required in order to obtain the profit rate. That the table in the *Measure of Value* proceeds solely in terms of *agricultural productivity and the corn wage*, it may be argued, is a deliberate simplification to express 'self-evident' propositions, for example that the profit rate necessarily falls with increased corn wages given productivity: 'If the increased reward of the labourer takes place without an increase of produce, this cannot take place without a fall of profits, as it is a self-evident truth, that given the quantity of produce to be divided between labour and profits, the greater the portion of it which goes to labour the less will be left for profits' (1823, p. 33). Conceivably a full-fledged treatment of the profit rate would have to take account of exchange values, but this does not seem to be the case. Throughout, the pamphlet assumes a given profit rate or a given change in the profit rate (1823, pp. 13–14, 24–5, 41–2, 51, 63–4), and only recognizes a *one-way* relation from distribution to relative values.[22] This suggests that Malthus maintained that

---

[21] Costabile, 1983, p. 161, uses Marxian terminology here: 'The market rate of profits can be below the "natural rate." Malthus's great merit was to have seen that there is a problem of realization in the market since there is no *ex ante* coordination between decisions to produce and decisions to buy.' She maintains that Malthus's opposition to Say's law did in fact derive, in a technical sense, from the labour-commanded procedures (pp. 144–5). Unfortunately her sections on 'Malthus's Critique of Say's Law', 'Prices and Effective Demand: Market Solutions' and 'Changes in the Level of Activity' lack adequate textual support from the *Measure of Value*.

[22] For example, the exchange ratio between capital- or time-intensive and labour-intensive products would vary 'in the progress of society' – a reduction in the profit rate is taken for granted here – although relative labour inputs are unchanged. The value of beef (a four- or five-year process according to Adam Smith) relative to corn (a one-year process) would fall more than 20% with a fall in the profit rate from 15 to 8% in the 'progress of society', although the labour input is constant, because of the longer period of production in the former case (pp. 10–11).

the profit rate is generated in 'agriculture' independently of value relationships, and is then used to bring the profit rates elsewhere into line, the
position emerging also in the *Principles*, as we have shown at length.

As remarked earlier (Section 2 above), a corn–profit calculation
requires that the wage basket be comprised solely of corn or else changes
in the relative prices of wage goods will affect the denominator of the
corn profit-rate expression. Allowing for a declining secular corn wage,
the falling profit rate still emerges in physical terms since the marginal
produce *necessarily* declines more rapidly than the wage, and at each
stage, the (lower) profit rate would presumably be applied to 'metal'
and 'cloth', dictating an appropriate reduction in their natural values,
that is a rise in the metal or cloth prices of corn. (Such changes will not
play further on the profit rate.)

6   Defence of the corn–profit interpretation

Here I shall consider a variety of criticisms of my interpretation of
Malthus, and take the opportunity to summarize the major themes of
this paper. Costabile (1983) disagrees with my interpretation on the following grounds: 'First of all, Malthus was the first to object to Ricardo's
determination of the rate of profits in terms of corn in 1815; he refused
the simplification of the one-sector models in the analysis of value and
distribution' (p. 152n). This observation is based on Malthus's early
insistence against Ricardo's *Essay on Profits* that 'the real capital of the
farmer which is advanced does not consist merely in raw produce but in
ploughs waggons threshing machines &c: and in the tea sugar clothes &c:
&c: used by his labourers' (Malthus to Horner, 14 March 1815, in
Ricardo, 1951, VI, p. 187); similarly: 'In no case of production, is the
produce exactly of the same nature as the capital advanced. Consequently
we can never properly refer to a material rate of produce, independent of
demand, and of the abundance or scarcity of capital' (to Ricardo, 5
August 1814, p. 117).[23] She asserts, moreover, that 'Malthus developed
all his theory of profits in terms of value', and she argues, thirdly, that
'the device of reducing inputs to dated quantities of labour would be
pointless, if it is to be applied only to one-sector models. Malthus's
corn–corn model in this example [of the table in the *Measure of Value*]
was only a temporary simplifying device, which was perfectly justified

---

[23] Costabile erroneously dates the second quote 1815 and implies that it follows the first.

since the main objective of the example was to illustrate the method of reduction to dated quantities of labour'.

Before dealing with these objections, a word is called for on Costabile's own interpretation. Costabile attributes to Malthus a Sraffa model, but it is the Sraffa of the *Production of Commodities* in which the profit rate emerges in the wage sector as the solution to a set of simultaneous equations given the real wage, commodity outputs and technology (1983, pp. 144, 156). On this view, the value of capital itself depends on the profit rate:

The rate of profits is determined as the ratio between the value of surplus product and the value of capital advanced. The latter value is determined on the basis of the device of reducing capital to dated labour (pp. 153–4).

... capital advanced in the wage sector is constituted by commodities whose production requires time.... Hence the value of capital depends on the time which its production required, as a profit element must be charged on it for that time. It follows that the value of capital must depend on the rate of profits, which on the other hand is precisely our unknown. But this difficulty can be overcome by using Malthus' resolution of inputs in dated quantities of labour. Malthus did not apply this device in the specific example, in *The Measure of Value*, we are referring to. But we are entitled to apply it, since Malthus, as we have shown, always calculated the value of inputs by this method (pp. 155–6).

This then is the main issue: Does the profit rate emerge for Malthus in the wage–goods sector *independently of value* as a ratio between physically homogeneous products, to be carried over in establishing the 'natural values' of other commodities each comprising the sum of dated quantities of labour (as I maintain), or does the determination of the profit rate itself require his value theory (as Costabile maintains)?

I turn now to Costabile's first observation that Malthus, in his early reaction to Ricardo, rejected a single-sector approach to profits. Now this is not quite the case. His early concern was that a decrease in the corn price of cloth during the course of progress acts to reduce wages estimated in corn (if cloth is a wage good) with a positive impact on the *total* corn surplus, i.e. *on rent and profits combined* not on profits alone (letters to Ricardo, 10 and 12 March 1815, in Ricardo, 1951, VI, pp. 182–3, 185–6, and to Horner, 14 March 1815, p. 187), a point emphasized by Ricardo (4 April, p. 207).[24] Even so, what is said in 1815 need not still apply in 1820 and thereafter. The fact is that the *Principles* maintains the dual

---

[24] Garegnani (1991, p. 104) also errs in his interpretation in this regard.

notions (1) that the profit rate as determined in agriculture governs the general profit rate by way of the terms of trade between corn and manufactures (1820, p. 300; 1836, p. 275; Section 3 above), and (2) that the decline in the agricultural profit rate with increasing land scarcity dictates a set of equilibrium costs throughout manufacturing (1820, p. 328; 1836, pp. 293–4; cf. 1820, pp. 334–5; 1836, pp. 296–7; Section 3 above). Finally, while the treatment of the *actual* – as distinct from the *limiting* – profit rate entails increasing 'competition of capital' in manufacturing, the agricultural profit rate itself reflects 'the amount of the produce obtained by a given amount of labour', the express assumption being that there exists 'an equal demand for all the parts of the same [agricultural] produce', precisely in order to allow the determination of profits 'by the excess of the *quantity* produced, above the advances necessary to produce it' (1820, p. 296n; 1836, p. 272n; Section 2 above).

There are certain additions to the second edition of the *Principles* (see Section 4 above) which formally deny the possibility of making physical calculations in profit-rate determination, but these do not vitiate the conclusion since the problem relates to the possibility of differentials in the price of corn between periods (t) and $(t + 1)$ due to 'abundant' or 'deficient' crops, an irrelevant matter in dealing with secular trends. A potentially more serious impediment to the application of the corn–profit model referred to in 1820 (pp. 211–12 above) is absent from the second edition. I conclude that we are very close to a corn–profit model in the first edition of the *Principles*, and that this model is if anything actually *reinforced* after 1820. It would scarcely be surprising, then, to find the determining role of the agricultural profit rate – in effect the solution to distribution prior to pricing – in the *Measure of Value*, which was written at the same time as many of the revisions.

As for Costabile's further observations, I agree of course that Malthus utilizes the device of reducing inputs to dated quantities of labour, and that the 1823 work extends beyond one-sector models, but this is recognized by my interpretation which has the profit rate as determined in agriculture applied to establish the 'natural values' of *other* commodities, without itself requiring the value dimension for its determination.

Costabile candidly recognizes that Malthus did not specifically refer to his device of resolving inputs to dated quantities of labour in arriving at the value of capital, a device which she believes is required to obtain the profit rate (p. 217 above). Her assertion that 'we are entitled to apply it' since Malthus 'always calculated the value of inputs by this method' is a contentious one. There are indeed statements by Malthus which apply the principle of compensation for the time labour is invested to 'the formation of capital' as well as to final products (e.g. 1823, p. 8, and – with reference to fixed capital – pp. 21, 53), but the question at issue is whether by this sort of extension Malthus specifically intended the system of Sraffa-1960 equations involving value of capital from which emerges the profit rate as solution. That Malthus intended Sraffa's own model would be something of an anachronism one might think, whereas there is an alternative reading – that all the allowances in question relate to the establishment of the 'natural values' of commodities *other than corn*, in which procedure the profit rate is taken as a *datum* derived on the basis of the special case of corn where a physical ratio is possible.

I turn to a second critic.[25] Prendergast (1986, p. 188n) reads Malthus's second edition of the *Principles not* as establishing the possibility of making a corn calculation, but to the contrary, as insisting (even in the case of homogeneous input and output) on a value calculation, and she suggests that this rejection of the estimation of profits by quantity may have been motivated by Torrens's objection to the formal definition in the 1820 *Principles* of the profit rate in terms of *value* ratios, insisting that profit is a surplus which would exist 'quite independently of value', originating 'not in the interchange of commodities nor in the quality of value which wealth thereby acquires, but in the power of human industry to produce a greater quantity of the necessaries of life than is sufficient to support the labourers by whom it is carried on' (*The Traveller*, No. 6624, 24 April 1820).[26] That Malthus read Torrens I do not dispute,[27] but one cannot presume that he read Torrens as proposing a corn output–input solution (which he himself rejected). Torrens seems to have been making

---

[25] I draw here on Hollander (1995).

[26] Cf. J. S. Mill's formulation of the same proposition introduced into the 4th edition (1857) of his *Principles*: 'We thus see that profit arises, not from the incidence of exchange, but from the productive power of labour; and the general profit of the country is always what the productive power of labour makes it, whether any exchange takes place or not...' (1965, II, p. 411).

[27] Ricardo (4 May 1820) brought the *Traveller* reviews to Malthus's attention, claiming that 'as his arguments are on my side I of course think his criticisms just' (1951, VIII, p. 185), but this need not refer to the proposition that profit is a surplus which would exist 'quite independently of value'. Torrens had insisted that Ricardo appreciated (*pace* Malthus) that the profit rate is affected not only by the difficulty of production on the land, but also by the real rate of wages, and by improvements; and he could not understand how Malthus had imagined that he had refuted Ricardo in these regards. In a further review, he objected to Malthus's arguments for agricultural protection, and to his criticisms of Ricardo on rent (the *Traveller*, 1 May 1820). It is to Torrens's defence of his position in these regards that Ricardo may have referred. (For a summary of the reviews see Robbins, 1958, pp. 282–3.)

a more general point about the source of profits, in fact of all non-wage incomes.[28]

Prendergast (p. 187n) wishes to know how I relate the 1823 and 1814/1815 correspondence (p. 216 above). The answer is two-fold. Malthus's concern in the early correspondence was with a 'rate of produce' or total surplus including *rent*, but in 1823 it was with a rate of *profits*. Secondly, the problem in the correspondence of a mixed wage basket is simply not raised in 1823 as an objection to the *physical* ratio procedure. Malthus frequently assumed a mixed wage basket and considered the impact of changes in the relative prices of manufactured and agricultural wage goods on worker's welfare. Nonetheless, in analysing the profit rate he intimates in the revisions to the *Principles* that the complexity of a mixed wage basket was not so great as to preclude a corn calculation (Section 4 above). Conceivably, a systematic replacement in the revised version of the *Principles* of the term '*real* wage' by '*corn* wage' in dealing with the secular trend of factor returns (e.g., p. 201 above) was intended to reflect this position. He was prepared to proceed for some purposes *as if* corn alone entered the wage basket.[29]

Malthus, it appears, withdrew his strongly stated position of early 1814 that (as expressed by Ricardo) 'the profits of the farmer no more regulate the profits of other trades, than the profits of other trades regulate the profits of the farmer' (in Ricardo, 1951, VI, p. 104). However, if account is taken of his distinction between the 'regulating' and the 'limiting' determinants of the profit rate, the original position would still hold in modified form as pertaining to the former set, where there is full scope for the principle of competition of capitals with special reference to *manufacturing* and allowing for an influence on agriculture since profit rates tend to an equality. Similarly, his insistence on causality running *from* the

---

[28] In a continuation of the review of the *Principles* for the *Traveller* of 1 May 1820, Torrens extended to *rent* his denial that value is essential, making out a case that rent could exist even were institutions not of the exchange variety: 'Rent, like profit has its origin in the power of human industry to produce a greater quantity of wealth than is necessary to support the labour by which it is carried on; and may appear though there should be neither markets nor market prices, neither exchange nor exchangeable value.' It would exist 'In a state of society, in which there was no division of employment, and in which each capitalist engaged his labourers in the immediate production of the several articles he consumed...' (see Robbins, 1958, pp. 282–3).

[29] Of course wholly to abandon the complexity of a mixed wage basket – and other non-wage components of capital stock – would undermine a wide range of Malthusian theory, including the criticism of Smith for his exact proportionality of corn and general prices and his own allowances for deviations between the corn and the general commodity wage. In my opinion he set the complexity aside in specific contexts only.

profit rate *to* proportionate wages (p. 209 above and footnote 14) would pertain specifically to the 'regulating' sphere where the profit rate is governed by aggregate demand–supply relation.[30]

7 A concluding note

It remains to note a circumstance that may lend some tangential support to the interpretation of Malthus offered here. In a pamphlet of 1822 on profits and exchangeable value, John Cazenove – who was later to edit the second edition of Malthus's *Principles* – himself maintained the determining role of the agricultural profit rate: 'In regard to the profit which is derived from manufacturing and mercantile capital, it is governed by the returns of agricultural capital. It is plain that no one would employ a capital in trade, or manufactures, unless it yielded him a profit equal to what it would if employed on the land; and he cannot expect it to yield him much more, as the competition of capital will always ultimately reduce profits, in all the various departments of industry, to nearly the same level' (1822, pp. 27–8). Now the agricultural rate itself is specifically defined in purely physical terms: 'The natural rate of profit... is measured by the proportion which the surplus produce of the worst soil bears to that which is employed in its production' (p. 29).[31] We are close to the notion of manufacturing profit rates coming into line by way of changes in the manufacturing terms of trade against corn, although Cazenove is not explicit on this detail. It is also pertinent for us that the section in question pays tribute to Malthus: 'Previously to the publication of Mr. Malthus' *Inquiry into the Nature and Origin of Rent* the question of profit seems to have been very imperfectly understood' (p. 26).[32] Cazenove's position and commendation are suggestive of the interpretation we have offered,

---

[30] I do not see how Prendergast can conclude that Malthus's (purported) rejection of a corn–profit calculation in the second edition on the grounds that to estimate profits by quantity neglected supply and demand 'seems to support Sraffa's conjecture regarding Ricardo's early theory of profits, that "the rational foundation of the principle of the determining role of profits in agriculture, is that in agriculture the same commodity, namely corn, forms both the capital and the product"' (p. 189). What Malthus maintained in the 1820s tells us *nothing* of what Ricardo maintained in 1815.

[31] Profit (like rent) had its source in 'the natural fertility of the earth, or its power of yielding more than is sufficient for the maintenance of those employed in its cultivation', although (unlike rent) it tended to fall secularly, since 'the surplus [net of rent] which remains after replacing the capital employed is smaller and smaller...' (p. 28).

[32] I owe both the reference to Cazenove and the corn–profit reading to Gordon (1985).

although the corn–profit case is spelled out fully in 1820 rather than in the 1815 *Inquiry* (but see p. 208 above).

References

Cazenove, J. (1822). *Considerations on the Accumulation of Capital and its Effects on Exchangeable Value*, London: J. H. Richardson.

Costabile, L. (1983). 'Natural Prices, Market Prices and Effective Demand in Malthus', *Australian Economic Papers*, **22**, pp. 144–70.

Faccarello, G. (1982). 'Sraffa versus Ricardo: The Historical Irrelevance of the "Corn–Profit" Model', *Economy and Society*, **11**, May, pp. 122–37.

Garegnani, P. (1991). 'The Labour Theory of Value: "Detour" or Technical Advance', in G. A. Caravale (ed.), *Marx and Modern Economic Analysis*, Vol. I, Aldershot: Edgar Elgar, pp. 97–118.

Gordon, B. (1985). 'John Cazenove (1788–1879): Critic of Ricardo, Friend and Editor of Malthus', Working Paper, Third HETSA Conference held at La Trobe University, Melbourne.

Hollander, S. (1979). *The Economics of David Ricardo*, Toronto: University of Toronto Press.

Hollander, S. (1995). 'Sraffa's Rational Reconstruction of Ricardo: On Three Contributions to the *Cambridge Journal of Economics*', *Cambridge Journal of Economics*, **19**, pp. 483–9.

Malthus, T. R. (1820). *Principles of Political Economy*, London: John Murray.

Malthus, T. R. (1823). *The Measure of Value Stated and Illustrated*, London: John Murray.

Malthus, T. R. (1824). 'Political Economy', *Quarterly Review*, **XXX**, No. LX, Article 1, pp. 297–334.

Malthus, T. R. (1836). *Principles of Political Economy*, 2nd edn, London: William Pickering.

Malthus, T. R. (1986 [1815]). *An Inquiry into the Nature and Progress of Rent*, in E. A. Wrigley and D. Souden (eds), *The Works of Thomas Robert Malthus*, London: William Pickering, Vol. 7, pp. 113–74.

Mill, J. (1966 [1804]). *An Essay on the Impolicy of a Bounty on the Exportation of Corn*, New York: A. M. Kelley.

Mill, J. S. (1965). *Collected Works of John Stuart Mill*, Vols. II and III, *Principles of Political Economy*, Toronto: University of Toronto Press.

Prendergast, R. (1986). 'Malthus's discussion of the corn-ratio theory of profits', *Cambridge Journal of Economics*, **10**, pp. 187–9.

Ricardo, D. (1951–73). *The Works and Correspondence of David Ricardo*, edited by Piero Sraffa, Vols, I–XI, Cambridge: Cambridge University Press.

Robbins, L. (1958). *Robert Torrens and the Evolution of Classical Economics*, London: Macmillan.

Skourtos, M. S. (1991). 'Corn Models in the Classical Tradition: P. Sraffa Considered Historically', *Cambridge Journal of Economics*, **15**, 215–28.

Smith, A. (1937 [1776]). *The Wealth of Nations*, New York: Modern Library.

Sraffa, P. (1951). Introduction to Vol. I of Ricardo, 1951–73.

Sraffa, P. (1960). *Production of Commodities by Means of Commodities*, Cambridge: Cambridge University Press.

Comment*

Pierangelo Garegnani

1. Professor Hollander's argument in his present paper is not easy to follow. The main reason lies, I believe, in that he does not make sufficiently clear what he means when he claims that

Sraffa's famous...interpretation of the early Ricardo...applies in fact to T. R. Malthus. (p. 198)

The difficulty arises in two main respects. The first is that Sraffa's interpretation, which Hollander deems instead to be applicable to Malthus, is taken to include 'the determining *role* of agricultural profits' (ibid., footnote 2). This is a principle which was undoubtedly *stated* by Ricardo in 1814–15 (1951–78, Vol. VI, p. 104), and no less undoubtedly *opposed* by Malthus at the time, so that it is not clear in what sense, chronological or otherwise, that principle can be envisaged to be a 'Malthusian conception'[a] (ibid. footnote 2). The second respect is that the claim itself seems to fizzle out at the end of the paper. There Hollander admits that as for the 'regulating determinants' of profits – i.e. for the actual determination of profits in any economy which is not in a final stationary state – Malthus in fact maintained all along his 'original negative position' that

the profits of the farmer no more regulate the profits of other trades, than the profits of other trades regulate the profits of the farmer (ibid., Section 6).

We shall here try our best to clear both obstacles, and arrive, as far as we can, at a reasonably unambiguous statement of Hollander's position. We shall then find, however, that by Malthus's own declaration[1] the corn calculations of profits in the *Principles of Political Economy* (1820, 1836)

---

* This comment has been conducted on what turned out to be a provisional draft of Professor Hollander's contribution. Scarcity of time for authors and editor alike has induced me to take care of the changes in Professor Hollander's published paper by means of a postscript and some footnotes distinguished by letters of the alphabet. I wish here to thank Professors R. Ciccone, H. Kurz, G. Mongiovi, F. Vianello and F. Petri for useful discussions on the question.

[a] Cf. however, the postscript, Section A, for the question as it emerges from Hollander's published version above.

[1] Cf. the passage in Malthus, 1820, pp. 316–17, quoted also in Paragraph 16 below.

and *The Measure of Value* (1823), on which Hollander ultimately rests his interpretation – far from reflecting a *Malthusian* conception of the determining role of agricultural profits were in fact intended to counter that conception which Malthus identified with Ricardo's theory of profit.

In Section 1, we shall inquire into the possible meaning of Hollander's claims in order to proceed, then, in Section 2, to a review of the essential lines of Malthus's theory of profits in the *Principles* and *Measure of Value*. We shall then be equipped to comment on Hollander's paper in our third and final section.

1   Hollander's claim

2. In fact, although in his paper Hollander argues at length his attribution to Malthus of the determining role of agricultural profits, he does not clarify how the description of that principle as a 'Malthusian conception' fits the fact that it was Ricardo who stated in 1814 that 'the profits of the farmer . . . regulate the profits of all other trades' (1951–73, Vol. VI, p. 104; also, e.g., Vol. IV, p. 23), and used that principle for his innovative theory of profits from 1813 to 1815. Hollander clearly does not mean that Ricardo *borrowed* that principle from Malthus – who, in fact, strenuously opposed it in those years by arguing, in Ricardo's words, that 'the profits of the farmer no more regulate the profits of other trades than the profits of other trades regulate the profits of the farmer' (Ricardo, 1951–73, Vol. VI, p. 104). Hollander's reference to the 'mature' Malthus of the *Principles* (Section 1) in fact makes clear that Malthus is supposed to have arrived at that principle *after* Ricardo. But then, will not Hollander's claim be the straightforward one that by 1820 Malthus had come to use corn calculations and agricultural profits in order better to counter Ricardo's theory, on what Hollander would now admit were Ricardo's own grounds? Even without the initial confirmation of Hollander's persisting opposition to Sraffa's interpretation of the early Ricardo (p. 199n), the wording about 'Malthusian conception' would suffice to convince us that this second possibility is not what he means either.

To sort out the question of what, then, can Hollander mean it seems necessary to take a step back to his book on Ricardo (1979), and to the (1973) article in which he first challenged Sraffa's interpretation.

3.[b] Our concern here is for a specific point, namely how Professor Hollander deals with what is perhaps the main piece of *direct* textual

---

[b] For the bearing of the changes in the published version of Hollander's paper published above (cf. p. 223, note a) on this and the following paragraphs of our comment, see Section A of the postscript below.

evidence[2] used by Sraffa for his interpretation: namely Malthus's letter to Ricardo of 4 August 1814. In that letter Malthus writes:

> In no case of production *is the produce exactly of the same nature as the capital advanced*. Consequently we can never properly refer to a *material rate of produce*, independent of demand, and of the abundance or scarcity of capital . . . it is the state of capital or the general profits of stock . . . which determines the particular profit upon the land; and . . . not the particular profits or rate of produce upon the land which determines the general profits of stock. (Ricardo, 1951–73, Vol. VI, pp. 117–18, quoted in Vol. I, p. xxxi; our italics)

Here Malthus criticises Ricardo for exactly the same calculation of the agricultural profit rate by means of a 'material rate' between quantities of corn, which Sraffa sees as the 'rational foundation' of Ricardo's principle

---

[2] *Indirect* evidence for Sraffa's interpretation is of course the fact that it makes sense of Ricardo's principle of the determining role of agricultural profits and of the corn calculations of his *Essay on Profits* (1815). Even more importantly, it explains how Ricardo *could* arrive at his novel theory of profits recognizing the determinacy of the profit rate once the real wage is given – what Stigler (1952, p. 190) called Ricardo's 'basic theorem of distribution' – despite sharing, at the time, Smith's view of other prices rising with the corn price and the wage, which was instead likely to lead him in an opposite direction, as it had done with his predecessors and contemporaries.

Hollander recognizes that prices moving with wages faced the Ricardo of his interpretation with 'a serious stumbling block' (1973, p. 265). Hollander seems, however, able to remove that block only by imagining an unlikely pendular movement of Ricardo, who would have moved from acceptance of the received position in 1810–11 (Ricardo, 1951–73, Vol. III, p. 270) to assuming *constancy* of manufacturing prices in 1813, in time to arrive on that basis at his novel theory of profits: this only in order to return to *changing* prices in 1814 (ibid., Vol. VI, pp. 108, 114) and finally to settle for *constant* prices in 1815 (ibid., Vol. IV, e.g. p. 21). In fact so far as I can see, no textual evidence is given by Hollander for Ricardo's supposed intermediate 1813 position, decisive for Hollander's thesis. (On the question, see Hollander, 1973, 265; 1979, 126–7; Garegnani, 1982, 66–8, 75–6; 1983, 176.) Difficulties in Professor Hollander's challenge of Sraffa's interpretation of Ricardo's early theory of profits have been argued in e.g. Eatwell (1975), Garegnani (1982, 1983), Langer (1982), De Vivo (1985, 1996), Blaug (1985), Prendergast (1986), Stigler (1981) and O'Brien (1981). Sraffa's interpretation seems to have been universally accepted at the time it was advanced (cf. e.g. Robbins, 1958, e.g. p. 61n; Stigler 1953, 1958; Hutchison 1952). It was only in the 1970s that criticism of Sraffa's interpretation of the early Ricardo began to appear, starting with Hollander (1973), followed by Rankin (1984), Peach (1984), Porta (1986) and others. A parallel stream of interpretations of Ricardo and classical economists along the lines of what Professor Samuelson labelled the 'canonical classical model' also developed around the middle 1970s at the hands of Levy (1976), Hicks and Hollander (1977), Samuelson (1978), Casarosa (1978), and others. It may perhaps be noted that by those years, with Sraffa (1960) and other works, the idea of the approach to prices and distribution of 'the old classical economists from Adam Smith to Ricardo' (Sraffa, 1960, v) as a 'paradigm' alternative to the dominant one had begun to emerge (on the relevance of this point, cf. e.g. Hollander 1987, pp. 4–6; 1995, pp. 4–5).

'that the profits of the farmer regulate the profits of all other trades' (Sraffa, 1951, p. xxxi–ii).

Now, in his attempt to reconcile that letter with his rejection of Sraffa's interpretation of Ricardo, Hollander recognises that Malthus's passage regarding the 'material rate of produce' answers the 'corn calculation' of the letter of 25 July 1814 by Ricardo, which Malthus was replying to on 5 August. He concludes, however, that:

In light of the consistent emphasis upon the role of the money wage rate in determining the general rate of profit – both immediately before and after the letter containing the *corn calculation* – it appears unjustified to interpret Ricardo's intentions in terms of a corn model. Ricardo's formulation of July represents a rather casual and inadequate restatement – the significance of which should not be exaggerated – of his basic and consistently maintained position. (1973, p. 266; for a statement similar to the first half of this passage see also 1979, p. 129)

This statement is not without ambiguities and it may in fact hide a change in Hollander's interpretation of Ricardo's letter between (1973) and (1979). However, the point which is of immediate interest to us is a different one: it is to bring out an important implication of Hollander's readings. The 'corn model' stated in Malthus's letter is not present in the same clear-cut form in Ricardo's July letter (where non-corn elements of capital are implied);[3] on the other hand, Hollander denies that Malthus had previously been instructed by Ricardo on the matter. Where, then, did Malthus get that 'corn model' from? Hollander's answer can only be that it was a piece of Malthus's own mind, suggested by Ricardo's July

---

[3] The relevant passage in Ricardo's letter is:

The capitalist who may find it necessary to employ a hundred days labour instead of fifty in order to produce a certain quantity of corn cannot retain the same share for himself unless the labourers who are employed for a hundred days will be satisfied with the same quantity of corn for their subsistence that the labourers employed for fifty had before. If you suppose the price of corn doubled, the capital to be employed estimated in money will probably be also nearly doubled (quoted in Hollander, 1973, p. 266; Ricardo's slip may be noted for which 'nearly doubled' should be read as 'nearly quadrupled').

Hollander's comment on this letter (see above in the text) can in fact be interpreted in two ways. Hollander may refer to an *actual use* of the 'corn model' by Ricardo, which however remained 'casual' because, after accidentally stumbling on it in July 1814, Ricardo quickly abandoned it as 'inadequate' (for Ricardo's alleged emphasis on money wages before and after 25 July, cf. Garegnani, 1982, pp. 71–3). Alternatively, Hollander may mean to deny *any* use of the 'corn model' by Ricardo, who *would have intended* just to *restate* in the July letter his 'consistently maintained' money–wage argument, but did it so inadequately as to

continued

'corn calculation', and used to reject an argument which *Malthus thought* underlay that 'calculation', whether or not it in fact did so.

This answer is not given explicitly in (1973). It is also not given in the part of (1979) dealing specifically with Malthus's letter (pp. 127–9). It does, however, indirectly emerge in that book, but only six hundred pages after the passage we referred to, and in the lines of Appendix G, quoted now by Hollander (p. 198 n2):

the determining role of agricultural profits and the solution to distribution prior to prices are *Malthusian conceptions* (1979, p. 722; our italics)

The ambiguity left in the pages on Malthus's August letter is here seemingly cleared by Hollander in a very strong form by attributing to Malthus not only a discovery of the 'corn model' in the course of his criticism of Ricardo, but also a positive use of the associated principle of the determining role of agricultural profits for his own theory – both things being apparently implied by Hollander in his reference to 'Malthusian conceptions'. In order to support such a striking overturn of Sraffa's interpretation, the reader finds in (1979) only two further lines to the effect that, in Malthus's *Measure of Value*,

the profit rate is determined in the agricultural sector independently of value. The profit rate thus calculated is then taken for granted in the discussion of value. (1979, p. 722)[4]

4. We can now return to the question we raised in Paragraph 2 about what Hollander may mean by the apparent paradox of describing as a 'Malthusian conception' the determining role of agricultural profits stated by Ricardo, and opposed by Malthus in 1814–15. What Hollander *can* mean is, it seems, something like the following. Ricardo arrived first at the farmer's profits principle but, unlike what Sraffa argues, he only

allow Malthus to misunderstand him. Indeed, as we indicated in the text above, there may be signs of a change in Hollander's position from the first to the second interpretation. In short, those signs are there in (1973, p. 266). Hollander refers to Ricardo's July corn calculation as an 'estimate [of the profit rate] in terms of a "material rate of produce" *to use Malthus's terminology*' (our italics), where Malthus is thus apparently seen to be *correct* in his interpretation of Ricardo in terms of a 'rate of produce'. In (1979) that passage disappears, and stress is instead laid on Ricardo's admission of non-corn elements of wages which had been ignored in (1973). Moreover, the expression 'Malthusian conception' first appears in an Appendix of (1979).

[4] We shall, of course, presently discuss the merits of those remarks, but we may already note how those lines of Appendix G (1979) prompted a critic to write:

in so far as Hollander judged it to be the case, one might have expected him to pose the question of relevance [of those lines in the Appendix] to the interpretation of the 1814–15 correspondence. He does not do it. (Prendergast, 1986, p. 187n) meant it as the rather general statement that *agricultural productivity* is decisive for the general rate of profits.[5] It would have been left to Malthus to arrive at the 'corn model' validating the proposition: in Hollander's view, that is, Ricardo failed to perceive, or to perceive the importance of, that rationale of the proposition about agricultural profits which he himself had reached.

However, that is not all. Hollander apparently contends that the 'corn model' later became an integral part of Malthus's positive theory of profits, and was no longer an instrument for criticising Ricardo, as it had been in 1814. Indeed in Malthus's later *Principles* (1820, 1836) and *Measure of Value* (1823), we frequently find calculations of the general rate of profits in terms of quantities in corn. By the audacious move of turning on its head Sraffa's reconstruction of the early Ricardo, Hollander seems to attempt to reconcile his own interpretation of Ricardo with those corn calculations by Malthus which, as we shall see, might otherwise emerge as just a more systematic prosecution of the 1814–15 critique of Ricardo, and thus threaten Hollander's interpretation even more seriously than Malthus's letter of 4 August 1814 does already.

5. However, if that is Professor Hollander's position when he describes the determining role of the agricultural profit rate as being a 'Malthusian conception' – and it is difficult to see what else *can* that position be[c] – it suffers, we shall claim, from two main misapprehensions. The first is a failure to distinguish between, on the one hand, Ricardo's *determining* role of agricultural profits (which requires, besides a wage consisting of corn, also that that wage be a *given* or an independent variable of the system), and on the other, corn calculations of profits like those we find in Malthus's *Measure of Value* which, as we shall see, merely *ascertain* or measure in agriculture a general rate of profits determined by demand and supply, where agriculture has no more role in that determination than has any other trade. The second misapprehension of Hollander regards instead a surprising treatment of Malthus's distinction between 'limitation' and regulation' of profits in his *Principles*.

---

[5] Hollander, 1973, p. 275; see also Garegnani, 1982, pp. 68–70, where I noted how, with that interpretation, Hollander apart from 'having to ascribe to Ricardo an incorrect use of words [when] those words could mean exactly what they say', is also prevented from explaining the disappearance of the proposition in Ricardo's *Principles* where it would apply equally well, if taken in Hollander's sense.

[c] In fact both these claims of Hollander's ('the corn model' as a piece of Malthus's mind, and its later positive use by that author) are made explicit by Hollander in the published version of his paper (cf. p. 223, note a above; see Section A of the postscript below).

It is therefore to Malthus's theory of profits and, in particular, to the two points just mentioned that we must now turn our attention first of all.

2 Malthus's theory of profits

6. The main lines of Malthus's argument on profits in his *Principles* (1820, 1826) and *Measure of Value* (1923) are comparatively simple. Malthus accepts Ricardo's 'basic theorem on distribution' concerning the determinacy of the rate of profits once the real wage and the margin of cultivation on the land are given. However, he generally replaces the wage with the rate of profits in the role of the independent variable and therefore takes the 'theorem' in the following form: once the rate of profits is given, the real wage rate (e.g. the corn wage) is also determined, and the two move in opposite directions. As a result, Malthus's explanation of profits in terms of 'the state of the supply and the demand' comes to be based on the *variability* of the real wage, indirectly determined by such a 'state'. In this way, while continuing to use Smith's phrases, Malthus in fact departs from Smith, who had failed to see with any clarity the necessary relation binding the two key distributive variables.

If, for the sake of definiteness, we refer to the second edition of the *Principles* (1836), what we find there about profits is a preliminary distinction between a 'limiting' and a 'regulating' principle of profits.[6] The first relates to the maximum rate of profits possible in the given conditions as to the fertility of the land last taken into cultivation, namely the rate of profits which would rule if the real wage, expressed in terms of 'corn' (generally evaluated in corn, rather than consisting of corn[7]), were at its strict subsistence level.[8] The second, or 'regulating', principle concerns instead the rate of profits as determined below that maximum level by the various circumstances which Malthus describes in terms of 'demand and supply'.

Now, by means of his 'limiting principle', Malthus tries in fact to encapsulate, so to speak, Ricardo's theory of a rate of profits independent

---

[6] Cf. Malthus, 1836, p. 271. In Malthus, 1820, 253–4 ff, we find a broadly equivalent distinction between 'two main causes' which influence 'the means of supporting labour'. More generally, Malthus (1820) does not seem to differ substantially from Malthus (1836) for what is of concern to us here.

[7] See point (iii) (p. 231) below.

[8] 'The command of a certain quantity of food is absolutely necessary to the labourer in order to support himself, and such a family as will maintain merely a stationary population' (Malthus, 1836, p. 274.)

of demand and supply, and then to reject it as due purely to the unjustified assumption of a *constant and minimum* corn wage. In the actual conditions of the economy, Malthus argues, the corn wage varies, and being always more or less above that minimum, it can fall as well as rise, as the profit rate correspondingly rises or falls, in response to the 'state of demand and supply' (1836, e.g. pp. 273, 276, 297). The only exception to that, and the only situation in which Ricardo's theory would come into its own, would be when, because of the extension of cultivation to less and less fertile lands, the economy reached a final stationary state where the wage and the rate of profits would be at their respective minima, for which population growth and capital accumulation would both have come to a halt. At that point it would no longer be possible for the real wage either to rise or to fall by the effect of demand and supply acting on the profit rate. There, but only there, argued Malthus, would the profit rate be determined in Ricardo's way, independently of 'demand and supply' (1836, e.g. p. 282).

7. Thus, in the actual conditions in which, in Malthus's view, the economy is likely to find itself for even a century to come (e.g. 1836, p. 282), the rate of profits and hence the wage (in particular the corn wage) will be determined in accordance with the 'regulating principle of profits'. The rate will be determined, that is, by what Malthus describes as 'the state of the supply and the demand' (1836, e.g. p. 280) or 'the principle of competition' (1836, e.g. pp. 294, 298) acting, as he tells us, through

the varying [labour commanded] value of the produce of the same quantity of labour. (1836, p. 276, see also p. 297)

For our present limited purpose it seems that we may summarize into the following four groups the circumstances which Malthus envisages as being covered by the above expressions.

(i) The circumstances which Malthus expresses as

abundance or scantiness of capital, including the funds for the maintenance of labour, as compared with the labour which it employs, (1836, p. 276)

and which he illustrates by his example of a sudden stop to population growth which would raise wages to the point at which the profit rate would be low enough to prevent any further accumulation (1836, pp. 276–8), or also by the further example of a 'uniform' progress of capital and population towards a final stationary state (1836, pp. 273–5).[9]

[9] It is perhaps interesting to note how Malthus takes that 'uniform' progress towards a final stationary state, not as an account of how things are likely to develop, but, rather, as a question which 'it may be curious' to consider 'before we proceed to the actual state of things' (cf. Hollander's different account of the question p. 201 above).

(ii) The circumstances relating to what we would describe today as 'aggregate demand' and 'aggregate supply' which, however, Malthus does not seem to distinguish clearly from those under (i). Thus, e.g., some pages after stating in the terms of the passage we quoted under (i) above the 'principal cause' coming under his 'regulating principle', he tells us

The different rates of profits during periods of peace and war ... are chiefly attributable to the abundance or scarcity of capital and produce compared with the demand, (1836, pp. 284–5)

and later Malthus speaks of a fall in the rate of profits resulting merely from a fall in the money price of corn due, he says, to a 'slack demand for *labour and produce*' (1836, p. 287, our italics; see also 1823, p. 55). However, the 'abundance or scantiness of capital ... as compared with the labour which it employs' of the passage under (i) would not seem to have much to do with 'the abundance or scarcity of capital and produce compared with the demand', or the 'slack demand for labour and produce'.

(iii) The relative price of the several wage goods, in particular that of corn in terms of manufactures. As Malthus puts it, the question concerns

a rise in the price of corn from increased demand, unaccompanied by a proportionate rise of most foreign and many home commodities

which

allows of some diminution in the corn wages of labour without a proportionate diminution of the comforts of the labourers (1836, p. 284)[10]

(iv) The price of the commodity when advanced as capital relative to the same when emerging as output (e.g. 1836, pp. 220, 265–6).[11]

These circumstances are mentioned by Malthus at various points in the *Principles*, and appear to be seen by him as all being expressions of the 'temporary or ordinary state of demand and supply' (1823, pp. 55–6;

[10] Also, e.g., 1836, p. 266, where a comparatively small consumption of manufactures by workers is clearly implied. We may note that any independent effect of circumstance (iii) on the profit rate is in fact illusory since, given the assumptions of the case, in particular the uniformity of the profit rate, relative commodity prices are *dependent* and not *independent* variables in any determination of the profit rate.

[11] Malthus also mentions among the circumstances affecting profits, improvements in agriculture (1836, pp. 282–3) and an 'increase of personal exertion among the labouring classes' (1836, p. 283), but these two factors may be seen as affecting the maximum, rather than the actual, rate of profits. Malthus, however, seems much concerned with showing how the maximum rate set by labour productivity on marginal land can be raised in the course of development, leaving more elbow room for 'demand and supply' in the actual determination of the profit rate.

also 1836, p. 290) and to provide the content of the 'regulating principle of profits'.

8. Thus, Malthus's 'regulating principle of profits', that is the *actual* determination of profits, appears to rest on a demand and supply determination of money prices relative to money wages (cf. our first quotation in Paragraph 7) which, by its very nature, gives to agriculture no more of a determining role than it gives to any other sector. Now, in order to understand how, as we shall see, Hollander may instead read into Malthus's theory a determining role to the agricultural rate of profits, it is useful to turn to the distinction we drew in Paragraph 5 above between the two possible meanings of a rate of profits calculated as a ratio between corn quantities.

In fact, one thing is (a) the *twin* assumptions which Sraffa sees in the early Ricardo, i.e. that the wage is given, and that it is given in terms of corn, where the first assumption, which Sraffa takes for granted, is as logically necessary as the second for Ricardo's conclusion that farmers' profits *determine* the general rate, and a quite different thing is (b) the possibility of *ascertaining* the general rate of profits in agriculture by means of a ratio between quantities of corn – whether the wages consist entirely of corn, or are merely evaluated in corn. In case (b), as in case (a), we reckon in terms of corn, but the meaning of the calculation is entirely different. Thus, even if 'demand and supply', in Malthus's sense above, are seen to determine the general rate of profit, and meaning (a) of the corn calculations is therefore excluded, yet, when 'the state of supply and demand' and hence the system of relative prices are known, the wage estimated in corn is also known, and we can, if we so wish, *ascertain* the ruling profit rate by a ratio between corn quantities. However, such a demand-and-supply-determined rate of profits could no more be said to 'determine' the other rates than that can be said of, e.g., the cloth-industry rate, which could also be ascertained, if we so wished, as a ratio between cloth quantities, once the non-cloth elements of capital are evaluated in cloth.[d] Indeed even if the wages *consisted* entirely of corn, only the third of the above four routes along which Malthus sees demand and supply as determining the rate of profits would be closed, and it would still be true that, as Malthus put it in his letter of 5 August 1814,

---

[d] In the version of his paper published above, Hollander writes that 'the logic of Sraffa's reconstruction does not require a constant corn wage' (p. 201). That logic requires, however, that the corn wage be an independent variable of the system, otherwise, as said in the text, agriculture could have no more determining role than, say, the cloth industry's rate.

it is the general profits of stocks... which determines the particular profit upon the land; and... not the particular profit... upon the land which determines the general profits of stock. (Vol. VI, pp. 117–18 and Paragraph 2 above).[12]

Clearly, if the assumption of corn wages is *necessary* to the logic of Ricardo's determining role of agricultural profits, it is not *sufficient*. Equally necessary is the assumption that the corn wage be an *independent variable* of the system, as it is in Ricardo's *Essay*, but it certainly is not in Malthus, where the corn wage depends on prices, and can accordingly be seen to be determined by 'demand and supply' together with the general profit rate.

9. Now, the above distinction between those two possible meanings of the corn calculations is particularly important in order to understand the analysis which Malthus conducts in his *Measure of Value*, and in the table appearing there (1823, p. 38).[13]

In that table several possible rates of profits are ascertained as ratios of corn quantities starting from the corresponding corn wage: these profit rates are then used to calculate the values of corn in terms of labour commanded. The table is thus similar in appearance to the one in Ricardo's *Essay* (1951–73, Vol. VI, p. 17) and might therefore seem to validate Hollander's interpretation of a determining role of agricultural profits in Malthus – it might seem to do so, that is, until we notice that *several* levels of the corn wage are allowed to correspond to the same state of agricultural productivity on the land, and that this is done just in order to show how 'demand and supply' can determine the rate of profits *independently* of the fertility of the land.

Such a demand-and-supply determination of the rate of profits is in fact argued to occur by way of determining the labour-commanded price of commodities produced by a given quantity of labour and, in particular, by determining the commanded-labour price of the corn so produced.[14] The reciprocal of the latter price, the corn wage, is thus determin*ed* by prices and rate of profits, and is not a determin*ant* of

---

[12] In fact, the heterogeneity between agricultural output and capital, although sufficient to reject the principle of the determining role of agricultural profits in Ricardo, is not necessary to validate Malthus's demand and supply theory of profits, as also shown, e.g., in the table of *The Measure of Value* (1823, p. 38), where Malthus can support his theory while assuming that corn wages are given independently of prices, *as if* they consisted entirely of corn.

[13] It is in fact to *that* text that Hollander first referred in (1979, p. 722) for his current interpretation of Malthus (Paragraph 3 above).

[14] 'The [labour commanded] value of the corn obtained by ten men depends mainly upon the rate of profits, which again depends mainly upon the demand and supply of corn compared with labour' (Malthus, 1823, p. 43).

them, as Hollander would need, and as a first reading of the table might suggest. Indeed, Malthus makes that quite clear by the caption he puts on the column giving the several alternative corn wages 'Yearly corn wages... *determined by the Demand and Supply*' (1823, p. 39, our italics). In fact the true causal chain runs the way opposite to that in which it may seem to run, and the way opposite to that in which it ran in Ricardo's *Essay*: it starts, that is, *from prices* to proceed to the general rate of profits and to reach, finally, the corn wage, and *not from the corn wage* to reach the agricultural rate of profits and then the general rate and the prices, as in Ricardo.

3   Hollander's paper

10. We are now equipped to comment on Hollander's paper. What we have just seen about Malthus's table in his *Measure of Value* offers a good starting point because it shows how Hollander may have been misled by that table when, in his 1979 book on Ricardo, he wrote:

Malthus does not put forward a 'theory of profits' in the *Measure of Value*... utilising value relationships; the profit rate is determined in the agricultural sector *independently of value*. The profit rate thus calculated is then taken for granted in the discussion of value. (1979, p. 722, our italics; cf. Paragraph 3 above)

Hollander has evidently followed Malthus's *expository* line running from the corn wage to profits and prices, and thus missing the *causal* line running in the opposite direction, with an agricultural profit rate most certainly *not* determined 'independently of value'.

Not surprisingly Hollander then has difficulties in dealing with the numerous passages of Malthus (1823) which contradict his interpretation. One example may suffice here.[15] Hollander quotes (Section 5) the following passage:

profits never, on any occasion rise or fall, unless *the value of the produce* of a given quantity of labour rises or falls either from the temporary or ordinary *state of the demand and supply*. (Malthus, 1823, p. 56; our italics)

The contradiction with Hollander's interpretation above, of Malthus's profit rate determined 'independently of value', could not be more striking. Hollander's defence is:

[Malthus's] proposition is misleading. It introduces 'the state of demand and supply' as if its relevance had been *demonstrated*, whereas all he had shown in

---

[15] A further instance is in footnote 17 below.

his table was a varying value of the produce in terms of its command over labour given agricultural productivity and the corn wage.[16] (p. 214; italics in the original)

It is not clear what Hollander means here about Malthus having failed to 'demonstrate' the relevance of value. The question in hand is to interpret Malthus, not assess the validity of his arguments. It is not whether Malthus has 'demonstrated' the relevance of value for his profit determination, it is whether Malthus *claims* that relevance or not, and Hollander in his passage in fact grants that Malthus does claim it. Thus, it seems, he grants that his own interpretation of a Malthus determining the profit rate 'independently of value' is not correct.[17]

11. If, in the *Measure of Value*, Hollander's interpretation of Malthus's theory of profits already runs into the difficulty we saw, the task of supporting it would seem to be even harder when we proceed to the *Principles*, where Malthus's theory of profits is fully spelled out, and no ambiguity can be created by an expository chain which is misleadingly distinct from the causal one. The task would indeed be an impossible one, were it not for one feature of Malthus's theory: his 'limiting principle of profits', a reflection of Ricardo's own theory, within which, therefore, the determining role of agricultural profits does come into its own, just as it did in Ricardo's early formulation. The difficulty for Hollander's interpretation is of course that, for Malthus, this agricultural rate is only the *maximum* rate – it is indeed introduced in order to argue it will *not* be the one generally ruling in the economy (Paragraph 6 above), which will instead be determined by the 'state of supply and demand' in accordance with the *'regulating* principle of profits'. Given this difficulty, it is not surprising that in Hollander's paper we find little

---

[16] We may note a slip in the passage. No variation of the labour-commanded value of the produce is possible when, as Hollander writes, *both* the corn wage and the agricultural productivity are given.

[17] After arguing that Malthus, by defending his labour-commanded standard, was thereby 'opening the door for the ... possibility of excess *general* commodity supply', Hollander reiterates

> Ricardo rejected the phenomenon on the wholly independent grounds of Say's Law. Nothing in the *Measure of Value* ... demonstrates the dependency of the profit rate on aggregate 'demand–supply ... Deficiency of aggregate demand is a matter of supplementary doctrine' (pp. 214–15).

However, again, what is relevant here is not whether or not a labour-commanded standard 'demonstrates', in some sense, the dependency of the profit rate on excess general commodity supply – it is whether or not Malthus did argue such a 'dependency', which is what Hollander, in fact, admits in the passage to be the case.

clarity about the above two 'principles' and their distinction.[e] With this, and an associated peculiar meaning attributed to Malthus's 'regulation of profits', we come to the second of the two misapprehensions (Paragraph 5 above) which appear to have led Hollander to the claims of his article.

12. Thus, the passages from Malthus's *Principles* quoted in the first pages of Hollander's paper and purporting to prove Malthus's 'adherence' to the determining role of farmer's profits do in fact refer to the 'limiting principle'. However, the only indication the reader may have in the first pages that the profit rate there referred to by Malthus is a maximum one, and *not* the ruling one, lies in a phrase cropping up in the Malthus quotation given in Section 2 (p. 199). The phrase is 'If then we suppose the *first cause* to operate singly' (our italics), where Hollander does not explain which is the 'second cause' Malthus is referring to[18] – namely the demand and supply of the 'regulating principle of profits'.

However, even more seriously misleading, if less obviously so, is the fact that the assumption of a *constant* (and minimum) corn wage, underlying as we saw (Paragraph 6) the 'limiting principle', and mentioned by Malthus in the passage describing 'the first cause', is surprisingly explained by Hollander as nothing but an 'expository preliminary' (p. 201) – as if that assumption were not the unfulfilled basic conditions which, in Malthus's view, prevents the rate of profits of the 'limiting principle' from constituting the normal rate of the 'regulating principle' (Paragraph 6 above).

13. Indeed, it can be said that Hollander's paper gives no real account of Malthus's distinction between 'limiting' and 'regulating' principles until its last page[f] (see Paragraph 15 below). Thus, when in Section 3 (p. 203) the existence of the distinction in Malthus is first mentioned, that is done by just saying:

[e] The same applies for the distinction between a 'real' and a 'natural' rate of profit in John Cazenove's *Considerations* (1822) to which Hollander refers in his 'Concluding Note' for support of his interpretation of Malthus: see Section C in the postscript to this comment.

[18] In the lines immediately preceding the passage in (1836) quoted by Hollander, Malthus had in fact concisely stated that 'the two main causes which affect these proportions [between the value of the advances and the value of the produce and, therefore, the rate of profits] are the productiveness ... of the last capitals employed upon the land ... This may be called the *limiting* principle of profits. And, secondly, the varying value of the produce of the same quantity of labour occasioned by the accidental or ordinary state of the demand and supply ... This may be called the *regulating* principle of profits' (1836, p. 271; italics in the original)

[f] The distinction is in fact on pp. 220–1 in the published version, where the 'Concluding Note' has been added..

the general profit rate was only 'limited', not *governed*, by agricultural productivity conditions. (p. 204; italics in the original)

and before the reader has had time to fully realize that what he would in fact need to know to assess Hollander's claims is what the profit rate is 'governed' by, and not what it is 'limited' by, he is rushed on to two more quotations concerning, again, the limiting profit rate and its extension from agriculture to manufactures.

What is even more surprising, however, is that when in Section 3 (p. 204), Malthus's own key word 'regulation' finally emerges in Hollander's text, with the associated notions of demand and supply, the word is curiously interpreted as if it concerned the process by which the rate of profits in manufactures would be 'brought into line' with an independently determined agricultural rate of profits, and it did not concern, as it instead does, and Hollander will recognize later (cf. Paragraph 15 below), the determination of the *general* rate of profits. The passage to which Hollander refers in Section 3 (p. 204) is in fact one in which, in the context of his criticism of Ricardo's theory of profits, Malthus had written:

It is obvious that, in this case, profits can only be *regulated* by the principle of competition, or of demand and supply, which would determine the degree in which the prices of commodities would fall; and their prices, compared with the uniform price of labour, would regulate the rate of profits. (1836, pp. 293–4, our italics; see also 1820, p. 328)

On this Hollander comments

It might, however, be fair to suppose that by *regulation* in this passage Malthus intended 'brought into line with' the agricultural profit rate. (p. 205)

This interpretation of Malthus's word 'regulation' is surprising.[g,19] Indeed an examination of the context of Malthus's passage confirms that by 'regulation' Malthus here, as elsewhere in the *Principles*, means

---

[g] In the published version of his paper (pp. 207–8 above) Hollander does introduce an explanation of this interpretation along the lines we had indicated in footnote 19 below: see Section B of the postscript.

[19] In (1997, p. 71), Hollander refers to a letter of 29 December 1814 to Ricardo, in which Malthus writes:

[Say] does not properly distinguish between necessaries of life and other commodities. The former create their own demand the latter not. (Ricardo, 1951–73, Vol. VI, p. 168)

The idea here expressed implies the growth of population, and is therefore meant for secular trends and rent, so that Malthus may have seen no inconsistency between it and his 'regulating' principle of profits, for which demand and supply determine the agricultural rate of profits by affecting the price of corn relative to the wage.

just what the word says, and the quoted passage itself makes sufficiently clear, namely the determination of the *general* profit rate, including therefore the agricultural profit rate, by 'the principle of competition or [...] of demand and supply'.[20] The agricultural profit rate is in fact there supposed to fall with those of the other sectors because of changes in the prices of the products relative to the wages. The fact that the labour-commanded price, while diminishing for manufactures, is supposed to rise in the case of corn, because the fall of profits is there more than compensated by a rise in the labour required to produce it (with the consequence of a fall in the corn wage thus determined by demand and supply), does not make any difference in that respect.[21]

14. It is of course to be expected that this reading of Malthus's 'regulating principle' should come into conflict with a large number of other passages in the *Principles* and should land Hollander into difficulties. One instance will suffice here.[22] In Section 3 (p. 206), Malthus is quoted by Hollander to the effect that:

[profits] may be much lower [than the state of the land will admit] from an abundant supply of capital compared with the demand for produce, while the soil is still rich: and practically they are very rarely so high as the actual state of the land combined with the smallest possible quantity of food awarded to the labourer would admit of. (1836, p. 297)

Here Malthus contrasts the *actual general* rate of his 'regulating principle' with the higher maximum rate of the 'limiting principle', thus contradicting Hollander's interpretation of the former principle as concerning the *adjustment* of the manufacturing to the agricultural rate. Hollander comments as follows:

It is not absolutely clear from this statement whether or not the impact on the profit rate of excess supply is limited to manufactures. It seems to be, but the question arises of how the agricultural rate then comes into line, a matter left in abeyance. (p. 206)

What in fact is not clear here is Hollander's passage and how Hollander may find Malthus's passage unclear. It is indeed difficult to see why

---

[20] It is curious to note that a few lines below those in which that interpretation of Malthus's concept of 'regulation' of profits is advanced, the correct content of that concept is in fact given without, however, using the expression 'regulation'. A quotation from Malthus is there introduced in which there is said to be an

emphasis on the priority of the agricultural profit rate as a *limiting* determinant... allowing scope for the operation of other forces – excess supply is specified in the 1836 version – keeping the *general return* below its potential. (pp. 205–6; our italics)

[21] Cf. e.g. Malthus's passage quoted in footnote 24 below.

[22] See the following footnote for further instances.

Malthus should confine to manufactures the impact of the 'abundant supply of capital' referred to: he had repeatedly stated in the *Principles*, not to mention the *Measure of Value*, that, given the fertility of the marginal land, it is the 'state of demand and supply', i.e. the 'abundant supply of capital', that determines the *general* rate of profits, by affecting the money price of the product relative to the wage in all sectors, and therefore in agriculture no less than in manufactures. Does that not also answer the second of Hollander's perplexities, as to 'how the agricultural rate then comes into line'? It is all but 'left in abeyance'[23] by Malthus that the agricultural rate, like all other rates, will 'come into line' through the money price of its product (corn) changing relative to the money wage rate.[24]

15. However, as we said above (Paragraph 1), it is Hollander himself who in his last page[h] (and earlier in footnote 14) clears some of the difficulties which his paper has raised for its readers. He does so by in fact granting that, in Malthus, there is no determining role for agricultural profits with respect to the economy in its actual, ordinary conditions. Thus, in Section

---

[23] Another passage in which Hollander struggles because of his interpretation of what Malthus means by 'regulation of profits' occurs on the following two pages. Malthus had written that 'powerful and certain' as the fall of the profit rate down to its final stationary level is, because of the rise in the quantity of labour necessary to produce the same food, 'yet [it] is so frequently counteracted and overcome by other causes as to leave very great play to the principle of the competition of capitals' (1820, pp. 274–5). At this, Hollander comments:

> Malthus neglects to specify whether increasing competition of capitals applies solely to manufactures, although that certainly seems to be his position. (p. 207)

What follows indicates that this time, for Hollander, it is again a question of the rate in manufactures 'coming into line' with that in agriculture as for the Malthus passage he reported earlier (see our Paragraph 13), rather than the opposite process allegedly 'left in abeyance' by Malthus and hinted at in the passage reported above. Clearly here, however, just as in both those other passages, Malthus refers to a play on 'the profit rate', i.e. on the *general* rate of profits, applying to agriculture as well as to manufactures. Still another passage by Malthus on 'the law of demand and supply' of the 'regulating principle' is similarly interpreted by Hollander as referring only to manufacturing rates 'coming into line' with the agricultural one, cf. a few lines below the quotation we gave in Section 13.

[24] Cf. e.g. Section 9 above on the table in (1823, p. 38), and the passages by Malthus in the preceding footnote. Indeed Malthus makes quite clear how the 'agricultural rate then comes into line' and he does so on the very same page from which Hollander has taken his quotation:

> Though the value of a given quantity of [corn estimated in terms of labour commanded] rises on account of the increased quantity of labour required to obtain it, yet the value of the diminished produce of the *same* quantity of labour [...] falls from the state of demand and supply. (Malthus, 1836, p. 297; italics in the original)

[h] Cf. footnote f above.

6, we finally find fully spelled out the distinction between Malthus's 'limiting' and 'regulating' principles – between, that is, what Hollander chooses to call the regulating and the limiting 'determinants'. We there find the admission that with respect to the former 'determinants', Malthus had continued to hold his original 1814 position for which:

the profits of the farmer no more *regulate* the profits of other trades, than the profits of other trades regulate the profits of the farmer. (p. 220; our italics)

We find there, to begin with, a recognition that in Malthus, 'regulating' profits means determination of the *general* rate of profit, including the agricultural rate, no less than the manufacturing one, and *not* the adjustment of the latter to an independently determined agricultural rate, as Hollander had apparently argued some pages before. And with the determining role of agricultural profits, 'the priority of distribution over pricing' (Section 1, p. 198) is also admitted there to apply only in the 'limiting case' (p. 211n).

Did Hollander, then, when he set out to 'demonstrate' the 'determining role of agricultural profits' and the 'priority of distribution over pricing' in Malthus (footnote 2 of his paper), only mean them to refer to what we are now told, with an unusual expression, to be the 'limiting determinants' as opposed to the 'regulating' ones? It would certainly have saved the reader some headaches to know from the beginning that, in the body of his article, by 'determination' Hollander always meant such 'limiting determination' and not what is usually understood by that word. Above all, that would have saved Hollander some unnecessary *tours de force* when he argued what it now follows is not correct, namely that Malthus's reference to the 'state of demand and supply' as the determinant of the profit rate in his *Measure of Value* was inconsistent with his Table there (see our quotations from Hollander at p. 235, fn. 17), or that by 'regulation' of the profit rate Malthus meant bringing the manufacturing rate into line with the agricultural one (see the quotations in Paragraphs 13–14 and footnote 23). Indeed, initial clarity in distinguishing between the two kinds of 'determinants' would also have saved Hollander from trying to find the 'limiting determinants' in the Table in *The Measure of Value*, (e.g. his Section 4; or 1979, p. 722) where, unlike in the '*Principles*', they are just not to be found.

16. However, once it is made clear that the agricultural rate of profits plays a role only as a 'limiting determinant', a second thing becomes clear: it is that the corn calculations which emerge in Malthus 1820, 1823, 1836, far from expressing a positive 'adherence' to a determining role of agricultural profits (Hollander, p. 198 above), are used, on the contrary, just in order *to deny* that Ricardian role under all ordinary conditions. This is the case in *The Measure of Value* (1823, p. 43), where the corn calculations of the *table* are meant to demonstrate that it is *not* the position of the least fertile land but 'demand and supply' that determine the general rate of profits, and *hence* the agricultural rate. This is no less clearly the case in both editions of the *Principles* where, as we noted (Paragraph 6), the limiting rate of profits is introduced just in order to show that it cannot be the ruling rate except in a future, distant stationary state.

That the purpose of Malthus' corn calculations was to *refute* Ricardo's theory of the independence of the profit rate from demand and supply, which Malthus identifies with Ricardo's early notion of the determining role of agricultural profits, is, in fact, quite clearly stated by Malthus himself in the following passage (also quoted by Hollander in Section 3 (pp. 206–7), where, however, he only comments on the 'considerable historiographical importance' of it):

The reader will be aware that *the reason why, in treating of profits, I dwell so much on agricultural profits* is, that . . . the argument against the usual view which has been taken of profits, as depending principally upon the competition of capital, is founded upon the physical necessity of a fall of profits in agriculture, arising from the increasing quantity of labour required to procure the same food; . . . *But I wish to shew*, theoretically as well as practically, that powerful and certain as this cause is, in its final operation . . . yet in the actual state of the world, its natural progress is . . . extremely slow . . . so that *at any one period of some length in the last or following hundred years*, it might most safely be asserted that profits had depended or would depend very much upon the causes which had occasioned a comparatively scanty or abundant supply of capital than upon the natural fertility of the land last taken into cultivation. (1820, pp. 316–17, our italics)

Clearly it was Ricardo who had first developed the 'argument against the usual view which has been taken of profits'. What better statement, then, of the fact that the reasoning founded on 'agricultural profits', i.e. on corn ('food') calculations, far from reflecting a 'Malthusian conception', as Hollander wishes to demonstrate, is instead Ricardo's own argument, which Malthus is in fact trying to refute by construing it as inapplicable to 'the actual state of the world . . . at any period of some length in the last, or following hundred years'? Above all, what better statement that such a Ricardo argument had been founded on a 'physical' link between wages and profits – a link, that is, between *corn* ('food') wages and corn produce – and not, as Hollander holds, on a value link between money prices of products and money wages?

Postscript

Three of the changes occurring between the draft of Hollander's paper to which I incorrectly referred my comment, and the published version of it are relevant for us here. We shall consider them under points A, B and C below.

A. The first change consists of the insertion in Section 1 (cf. p. 198) of the following lines, between the words '... applies in fact to T. R. Malthus' and ' – the mature Malthus...':

Faccarello has observed: 'If indeed such a corn–profit model was really formulated, it took shape, for a brief period of time, in Malthus's fancy' (1982, p. 134), an allusion to the possible attribution *to Ricardo* by Malthus of such a model in the early correspondence. I shall demonstrate, rather, a positive adherence by Malthus [– the mature Malthus...].

Two points are made explicit in these lines, which I had instead to infer from Hollander's earlier publications in Paragraphs 3 and 4 of my Comment. The first is the view, to which Hollander subscribes in those lines, according to which the idea of the agricultural rate of profits as a 'material rate' between corn quantities, which Malthus attributes to Ricardo in the letter of 5 August, would instead have taken shape 'in Malthus's fancy'. The second point regards the evolution of Malthus's thought for which his opposition in 1814–15 to the notion of the determining role of agricultural profits advanced by Ricardo, would, by 1820, have given way to a 'positive adherence' to it.

In the face of these explicit statements, my argument in Paragraphs 3 and 4 is no longer needed for its upshot (which is confirmed by those lines). However, it provides a necessary background to Hollander's present position with regard, especially, to the second of the two points above, which in my opinion still needs some preliminary clarification.

On the other hand, since Hollander does not refer to them, we do not need to enter here into the detailed arguments by which Faccarello arrives at his conclusions about Malthus's letter of 5 August 1814. It can, however, be mentioned that the main argument appears to be a passage of Ricardo's *Essay* (1815) where the classical author argues the *constancy* of manufacturing prices in the face of a change of the corn price and the money wage (Faccarello, 1982, p. 131). Now, that passage and similar ones in the *Essay* are well known to mark an important *change* in the position of Ricardo. The previous position, documented in 1810–11 and up to 25 July 1814 (1951–73, Vol. VI, p. 114; cf. also Paragraph 3 footnote 1 in my Comment), subscribed instead to the generally accepted view about manufacturing prices *rising* with the corn price and the wage. That 1815 quotation by Faccarello is therefore of little help in interpreting the Ricardo of July 1814, to whom Malthus was writing on 5 August.

B. A second relevant change in the published version is the insertion of the present last page of Section 3, starting from '... and it probably reflects the notion that...' (cf. p. 207). An explanation, missing before, is there given by Hollander for his surprising interpretation of some of Malthus's passages on the 'regulation of profits' as referring to an adjustment of the profit rate in manufactures to an independently given agricultural rate (Paragraphs 13 and 14 of my comment). That explanation, though more detailed, follows the lines I had quoted at p. 237, fn. 19, from Hollander (1997).

What should first of all be made clear on this point is that there is no question in Malthus of any sort of 'Say's law' (Hollander, Section 3) sheltering the agricultural profit rate from the influence of what we would today call aggregate demand and supply. If the numerous references given in my Comment (Paragraphs 7 and 9) were not to suffice, the point may be clinched by a very explicit passage by Malthus:

> It is consistent with theory... that high corn wages... should frequently occur with a very slack demand for labour... when the value of the whole produce falls from excess of supply compared with the demand. (1823, p. 55, referred to in Paragraph 5 above)

where we unambiguously have a low labour commanded price of corn (i.e. a high corn wage) and hence an agricultural profit rate which is low because of an excess in the supply of corn.

The fact is that the passage from Malthus (1815) quoted by Hollander at p. 208 above, and the similar passages in (1820, 1836), occur in connection with the *rent of land*. Malthus attempts there to argue that rent arises, not from a 'monopoly', but from the fertility of the land which 'God has bestowed on man' (1815, p. 16). However, he seems troubled by the objection that the comparative abundance of necessaries brought about by such a 'gift of God' should, like the abundance generated by, say, a machine, result in a fall of prices down to their costs in wages and profits, and not into a *price exceeding costs*, as is the case for those fertile lands. Malthus then seems somehow restrained from noting that the only costs relevant for corn prices are those incurred on the least fertile land, where the price does in fact adjust to such costs. He attempts instead to justify *that excess price* by a demand for corn generated by that very corn output through increases in population. Whether or not any sense might be made of such an argument, one thing is clear: it is that Malthus does *not* use it in connection with agricultural *profits*, which are seen instead as part of the *costs* which the price of corn exceeds (e.g. 1815, p. 17), and are therefore determined by demand and supply in the way we saw (cf. e.g. Malthus, 1815, p. 17).

C. The third and last change we need to note in the published version is the addition of the 'Concluding note' (Section 7). Hollander's belief in the support he can derive from Cazenove (1822) for his interpretation of Malthus seems, however, to suffer from a shortcoming similar to that of his interpretation of Malthus's *Principles*: a failure, that is, to distinguish clearly between a limiting rate of profits and the ruling one.

In fact, in (1822) Cazenove draws a distinction between the 'real' or 'actual' rate of profits, and a 'natural' rate – marking an upper limit to the former (ibid., p. 31)[25] – which is parallel to the distinction drawn by Malthus between 'regulating' and 'limiting' principles of profits. It is indeed the 'natural rate' only which Cazenove sees as determined in agriculture (ibid., p. 29). The 'real' or 'actual' rate – the rate ruling in the economy, including agriculture – is determined instead by demand and supply, as in Malthus: namely, in Cazenove's words, by the 'exchangeable value' of the 'mass of the commodities' and therefore by 'the proportion which the supply of them bears to the demand of those who are willing to pay the whole costs of their production' (ibid., p. 30). The Malthusian Cazenove thus sees the 'real' general rate of profits as determined by demand and supply, and not by the agricultural 'natural' rate.

References

Blaug, M. (1985). 'What Ricardo said and what Ricardo meant', in G. Carvale (ed.), *The Legacy of Ricardo*, Oxford: Blackwell.

Casarosa, C. (1978). 'A new formulation of the Ricardian system', in *Oxford Economic Papers*, March, pp. 38–63.

Cazenove, J. (1822). *Considerations on the Accumulation of Capital and its Effects on Exchangeable Value*, London: J. H. Richardson.

De Vivo, G. (1985). 'Robert Torrens and Ricardo's corn-ratio theory of profits', *Cambridge Journal of Economics*, 9, pp. 89–92.

De Vivo, G. (1996). 'Ricardo, Torrens and Sraffa: a summing up': reply to Hollander, *Cambridge Journal of Economics*, 20, pp. 387–92.

Eatwell, J. (1975). 'The interpretation of Ricardo's "Essays on Profits"', *Economica*, May.

Faccarello, G. (1982). 'Sraffa versus Ricardo: the historical irrelevance of the "corn–profit" model', *Economy and Society*, 11, May, pp. 122–37.

Garegnani, P. (1982). 'On Hollander's interpretation of Ricardo's early theory of profits', *Cambridge Journal of Economics*, 6, pp. 65–77.

---

[25] Thanks are due to Professor Hollander for kindly providing me with a copy of the relevant pages of Cazenove's 1822 booklet.

Garegnani, P. (1983). 'Ricardo's early theory of profits and its "rational foundation": a reply to Professor Hollander', *Cambridge Journal of Economics*, 7, pp. 175–8.

Hicks, J. R. and Hollander, S. (1977). 'Mr. Ricardo and the moderns', *Quarterly Journal of Economics*, 9, pp. 351–69.

Hollander, S. (1973). *The Economics of Adam Smith*, London: Heinemann.

Hollander, S. (1979). *The Economics of David Ricardo*, Toronto: Heinemann.

Hollander, S. (1987). *Classical Economics*, Oxford: Blackwell.

Hollander, S. (1997). *The Economics of Thomas Robert Malthus*, Toronto: Toronto University Press.

Hutchison, T. W. (1952). 'Some questions about Ricardo', *Economica*, pp. 415–32.

Langer, G. F. (1982). 'Further evidence for Sraffa's interpretation of Ricardo's early theory of profits', *Cambridge Journal of Economics*, 6, pp. 397–400.

Levy, D. (1976). 'Ricardo and the Iron Law: a correction of the record', *History of Political Economy*.

Malthus, T. R. (1820). *Principles of Political Economy*, London: John Murray.

Malthus, T. R. (1823). *The Measure of Value Stated and Illustrated*, London: John Murray.

Malthus, T. R. (1836). *Principles of Political Economy*, 2nd edition, London: William Pickering.

O'Brien, D. P. (1981). 'Ricardian economics and the economics of Ricardo', *Oxford Economic Papers*, November.

Peach, T. (1984). 'David Ricardo's early treatment of profitability', *Economic Journal*, 9, pp. 733–51.

Porta, P. (1986). 'Understanding the significance of Piero Sraffa's standard commodity: a note on the Marxian notion of surplus value', *History of Political Economy*, Fall, pp. 443–54.

Prendergast, R. (1986). 'Malthus' discussion of the corn ratio theory of profits', *Cambridge Journal of Economics*, 10, pp. 187–9.

Rankin, S. (1984). 'The wage basket in Ricardo's *Essay on Profits*', *Cambridge Journal of Economics*, 8, pp. 83–6.

Ricardo, D. ([1815] 1951). 'An essay on the influence of a low price of corn on the profits of stock'; reprinted in Ricardo (1951–73), vol. IV, pp. 9–41.

Ricardo, D. (1951–73). *The Works and Correspondence of David Ricardo*, edited by P. Sraffa with the collaboration of M. D. Dobb, vols. I–XI, Cambridge: Cambridge University Press.

Robbins, L. (1958). *Robert Torrens and the Evolution of Classical Economics*, London: Macmillan.

Samuelson, P. A. (1978). 'The canonical classical model of political economy', *Journal of Economic Literature*, 16, pp. 1415–34.

Sraffa, P. (1960). *Production of Commodities by Means of Commodities: Prelude to a Critique of Economic Theory*, Cambridge: Cambridge University Press.

Stigler, G. J. (1952). 'The Ricardian theory of value and distribution', *Journal of Political Economy*, 60, June.

Stigler, G. J. (1953). 'Sraffa's Ricardo', *American Economic Review*, September, pp. 302–26.

Stigler, G. J. (1981). Review of Hollander's *The Economics of Ricardo*, in *Journal of Economic Literature*, No. 3, pp. 100–2.

Rejoinder to Professor Garegnani's Comment*

Samuel Hollander

1. Professor Garegnani says of my thesis that Sraffa's interpretation of the early Ricardo applies in fact to Malthus, that it 'seems to fizzle out at the end of the paper' (Garegnani, Section 1). There 'Hollander admits that as for the "regulating determinants" of profits – i.e. for the actual determination of profits in any economy which is not in a final stationary state – Malthus maintained all along his "original negative position" that "the profits of the farmer no more regulate the profits of other trades, than the profits of other trades regulate the profit of the farmer"'. Now if indeed my claim fizzles out, it does so not at the end of the paper, but much earlier, where I introduce what Garegnani is pleased to call my 'admission': 'Despite all this, the general profit rate was only "*limited*", not *governed* by, agricultural productivity conditions, the latter imposing a maximum which the general profit rate can never exceed' (Hollander, Section 3). Garegnani (Section 13) notes this statement, but nonetheless insists that my paper 'gives no real account of Malthus's distinction between "limiting" and "regulating" principles until its last page' (also Section 15). I find his complaint unjustified. The 'regulating' principle is distinctly elaborated by me in detail in Section 3 in the discussion of Malthus on 'Profits as affected by the causes practically in operation'. In short, I make it absolutely clear that my 'Sraffian' claim for Malthus refers to the 'limiting' rate; it is not a matter of belated 'admission' but a simple statement of fact.[1]

2. Professor Garegnani, we have seen, takes for granted that the 'limiting' principle is effective only 'in a final stationary state'. This is misleading.

---

* That Professor Garegnani commented originally on an early (1993) draft of my paper is no fault of mine. The final draft, as printed above, had been in the hands of the editor since February 1996 whereas Garegnani's original comments were sent to me only in May 1998 and a second version, printed above, in August 1998. [After Professor Hollander had drawn Professor Garegnani's attention to the fact that he had commented on an early draft of the paper, the latter contacted me asking what was to be done. In the interest of avoiding any further delay of the publication of the book, I asked Professor Garegnani to take care of the necessary change in the way he did. H.D.K.]

[1] Garegnani will not be able to fault my *Economics of Thomas Robert Malthus* where I head the relevant section: 'The Determining Role of the Agricultural Profit Rate: A "Corn Profit" Model' (1997, p. 446).

For Malthus, the limiting principle defines the maximum general profit rate '*at all times, and on every supposition*' (see Hollander, p. 205; emphasis added). The 1836 expansion of this point is striking: 'the great limiting principle' which 'determines the *range* of possible profits; how high they may by possibility rise, and how low they may by possibility fall . . . *is indeed always ready to act*' (emphasis added)', and – this in both versions 'if not overcome by countervailing tendencies' – 'will necessarily lower the rate of profits on the land, from which it will extend to *all other departments of industry*' (emphasis added). Thus while it is only in the final stationary state that the 'limiting' rate will *necessarily* dictate the actual rate, because in that state the maximum and minimum profit rates coincide, nonetheless throughout the course of accumulation and population growth those limits will be approaching each other, dictating an ever-narrower range over which there is scope for other forces to play a part, so that the agricultural sector must be actively playing out its role; furthermore, if – as is conceivable – those 'regulating' forces should happen to be either inactive or cancel out, the 'limiting' force is 'always ready to act'. That the declining agricultural rate is in fact at play is clear from the explicit statement that '[t]his continued accumulation of capital and increasing difficulty of procuring subsistence would unquestionably lower profits' (1820, p. 328; 1836, p. 293, cited in Hollander, Section 3).

It is easy then to appreciate why Malthus bothers to set out in his chapter on Profits by expounding the entire growth path assuming away all 'countervailing tendencies', proceeding, that is to say, *as if* the limiting (maximum) rate was the effective rate. I therefore attribute to Malthus's agricultural sector a more pervasive significance than does Garegnani, who reads the term 'final operation' (Garegnani, Section 16) too narrowly.

3. I turn now to what appears to be an error on Garegnani's part relating to the *substance* of the limiting principle. Garegnani believes that the maximum achievable profit rate is given by the agricultural rate pertaining when the corn wage is at its *minimum* possible level: 'the assumption of a *constant* (and minimum) corn wage, underl[ies] as we saw (Paragraph 6) the "limiting principle"', and is 'the unfulfilled basic condition which, in Malthus's view, prevents the rate of profits of the "limiting principle" from constituting the normal rate of the "regulating principle"' (Garegnani, Section 12). Here (as in his 'Paragraph' 6) Garegnani confuses *fluctuations* in the corn wage given agricultural productivity, with the *downward secular trend* in the corn wage which proceeds simultaneously with the downward trend of the profit rate until the respective minima of the returns to the variable factors are attained. This latter feature is the essence of the canonical classical growth model

(Samuelson, 1978; Hollander, 1998). Several of Garegnani's complaints simply reflect this error. In particular, he finds it 'surprising' that I refer to Malthus's provisional assumption of a constant (and minimum) corn wage in the secular case 'as nothing but an expository preliminary' (Garegnani, Section 12), whereas this statement reflects Malthus's position *precisely*, as will be confirmed in the next paragraph.

To dispel a pervasive misreading – for Garegnani is in quite good company – I must carry the reader patiently through Malthus's text on profits: Section I in the 1820 edition, 'Of Profits as Affected by the Increasing Difficulty of Procuring the Means of Subsistence', corresponding to Section II in the 1836 edition, 'Of the Limiting Principle of Profits'. Note first that Malthus sets off by supposing that 'the wages [1836: the corn wages] of the individual labourer were always the same' (1820, p. 295; 1836, p. 271), but a few paragraphs later, although always in the *same* section dealing with the 'Limiting Principle', he then *abandons the 'supposition'*:

But a moment's consideration will shew us, that the supposition here made of a constant uniformity in the real [1836: corn] wages of labour is not only contrary to the actual state of things, but involves a contradiction. (1820, p. 297; 1836, p. 272)

For the (corn wage) is necessarily a variable, governed by a decelerating (common) growth rate of capital and population – a case of dynamic equilibrium:

We may however, if we please, suppose a uniform progress of capital and population, by which is not meant in the present case the same *rate* of progress permanently, which is impossible; but a uniform progress towards the greatest practicable amount, without temporary accelerations or retardations. And before we proceed to the actual state of things, it may be curious to consider in what manner profits would be affected under these circumstances. (1820, pp. 297–8; 1836, p. 273)

Malthus then clarifies that, under the supposed conditions, the secular corn wage necessarily falls, but at a shallower rate than the marginal product, so that the profit rate tends downwards simultaneously with the corn wage:

if poorer lands which required more labour were successively taken into cultivation, it would not be possible for the corn wages of each individual labourer to be diminished in proportion to the diminished produce; a greater proportion [1836: *proportion*] of the whole would necessarily go to [1836: to pay] labour; and the rate of profits would continue regularly falling till the accumulation of capital had ceased.

Such would be the necessary course of profits and wages in the progressive accumulation of capital, as applied to the progressive cultivation of new and less fertile land, or the further improvement of what had before been cultivated; and on the supposition here made, the rates both of profits and of real wages would be highest at first, and would regularly and gradually diminish together, till they both came to a stand at the same period, and the demand for an increase of produce ceased to be effective. (1820, p. 299; 1836, p. 274)

Now it is only in the *following* Section (II in 1820: 'Of Profits as Affected by the Proportion which Capital bears to Labour'; III in 1836: 'Of the Regulating Principle of Profits') that Malthus takes up the matter of *wage fluctuations*:

The second main cause which, by increasing the amount of advances, influences profits, is the proportion which capital bears to labour.

This is obviously a cause which alone is capable of producing the very greatest effects; and on the supposition of adequate variations taking place between the supplies of capital and the supplies of labour, all the same effects might be produced on profits as by the operation of the first cause, and in a much shorter time. (1820, p. 301)

The second cause which affects profits, is the varying value of the produce of the same quantity of labour on the same value of capital, determined by the state of the demand and supply. This may be called the regulating principle of profits, as within the extreme limits prescribed by the state of the land, all the variations of profits, whether temporary or durable are regulated by it.

Such variations in the value of produce are occasioned principally by the abundance or scantiness of capital, including the funds for the maintenance of labour, as compared with the labour which it employs.

This is obviously a cause which, by awarding a greater or a smaller *proportion* of the produce to the labourer, must have a powerful influence on profits; and if considerable variations were to take place in the supplies of capital and produce and the supplies of labour, in a rich and unexhausted soil, the same effects might be produced on profits as by the operation of the first cause, and in a much shorter time. (1836, p. 276)

In my original statement (Hollander, Section 2) I gave page references to some of these texts and reproduced some extracts. Professor Garegnani has not yet absorbed their import, for which reason I have considered it necessary to expand the citations.

4. Professor Garegnani represents Malthus as treating the rate of profit as *independent* variable – governed by 'the state of supply and demand' – and the real wage as *dependent* variable:

The main lines of Malthus's argument on profits in his *Principles* (1820, 1836) and *Measure of Value* (1823) are comparatively simple. Malthus accepts Ricardo's 'basic theorem on distribution' concerning the determinacy of the rate of profits once the real wage and the margin of cultivation on the land are given. However, he generally replaces the wage with the rate of profits in the role of the independent variable and therefore takes the 'theorem' in the following form: once the rate of profits is given, the real wage rate (e.g. the corn wage) is also determined, and the two move in opposite directions. As a result Malthus's explanation of profits in terms of 'the state of the supply and the demand' comes to be based on the *variability* of the real wage, indirectly determined by such a 'state'. In this way, while continuing to use Smith's phrases, Malthus in fact departs from Smith, who had failed to see with any clarity the necessary relation binding the two key distributive variables. (Garegnani, Section 6)

That 'demand and supply' or 'the principle of competition' determine the profit rate, which rate then governs the corn wage, is repeated by Garegnani in his Sections 7 and 8. In his Section 8 he says of the corn wage rate that it 'depends on prices, and can accordingly be seen to be determined by "demand and supply" *together with* the general profit rate' (my emphasis), but this presumably is a slip.

I do sympathize with Professor Garegnani, who struggles to make sense of Malthus – not only of me! – particularly the statement in the second edition of the 'regulating principle' that the profit rate 'will be determined ... by what Malthus describes as "the state of the supply and the demand" ... or "the principle of competition"' (Garegnani, Section 7). His repeated 'seems' and 'appears' in this context are indicative of his uncertainty, yet he concludes by positively *identifying* the position that the profit rate is determined (1) by 'the abundance or scantiness of capital including the funds for the maintenance of labour, as compared with the labour which it employs', and (2) by 'the abundance or scarcity of capital and produce compared with the demand', despite an apparent realization that by (2), Malthus intended the 'aggregate demand–aggregate supply' issue. For my part, I think it best to keep separate the effects on profits due to real-wage changes brought about in the labour market from those due to real-wage changes brought about by way of alteration in final commodity prices. That it is misleading entirely to efface the former in any exposition of Malthus's full position, as Garegnani does, will become clear in what follows.

As we have indicated, Professor Garegnani seeks to remove Malthus as far as possible from a position where the profit rate is *determined* by the corn wage of labour – a first stage in any structure involving an agricultural rate of profit, and though he has interesting things to say (in principle) on a *determining* role of agricultural profits *versus* a corn-calculation *measure* of the general profit rate (Garegnani, Sections 5 and 8), he is unconvincing in his specific applications to Malthus's *Measure of*

Value. For he maintains not only that for Malthus the corn wage is 'determin*ed* by prices and rate of profits, and is not a determin*ant* of them, as Hollander would need, and as a first reading of the table [of the *Measure of Value*] might suggest', but also that 'Malthus makes that quite clear by the caption he puts on the column giving the several alternative corn wages [:] "Yearly corn wages... *determined by the Demand and Supply*"' (Section 9). The problem is that Garegnani takes the term 'demand and supply' to apply to the *product* market, whereas it evidently applies to the *labour* market. Consider, for example, Malthus's exercise involving the effect on the profit rate of an increase in the corn wage (given productivity) due to a reduction in the national labour supply: 'If the increased reward of the labourer takes place without an increase of produce, this cannot happen without a fall of profits, as it is a self evident truth, that given the quantity of the produce to be divided between labour and profits, the greater the portion of it which goes to labour the less will be left for profits' (1823; 1986, Vol. 7, p. 197). Conversely, '[i]f instead of labourers being sent out of the country, labourers were imported... [a] smaller quantity of produce would be awarded to the labourer and profits would rise'. There is no doubt that the labour market alone is at play.

I do not deny that Malthus in his *Measure of Value* sometimes brings in demand and supply for products, *but even here the effect of any change in the corn price on the profit rate works via the corn wage.* This is crystal clear in the discussion of the quantitative significance of a varying corn wage relative to diminishing returns as determinants of the profit rate:

A fourth result shown in the Table is, that the value of the corn obtained by ten men depends mainly upon the rate of profits, *which again depends mainly upon the demand and supply of corn compared with labour [i.e., the corn wage].* If corn be in such demand, that notwithstanding the fertility of the soil, a small quantity of it comparatively will purchase the labour required, profits will be very high, and the value of the produce will greatly exceed the constant value of the wages of the labour advanced; but if the supply of corn be so great, compared with labour, that a large quantity of it is required to purchase the given quantity of labour, profits will be low, and the excess of the value of the produce above the constant value of the advances in wages will be considerable (1823; 1986, Vol. 7, p. 202; emphasis added).

5. Professor Garegnani, we have seen, makes the unjustified complaint that I do not sufficiently indicate that my attribution to Malthus of a corn–profit model applied to the *limiting* not the *regulating* case. For my part – and this is *my* main complaint – I find that Garegnani has not taken seriously what Malthus has to say about that limiting case. He

simply does not deal with my citations from 1820, p. 300, and 1836, p. 275 (Hollander, Section 3), *which have the manufacturing rate coming into line with the agricultural rate by way of changes in the terms of trade between manufactures on the one hand, and corn and labour on the other.* He would also do well to consider carefully the full text of 1820, pp. 316–17, referring to 'the physical necessity of a fall in profits, arising from the increased quantity of labour necessary to produce the same food', rather than rely on his reduced-form version given in his Section 16. The omitted passage – he will find it conveniently in Hollander, pp. 206–7 – reads thus:

it is certain that if the profits on land permanently fall from this or any other cause, profits in manufactures and commerce must fall too as it is an acknowledged truth that in an improved and civilized country, the profits of stock ... must be nearly on a level in all the different branches of industry to which capital is applied.

Now I am fully disposed to allow the truth of this argument as applied to agricultural profits, and also its natural consequences on all profits. This truth is indeed necessarily involved both in the *Principles of Population* and in the theory of rent which I published separately in 1815 (1820, pp. 316–7).[2]

The task I set myself was to understand *precisely how the manufacturing rate is supposed to come into line with the posited agricultural rate.* Garegnani should do the same.

6. Professor Garegnani's neglect of the one-way relation of the 'limiting case' – which, I repeat, is not restricted to the stationary-state case (see above, Paragraph 2) – is responsible for his complaint that, at one key juncture, I use the word 'regulation' illegitimately (Garegnani, Section 13). The passage in question from the *Principles* (1820, p. 328; 1836, pp. 293–4) – as I point out (Hollander, Section 3) – relates specifically to the implications of growth subject to diminishing returns where all problems relating to aggregate demand are set aside; it appears in the final section of the chapter on Profits devoted to the Ricardian theory, and is designed to show that using Malthus's *measure of value* – a commodity produced by 'unassisted labour' and thus dictating an *invariable* money wage – all of Ricardo's results for the profit rate nonetheless follow. The analysis starts with the declaration: 'This continued accumulation of capital and increasing difficulty of procuring subsistence would unquestionably lower profits' – note, in passing, that there is no question here of a stationary-state position – and it is this lower profit rate that Malthus *assumes* in

---

[2] I register a mild protest at Garegnani's remark that I only comment that this passage has 'considerable historiographical importance' (Section 16). In fact I proceed to a full paraphrase of the passage.

analysing the effect on prices in the manufacturing sectors. 'Regulation' can then only mean 'brought into line with' the agricultural profit rate. My case may be confirmed by considering closely the concluding sentence of the full passage: 'It is obvious that, in this case [i.e. given the money wage rate], profits can only be regulated by the principle of competition, or of demand and supply, which would determine the degree in which the prices of commodities would fall; and their prices, compared with the uniform price of labour, would mainly regulate [1836: would regulate] the rate of profits'. If we keep in mind that corn, as Malthus indicates earlier in the passage, 'would rise in money price', it is clear that the allusion to 'demand and supply lowering prices' must refer specifically to non-agricultural products, with the term 'regulation' used in the sense I originally maintained.

7. I turn to Professor Garegnani's Supplementary Point A. That Malthus, in 1814–15, did *not himself subscribe to a corn–profit model* is not in dispute; I express no doubt about that in any of my formulations and do not understand the heavy weather made of all this by Garegnani. I am pleased, though, that my reference to Faccarello has cleared the air for him. Did Malthus attribute such a model *to Ricardo* in that early correspondence? He *may* have done, although the evidence is sketchy; but if he did it was (as Faccarello puts it) a matter of his 'fancy', since we believe that such a model is not to be found in Ricardo.

I notice at this point Professor Garegnani's query earlier in his text: 'Where, then, did Malthus get that "corn model" from?' (Garegnani, Section 3). He provides an answer on my behalf: 'Hollander's answer can only be that it was a piece of Malthus's own mind, suggested by Ricardo's July [1814] "corn calculation", and used to reject an argument which *Malthus thought* underlay that "calculation", whether or not it in fact did so'. I accept that Malthus's corn model may simply have been his own invention, but I am not at all convinced that in preparing his *Principles* and thereafter he had the 1814 correspondence laid out before him; after all, he did not have access to Sraffa's splendid edition of the *Works and Correspondence of David Ricardo*. Malthus's odyssey from 1814/15 to 1820 is recorded in Hollander, 1997, Part I; it is far too complex a story to relate here.

Returning to Point A, I see that Garegnani alludes to 'the notion of the determining role of agricultural profits advanced by Ricardo' as if this were no longer a matter in dispute. A nice debating ploy. Let me then take this opportunity to direct readers' attention to Ricardo's *own* response to Malthus's objection of 1814 that since 'in no case of production, is the produce exactly of the same nature as the capital advanced', a 'material rate of produce, independent of demand, and of the abundance or scarcity of capital' was ruled out. His response insists that societies *do* 'estimate their profits by the material production', in contrast with individuals *who are subject to money illusion*:

Individuals do not estimate their profits by the material production, but nations invariably do. If we had precisely the same amount of commodities of all descriptions in the year 1815 that we now have in 1814 as a nation we should be no richer, but if money had sunk in value they would be represented by a greater quantity of money, and individuals would be apt to *think* themselves richer. (11 August 1814; Ricardo 1951–73, Vol. VI, p. 121)

It is conspicuous that Ricardo did not defend himself by insisting on the homogeneity of input and output, for in fact, by 'materiality' he intended the specific sense of the avoidance of money illusion. I trust that this comment will awaken some doubts in the mind of my critic regarding Ricardo's true position.

8. With respect to Point B, I would point out that my entire position is stated for the secular case only, not that involving short-run fluctuations in the corn price. Malthus obviously recognized corn-price reductions with excellent harvests so that Garegnani's citations are irrelevant to my position.

As for the secular case, I do not see how the downward trend in prices due to increasing 'competition of capitals' can apply to agriculture considering Malthus's proposition that aggregate demand and supply of food move in unison. Garegnani, of course, insists that such logic could not protect agricultural profits since they are determined by 'demand and supply' and depressed by competition of capitals as in any other sector, but there is more to Malthus than Garegnani allows. In what follows, I shall draw on Hollander, 1997, Chap. 8; also 1998, Chap. 18.

Malthus spelled out three 'causes' of rent:

The causes of the high price of raw produce [1820: the causes of the [1836: ordinary] excess of the price of raw produce above the costs of production] may be stated to be three. First, and mainly, that quality of the earth [1836: soil], by which it can be made to yield a greater portion [1836: quantity] of the necessaries of life than is required for the maintenance of the persons employed on the land. 2ndly, that quality peculiar to the necessaries of life, of being able [1820: when properly distributed] to create their own demand, or to raise up a number of demanders in proportion to the quantity of necessaries produced. And, 3rdly, the comparative scarcity of the most fertile land [1820: The comparative scarcity of fertile land, either natural or artificial]. (1815, p. 8; 1820, pp. 139–40; 1836, p. 140)

It was the first characteristic that generated a physical surplus – *the concern extends beyond rent proper* – without which, however scarce land might be, 'neither rent, nor any essential surplus produce of the land in the form of high profits [1820: and high wages] could have existed' (1815, p. 9; 1820, p. 140; 1836, p. 141). In the *Principles*, the emphasis is, in fact, formally placed on the *maximum rent potential* allowing that this surplus might take the form of high wages and profits:

On the other hand, it will be allowed, that in whatever way the produce of a given portion of land is divided, whether the whole is distributed to the labourers and capitalists, or a part is awarded to a landlord, the *power* of such land to yield rent is exactly proportioned to its [1836: natural or acquired] fertility, or to the general surplus which it can be made to produce beyond what is strictly necessary to support the labour and keep up the capital employed upon it. (1820, p. 140; 1836, p. 141)

However, this physical potential, the 'foundation or main cause of all rent', had to be supplemented since (in 1815) 'if the necessaries of life ... had not the property of creating an increase of demand proportioned to their increased quantity, such increased quantity would occasion a fall in their exchangeable value'. Here we see the sharpest contrast between the secular case and the short-run allowances for reductions in the corn price due to excellent harvests. Or again (in the *Principles*): 'this surplus, necessary and important as it is, would not be sure of possessing a value which would enable it to command a proportionate quantity of labour and other commodities, if it had not a power of raising up a population to consume it, and, by the articles produced in return, of creating an effective demand for it'.

Malthus's primary concern then was with the *total surplus* or excess of corn output over internal (agricultural) consumption, and its *value* counterpart – the first accounted for by a providential quality in land, the second by the population reaction to food which ensures appropriate demand. The third or land-scarcity condition accounts only for the surplus taking the specific form of rent narrowly defined. Were land free, 'the effects would show themselves in excessive profits and excessive wages' (1815, p. 11; 1820, p. 144; 1836, p. 143), *but those excessive returns too were to be explained (a) by the providential surplus of corn output over minimum internal consumption, and (b) by a corresponding value excess ensured by population growth in almost automatic response to any increase in the food supply*.

I stated my case in Section 3 with due circumspection. Even so, it seems to me far stronger than Professor Garegnani allows: pressure on the profit rate, not only rent proper, from falling prices due to increasing aggregate supplies seems to be ruled out by Say's law, in the sense that 'supply creates its own demand', applied to agriculture.[3]

9. Garegnani's Point C yields more than he apparently realizes. Since my entire case turns on the 'limiting rate', it is enough for my purposes that Cazenove sees the 'natural rate' – Malthus's 'limiting rate' – as determined in agriculture. *That he does, Garegnani explicitly allows*: 'It is indeed the "natural rate" only which Cazenove sees as determined in agriculture'. Not only does Cazenove state that the manufacturing profit rate 'is governed by the returns on agricultural capital', but we have seen too his position that the agricultural rate 'is measured by the proportion which the surplus produce of the worst soil bears to that which is employed in its production' – a physical ratio. For all that, I claim no more than possible 'tangential support' from Cazenove for my interpretation of Malthus (Hollander, Section 7).

10. What is the historiographical significance of all this? I read the Malthus texts that have engaged us as fitting into a sort of 'physiocratic-based' paradigm which Sraffa and neo-Ricardians generally identify rather with the origins of a Ricardo–Marx–Sraffa sequence. I am not surprised, therefore, at Professor Garegnani's strong objections, but I would *myself* insist that there is much more to Malthus than the corn–profit model, and that the weighting to be given to it remains *sub judice*. My point is that, nonetheless, it cannot simply be neglected.

Additional Rererences

Hollander, S. (1997). *The Economics of Thomas Robert Malthus*, Toronto: University of Toronto Press.

Hollander, S. (1998). 'The Canonical Classical Growth Model: Content, Adherence and Priority', *Journal of the History of Economic Thought*, **20**, pp. 253–77.

Samuelson, P. A. (1978). 'The Canonical Classical Model of Political Economy', *Journal of Economic Literature*, **16**, pp. 1415–34.

---

[3] It is Ricardo who originally coined Malthus's proposition this way: 'Mr. Malthus appears to me to be too much inclined to think that population is only increased by the previous provision of food – "that it is food that creates its own demand" – that it is by first providing food, that encouragement is given to marriage, instead of considering that the general progress of population is affected by the increase of capital, the consequent demand for labour, and the rise of wages; and that the production of food is but the effect of that demand' (Ricardo, 1951–73, Vol. I, pp. 405–6). In rejecting Malthus's position on corn pricing in his *Notes on Malthus*, Ricardo draws attention to the subjective dimension: 'The question is not about the number of demanders but of the sacrifices that they are willing to make to obtain the commodity demanded. On that must its value depend' (Vol. II, p. 114).

CHAPTER 6

The Hayek–Keynes–Sraffa controversy reconsidered

Heinz D. Kurz

1   Introduction

Piero Sraffa's debate with Friedrich August von Hayek subsequent to the publication of Hayek's *Prices and Production* in 1931 (Hayek, 1931b) has met with serious difficulties of understanding and was subject to vastly diverging interpretations. In a letter to Oskar Morgenstern, Frank Knight wrote: 'I wish he [Hayek] or someone would try to tell me in a plain grammatical sentence what the controversy between Sraffa and Hayek is about. I haven't been able to find anyone on this side who has the least idea' (quoted in Lawlor and Horn, 1992, p. 319, fn.). This view is echoed in the introduction to Vol. 9 of *The Collected Works of F. A. Hayek*, entitled *Contra Keynes and Cambridge*, in which the editor maintains that 'the Hayek–Sraffa duel lacks clarity' (Caldwell, 1995, p. 37).[1] Other

This paper draws partly on Kurz (1995). Earlier versions of the paper were given in a seminar at the University of Graz, at a meeting of the post-Keynesian study group at University College, London, during the 'European Summer School on Structural Change and Economic Dynamics', 8–14 July 1995, at Selwyn College, Cambridge, in a workshop at Malvern (UK) and in seminars at the École Normale Supérieure de Fontenay-Saint-Cloud, Paris, the University of Paris II – Panthéon, the University of Nice and the University of Rome III. I should like to thank the participants for useful discussions. I am particularly grateful to Christian Gehrke, Piero Garegnani, Edward J. Nell, Neri Salvadori and Ian Steedman for detailed comments and suggestions. It goes without saying that any remaining errors or misinterpretations are entirely my responsibility.

[1]   To this he adds the observation that *Prices of Production* 'is not an easy book to read', and then draws a parallel to Sraffa's *Production of Commodities by Means of Commodities* – in Caldwell's opinion 'a paradigmatic example of concisely obscure academic writing'. He continues to speculate that 'Sraffa's own treatise...is apt to produce in the reader of today a reaction not unlike that caused by reading *Prices and Production* without benefit of Hayek's earlier work' (ibid., p. 37 and p. 37, fn.).

interpreters opined that despite the heat that emanated from the controversy, the positions advocated by the adversaries, far from being the two sides of a debate, passed each other without touching, like ships in the night (cf. for example, McCloughry, 1982). Since Sraffa's critique of Hayek's monetary theory of overinvestment was formulated at an important stage of his investigations in the theory of value and distribution, it is perhaps useful to reconsider this debate. His contribution may be expected to reveal his understanding of traditional marginalist doctrines and bear witness to his remarkable analytical skills and impeccable logic. As will be seen, this expectation is indeed met.

The structure of the paper is as follows. Section 2 summarizes Hayek's argument in *Prices and Production*. Section 3 deals briefly with the controversy between Keynes and Hayek subsequent to the latter's publication of the first part of a critical review of Keynes' *Treatise on Money*. Section 4 turns to the debate between Sraffa and Hayek which brought, in the words of Ludwig Lachmann, 'the opening shots in a battle between two rival schools of economic thought' (Lachmann, 1986, p. 226). Section 5 outlines the subsequent debates, first in the 1930s and then in more recent times after Hayek had been awarded the Nobel prize in economics in 1974. Section 6 draws some conclusions.

2   Hayek's *Prices and Production*

When Hayek was invited to give four lectures at the London School of Economics during the session 1930–31, he devoted them to the theory of industrial fluctuations, placing special emphasis on the role of money and the banking system.[2] In 1927, Hayek had been appointed to the position of the Director of the Austrian Institute of Business Cycle Research (Österreichisches Institut für Konjunkturforschung). Most of his earlier work in economics was in the fields of monetary and business cycle theory. For example, in 1928 he had published an essay on 'Das intertemporale Gleichgewichtssystem der Preise und die Bewegungen des

---

[2] Lionel Robbins, the newly appointed and ambitious head of the Department of Economics, was keen to establish the LSE as a centre for economic theory. He was also looking for allies to support him in the recently established Economic Advisory Council to which Keynes had invited him, but in which he had assumed, to Keynes' disappointment, a dissenting minority position. In these conditions the rising Austrian economist seemed to be the perfect choice to challenge Keynes and his followers in Cambridge. As Joan Robinson (1978, pp. 2–3) put it: 'Professor Robbins sent to Vienna for a member of the Austrian school to provide a counter-attraction to Keynes.' See on this also Lachmann (1986), Caldwell (1995) and Dahrendortf (1995).

"Geldwertes" ' (Hayek, 1928), and one year later a book entitled
Geldtheorie und Konjunkturtheorie (Hayek, 1929).[3] Therefore, and given
the little time he had to prepare his LSE lectures, it was quite natural for
him to have developed some ideas along the lines of his previous work.
Hayek's lectures were published in 1931 under the title *Prices and
Production* (Hayek, 1931b).

Prices and Production had two aims: one constructive, the other
critical. The constructive aim consisted of a further elaboration of
Hayek's own theory of the trade cycle, and especially of the crisis.
According to this theory, the crisis has its origin in a lack of capital,
which in turn is the result of a preceding inflation and the 'misdirections of production' caused by it. The critical task consisted of refut-
ing alternative theories of the business cycle. The main targets of
Hayek's criticism were those theories which explained the crisis in
terms of a deficient effective demand and the ensuing deflationary
tendencies. The four lectures deal with the following subjects.
Lecture I, 'Theories of the Influence of Money on Prices', is devoted
to a brief history of attempts to come to grips with the role of money
and the banking system for the volume and the direction of production; Sraffa, in his otherwise acerbic and uncompromising review of
Hayek's book, calls the introductory lecture 'excellent' and 'a model
of clearness' (Sraffa, 1932a, p. 42). Lecture II, 'The Conditions of
Equilibrium Between the Production of Consumers' Goods and the
Production of Producers' Goods', expounds the foundation on which
Hayek's construction is erected: the Austrian theory of production
and distribution. The emphasis is on Böhm-Bawerk's concept of the
'average period of production' as an expression of the capital intensity
of production, and the idea of an inverse relationship between the
money rate of interest and the length of the production period chosen
by cost-minimizing producers. Lecture III, 'The Working of the Price
Mechanism in the Course of the Credit Cycle', contains Hayek's
explanation of the trade cycle which revolves around the impact of
changes in the money rate of interest on relative prices and the
adjustment process triggered by such changes. Lecture IV, 'The
Case For and Against an "Elastic" Currency', draws some conclusions for economic policy. In what follows I shall briefly summarize
the argument in the first three lectures.

---

[3] An English translation of a revised version of his book was published in 1933 under the
title *Monetary Theory and the Trade Cycle* (Hayek, 1933).

2.1   Tracing the sources of his own doctrine in the history of economic thought

Hayek discerns four stages in the development of the analysis of the impact of money on prices and production. In the first stage we encounter the more 'mechanistic' forms of the quantity theory of money, one of which was advocated towards the end of the 17th century by John Locke. These mechanistic forms are said to have been resuscitated at the beginning of the 20th century by Irving Fisher's 'equation of exchange'. To Hayek, any reasoning in terms of *aggregate* magnitudes such as the total quantity of money, the general price level and the total amount of production is ill-conceived, 'For none of these magnitudes *as such* ever exerts an influence on the decisions of individuals; yet it is on the assumption of a knowledge of the decisions of individuals that the main propositions of non-monetary economic theory are based.'[4] Monetary theory therefore ought to adopt the 'individualistic' method, which 'the modern "subjective" theory has advanced beyond the classical school in its consistent use' (1931b, p. 4). It follows that attention should focus on *relative* prices rather than on the general price level.

In the second stage we witness attempts to integrate monetary theory and general economic theory, and 'to trace the actual chain of cause and effect between the amount of money and prices' (ibid., p. 8). A start was made by Richard Cantillon in a 'brilliant' chapter of his *Essai sur le Commerce*, published in 1755, in which he clearly spelled out that an increase in the quantity of money may have distributive effects, which need not be neutral with respect to the volume and composition of production. For example, if consequent upon an increase in money supply the incomes of those with a high propensity to save and invest rise first, then the increase may have an impact on productive activity and growth.[5] This type of analysis was refined by David Hume and, more recently, by J. E. Cairnes. The most advanced versions in this tradition are said to be

---

[4] It comes as a surprise that despite his negative assessment of the quantity theory of money, Hayek is 'ready to concede that so far as it goes it is true, and that, from a practical point of view, it would be one of the worst things which could befall us if the general public should ever again cease to believe in the elementary propositions of the quantity theory' (Hayek, 1931b, p. 3). The passage immediately following reads: 'What I complain of is not only that this theory in its various forms has unduly usurped the central place in monetary theory, but that the point of view from which it springs is a positive hindrance to further progress. Not the least harmful effect of this particular theory is the present isolation of the theory of money from the main body of general economic theory' (ibid., pp. 3–4).

[5] We shall see below that Hayek should have remembered Cantillon's argument when developing his own doctrine.

the 'income theories' of the value of money of Friedrich von Wieser, Albert Aftalion and Ludwig von Mises. 'In the form it has received at the hands of Professor Mises, it belongs already to the third and fourth of our main stages of development' (ibid., p. 10). The reference is to Mises' *Theorie des Geldes und der Umlaufsmittel*, published in 1912 (Mises, 1912).[6] While their achievements relative to the first stage are obvious, in Hayek's opinion these theories 'suffer from a not unimportant defect', that is,

they do not help us to make any *general* statements about the effects which any change in the amount of money must have. For, as I shall show later, everything depends on the point where the additional money is injected into circulation (or where money is withdrawn from circulation), and the effects may be quite opposite according as the additional money comes first into the hands of traders and manufacturers or directly into the hands of salaried people employed by the State. (Hayek, 1931b, p. 11).[7]

It is Hayek's aim to overcome this defect and to develop a general analysis of the effects of changes in monetary policy, emphasizing especially the difference between producers' credits and consumers' credits.

The third stage is characterized by a study of the impact of the quantity of money on the rate of interest and, via the rate of interest, on the composition of demand for consumption goods and capital goods, respectively. In Hayek's judgement, two particular ideas are developed in this stage. The first comes from Henry Thornton, who, in the famous *Bullionist Controversy* in England at the beginning of the last century, advocated the view that if the Bank of England would keep its interest rate low enough, the circulation of paper money might expand beyond all limits. Thornton thus rejected the idea that natural forces would regulate the circulation of the Bank and ward off the danger of a sudden and swift depreciation of the currency.[8] The second is due to Thomas Robert Malthus, and concerns an early version of the concept of 'forced' or

---

[6] Hayek's indebtedness to Mises is expressed in various ways. Most importantly perhaps, Lecture III, which contains Hayek's own theory of the credit cycle, is headed by the following quotation from Mises' book (cf. Hayek, 1931b, p. 65). 'The first effect of the increase of productive activity, initiated by the policy of the banks to lend below the natural rate of interest is... to raise the prices of producers' goods while the prices of consumers' goods rise only moderately.... But soon a reverse movement sets in: prices of consumers' goods rise and prices of producers' goods fall, i.e. the loan rate rises and approaches again the natural rate of interest' (Mises, 1912, p. 431; Hayek's translation).

[7] Unless otherwise stated, emphases in quotations are by the authors' quoted.

[8] A low interest rate was taken to lead to an expansion of investment, hence to a high demand for loans, and so to a supply that exceeds what can be supported by bank capital.

'compulsory' saving which plays a central role in Hayek's own analysis. Malthus had admitted that an increase in money supply might stimulate capital accumulation. The additional money would lead to a rise in prices from which the 'industrious classes' would benefit to the detriment of the 'unproductive classes'. This redistribution of income may entail a problem of effective demand. For, Malthus argued, if capital accumulated too rapidly, the increase in production would tend to exceed the increase in effective demand and thus a general glut of commodities would obtain.[9] Hayek comments on this: 'The recognition of this tendency of an increased issue of notes to increase the national capital does not blind Malthus to the dangers and manifest injustice connected with it' (ibid., p. 19).

It was only with Knut Wicksell's *Geldzins und Güterpreise* (Wicksell, [1898] 1936), a contribution of 'signal importance', that Thornton's analysis was rediscovered and combined with a theory of the influence of money supply on capital formation (ibid., p. 20). Wicksell's success in this regard, Hayek contends, was essentially due to 'the fact that his attempt was based on a modern and highly developed theory of interest, that of Böhm-Bawerk'. He adds:

But by a curious irony of fate, Wicksell has become famous, not for his real improvements on the old doctrine, but for the one point in his exposition in which he definitely erred: namely, for his attempt to establish a rigid connection between the rate of interest and the changes in the general price level. (ibid., p. 20).

If there was no money, Wicksell's 'natural' rate of interest – Hayek prefers the term 'equilibrium' rate – would assume a level such that the *in natura* demand for capital, i.e. investment, would be equal to the *in natura* supply of capital, i.e. savings. In a money economy, the money rate may differ from the equilibrium rate because demand and supply do not meet in their 'natural form', but in the form of money, 'the quantity of which available for capital purposes may be arbitrarily changed by the banks' (ibid., p. 21). With the money rate falling short of (exceeding) the natural rate, there will be a process of inflation (deflation). Wicksell also coined the term 'forced saving'. Von Mises built on the foundations laid out by Wicksell, emphasizing the different influences which a divergence between the two rates has on the prices of consumption and of capital

---

[9] Since Malthus held the view that any act of saving would lead to an act of investment of the same size, Ricardo was at a loss to understand how Malthus could ever arrive at the opinion that aggregate effective demand may fall short of aggregate productive capacity. See Ricardo's *Notes on Malthus* (Ricardo, *Works*, Vol. II).

goods, respectively. In this way, Hayek concludes, Mises 'has succeeded in transforming the Wicksellian theory into an explanation of the credit cycle which is *logically satisfactory*' (ibid., p. 22; emphasis added).

As yet there is little to be said about the fourth stage, which is only just coming into being, with Hayek as its main creator. Therefore, the question is not what *is*, but what *ought to be and what not*. A negative determination should start from Wicksell's theory. In Hayek's opinion, his main error was to assume that the natural rate of interest 'was a rate which simultaneously restricted the demand for real capital to the amount of savings available *and* secured stability of the price level' (ibid., p. 23). From this perspective, a money rate that equals the equilibrium rate means that money is 'neutral'. Hayek objects: other than in a stationary state, banks can *either* equilibrate the demand for and the supply of capital *or* they can keep the price level stable, but they cannot do both at the same time (cf. ibid., p. 24). Thus, in times of a growing (shrinking) production, the equality between the two interest rates would imply falling (rising) prices. Wicksell's analysis, Hayek concludes, has led into a dead end. A fresh start is needed. This brings us to Hayek's positive determination of the project under consideration. We begin with an investigation of his method of analysis and the notion of equilibrium he adopts, and then turn to the theory of production and capital that underlies his approach.

2.2   Hayek's method and his notion of equilibrium

Hayek starts from two propositions which in his opinion cannot sensibly be questioned. First, while a change in the quantity of money may, or may not, have an impact on the price *level*, it will most certainly have an impact on *relative* prices. Second, the volume and direction of production depends on relative prices. A constant price level must therefore not be mistaken to imply constant conditions in the real sphere of the economy. Hayek pleads for the abandonment of the 'useless' and 'superfluous' concept of a general value of money. Monetary theory of the fourth stage will rather be characterized by an investigation of '*how the relative values of goods as sources of income or as means of satisfaction of wants are affected by money*' (ibid., p. 27). In this context Hayek introduces the notion of 'intertemporal equilibrium', which he had developed three years earlier (cf. Hayek, 1928):

This view of the probable future of the theory of money becomes less startling if we consider that the concept of relative prices includes the prices of goods of the same kind at different moments, and that here, as in the case of interspatial price relationships, only one relation between the two prices can correspond to a condition of 'intertemporal' equilibrium, and that this need not, *a priori*, be a relation of identity or the one which would exist under a stable price level (Hayek, 1931b, p. 26).

This passage has been interpreted as implying that along with the old *theory*, Hayek also jettisoned the received long-period *method* of analysis, centred around the notion of a competitive equilibrium characterized by a uniform rate of interest on the capital invested in the different industries and uniform rates of remuneration for all homogeneous primary factors of production. Scrutiny shows, however, that apart from the passage just quoted, the new notion of intertemporal equilibrium, developed almost simultaneously by Hayek and Erik Lindahl, a student of Wicksell's, plays hardly any role in *Prices and Production*.[10] Hayek's analysis in that book is indeed quite traditional, that is, firmly entrenched in contemporary long-period neoclassical and Austrian modes of thought centred around the notion of *the* 'equilibrium rate of interest'.

In 1926, Adolph Löwe (later Lowe) had published an article asking the question (and answering in the affirmative) whether, in order to do business cycle theory, one has to dispense with what was then called the 'static theory' and the notion of *long-period equilibrium* characterized by full employment of labour and full capacity utilization (Löwe, 1926). In *Geldtheorie und Konjunkturtheorie*, Hayek discussed in great detail Löwe's radical position. In *Prices and Production* there is not a single reference to the controversy or to Löwe, but Hayek's point of view is unaltered: an explanation of fluctuations in production that claims to be complete must start 'where general economic theory stops; that is to say at a condition of equilibrium when no unused resources exist' (Hayek, 1931b, p. 31). This starting point is also said to draw attention to an important aspect which might otherwise tend to get overlooked, namely 'changes in the methods of using *existing* resources'. Hayek expounds: 'Changes in the direction given to the existing productive forces are not only the main cause of fluctuations of the output of individual industries; the output of industry as a whole may also be increased or decreased to an enormous extent by changes in the use made of existing resources' (ibid., p. 32; emphasis added).[11] Yet Hayek chooses a long-period equili-

---

[10] In one other place Hayek addresses the problem of the influences of a change in relative prices on interest rate differentials (ibid., p. 60) without, however, employing the notion of intertemporal equilibrium. One rather gets the impression that in view of the highly complicated nature of these influences, that notion would be of little or no use.

[11] It remains unclear how these 'enormous' changes in output of industry as a whole would come about.

brium not only as the starting point of his analysis; he also sees reasons to think that any disturbance of such an equilibrium would call into action self-interested agents whose activities would gradually bring the system back to a long-period equilibrium. Hence, the business or credit cycle discussed by Hayek is nothing but a sequence of transitional processes between long-period equilibria. In conditions of free competition, as assumed by Hayek, each of these equilibria is defined by a full adjustment of the size and composition of production and the social capital stock to the other data of the system, such that a uniform rate of interest obtains. The notion of equilibrium adopted by Hayek both in *Geldtheorie und Konjunkturtheorie* and in *Prices and Production* is that of traditional marginalist theory.[12] The latter determines all dependent variables of the system, that is, all prices and quantities produced, in terms of supply and demand, conceived of as functional relationships between the price of a commodity and its quantity. In *Geldtheorie und Konjunkturtheorie*, Hayek made it clear that his point of reference was the Lausanne theory of Walras and Pareto.[13] That theory commonly starts from the following three sets of data:

  (i)   the (intertemporal) tastes of consumers;
  (ii) the technical alternatives of production;
  (iii) the endowment of the economy with goods of all kinds, in par-
        ticular its endowment with labour, land and 'capital', and the
        distribution of property rights amongst agents.

For obvious reasons, in order to be compatible with a long-period equilibrium, the 'quantity of capital' in given supply could only be specified as a sum of *value* expressed in some standard of value (cf, for example, Kurz and Salvadori, 1995, Chap. 14).

Should any one of these data change, then in general the equilibrium allocation of goods and the corresponding system of normal prices and

---

[12] The notion of long-period equilibrium surfaces repeatedly in *Prices and Production*. For example, we read about the equalization of the rate of interest: 'It is clear that producers' goods which are in different stages of production cannot, for any length of time, bring in different returns or obtain different prices in these different stages. On the other hand, it is no less clear that temporary differences between the prices offered in the different stages of production are the only means of bringing about a shift of producers' goods from one stage to another' (ibid., p. 67). Hayek also refers to the classical concept of 'gravitation' (ibid., p. 73; see also pp. 68–9 and 71).

[13] Ludwig Lachmann (1986, p. 227) characterized Hayek's approach succinctly as follows: 'For Hayek Paretian general equilibrium was the pivot of economic theory, the centre of gravity towards which all major forces tended. For him the task of trade cycle theory was to show how it came about that these major forces were temporarily impeded and their effects delayed'.

income distribution would also change. We shall see that Hayek conceives the problem of economic fluctuations as a change or 'disturbance' in one of these data and the adjustment processes triggered by it until the economy reaches a new equilibrium. In this context it is worth mentioning that Ludwig von Mises advocated basically the same idea. On the occasion of a conference organized by the Verein für Socialpolitik, the German association of economists, on 'Probleme der Wertlehre' (problems of value theory) in Dresden in 1932, which was also attended by Hayek, Mises stressed:

One must not commit the error of believing that the static method can only be used to explain the stationary state of an economy, which, by the way, does not and never can exist in real life; and that the moving and changing economy can only be dealt with in terms of a dynamic theory. The static method is a method which is aimed at studying changes; it is designed to investigate the consequences of a change in *one* datum in an otherwise unchanged system. This is a procedure which we cannot dispense with. (Mises in Mises and Spiethoff, 1933, p. 117)

This description also applies to Hayek's method in *Prices and Production* (and in his previous book). The consequences of a change in one datum, for example consumers' time preferences, are ascertained in terms of the static method. These consequences are considered to be *independent* of the process of transition, which can only be studied in terms of a dynamic analysis. In this view dynamic analysis is seen to be mainly at the service of static analysis. Against Löwe's radical program, Hayek puts forward a conservative one. The opinion to be found in the literature (e.g. McCloughry, 1982) that in *Prices and Production* Hayek had abandoned the traditional notion of equilibrium finds no support in Hayek's book.

As to the changes in data and their effects contemplated by Hayek in *Prices and Production*, it should be noted that he restricts his attention to a small subset of all possible cases. While in *Geldtheorie und Konjunkturtheorie* Hayek, following Wicksell's lead in *Geldzins und Güterpreise*, had expressed the opinion that the main elements causing economic fluctuations are improved expectations of entrepreneurs as regards the profitability of investment due to technological and organizational inventions (cf, for example, Hayek, 1929, pp. 80–81), this aspect is altogether absent in *Prices and Production*. Hayek explicitly rules out changes in data (ii):

What I have here in mind are *not* changes in the methods of production made possible by the progress of technical knowledge, but the increase of output made possible by a transition to more capitalistic methods of production, or, what is the same thing, by organising production so that, at any given moment, the available resources are employed for the satisfaction of the needs of a future more distant than before. It is to this effect of a transition to more or less 'round-about' methods of production that I wish particularly to direct your attention. For, in my opinion, it is only [!] by an analysis of this phenomenon that in the end we can show how a situation can be created in which it is temporarily impossible to employ all available resources. (Hayek, 1931b, pp. 32–3; see also p. 67)[14]

There remain changes in data (i) and (iii). We shall see that Hayek focused attention exclusively on changes in tastes, that is, in time preferences, expressed in a change in the propensity to save. It will turn out to be a major shortcoming of his analysis that he tended to neglect how monetary policy, via affecting data set (iii), thereby affects equilibrium, and how the sets of data (i) and (iii) are interrelated. It should also be mentioned that Hayek assumes a labour supply which is given and constant, that is, independent of the money wage rate and prices on one hand and intertemporal preferences on the other. One could say that the 'subjective method', which Hayek praised at the beginning of his book, is suspended with regard to significant parts of his analysis.

2.3   Austrian capital theory

Hayek based his construction on Böhm-Bawerk's theory of capital and interest (cf Böhm-Bawerk, [1889] 1921). Before we briefly summarize this theory, as presented by Hayek, it should be mentioned that this part of his analysis met with substantial difficulties of understanding in large parts of the English and the American profession. Two example suffice to illustrate this. In a letter to Keynes of 4 October 1931 on the ongoing debate about saving and investment, D. H. Robertson lamented: 'This 3-cornered debate [Robertson meant Keynes, Hayek and himself], all of us talking different dialects, has become so complicated', requiring one to know all three dialects, including 'the "goods of higher and lower orders" tongue of Vienna!' (Robertson in Keynes, *CW*, Vol. XIII, p. 271). Hawtrey also attacked Hayek for having entangled his argument 'with the intolerably cumbersome theory of capital derived from Jevons and Böhm-Bawerk', which is said to be 'singularly ill-adapted for use in monetary theory' (Hawtrey, 1932, p. 125).[15]

---

[14] Hayek's neglect of the role of technical progress in the theory of economic fluctuations met with severe criticism; see, for example, Hawtrey (1932, pp. 121–2). It may also explain why Schumpeter did not think highly of Hayek's construction.

[15] What to some people was a source of toil and trouble, to others was a source of 'fascination' (see Kaldor, 1942, p. 359). On Böhm-Bawerk's theory of capital and interest, see, for example, Kurz (1994).

In the Austrian view, the process of production is a time-consuming, unidirectional process leading from the services of the 'original' factors of production, labour and land, via one or several 'intermediate products' to consumption goods. Scrutiny shows that Hayek's argument is based on the following assumptions, most of which are implicit: (a) there is only a single consumption good (or basket of consumption goods with fixed proportions); (b) there is essentially only a single original factor of production, homogeneous labour, i.e. land is taken to be a free good; (c) there is only single production, i.e. joint production and fixed capital are set aside;[16] (d) there are constant returns to scale with regard to each production process; (e) the amount of labour per unit of time is constant with regard to each process, i.e. there is a steady flow of labour inputs from the beginning of a process to its end, when the consumption good becomes available, and hence the processes contemplated are of the *steady flow input–point output* type. In addition he assumed: (f) that labour and 'non-specific' intermediate products are transferable between processes of production at negligible cost;[17] (g) throughout Lecture II that the rate of interest is zero; (h) that the total labour supply is given and constant; (i) that there is free competition, i.e. there are no barriers to entry to or exit from any one of the markets. Hayek appears to have been of the opinion that each of the assumptions (a)–(e) could be removed without endangering the basic message of the Austrian theory of production and capital. In one place he writes: 'It would be open to us to deal with the difficulties by the aid of higher mathematics. But I, personally, prefer to make it amenable to a simpler method' (ibid., p. 39). His illustration of the theory in terms of his (in)famous triangles has caused many readers headaches, and Hayek himself discloses one of the potential reasons for it. He stresses: 'it should be noticed that... the figure[s] represent values and not physical production' (ibid., p. 38).

---

[16] Hayek pointed out that there is 'some difficulty in regard to the way in which durable goods...are to be taken account of in our schematic representation'. In these circumstances he felt it was 'more convenient to regard only that part of these durable goods which is currently used up and renewed as entering into the total of intermediate products existing at any moment' (Hayek, 1931b, p. 37, fn.). He left it at that and did not discuss how that 'part' was determined. The neglect of fixed capital implies that an important aspect of the business cycle, and the main reason for the elasticity of the industrial system, was missed by Hayek: the variability of the degree of capital utilization. In Hayek there are only the following extremes: either capital goods are used or they are superfluous and thus lost.

[17] This assumption is clearly in the tradition of Walras and not of Marshall. As is well known, Keynes followed the latter in assuming that the transfer of most durable capital goods between firms is generally prohibited by high costs.

On the basis of assumptions (a)–(e), the technical alternatives available to cost-minimizing producers can be ordered as follows. For a given amount of labour, which Hayek equated with full employment of labour, the input flow can be more or less long and correspondingly more or less narrow. The longer it is, the larger is the average time a unit of labour is invested in the production process. This leads to Böhm-Bawerk's concept of the 'average period of production'. It is defined as the weighted average of the periods of time over which the amounts of labour remain invested until the output of the consumption good is obtained, with the respective amounts of labour serving as weights. By means of this device the Austrian capital theorists thought it possible to replace a vector of physically heterogeneous intermediate products with a scalar, the average period of production, τ, which is supposed to be independent of distribution and prices. 'Capital' was thus taken to be reducible to a single variable dimension: the length of time. The available technical alternatives could now be unambiguously ordered according to their 'capitalistic' character, or capital intensity: 'As the average time interval between the application of the original means of production and the completion of the consumers' goods increases, production becomes more capitalistic, and *vice versa*' (ibid., p. 38). This order of the technical alternatives is said to be subject to what Böhm-Bawerk called the 'law of the superiority of more round-about processes of production' (cf. Böhm-Bawerk, [1889] 1921, pp. 338–62): the longer the average period of production, the larger the consumption output per unit of labour, with the increase in output becoming smaller for longer average periods. In Hayek's words:

We must therefore be content to accept it as one of the definite conclusions of this theory that – other things remaining the same – these margins must grow smaller as the roundabout processes of production increase in length and *vice versa*. (ibid., p. 69)[18]

Assuming that there is a continuum of non-dominated processes of production, and setting aside all problems related to the heterogeneity of

---

[18] Recently Thalenhorst and Wenig (1984) attempted to translate Hayek's theory of the business cycle in *Prices and Production* into 'mathematical economics'. According to their own statement they were keen to effectuate this translation 'in the spirit and tradition of Hayek and the Austrian School' (ibid., p. 214). In this light it is all the more surprising that they assume 'that the marginal productivity of the duration of a process is not only positive but also increasing' (ibid., p. 216). This assumption is not only not 'Austrian', it also does not make sense economically. Even in the case in which the marginal product is constrained from above there are only two possibilities: either the money rate of interest is equal to or larger than this upper limit, and then the optimal
continued

capital goods and the presence of compound interest, let y be consumption output per unit of labour employed and τ the average period of production; then the technical alternatives given in data set (ii) may conveniently be summarized by the following *temporal production function*

$$y = f(\tau) \quad \text{where } \frac{dy}{d\tau} > 0 \text{ and } \frac{d^2y}{d\tau^2} < 0 \tag{1}$$

Figure 1(a) illustrates the postulated relationship. The possibility of 'non-capitalistic' production involves $f(0) = y_{min} > 0$, i.e. a positive value on the ordinate from which the function starts. As is well known, implicit in the production function (Equation 1) is an inverse relationship between the real wage rate, w, that is the amount of the consumption good paid to workers per unit of labour, and the 'equilibrium' rate of interest, r,

$$r = r(w), \quad \text{where } \frac{dr}{dw} < 0 \tag{2}$$

The w–r frontier, or wage–interest frontier, is illustrated in Figure 1(b). It is convex to the origin; the minimum wage rate, w_{min}, equals y_{min} and defines the maximum rate of interest, r_{max}, compatible with the technical conditions under consideration.[19] With a rise (fall) in the wage rate, to which corresponds a fall (rise) in the natural rate of interest, cost-minimizing producers would lengthen (shorten) the average period of production.

As we have seen (cf the passage from *Prices and Production* quoted towards the end of Subsection 2.2), this inverse relationship between τ and r is at the heart of Hayek's theory of economic fluctuations. In his view, a transition between processes of production characterized by

average period of production is nil, that is, the 'non-capitalistic' production prevails, or the money rate of interest is smaller, and then the 'average' period is infinite. (It is not clear how the second constellation could represent a sensible economic equilibrium.) Therefore, the money rate of interest plays the role attributed to it by Hayek in an extreme way: changes in its level have either no impact at all, which is the case when the money rate stays in the interval between zero and the upper limit of the marginal product, or they prompt agents to shift from a production with no intermediate products to one with an infinite number of such products.

[19] On the assumption that $f(0)$ is large enough for the upkeep of the worker and his family, it gives the reservation price of *wage* labour: if firms offered a wage rate below it, no worker would be willing to sell his labour power but would rather use it in a self-employed way producing the consumption good without produced means of production. Hayek, however, doubts that $f(0)$ is large enough: 'as a general rule the single workman will not be able to produce enough for a living without the help of capital and he may, therefore, temporarily become unemployable' (ibid., p. 84).

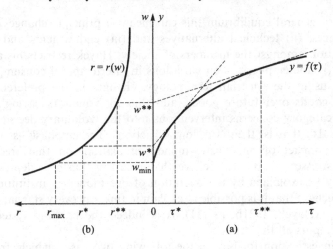

Figure 1

different lengths necessitates certain changes in what Hayek calls the 'structure of production' (ibid., p. 35). Whichever cause prompts a change in the adopted technique, it perturbates the going intertemporal coordination of the different stages of production, and forces upon the economy a more or less costly adjustment process until a new equilibrium structure of production is obtained. The main question Hayek raises is: When does the *process substitution* under consideration converge to a new equilibrium, and when not? The problem of the business cycle is thus reduced to a very narrow question: Starting from the results of the 'static' Austrian theory of the choice of technique of cost-minimizing producers, Hayek is concerned with the transition between alternative techniques and the causes or 'disturbances' that prompt these transitions. In one place he writes that business cycles are 'nothing but contrary fluctuations in the capitalistic structure of production' (Hayek, 1931c, pp. 91–2, fn.) – an opinion which must have come as a surprise to many people at a time when several countries still suffered from the Great Depression.

2.4   'Natural' and 'artificial' disturbances

Hayek distinguishes between two categories of causes that may bring about a change in the processes of production: 'natural' and 'artificial' ones. The first category concerns changes in what he calls the 'fundamental' data of the economic system. As we have seen, in the Lausanne theory of general equilibrium this can mean in principle changes in (i) preferences, (ii) technical alternatives and (iii) endowments and their distribution amongst the members of society. Hayek restricts his attention to (i): the emphasis is on variations in intertemporal consumption, that is, using the Austrian terminology, changes in the preference of present goods over future goods, and thus in 'voluntary saving'. The second category concerns interventions into the 'voluntary decisions of individuals', that is, their 'freedom of action'. The emphasis is on the *negative* impact of an 'elastic money circulation' on that freedom. Hayek stresses: 'Though I believe that recurring business depressions can only be explained by the operation of our monetary institutions, I do not believe that it is possible to explain in this way every stagnation of business' (Hayek, 1931b, p. 111). It is indeed the banking system on which he puts all the blame.[20]

His investigation focuses on the following two cases, which, from a 'practical' point of view, he considers to be the most important ones: an increase in savings, given the amount of money in circulation, on the one hand, and an increase in the amount of money due to the creation of new producers' credits, given the amount of 'voluntary' savings, on the other. In the first case a new and stable equilibrium is taken to result, reflecting the changed preferences of agents and characterized by a different structure of production with a longer average period of production. Things are different in the second case, in which a money rate of interest below the equilibrium rate leads to a change in demand in favour of intermediate products relative to consumption goods. However, since the fundamental data of the system are said to be the same as before, after a shorter or longer period of derangement and assuming that the banking system will eventually correct its error, the system will return to the old equilibrium. Let us look at Hayek's discussion of the two cases more carefully.

'Voluntary' saving

In the literature, there is some uncertainty about what Hayek meant when he talked about an increase in 'voluntary' saving. What is clear, though, is that he meant the decision to forgo present for future consumption. Hence Hayek's conception of 'saving' implies a definite, known, increase in future consumer demand to the detriment of present

---

[20] In this context it deserves to be mentioned that Hayek does not include money among the endowments of individual agents. His approach differs markedly from the more recent analyses of, for example, Patinkin or Ostroy and Ross, who reckon cash balances among endowments. As Sraffa was to object, in Hayek money is not considered a store of value.

consumer demand, but did he mean *gross* or *net* saving? In the first case, the equilibria contemplated by him would be stationary states, in the second case, the equilibria of systems growing at different speeds. While some of Hayek's formulations seem to point in the second direction, there is sufficient evidence that he means only transitions from one stationary state of the economy to another one. In fact, in systems with a constant labour supply and no technical progress there can be no growth (at a non-diminishing rate): instead the system is approaching asymptotically a stationary state characterized by a higher consumption per capita. An increase in savings therefore means a changed proportion in which income will be spent on consumption goods and on capital goods, which involves a change in *gross* savings. Net savings will be positive only during the transitory phase, that is, until the larger capital intensity has been built up which allows for a larger consumption output per worker.[21,22] In the new equilibrium, the real income and the value of the periodically worn out capital goods, both expressed in units of the consumption good, will be larger. To replace the capital goods, gross investment and gross savings must also be larger than in the initial situation. This transition between two stationary equilibria is illustrated in Figure 2.

Other things being equal, higher savings imply a lower equilibrium rate of interest. $S_0^b(i, K)$ gives the gross saving function in the initial situation, and $S_0(i, K)$ the corresponding net saving function; $S_1^b(i, K)$ and S_1 (i, K) refer to the situation after the increase in the propensity to save. (In what follows, attention will focus on net saving.) Savings are accordingly seen to depend on the money rate of interest, i, and the size of the existing capital stock (in value terms), K. For a given rate of time preference of consumers, π^*, they are the more prepared to abstain from present consumption, the more future consumption they can

[21] The interpretation that Hayek had in mind a growing system was put forward by Hicks, who argued that Hayek's analysis 'does not belong to the theory of business cycles, which was in the centre of attention of economists in the 1930s, but is a forerunner of the growth theory of more recent years' (Hicks, 1967, pp. 210–11). Streissler radicalized Hicks's idea and maintained that here is a 'close relationship' between Hayek's model and the von Neumann model (Streissler, 1969, p. 246). There is, however, no evidence in support of this claim. For an interpretation of the von Neumann model and how it probably relates to the work on general equilibrium carried out in Vienna in the 1930s, see Kurz and Salvadori (1993).

[22] As indirect evidence that Hayek was concerned with once and for all changes in gross rather than net magnitudes, it may be noted that in his *Pure Theory of Capital* Hayek was very dismissive of 'net' saving and investment concepts; cf Hayek (1941). I am grateful to Ian Steedman for having drawn my attention to this fact.

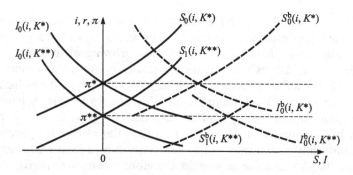

Figure 2

expect, that is, the larger is the interest paid on savings: $\partial S/\partial i > 0$.[23] In the initial situation, net savings are positive (negative) if the money rate of interest, i, is above (below) the rate of time preference, π^*. In stationary equilibrium money rate, time discount rate and natural rate are all equal, that is, $i = r = \pi^*$; the corresponding value of social capital is K^*. Hayek first assumes that the people that save are the same people that invest. This implies that there is no distinction between a saving and an investment function and hence no market for liquid funds. If now the rate of time preference falls to a level π^{**}, then there will be positive net savings, since $\pi^{**} < r = \pi^*$. Investing these savings entails a more 'capitalistic' structure of production and, due to a falling marginal product of lengthening the average period or production, *pari passu* a falling equilibrium rate of interest. This process continues until at a value of social capital $K^{**} > K^*$, a new equilibrium obtains, where $r = \pi^{**}$. In the case in which savers and investors are different people, investment behaviour must be dealt with. From the given assumptions about production and distribution, Hayek, in the conventional marginalist manner, derives functions for gross and net investment, $I^b(i, K)$ and $I(i, K)$, in which investment is elastic with respect to the money rate of interest and the size of the capital stock in existence, that is, focusing attention on net investment, $\partial I/\partial i < 0$ and $\partial I/\partial K < 0$ (cf. Hayek, 1931b, pp. 75–81; see also Milgate, 1988). With a fall in the rate of time preference and the consequent increase in saving, there will be an excess supply in the market for liquid funds. This pushes the

---

[23] Since according to Hayek the rate of time preference can safely be assumed to differ amongst agents, the diagram represents only the aggregate situation, *given the distribution of income*: π^* is that rate of discount at which net savings at this distribution of income are nil.

money rate of interest down and stimulates investment. With a growing value of social capital and a correspondingly decreasing marginal productivity of capital, the investment function moves towards the origin, until voluntary net saving and planned net investment reach a new equilibrium, both being equal to zero, at a lower equilibrium rate of interest which is equal to π^{**}.

For a given quantity of money in circulation and a given velocity of circulation, the change contemplated in the two cases consists 'in a stretching of the money stream flowing from the consumers' goods to the original means of production. It has, so to speak, become longer and narrower' (ibid., p. 48). This reflects the prolongation of the 'average period of production'. To the new equilibrium corresponds a new system of relative prices, that is, the prices of the intermediate products that are now being produced, expressed in terms of the consumption good. This new price system, or 'price fan' as Hayek calls it (ibid., p. 73), reflects both the now adopted technique of production and the associated distribution of income. On the assumption that in the old equilibrium Y^* units of the consumption good were produced by L units of labour uniformly spread over t periods of time (of uniform length), whereas in the new equilibrium Y^{**} units of the consumption good are produced by the same amount of labour uniformly spread over T periods, we obtain, assuming that wages are paid at the end of each time period, the following two reduction equations:

$$Y^* = l_0 w^* + l_0 w^* (1 + r^*) + l_0 w^* (1 + r^*)^2 + \ldots + l_0 w^* (1 + r^*)^t$$

$$= l_0 w^* \frac{(1 + r^*)^t - 1}{r^*} \tag{3}$$

$$Y^{**} = l_1 w^{**} + l_1 w^{**} (1 + r^{**}) + l_1 w^{**} (1 + r^{**})^2 + \ldots + l_1 w^{**} (1 + r^{**})^T$$

$$= l_1 w^{**} \frac{(1 + r^{**})^T - 1}{r^{**}} \tag{4}$$

with $l_0 = L/t$ and $l_1 = L/T$. The wage rate clearing the labour market in the initial (new) equilibrium is w^* (w^{**}); the corresponding equilibrium rate of interest is r^* (r^{**}). According to the logic of the Austrian approach: $T > t$; $Y^{**} > Y^*$; $w^{**} > w^*$; $r^{**} < r^*$. The price of the first (second, ...) intermediate product in the old equilibrium, expressed in terms of the consumption good, is equal to the first term (the first two terms, ...) on the right-hand side of Equation (3), divided by Y^*. Similarly for the price of the first (second ...) intermediate product in the new equilibrium,

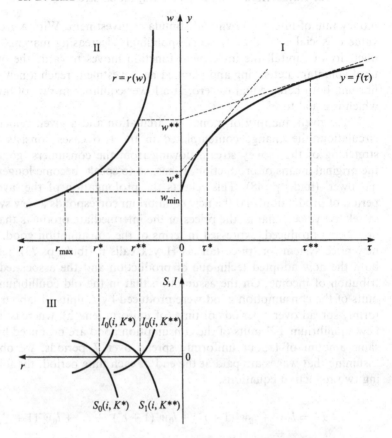

Figure 3

where the reference is now to Equation (4), of course. Each of these two equations therefore contains a complete system of equilibrium prices, or 'price fan'.

We may finally illustrate the relationships under discussion in terms of a single diagram: quadrant I of Figure 3 gives the production function, quadrant II the wage–interest frontier, and quadrant III the (net) saving and (net) investment functions. The values of the variables representing the old equilibrium have a single asterisk, while those of the new equilibrium have two asterisks.

During the transition between the old and the new equilibria the old equilibrium price fan no longer holds, but the new one has not yet become established. Hence there is, in Hayek's words, a 'disequilibrium'.

An increase in the propensity to save shifts demand away from consumption and towards intermediate products. Consequently, the prices of intermediate products will rise relative to the consumption good. On the assumption that the wage rate is independent of the stage of production in which labour is employed, an assumption which is implicit in Hayek, the disequilibrium is reflected in interest rate differentials.[24] In the case under consideration, the change in relative prices increases profitability in the early stages of production and depresses it in the later ones. This provides an incentive to the restructuring of the process of production which continues until a new equilibrium characterized by an interest rate that is again uniform is reached via a reallocation of labour (and of non-specific capital goods) across the different and now more numerous stages of production.

'Forced' saving

The second case is meant to illustrate Hayek's belief 'that recurring business depressions can only be explained by the operation of our monetary institutions' (ibid., p. 111). The story starts again with a shift in demand towards means of production, but this time that shift is 'artificially' brought about by means of more favourable terms at which banks are willing to lend money to producers. Hayek's comparison of the two cases reads:

When a change in the structure of production was brought about by saving, we were justified in assuming that the changed distribution of demand between consumers' goods and producers' goods would remain permanent, since it was the effect of voluntary decisions on the part of individuals. . . . But now this sacrifice is not voluntary, and is not made by those who will reap the benefit from the new investments. It is made by consumers in general who, because of the increased competition from the entrepreneurs who have received the additional money, are forced to forgo part of what they used to consume. (ibid., pp. 52-3)

It is now the totality of consumers that are taken to be subject to 'forced saving'. Figure 4 illustrates the case. In the initial stationary state of the economy, net savings and net investment are equal to one another and are equal to zero, since $i = r = \pi^*$. With the money

---

[24] Otherwise, wage differentials would also have to be taken into account. They appear in fact to be quite important, since the increase in the demand for intermediate products involves an increase in the demand for labour employed in the early stages of production relative to that in stages that are close to the completion of the consumption good. An increase in the wages of labour in the former stages relative to the later ones attracts workers from the latter and thus contributes to a 'restructuring of production'.

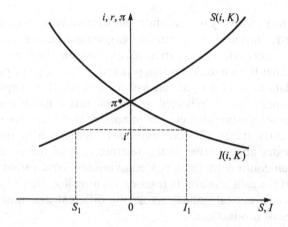

Figure 4

rate of interest reduced by banks to i' there will be a net investment of I_1 and an excess demand for investment goods equal to $I_1 - S_1$. This excess demand is financed by the creation of new credit. At the lower money rate of interest, profit maximizing firms are prompted to adopt more 'round-about' processes of production. The excess demand for means of production exerts an upward pressure on their prices. Profitability in the early stages of production rises and thus attracts primary and non-specific intermediate factors presently employed in stages of a lower order, that is, closer to the maturing of the consumption good. However, 'this application of the original means of production and non-specific intermediate products to longer processes of production will be effected without any preceding reduction of consumption' (ibid., p. 78). Rather, the rate of output of consumables is bound to fall *as a consequence* of all this, involving an 'involuntary' curtailment of consumption. At the same time the competition amongst producers for the original factor of production, labour, intensifies, pulling up wages. The result is a 'crisis' which puts into sharp relief the 'misdirections of production' (ibid., p. 89). With their increased money incomes the consumers, whose intertemporal preferences have not changed, will increase the demand for consumption goods, thereby bidding up the price(s) of the consumer good(s) relative to the prices of the means of production. This, in turn, signals the entrepreneurs that a less 'capitalistic' production is optimal. The development may be precipitated by an alteration in the policy of the central bank to curb inflation. As a consequence, 'production will become less capitalistic, and that part of the new capital which was sunk in equipment adapted only to the more capitalistic processes will be lost' (ibid., p. 53). In the German version of his book Hayek concluded:

The existence of unused productive capacity is therefore nothing less than a proof that capital is available in abundance, whereas consumption is insufficient: Quite on the contrary, it is a sign that these productive capacities cannot be used, because the current demand for consumption goods is too urgent to allow us to invest the available productive resources in time consuming processes of production, for which we do not have the necessary equipment (due to 'misdirections of capital'). (Hayek, 1931c, p. 94)

In terms of Figure 4, this means that in the medium or long run the unchanged 'fundamental' forces will prevail: after a costly round trip the system will return to the original equilibrium with both the money rate and the equilibrium rate equal to π^*.

These considerations provide Hayek with a foil against which he criticizes alternative conceptualizations of the business cycle and a policy of an elastic money supply. Against the view that a crisis could effectively be fought by the creation of 'artificial demand', he objects that this would aggravate the difficulties rather than mitigate them, because a part of the available resources 'is again led into a wrong direction and a definite and lasting adjustment is again postponed'. He concludes:

The only way permanently to 'mobilise' all available resources is, therefore, not to use artificial stimulants – whether during a crisis or thereafter – but to leave it to time to effect a permanent cure by the slow process of adapting the structure of production to the means available for capital purposes. (Hayek, 1931b, p. 87)

3   The controversy between Keynes and Hayek

Hayek's book caused a considerable stir: immediately its author was involved in several controversies, which were themselves part of a larger debate about saving and investment and, somewhat later, about capital theory. The debate on saving and investment centred around the following contributions: Dennis Robertson's *Banking Policy and the Price Level* (Robertson, 1926), Keynes' *Treatise on Money* (1930; *CW*, Vols. V and VI) and his *General Theory of Employment, Interest and Money* (1936; *CW*, Vol. VII), and Hayek's *Prices and Production* (1931b) and his *Monetary Theory and the Trade Cycle* (1933). Numerous economists participated in the debate, some of whom had already made a name for themselves, while others were about to do so. The quest for truth competed with other motives, including the desire to win out against alternative schools of economic thought and establish a dominant position in the field of economics.[25]

The steady rise of Keynes and his group in Cambridge to intellectual and academic dominance in economics was not accepted without resistance. Some economists at the London School of Economics especially, with Lionel Robbins as the main driving force, took up the challenge. Robbins asked Hayek to join their forces and to enter the 'battlefield'. In August 1931 and February 1932 Hayek published a highly critical review article of Keynes' *Treatise on Money* (Hayek, 1931a, 1932a) in two instalments in *Economica*, the LSE journal. In Hayek's view, Keynes' analysis was unclear, muddled, contradictory and devoid of any solid capital theoretic foundations, indeed any such foundations at all. Apparently, Keynes was embarassed when he saw the first part of the review. At the end of his copy of the review he noted: 'Hayek has not read my book with that measure of "good will" which an author is entitled to expect of a reader. Until he can do so, he will not see what I mean or know whether I am right. He evidently has a passion which leads him to pick on me, but I am left wondering what that passion is' (Keynes, *CW*, Vol. XIII, p. 243).[26] Keynes answered the first part of Hayek's attack in the same issue of *Economica* with a piece entitled 'The Pure Theory of Money. A Reply to Dr Hayek' (Keynes, [1931] *CW*, Vol. XIII, pp. 243–56), followed by a reply by Hayek (1931d).

3.1   Keynes: attack is the best defence

Before we turn to Keynes' anti-critique, it should be recalled that at the time of the *Treatise* Keynes still moved essentially within the confines of that variant of traditional marginalist theory which had Marshall's long-period analysis as its backbone. Characteristic features of this theory were the assumed dichotomy between a 'real' and a 'monetary' sphere of the economy and a concept of equilibrium which is exclusively determined by real factors. Put in a nutshell, Keynes tried to enlarge the framework of this analysis by allowing monetary factors a larger role

---

[25] For accounts of the different aspects of the debate, see, for example, Colonna (1990a,b), Klausinger (1991), Foss (1994) and Kurz (1995).

[26] An indirect answer to this question is contained in a letter by O. Meredith to Keynes of 8 December 1931. He calls Hayek 'a pedant trained in Austrian economics and eager to show (not without some encouragement from London) that "Codlin is the friend, not Short"! I.e. that your work was spoiled by being cast in the mould of Marshall instead of in that of Böhm-Bawerk' (cf. Keynes, *CW*, Vol. XIII, p. 267). (The reference is to Charles Dickens's *The Old Curiosity Shop*, Chapter XIX.)

to play. In accordance with the conventional point of view, he was of the opinion that these factors prevented the 'perfect' functioning of the market mechanism. However, while deviations from long-period equilibrium were commonly considered to be short-run phenomena, Keynes argued that they could persist for longer periods of time, with the 'natural' rate of interest therefore differing from the money rate more permanently. Therefore, it was hardly surprising that his critics found it difficult to see much of a novelty in the *Treatise*. Keynes himself appears to have felt this. In his reply to Hayek he opined that 'those who are sufficiently steeped in the old point of view simply cannot bring themselves to believe that I am asking them to step into a new pair of trousers, and will insist on regarding it as nothing but an embroidered version of the old pair which they have been wearing for years' (*CW*, Vol. XIII, p. 247).

This was essentially also the view of Hayek, who in his review tried to nail down Keynes to the old doctrine and displayed a lack of understanding for the new elements in his analysis. Keynes, on the other hand, was at a loss to understand how Hayek could fail to grasp what he was trying to do. The Austrian, we read in one place, 'has seriously misapprehended the character of my conclusions. He thinks that my central contention is something different from what it really is' (ibid., p. 244). In order to clarify the differences of opinion between himself and Hayek, Keynes decided to enter into a discussion of Hayek's recently published *Prices and Production*, in which his critic's own point of view is said to become much clearer than in the review article. In this way Keynes' reply to Hayek's criticism of the *Treatise* is swiftly transformed into a criticism of *Prices and Production*: from the second page onwards, Keynes' answer aims exclusively at pointing out differences between him and Hayek and putting into sharp relief what he considered Hayek's main errors and misconceptions. Keynes' argument can be summarized as follows. The quantity of money can, under certain circumstances, vary without disturbing the equality between saving and investment. Therefore, it cannot be excluded that Wicksell was right in maintaining that the banking system is simultaneously able to guarantee a stable price level and that equality. An increase in the quantity of money is not a necessary condition for investment to exceed saving, and the addition to that quantity is not a measure of the difference between the two magnitudes. 'In my view', Keynes wrote, 'saving and investment (as I define them) can get out of gear without any change on the part of the banking system from "neutrality" as defined by Dr Hayek, merely as a result of the public changing their rate of saving or the entrepreneurs changing their rate of investment, there being no automatic mechanism in the economic system (as Dr Hayek's view would imply there must be) to keep the two rates equal, provided that the effective quantity of money is unchanged' (*CW*, Vol. XIII, p. 251). Hayek's book is said to be 'one of the most frightful muddles I have ever read, with scarcely a sound proposition in it beginning with page 45.... It is an extraordinary example of how, starting with a mistake, a remorseless logician can end up in Bedlam'. Keynes admitted that he had not built his own analysis on a satisfactory theory of capital and interest, simply because 'there is no such theory at present'. Hayek's own statement of such a theory in Lecture II is dismissed on the ground that it contains nothing but 'a series of baffling *non-sequiturs*'. Keynes added: 'If I am wrong, I hope that some authority, such as Professor Robbins, who is confident that he understands what Dr Hayek means in pages 45–64 of his book, will act as an interpreter' (ibid., pp. 252–3).

3.2   Hayek's reply

In his rejoinder, Hayek did not hide his embarassment at Keynes' response: rather than answering his objections, Keynes is said to have chosen to denounce his adversary. Hayek indicated, however, that this was perhaps the only sort of defence open to 'an author who has been shown that almost all his fundamental concepts are ambiguous, and that some are even defined in several flatly contradictory ways' (Hayek, 1931d, p. 399). Hayek reiterated the objection that Keynes' analysis was devoid of a proper capital theoretic foundation, and added:

Mr. Keynes seems never to have been concerned to study the fundamental non-monetary problems of capitalistic production. He now contends that we have no satisfactory theory of capital.... [T]he obvious answer, of course, is that even if we have no quite satisfactory theory we do at least possess a far better one than that on which he is content to rely, namely that of Böhm-Bawerk and Wicksell. That he neglects this theory, not because he thinks it is wrong, but simply because he has never bothered to make himself acquainted with it, is amply proved by the fact that he finds unintelligible my attempts to develop certain corollaries of this theory – corollaries which are not only essential for the very problem we are discussing, but which, as experience has shown me, are immediately intelligible to every student who has ever studied Böhm-Bawerk or Wicksell seriously. (ibid., pp. 401–2)

After the polemics in *Economica*, Keynes and Hayek exchanged several letters in which most of the discussion centred around the problem of how to define saving and investment. In the course of this correspondence, Keynes increasingly showed signs of tiredness. In a note to Piero Sraffa and Richard Kahn of 1 February 1932, he wrote: 'What is the next move? I feel that the abyss yawns – and so do I.' To this he added: 'Yet I can't help feeling that there is something interesting in it' (*CW*, Vol. XIII, p. 265). This remark reflects once more the difficulties he had in coming to grips with Hayek's approach.

To conclude, Keynes was not able to effectively counter Hayek's attack, and he himself appears to have clearly felt his ineptness. Another Cantabrigian had to take on the task of freeing Keynes from the impasse: invited by Keynes, who then edited the *Economic Journal*, Piero Sraffa published a paper entitled 'Dr. Hayek on Money and Capital' in the March issue of 1932 of that journal (Sraffa, 1932a). The June issue carried Hayek's reply (Hayek, 1932b) and Sraffa's rejoinder (Sraffa, 1932b).

4   The debate between Sraffa and Hayek

Before we enter into a discussion of the debate between Sraffa and Hayek, a few words should be said about the state of the development of Sraffa's own analysis of value and distribution at the time of his criticism of Hayek's book. As Sraffa wrote – and as his papers in the Wren Library of Trinity College, Cambridge, confirm – 'central propositions' of his later book *Production of Commodities by Means of Commodities* had been already worked out in the late 1920s (Sraffa, 1960, p. vi). The production equations he then studied showed that both the classical labour theory of value and the marginalist supply and demand theory were generally unable to explain 'normal', long-period prices. Both theories relied on what Sraffa was then to call 'metaphysical' concepts – 'labour' in one case and 'utility' in the other – and suffered from a logical defect stemming from an inadequate treatment of the problem of distribution. We also know that Sraffa, unlike several of his Anglo-Saxon and American colleagues, including Keynes, was familiar with both Vilfredo Pareto's theory of general equilibrium and the Austrian theory of capital and interest of Böhm-Bawerk and Wicksell. Sraffa may indeed have been one of the few scholars in Britain who was not taken by surprise by Hayek's book because of the sources it tapped. It is the working hypothesis of what follows that Sraffa knew perfectly well what Hayek was talking about.

4.1   Sraffa's attack

In Sraffa's review article there is next to nothing on his own theoretical position at that time. Sraffa did not use the article as a welcome opportunity to expound his findings in the theory of value and distribution or to apply them to the problem under consideration. This abstinence on Sraffa's part is also reflected in Hayek's complaint at the beginning of his reply that Sraffa failed to make 'his own position' clear (Hayek, 1932b, p. 237). Sraffa, in fact, defines his task as a critic as 'the somewhat monotonous one of discovering, for each step of Dr. Hayek's parallel analyses [reference is to the two cases of "voluntary" and "forced" saving, or rather, a barter and a monetary economy], which is the error or irrelevancy which causes the difference' (Sraffa, 1932a, p. 45). Sraffa's criticism is therefore purely internal: he scrutinizes the consistency of Hayek's argument in the context of the latter's own approach. This is clearly expressed by Sraffa's main objection to Hayek: 'Dr. Hayek as it were builds up a terrific steam-hammer in order to crack a nut – and then he does not crack it. Since we are primarily concerned in this review with the nut that is not cracked, we need not spend time criticising the hammer' (ibid.). The 'steam-hammer' Sraffa talks of is, of course, the Austrian theory of capital and interest. The demonstration that it cannot be sustained was postponed to Sraffa's book (cf Sraffa, 1960, p. 38).[27]

According to Sraffa, Hayek's project to integrate monetary theory with general economic theory was laudable. It was also right to focus attention on the impact of money on relative prices. Hayek's execution of his project was, however, a complete failure, as seen by Sraffa. Rather than clearing up the muddle in the existing literature, the book is said to add to it. The difficulties begin with Hayek's concept of money 'neutrality'. Money is taken to be 'neutral' if it leaves undisturbed production, relative prices, and thus also the natural rate of interest as it would obtain in a barter economy. Yet instead of investigating under which monetary system the neutrality as specified would obtain, Hayek addresses 'the wholly different problem of proving that only one particular banking policy (that which maintains constant under all circumstances the quantity of money multiplied by its velocity of circulation) succeeds in giving full effect to the "voluntary decisions of individuals," especially in regard to saving, whilst under any other policy these decisions are "distorted" by the "artificial" interference of banks' (Sraffa, 1932a, p. 43). Hayek thus implicitly assumes – wrongly, as Sraffa was to argue – that the kind of distortions contemplated by him cannot occur in a barter economy.

---

[27] Sraffa contents himself with the following aside. Hayek's discussion of the relationship between the quantity of capital and the length of the (average) period of production obscures rather than clarifies the main issue: 'a maze of contradictions makes the reader so completely dizzy, that when he reaches the discussion of money he may out of despair be prepared to believe anything' (Sraffa, 1932a, p. 45).

In Hayek's construction, Sraffa points out, money has only a single function: that of a *means of exchange*. Every introductory textbook in monetary economics tells one that in addition money performs the functions of a unit of account and, more importantly, of a *store of value*. Not so in Hayek's story: 'There are no debts, no money-contracts, no wage-agreements, no sticky prices in his suppositions. Thus he is able to neglect altogether the most obvious effects of a general fall, or rise, of prices' (ibid., p. 44). His objection to the vague concept of 'the general price level' misleads him into throwing the baby out with the bathwater and ignoring altogether the role of money as a store of value, that is, that money is itself one of the commodities. 'Having thus reduced money to utter insignificance', Sraffa remarks, 'amounts to assuming away the very object of the inquiry' (ibid., p. 44). This then leads Sraffa to ask: How is it possible that an economy with 'emasculated' money can behave differently from an economy without money, i.e. a barter economy? What is wrong with Hayek's argument, or which element that is extraneous to the discussion does he introduce that causes the difference? At this point Sraffa emphasizes again the purely internal nature of his criticism: 'But from the beginning it is clear that a methodological criticism [which Sraffa does not provide] could not leave a brick standing on the logical structure built up by Dr. Hayek' (ibid., p. 45).

After this criticism of Hayek's stage set, Sraffa turns to the *dramatis personae* of the play. Here his objection is that there is great confusion about which role is ascribed to which actor. For example, in one act the 'consumers' are the same individuals as the 'entrepreneurs', while in another act they are distinct from them (ibid., p. 45 fn.). At one time the decisions to save are taken by the 'consumers', at another by the 'entrepreneurs', and at still another even by the 'industries' (cf Hayek, 1931b, p. 58). In this last case Hayek seems to have forgotten what he praised in the 'subjective' method, namely, that the theory must not rely on relationships between aggregates. Clearly, only if consumers and entrepreneurs are *identical* can the consumers' decisions to save *uno actu* involve a decision about the proportions in which the total gross income is divided between the purchase of consumers' goods and that of producers' goods, and only if they are *distinct* is Hayek's distinction between consumers' credits and producers' credits, which plays a crucial role in his reasoning, sensible (cf. Sraffa, 1932a, p. 45 fn.).

Sraffa then scrutinizes Hayek's polar cases of 'voluntary' and 'forced' saving. At first sight the two seem to be similar: entrepreneurs will be engaged in lengthening the average period of production, capital will be accumulated and relative prices will change. There appears to be only a single difference: while in the former case money prices will fall, in the case in which the process is triggered by banks expanding circulation they will rise. This prompts Sraffa's comment: 'It would appear that the parallelism is due to our having ignored the secondary effects of a general fall or rise of prices. But Dr. Hayek has undertaken to avoid the concept of "value of money"; and at the same time he must impress us with the benefits of voluntary saving, and the evils of inflation' (ibid., p. 47).

Yet, as we have seen, this is not the end of Hayek's story. According to him, in the former case a *new* equilibrium will be established, characterized by a larger 'quantity of capital' per unit of labour and a higher consumption output per unit of labour, whereas in the latter case the economic system is bound to return to the *old* equilibrium. The change in economic conditions due to 'forced saving' cannot be permanent. Eventually, the money receipts of consumers will rise again, which will allow them to expand consumption 'to the usual proportion'. This implies that capital has to be reduced to its former quantity – a process that 'necessarily takes the form of an economic crisis' (Hayek, 1931b, p. 53). To this reasoning Sraffa objects that Hayek failed to show that the damage done to those whose real income was curbed during the inflation will be made good. This is a necessary, albeit not sufficient, condition in order for the system to return to the original equilibrium:[28]

One class has, for a time, robbed another class of a part of their incomes; and has saved the plunder. When the robbery comes to an end, it is clear that the victims cannot possibly consume the capital which is now well out of their reach. If they are wage-earners, who have all the time consumed every penny of their income, they have no wherewithal to expand their consumption. And if they are capitalists, who have not shared in the plunder, they may indeed be induced to consume now a part of their capital by the fall in the rate of interest; but not more so than if the rate had been lowered by the 'voluntary savings' of other people. (Sraffa, 1932a, p. 48).

Seen from the vantage point of Paretian general equilibrium theory, which Hayek had endorsed, Sraffa's criticism amounts to the objection that the process of inflation (as well as that of deflation) is commonly associated with a change in agents' endowments, that is, it affects one of the fundamental data determining general equilibrium: even with preferences and the set of technological alternatives remaining the same, the system will end up in a different equilibrium due to the redistribution of resources.[29] To this is added a further objection which shows that Hayek's attempt to identify his two cases as pure cases is ill-conceived. Since it can safely be

[28] In addition, it is required that the banking system increases the money rate of interest to its former level.

[29] Hayek could have avoided this slip had he remembered the reasons for his praise of Cantillon in the first lecture.

assumed that those who gained during the inflation will carry out 'voluntary saving', the picture gets blurred. For example, on the assumption that the rate of time preference of those that gain from inflation is smaller than the rate of time preference of those that lose, and on the Hayekian premise that in the long run the preferences of agents will prevail, the system will gravitate to a *new* equilibrium just as the system did in Hayek's case of saving that was allegedly exclusively 'voluntary'.[30] In short, Hayek discusses processes of transition between equilibria, where the final state is taken to be known prior to, and independently of, the path the system takes after it has been removed from its old equilibrium position. He thus ignores the possibility that *en route* various events may occur that push the system to a final state that is different from the initial one.[31] This demonstrates at the same time that Hayek's sharp distinction between the case of 'voluntary' and 'forced' saving breaks down, and with it the main thrust of his argument. 'Dr. Hayek', Sraffa writes in one place, 'who extols the imaginary achievements of the "subjective method" in economics, often succeeds in making patent nonsense of it' (ibid., p. 47 fn.). In the present context Hayek is said to ignore the effect of the redistribution of wealth due to an expansion of circulation and its implications for the long-run equilibrium to which the system will gravitate.

So far the discussion concerned the 'artificial stimulant' of inflation in the shape of producers' credits. Now, what about consumers' credits? Are they, in Hayek's view, equally incapable of moving the system to an

---

[30] A closer look at that case would show, however, that elements of 'forced saving' can be avoided only at the cost of singularly bold assumptions concerning each agent's capacity to anticipate the impact of a change in other agents' intertemporal preferences. In order for his case of 'voluntary saving' to preserve its purity, it would seem that Hayek is forced to suppose a very strong form of rational expectations (cf. Hayek, 1931b, p. 75). This appears to have been overlooked by some of the people who attempted to defend Hayek against the interpretation of his doctrine as foreshadowing rational expectations (see, for example, Butos, 1986).

[31] Caldwell (1995, p. 38) claims that 'what was really at issue between them [i.e. Hayek and Sraffa] here is the self-adjusting nature of the market system. Hayek assumed that the adjustment mechanism, formally described in what he called "equilibrium theory", works faultlessly in a world in which money is absent.... Sraffa questioned the initial and crucial premise of a self-adjusting system. This is the bedrock-level conflict that underlies their arcane dispute about how best to model a monetary economy'. This interpretation is at best misleading, if not wrong. As will also be seen below, nowhere in his criticism of Hayek's approach did Sraffa question the equilibrating tendencies at work, as Caldwell maintains. Rather, he saw reason to question Hayek's view as to how these tendencies would make themselves felt and to which equilibrium position they would push the economic system. In short, the 'bedrock-level conflict' was not whether or not the system was self-adjusting, but to which state the system would converge. Only the latter question was in dispute between the two.

equilibrium that is different from the original one? Interestingly, to Hayek the two cases are not analogous. He sees reason to assume that an increase in consumers' money as opposed to an increase in producers' money has a permanent effect, because it tends 'to frustrate the effect of saving' (Hayek, 1931b, p. 57). Accordingly, inflation through consumers' credits would effectively decrease capital and thus push the system to a new final state with a lower consumption output per capita. Sraffa's dry comment reads: 'Thus Dr. Hayek will have it both ways' (Sraffa, 1932a, p. 48). Hayek's claim that the two cases are not analogous finally reveals the 'error or irrelevancy' which is responsible for the fact that, contrary to what one would expect, a rise or fall in the quantity of 'emasculated' money can make a difference. As Sraffa stresses: 'an extraneous element, in the shape of the supposed power of the banks to settle the way in which money is spent, has crept into the argument and has done all the work. As Voltaire says, you can kill a flock of sheep by incantations, plus a little poison' (ibid., p. 49).

Sraffa's next main criticism concerns Hayek's view, which he took from Wicksell, that the difference between the actual rate and the 'natural' or 'equilibrium' rate is a characteristic of a money economy. This is said to be a confusion. To see this one ought to recall Wicksell's definition according to which the rate of interest measures the excess in real terms yielded in an exchange of physically homogeneous goods over time:

If money did not exist, and loans were made in terms of all sorts of commodities, there would be a single rate which satisfies the conditions of equilibrium, but there might be at any moment as many 'natural' rates of interest as there are commodities, though they would not be 'equilibrium' rates. The 'arbitrary' action of the banks is by no means a necessary condition for the divergence; if loans were made in wheat and farmers (or for that matter the weather) 'arbitrarily changed' the quantity of wheat produced, the actual rate of interest on loans in terms of wheat would diverge from the rate on other commodities and there would be no single equilibrium rate. (ibid., p. 49)

Sraffa illustrates his argument in terms of two economies, one with and the other without money, and introduces in this context the concept of the *own-rate of interest*, or, as he prefers to call it, the 'commodity rate of interest'.[32] In both economies, loans are made in terms of all commod-

---

[32] The concept of own-rates of interest can be traced back to Irving Fisher's *Appreciation and Interest*, published in 1896 (cf Fisher, 1991). It was then dealt with in Fisher's 1907 book *The Rate of Interest* (cf Fisher, 1907). Keynes made use of Sraffa's concept in Chapter 17 of the *General Theory* (*CW*, Vol. VII), in which he tried to put forward an argument in terms of a preference for liquidity on the part of economic agents that was

continued

ities for which there are forward markets. Assume that in the money economy a cotton spinner borrows at time t a sum of money for θ periods (months) and uses the sum to purchase on the spot market a quantity of raw cotton at price p^t, which he simultaneously sells θ periods forward at price $p^{t+\theta}$. This means that the cotton spinner 'is actually "borrowing cotton"' for the given time span of θ periods. Sraffa expounds: 'The rate of interest which he pays, per hundred bales of cotton, is the number of bales that can be purchased with the following sum of money: the interest on the money required to buy spot 100 bales, plus the excess (or minus the deficiency) of the spot over the forward prices of the 100 bales' (ibid., p. 50). Let $i_{t,\theta}$ designate the money rate of interest for θ periods, then the sum of money, M, referred to is given as

$$M = (1 + i_{t,\theta})p^t - p^{t+\theta}$$

The own-rate of interest of cotton between t and $t + \theta$, $\rho_{t,\theta}$, is then defined as the quantity of cotton which can be purchased with that sum of money at the given forward price, that is,

$$\rho_{t,\theta} = \frac{M}{p^{t+\theta}} = \frac{(1 + i_{t,\theta})p^t - p^{t+\theta}}{p^{t+\theta}} = \frac{(1 + i_{t,\theta})p^t}{p^{t+\theta}} - 1$$

Sraffa adds:

In equilibrium the spot and forward price coincide, for cotton as for any other commodity; and all the 'natural' or commodity rates are equal to one another, and to the money rate. But if, for any reason, the supply and the demand for a commodity are not in equilibrium (i.e. its market price exceeds or falls short of its cost of production), its spot and forward prices diverge, and the 'natural' rate of interest on that commodity diverges from the 'natural' rates on other commodities. (ibid., p. 50)

Essentially the same can be said of a non-money economy: out of equilibrium, 'natural' rates of interest will be different for at least some commodities. Hayek's opinion that in a 'disequilibrium' caused by a sudden increase in money supply (or in the propensity to save) the natural rate of interest would be above (below) the money rate does not make

meant to explain a downward rigidity of the money rate of interest. The 'liquidity premium' is taken to prevent the money rate of interest from falling to that level at which a volume of investment would be forthcoming, which, via the multiplier, would lead the system to full employment. Sraffa, as we know from his yet unpublished papers, did not think highly of Keynes' argument. His main criticism was that the benefits involved in *holding* a commodity (including money) have no relation to its own-rate of interest, and that no properties of that commodity – apart from an expected price change – have any relations to the difference between its rate and other rates.

sense, because out of equilibrium there is no such thing as *the* 'natural' rate; there may be 'as many "natural" rates as there are commodities' (ibid.).

This observation then leads to the question of how the system gets re-equilibrated. Sraffa stresses 'that, under free competition, this divergence of rates is as essential to the effecting of the transition as is the divergence of prices from the costs of production; it is, in fact, another aspect of the same thing'. As to the gravitation of market prices to costs of production (inclusive of interest), Sraffa addresses Hayek's case in which

> there is a change in the distribution of demand between various commodities; immediately some will rise in price, and others will fall; the market will expect that, after a certain time, the supply of the former will increase, and the supply of the latter fall, and accordingly the forward price, for the date on which equilibrium is expected to be restored, will be below the spot price in the case of the former and above it in the case of the latter; in other words the rate of interest on the former will be higher than on the latter. (ibid., p. 50)

This will prompt profit-seeking producers of the former commodities to expand output and of the latter commodities to reduce it. In this way production will adjust to demand until a new equilibrium obtains in which all commodity rates of interest are uniform and, in the case of a money economy, equal to the money rate of interest. The concept of equilibrium under discussion is the traditional long-period concept as it was informed by the earlier classical economists and advocated by all marginalist authors until the late 1920s, including Walras, Böhm-Bawerk and Wicksell. More important, it is precisely the concept adopted by Hayek in *Prices and Production*. Therefore, the view to be found in the literature that Sraffa's criticism of Hayek was not pertinent because his notion of equilibrium was different from that used by Hayek cannot be sustained.[33]

Sraffa refutes Hayek's opinion that there will only be a destruction of capital in the case of 'forced', but not in that of 'voluntary', saving: 'With or without money, if investment and saving have not been planned to match, an increase of saving must prove to a large extent "abortive"'. That is, both a sudden relative increase and a sudden relative decrease in the demand for consumption goods may cause a derangement of the system and dissipate some of the existing plant and equipment. Moreover, Sraffa objects, using a distinction of Robertson's, that savings

---

[33] This view is reiterated by Caldwell (1995, p. 39): 'Ludwig Lachmann later remarked sagely [?]...that Hayek and Sraffa were operating with two very different notions of equilibrium.' The reference is to Lachmann (1986). However, no evidence is given in support of this view. Similarly, McCloughry (1982).

may be seen as an 'inducement' to investment, but cannot in general be considered its 'source', which raises, among other things, the problem of effective demand, which is totally ignored by Hayek in his analysis (cf. ibid., p. 52).

Sraffa also defends Wicksell's concept of 'neutral' money against the criticism levelled at it by Hayek. Since Wicksell was concerned with the stabilization of the price-level – the price of a composite commodity – his idea of adjusting the bank rate to the 'natural' rate can be given the following interpretation: the reference is not to a single 'natural' rate, but to a weighted average of the 'natural' rates of the commodities entering into the price index, with the weights used in constructing this index applied to the interest rates. 'What can be objected to Wicksell is that such a price-level is not unique, and for *any* composite commodity arbitrarily selected there is a corresponding rate that will equalise the purchasing power, in terms of that composite commodity, of the money saved and of the additional money borrowed for investment' (ibid., p. 51).

4.2   Hayek's reply and Sraffa's rejoinder

Hayek's reply is of similar length to Sraffa's review (cf Hayek, 1932b). He accuses Sraffa of not 'making his own position quite clear' and characterizes his attitude as

a curious mixture of, on the one hand, an extreme theoretical nihilism which denies that existing theories of equilibrium provide any useful description of the non-monetary forces at work; and, on the other hand, of an ultra-conservatism which resents any attempt to show that the differences between a monetary and a non-monetary economy are not only, and not even mainly, 'those characteristics which are set forth at the beginning of every textbook on money'. (ibid., p. 238)

Hayek summarizes his theory in the following two statements, the former of which is in full harmony with the then received doctrine: first, 'so long as we neglect monetary factors, there is an inherent tendency towards an *equilibrium* of the economic system'; second, 'monetary factors may bring about a kind of *disequilibrium* in the economic system – which could not be explained without recourse to these monetary factors' (ibid., p. 238; emphases added). He then addresses Sraffa's objections against 'two cardinal points in my theory': (i) the notion of a money rate of interest which differs from the 'equilibrium' rate; and (ii) 'the tendency for capital accumulated by "forced saving" to be, at least partly, dissipated as soon as the cause of the "forced saving" disappears'. Hayek adds that 'it is upon the truth of this [latter] point that my theory stands or falls' (ibid., p. 239). He deals with these points in reverse order.

As regards the question how much additional demand for capital goods will result from the injection of producers' credits, Hayek admits that it all depends on how quickly the incomes of primary factors, i.e. wages, tend to rise.[34] He implicitly concedes that his argument in the book was based on the assumption that wages do not rise immediately: 'But they will rise to the full extent only when the new money has passed backwards through the successive stages of production until it is finally paid out to the factors' (ibid., p. 242). In addition, he accepts Sraffa's criticism that the share of profits need not rise with an increase in the capital–output ratio (ibid., pp. 242–3). Most importantly, he admits that the system need not return to its old equilibrium position, since 'entre-preneurs may not consume part of the extra profit made during that [inflationary] period, but may invest it. In such a case, the shift of incomes from a class less inclined to save to a class more so inclined will ultimately have produced some real saving' (ibid., p. 242). Hence, he is forced to abandon his previous opinion that the 'artificial stimulant' of inflation cannot do any good and cause an accumulation of capital. He tries, however, to play down the importance of this concession by contending that the dissipation of capital during the crisis will eventually lead 'to something approaching the former state' (ibid., p. 243). Given this con-cession, it comes somewhat as a surprise that he can call Sraffa's respec-tive criticism (cf. 'one class has, for a time, robbed another class of a part of their incomes; and has saved the plunder') 'a surprisingly superficial objection', and add: 'Is Mr. Sraffa really unfamiliar with the fact that capital sometimes falls in value because the running costs of the plant have risen...? And would he really deny that, by a sudden relative increase in the demand for consumers' goods, capital may be destroyed against the will of its owners?' (ibid., p. 244). As Sraffa's review shows, his answer to both questions is 'No'.

As regards the first 'cardinal point', Hayek cannot but accept Sraffa's argument that generally there will be a multiplicity of 'natural' or own-rates of interest. This observation must have hit Hayek very hard, since it meant either or both of two things: that he had not properly understood the concept of 'intertemporal prices' developed by himself (Hayek, 1928), or that he was unable to apply it to the questions dealt with in *Prices and Production*. To be told by someone who could not be expected to have known Hayek's earlier paper[35] what the implications of this paper were

---

[34] On the problem of various time lags in Hayek's approach, see Hicks (1967) and Cottrell (1994).

[35] To the best of my knowledge, there is indeed no evidence in Sraffa's papers in the Wren Library of Trinity College, Cambridge, that he was familiar with Hayek's 1928 article.

for his own analysis in *Prices and Production* must have been utterly frustrating to Hayek – all the more so, since the lesson taught totally undermined his concept of 'neutral' money, as we shall see in a moment. In these circumstances, Hayek's response to Sraffa's criticism is of particular interest. He does not attempt to do away with it by referring to his paper and pointing out that all this was well known to him when writing the book. Rather, he avoids admitting his neglect by not mentioning his paper at all. Instead he chooses a forward strategy, maintaining 'that, in this situation, there would be *no single rate* which, applied to all commodities, would satisfy the conditions of equilibrium rates, but there might, at any moment, be as many "natural" rates of interest as there are commodities, *all* of which would be *equilibrium rates*' (Hayek, 1932b, p. 245). This is a surprising statement in the light of Hayek's earlier insistence that a credit expansion is bound to bring about a *disequilibrium* in the economy.[36] Yet, rather than explaining the meaning of this statement, Hayek contents himself with the following remark: 'The inter-relation between these different rates of interest is far too complicated to allow of detailed discussion within the compass of this reply' (ibid., pp. 245–6). The obvious reference to his 1928 paper is missing.

In the concluding section of his rejoinder, Hayek addresses what he calls Sraffa's 'absurd suggestion' (ibid., p. 248) that with the new definition of savings in the German edition of his book (cf. Hayek, 1931c) he 'has landed himself right in the middle of Mr. Keynes' theory' (Sraffa, 1932b, p. 53). He writes: 'That Mr. Sraffa should have made such a suggestion, indeed, seems to me only to indicate the new and rather unexpected fact that he has understood Mr. Keynes' theory even less than he has my own' (Hayek, 1932b, p. 249). It is remarkable that to this the editor of the *Economic Journal* added a footnote, in square brackets, saying: 'With Prof. Hayek's permission I should like to say that, to the best of my comprehension, Mr. Sraffa has understood my theory accurately. – J. M. KEYNES' (ibid.).

Sraffa's rejoinder is short and acerbic (Sraffa, 1932b). As regards point (ii) he repeats his previous objection, calling 'forced saving' a 'misnomer for spoliation', since those who had gained by the inflation and chose to save the spoils had no reason at a later stage to revise the decision, whereas those on whom forced saving had been inflicted would have no say in the

---

[36] Hayek's response, it could be argued, shows that he was prepared to abandon the long-period notion of equilibrium, but only in the face of criticism which could not be answered. Hence, rather than having adopted the notion of intertemporal equilibrium at the very beginning of his enterprise, Hayek had recourse to it only when no other possibility was open to him.

matter. 'This appeal to common sense has not shaken Dr. Hayek: he describes it as "surprisingly superficial", though unfortunately he forgets to tell me where it is wrong' (ibid., p. 249). According to Sraffa, 'the point of the dispute' is Hayek's assumption, reiterated in his reply, that incomes will eventually rise *in proportion* to the additional money which has become available for investment. 'I contend that this will not happen.' Sraffa adds: 'Once more Dr. Hayek himself provides me with the argument against his theory' (ibid., p. 250). This assumption is said to contradict the following assumptions of his analysis: capital will be accumulated in proportion to the quantity of money issued in the form of loans to producers, the number of stages of production will increase in proportion to the quantity of capital, and the quantity of payments to be made will increase in proportion to the number of stages. Sraffa concludes that 'as a result, the quantity of payments to be made increases in proportion to the quantity of money, and the whole of the additional money is absorbed in cash holdings for performing such payments' (ibid.). Again, what is at stake is the internal coherence of Hayek's argument; in this context it is of no import whatsoever 'what I "really believe"' (ibid.).

As regards the other cardinal question (i), Sraffa notes with satisfaction that Hayek 'now acknowledges the multiplicity of the "natural" rates'. However, he should then also draw the consequences for his ideal maxim for monetary policy. On his proposition that they '*all* . . . would be equilibrium rates' Sraffa comments: 'The only meaning (if it be a meaning) I can attach to this is that his maxim of policy now requires that the money rate should be equal to all these divergent natural rates' (ibid., p. 251).

In view of this devastating final judgement passed on Hayek's concept of 'neutral money', it is hardly surprising that even authors who were broadly sympathetic to Hayek's analysis felt that, in the debate with Sraffa, Hayek's stature as an economic theorist had been seriously damaged (see, for example, Lachmann, 1986).

The attacks of Keynes and Sraffa on Hayek initially contributed to the latter's prestige in the scientific community, because if someone was able to challenge Keynes he had to be taken seriously. However, in the medium run they proved detrimental to his stature as an economic theorist. It was particularly Sraffa's attack which, according to the gradually emerging view, had dealt a serious blow to Hayek's doctrine. Former followers of Hayek turned away from him, others even became adversaries to his ideas.[37] Joseph Alois Schumpeter wrote to Sraffa

---

[37] On the erosion of the 'Robbins Circle' at the LSE, see Hicks (1982, p. 3) (see also Kaldor, 1942, p. 359).

after the publication of his debate with Hayek: 'I am fully in agreement with you'; and on the occasion of the publication of Sraffa's 1960 book (cf. Sraffa, 1960), George Shackle, in a letter to Sraffa, called the latter's criticism of Hayek 'a milestone' in economic analysis.

Hayek undertook another single greater effort to turn the defeat into a victory. About his *Pure Theory of Capital*, published in 1941 (Hayek, 1941), he says that it may perhaps have been more aptly called 'Introduction to the Dynamics of Capitalist Production'. He expounds: 'The whole of the present discussion is essentially preparatory to a more comprehensive and more realistic study of the phenomena of capitalistic production' (ibid., p. 3). One might say that the *Pure Theory* compares to the planned study as the first two chapters of *Prices and Production* compare to the subsequent two. This study was never completed by Hayek, and a reading of the *Pure Theory* shows why. Hayek clearly understood that he had erred in assuming that the problem of the business cycle could be tackled in terms of Böhn-Bawerk's theory of capital. His attempt to save that theory had turned out to be enormously difficult, and in the end futile: the theory was beyond remedy and the alternative construction that he sought to put in its place was too complex to allow one to derive simple and clear-cut results.[38] The 'steam-hammer', to use Sraffa's expression, was no longer at Hayek's disposal: a new attempt at 'cracking the nut' was illusory.

5   The subsequent debates

Hayek's book produced a considerable stir. In the years following its publication it was reviewed in all leading economic journals by leading experts on capital theory, trade cycle theory or monetary theory. Reviews came from, among others, Ralph G. Hawtrey (1932), Arthur W. Marget (1932), George L. Shackle (1933–34), Alvin Hansen and Herbert Tout (1934), Gustav Åkerman (1934), Otto Conrad (1934), Costantino Bresciani-Turroni (1934), Hans Neisser (1934) and Ragnar Nurkse (1934–35); Hayek's approach was also dealt with in the monographs on alternative theories of business cycles by Wilhelm Röpke (1936) and

[38] In this connection, see also the assessments of the *Pure Theory of Capital* by Lutz (1967, Chap. 4), Shackle (1981) and Steedman (1994). In Caldwell's opinion, Hayek with his *Pure Theory* 'had been able to clear away Böhm-Bawerk's "average period of production" and replace it with the far more complex notion of a structure of production, thereby securing the capital-theoretic foundation of Austrian theory' (Caldwell, 1995, p. 42); it is, however, not clear how the capital-theoretic foundation of Austrian theory could have been 'secured' by demolishing Austrian capital theory.

Gustav Haberler ([1937] 1958). While Sraffa's criticism at first met with considerable difficulties of understanding, as time went on major elements of it were explicitly or implicitly accepted in the relevant literature.[39] With the publication of Keynes' *General Theory* in 1936, the interest in Hayek's approach to the theory of money and crises lost momentum as rapidly as it had gained it at the beginning of the decade. It was only after Hayek had been awarded the Nobel prize in economics in 1974 that his early work on monetary theory and the trade cycle received renewed attention. Lucas (1981, p. 216) thought he could see in Hayek a precursor of the theory of 'rational expectations', and with the rise of Austrian ideas in some circles of economists the Hayek–Sraffa debate was scrutinized again. In what follows, I shall briefly deal with the controversy between Desai and McCloughry on that debate (cf. Desai, 1982; McCloughry, 1982).

Desai correctly argues that Hayek failed to develop a satisfactory notion of a monetary equilibrium; his concept of a 'neutral' money represents but a 'utopian ideal' (Desai, 1982, p. 164). In his comment on Desai's paper, McCloughry confirms this view. McCloughry, on the other hand, once again contends that Hayek and Sraffa, while obviously discussing the same model, 'are in fact not thinking within the same framework' (McCloughry, 1982, p. 172). Since it is intrinsically difficult, if not impossible, to know what and how people think, we must rely on the observable results of their acts of thinking. McCloughry provides the following cases in support of his view. First, there is the problem of the notion of 'inflation' in the two authors. While Sraffa is said to conceive of inflation as a problem of the 'distribution of income', Hayek sees it as a problem of the 'allocation of resources' (ibid., p. 173). In fact, it is both. Hayek in his reply to Sraffa admits that inflation has the distributive effects pointed out by Sraffa. Hence, the case mentioned by McCloughry does not indicate any difference in perspective, or 'vision', but simply an omission on Hayek's part which he, Hayek, would readily concede to his critic. Second, there is the problem of the notion of 'equilibrium'. McCloughry maintains: 'Hayek is thinking not in the traditional long-period framework, *but in terms of intertemporal equilibrium*' (ibid., p. 174). However, as we have seen there is no evidence in support of this opinion except that Hayek is forced into that position when confronted

---

[39] For a summary statement of the opinions expressed in the works mentioned, see Kurz (1995, Part 5); for a historical study of the impact of Hayek's book, see also Colonna (1990a) and the book edited by Colonna and Hagemann (1994). (It is a shortcoming of the latter contribution that the debate between Sraffa and Hayek and its impact on the subsequent discussion is not dealt with in detail.)

with Sraffa's critique. Instead, Hayek adopted the conventional long-period notion of equilibrium, centred around the uniformity of the rate of interest, as he had found it in such authors as Böhm-Bawerk and Wicksell. It may be conjectured that had he himself felt the need to point out a difference between the notion of equilibrium adopted by him and that used in Sraffa's criticism, he would in all probability have said so. The best opportunity to have done so was perhaps when Sraffa introduced the concept of own-rates of interest in the debate. The fact that Hayek did not take issue with Sraffa's interpretation as regards the supposed notion of equilibrium might be sufficient to dispel the opinion that the two disagreed fundamentally on this matter. Finally, McCloughry contends that the Hayek–Sraffa debate saw a clash of two different 'Weltanschauungen' (visions of the world), which is said to have prevented a fruitful communication (ibid., p. 181). This interpretation is no more acceptable than the previous two. Only a single 'Weltanschauung' (to retain McCloughry's term) was under consideration, namely Hayek's. It did not pass Sraffa's test of logical coherence and consistency. Sraffa did not confront Hayek with a different 'Weltanschauung', but with the logical implications of the latter's own 'Weltanschauung' which he had overlooked. Sraffa was able to show that Hayek was not standing firm on his own gound. That was all.

6   Conclusion

While the execution of Hayek's bold project must be considered a failure, the project itself deserves to be praised, as even Hayek's most uncompromising critic, Sraffa, admitted. To date, several economists have attempted, without much success, to integrate monetary theory and the theory of value and distribution. A start was made by Knut Wicksell in *Interest and Prices* (Wicksell, [1898] 1936). Hayek's contribution consisted essentially of a development of Wicksell's analysis by way of its criticism and further elaboration. None of the existing traditions in economics has so far succeeded in accomplishing the task. Hayek's problem is therefore still on the agenda.

In the debate Sraffa demonstrated anew, after his criticism of Marshallian partial equilibrium analysis in the mid-1920s, his extraordinary analytical skills and impeccable logic. In addition, he displayed a thorough understanding of different traditions of economic thought, including contemporary general equilibrium theory, Austrian capital theory and Wicksellian price and interest theory. The debate with Hayek appears to have left its traces on Sraffa's mature work: *Production of Commodities by Means of Commodities* (Sraffa, 1960). It may be contended that the famous passage in which he argued that the rate of profits is 'susceptible of being determined from outside the system of production, in particular by the level of the money rates of interest' (ibid., p. 33) echoes this debate. Seen from this vantage point, the passage implies, contrary to Hayek's argument in *Prices and Production*, that monetary policy will generally have a lasting impact on income distribution and the 'real' system at large, not least by influencing the choice of technique of cost-minimizing producers. Hence, the 'real' and the 'monetary' sphere are seen as intimately intertwined. At the same time, Sraffa clarified that there is no presumption that a fall (rise) in the rate of interest will lead to the adoption of more (less) 'round-about' or 'capital-intensive' methods of production, as Hayek had claimed. It appears to be an interesting task to investigate whether following up Sraffa's above remark leads us any further in the direction of the long-sought integration of monetary theory and the theory of value and distribution.

References

Åkerman, L. (1934). 'Preise und Produktion', Review in *Zeitschrift für Nationalökonomie*, **5**, pp. 372–9.

Böhm-Bawerk, E. v. (1921). *Kapital und Kapitalzins. Zweite Abtheilung: Positive Theorie des Kapitales*, 1st edn, Innsbruck, 1889: Wagner. 4th edn in two volumes, Jena, 1921.

Bresciani-Turroni, C. (1934). 'Monetary Theory and the Trade Cycle', Review in *Economica*, **11**, pp. 344–7.

Butos, W. N. (1986). 'Hayek and General Equilibrium Analysis', *Southern Economic Journal*, **52**, pp. 332–43.

Caldwell, B. (1995). 'Introduction', in Hayek, F. A. (1995). *The Collected Works of F. A. Hayek*, Vol. IX: *Contra Keynes and Cambridge. Essays, Correspondence*, edited by B. Caldwell, London: Routledge, pp. 1–46.

Colonna, M. (1990a). 'Introduzione', in Hayek, F. A. (1990). *Prezzi e produzione. Il dibattito sulla moneta*, Italian translation of the 2nd edition of Hayek (1931b) and other works, edited with an introduction by M. Colonna, Naples and Rome: Edizioni Scientifiche Italiane, pp. XVII–L.

Colonna, M. (1990b). 'Hayek on Money and Equilibrium', *Contributions to Political Economy*, **9**, pp. 43–68.

Colonna, M. and Hagemann, H. (eds) (1994). *Money and Business Cycles*, Vol. I of *The Economics of F. A. Hayek*, Aldershot: Edward Elgar.

Conrad, O. (1934). 'Preise und Produktion. Eine Auseinandersetzung mit Friedrich A. Hayek', *Jahrbücher für Nationalökonomie und Statistik*, **140**, pp. 385–403.

Cottrell, A. (1994). 'Hayek's Early Cycle Theory Re-examined', *Cambridge Journal of Economics*, **18**, pp. 197–212.

Dahrendorf, R. (1995). *LSE: A History of the London School of Economics and Political Science*, Oxford: Oxford University Press.

Desai, M. (1982). 'The Task of Monetary Theory: The Hayek–Sraffa Debate in a Modern Perspective', in M. Baranzini (ed.), *Advances in Economic Theory*, Oxford: Basil Blackwell, pp. 149–170.

Fisher, I. (1907). *The Rate of Interest*, New York: Macmillan.

Fisher, I. (1991). *Appreciation and Interest*, first published in 1896, reprinted New York: Augustus M. Kelley.

Foss, N. J. (1994). *The Austrian School and Modern Economics: Essays in Reassessment*, Copenhagen: Handelshøjskolens Forlag.

Haberler, G. (1937). *Prospérité et dépression. Étude théorique des cycles économiques*, Geneva: Société des Nations. English translation as *Prosperity and Depression*, 5th edn, London, 1964: George Allen & Unwin.

Hansen, A. H. and Tout, H. (1934). 'Annual Survey of Business Cycle Theory: Investment and Saving in Business Cycle Theory', *Econometrica*, 2, pp. 119–47.

Hawtrey, R. G. (1932). 'Prices and Production', Review in *Economica*, 12, pp. 119–25.

Hayek, F. A. (1928). 'Das intertemporale Gleichgewichtssystem der Preise und die Bewegungen des "Geldwertes"', *Weltwirtschaftliches Archiv*, 2, pp. 33–76. English translation by W. Kirby entitled 'The System of Intertemporal Price Equilibrium and Movements in the "Value of Money"', in I. M. Kirzner (ed.), *Classics in Austrian Economics. A Sampling in the History of a Tradition*, Vol. III, London, 1994: Pickering and Chatto, pp. 161–98.

Hayek, F. A. (1929). *Geldtheorie und Konjunkturtheorie*, Wien and Leipzig: Hölder, Pichler und Tempsky.

Hayek, F. A. (1931a). 'Reflections on the Pure Theory of Money of Mr. J. M. Keynes', *Economica*, 11, pp. 270–95.

Hayek, F. A. (1931b). *Prices and Production*, 1st edn, London: George Routledge; 2nd edn, London, 1935.

Hayek, F. A. (1931c). *Preise und Produktion*, Vienna: Julius Springer.

Hayek, F. A. (1931d). 'A Rejoinder to Mr. Keynes', *Economica*, 11, pp. 398–403.

Hayek, F. A. (1932a). 'Reflections on the Pure Theory of Money of Mr. J. M. Keynes', *Economica*, 12, pp. 23–44.

Hayek, F. A. (1932b). 'Money and Capital: A Reply', *Economic Journal*, 42, pp. 237–49.

Hayek, F. A. (1933). *Monetary Theory and the Trade Cycle*, London: Jonathan Cape. English translation of a revised version of Hayek (1929).

Hayek, F. A. (1941). *The Pure Theory of Capital*, Chicago: Routledge and Kegan Paul.

Hicks, J. R. (1967). 'The Hayek Story', in J. R. Hicks, *Critical Essays in Monetary Theory*, Oxford: Clarendon Press, pp. 203–15.

Hicks, J. (1982). *Money, Interest and Wages*, Vol. II of Hicks's *Collected Essays on Economic Theory*, Oxford: Basil Blackwell.

Kaldor, N. (1942). 'Professor Hayek and the Concertina Effect', *Economica*, 9, pp. 359–82.

Keynes, J. M. (1973). *The Collected Writings of John Maynard Keynes*, edited by D. Moggridge, Vols V–VII and XIII, London: Macmillan. Referred to as *CW*, volume number, page number.

Klausinger, H. (1991). *Theorien der Geldwirtschaft. Von Hayek und Keynes zu neueren Ansätzen*, Berlin: Duncker & Humblot.

Kurz, H. D. (1994). 'Auf der Suche nach dem "erlösenden Wort"': Eugen von Böhm-Bawerk und der Kapitalzins', in B. Schefold et al. (eds), *Eugen von Böhm-Bawerks 'Geschichte und Kritik der Kapitalzins-Theorieen'. Vademecum zu einem Klassiker der Theoriegeschichte*, Düsseldorf: Verlag Wirtschaft und Finanzen, pp. 45–110.

Kurz, H. D. (1995). 'Über "natürliche" und "künstliche" Störungen des allgemeinen wirtschaftlichen Gleichgewichts: Friedrich August Hayeks monetäre Überinvestitionstheorie in "Preise und Produktion"', in B. Schefold et al. (eds), *Friedrich A. von Hayeks 'Preise und Produktion'. Vademecum zu einem Klassiker der Marktkoordination*, Düsseldorf: Verlag Wirtschaft und Finanzen, pp. 67–119.

Kurz, H. D. and Salvadori, N. (1993). 'Von Neumann's Growth Model and the "Classical" Tradition', *The European Journal of the History of Economic Thought*, 1, pp. 129–60.

Kurz, H. D. and Salvadori, N. (1995). *Theory of Production. A Long-Period Analysis*, Cambridge, Melbourne and New York: Cambridge University Press.

Lachmann, L. M. (1986). 'Austrian Economics under Fire: The Hayek–Sraffa Duel in Retrospect', in W. Grassl and B. Smith (eds), *Austrian Economics: Historical and Philosophical Background*, London: Croom Helm, pp. 225–42.

Lawlor, M. S. and Horn, B. (1992). 'Notes on the Sraffa–Hayek Exchange', *Review of Political Economy*, 4, pp. 317–40.

Löwe, A. (1926). 'Wie ist Konjunkturtheorie überhaupt möglich?', *Weltwirtschaftliches Archiv*, 24, pp. 165–97.

Lucas, R. E. (1981). 'Understanding Business Cycles', in K. Brunner and A. Meltzer (eds), *Stabilization of the Domestic and International Economy*, Amsterdam, 1977: North Holland. Reprinted in R. E. Lucas, *Studies in Business Cycle Theory*, Cambridge, MA, 1981.

Lutz, F. A. (1967). *Zinstheorie*, 2nd edn, Tübingen: Mohr.

Marget, A. W. (1932). 'Prices and Production and Preise und Produktion', Review in *Journal of Political Economy*, 40, pp. 261–6.

McCloughry, R. (1982). 'Neutrality and Monetary Equilibrium', in M. Baranzini (ed.), *Advances in Economic Theory*, Oxford: Basil Blackwell, pp. 171–82.

Milgate, M. (1988). 'Money, Capital and Forced Saving', *Cambridge Journal of Economics*, 12, pp. 43–54.

Mises, L. v. (1912). *Theorie des Geldes und der Umlaufsmittel*, Munich and Leipzig: Duncker & Humblot. 2nd edn 1924. English translation of the 2nd edn as *The Theory of Money and Credit*, London, 1934: Jonathan Cape.

Mises, L. v. and Spiethoff, A. (eds) (1933). *Probleme der Wertlehre*, Part II, Schriften des Vereins für Socialpolitik, Munich and Leipzig: Duncker & Humblot.

Neisser, H. (1934). 'Monetary Expansion and the Structure of Production', *Social Research*, 1, pp. 434–57.

Nurkse, R. (1934–35). 'The Schematic Representation of the Structure of Production', *Review of Economic Studies*, 2, pp. 232–44.

Ricardo, D. (1951 et seq.). *The Works and Correspondence of David Ricardo*, 11 vols, edited by P. Sraffa with the collaboration of M. H. Dobb, Cambridge: Cambridge University Press. Referred to as *Works*, volume number.

Robertson, D. (1926). *Banking Policy and the Price Level*, London: P. S. King.
Robinson, J. (1978). 'The Second Crisis of Economic Theory', in J. Robinson, *Contributions to Modern Economics*, New York: Academic Press.
Röpke, W. (1936). *Crises and Cycles*, London: William Hodge.
Shackle, G. L. S. (1933–34). 'Some Notes on Monetary Theories of the Trade Cycle', *Review of Economic Studies*, 1, pp. 27–38.
Shackle, G. L. S. (1981). 'F. A. Hayek', in D. P. O'Brien and J. R. Presley (eds), *Pioneers of Modern Economics in Britain*, London: Macmillan, pp. 234–61.
Sraffa, P. (1932a). 'Dr. Hayek on Money and Capital', *Economic Journal*, 42, pp. 42–53.
Sraffa, P. (1932b). 'A Rejoinder', *Economic Journal*, 42, pp. 249–51.
Sraffa, P. (1960). *Production of Commodities by Means of Commodities*, Cambridge: Cambridge University Press.
Steedman, I. (1994). 'On the *The Pure Theory of Capital* by F. A. Hayek', in M. Colonna, H. Hagemann and O. Hamouda (eds), *Capitalism, Socialism and Knowledge*, Vol. II of *The Economics of F. A. Hayek*, Aldershot: Edward Elgar, pp. 3–25.
Streissler, E. (1969). 'Hayek on Growth: A Reconsideration of his Early Theoretical Work', in E. Streissler et al. (eds), *Roads to Freedom. Essays in Honour of Friedrich A. von Hayek*, London: Routledge and Kegan Paul, pp. 245–85.
Thalenhorst, J. and Wenig, A. (1984). 'F. A. Hayek's "Prices and Production" Re-analyzed', *Jahrbücher für Nationalökonomie und Statistik*, 199, pp. 213–36.
Wicksell, K. (1936). *Interest and Prices. A Study of the Causes Regulating the Value of Money*, London: Macmillan. First published in German in 1898 as *Geldzins und Güterpreise*, Jena: Gustav Fischer.

PART III

Long-period theory and the problem of capital

CHAPTER 7

The capital theory controversy

Edwin Burmeister

Sraffa played a key role in the 'capital theory controversy' that arose in the 1960s. Involving economists centred primarily in Cambridge, US (more particularly at MIT), and in Cambridge, UK (though, of course, involving economists from elsewhere), the capital theory controversy has, for some, meant the abandonment of neoclassical economics, while for others it has been a tempest in a teapot occasioned by some prominently published errors but necessitating only minor alterations to the core of neoclassical economics. While the fervour of the debate has passed since the mid-1960s and early 1970s, its meaning and ramifications remain muddy to most economists. It is my hope that the perspective gained by the passage of time can help clarify the issues involved. To that end, I will begin with a brief sketch of the historical background of the controversy, and will then summarize what we have learned. Rather than explore numerous dead-end paths, my focus will be on those results that, in my opinion, remain important today. These are few enough, so my message will be concise. I will conclude by suggesting a broader view of the matter that raises some questions about the appropriate role of assumptions and approximations in economic science.

The controversy begins, for our purposes, in Cambridge, UK, with the publication of (i) Piero Sraffa's *Production of Commodities by Means of Commodities* in 1960, and (ii) Joan Robinson's *Essays in the Theory of Economic Growth* in 1962.[1] The essential argument in these works was that economic theory based on a single capital good must change radically to accommodate the existence of heterogeneous capital goods – the fact that there are many physically different machines used for

[1] In this work, Robinson developed a line of reasoning she began in 1953 (see Robinson, 1953–1954, 1956).

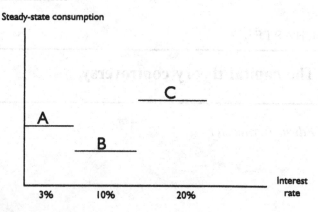

Figure 1. Failure of 'the neoclassical parable'.

production. While it remains for the economic historians to detail the contemporary response, the Sraffa–Robinson messages did not immediately prompt the uproar that later ensued. Indeed, my sense was that the Cambridge, US, response around 1963 was an acknowledgement that some technical complications would result from heterogeneous capital goods, but that these complications were essentially trivial.

The only solid evidence for this opinion is the 'neoclassical parable' as illustrated in a chapter appendix to the sixth edition of Samuelson's well-known principles text. Clearly acknowledging the issue by asking, 'Can our account of interest determination avoid the use of . . . [the] simplifying concept of a stock of homogeneous capital?' Samuelson answers that '[i]f the realistic problem of uncertainty about the future and the risks thereby implied could be ignored, advanced treatises can show rigorously how *an equilibrium interest-rate pattern can be defined in such a heterogeneous model* (emphasis added)'.[2]

So far so good, but Samuelson followed this correct statement with a discussion of diminishing returns and a diagram demonstrating the belief, based primarily on the one-capital-good models of Irving Fisher and Robert Solow, that across steady-state equilibria, larger quantities of 'aggregate capital' are associated with lower interest rates and higher levels of consumption.

The latter assertion is wrong. As is now well known, when there is more than one capital good, the situation illustrated in Figure 1 can occur. Here it is assumed that the growth rate is zero, so that maximum

---

[2] See Samuelson, 1964, pp. 594–600, 'Appendix to Chapter 28: Interest and Capital'.

steady-state consumption is at the Golden Rule point where the interest rate equals zero. Based on the results from one-capital-good models, one would expect steady-state C to have lower consumption since it is associated with higher interest rates, but in fact the opposite is true: despite the higher interest rate, steady-state C is associated with higher consumption. Without the elimination of such 'paradoxical consumption behaviour', one cannot define a well-behaved aggregate production function (having only one 'capital' input) appropriate for use in a world of heterogeneous capital goods.

Samuelson undoubtedly did not think that the story stated in his sixth edition was literally true – that is why he often called it a parable. However, at the time the prevailing belief among Cambridge, US, economists (myself included) was that if one imposed some mild technical regularity conditions on a technology with heterogeneous capital goods, the fundamental insight of the parable that 'Across steady-state equilibria, larger quantities of "aggregate capital" are associated with lower interest rates and higher consumption' could be rendered true as a theorem, allowing the rigorous definition of an aggregate production function so often used in empirical work.

A related but, with hindsight, distinct problem arising in models with heterogeneous capital goods was the question of the re-switching of techniques, as shown in Figure 2. A brief discussion of this issue will suffice here; the reader who is interested in details is referred to my 1980 book or to other references.[3] Let a particular list of the quantities of inputs and outputs that are technologically feasible be called a *technique of production*. If a particular production technique, call it A, represents a steady-state equilibrium at an interest rate r_1, and if another technique represents a steady-state equilibrium at a higher interest rate $r_2 > r_1$, then, if it is possible for technique A to again represent a steady-state equilibrium at some higher interest rate $r_3 > r_2$, technique A is said to *recur* and *re-switching of techniques* is said to exist.

One of the technical regularity conditions often imposed on Sraffa-type technologies with heterogeneous capital goods was the assumption that the technology was *indecomposable* – that every capital good and labour be required, either directly or indirectly, as an input to produce output of every other good. It was conjectured by some that this condition was sufficient to preclude re-switching, and even to validate the

---

[3] See Burmeister (1980). Definitions can also be found in the original Levhari paper (Levhari, 1965) and in Bruno, Burmeister and Sheshinski (1966). See also Levhari and Samuelson, 1966, and Samuelson, 1966.

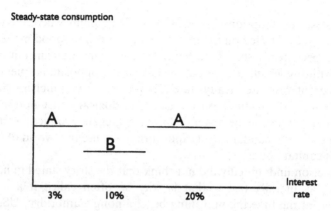

Figure 2. The re-switching of techniques.

results from a world with only one capital good to the more complex world of many capital goods.

This conjecture received widespread attention after the 1965 publication of a chapter from David Levhari's MIT dissertation with its now famous 'Levhari error' (Levhari, 1965). As a very small part of an otherwise outstanding dissertation, Levhari offered a 'proof' for the proposition that if the technology was indecomposable – that is, if *every* technique of production was itself indecomposable – then the re-switching of techniques could not occur. It is clear now that, even if this proposition was true, it could only resolve the re-switching problem shown in Figure 2 and would not eliminate the more troubling behaviour shown in Figure 1. Indeed, even Joan Robinson came to believe that re-switching was not a central issue, as clearly stated in her 1975 article 'The Unimportance of Reswitching' (Robinson, 1975). That is, while re-switching *revealed* examples that contradicted one-capital-good results, re-switching *per se* is not a central issue because eliminating it is not sufficient for the validation of one-capital-good results.

Levhari misused an inequality result from linear programming, and his 'proof' was wrong. Much more importantly, the proposition itself was false. At the First World Congress of the Econometric Society in Rome, in August 1965, Luigi Pasinetti presented a counter-example which made it clear that re-switching was possible even with an indecomposable technology.

If Pasinetti's counter-example and the realization of 'Levhari's error' were not enough to marshal the forces against neoclassical economics and its parable, the evidence presented shortly thereafter that the behaviour illustrated in Figure 1 was also possible was further ammunition for the assault: *The neoclassical parable could be wrong even in models that did not exhibit re-switching*. Somewhat ironically, this result was not discovered in Cambridge, UK, but in Cambridge, US, by Michael Bruno, myself and Eytan Sheshinki (1966). By the fall of 1965, such questions involving models of heterogeneous capital goods became known as 'the capital controversy'. *The Quarterly Journal of Economics* deemed the issues to be of sufficient importance to publish a special *Symposium* issue in November 1966.

Another group of participants on the sidelines of the debate deserves mention before we turn our attention to what we have learned. Many Austrian economists were little concerned with the 'technical work' being done at *either* Cambridge. They had learned from Böhm-Bawerk that roundabout production processes, i.e. those which take more time to produce output, are technologically superior. Thus, argued Leland Yeager in 1976, rather than the flawed concept of an aggregate capital stock, one needed only an index of roundaboutness: time itself would provide the key to aggregation.

However, my own work had already demonstrated that the Austrian approach to capital theory could solve none of the re-switching related problems, as this approach merely represented a special case of Leontief–von Neumann methods.[4] According to the Austrian model, replacing the interest rate in Figures 1 or 2 with some index of roundaboutness should result in *increasing* steady-state consumption since a more roundabout process is technologically superior and thus produces additional output. I proved that there does not exist *any* index of 'roundaboutness' that rules out the behaviour in Figures 1 or 2.[5] Thus an Austrian approach gives rise to exactly the same type of problems that are encountered in the heterogeneous capital good models studied in both Cambridges.

It is important, for the record, to recognize that key participants in the debate openly admitted their mistakes. Samuelson's seventh edition of *Economics* was purged of errors. Levhari and Samuelson published a paper which began, 'We wish to make it clear for the record that the nonswitching theorem associated with us is definitely false. We are grateful to Dr. Pasinetti...' (Levhari and Samuelson, 1966). Leland Yeager and I jointly published a note acknowledging his earlier error and attempting to resolve the conflict between our theoretical perspectives (Burmeister and Yeager, 1978).

---

[4] A proof of this result is contained in Burmeister (1974).

[5] See Burmeister (1974).

However, the damage had been done, and Cambridge, UK, 'declared victory': Levhari was wrong, Samuelson was wrong, Solow was wrong, MIT was wrong and therefore neoclassical economics was wrong. As a result there are some groups of economists who have abandoned neoclassical economics for their own refinements of classical economics.[6] In the United States, on the other hand, mainstream economics goes on as if the controversy had never occurred. Macroeconomics textbooks discuss 'capital' as if it were a well-defined concept – which it is not, except in a very special one-capital-good world (or under other unrealistically restrictive conditions).[7] The problems of heterogeneous capital goods have also been ignored in the 'rational expectations revolution' and in virtually all econometric work.

While this very brief historical sketch does not do justice to the complexity of the debate, let me now turn to some results that, to me at least, still seem important enough to remember:

1. Neither the extreme of abandoning neoclassical economics nor ignoring the complexities of heterogeneous capital goods is justified. The fact that the Levhari proposition is wrong and the fact that the error in his 'proof' led to the discovery that the neoclassical parable is wrong are not sufficient reasons for concluding that all of neoclassical economics is wrong. Certainly a careful comparison of the relevant appendices in Samuelson's sixth and seventh editions will reveal how very little hinged on the earlier error. In fact, as emphasized by Samuelson, the *fundamental* neoclassical proposition is that there exists a negatively sloped, concave trade-off between consumption today and consumption tomorrow – a result arising in Irving Fisher's one-capital-good model. *This proposition remains valid despite the existence of heterogeneous capital goods.* Moreover, although almost all of the re-switching debate was concerned with non-joint production technologies having only one primary factor (labour), these assumptions can be weakened without altering the truth of this fundamental inter-temporal consumption trade-off. (Even with only one capital good, however, the situation depicted in Figure 1 can arise in joint production economies.)[8] Moreover, the result generalizes easily to many time periods and allows one to study the properties of dynamic paths for heterogeneous capital good models as, for example, in my

---

[6] The papers in Bharadwaj and Schefold (1989) exemplify this line of inquiry.

[7] See, for example, Chapters 9 and 10 in Barro's widely-used textbook (Barro, 1990).

[8] More precisely, it is possible for steady-state consumption to rise with an increase in the interest rate. An additional complication is that multiple steady states can exist for a given interest rate.

paper, 'Sraffa, Labor Theories of Value and the Economics of Real Wage Determination' (Burmeister, 1984).

2. It is evident now that the comparison of alternative steady-state equilibria is fundamentally a flawed economic exercise. As noted above, different techniques such as A, B and C (in Figure 1 or Figure 2) entail *different stocks of capital goods*, both different types and different quantities. In general, one cannot move from B to A or C in one time period because it may take longer for the capital stocks to adjust to the types and levels of goods appropriate for the new production technique. A comparison of the steady-state equilibria represented by A, B and C seems to suggest that when starting at the steady-state equilibrium achieved using technique B, for example, one could choose whether to remain there or to move immediately to the steady-state equilibrium represented by technique C, but this choice is not feasible. Instead, the economically relevant choices are either to stay at B, or to follow any one of the feasible paths that start from B. Since the comparison of steady-state equilibria, in effect, compares infeasible alternatives, it is not surprising that paradoxical results may sometimes emerge. When one does study the dynamic properties of feasible paths, *no* paradoxes arise and the insights of neoclassical economics are left intact (though, of course, not all the insights from a one-capital-good simplification of neoclassical economics).

3. Under quite general conditions, a *necessary and sufficient* condition for an economy never to exhibit the paradoxical consumption behaviour illustrated by Figure 1 is that the economy be *regular* in the sense of Burmeister (1976).

Using the self-evident notation in the latter paper, an economy is called *regular* if

$$\sum_{i=1}^{n} p_i \left(\frac{dk_i}{dr}\right)\bigg|_{(r^*,p^*)} < 0$$

at every steady-state equilibrium point (r^*, p^*). In discrete technologies,

$$\frac{dk_i}{dr} \quad \text{above is replaced by} \quad \frac{\Delta k_i}{\Delta r}$$

and p_i is evaluated at the switch-point rate of interest, r^*.

Moreover, when an economy is regular, there exists an index of aggregate capital stock, K, and an aggregate production function

$$C = F(K)$$

defined only across steady-state equilibria. Thus, this aggregate production function gives steady-state consumption as a function of the index of capital. This function has the properties

$$F'(K) = r$$

and

$$F''(K) < 0$$

and therefore is 'well-behaved'. Proofs are contained in Burmeister (1977, 1979).

It is important to note that this aggregate production function is useful *only* for comparing alternative steady-state equilibria and cannot be used for studying more general dynamic paths.

4. An unresolved question remains: To what extent can we comfortably rely upon one-capital-good models for empirical work and policy recommendations? Of course, *all* theories are distortions of reality – otherwise they would not be theories. The practical issue is not whether or not the assumptions we make to build a model distort reality; they must. Rather the practical issue is whether or not the impact of these distortions is sufficiently small for us to take particular implications as approximately true and therefore to use them to answer questions of practical importance.

Methodology that relies upon one-capital-good models may, for some questions at least, lead to serious mistakes – either by way of faulty explanations or by way of bad policy implications. One study that sheds some light on this issue is by Franklin M. Fisher, who concluded that the old, traditional methods of relying on an index of the capital stock, treating it as if it measured the quantity of a single capital good, and then estimating a Cobb–Douglas 'aggregate production function' work surprisingly well, at least whenever (for whatever reason) labour's share is approximately constant,[9] but this limited result is of little comfort, and this whole area would benefit from further research.

5. The real problem, of course, is that those interested in doing empirical work have few alternatives available to them. Even if we had appropriate data on the stocks of different types of capital goods over time – and we do not – realistic econometric models allowing for heterogeneous capital goods would necessarily involve new complexities. No doubt this would become a flourishing research area if appropriate capital goods data were available, but there is no point in specifying sophisticated models that cannot be estimated. Thus the approximate answers provided by one-capital-good models are likely to prevail, lacking both clear evidence why they should not and any viable alternative.

---

[9] See Fisher (1971).

In conclusion, there are meaningful and potentially important questions about the implications of heterogeneous capital goods that remain to be answered. A particular model might yield approximate but acceptable answers for some sets of questions and yet give awful answers to other questions. For example, by ignoring friction, Newton was able to provide very accurate (though approximate) answers to questions such as, 'How long will it take a sphere to roll down a smooth inclined plane?' Obviously this model distorts reality by ignoring friction, and it is totally inappropriate for studying the effects of how long it takes an automobile to stop when the brakes are applied.

So it is with economics. There are full-employment models that may give perfectly acceptable answers to questions about the effect of money supply growth on inflation, but such models obviously cannot answer questions about the costs of alternative unemployment insurance plans. Likewise, single-capital-good models that yield acceptable answers under some circumstances nevertheless may be inadequate in other circumstances, such as for the study of a developing economy. However, in all cases, whether or not a particular model is satisfactory *cannot* be answered independently of what question it is intended to answer, and even then the suitability of approximate answers cannot be evaluated without knowing to what *purpose* those answers are going to be put.

In our further attempts to understand the effects of heterogeneous capital goods, we just begin to be clear about the precise uses we intend for each model we build. For some purposes it may turn out that a one-capital-good setting is appropriate, while for others explicit recognition of heterogeneous capital may be crucial. It would be unfortunate if the insights we have gained from the work of Sraffa and Robinson were forgotten.

For such lines of inquiry to continue and to command the serious attention of modern economists, it is essential that we do two things.

First, we must identify interesting economic questions whose correct answers require a model with heterogeneous capital goods.

Second, we must find ways to give such models empirical and policy content.

References

Barro, R. J. (1990). *Macroeconomics*, 3rd edn, New York: John Wiley.
Bharadwaj, K. and Schefold, B. (eds) (1989). *Essays on Piero Sraffa: Critical Perspectives on the Revival of Classical Theory*, London: Unwin Hyman.

Bruno, M., Burmeister, E. and Sheshinski, E. (1966). "The Nature and Implications of the Reswitching of Techniques", *The Quarterly Journal of Economics*, **LXXX**(4), pp. 526–53.

Burmeister, E. (1974). 'Synthesizing the Neo-Austrian and Alternative Approaches to Capital Theory: A Survey', *Journal of Economic Literature*, June.

Burmeister, E. (1976). 'Real Wicksell Effects and Regular Economies', in M. Brown, K. Sato and P. Zarembka (eds), *Essays in Modern Capital Theory*, Amsterdam: North-Holland, pp. 145–64.

Burmeister, E. (1977). 'On the Social Significance of the Reswitching Controversy', *Revue d'Economie Politique*, March–April, pp. 330–50.

Burmeister, E. (1979). 'Professor Pasinetti's "Unobtrusive Postulate", Regular Economies, and the Existence of a Well-Behaved Aggregate Production Function', *Revue d'Economie Politique*, September–October, pp. 644–52.

Burmeister, E. (1980). *Capital Theory and Dynamics*, New York: Cambridge University Press.

Burmeister, E. (1984). 'Sraffa, Labor Theories of Value, and the Economics of Real Wage Determination', *Journal of Political Economy*, June.

Burmeister, E. and Yeager, L. B. (1978). 'Continuity and Capital Reversal: Reply', *Economic Inquiry*, January.

Fisher, F. M. (1971). 'Aggregate Production Function and the Explanation of Wages: A Simulation Experiment', *Review of Economics and Statistics*, **LIII**(4), pp. 305–25.

Levhari, D. (1965). 'A Nonsubstitution Theorem and Switching of Techniques', *The Quarterly Journal of Economics*, **LXXIX**(1), pp. 98–105.

Levhari, D. and Samuelson, P. A. (1966). 'The Nonswitching Theorem is False,' *The Quarterly Journal of Economics*, **LXXX**(4), pp. 518–19.

Robinson, J. (1953–1954). 'The Production Function and the Theory of Capital', *Review of Economic Studies*, **XXI**, pp. 312–20.

Robinson, J. (1956). *The Accumulation of Capital*, New York: St Martin's Press.

Robinson, J. (1962). *Essays in the Theory of Economic Growth*, New York: St. Martin's Press.

Robinson, J. (1975). 'The Unimportance of Reswitching', *The Quarterly Journal of Economics*, **LXXXIX**(1), pp. 32–9.

Samuelson, P. A. (1964). *Economics: An Introductory Analysis*, 6th edn, New York: McGraw-Hill.

Samuelson, P. A. (1966). 'A Summing Up', *The Quarterly Journal of Economics*, **LXXX**(4), pp. 568–83.

Sraffa, P. (1960). *Production of Commodities by Means of Commodities*, Cambridge: Cambridge University Press.

Yeager, L. B. (1976). 'Towards Understanding Some Paradoxes in Capital Theory', *Economic Inquiry*, September, pp. 313–46.

CHAPTER 8

Wicksell and Douglas on distribution and marginal productivity

Christian Bidard

1 Production function and distribution

The hottest issue[1] between the 'neo-Ricardian' and the 'neoclassical' schools has been the debate on capital theory, which mainly took place in the 1960s. As told from a neo-Ricardian standpoint, the dominant neoclassical school represents the technical capabilities of an economy by assuming the existence of a functional relationship (the production function F) between the amounts of 'factors' (capital K and labour L, land being ignored for the sake of simplicity) and their net product Q, i.e. $Q = F(K, L)$. Function F is assumed to be well behaved (homogeneous and concave). A number of properties are derived from this conception, concerning distribution and its influence on the choice of technique $k = K/L$, output per worker $q = Q/L$, etc. However, it can shown analytically that several of these consequences are plainly wrong. To stick to the most famous argument, the neoclassical law of substitution between factors ('the higher the remuneration of a factor, the lower its use') is incompatible with the re-switching phenomenon, i.e. the possibility that the same technique is operated at both low and high rates of profit whereas it is dominated by another at an intermediate level: whatever the technique one classifies as more capitalistic, one of the two switchings contradicts the lesson of the law of substitution (see Sraffa, 1960). The reader may refer to Harcourt's classical book (1972) for a record of similar 'paradoxes' and the neo-Ricardian criticism of marginalist theory.

It can hardly be denied that economists do use production functions $Q = F(K, L)$ and their. alleged properties in their current practice,

---

[1] With acknowledgements to C. Benetti, H. D. Kurz, P. A. Samuelson and I. Steedman for helpful comments.

whether they are theoreticians or econometricians. The theoretical foundation of this tool, which is undermined by the neo-Ricardian critique, was given by J. B. Clark (1889), who stated the law connecting distribution and marginal productivity: in a competitive economy at equilibrium, each factor is paid according to its marginal productivity. A further step was achieved when Cobb and Douglas (1928) later used the observed distribution of the product between profits and wages to infer marginal productivities, and hence to get some information on production function F itself. More precisely, let us assume that the production function is written $Q = aK^{\alpha}L^{1-\alpha}$ (or $q = ak^{\alpha}$ if quantities per head are considered) for some unknown coefficient α. According to Clark's law, capital receives portion KF_K'/Q of the net product, while labour receives LF_L'/Q. Due to the specific form here assumed for the production function, its exponents α and $1 - \alpha$ represent the shares of national income going to profits and wages, respectively. Observing the distribution thus allows one to determine the production function.

Obviously, the choice of a Cobb–Douglas type function is only made for the sake of simplicity and is not a theoretical issue: alternative functions (CES, VES, etc.) may be used for general or specific purposes, e.g. to check the occurrence or not of 'factor intensity reversals', which play a role in the pure theory of international trade but cannot happen for Cobb–Douglas functions (Samuelson, 1948; Arrow et al., 1961; Minhas, 1962). We too will adopt a Cobb–Douglas production function.

No less obviously, adopting a 'neo-Ricardian standpoint' and a 'Cobb–Douglas production function' simultaneously promises a difficult fatherhood. This strange idea requires some explanations, first on its possibility, secondly on its purpose.

The paradoxes of capital theory such as the re-switching phenomenon show that, in general, no such thing as a production function in Clark's sense exists. However, this statement does not exclude the fact that, in some cases where certain paradoxes do not appear, a production function is conceivable. Section 2 shows that Wicksell's model belongs to such a category, and this is why it will serve as a basic framework for our developments. Wicksell's contribution, anterior to Cobb and Douglas's work, is historically important as being the seminal study to mention difficulties with capital theory.[2] Despite its specificity due to its

---

[2] Wicksell invented the 'Cobb–Douglas' production function long before Cobb and Douglas. Samuelson, a former pupil of Douglas, notices this fact and, aware of the debates on capital theory, gives an assessment of Douglas's work under the explicit but heroic assumption that the difficulties with capital are eliminated (see the references to Douglas (1934), Samuelson (1979), Velupillai (1973) and Wicksell (1900)).

Austrian embedding, which ignores interindustrial relationships (i.e. the production of commodities by means of commodities) and only takes delay of production into account (roundaboutness of techniques), it exhibits a case where, contrary to Clark's statement, the remuneration of capital is *not* equal to its marginal productivity. An increase of capital is, Wicksell explained, partly physically efficient and partly 'improductively absorbed' by price movements.

Our aim is not to study the various paradoxes of capital theory, which nowadays are well known, but to concentrate on Clark's theory of marginal productivity. The precise question we try to answer is: how much is Clark's theory wrong? From a logical standpoint, where the only marks are the binary magnitudes zero or one, the theory holds true for Clark's one-good static model and in a few exceptional cases, whereas its value is null otherwise; this result will not be disputed here. The machinery we have is constructed for another purpose: it aims to give some hint of the quantitative error due to the adoption of Clark's law instead of Wicksell's result. An answer is made possible because our model is two-fold: when considered as a Cobb–Douglas production function and committed to neoclassical hands, the observation of the share of profit in national income combined with an *inappropriate* treatment of capital will secrete a wrong estimation, $\hat{\alpha}$, for the exponent of k. However, if it is represented as a Wicksellian model and delivered to neo-Ricardian minds, it is treated differently and appears as equivalent to a Cobb–Douglas function with a right estimation for exponent α. The gap between $\hat{\alpha}$ and α is a measure of the distance between the quantitative implications of a wrong and a right theoretical framework.

2 Wicksell's forest

Wicksell's model is of the Austrian type (see also Wicksell, 1934). Substituting labour for grapefruit and calling wood its output (the example is not more realistic, but more sober), it is assumed that the process begins as one worker plants acorns. After a period of production t (the process is expressed in continuous time, hence t is a real number whose exact value will result from the capitalist's choice of technique) a quantity $q = q(t)$ of wood is obtained by felling the forest, no labour being required for this last operation. All quantities, including the wage w per worker, are expressed in terms of wood, and the instantaneous profit rate is denoted by r. Constant returns and steady state being assumed, the quantities are reduced to quantities per head. Wicksell's equations are

$$q = q(t) \tag{1}$$

$$w = q(t)e^{-rt} \tag{2}$$

$$k = q(t)(1 - e^{-rt})/r \tag{3}$$

$$r = q'(t)/q(t) \tag{4}$$

Equation (2) expresses that the real cost per worker is exactly covered by the present value of the product ('ni bénéfice, ni perte', according to Walras's dictum). Equation (3) results from Equations (1) and (2) and identity $q = rk + w$, or directly, capital per head is equal to the present value of successive investments: $k = \int_{-t}^{0} we^{-ru}du$. In a neo-Ricardian spirit that Wicksell did not have, Equation (4) flows from the property that, at a given rate of profit, the dominant technique maximizes the real wage. Here, a technique is specified by the choice of t, and Equation (4) emerges as the solution to $\max_t w(t)$, $w(t)$ being defined by Equation (2). The alternative way is to write a no-arbitrage condition between waiting and borrowing at equilibrium: $q(t + dt) - q(t) = rq(t)dt$.

Equation (4) determines the solution $t = t(r)$, then $q = q(r)$, $w = w(r)$ and $k = k(r)$ are obtained from Equations (1), (2) and (3). Inequalities

$$\frac{dr}{dt} < 0, \qquad \frac{dk}{dr} < 0, \qquad \frac{dq}{dr} < 0, \qquad \frac{dw}{dr} < 0 \tag{5}$$

hold (the property is general: for instance, the first inequality does not rely on the assumption that function q'/q in Equation (4) be decreasing, as shown in Bidard (1991, Chap. VII)), and therefore Wicksell's model behaves according to the Austrian laws and most neoclassical 'parables': capital per head is positively correlated with the duration of production ($dk/dt > 0$) and negatively with its remuneration ($dk/dr < 0$); re-switching is excluded, as t is a decreasing function of r. Finally, inequality $dw/dr < 0$ states the general Ricardian trade-off between wages and profits.

As $q = q(r)$ and $k = k(r)$ are decreasing functions of r (or increasing functions of t), variable r may be eliminated between these two functions and q appears as an increasing function of k, i.e. $q = f(k)$. Function f, which is the production function in the neoclassical sense, derives from $q = q(t)$, the production function in the Austrian sense. Wicksell's main discovery in this field was that the value of its derivative, i.e. the marginal productivity of capital, differs from the profit rate: inequality

$$dq/dk < r \tag{6}$$

holds, a result in sharp contrast with Clark's law.

Given a production function $q = q(t)$ in the Austrian sense, an explicit form of its associated production function $q = f(k)$ in the neoclassical sense is rarely found. However, calculations remain simple when

$$q = at^\beta \qquad (\beta > 0) \tag{7}$$

is the wood product per worker after waiting t. Starting with Equation (4), Equations (2)–(4) are then written

$$w = ae^{-\beta}t^\beta \tag{8}$$

$$k = a\beta^{-1}(1 - e^{-\beta})t^{\beta+1} \tag{9}$$

$$r = \beta t^{-1} \tag{10}$$

Elimination of t between Equations (7) and (9) leads to the neoclassical production function $q = f(k)$, where

$$q = \left[\frac{\beta a^{1/\beta}}{1 - e^{-\beta}}\right]^{\frac{\beta}{1+\beta}} k^{\frac{\beta}{1+\beta}} \tag{11}$$

Inequalities (5) are easily checked. As for the marginal productivities, inequality (6) is confirmed as

$$\frac{dq}{dk} = \frac{\partial Q}{\partial K} = \frac{\beta}{(1 + \beta)(1 - e^{-\beta})} r < r \tag{12}$$

and it follows from Equations (8), (9) and (11) that

$$\frac{\partial Q}{\partial L} = \frac{e^\beta}{1 + \beta} w > w \tag{13}$$

i.e. the marginal productivity of labour is greater than the real wage. Of course, equality $K\partial Q/\partial K + L\partial Q/\partial L = Q$ holds good.

3   Quantitative error due to wrong theory

We are now in a position to set the problem precisely. The economy we are considering is of the Wicksell type, the Austrian production function $q = q(t)$ depending on some parameter. We are not directly interested in function $q = q(t)$, but in estimating its associated neoclassical counterpart, the production function $q = f(k)$. It is (rightly) assumed that the neoclassical function belongs to the Cobb–Douglas family: $q = ak^\alpha$, the value of α being unknown. The question is to find the exponent on the basis of one observation, the share π of profits in national income.

The right (neo-Ricardian) calculation is: Equations (7) and (11) show that a Cobb–Douglas structure for $q = f(k)$ derives from a structure as a power of t for the Austrian production function; more precisely q is proportional to k^α if the wood output at date t is proportional to t^β where $\alpha = \beta/(1 + \beta)$, that is $\beta = \alpha/(1 - \alpha)$. Equations (7), (9) and (10) then show that the share of profits in national income is $\pi = rk/q = 1 - e^{-\beta} = 1 - \exp(-\alpha/1 - \alpha)$. Therefore, the value of α, knowing π, is

$$\alpha = \frac{-\ln(1 - \pi)}{1 - \ln(1 - \pi)} \tag{14}$$

Conversely, an economist who has faith in Clark's law will erroneously conclude that the exponent is

$$\hat{\alpha} = \pi \tag{15}$$

Naturally, if other data are available, he should recognize that something is going wrong. For instance, if the marginal productivity of capital and its remuneration can be measured directly, our man will be surprised by the result and can react either by rejecting the model, or searching for some statistical distortion in the data or even (why not?) reading Wicksell.

Figure 1 shows a diagram of the right and wrong estimations (Equations (14) and (15)) of the exponent as a function of the share of profits. If $\alpha = 0.25$ is the right value of the Cobb–Douglas exponent, its neoclassical estimate is $\hat{\alpha} = 0.284$, i.e. the relative error amounts to 13%. This method leads one to consider that capital is more productive than it really is: $\hat{\alpha}(\pi) > \alpha(\pi)$. Inequality (12) explains this phenomenon: the marginal productivity is overestimated when identified with the remuneration of capital. The distortion, due to the negative Wicksell effect, might not

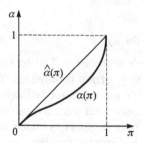

Figure 1. Exponent of the C–D function and share of profits, or right *vs.* wrong theory.

have a systematic direction if the underlying model of the economy were more general than the one considered here. The econometricians who proceed to the evaluation of production functions used to take imperfections into account in order to explain and reduce the gap between the working of the abstract model and economic reality:

Paul Douglas was adept at explaining away most errors of fit. We students used to jest admiringly that his multiple correlation coefficients of 0.97 probably overflowed above 1.00 once he turned his serious attention to explaining observed squared errors; thus, the recorded depression C_t *in place* was probably in excess of the true capital stock *used,* ... etc. (Samuelson, 1979, p. 929)

The serious problem is that *theory* itself hides some pitfalls, even in a model with perfect observations and no friction at all.

4 Conclusion

To estimate a production function is a standard practice for econometricians. Having selected a case which avoids many of the intricacies of capital theory, we have shown that relying on Clark's law of distribution leads to a systematic error in the estimations. As for the implications for pure theory, it is also clear that all conclusions derived from the 'neoclassical' model should at least be re-examined.

References

Arrow, K. J., Chenery, H. B., Minhas, B. S. and Solow, R. M. (1961). 'Capital–Labor Substitution and Economic Efficiency', *Review of Economics and Statistics*, **43**, pp. 225–50.
Bidard, Ch. (1991). *Prix, Reproduction, Rareté*, Paris: Dunod.
Clark, J. B. (1889). 'The Possibility of a Scientific Law of Wages', *Publications of the American Economic Association*, **4**(1), pp. 37–69.
Cobb, C. W. and Douglas, P. H. (1928). 'A Theory of Production', *American Economic Review*, **18**, Supplement, pp. 139–65.
Douglas, P. H. (1934). *The Theory of Wages*, New York: Macmillan.
Harcourt, G. C. (1972). *Some Cambridge Controversies in the Theory of Capital*, Cambridge: Cambridge University Press.
Minhas, B. S. (1962). 'The Homohypallagic Production Function, Factor-Intensity Reversals, and the Heckscher–Ohlin Theorem,' *Journal of Political Economy*, **70**(2), pp. 138–56.
Samuelson, P. A. (1948). 'International Trade and the Equalization of Factor Prices', *The Economic Journal*, **58**, pp. 163–84.
Samuelson, P. A. (1979). 'Paul Douglas's Measurement of Production Functions and Marginal Productivities', *Journal of Political Economy*, **87**(5), 923–39.
Sraffa, P. (1960). *Production of Commodities by Means of Commodities. Prelude to a Critique of Economic Theory*, Cambridge: Cambridge University Press.

322   **C. Bidard**

Velupillai, K. (1973). 'The Cobb–Douglas or the Wicksell Function', *Economics and History*, **16**, pp. 111–113.

Wicksell, K. (1900). 'Marginal Productivity as the Basis of Distribution in Economics', *Ekonomisk Tidskrift*. English translation in *K. Wicksell: Selected Papers in Economic Theory*, E. Lindahl (ed.), London: Unwin and Allen, 1958.

Wicksell, K. (1934). *Lectures on Political Economy*, Vol. I, London: Routledge and Kegan Paul.

CHAPTER 9

On the probability of re-switching and capital reversing in a two-sector Sraffian model

Lynn Mainwaring and Ian Steedman

1   Introduction

In his classic *Production of Commodities by Means of Commodities* (1960), Piero Sraffa claimed (in Chapter XII) that a technique of production which was most profitable at one rate of profit (interest) could become inferior to another technique at a higher rate and then reappear as the most profitable at a yet higher rate. This phenomenon, known as the 're-switching' of techniques, has profound implications for the logic of using aggregate concepts of capital and the standard monotonic relationships between 'factor' quantities and prices derived therefrom (see Harcourt, 1972, and, for a recent exposition, Ahmad, 1991). Sraffa's claim was the subject of intense debate in a symposium (1966) in the *Quarterly Journal of Economics*, and subsequently in papers by Galloway and Shukla (1974), Garegnani (1970, 1976), Sato (1976) and Laibman and Nell (1977). The outcome established categorically the possibility of re-switching in general multisector models of production, but despite these demonstrations of 'possibility', the question of 'probability' has received far less attention.

Apart from some early statements of (generally quite weak) sufficiency conditions for non-re-switching (e.g. Bruno, Burmeister and Sheshinski, 1966, p. 544), there have been few explicit attempts in the theoretical literature to deal with this question. One of the first was by Eltis (1973,

We should like to thank Christian Bidard, Roberto Ciccone, Heinz Kurz and Neri Salvadori for comments on previous drafts, Walter Eltis and Paul Samuelson for encouraging our investigations, and Neil Manning for computational advice.

Chap. 5), who considered the matter in relation to the two-sector model of Hicks (1965) and to his own particular variant of the model.[1] Eltis does not derive an explicit measure of probability but, using numerical examples, concludes that 'the range of values [of the technical coefficients] where there will be reswitching is generally quite narrow, but this is not always the case' (p. 113). A more detailed investigation of the two-sector 'Samuelson–Hicks–Spaventa' model (Samuelson, 1962; Hicks, 1965; Spaventa, 1968) has been undertaken by D'Ippolito (1987). That paper directly considers the probability not of re-switching but of 'real capital reversing': i.e. it asks what is the probability that at a switch-point an increase in the rate of profit, r, will lead (contrary to the neoclassical view) to an increase in the value of capital per worker. Real capital reversing and re-switching are not the same, but the two are often closely related (as we shall see in Section 6) and D'Ippolito's findings are, in any case, of interest in their own right. Assuming that all mathematically feasible technical combinations (with non-negative productivity) exist with equal probability, he finds that the probability of capital reversal is zero for a switch at $r = 0$, but rises as the switching value of r rises, tending to 0.25 as the switch rate tends to infinity. For switching rates of profit below twenty per cent, the probability is less than 6.5 per cent. The Samuelson–Hicks–Spaventa model has a structure which differs in important respects from that of the two-sector Sraffian model investigated in this paper, and a comparison of our findings and those of Eltis and D'Ippolito will be made in Section 7.

In the Sraffian context, Schefold (1976) argued that re-switching in the two-sector model is 'easily possible'. What he meant by this is that re-switching is not a mathematical fluke, i.e. it can occur with finite probability. He was not, however, able to propose a formula that could express the probability 'as a percentage... in function of some economic property of the system' (p. 42). D'Ippolito (1989) has also turned his attention to the Sraffian model in an ambitious assessment of the probability of capital reversing in a multi-sector model. In this case he was unable to obtain an answer by analytical means, but using Monte Carlo methods, with 1200 trials for each combination of switching rate of profit and number of industries, he again found generally low probabilities.

Our brief reflections on theoretical attempts to establish the probability of re-switching point to the difficulty of obtaining a simple and easily interpretable formula. This is not entirely surprising. Even a two-sector,

---

[1] In an Austrian framework, similar conclusions are reached by Hicks (1973, Chap. IV) and Laing (1991). (The application to the Austrian and other models of the basic methodology of this paper is considered in Appendix II.)

single-products Sraffian technique, which is the subject of our investigations, is defined by six coefficients, from which the wage–profit curve may be derived. However, fixing a potential switch-point on that curve requires specifying in advance either the wage rate, the rate of profit or the price ratio. The probability formula will thus be a function of seven parameters. In what follows we are able to derive such a formula, but it is not as transparent as one might wish. Nevertheless, it is sufficiently tractable to permit the derivation of some fairly clear-cut results by use of numerical simulations. Unlike the random selections made by D'Ippolito, these can be pursued in a systematic manner so that the behaviour of the probability with respect to technology characteristics and the independent variable can be uncovered.

In Sections 2–5 we examine the probability that two techniques are equi-profitable at two distinct rates of profit. Double equi-profitability does not necessarily imply that the two techniques re-switch, since it is possible that at one or the other switch-point the two techniques are dominated by a third. In the accepted definition of re-switching the two switch-points must form part of the w–r *frontier* (which consists of those parts of the individual w–r curves that dominate competing w–r combinations). However, to avoid tedious circumlocutions, the discussion proceeds on an interim assumption of no third-technique dominance. Thus, for the purpose of these sections, double equi-profitability will be taken to be synonymous with re-switching. Of course, matters cannot be left to rest like that, and the significance of the distinction will be explored in Section 6.

2   Basic properties of the two-sector model

Consider a technique $\alpha = \{A_1, A_2, a\}$ where[2]

$$[A_1 \ A_2] = A = \begin{bmatrix} a_{11} & a_{12} \\ a_{21} & a_{22} \end{bmatrix} \quad \text{and} \quad a = [a_1 \ a_2]$$

a_{ij} is the input of commodity i per unit of j, A_j the column vector of such inputs, and a_j the input of labour per unit of j. Choose good 2 as the system's *numéraire*, and let p be the corresponding price of good 1, r the uniform rate of profit and w the uniform wage rate (paid *post factum*). The price equations for α are then

$$p = (1 + r)(pa_{11} + a_{21}) + wa_1 \tag{1}$$

---

[2] $\{A_i, a_i\}$ is defined as a method for the production of good i and a combination of methods $\{A, a\}$ as a technique of production.

$$1 = (1 + r)(pa_{12} + a_{22}) + wa_2 \tag{2}$$

which may be solved to give

$$p = p(r) = \frac{[1 - a_{22}(1 + r)]a_1 + a_2 a_{21}(1 + r)}{[1 - a_{11}(1 + r)]a_2 + a_1 a_{12}(1 + r)} \tag{3}$$

$$w = w(r) = \frac{[1 - a_{11}(1 + r)][1 - a_{22}(1 + r)] - a_{12} a_{21}(1 + r)^2}{[1 - a_{11}(1 + r)]a_2 + a_1 a_{12}(1 + r)} \tag{4}$$

where w is, of course, expressed in terms of good 2. The system is productive (yields $w > 0$ at $r = 0$) if

$$a_{ii} < 1 \tag{5.1}$$

and

$$(1 - a_{11})(1 - a_{22}) > a_{12} a_{21} \tag{5.2}$$

Equation (4) describes the wage–profit curve or $w(r)$ function for α. Simple differentiation shows that $w'(r) < 0$, with $w(R) = 0$ at $r = R > 0$ for a productive system. It is also seen that

$$w''(r) \lesseqgtr 0 \quad \text{as} \quad \frac{a_{21} a_2 + a_{11} a_1}{a_{22} a_2 + a_{12} a_1} \gtreqless \frac{a_1}{a_2} \tag{6}$$

Returning to the price ratio, $p(r) > 0$ for all $r(0 \leq r \leq R)$ if Inequalities (5.1) and (5.2) hold. Moreover,

$$p'(r) \gtreqless 0 \quad \text{as} \quad \frac{a_{21} a_2 + a_{11} a_1}{a_{22} a_2 + a_{12} a_1} \gtreqless \frac{a_1}{a_2} \tag{7}$$

From Inequalities (6) and (7), it follows that $p'(r) > 0$ when $w''(r) < 0$, i.e. prices rise with r if the wage–profit curve is concave to the origin. It is then easy to see that had good 1 been chosen as the *numéraire* of system α, the curvature of $w(r)$ and the sign of $p'(r)$ would have been reversed. Since the choice of *numéraire* is arbitrary with respect to re-switching (see Ahmad, 1991, Chap. 10), nothing is lost if, in subsequent sections, we concentrate on the case of a concave $w(r)$. In the meantime, attention should be drawn to the important borderline case $p'(r) = w''(r) = 0$. Here we have what Sraffa called equal 'proportions of labour to means of production' (1960, Chap. III) (EPLMP, henceforth) in which prices are equal to ratios of directly and indirectly embodied labour, at all r. (This is equivalent to Marx's 'equal organic compositions of capital'.)

A switch-point may be defined as a rate of profit at which two techniques, say α and β, are equi-profitable and can co-exist. This implies that both yield the same wage rate and price ratio at the switch-point. According to the theorem of Bruno, Burmeister and Sheshinski (1966), equi-profitable techniques at a switch-point differ (flukes apart) in only one method. That is to say, matrix B of technique β differs from A in only one column, and vector b differs from a in the corresponding element. Thus, if A and B differ in the method for the production of good 2, then $\beta = \{A_1, B_2, a_1, b_2\}$ and the price equations for β are given by Equation (1) and (using the same *numéraire*)

$$1 = (1 + r)(pb_{12} + b_{22}) + wb_2$$

Naturally, for system β, we have that $p'_\beta(r) \gtrless 0$ as $w''_\beta(r) \lessgtr 0$. As noted by Woods (1988), relations (6) and (7) immediately rule out the possibility of re-switching in certain cases. For re-switching to be possible it is necessary that sign $w''_\alpha(r) \neq$ sign $w''_\beta(r)$, i.e. that the wage–profit curves have qualitatively the same curvature. This is so because of the fundamental property of a switch-point that $p_\alpha(r) = p_\beta(r)$. Re-switching thus requires that the price ratios of the two systems be equal at two distinct rates of profit. Yet qualitative differences in $w(r)$ curvatures imply that sign $p'_\alpha(r) \neq$ sign $p'_\beta(r)$ and so a double intersection of these monotonic price functions is impossible. This means that a concave $w(r)$ function can never re-switch with a convex one; nor can a function with either kind of curvature re-switch with a straight-line (EPLMP) function.[3]

3   Evaluating the probability

Let α be a technique with a concave-to-the-origin $w(r)$ function and hence, with good 2 as *numéraire*, $p'(r) > 0$. In addition to the choice of *numéraire*, we are also at liberty to choose the units of measurement of the two goods. This is done by setting

$$p(R) = 1 \tag{8}$$

The choice of units does, naturally, have implications for the numerical value of the technical coefficients. (If good 1 is measured in half-ounces instead of ounces, then a_{12} will be doubled numerically and a_{12} will be halved.) The consequence of Equation (8) is that a restriction is now placed on the relationship between coefficients. Inserting Equation (8) into Equations (1) and (2) and recalling that $w(R) = 0$ gives

$$a_{11} + a_{21} = a_{12} + a_{22} = (1 + R)^{-1} \tag{9}$$

---

[3] This statement is true of single-product Sraffa systems of any order, since a technique in which the price vector recurs at distinct rates of profit must have EPLMP (Mainwaring, 1978). Salvadori and Steedman (1988) point out that it is not possible for two EPLMP systems to switch once, let alone re-switch.

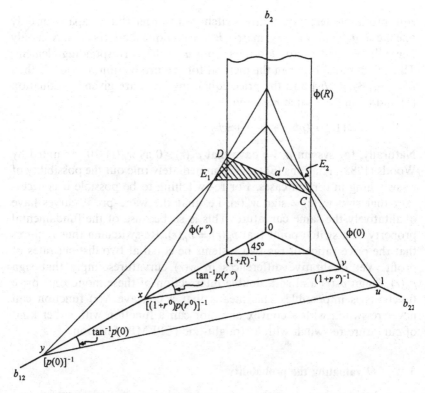

Figure 1

Next consider a technique $\beta = \{A_1, B_2, a_1, b_2\}$ which differs from α in the second method and is therefore eligible to switch with α. If such a switch occurs at a rate of profit r^0, then the two techniques are equi-profitable at that rate, so that using the wage rate and prices of α yields, for method 2 of β, the price equation

$$1 = w(r^0)b_2 + (1 + r^0)[p(r^0)b_{12} + b_{22}] \qquad (10)$$

For $r^0 (0 \le r^0 < R)$, Equation (10) describes a downward-sloping plane, $\phi(r^0)$, in (b_2, b_{12}, b_{22})-space (see Figure 1, which is an elaboration of a figure in Schefold, 1976). (For $r^0 = R$, $\phi(R)$ is vertical and hence unbounded along the b_2-axis.) Since the method (A_2, a_2) satisfies Equation (10), by the definition of a switch-point, $\phi(r^0)$ must pass through the point $a' = (a_2, a_{12}, a_{22})$. It has intercepts on the b_{12} and b_{22} axes at $x = [(1 + r^0)p(r^0)]^{-1}$ and $v = (1 + r^0)^{-1}$, respectively. The tangent of the angle described by the intersection of $\phi(r^0)$ with the (b_{12}, b_{22})-plane and the b_{12} axis is thus equal to the price ratio $p(r^0)$. Any point within $\phi(r^0)$ describes a possible method for the production of good 2 that is equi-profitable with (A_2, a_2), and hence a technique β which switches with α at r^0.

Taking an alternative value of r, say r', the plane $\phi(r')$ likewise describes all potential methods (B_2, b_2) which switch with α at r'. The straight line intersection of $\phi(r^0)$ and $\phi(r')$ then defines the set of methods (and hence techniques) which double-switch at the two rates of profit r^0 and r'. The line $E_1a'E_2$, for example, defines the set of techniques which are equi-profitable with α at $r = r^0$ and $r = 0$. Likewise, $Da'C$ is the set of methods which double-switch at r^0 and R. Given an initial switch at r^0, varying r from 0 to R yields an infinity of intersections of $\phi(r^0)$ and $\phi(r)$ which, when integrated, is described by the shaded area $CE_2a'E_1D$ on the $\phi(r^0)$-plane.

The probability, $\psi(r^0)$, that a technique which switches with α at r^0 will also switch at some other rate of profit, $r^s(0 \leq r^s \leq R)$, is taken to be the ratio of the area $CE_2a'E_1D$ to the area of $\phi(r^0)$. We recognize that conceptual difficulties can arise about expressing the probability as a ratio of two sets each of which contains an infinite number of points. In particular, it may be objected that not all points within these sets are equally likely to present themselves as eligible alternatives to α, and, indeed, we shall see in Section 5 that a problem of this sort arises when $r^0 = R$. In general, however, there is no reason to suppose that the distribution of eligible points in the 're-switch set' $CE_2a'E_1D$ is more dense or less dense than that of the 'switch set' $\phi(r^0)$. While recognizing the difficulties of the proposed probability measure, we proceed on the grounds that it does have intuitive appeal. Others are, of course, welcome to advocate superior measures. We should add that our argument in no way presupposes the particular choice of units implicit in Equation (8), or any other choice of units.

Two limiting cases can immediately be identified. If technique α has EPLMP (implying that $p(r)$ is constant), then the intersections of all $\phi(r)$ with the (b_{12}, b_{22})-plane are parallel straight lines. The set $CE_2a'E_1D$ thus collapses to a line and the probability of re-switching is zero. This merely confirms what we know already. The probability is also zero if the initial switch occurs at R. In this case the re-switch set is of finite dimension, but is infinitesimal in relation to the unbounded set $\phi(R)$. The reason why $\phi(R)$ is unbounded is that at $w = 0$, b_2 can be varied from zero to infinity without affecting the profitability of β. This is, of course, an exceptional case, relying as it does on a zero wage rate. (We shall see in Section 5 that this case causes problems in relation to our measure of probability.)

The probability is defined as a ratio of areas which, in Figure 1, are drawn in three-dimensional space. However, a vertical projection of the

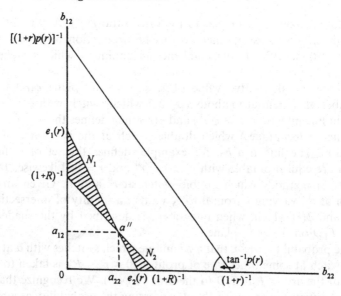

Figure 2

$\phi(r)$ onto the (b_{12}, b_{22})-plane preserves this ratio while allowing it to be represented in two dimensions (Figure 2). Here points $e_i(r)$ correspond to the E_i of Figure 1 and are the projections onto the b_{i2} axis of the intersections of the edges along the (b_2, b_{12})-planes of $\phi(r)$ and $\phi(0)$. They are given (dropping the 0 superscript) by

$$e_1(r) = \frac{w(0) - w(r)}{w(0)(1 + r)p(r) - w(r)p(0)} \tag{11}$$

$$e_2(r) = \frac{w(0) - w(r)}{w(0)(1 + r) - w(r)} \tag{12}$$

respectively. The shaded sets in Figure 2 have a combined area[4]

$$N = N_1 + N_2 = [(1 + R)^{-1}(a_{12} - a_{22}) + e_1(r)a_{22} - e_2(r)a_{12}]/2$$

The vertical projection $\varphi(r)$ of $\phi(r)$ onto the (b_{12}, b_{22})-plane has an area $[(1 + r)^2 p(r)]^{-1}/2$, so that the probability of re-switching given a switch at r is

[4] Note that $p'(r) > 0$ implies that $d(e_2/e_1)/dr > 0$, which in turn means that $e_2 < (1 + R)^{-1}$.

$$\psi(r) = N/\varphi(r) = [(1 + R)^{-1}(a_{12} - a_{22}) + e_1(r)a_{22} - e_2(r)a_{12}]$$
$$\cdot (1 + r)^2 p(r)$$

$$(13)$$

This is potentially a very complicated expression, its sub-functions $e_i(r)$ being dependent, via $w(r)$ and $p(r)$, on the full set of technical coefficients of α. The formula can be re-stated using alternative *numéraires* (e.g. labour or Sraffa's 'standard commodity'), but no such juggling can reduce its complexity.[5]

4   Numerical estimation of $\psi(r)$

Because Equation (13) does not yield easy analytical insights, except in special cases, investigation of its properties will be pursued by means of numerical simulations. We shall see that the behaviour of $\psi(r)$ depends, in a significant way, on the magnitude of the coefficient a_{22}, and simulation results are first presented for the case $a_{22} = 0$.

The simulation procedures are as follows. For the case $a_{22} = 0$, an EPLMP 'base' technology for α is specified. A base technology accords to a particular system productivity, as measured by R. Ease of calculation has led us to concentrate on the case $R = 1$, but the effect of varying system productivity is examined by looking (more briefly) at base techniques which imply $R = 0.4$ and $R = 3$. For these base technologies, the $w(r)$ functions are straight lines and $\psi(r)$ is zero for all $r(0 \leq r \leq R)$. Starting from a given base, the technical coefficients are varied systematically in different directions so as to generate concave $w(r)$ curves, and, for each new combination of coefficients, the $\psi(r)$ function is plotted (in Figures 3–5). First we vary the composition of a, then of A_1 and finally we combine variations in a and A_1. It may be noted that *scale* changes in A_1 affect system productivity and hence imply different 'base' technologies. Thus, for a given base, only changes in the proportions of a_{11} and a_{21} are relevant. Scale changes in the a vector need not be considered at all, because they are Harrod-neutral and result in inversely proportional changes in $w(r)$. Thus Equations (11), (12) and, hence, (13) are invariant

---

[5] It may be observed directly from Figure 2 that if a re-switching method has $b_{22} > a_{22}$, then it must also have $b_{12} < a_{12}$. This illustrates Pertz's (1980) necessary condition for re-switching, that the difference vector $A_2 - B_2$ must have some positive and some negative elements. Whilst this condition clearly prevents N from trespassing on certain points within $\varphi(r)$ it does not, on its own, place more than very weak bounds on the magnitude of $\psi(r)$.

to scale changes in a. Throughout the following, a is scaled to yield $w(0) = 1$ for each technique.

Similar procedures are then followed for various positive values of a_{22}.

For each technique generated by these variations an index of concavity, $\sigma = w(0.5R)/w(0)$, is calculated in order to see if there is any relationship between the behaviour of $\psi(r)$ and the curvature of the $w(r)$ relation.[6] (For the EPLMP case, $\sigma = 0.5$.)

Case (i): $a_{22} = 0$

The first EPLMP base technology for this case is

$$\left[\frac{A}{a}\right] = \begin{bmatrix} 0.25 & 0.5 \\ 0.25 & 0 \\ \hline 0.5 & 0.5 \end{bmatrix}$$

yielding $w(0) = p(R) = R = 1$, and $\psi(r) = 0$ for all r. Variations from this base are recorded in Table 1, the individual techniques being numbered in the No. column. The concavity index is also recorded. Techniques 1–4 vary $[a_1\ a_2]$ given the base values of a_{11} and a_{21}. For these pure compositional variations in a, concavity is greatest when $a_1 = 0$ (which means, of course, that sector 1 is completely 'robotized'). Once this point is reached, concavity can only be increased further by changing the proportions of the A_1 vector. Techniques 5–8 have increasing ratios a_{11}/a_{21} (with $a_1 = 0$,

Table 1. $R = 1$ ($a_{12} = 0.5$)

$a_{11} = 0.25, a_{21} = 0.25$				$a_1 = 0$			
No.	a_1	a_2	σ	No.	a_{11}	a_{21}	a_2	σ
1	0.5	0.5	0.5	5	0.375	0.125	0.9	0.75
2	0.333	0.611	0.54	6	0.45	0.05	0.954	0.87
3	0.167	0.722	0.60	7	0.49	0.01	0.99	0.97
4	0	0.833	0.66	8	0.499	0.001	0.999	0.997

[6] The σ index is obviously not unique, and deviations measured at other r-values might give a different ranking of curvatures. The same is true of indexes based on the second derivative or on the area enclosed by the $w(r)$ curve and the w-, r-axes. These have the additional disadvantage of difficulty of calculation. Basing an index on Inequality (6) is equally problematic since the index becomes infinite when $a_1 = 0$ even though concavity is still free to vary an account of the a_{ij}.

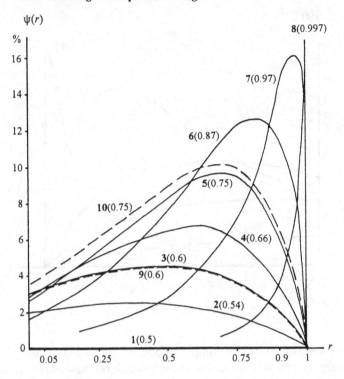

Figure 3

in all cases). When $a_{11} = 0.5$, the system is decomposable and $\psi(r)$ collapses to zero. However, interesting variations in $\psi(r)$ occur close to this limit.

For these variations in a and A_1, $\psi(r)$ functions are plotted as continuous lines in Figure 3, which also indicates the corresponding σ-indexes. Together they display a distinct pattern. First, given σ, $\psi(r)$ rises with r, then falls to zero at R. (That $\psi(R) = 0$ has already been deduced analytically.) Secondly, the r at which $\psi(r)$ is maximized increases as σ increases. Thirdly, $\psi(r)_{\max}$ is greater, the greater is σ. Finally, for very low values of r, $\psi(r)$ first rises with σ and then falls. The most extreme concavity considered is $\sigma = 0.997$, and $\psi(r)$ then reaches 17 per cent at $r = 0.994$.

Starting from the base techniques, concavity has been increased first by raising a_2/a_1 (to the point of robotizing sector 1), and then by raising a_{11}/a_{21}. Taking a high a_2/a_1, concavity can be reduced by lowering a_{11}/a_{21} below its base value. Likewise, with high a_{11}/a_{21}, reducing a_2/a_1

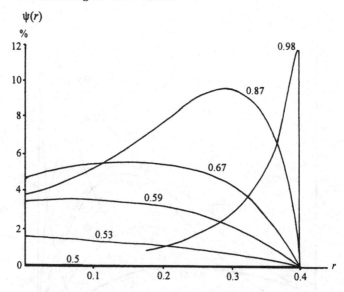

Figure 4

also reduces concavity. Techniques 9 and 10 (recorded in Table A1 of Appendix I) are generated by these procedures and have concavity indexes which are the same as techniques 3 and 5. Their $\psi(r)$ functions are plotted in Figure 3 as pecked lines. It can be seen that σ is not a perfectly accurate predictor of the shape of $\psi(r)$: although the $\psi(r)$ functions for techniques 3 and 9 are very close, those for 5 and 10 differ more significantly. Nowhere, however, is the probability difference greater than one per cent.

The procedures described so far relate to a base technology yielding $R = 1$. Tables A.2 and A.3, in Appendix I, record variations of base techniques with $R = 0.4$ and $R = 3$. The corresponding $\psi(r)$ functions are plotted in Figures 4 and 5. As expected, qualitatively the same kinds of patterns emerge in the three cases distinguished by R-value. However, the variations in $\psi(r)$ behaviour become more exaggerated as R increases. Thus, at equivalent levels of σ, for $r \simeq R$, $\psi(r)$ rises as R rises, and for $r \simeq 0$, $\psi(r)$ falls as R rises.

Case (ii): $a_{22} > 0$

For the case $R = 1$, $\psi(r)$ functions were also derived for a number of positive values of a_{22}. An implication of Inequalities (6) and (7) is that, as

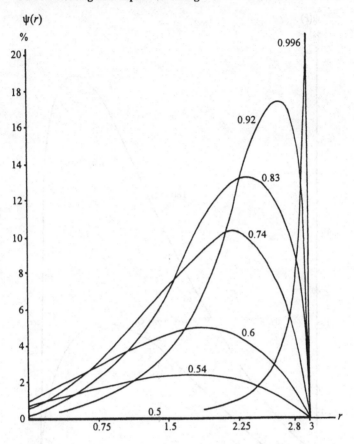

Figure 5

a_{22}/a_{11} is raised, *ceteris paribus*, concavity is reduced. Moreover, at higher and higher values of a_{22}, the scope for generating greater concavity by an appropriate choice of the other coefficients is reduced. It might thus be thought, on the basis of the findings of the preceding sub-section, that in this case higher values of a_{22} would generate $\psi(r)$ curves with generally modest maxima. It turns out, however, that precisely the opposite happens.

A sample of techniques is reported in Table A.4 in Appendix I. Techniques 11–13 have $a_{22} = 0.25$, and plots of their $\psi(r)$ functions in Figure 6 are generally consistent with the results for $a_{22} = 0$. Techniques 14–18 have a_{22}-values in excess of 0.4. Inspection of the corresponding $\psi(r)$ curves show that (even approximate) predictions can no longer be

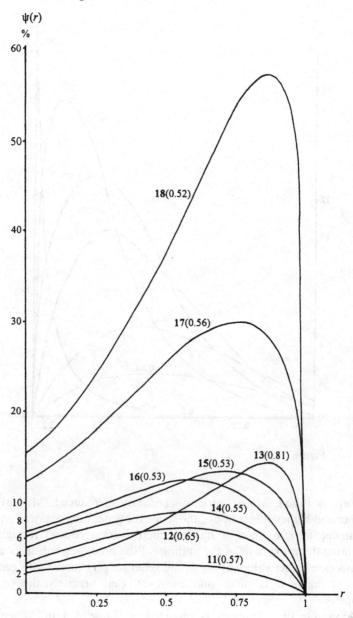

Figure 6

based on σ alone. It appears that, for high values of a_{22}, very small increases in σ generate large upward shifts in the $\psi(r)$ function. For given values of σ, small increases in a_{22} (at the upper end of its range) also generate large increases in $\psi(r)$. Technique 18 (with $a_{22} = 0.49$) yields a modest $\sigma = 0.52$, yet its $\psi(r)$ function starts at over 15 per cent and peaks at 58 per cent.

In terms of the hope that concavity might provide an easily observable predictor of the likelihood of re-switching, these findings are a set-back. More importantly, they also appear to undermine the conclusion that $\psi(r)$ tends, on the whole, to be rather low. We can see that, even at r close to zero, it is possible to generate re-switching probabilities of around 15 per cent,[7] but this begs further questions. One of these is postponed to the next sub-section; one is dealt with immediately.

What we have done up to now is to take an arbitrary technique (α) and calculate the corresponding $\psi(r)$, but what is the probability of the existence of a given α? Purely for illustrative purposes, suppose that for a technique of given productivity (say, $R = 1$) any combination of the elements of the respective vectors, a, A_1 and A_2 is equally likely.[8] Thus, for example, since $a_{12} + a_{22} = 0.5$, the probability that $a_{22} \geq 0.49$ is 0.02. By similar reasoning for the other coefficients, the probability of the existence of technique 18 is 0.000008. Generally speaking, $\psi(r)$ functions which lie above ten per cent over the great part of their range require a_{11}, a_{22} and $a_2/(a_1 + a_2)$ to be simultaneously in excess of 0.4 (although, as techniques 15 and 16 illustrate, there is some trade-off between a_{11} and a_1). The probability of this combination is less than one per cent. Reasoning along these lines leads to the tentative conclusion that there is a very low probability of the existence of a technique for which the probability of re-switching is very high; or, more succinctly, very high $\psi(r)$ functions are generated by very unlikely αs.

[7] The sensitivity of $\psi(r)$ to α_{22} should be put into context by recalling that we have limited our considerations to concave $w(r)$ curves with commodity 2 as *numéraire*. Convex $w(r)$ curves would arise if either the *numéraire* were changed, or if the commodity indexes were reversed. Changing the *numéraire* does not change the switching behaviour of the technology and we should, in that case, continue to focus on the critical rôle of a_{22}, although raising a_{22} would then have the effect of reducing convexity rather than concavity. Relabelling goods does not affect switching properties either, but in that case the critical coefficient would be a_{11} (provided, now, that the method for producing commodity 1 is displaced at the switchpoint).

[8] This is consistent with the definition of $\psi(r)$, which also assumes that all mathematically feasible coefficient combinations have equal probability, and with the approach of D'Ippolito (1987).

'Close' switch-points

$\psi(r^0)$ measures the probability of a technique which switches at r^0 re-switching at r^s anywhere in the domain $(0 \le r^s \le R)$. Suppose we wish to know the probability $\hat{\psi}(r)$ of a switch and re-switch falling in a restricted domain $(0 \le r^0, r^s \le \hat{r} < R)$. Then in Figure 2, the shaded areas N_i would be defined along the axes not by the difference $[e_i(r) - (1 + R)^{-1}]$, but by $[e_i(r) - e_i(\hat{r})]$. All simulations were repeated over restricted domains $(0, 0.5R)$. Typically, $\hat{\psi}(r)$ was found to be between one-third and one-half of $\psi(r)$, the highest recorded ratio being 0.54. Interestingly, those techniques which generate very high $\psi(r)$ had proportionately low $\hat{\psi}(r)$. (The ratio $\hat{\psi}(r)/\psi(r)$ for technique 17 is approximately one-sixth; that for 18, approximately one-third.) Given the typical assumption that $w_{min} > 0$, it is of interest that a restriction of the switch/re-switch domain appears to reduce probability, generally more than in proportion to the degree of restriction.

5   The probability of re-switching at any two rates of profit

Up to now we have been concerned (in the unconstrained case) with the question: Given that a technique β can switch with a pre-specified technique α at some given rate of profit r^0, what is the probability, $\psi(r^0)$, of β switching with α at some other $r = r^s(0 \le r^s \le R)$? It would be natural to extend the enquiry to ask a more general question: What is the probability, ψ, of finding a technique which switches with α at *any* two rates of profit? In geometrical terms, this would require the picture drawn in Figure 1 to be repeated for each of the infinitely many fixed planes $\phi(r)$ $(0 \le r < R)$. The shaded area $CE_2 a' E_1 D$ would then have as its counterpart a solid consisting of two non-convex cones with apexes touching at a'. To see this, consider Figure 7, which is a vertical slice along the (b_2, b_{22})-planes of Figure 1. The line $t^0 v^0$ defines the edge of $\phi(r^0)$ in this plane. The intersection of $t^0 v^0$ and all other edges $\phi(0) \ldots \phi(R)$ is the segment $e^0 c^0$ (corresponding to $E_2 C$ in Figure 1), defining the re-switch set, in this plane, conditional on an initial switch at r^0. The broken lines in Figure 7 show other edges and their corresponding re-switch segments in bold. Continuous variation thus generates the darkly shaded area qmn (also shown magnified) as the re-switch space in this plane, i.e. the set of all $(b_2, 0, b_{22})$ capable of switching with α. A vertical slice through the (b_2, b_{12})-plane could be similarly interpreted. A slice along the b_2-axis through a' would reduce the re-switch space to a single point (a'). As the slice swings from the

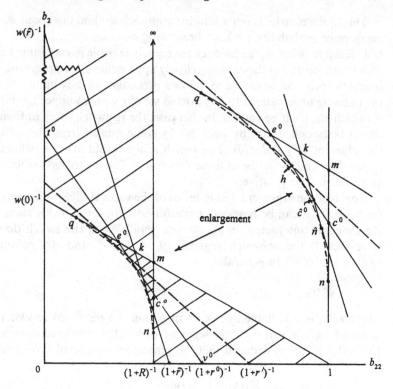

Figure 7

axial planes to a', the re-switch space collapses linearly to a point, thus defining the pair of cones described above. The volume of these cones could then be taken as the numerator in a generalized measure of probability.

A problem immediately arises, however, with respect to the denominator, i.e. the volume of a solid corresponding to the plane $\phi(r^0)$ in Figure 1 (and represented in Figure 7 by the lightly shaded area), for this solid is unbounded along the b_2-axis. This is because the denominator includes all of the techniques which are, in principle, eligible to switch with α at any $r(0 \leq r \leq R)$. It has already been noted that at R (when $w = 0$), the labour coefficient b_2 is free to take on any value without affecting the economic (as opposed to the technical) properties of the technique. There is therefore an unbounded set of eligible switching techniques, but a strictly bounded set of re-switching techniques. Simply taking the ratio of these volumes would yield $\psi = 0$.

This, quite clearly, is not a sensible approach to thinking about ψ. The measure of probability we have been using assumes that all mathematically feasible switching techniques are equally feasible in economic terms. This is obviously not the case as r closely approaches R. A pragmatic way round the problem would be to follow a procedure already hinted at, that of confining observations to a restricted set of r with an upper bound $\hat{r} < R$ (which can itself be varied). In that case, the re-switch space in Figure 7 would be bounded, not by qmn, but by some smaller 'triangle', $qk\hat{n}$, on the edges of $\phi(\hat{r})$ and $\phi(0)$. The switch space would also be defined by these edges and would be of finite dimension. The 'restricted' probability $\hat{\psi}$ would thus be positive.

Consider the argument first in terms of the vertical slice in Figure 7, i.e. for $b_{12} = 0$. (It can be repeated, *mutatis mutandis*, for all other slices and the outcome 'integrated' in an obvious way.) When the switch domain is restricted, the re-switch segment at r^0 is $e^0\hat{c}^0$ and, by definition, $\hat{\psi}(r^0) = e^0\hat{c}^0/t^0v^0$. In general,

$$\hat{\psi}(r)_{|b_{12}=0} = e\hat{c}(r)/tv(r)$$

where $e\hat{c}(r)$ is a variable line segment within the restricted re-switch set $qk\hat{n}$ and $tv(r)$ a variable line segment within the restricted switch set. From this it can be deduced that the generalized restricted probability is

$$\hat{\psi}_{|b_{12}=0} = \frac{1}{2}\int_0^{\hat{r}} e\hat{c}(r)\mathrm{d}r / \int_0^{\hat{r}} tv(r)\mathrm{d}r \tag{14}$$

where the numerator of this expression is half the area of the re-switch space. To see how this expression is arrived at, return to $e^0\hat{c}^0$. As $\phi(r)$ varies from $\phi(0)$ to $\phi(\hat{r})$, each edge describes an intersection on $e^0\hat{c}^0$, such as a point h. Point h refers to a technique $(b_2^h, 0, b_{22}^h)$ which switches with α at r^0 and re-switches at r'. It represents *one* technique capable of re-switching with α. Similarly, every other point on $e^0\hat{c}^0$ will be a point on the re-switch segment $e\hat{c}(r)$ of some plane other than $\phi(r^0)$. Indeed, each point in the re-switch space will be on exactly two re-switch segments. This follows from the definition of a re-switch – each alternative technique must coexist with α at two distinct rates of profit. Outside the re-switch set the edges do not intersect and each point is equi-profitable with α at only one rate of profit. That is why in Equation (14) the infinite sum of re-switch segments $e\hat{c}(r)$ is divided by two to obtain the number of distinct re-switching techniques. Expressions similar to Equation (14) can be obtained for $b_{12} > 0$, and these can then be integrated to obtain a finite ratio of solids. It may be noted that as $\hat{r} \to R$, the denominator in Equation (14) approaches infinity, giving $\psi(r) = 0$.

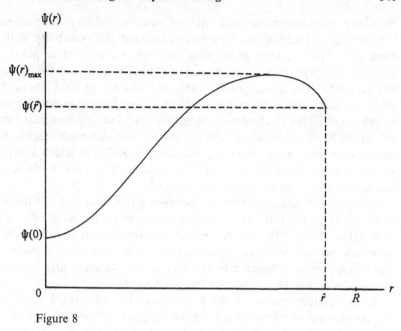

Figure 8

There seems to be little point in trying to develop this insight into a formula corresponding to Equation (13) since the result would be considerably less transparent than Equation (13) which itself is only interpretable with numerical assistance. Nevertheless, some deductions can be made. Figure 8 shows a $\hat{\psi}(r)$ function for α (which lies below the $\psi(r)$ function because of the restriction $\hat{r} < R$). It follows from the preceding argument that $2\hat{\psi}$ is a weighted average of all $\hat{\psi}(r)$, with weights $tv(r)/\int_0^{\hat{r}} tv(r)dr$. Thus $2\hat{\psi}$ cannot exceed $\hat{\psi}(r)_{max}$ and cannot be less than $\min[\hat{\psi}(0), \hat{\psi}(\hat{r})]$.

The conclusion is that the probability of finding a technique which re-switches with α at any two rates r, $r^s \leq \hat{r}$ is one-half of the weighted average of probabilities of finding a technique which switches at each $r(0 \leq r \leq \hat{r})$ and re-switches at some other $r^s(0 \leq r^s \leq \hat{r})$. If the latter is in the region of 2.5 per cent when $\hat{r} = 0.5R$, then $\hat{\psi}$ will be about 1.25 per cent.

6   Switch-point domination and capital reversing

Up to now we have used the term 'switch-point' to mean a rate of profit at which two techniques, α and β, are equi-profitable and the term 're-switching' is synonymous with 'double equi-profitability' (henceforth: DEP). This is because we have not considered the possibility that a third technique, γ, may be superior to both α and β at a 'point of equi-profitability' (PEP). This is a matter to which we must now turn our attention. The investigation is only of interest if at least one (α, β)-PEP is undominated (otherwise we might as well have begun with the γ switch-point). There is, however, no reason to exclude the possibility that one of the PEPs is dominated. The matter is of particular relevance to the question of 'real capital reversing' (henceforth: RCR) in which a switch on the frontier from one technique to another, as r rises, leads to an increase in the value of capital per worker.[9]

Re-switching, as conventionally understood (i.e. both PEPs on the w–r frontier), is a sufficient but not necessary condition for RCR. We shall now argue that DEP, a more general concept than re-switching, is a necessary but not sufficient condition for RCR. However, in order to forestall a possible objection to this conclusion, we must first consider, in order to eliminate, a potential exception to the result.

In production systems of the Samuelson–Hicks–Spaventa type, one can construct a w–r frontier (or a finite segment of that frontier) which is a 'true envelope' of the individual w–r curves; that is, a movement along the w–r frontier implies a continuous change of technique. As a consequence, it is possible in such systems to generate RCR even if no pair of techniques displays DEP (see, for example, Spaventa, 1970). In the present Sraffian model, point a' in Figure 1 would correspond to a point (α') on the w–r frontier, but since, by the definition of a continuous frontier, no other technique coexists with α at r^0, then, of the infinity of potential switching techniques defining $\phi(r^0)$ in Figure 1, none is, in fact, available. On our definition of probability, this must be judged as an outcome of zero probability.

If we confine our attention to cases of 'discrete' technique change along the w–r frontier, DEP becomes a necessary but insufficient condition for RCR. The point is illustrated in Figure 9 (i) and (ii), where α and β are equi-profitable at r^0 and r^s. The former is at the frontier (hence a true switch-point) but the latter is not. Even so, since α and β differ in

---

[9] Since the two techniques have the same set of prices at the switch-point, the change in the value of capital per worker is due entirely to the difference in the physical compositions of the capitals of the two techniques. This form of capital reversing (with which we are solely concerned) is known as a negative real Wicksell effect (see Harcourt, 1972). (Changes in the value of capital may also arise as r varies with a single technique in use, but these are due to the revaluation of stocks of capital of given physical composition – the so-called price Wicksell effect.)

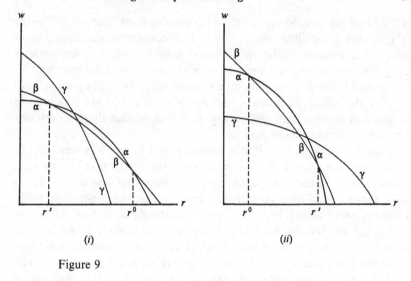

Figure 9

only one method, they must have common prices at the PEPs. At r^s, therefore, the PEP has all the properties of a true switch-point except that α and β are dominated by γ. (This statement may not apply to the intersection of the $w(r)$ curves of β and γ, since these techniques need have no methods in common.) Assuming that the growth rate is zero – an assumption maintained throughout this section – Figure 9 (i) illustrates a case of DEP with RCR and Figure 9 (ii) a case of DEP without RCR.[10] Real capital reversing cannot occur unless two techniques display DEP, but since DEP can occur without RCR, it follows immediately that the probability of RCR – conditional on a given frontier switch at r^0 – is less than the conditional probability, $\psi(r^0)$, of DEP.

This naturally raises the question of the relationship between the probability of DEP and the probability of re-switching proper, once the possibility of dominance is admitted. This is a very tricky question that seems (to us) to have no clear-cut answer. Without going into details, it can be shown (in Figure 1) that all points (representing potential techniques) in the three-dimensional wedge $E_1 E_2 uvxy E_1$ will dominate a technique which has DEP with α at $r^s < r^0$. The problem for any attempt at probability measurement is that while the sets of EP and DEP techniques (the

---

[10] The value of capital per worker in the case of a zero growth rate is given by the slope of a line from the vertical intercept of the $w(r)$ curve to the point on that curve corresponding to the given rate of profit. Thus at a PEP, the technique with the greater $w(0)$ has the higher value of capital per worker.

'switch' and 're-switch' sets of the previous sections) occupy the plane $\phi(r^0)$, the set of possible dominating techniques occupies a three-dimensional space. In terms of the $w(r)$ curves of Figure 9, what we are saying is that given two curves, belonging to α and β, with a frontier switch at r^0, we can find infinitely many coefficient combinations yielding techniques γ, δ, ..., etc., which dominate α and β at r^s, but it does not follow from the fact that there are infinitely many, in principle, that there is even one in practice – though there may be!

In the previous sections it was assumed that both PEPs were on the frontier and the probability measures were subject to that assumption. Although it is difficult to specify the probability that one PEP is dominated, that probability is greater than zero, so that the conditional probability of re-switching proper is correspondingly less than $\psi(r^0)$, the conditional probability of DEP. A reader who objects (for whatever reason) that it is wrong to take account of third-technique dominance would have to concede that the long-accepted proposition that RCR can occur without re-switching proper is uninteresting because, in the Sraffian model, that proposition depends precisely on the existence of a dominating technique.

7   Conclusion

The central findings of the paper are summarized in Figures 3–6. For relatively low values of a_{22}, intermediate-concavity $w(r)$ functions are associated with techniques for which $\psi(r)$ averages approximately four–five per cent. Increases in concavity reduce $\psi(r)$ over the lower part of the function's domain and increase it over the upper part. When a_{22} is relatively high, $\psi(r)$ becomes very sensitive to both increases in a_{22} and increases in concavity and, in this case, it is possible to generate $\psi(r)$ values exceeding fifty per cent. If, however, it is assumed that techniques are distributed uniformly over all coefficient combinations consistent with a given productivity level (as measured by R), the probability of finding techniques generating very high $\psi(r)$ is, itself, very low. Moreover, imposing the condition $w > 0$ means that the switching domain is restricted. It appears that such a restriction typically reduces the re-switching probability, $\hat{\psi}(r)$, more than in proportion to the degree of restriction. The probability, $\hat{\psi}$, of a technique re-switching at any two rates of profit in a restricted domain is smaller still. Finally, we have seen that when account is taken of the possibility of switch-point domination, the probability of 'true' re-switching (i.e. frontier re-switching as opposed to double equi-profitability) is further reduced. (We have also seen that the probability of real capital reversing is less than that of double equi-profitability.) We are thus led to conclude that the probability of (frontier) re-switching at any two rates of profit in a restricted domain is very small – typically less than one per cent.

These findings appear to be consistent with those obtained (via a less systematic investigation) by Eltis (1973) in the Samuelson–Hicks–Spaventa framework, and by Hicks (1973) and Laing (1991) in an Austrian context. There is, however, an interesting difference between the Sraffa and the Samuelson–Hicks–Spaventa models. In the latter case, Eltis concludes (p. 114) that re-switching 'is most likely to occur where techniques of production are fundamentally different'. In that model we know that techniques can re-switch even if one has a concave $w(r)$ function and the other a convex function. There is an intuitive sense in which double-intersection is more likely if $w(r)$ functions have differently signed second derivatives, so that Eltis' conclusion is, perhaps, not surprising. In the two-sector Sraffa model, re-switching is only possible between techniques whose $w(r)$ functions have second derivatives of the same sign and the general continuity properties of the model suggest, intuitively, that re-switching is more likely the more *alike* are the respective techniques. This is consistent with Figure 1, where techniques in the shaded re-switch set have (relative to a point a') either higher b_{22} and lower b_{12}, or higher b_{12} and lower b_{22}. If one b_{i2} is higher while the other is lower then, at least in 'value-capital' terms, the techniques are similar (as compared with cases in which both b_{i2} are higher or lower). In this respect, the Sraffa and Samuelson–Hicks–Spaventa models give contradictory conclusions, and this naturally raises the question (which we shall not pursue) of which model gives the better representation of reality.[11]

Our findings also have implications for some empirical results on $w(r)$ functions by Ochoa (1989) and Petrovic (1991). These claim to show that actual $w(r)$ functions generally have low curvature, and this is used to support the view that re-switching is unlikely in practice. Petrovic is quite explicit upon this, concluding that 'theoretical results which rely on pronounced curvature of wage–profit curves are not empirically sound. In particular, much discussed phenomena of capital reversal and double

---

[11] There is another difference worth noting. Given the close relationship between DEP and RCR, noted in the previous section, it would not be surprising if functions relating the probability of RCR to r in the Sraffa model have a similar appearance to the $\psi(r)$ functions. D'Ippolito (1987) finds, in his investigations into the Samuelson–Hicks–Spaventa model, that the probability of capital reversing is zero at $r = 0$ and rises monotonically to a limit (of fifty per cent in the highest case and 25 per cent in the median case) as r approaches infinity. (His median case assumes the equi-profitability of technical combinations.)

switching turn out to be highly improbable events in any actual economy' (p. 108). Putting aside the considerable problems of deriving $w(r)$ functions empirically, we note simply that the highest re-switching probabilities were generated in our simulations by $w(r)$ functions of low concavity. That this is so in a two-sector model should make us particularly wary of claiming a simple relationship between probability and curvature in theoretical or actual multi-sector economies.

This brings us naturally to the question of the wider applicability of our results. To repeat the present kind of exercise for three or more sectors would be a horrendously complicated task. There is, however, some evidence for multi-sector systems, at least for capital reversing. D'Ippolito's (1989) paper records the percentage of randomly generated techniques displaying capital reversing at various switching rates of profit for systems of up to thirty sectors. There is no discernable tendency for this percentage (which is less than unity for $r = 0.1$) to rise or fall as system dimensions increase. Given the close connection between the two phenomena, this suggests that the re-switching probability is also likely to be independent of the number of sectors (excepting one-sector systems, of course).

What remains is to consider the implications of these findings for capital theory. What we have suggested is that the probability of re-switching is generally low, but what does 'low' mean in this context? One per cent may seem insignificant to some but not to others. Some may take a pragmatic view that phenomena which occur with 'low' probability may be ignored for practical purposes, while others may argue that, however low the (positive) probability, it is still sufficient to undermine any theoretical construction which relies on, or postulates, the complete absence of re-switching. Sraffa would probably have taken the latter view.[12] If so, then close followers of Sraffa may continue to stress that re-switching is a distinct theoretical possibility, while pragmatic defenders of orthodoxy may rest content with the cumulating evidence that its probability is small.

[12] Consider the report of Sraffa's contributions to the discussion of Hicks' paper at the Corfu Conference on Capital (Lutz and Hague, 1961, pp. 305 and 306) (emphasis added):

> Mr Sraffa thought that one should emphasize the distinction between two types of measurement. First, there was the one in which statisticians were mainly interested. Second there was measurement in theory. The statisticians' measures were only approximate and provided a suitable field for work in solving index number problems. *The theoretical measures required absolute precision.* Any imperfections in these theoretical measures were not merely upsetting, but knocked down the whole theoretical basis.

and

continued

Appendix I

Figures 3–6 show the graphs of $\psi(r)$ functions for the techniques recorded in Table 1 and Tables A1–A4 below.

Table A1. $R = 1$ ($a_{22} = 0$) (see Figure 3)

No.	a_1	a_2	a_{11}	a_{21}	σ
9	0.1231	0.7356	0.2	0.3	0.6
10	0.1072	0.8585	0.45	0.05	0.75

Table A.2. $R = 0.4$ ($a_{12} = 0.7143$, $a_{22} = 0$) (see Figure 4)

$a_{11} = 0.3571$,	$a_{21} = 0.3571$		$a_1 = 0$			
a_1	a_2	σ	a_{11}	a_{21}	a_2	σ
0.2857	0.2857	0.5	0.5357	0.1786	0.7255	0.67
0.1905	0.3915	0.53	0.6786	0.0357	0.9209	0.87
0	0.6031	0.59	0.712	0.0023	0.9995	0.98

Table A.3. $R = 3$ ($a_{12} = 0.25$, $a_{22} = 0$) (see Figure 5)

$a_{11} = 0.125$,	$a_{21} = 0.125$		$a_1 = 0$			
a_1	a_2	σ	a_{11}	a_{21}	a_2	σ
0.75	0.75	0.5	0.1875	0.0625	0.981	0.83
0.5625	0.8036	0.54	0.225	0.025	0.992	0.92
0.375	0.857	0.6	0.249	0.001	0.9997	0.996
0	0.9643	0.74				

> *Mr Sraffa* took the view that if one could not get the measures required by the theorists' definitions, this was a criticism of the theory, which theorists could not escape by saying that they hoped their theory *would not often fail*. If a theory failed to explain *a* situation, it was unsatisfactory.
>
> Although Sraffa is talking here of the measurement of capital, his insistence on the need for 'absolute precision' in theory has obvious implications for the question of re-switching.

Table A.4. $R = 1$ (see Figure 6)

			$a_{12} = a_{22} = 0.25$		
No.	a_{11}	a_{21}	a_1	a_2	σ
11	0.25	0.25	0.14316	0.61895	0.57
12	0.45	0.05	0.14679	0.66055	0.65
13	0.49	0.01	0	0.7451	0.81

			$a_{12} = 0.1,\quad a_{22} = 0.4$		
	a_{11}	a_{21}	a_1	a_2	σ
14	0.4	0.1	0.2	0.55	0.55

			$a_{12} = 0.05,\quad a_{22} = 0.45$		
	a_{11}	a_{21}	a_1	a_2	σ
15	0.5	0	0.34375	0.5156	0.53
16	0.35	0.15	0.0886	0.5316	0.53
17	0.5	0	0.1774	0.5323	0.56

			$a_{12} = 0.01,\quad a_{22} = 0.49$		
	a_{11}	a_{21}	a_1	a_2	σ
18	0.49	0.01	0.01	0.5096	0.52

Appendix II

Whilst passing reference has been made, in the main text, to other models of production, our own analysis there has been conducted exclusively within the framework of a two-sector Sraffian model. The purpose of this appendix is to indicate how the interested reader might extend our analysis to other simple representations of production. In the interest of brevity, however, we shall provide only a sketch-map, leaving the reader to pursue the details of the path.

An 'Austrian' model

Let $(\lambda_2, \lambda_1, \lambda_0)$ be the labour inputs to an 'Austrian' production process 2, 1 and 0 years before the consumption commodity becomes available. An alternative process (ℓ_2, ℓ_1, ℓ_0) will yield the same real wage at profit rate $r^0 > 0$ if

$$\ell_2(1 + r^0)^2 + \ell_1(1 + r^0) + \ell_0 = \lambda_2(1 + r^0)^2 + \ell_1(1 + r^0) + \ell_0$$

$$(A1)$$

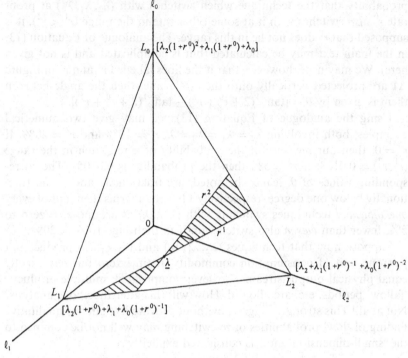

Figure A1

Equation (A1) defines – given λ_2, λ_1, λ_0 and r^0 – a downward-sloping plane in (ℓ_2, ℓ_1, ℓ_0)-space, which passes through $(\lambda_2, \lambda_1, \lambda_0)$ whatever may be the value of r^0. The section of the plane belonging to the positive orthant (including its edges) represents all those techniques (ℓ_2, ℓ_1, ℓ_0) which switch with $(\lambda_2, \lambda_1, \lambda_0)$ at profit rate r^0. The intercept on the ℓ_0-axis always rises and that on the ℓ_2-axis always falls as r^0 (notionally) increases (see Figure A1). The intercept on the ℓ_1-axis always increases with r for sufficiently large r^0; for simplicity, we suppose here that $\lambda_2 \geq \lambda_0$ for then the ℓ_1 intercept is increasing for all $r^0 > 0$.

Now consider the corresponding (ℓ_2, ℓ_1, ℓ_0) plane for $0 \leq r^1 \neq r^0$; it will necessarily intersect that for r^0 in a straight line passing through $(\lambda_2, \lambda_1, \lambda_0)$. So, again, will the (ℓ_2, ℓ_1, ℓ_0) plane for $r^1 < r^2 \neq r^0$. In Figure A1 – cf. Figure 3 in Laing (1991) – the lines labelled r^1 and r^2 represent these intersections with the plane $L_2 L_1 L_0$, which is the relevant plane for profit rate r^0. Much as in Figure 1 of the main text, the hatched area in Figure A1 divided by the area of $L_2 L_1 L_0$ may be taken as the probability that the technique which switches with $(\lambda_2, \lambda_1, \lambda_0)$ at profit rate r^0 *also* switches with it at some other rate in the range $(r^1 < r^2)$; it is supposed that r^0 does not lie in this range. The analogue of Equation (13) in the main text may be calculated (but is complicated and is not given here). We may note, however, that if the lines labelled r^1 and r^2 in Figure A1 are projected vertically onto the $\ell_1\ell_2$ plane, then the angle between them is given by $\theta = [\tan^{-1}(2 + r^0 + r^2) - \tan^{-1}(2 + r^0 + r^1)]$.

Using the analogue of Equation (13), we may give two numerical examples, both involving $\lambda_2 = \lambda_1 = \lambda_0 = \lambda$, $r^1 = 10\%$ and $r^2 = 20\%$. If $r^0 = 0$, then our measure of the probability of a re-switch in the range $(r^1, r^2) = 0.0108$; if $r^0 = 5\%$ then the probability is 0.0105. (The corresponding values of θ, it may be noted, are fractionally above and fractionally below one degree, respectively.) In broad terms then, out of every *one thousand* techniques switching with $(\lambda, \lambda, \lambda)$ at around $r^0 = $ zero to 5%, fewer than *eleven* also switch with it in the range 10% to 20%.

Suppose now that techniques $(\lambda_2, \lambda_1, \lambda_0)$ and (ℓ_2, ℓ_1, ℓ_0) produce not just one unit of consumption commodity at time zero but *any* exactly equal physical output streams, however complicated; multiple products, 'fallow' periods, etc. are allowed. How will this alter the above analysis? Not at all! This strongly suggests (without proving it) than our qualitative finding of 'low' probabilities of re-switching may well not be confined to the 'small-dimension' models considered explicitly.

The 'corn–tractor' model

The familiar Samuelson–Hicks–Spaventa model has four coefficients for each technique; in Hicks' notation (a, b, α, β), but b and α only ever appear in the product (αb), so that, in effect, there are only three coefficients. Moreover, each of $[a, (\alpha b), \beta]$ is dimensionally the same for every technique. (For every technique, 'a' is a pure number, and 'αb' and 'b' are both amounts of labour per unit of corn.) Can one, then, construct a figure, similar to Figures 1 and A1, showing all the techniques which switch with a given technique at a specified rate of profit, r^0? In principle, one can – but unfortunately the techniques in question now lie not on a plane but on a much more complicated surface, as shown in Figure A2.

The axes in Figure A2 are labelled so as to make the figure as reminiscent as possible of Figures 1 and A1; w^0 is the given real wage. Our surface still intersects the '$a = 0$' and the '$\beta = 0$' planes in straight lines. The intersection with '$\alpha b = 0$', however, consists of two straight lines, as shown, and a typical cross section, for $0 < \alpha b < [(1 + r^0)w^0]^{-1}$ is shown by CS. Similarly to Figures 1 and A1, the intercept with the 'β' axis rises

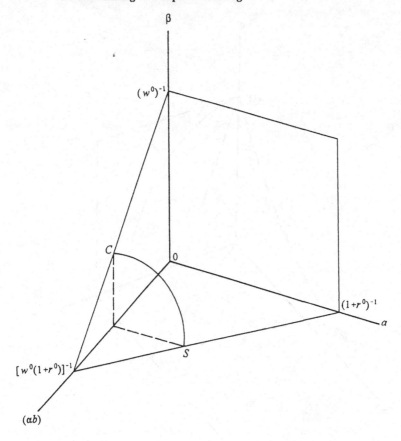

Figure A2

and that with the 'a' axis falls as the given value of the profit rate is increased. The intercept with the 'αb' axis always rises with $r(r \geq 0)$ if

$$(\alpha b) > R^2 (\alpha \beta)$$

for the given technique, R being the maximum rate of profit which it permits. If, for example, $R = 25\%$, our condition becomes $16(\alpha/\beta) > (a/b)$, which most readers will, perhaps, happily accept as plausible.

If to Figure A2 we now add the surface for $0 \leq r^1 < r^2 < r^0$ or $r^0 < r^1 < r^2 < R$, we shall obtain two 'horn-like' areas on the surface already shown in that figure, their common apex being at $(\alpha b, a, b)$ for the given technique – cf. Figures 1 and A1. The probability that a

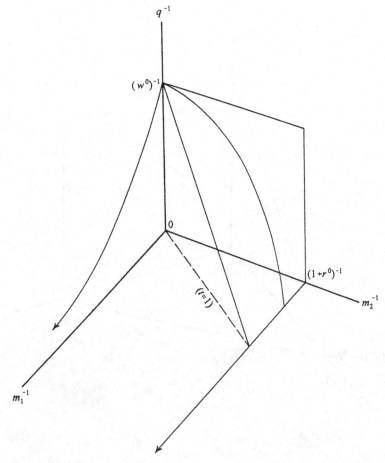

Figure A3

technique switching at r^0 will also switch in the range (r^1, r^2) is then given by a ratio of areas, as before, but both are those of curved surfaces.

The 'Lowe–Mathur' model

Both Adolph Lowe (1976) and Gautam Mathur (1965) employed yet another model characterized by three coefficients. One 'basic' machine and one unit of labour can produce either m_2 'basic' machines or m_1 'intermediate' machines. One 'intermediate' machine and one unit of labour can produce q units of the consumption commodity. The techniques of this kind which switch with a given such technique, at a given rate of profit, are contained by a surface such as that shown in Figure A3. (For ease of comparison with Figures 1, A1 and A2, the 'output coefficients' (m_2, m_1, q) have been represented by the 'input coefficients' $(m_2^{-1}, m_1^{-1}, q^{-1})$.) This surface is different again, although it resembles that in Figure A2 for $m_1^{-1} = 0$ (cf $\alpha b = 0$). For $m_1^{-1} = t m_2^{-1}$, q^{-1} is linear in m_2^{-1} when $t = 1$, concave when $t < 1$ and convex when $t > 1$. Any reader who has followed thus far can easily complete the argument by introducing surfaces for other rates of profit and considering their intersections with that shown in Figure A3.

References

Ahmad, S. (1991). *Capital in Economic Theory*, Aldershot: Edward Elgar.
Bruno, M., Burmeister, E. and Sheshinski, E. (1966). 'The Nature and Implications of the Reswitching of Techniques', *Quarterly Journal of Economics*, **80**, pp. 526–53.
D'Ippolito, G. (1987). 'Probabilità di Perverso Compartamento del Capitale al Variare del Saggio dei Profitti: Il Modello Embrionale a Due Settori', *Note Economiche*, **2**, pp. 5–37.
D'Ippolito, G. (1989). 'Delimitazione dell'Area dei Casi di Comportamento Perverso del Capitale in u Punto di Mutamento della Tecnica', in L. L. Pasinetti (a cura di), *Aspetti Controverssi della Teoria del Valore*, Bologna: Il Mulino.
Eltis, W. (1973). *Growth and Distribution*, London: Macmillan.
Galloway, L. and Shukla, V. (1974). 'The Neoclassical Production Function', *American Economic Review*, **64**, pp. 348–58.
Garegnani, P. (1970). 'Heterogeneous Capital, the Production Function and the Theory of Distribution', *Review of Economic Studies* **37**, pp. 407–36.
Garegnani, P. (1976). 'The Neoclassical Production Function: A Comment', *American Economic Review*, **66**, pp. 424–7.
Harcourt, G. C. (1972). *Some Cambridge Controversies in the Theory of Capital*, London: Cambridge University Press.
Hicks, J. R. (1965). *Capital and Growth*, Oxford: Oxford University Press.
Hicks, J. R. (1973). *Capital and Time: A Neo-Austrian Theory*, Oxford: Oxford University Press.
Laibman, D. and Nell, E. J. (1977). 'Reswitching, Wicksell Effects and the Neoclassical Production Function', *American Economic Review*, **67**, pp. 878–88.
Laing, N. F. (1991). 'The Likelihood of Capital-Reversing and Double-Switching', *Bulletin of Economic Research*, **43**, pp. 179–88.
Lowe, A. (1976). *The Path of Economic Growth*, London: Cambridge University Press.
Lutz, F. A. and Hague, D. C. (eds) (1961). *The Theory of Capital*, London: Macmillan.
Mainwaring, L. (1978). 'The Interest Rate Equalisation Theorem with Nontraded Goods', *Journal of International Economics*, **8**, pp. 11–19.
Mathur, G. (1965). *Planning for Steady Growth*, Oxford: Blackwell.

Ochoa, E. M. (1989). 'Values, Prices and Wage Profit Curves in the US Economy', *Cambridge Journal of Economics*, 13, pp. 413–29.

Pertz, K. (1980). 'Reswitching, Wicksell Effects and the Neoclassical Production Function: A Note', *American Economic Review*, 70, pp. 1015–17.

Petrovic, P. (1991). 'Shape of a Wage–Profit Curve: Some Methodology and Empirical Evidence', *Metroeconomica*, 42, 93–112.

Salvadori, N. and Steedman, I. (1988). 'No Reswitching? No Switching!', *Cambridge Journal of Economics*, 12, pp. 481–6.

Samuelson, P. A. (1962). 'Parable and Realism in Capital Theory: The Surrogate Production Function', *Review of Economic Studies*, 29, pp. 193–206.

Sato, K. (1976). 'The Neoclassical Production Function: Comment', *American Economic Review*, 66, pp. 428–33.

Schefold, B. (1976). 'Relative Prices as a Function of the Rate of Profit: A Mathematical Note', *Zeitschift für Nationalökonomie*, 36, pp. 21–48.

Spaventa, L. (1968). 'Realism without Parables in Capital Theory', in *Recherches Récentes sur la Fonction de Production*, Centre d'Etudes et de Récherches, Universitaire de Namur, pp. 15–45.

Spaventa, L. (1970). 'Rate of Profit, Rate of Growth and Capital Intensity in a Simple Production Model', *Oxford Economic Papers*, 22, pp. 129–47.

Sraffa, P. (1960). *Production of Commodities by Means of Commodities*, London: Cambridge University Press.

Symposium (1966). 'Paradoxes in Capital Theory', *Quarterly Journal of Economics*, 80, pp. 503–83.

Woods, J. (1988). 'On Switching of Techniques in Two-Sector Models', *Scottish Journal of Political Economy*, 35, pp. 84–91.

Comment on Mainwaring and Steedman*

Neri Salvadori

Let (A, l) be a technique defined by the usual input–output coefficients (A is the $n \times n$ material input matrix and l is the $n \times 1$ labour input vector, the output matrix being the $n \times n$ identity matrix I). Let S be the set of

* The main idea of this comment was mentioned at the International Workshop *Can one Responsibly Base Macroeconomic Policy on One-Good or One-Agent Models?* at Terza Università degli Studi di Roma, 18–19 May 1995. The workshop was attended by, among others, Christian Bidard, Pierangelo Garegnani, Bertram Schefold and Ian Steedman, who also contributed to the present volume. I would like to thank Heinz Kurz for comments and encouragement (the usual caveat does *not* apply). I also benefited from reading an unpublished manuscript by Fabio Petri prior to attending the workshop. I would like to thank him for giving me this opportunity.

points (b, m) in the space R^{n+1} such that (b, m) can be interpreted as a process producing commodity n, and such that the technique (B, m), built up by process (b, m) and all processes of technique (A, l) except the last one, at $r = r_0$ determines a price vector equal to the price vector determined by technique (A, l) at r_0. (For the sake of simplicity, let us express all prices in terms of 'labour commanded', that is, use labour as the numéraire.) Obviously, S depends on (A, l) and r_0. Let R be a subset of S such that if (b, m) is in R, techniques (B, m) and (A, l) have again the same price vector at some $r' > r_0$.

Mainwaring and Steedman argue that the ratio between the 'size' of R and the 'size' of S can be interpreted as a measure of the probability of re-switching. They are aware of the difficulty of this conceptualization:

We recognize that conceptual difficulties can arise about expressing the probability as a ratio of two sets each of which contains an infinite number of points. In particular, it may be objected that not all points within these sets are equally likely to present themselves as eligible alternatives to [technique (A, l)]... In general, however, there is no reason to suppose that the distribution of eligible points in the 're-switch set' [R] is more dense or less dense than that of the 'switch set' [S]. While recognizing the difficulties of the proposed probability measure, we proceed on the grounds that it does have intuitive appeal. (p. 329)

This position is difficult to sustain. The probability of re-switching is certainly independent of the *description* of the techniques involved. However, the definition of probability used by Mainwaring and Steedman is not independent of the description adopted. In order to clarify this point, it suffices to recall that technique (A, l) may alternatively be described by any of the following $nx(n + 1)$ matrices.[1]

$$(l, Al, A^2l, \ldots, A^n l) \tag{1}$$

$$((I - A)^{-1}A, (I - A)^{-1}l) \tag{2}$$

$$([I - (1 + r_1)A]^{-1}l, [I - (1 + r_2)A]^{-1}l,$$
$$[I - (1 + r_3)A]^{-1}l, \ldots, [I - (1 + r_{n+1})A]^{-1}l), \tag{3}$$

where $-1 < r_1 < r_2 < r_3 < \ldots < r_{n+1} < R$, and R is the maximum rate of profit of the technique under consideration.

In general any one-to-one transformation of matrix A and vector l can be a valid description of the technique. Note that for each of these transformations we can apply the method used by Mainwaring and Steedman

---

[1] See Kurz and Salvadori (1995, Chap. 6). Descriptions (2) and (3) are known from Pasinetti (1973) and Bidard and Salvadori (1995), respectively. Kurz and Salvadori (1995, p. 175) emphasize that still other significant descriptions of technique (A, l) can be provided.

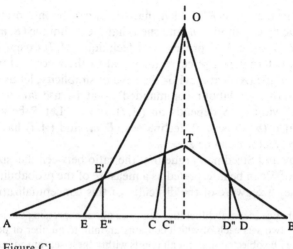

Figure C1

and argue that in general 'there is no reason to suppose that the distribution of eligible points in the "re-switch set" [R] is more dense or less dense than that of the "switch set" [S]. While recognizing the difficulties of the proposed probability measure, we proceed on the grounds that it does have intuitive appeal.' This difficulty of their measure becomes obvious once it is understood that by an appropriate one-to-one transformation the 'probability' can either be made to get very close to zero or to get very close to unity. In this short comment I will not attempt to show this fact for the special case studied by Mainwaring and Steedman. Instead I shall provide a simple diagram illustrating that this result can indeed be obtained in an even simpler case.[2]

Let the segments AB and CD of Figure C1 represent S and R, respectively. Then draw the polygonal ATB and fix the point O on the vertical line through T in such a way that the polygonal ATB is inside the triangle AOB (except for points A and B). Let F be a transformation which associates to any point E on AB the point E'' obtained by the orthogonal projection of the point where the ray OE cuts the polygonal ATB, E', on the segment AB itself. It is easily shown that this transformation is one-to-one, and that it transforms segment AB in itself and segment CD in $C''D''$. Call the segment $C''D''$ $R' = F(R)$. It is immediately clear that the

---

[2] The interested reader can take the triangle depicted in Figure 2 by Mainwaring and Steedman as segment AB in Figure C1, and an appropriate pair of pyramids instead of triangles AOB and ATB.

'size' of R' is smaller than the size of R. Moreover, since a one-to-one transformation of a one-to-one transformation is one-to-one, we can iterate this procedure in order to determine the sets $R'' = F(F(R)) = F(R')$, $R''' = F(F(F(R))) = F(R'')$, ..., and so on until we do not find a transformation such that the ratio between the 'size' of $R^* = F(F(F(...(R)))...)$ and the 'size' of S is smaller than a pre-assigned $\epsilon > 0$. Finally, since the inverse of a one-to-one transformation is one-to-one, we can determine a one-to-one transformation G such that $G(S) = S$ and $G(R) = F^{-1}(F^{-1}(F^{-1}(...(R)))...) = R^{**}$ is such that unity minus the ratio between the 'size' of R^{**} and the 'size' of S is smaller than a pre-assigned $\epsilon > 0$.

I would like to conclude this comment with a few remarks. I have *not* tried to show that the probability of re-switching is high. I have only shown that it cannot be determined in the way suggested by Mainwaring and Steedman. However, I think that more than one of their results survives the above criticism. First, if the 'probability' of re-switching found by Mainwaring and Steedman were nought or unity, then it would be nought or unity with any other possible description of technique. This seems to suggest that the probability of re-switching is actually positive and lower than unity. Second, the analysis supplied by Mainwaring and Steedman could be completed by an appropriate assumption on the probability distribution around the existing technique. (With a one-to-one transformation of the parameters describing the technique, the probability distribution would also be transformed in a one-to-one way.) However, this probability distribution cannot be justified simply in terms of the argument that since there is no information on it, the equi-probable distribution is the most appealing one. This procedure seems to be appropriate in the case of a finite universe (for instance the thirty-seven numbers of the roulette wheel or the two sides of a coin), but certainly not in the case of an infinite one.

References

Bidard, Ch. and Salvadori, N. (1995). 'Duality between Prices and Techniques', *European Journal of Political Economy*, **11**, pp. 379–89.

Kurz, H. D. and Salvadori, N. (1995). *Theory of Production. A Long-Period Analysis*, Cambridge: Cambridge University Press.

Pasinetti, L. L. (1973). 'The Notion of Vertical Integration in Economic Analysis', *Metroeconomica*, **25**, pp. 1–29.

Comment on the LM–IS diagrams

Christian Bidard and Lucette Carter

From an abstract point of view, Mainwaring and Steedman's method first defines a space S and associates a point s in S to a couple of techniques which admit a switch point. In the case of re-switching, the point s belongs to a subset R of S. The magnitude of R with regard to S is then measured, the result being considered as the probability of re-switching (a conditional probability, given the existence of one switch point at least). Because of the geometrical representation, space S, which is imbedded into a Euclidean space, inherits the Lebesgue measure L, and the probability of re-switching is identified with $L(R)/L(S)$.

The reference to the Lebesgue measure is somehow arbitrary. Moreover, one may imagine other geometric representations (S', R') for which the ratio $L(R')/L(S')$ would be different, and therefore the above probability has no intrinsic meaning. More precisely, the nature of the problem itself requires a definition of its probabilistic structure at the very beginning. This note sketches an alternative approach to the question.

Assume first that the initial process operating in the second industry is given, and that an alternative process is picked up at random from a 'method-tank'. If the tank contains finitely many processes, an exhaustive description can be made; otherwise, the characteristics (a'_{12}, a'_{22}, a_2) of the alternative processes can be seen as random variables depending on a parameter $\omega \in \Omega$.

Let a switch point between the old and the new process be characterized by value $\lambda = (1 + r)^{-1}$. At a switch point λ, one price vector (p_1, p_2, w) is compatible with three operated processes, and, equality

$$(p_1 \ p_2 \ \lambda w_2) \begin{bmatrix} \lambda - a_{11} & -a_{12} & -a'_{12} \\ -a_{21} & \lambda - a_{22} & \lambda - a'_{22} \\ -a_1 & -a_2 & -a'_2 \end{bmatrix} = 0$$

holds. By setting $\Delta a_{12} = a'_{12} - a_{12}$, $\Delta a_{22} = a'_{22} - a_{22}$, $\Delta a_2 = a'_2 - a_2$, a switch point λ is a feasible value which is a root of the second-degree equation

358

$$\det \begin{bmatrix} \lambda - a_{11} & -a_{12} & \Delta a_{12} \\ -a_{21} & \lambda - a_{22} & \Delta a_{22} \\ -a_1 & -a_2 & \Delta a_2 \end{bmatrix} = 0 \qquad (1)$$

This algebraic criterion (Bidard, 1991) avoids the calculation of prices and shows that the switch points are random variables derived from the technical characteristics of the processes. No switching occurs if the solutions λ_1 and λ_2 to Equation (1) are complex. When they are real, with $\lambda_1 \geq \lambda_2$, the feasible values are defined by their lower bound Λ, the Perron–Frobenius value of the initial technical matrix, and therefore the conditional probability

$$P = \mathrm{prob}(\lambda_1 \text{ and } \lambda_2 \text{ feasible} | \lambda_1 \text{ or } \lambda_2 \text{ feasible})$$

is more simply written as

$$P = \mathrm{prob}(\lambda_2 \text{ feasible} | \lambda_1 \text{ feasible}) \qquad (2)$$

To sum up, the probability of re-switching is given by Equation (2), λ_1 and λ_2 ($\lambda_1 \geq \lambda_2$) being the real roots of the second-degree equation (1).

The numerical estimations clearly depend on the characteristics of the method tank. Various types have been experimented with.

- The 'no-knowledge' assumption. Let a_2' be given for the sake of simplicity. In the absence of any information on the available methods, one may assume that they are uniformly distributed over a domain defined by the non-negativity ($a_{12}' \geq 0$, $a_{22}' \geq 0$) and the viability constraints (a_{12}' and a_{22}' are upper bounded). This formalization differs from the LM–IS hypothesis which sets a uniform distribution on space S, not on the initial data themselves.
- Substitution between capital goods. For a given labour input, let one capital good be substituted 'in average' for the other. E.g., for a given $a_{22}'(\omega)$, $a_{21}'(\omega)$ is uniformly distributed over interval $[0, 1 - a_{22}'(\omega)]$: high values of $a_{22}'(\omega)$ are likely to induce small values of $a_{21}'(\omega)$.
- Substitution between 'capital' and labour. Similarly, the distribution may be such that a negative correlation exists between labour and some index of aggregate capital.

The introduction of such a stochastic substitution has no great influence on the probability of re-switching. This is because the switching phenomenon itself requires that one technique uses more of some input and less of some other. When attention is restricted to families of methods which favour substitution, the number of switchings and re-switchings are both significantly increased with regard to other families, but not necessarily their ratio, which is the expression of the conditional probability.

Some extensions and variants are given below.

- The initial process itself can be chosen at random, instead of being given, or the two processes can be chosen at random in their respective tanks.
- Re-switching, even if possible on paper, is not economically realistic if it occurs for too low or too high values of the rate of profit. Attention must be restricted to switchings and re-switchings within a plausible range, i.e. $\lambda_i \in [\lambda_{min}, \lambda_{max}]$. The smaller the range, the smaller the conditional probability of re-switching.

Various distributions of probability have been tested according to these lines by means of the Monte-Carlo method. The results confirm the order of magnitude given by previous experimentations: re-switching occurs in a few per cent of the cases of switching.

Two conclusions are drawn from this study.

- The LM–IS method introduces the probabilistic structure too late in the argument, but it helps intuition and provides an interesting visualization of the phenomenon.
- If it were true that the 'paradoxes' of the theory of capital, and not only re-switching, happen rarely, the neoclassical parables would still remain invalid in pure theory. They could, however, be considered as satisfactory for practical purposes, thus relegating the whole debate on capital to a mere academic dispute. Other aspects of the question, including the capital reversals which we have not examined here, should, of course, be explored.

References

Bidard, C. (1991). *Prix, Reproduction, Rareté*, Paris: Dunod.
Mainwaring, L. and Steedman, I. (1995). *On the Probability of Re-switching and Capital Reversing in a Two-Sector Sraffian Model*, this volume.

PART IV

Intertemporal equilibrium theory and the problem of capital

CHAPTER 10

Paradoxes of capital and counterintuitive changes of distribution in an intertemporal equilibrium model

Bertram Schefold

1   Two parables

Is the problem of capital theory one of aggregation which only concerns macroeconomic production functions or does it apply to all versions of the neoclassical theory of distribution? The generality of the critique was often questioned around 1970, when one heard the objection: 'Re-switching poses a problem for the marginal productivity theory of distribution, but general intertemporal equilibrium theory is not affected; Arrow and Debreu have proved the existence of equilibrium.' The assertion is simplistic, but is still made.

C. Bliss (1970, p. 437), in an editorial comment on an article by Garegnani (Garegnani, 1970), expressed this opinion in the following form:

Prof. Garegnani in his paper makes a claim which, to economists familiar with the modern theory of general equilibrium, will seem rather surprising. He supposes an economy with many capital goods in stationary long-run equilibrium at rate of interest r^*. He then asks himself whether, following a change in demand leading to 'a tendency to positive net saving', there exists a new equilibrium of supply and demand consistent with the new demand functions. He concludes that no such equilibrium need exist.... Now an equilibrium of supply and demand certainly might not exist, but we know from the work of G. Debreu ... that the conditions required for existence are rather weak ... these conditions obtain in Garegnani's model.

363

Bliss then criticizes the fact that Garegnani uses long-period prices where, in the transition, short-run equilibria are involved. In his Reply, Garegnani (1970, p. 439) said that he wanted

to focus the analysis on one central deficiency, and show that, *even if the process of transition could be assumed to work smoothly*..., it might still lead to no new long-run equilibrium, or to no plausible one, because the fall of r might be accompanied by a *decrease* and not an increase in the proportion of 'capital' to labour in the economy.

A straight answer was given by E. Burmeister (1980), who introduced the distinction between 'regular' and other economies. According to him, the phenomenon of re-switching had 'triggered the discovery of paradoxical consumption behaviour'; in economies that were not regular, consumption per head could fall with increases in the rate of interest (Burmeister, 1980, p. 124). He then found that, on optimal capital accumulation paths, regular points were stable and irregular ones unstable (Burmeister, 1980, p. 126).

In a sense, this is in fact the essence of the matter. We shall confirm that re-switching is associated with movements of factor prices that run in the opposite direction to what is conventionally deemed necessary to attain equilibrium. Relevant, however, are only those equilibria that not only exist, but are also stable.

A comprehensive and exact analysis of this point presupposes a clarification of different equilibrium concepts; the relationship between classical and neoclassical long-run equilibria and intertemporal equilibria is of particular relevance here. The paradoxes of capital theory appear in different forms; their likelihood and relevance should be assessed. Our present task is to show how they manifest themselves in intertemporal equilibrium. We shall focus on the most important and characteristic cases and omit most of the proofs which are given elsewhere.[1]

We want to show that the so-called paradoxes of capital theory relate to the neoclassical theory of distribution, employment and accumulation itself; they do not depend on any attempt to aggregate capital. They

---

[1] This paper provides a summary and an extension of chapter 18.2 in Schefold (1997). The first part of that chapter (18.1) was first written and presented in French; it appeared as a paper in *Cahiers d'Economie Politique*, 22, 1993, pp. 25–44, and was mainly concerned with the conceptual distinctions. The second part contains the proofs which are here omitted. The method of analysis proposed there is perhaps not easy to grasp; this may justify the present second attempt at an explanation. Work on the model underlying this paper began after I had taken inspiration from the Siena Conference, 5–7 April 1990 (Schefold, 1990, pp. 155–60). The present version was first presented at the EAEPE Conference in Antwerp (1996).

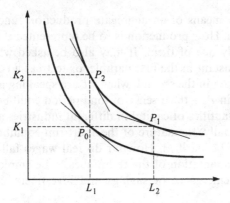

Figure 1. Two parables: 'Immigration' shows the increase in population from L_1 to L_2, with K_1 given, and 'Accumulation' shows the increase from K_1 to K_2 with L_1 given.

concern 'microeconomics' as much as 'macroeconomics'. We shall work our way towards the construction of examples of intertemporal equilibria which present the same problems as those encountered when the construction of the 'surrogate production function' was questioned by the discovery of re-switching.

The interdependence of the neoclassical theories of capital and distribution, employment and accumulation was made clear by means of various 'parables'; we start by recalling two of them. Production in an economy is assumed to be represented by a well-behaved production function. There is a certain level of population L_1 and of capital accumulation K_1; both are fully employed. The ratio of the wage rate to the rate of interest is equal to the absolute value of the slope of the tangent to P_0 in Figure 1.

According to the first parable, an immigration takes place so that the short-period equilibrium is disturbed and real wages fall relative to the rate of interest. Less mechanized techniques become profitable. If they are introduced, a new full employment equilibrium, with a higher level of output but at the same level of capital accumulation, is attained at P_1. In the accumulation scenario, by contrast, population remains constant. Temporarily, more is saved and less is consumed. The savings are invested and the consequent accumulation of capital leads to equilibrium point P_2 in Figure 1. Again, consumption has risen – indeed, consumption per head – and the greater availability of capital allows the long-run rate of interest to fall relative to the initial position.

These parables, told by means of an aggregate production function, leave many questions open. How production is to be represented if capital is heterogeneous is only one of them. It may also be asked what it means to keep 'capital' constant in the first parable, or to treat a certain amount of capital as a datum in the second, when we are speaking about a long-period equilibrium in P_1 – the essence of long-period equilibrium, after all, is that relative quantities of capital in different industries adapt to long-run conditions. Finally, the nature of the short-run equilibria in each transition remains to be clarified. How far do real wages fall with immigration, prior to the adaptation of the techniques to be employed? What exactly causes the emergence of savings and investment in the second parable?

Intertemporal equilibrium provides specific answers to each of these questions. Transitions are represented by subdividing the time between the initial and the terminal state into 'many' periods, and an intertemporal equilibrium with perfect foresight allows the transition to be represented not as the emergence of a new long-period equilibrium after an unforeseen disturbance of an initial long-period equilibrium, but as a process in which all events are anticipated and a market brings forward demands and supplies into equilibrium at the beginning of the first period. The given amounts of capital have to be represented as endowments of capital goods. Over time, the anticipated change is absorbed and, eventually, a permanent state (after 'immigration' or after 'accumulation') can be reached.

However, let us first look at the representation of the heterogeneity of capital goods in a comparison of stationary long-period equilibria. A_α is an indecomposable and productive input–output matrix and l^α the associated positive labour vector; long-run prices p^α, with rate of interest r and wage rate w_α, are then given by

$$(1 + r)A_\alpha p^\alpha + w_\alpha l^\alpha = p^\alpha$$

These equations define a wage curve pertaining to technique α if some numéraire (usually the vector of net output) is given. If the wage curves of two techniques α and β for the production of the same goods were linear – as was assumed in the construction of the surrogate production function – we could represent the parables as in Figure 2. As is well known, the slope of linear wage curves measures the capital–labour ratio. The immigration scenario implies a movement from a technique with a high capital–labour ratio – say, Q_1 on the wage curve w_α – to a technique with a low capital–labour ratio – say, point Q_2 on the wage curve w_β. Consumption per head, equal to output per head in the stationary state, falls. It is equal to $w_\alpha(0)$ and $w_\beta(0)$, respectively, since we choose

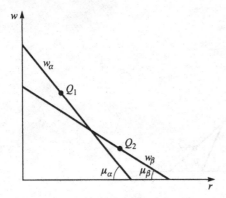

Figure 2. Linear wage curves, representing techniques with a high capital–labour ratio, $k_1 = tg\mu_\alpha$, at Q_1, and a low capital–labour ratio, $k_2 = tg\mu_\beta$, at Q_2. The transition from Q_1 to Q_2 corresponds to the 'immigration parable'; that from Q_2 to Q_1 to the 'accumulation parable'.

net output as the numéraire. Note that the accumulation scenario, in this context, is a movement from Q_2 to Q_1. We assume in both cases – immigration and accumulation, here and below with re-switching – that the change of technique implies a change in the capital–labour ratio which is just sufficient to absorb the increase in the amount of the variable factor, given the amount of the constant factor.

Re-switching in the simplest case is depicted in Figure 3. It is well known that wage curves are – except in fluke cases primarily associated with the labour theory of value – not straight. The capital–labour ratio is, for a wage curve such as w_β at a point such as Q_1^*, determined by

$$k_\beta = tg\mu_\beta = \frac{w_\beta(0) - w_\beta(r)}{r} = \frac{P/L}{P/K} = K/L$$

since $w_\beta(0)$ is the price of net output per head in the stationary state. The immigration scenario now is a movement like that from Q_2^* to Q_1^*: in order to preserve full employment by moving from a technique with a high capital–labour ratio to one with a low capital–labour ratio ($tg\mu_\alpha = k_\alpha > tg\mu_\beta = k_\beta$), the real wage has to be raised in reaction to the immigration of labour. This counterintuitive move of a factor price allows full employment to be restored after the immigration if technique β is the only alternative to technique α and if the amount of capital is somehow given and somehow kept constant during the transition. Note that the accumulation scenario again involves a movement in the opposite direction from Q_1^* to Q_2^*, since accumulation leads to an increase of

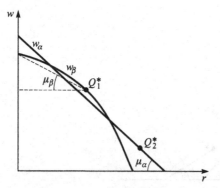

Figure 3. Two wages curves with re-switching. A transition from a higher to a lower capital–labour ratio ('immigration scenario') now involves a movement from Q_2^* to Q_1^*; the 'accumulation scenario' starts from a low capital–labour ratio ($tg\mu_\beta$) at Q_1^* and moves to a high capital–labour ratio ($tg\mu_\alpha$) at Q_2^*. Both cases involve 'perverse' factor prices movements.

capital per head. Accumulation paradoxically is associated with a rising rate of interest.

The main point in the debate about re-switching was that it involved such counterintuitive moves of factor prices. Our task is to represent the transitions in an intertemporal model.

2   An intertemporal equilibrium model with a linear spectrum of techniques

The intertemporal model is based on a spectrum of techniques (A, B, l), where A is the input matrix (with semi-positive rows), B the output matrix (with semi-positive columns) and l the (positive) labour vector, composed of a finite number of methods of production, to produce n goods which are both consumption goods and capital goods. Time is divided into periods of production $1, \ldots, T$. Endowments of capital goods are available at the end of period 0. In each period of production, a positive amount, L_t, of labour is available. Activity levels are given by row vectors q^t, $t = 0, \ldots, T$. Similarly, we have consumption vectors c^t, $t = 0, \ldots, T$.

At the end of period $t - 1$, an output of $q^{t-1}B$ is available. It divides into consumption, c^{t-1}, and the inputs for production in period t, $q^t A$. At the end of period $t - 1$, goods will be sold at prices p^{t-1}. At the end of period t, a wage according to wage rate w_t will be paid.

At the beginning of the first period, a stock $q^0 B > 0$ will be given. At the end of period t, a final stock of goods f will be required to exist: $f \geqq 0$. The assumption of a positive final stock of goods will often be made in order to prevent the economy from shrinking to nil in the last period and to allow – albeit in an arbitrary manner – for the possibility of a stationary state with a finite horizon.

There is one consumer, characterized by a utility function $U = U(c^0, c^1, \ldots, c^T)$, which is positive and strictly concave. We assume positive first and negative second partial derivatives in each variable c^t; $t = 0, \ldots, T; i = 1, \ldots, n$.

A programme $z = (c^0, c^1, \ldots, c^T; q^1, \ldots, q^T) \geq 0$ is called *feasible* if

$$q^{t-1} B \geqq c^{t-1} + q^t A; \qquad t = 1, \ldots, T$$

$$q^T B \geqq c^T + f$$

$$L_t \geqq q^t l; \qquad t = 1, \ldots, T$$

We assume that the set Z of feasible programmes contains at least one for which consumption is positive. Z is clearly convex and compact.

An *optimum* is a programme $\bar{z} \in Z$ if

$$U(\bar{c}^0, \bar{c}^1, \ldots, \bar{c}^T) \geqq U(c^0, c^1, \ldots, c^T)$$

for all $z \in Z$.

An *equilibrium* is a programme $z = (\bar{c}^0, \bar{c}^1, \ldots, \bar{c}^T, \bar{q}^1, \ldots, \bar{q}^T) \geq 0$, together with prices and wage rates $u = (p^0, \ldots, p^T, w_1, \ldots, w_T) \geq 0$ such that, with $\bar{q}^0 = q^0$,

(a) the following equilibrium conditions hold:

Reproduction feasible   Rule of free goods

$$\bar{q}^{t-1} B \geqq \bar{c}^{t-1} + \bar{q}^t A \qquad (\bar{q}^{t-1} B - \bar{c}^{t-1} - \bar{q}^t A)p^{t-1} = 0; \qquad t = 1, \ldots, T$$

$$\bar{q}^T B \geqq \bar{c}^T + f \qquad (\bar{q}^T B - \bar{c}^T - f)p^T = 0$$

$$L_t \geqq \bar{q}^t l \qquad (L_t - \bar{q}^t l)w_t = 0; \qquad t = 1, \ldots, T$$

Competition   Maximization of profits

$$Bp^t \leqq Ap^{t-1} + w_t l \qquad \bar{q}^t(Bp^t - Ap^{t-1} - w_t l) = 0; \qquad t = 1, \ldots, T$$

(b) and such that the condition of the maximization of utility of the household is fulfilled:

$$U(\bar{c}^0, \ldots, \bar{c}^T) \geqq U(c^0, \ldots, c^T)$$

in the set H of all $(c^0, \ldots, c^T) \geqq 0$

such that $c^0 p^0 + \ldots + c^T p^T \leqq q^0 B p^0 - f p^T + w_1 L_1 + \ldots + w_T L_T$

i.e., such that utility is maximized among all consumption bundles which can be bought with the budget of the household.

It should be noted that overproduction of goods will not occur because goods will later be assumed to be consumption goods as well as means of production. The wage rate, however, may be zero if full employment is not attained. The rule of free goods applies to the labour market. Competition prevents prices from rising above costs; maximization of profits implies that unprofitable processes are not used. The budget equation expresses the fact that all prices are discounted to period zero where the cost of the acquisition of future goods can be compared with expected incomes from work and from the ownership of the endowments (net of the capital to be left over after the last period). We now have:

> **Theorem 1:**   *There is an optimum. It is uniquely determined. Each optimum is an equilibrium.*

> **Theorem 2:**   *An equilibrium exists. It is uniquely determined. Each equilibrium is an optimum.*

We are interested in this relatively simple model of intertemporal equilibrium because it provides a link with the linear models familiar from the debate on capital theory. We shall soon see that the competitive price system described by conditions (a), together with the conditions of reproduction, contains stationary or steadily growing Sraffa systems (with constant returns to scale) as special cases. However, we shall also see that the price paths described by conditions (a) converge under fairly general conditions towards solutions with a uniform rate of profit or interest, so that it can also be argued that the intertemporal equilibrium then describes a process of convergence of 'market prices' to the 'normal prices' of the long period. We shall use this property of intertemporal equilibrium in order to construct the transitions between techniques which involve re-switching.

Allocation is guided by the preferences of individuals according to neoclassical equilibrium theory. The usual view, then, is that the equilibrium tends towards a certain state, determined by preferences but conditioned by the availability of endowments and technology. Terminal states change because of exogenous shocks, like a change in factor supply (as in our immigration parable), a change of preferences (there may be a change in the desire to accumulate, as in one possible interpretation of the accumulation parable), or an innovation, leading to evolutionary change. Shocks imply that an existing equilibrium is disturbed and replaced by another.

However, preferences in an intertemporal equilibrium can also be such that transitions which take place between states are foreseen. The system may be near a stationary state during the first couple of periods, and then a transition towards another stationary state begins which is – in general not completely – reached after a finite number of further periods. The entire transition is then a process taking place in equilibrium. As we shall show, the immigration scenario may be represented as such an equilibrium transition from Q_2^* to Q_1^*, with full employment maintained because technique β is available as a less capital-intensive technique. This implies a rise of the real wage in the case of re-switching.

If, as in our intertemporal equilibrium model, there is only one consumer, such a transition might be regarded as planned. The association of a larger supply of labour with a rise of the real wage would then seem to be not a paradoxical factor price movement in the presence of a sudden and unforeseen immigration, but the normal response of the consumer who supplies more labour in the face of a rising real wage.

However, even here, with only one consumer, the paradox would remain that firms would install a less capital-intensive technique in response to the rise of the real wage, and, generally speaking, it would have to be remembered that the one-consumer model stands only as a simplification for a model with many consumers and many agents. Foresight for them only means that they deal in forward markets, knowing their future preferences and choices in response to different conceivable prices, but it does not mean that they foresee the outcome of the market process. I considered the possibility of using a model with many consumers in order to render this limitation of perfect foresight clear and to avoid the mistaken impression that the consumer acts as a central planner in the formation of equilibrium, but then I chose to avoid the formal complications. It seems sufficient to assume that the consumer plans in reaction to prices formed on the market, but that he does not know the 'macroeconomic' outcome of the market process in advance. The consumer acts as a central planner only in the determination of the optimum. By contrast, the consideration of equilibrium makes sense only if the consumer's choices depend on prices. He follows the usual logic of microeconomics; the transitions to be represented should be interpreted in this light.

The producers are many and of indefinite number since we have introduced a technology with constant returns to scale. Re-switching (and employment opportunity reversals – a similar, more general phenomenon, discussed in the parallel paper) can occur in response to factor price changes, with producers maximizing their profits. They do not lower the capital–labour ratio in the immigration parable with re-switching because they consciously plan to preserve full employment, but because technology happens to be such that a rising real wage induces the choice of a technique which happens to preserve full employment. The point is to show that, in spite of all these favourable assumptions, the paradox of counterintuitive factor price movements is possible, and this even with only one consumer (usually, it is the multiplicity of consumers which is thought to lead to instability, whereas here the problem is rooted in production).

3   The utility function

The question now is whether utility functions exist which generate the kind of transition we have in mind. Such a utility function would only have to fulfil the condition that marginal utilities are equal to prices, as determined by the conditions of reproduction. This results from the following corollary:

> **Corollary:**   *Let a strictly concave utility function U and a programme* $\bar{z} = (\bar{c}^0, \dots, \bar{c}^T, \bar{q}^1, \dots \bar{q}^T)$ *with prices u be given which fulfil the equilibrium conditions (a), for which we have in* $(\bar{c}^0, \dots, \bar{c}^T)$
>
> $$\frac{\partial U}{\partial c_i^t} = p_i^t; \qquad t = 0, \dots, T; \qquad i = 1, \dots, n$$
>
> *Then $\bar{z}$ is an optimum with respect to U and $(\bar{z}, u)$ is an equilibrium.*

If prices are given by the equilibrium conditions (a), a utility function is in fact easily found such that marginal utilities are equal to prices if quantities are in equilibrium. For we have (the normalization condition makes no problem) the following:

> **Example:**   *Let a programme $\bar{z}$ with prices u be given such that the equilibrium conditions (a) are fulfilled, with $\Sigma p_i^t < 1$, $\bar{c}_i^t < 1$. The utility function*
>
> $$U^* = \prod_{i,t}(1 + c_i^t - \bar{c}_i^t)^{p_i^t}$$
>
> *renders $\bar{z}$ an optimum and $(\bar{z}, u)$ an equilibrium.*

The trick, therefore, is as follows. Suppose we know the prices and quantities of a programme, fulfilling conditions (a) of equilibrium. Conditions (b) will then also be fulfilled if these equilibrium prices and quantities are treated as parameters in the function U^*, and equilibrium is defined with U^* given.

U^* is not homothetic, but the rates of intertemporal substitution turn out to be independent of the scale of consumption in stationary states. The rates of intertemporal substitution $\rho_i^t = (\partial U^*/\partial c_i^{t-1})/(\partial U^*/\partial c_i^t) - 1$ in the stationary state are the same for all commodities and may be regarded as 'the' rate of time preference in this model. The rate of time preference is not an unambiguous concept outside the stationary state, however.

4 Accumulation

We shall start our investigation by analysing the logic of price formulation and of the choice of technique which is implicit in the equilibrium conditions (a). Because of competition, prices fulfil

$$Bp^t \leqq Ap^{t-1} + w_t l$$

We now assume single production and consider a programme with positive consumptions; reproduction is feasible. Prices are positive (interior solution) but the wage rate may be zero. For each good it is necessary to activate at least one process producing it. There therefore has to be at least one profitable process for each good, according to the profit maximizing condition. For each good we choose one profitable process producing it. Taken together, those profitable processes form a square system A_σ, l^σ such that

$$p^t = A_\sigma p^{t-1} + w_t l^\sigma$$

This technique σ will then be called 'temporarily dominant', i.e. dominant in period t. All other processes, not in technique σ, in the spectrum of techniques (A, B, l), will then make losses and only exceptionally be as profitable as processes in σ. This means that any other square system forming a technique α, chosen from the spectrum of techniques (A, B, l), must fulfil

$$p^t \leqq A_\alpha p^{t-1} + w_t l^\alpha$$

This formulation makes it clear that the dynamic of the choice of techniques and of the formation of prices appears to be entirely determined, once prices p^0 'in the beginning' are known, and once distribution is given in the form of a fixation of wage rates in each period. Initial prices p^0 and distribution are endogenous variables in the determination of equilibrium, but we treat them as exogenous in much of what follows because we are interested in the inductive, forward-looking determination of prices according to the equilibrium conditions (a) in the case of single production. This determination is particularly simple if there is unemployment and wage rates are equal to zero: given p^0, (A_σ, l^σ) will be chosen through cost minimization as the technique temporarily dominant in the first period, and p^1 is determined. In the subsequent period, p^1 will determine whether A^σ remains temporarily dominant or whether another combination of processes is (temporarily) superior. Once this is known, p^2 is determined. The procedure is analogous if wage rates are positive and given in each period. Technique σ is the cost-minimizing technique; it is convenient to combine the determination of prices and cost-minimization by writing

$$p^t = A_\sigma p^{t-1} + w_t l^\sigma \leqq A_\alpha p^{t-1} + w_t l^\alpha$$

for all rival systems α in the spectrum.

The system of quantities influences the dynamics of the choice of technique via distribution. Distribution may be regarded as determined endogenously by the rates of intertemporal substitution (time preference in the stationary state) if full employment obtains, otherwise the own rates of interest may, given p^0, be considered as determined conversely by technology alone. In order to justify this assertion, we shall first of all make a convention which will allow us to regard paths with less than full employment as plausible. It we have unemployment, we must assume that the workers who are employed receive a minimum wage in order to be able to work. We assume, following Sraffa's lead (Sraffa, 1960, p. 19) that the minimum wage of the workers is represented in the coefficients of the input–output matrix. Hence, a positive wage represents something like a luxury wage. If there is unemployment, the unemployed retreat to an invisible subsistence economy.

The role of distribution will become easier to grasp once we introduce undiscounted prices. For each period, we define a new price vector and a new wage rate through $\tilde{p}^t = p^t/sp^t$, $\tilde{w}_t = w_t/sp^t$. Then we have $\tilde{p}^t = (1 + r_s^t)A_\sigma\tilde{p}^{t-1} + \tilde{w}_t l^\sigma$, where s is the basket of goods used as numéraire and where r_s^t is the own rate of interest in terms of s: $1 + r_s^t = sp^{t-1}/sp^t$. If $w_t > 0$, we can also define $\hat{p}^t = p^t/w_t$, i.e. we can define prices in terms of the wage rate. Then we obtain, after division by w_t,

$$\hat{p}^t = (1 + r_w^t)A_\sigma\hat{p}^{t-1} + l^\sigma$$

with $1 + r_w^t = w_{t-1}/w_t$ (r_w^t is the own rate of interest in terms of the wage-rate). It should be noted that, conversely, discounted prices can be calculated from a sequence of undiscounted prices and own rates. For instance, if undiscounted prices are given in terms of the wage-rate, $\hat{p}'$ and r'_w, one obtains discounted prices by formally choosing some value for w_0, for instance $w_0 = 1$. Then we obtain

$$w_1 = 1/(1 + r'_w), \qquad p^0 = \hat{p}^0$$

$$p^1 = \hat{p}^1 w_1 = \hat{p}^1 w_0/(1 + r'_w) = \hat{p}^1/(1 + r'_w), \qquad \text{etc.}$$

The intertemporal rates of substitution are equal to the own rates of interest in equilibrium. Thus, $\rho'_i = r'_i$. In particular, the own rate of interest of a numéraire r'_s in each period t, and prices of the preceding period determine both the wage–rate $\tilde{w}_t$ and the n prices $\tilde{p}'$, if we add the condition for the normalization of prices to the n price equations,

$$\tilde{p}' = (1 + r'_s)A_\sigma \tilde{p}^{t-1} + \tilde{w}_t l^\sigma, \, s\tilde{p}' = 1$$

If techniques are compared in terms of long-term prices, at a given rate of profit, that technique will be superior which yields the highest wage in terms of any numéraire. It is called 'dominant in the long-run'. Any inferior technique, estimated in terms of the prices of the technique which is dominant in the long-run, i.e. estimated in terms of long-period prices, will show losses relative to normal profits, defined by the uniform rate of profit. Conversely, if a superior method of production is estimated in terms of the prices of an inferior technique, surplus profits will indicate that it would be worthwhile to adopt the superior method (Schefold, 1978, p. 40).

However, the technique which is temporarily dominant need not be the one which is dominant in the long-run, since it is estimated in terms of intertemporal prices which converge only gradually towards long-run prices. The competitive process therefore leads to the selection of the method which is dominant in the long-run – if at all – only after a number of periods which is sufficiently large for intertemporal prices to have approached the long-run normal prices.

5 Turnpike properties of intertemporal prices

We may assume that the theory of the choice of technique using long-run normal prices is known. It suffices for our later purposes to suppose that a productive technique exists which is dominant in the long run. What we need is a theorem which guarantees the convergence of the time path of intertemporal prices and of the selection of methods of production which follows from those prices towards a technique which is dominant in the long run. Such a convergence does not obtain under all conditions; we prove it under the condition that distribution is given. It is enough to consider the case of productive indecomposable matrices (for Theorem (b), they must be primitive as well).

> **Theorem (a):**   *Let a sequence of intertemporal prices be given which defines the temporarily dominant technique in each period. We assume it to be indecomposable and such that $w_t > 0$, $t = 0$, $1, 2, \ldots$ (full employment). The own rate of interest in terms of s is assumed to be constant; therefore $r_s^t = r$, $t = 1, 2, \ldots$. The technique which is dominant in the long run at r, δ, is defined as the technique for which w, in terms of long-run normal prices*
>
> $$p = (1 + r)A_\delta p + wl^\delta, \qquad sp = 1$$
>
> *is largest (it is also assumed that $r < R_\delta$, R_δ being the maximum rate of profit of technique δ). (This technique is known to minimize costs in terms of its own long-run prices.) Then we have: Whatever the $p^0 \geq 0$ in the sequence of intertemporal prices, there is a t' such that δ is temporarily dominant for all $t > t'$ and $\tilde{p}^t$ converges to p and $\tilde{w}^t$ to w.*

> **Theorem (b):**   *Let $w_t = 0$, $t = 1, 2, \ldots$ (unemployment, except for flukes), the other assumptions remaining the same. The technique which is dominant in the long run is now defined as that for which the maximum rate of profit R_δ in*
>
> $$p = (1 + R_\delta)A_\delta p, \qquad sp = 1$$
>
> *is largest among all techniques. (This technique is known to minimize costs.) Then there is a t' such that δ is temporarily dominant for all $t > t'$ and $\tilde{p}^t$ converges to p and r_s^t to R_δ.*

A comparison in terms of long-run normal prices thus allows an immediate decision on which of two given techniques in the spectrum is superior, using the criterion of the higher wage rate at the given rate of profit. However, if we consider a process of adaptation, using intertemporal prices, the adoption of the best technique will in general take place only after a certain time lag. This 'lagging behind' may involve several changes of methods of production before the system eventually settles down, with intertemporal prices approaching long-run normal prices pertaining to the technique which is dominant in the long run. From a merely technical point of view, one could imagine sudden transitions from one stationary state to another; examples will be considered below, where quantities change in such a way that one technique is replaced by another between two periods. The new stationary state is reached at once because consumption adapts (and the utility function is such that the consumer wants this to happen), but prices adapt only gradually. A sudden change from one set of long-run prices to another would involve surplus profits and losses, and that is ruled out in intertemporal equilibrium.

However, even if prices do not change at once, we do have convergence of prices to long-run conditions. It is easy to see that convergence may not obtain if the assumptions of our theorem are not fulfilled. If distribution oscillates, the system may never settle down to the use of a permanent technique.

6 A spectrum of techniques with re-switching

A change of distribution may induce a change of technique. It is the central neoclassical idea that an increase in the rate of interest leads to the use of less capital and, with the accompanying reduction of the wage rate, the use of more labour. This is reflected in our system as well, if the change of methods of production is such that we can speak unambiguously of 'more' or 'less' capital, independently of relative prices. If we have an increase of r and a reduction of w, a transition from a method a_1 to a method a_0 with $a_0 < a_1$ and with $l_0 > l_1$ will be unambiguous. Two such techniques have only one switch point in common (Schefold, 1976a, p. 811). Consider the switch point between two techniques α, β where long-run prices $p = p^\alpha = p^\beta$, $w = w^\alpha = w^\beta$, and therefore

$$(l + r)a_0 o + wl_0 = (1 + r)a_1 p + wl_1$$

$$w(l_0 - l_1) = (1 + r)(a_1 - a_0)p$$

If r is raised and w is lowered, and if relative prices change little, a cost advantage will appear on the left-hand side of both equations. This means that the switch implies a transition to a less capital-intensive technique, which can here be defined as such unambiguously (independently of distribution and prices) because $a_1 > a_0$.

Re-switching may occur only where $a_1 - a_0$ has both positive and negative components. The second equation shows that it presupposes a considerable change in relative prices.

How likely is re-switching? This question is at last being dealt with in the literature (Schefold, 1976b; D'Ippolito, 1987; Mainwaring and Steedman, 1994). The papers referred to suggest that the measure of the set of techniques allowing re-switching is generically positive, but not large compared with the measure of all conceivable productive techniques. Re-switching may be rather unlikely, but there are many related phenomena of capital theory, some of which are more 'likely' to occur. There is some discussion of the likelihood of re-switching and of related effects (employment opportunity reversals) in my parallel paper referred to in the beginning.

7   The two parables as intertemporal equilibria

7.1   Preliminary exercise: Steady state with constant rate of profit

We first confirm that steady states of finite duration may be represented as intertemporal equilibria. Let only technique α be given. Net output is represented by $d = c^t$; $t = 0, \ldots, T$; therefore $q^t = q = d(I - A_\alpha)^{-1}$ and the labour force must fulfil $q^t l = ql = L_t$; $t = 1, \ldots, T$. We define $f = q^T - c^T = q - d$. We assume that the initial endowments are such that the stationary state is possible: $q^0 = q$.

Diverse price systems are compatible with this artificial stationary state, according to the utility function. We suppose that r is given, $0 \leqq r < R_\alpha$, and we choose undiscounted prices $\tilde{p}^t = p^\alpha(r)$, $\tilde{w}_t = w_\alpha(r)$, $d\tilde{p}^t = 1$. We transform them into discounted prices by putting $p^0 = p^\alpha$, $p^t = (1 + r)^{-t}\tilde{p}^t$, $w_t = (1 + r)^{-t}\tilde{w}_t$.

We then choose, e.g. according to the example provided, a utility function U for which we have in $(c^0, \ldots, c^T)$ that marginal utility equals price, i.e. $\partial U/\partial c_i^t = p_i^t$ for all commodities in all time periods considered. According to the Corollary, the stationary state is then an optimum and an (intertemporal) equilibrium.

7.2   Increasing supply of labour and rising rate of profit: 'Demechanization' as a 'normal' reaction

We now want to show under what conditions the central neoclassical idea of a substitutability of labour for 'capital' may be represented in our framework. A numerical example is provided in the Appendix.

To this end, let our economy be in a stationary state for some time as in the previous case, i.e. for $t = 1, \ldots, t'$, with $c^{t-1} = d$, $q^t = d(I - A_\alpha)^{-1} = q = q^0$, and with $\tilde{p}^0 = \tilde{p}^t = p^\alpha$ and $r = r_1$, as in Q_1 in Figure 2; of course, $q^t l = L_t$; $t = 1, \ldots, t'$. Suppose there is a less capital-intensive technique (a_0, l_0) with $a_0 < a_1, l_0 > l_1$, which is not profitable in P_1, however; this means that for $t = 1, \ldots, t'$ we have

$$(1 + r_1)a_0\tilde{p}^{t-1} + \tilde{w}_t l_0 > (1 + r_1)a_1\tilde{p}^{t-1} + \tilde{w}_t l_1 = \tilde{p}_1^t$$

Because of $a_0 < a_1$, $l_0 > l_1$, it is clear – independently of prices! – which technique employs less capital per man. At the end of period t' we still have $\tilde{p}' = p^\alpha$, but in the subsequent period, a change of distribution occurs, and accordingly also of technique and of consumption, because our representative consumer will have more labour at his disposal than before: $L_{t'+1}$ exceeds $L_{t'}$. One expects a fall of wages and a rise of the rate of profit, at least in neoclassical theory, for a classical economist would not be surprised if distribution remained constant and persistent unemployment developed. In an intertemporal equilibrium, the adaptation of intertemporal prices will be gradual; own rates of interest rise first. We assume that $r_s^{t'+1} = r_2$, corresponding to point P_2 in Figure 1, and that r_s^t remains constant thereafter.

We saw in Section 6 above that this 'normal' reaction in distribution entails a 'normal' reaction in the choice of technique if $a_0 < a_1$, $l_0 > l_1$. We now consider quantities, assuming that the technique changes between t' and $t' + 1$. For simplicity, we keep gross outputs constant. Hence we have $c^{t'} = q^{t'} - q^{t'+1}A_\beta = q(I - A_\beta)$. If the difference between any two techniques is not too large, we can be certain that consumption remains positive. As a matter of fact, in this case, c^t will remain constant, after having *risen* in both components, since $a_0 < a_1$. Therefore, the transition also corresponds to that from P_0 to P_1 in Figure 1, where total output (but not output per head) rises. On the other hand, we assume immigration to be such that $L_t = ql^\beta$, $t = t' + 1, \ldots, T$; $ql^\beta > ql^\alpha$. This transition will take place at once if the rise of $r_s^{t'+1}$ relative to r_s^t is – and can be – sufficiently large. The effect of 'lagging behind' which we mentioned earlier is here not very likely to happen because less capital is being used in a physical sense and more labour, so that the introduction of the new technique primarily depends on the change in the distributive variables themselves and not so much on a consequent change of relative prices. If r_2 corresponds to point Q_2 in Figure 2, we must have for $t = t' + 1$ to $t = T$, starting with $\tilde{p}^{t'} = p^\alpha$,

$$\tilde{p}^t = (1 + r_2)A_\beta\tilde{p}^{t-1} + \tilde{w}_t l^\beta$$

where

$$(1 + r_2)a_1\tilde{p}^{t-1} + \tilde{w}_t l_1 > (1 + r_2)a_0\tilde{p}^{t-1} + \tilde{w}_t l_0 = \tilde{p}_1^t;$$

$$t = t' + 1, \ldots, T$$

The path so constructed is again turned into an equilibrium by replacing the undiscounted prices by discounted prices and by choosing an appropriate utility function. The rise of the consumption vector with the change of technique does not imply a rise of consumption per head, since labour also rises. If we measure in terms of normal prices at $r = 0$, using s as a numéraire common to the price systems α and β, we obtain

$$\frac{c'p^\sigma}{ql^\sigma} = \frac{w_\sigma q(I - A_\sigma)(1 - A_\sigma)^{-1}l^\sigma}{ql^\sigma} = w_\sigma(0); \qquad \sigma = \alpha, \beta$$

and hence the labour value of consumption per head falls in the transition from α to β.

7.3   Re-switching: Gross outputs given

In the preceding case and in this example, gross output levels are constant, the technique changes with immigration between periods t' and $t' + 1$, and consumption changes once at the end of period t'. In the preceding case, undiscounted prices are long-run prices of technique α up to the end of period t', and they start to adapt to the long-run prices of technique β from period $t' + 1$ onwards. A 'lagging behind' effect requires an earlier start of the adaptation of prices in the case now to be discussed. (A numerical example is provided in the Appendix.)

To see this, we assume that the alternative technique, β, is chosen such that (a_0, l_0) with $l_0 > l_1$ superior at r_1, corresponding to Q_1^* in Figure 3. There are two switch points: one between $r = 0$ and $r = r_1$, corresponding to Q_1^*, and the other between r_1 and r_2, corresponding to Q_2^*. We have the same stationary state as before in Q_2^* such that $c^{t-1} = d$, $q = q^t = d(I - A)^{-1}$, with $q^0 = q$ and with $q^t l = L_t$ for $t = 1, \ldots, t'$. Afterwards, consumption changes to $c^t = q(I - A_\beta)$ for $t = t', \ldots, T$. We fix $f = qA_\beta$.

Since $a_1 - a_0$ has one positive and one negative component – otherwise, re-switching would not be possible – one component of $c^{t'}$ will rise and one will fall. It remains true, however, that $c^{t'} > 0$ if (a_0, l_0) is sufficiently close to (a_1, l_1) – here we need the assumption, mentioned above, that (a_0, l_0) is 'close' to (a_1, l_1), which is positive. We assume again that the increased labour supply at the disposal of the consumer happens to be such that full employment is possible, i.e.

$$q^1 l^\alpha = L_1 = \ldots = q^{t'} l^\alpha = L_{t'} < q^{t'+1}l^\beta = L_{t'+1} = \ldots = L_T$$

Turning now to prices, we have to be aware that a 'lagging behind' in the introduction of the new technology is to be expected in the case of re-switching. For re-switching, contrary to the example discussed in the previous subsection, demechanization presupposes in an essential way that not only distribution changes but also relative prices. Re-switching cannot happen if relative prices are constant for given techniques and wage curves are straight lines. We know, on the other hand, from the theorems on the convergence properties of intertemporal prices, that the technique which is dominant in the long run must become temporarily dominant after a finite number of periods.

The solution to the problem of constructing a time path with re-switching, therefore, is as follows. We start with a stationary system for which $\tilde{p}^0 = \tilde{p}^t = p^\alpha$, $\tilde{w}_t = w_\alpha$, $r_s^t = r_2$; $t = 1, \ldots, t''$, with t'' *smaller* than t', i.e. the change in distribution has to happen in a period t'', with $r_s^t = r_1$; $t > t''$, and t'' has to be calculated to be such that for $t'' \leq t < t'$

$$\tilde{p}_1^{t+1} = (1 + r_1)a_1\tilde{p}^t + \tilde{w}_{t+1}l_1 < (1 + r_1)a_0\tilde{p}^t + \tilde{w}_{t+1}l_0$$

In other words, method (a_1, l_1) must remain profitable after the change of distribution until the change of technique occurs because of immigration (which sets the date for the change of technique). Thereafter we have (excluding repeated switches between (a_1, l_0) and (a_0, l_0) at r_1 by assumption)

$$(1 + r_1)a_1\tilde{p}^t + \tilde{w}_{t+1}l_1 > (1 + r_1)a_0\tilde{p}^t + \tilde{w}_{t+1}l_0 = \tilde{p}_1^{t+1}$$

In consequence of the transition to the new method, the old method must appear to be unprofitable. We therefore have first what we shall call an 'anticipated change in distribution', then an adaptation of relative prices, then the choice of the new method of production (this date is fixed exogenously through immigration) and finally an adaptation of prices to the new steady state – an adaptation which will be the better the larger is T. I do not rule out that other cases, with a simultaneous change of distribution and of the method of production, i.e. with $t' = t''$, can be constructed, but the path proposed here seems to be characteristic, as is confirmed by numerical examples; one is given in the Appendix.

One has again to convert undiscounted prices into discounted ones and to apply the Corollary in order to obtain the intertemporal equilibrium with re-switching. The increase in employment which corresponds to the transition which we have considered is possible because less capital is being used in terms of intertemporal prices. This simply follows from the fact that $l_0 > l_1$, with activity levels being kept constant, and with the wage rate having been raised, so that the saving in cost must be due to the diminished cost of capital, although the input of one commodity per unit of output rises. (This consideration also confirms that re-switching is associated with a strong change of relative prices.)

Clearly, this equilibrium is highly implausible. The assumption of perfect foresight is particularly difficult to sustain. The lagging behind implies that the market participants have to set the price signals to themselves, by changing distribution in anticipation of the immigration, so as to ensure that the change of technique occurs at a suitable time. It is implausible from a common sense point of view, but also with regard to customary assumptions in stability analysis, that the real wage rises in consequence of an anticipated increase in the supply of labour. It is even more implausible from the point of view of neoclassical theory that capital diminishes, measured in the short-run prices, as the rate of interest is lowered. The equilibrium exists formally because the various anomalies compensate each other. What the construction really means is that the underlying theory is flawed: if the equilibrium exists, it presupposes implausible preferences and, if these are accepted, it is unstable. (A preliminary analysis of stability is proposed in the parallel paper.)

We might also have constructed this path on the assumption that net output was kept constant during the transition, i.e. such that $q^t = d(I - A_\alpha)^{-1}$ prior to, and $q^t = d(I - A_\beta)^{-1}$ after, the change of technique, with $c^t = d$ for all time periods except t', where we have $q^{t'} = c^{t'} + q^{t'+1} A_\beta$, and therefore $c^{t'} = d(I - A_\alpha)^{-1} - d(I - A_\beta)^{-1} A_\beta$. We then obtain $d(I - A_\alpha)^{-1} l^\alpha < d(I - A_\beta)^{-1} l^\beta$, i.e. the required increase in employment, if and only if $w_\alpha(0) > w_\beta(0)$.

The advantage of keeping net output constant is two-fold. First it allows the separation of the effect of a change of time preference from the effect of a change in the composition of output (taste). Here, we only have the former. Second, it implies that we can measure the capital–labour ratio on the wage curve, following the well-known procedure indicated in Figure 3, with the result that we observe a lowering of the capital–labour ratio in the transition from P_1 to P_0. We may therefore say that the intertemporal equilibrium shows a transition from one steady state to another (provided T is sufficiently large) such that a rising real wage rate is not only associated with a rise in the demand for labour through a 'perverse' substitution effect, but also that the fall of the rate of interest is associated with a fall of the intensity of capital, measured in normal prices. This confirms the earlier assertions that the comparison in terms of steady states is applicable to intertemporal equilibrium situations.

7.4 Without full employment: At the 'maximum rate of profit'

What happens if the technical methods available, given initial endowments, do not allow the available supply of labour to be absorbed by means of the appropriate substitution of techniques? This would happen, for instance, in the situation indicated by Q_2^* in Figure 3 if the technique corresponding to Q_1^* was not available, or if the consumer was not ready to reduce his time preference so as to make the transition to Q_1^*. Obviously, the wage must now fall to the subsistence level for those still employed. The path of prices, once started, turns out to be defined independently of utility considerations, according to Theorem (b). Prices are determined by $A_\alpha p^t = p^{t+1}$, and the own rates of interest must approach the maximum rate of profit, as long as full employment is not restored.

Without alternative methods of production of the form we described as 'demechanization', there would be little hope for stabilization in this case, according to the logic of neoclassical theory, if a new stationary state is to be approached quickly. In order to return to full employment, with only technique α available, accumulation with unchanged methods of production would be necessary, i.e. it would be necessary to raise activity levels q^{t+1} relative to q^t repeatedly by curtailing consumption per head, c^t, where $q^t = c^t + q^{t+1}A$. Whether this growth was balanced or not, the full employment ceiling might eventually be reached. With own rates of interest tending to R_α, the rates of intertemporal substitution would be higher than before the immigration. A higher rate of interest means that a higher amount of consumption today has to be sacrificed to obtain a given amount tomorrow, i.e. savings, in fact, increase. Whether this effect would suffice to generate savings which, if invested, lead back to full employment cannot be said without specifying a utility function.

I interpose a terminological remark. A partial use of an endowment (e.g. of an inferior piece of land) is consistent with the full employment of resources in the language of general equilibrium. If $L_t > q_t l$ in our model, there is still full employment in that sense, but $w_t = 0$. We have nevertheless usually spoken of unemployment of labour in this case since workers are only partially employed and receive a subsistence wage, thought to be contained in the input coefficients of A_α.

Persistence of $w_t = 0$ is thus consistent with neoclassical premises, even if the convergence of $p_i^t = r_i^t$ to R_α results in some saving and some rise of q_t. Hence, the necessity for neoclassical theory to stress substitution of less mechanized methods of production as the way to full employment with $w_t > 0$. In fact, it is *the* relevant way to true full employment within that theory (Keynes' theory of effective demand is another matter), since every increase of the rate of interest is sure to lead to more employment through demechanization if less mechanized techniques become available. However, this leads back to the question of whether the spectrum of techniques is essentially like that of the surrogate production function.

7.5   Mechanization: Growth with a constant labour force

We want to return to the problem of re-switching, but now the labour force is to be kept constant and we want to examine what re-switching implies for the process of accumulation. In order to clear the ground for this savings scenario, we first examine a case of mechanization which is induced by the desire to save, not by a reduction of the labour force. The alternative to the existing technique, α, now consists of the introduction of a process (a_0, l_0) such that $l_0 < l_1$ and $a_0 > a_1$. The alternative technique, β, is therefore unambiguously more mechanized. The movement is like that from Q_2 to Q_1 in Figure 2, but note that α denotes the more mechanized technique in Figure 2, not β, as – because of the sequence – in the text of this section! We are looking for a transition at the end of period t' such that employment is kept constant. This means $q^{t'+1}l^{\beta} = q^{t'}l^{\alpha} = L$ and, more generally, $q^{t}l^{\alpha} = L$; $t = 1, \ldots, t'$; and $q^{t}l^{\beta} = L$; $t = t' + 1, \ldots, T$. We assume that consumption is stationary up to the beginning of period t': $c^{t} = d$; $t = 0, \ldots, t' - 1$; and that the proportion in which goods are consumed is kept constant after the change, and therefore $c^{t} = \mu d$; $t = t' + 1, \ldots, T$. As in the earlier examples, $q^{0} = q^{1}$ and $f = q^{T} - \mu d$ to secure the stationarity of the system at its beginning and at the end. From

$$L = q^{1}l^{\alpha} = d(I - A_{\alpha})^{-1}l^{\alpha} = q^{T}l^{\beta} = \mu d(I - A_{\beta})^{-1}l^{\beta}$$

we obtain, using $w_{\alpha} = 1/d\hat{p}(r)$ in terms of standard d (not in terms of standard s):

$$\mu = \frac{d(I - A_{\alpha})^{-1}l^{\alpha}}{d(I - A_{\beta})^{-1}l^{\beta}} = \frac{d\hat{p}^{\alpha}(0)}{d\hat{p}^{\beta}(0)} = \frac{w_{\beta}(0)}{w_{\alpha}(0)}$$

Mechanization means that the wage curves $w_{\alpha}(r)$ and $w_{\beta}(r)$ intersect once and only once. We start at a rate of profit r_2 on the right of the point of intersection and move to a rate of profit r_1 on the left of it (the reverse of the case of demechanization above). Therefore, $w_{\beta}(0) > w_{\alpha}(0)$, $\mu > 1$ and $c^{0} = \ldots = c^{t'-1} < c^{t'+1} = \ldots = c^{T}$. For $c^{t'}$, we obtain

$$c^{t'} = q^{t'} - q^{t'+1}A_\beta = q^{t'} - q^{t'+2}A_\beta = q^{t'} + c^{t'+1} - q^{t'+1}$$

$$= \mu d + d(I - A_\alpha)^{-1} - \mu d(I - A_\beta)^{-1}$$

$$= d + \epsilon d - \epsilon d(I - A_\beta)^{-1} + d(I - A_\alpha)^{-1} - d(I - A_\beta)^{-1} < d$$

using $\epsilon = \mu - 1 > 0$, $A_\beta \geq A_\alpha$, and therefore $(I - A_\beta)^{-1} > (I - A_\alpha)^{-1} = I + A_\alpha + \ldots > I$. This is the true neoclassical parable: the society decides to accumulate. The decision is expressed in a lowering of time-preference. The own rates of interest fall from r_2 to r_1. The change of distribution induces a change of technique (for the reasons expounded earlier, we may suppose that both changes occur simultaneously, without 'lagging behind'). More capital, in physical terms (therefore also in price terms), is required, and less labour is needed per unit of output. To preserve full employment, this accumulation takes place at the expense of a once-and-for-all reduction of the level of consumption (again, both in physical terms, $c^{t'} < c^{t'-1} < c^{t'+1}$ and in price terms). As a result, consumption will permanently be higher, vindicating the sacrifice.

Undiscounted prices are equal to the long-run prices of α at r_2 from $t = 0$ to t'. In period $t' + 1$, we have (reckoning all prices in terms of the same standard d and assuming that there is no lagging behind, as is likely in this case)

$$\tilde{p}^{t'+1} = (1 + r_1)A_\beta\tilde{p}^{t'} + \tilde{w}_{t'+1}l^\beta, \quad \text{with } \tilde{p}^{t'} = p^\alpha(r_2)$$

and

$$\tilde{p}_1^{t'+1} < (1 + r_1)a_1\tilde{p}^{t'} + \tilde{w}_{t'+1}l_1$$

Prices $\tilde{p}^t$ then converge towards $p^\beta(r_1)$ for $t = t' + 1, t' + 2, \ldots$. It is also useful in this case to evaluate the change in terms of long-run prices, if d is chosen as our standard of prices. Net consumption (or net income) per head in terms of long-run prices is then, for $t = 0, \ldots, t' - 1$, equal to

$$y_t = \frac{dp^\alpha(r_2)}{q^t l^\alpha} = \frac{1}{L} = \frac{1}{d(I - A_\alpha)^{-1}l^\alpha} = w_\alpha(0)$$

and for $t = t' + 1, \ldots, T$ is equal to

$$y_t = \frac{\mu dp^\beta(r)}{q^t l^\beta} = \frac{\mu}{L} = \frac{\mu}{\mu d(I - A_\beta)l^\beta} = w_\beta(0)$$

Since $w_\beta(0) = (1 + \epsilon)w_\alpha(0)$, there is a permanent gain in net income. The capital–labour ratio rises from $k_\alpha = (y_1 - w_\alpha(r_2))/r_2 = (w_\alpha(0) - w_\alpha(r_2))/r_2$ unambiguously to $k_\beta = (y_T - w_\beta(r_1))/r_1 = (w_\beta(0) - w_\beta(r_1))/r_1$, if the wage curves do not deviate a great deal from straight lines, as in

Figure 2. This means, once more, that the neoclassical parable presupposes that relative prices do not change (or do not change much) with distribution. The fall in the rate of profit leads to a rising intensity of capital.

7.6   *Re-switching with a constant labour force: Accumulation at a rising rate of profit*

The fundamental idea must be the same as in the preceding case: the consumer wishes to attain a permanently higher level of consumption through accumulation at the same level of employment. Re-switching, however, will make this possible only through a 'perverse' movement of factor prices. If our notion of equilibrium included the requirement that factor prices and factor supplies be normally related, an equilibrium with re-switching (rising rate of interest with rising intensity of capital) would be just as impossible as the immigration scenario (rising supply of labour at a rising rate of wages). Since the concept of general equilibrium of supply and demand is wider, we must say that an equilibrium with re-switching exists, but that it is implausible and, in a sense, unstable.

We suppose that initially the economy is in stationary equilibrium as at Q_1^* in Figure 3 (note, however, that the technique which is less mechanized at Q_1^* is denoted by β in the diagram, not by α, as – because of the sequence – in the text of this section!), using a technique called α which consists of processes 1 and 2; technique β uses process 0 and employs less labour: $l_0 < l_1$. The figure can be used for the long-term comparison because consumption is still assumed to change proportionally in the transition from technique α, with $c' = d$ in Q_1^*, to technique β, with $c' = \mu d$ in Q_2^*. As in the previous case of mechanization, full employment entails a rise of consumption, for, with employment kept constant,

$$L = q^1 l^\alpha = d\,(I - A_\alpha)^{-1} l^\alpha = 1/w_\alpha(0) = q^T l^\beta = \mu d(I - A_\beta)^{-1} l^\beta = \mu/w_\beta(0).$$

Since there is a switch not only between Q_2^* and Q_1^* but also between Q_1^* and zero, we have $w_\beta(0) > w_\alpha(0)$ and $\mu > 1$. As in the previous case, $c^0 = \ldots = c^{t'-1} < c^{t'+1} = \ldots = c^T$. The fall of $c^{t'}$ is now not quite unambiguous; one again obtains, by the same transformation and using $\mu = 1 + \epsilon$,

$$c^{t'} = d + \epsilon d - \epsilon d(I - A_\beta)^{-1} + d(I - A_\alpha)^{-1} - d(I - A_\beta)^{-1}$$

We should be sure to have $c^{t'} < d$ if $A_\beta \geq A_\alpha$ and $(I - A_\beta)^{-1} > (I - A_\alpha)^{-1}$, but re-switching is not possible if $a_0 - a_1$ is either positive or negative. However, since clearly $d(I - A_\beta)^{-1} > d$, we expect $c^{t'} < d$.

We conclude that the transition from Q_1^* to Q_2^* so far is like mechanization: a drop of consumption in one period allows a permanent gain in all later periods, at constant employment, through a transition to another technique which exhibits a higher capital–labour ratio, measured in long-term prices. The sacrifice of consumption ($c^{t'} < c^{t'-1}$) is tantamount to an increase in real gross saving in t' from $q^{t'-1} - c^{t'-1}$ to $q^{t'} - c^{t'}$, since $q^{t'} = q^{t'-1}$, and results in a permanent gain.

Lagging behind is likely. Prices are stationary from $t = 0$ to $t = t'' < t'$. In t'', distribution changes because r_1 rises to r_2. If prices have adapted sufficiently by the time we reach t', we may also be sure that savings in price terms $(q^{t'} - c^{t'})p^{t'}$ have increased in t' relative to $t' - 1$. Undiscounted prices start to gravitate to long-run prices of technique β at rate of interest r_2 from $t' + 1$ onwards. Undiscounted prices are then converted to discounted prices.

The paradox is in the fact that the more capital-intensive technique is chosen at the higher rate of interest. The parallel paper proposes a more specific analysis of this cause for instability.

8 Conclusion

It has been shown that transitions involving re-switching and employment opportunity reversals can be represented within intertemporal equilibrium models. In our examples, the paradoxical relations between the distributive variables and the intensity of capital do not preclude the existence of equilibria, but with properties which run counter to generally accepted notions of stability. A rising supply of labour is absorbed by raising the real wage rate; accumulation at constant full employment is made possible with a rise of the rate of interest, in a given state of knowledge. If normal reactions prevail, the factor prices should move away from these equilibria which we have constructed. The conclusion seems inevitable: intertemporal equilibrium does not provide a stronghold which could be better defended against the critiques derived from capital theory than the older notions of long-period neoclassical equilibrium. They stand or fall together.

References

Bliss, C. J. (1970). 'Comment on Garegnani', *Review of Economic Studies*, **37**, pp. 437–8.

Burmeister, E. (1980). *Capital Theory and Dynamics*, Cambridge: Cambridge University Press.

D'Ippolito, G. (1987). 'Probabilità di perverso comportamento del capitale al variare del saggio dei profitti', *Note Economiche*, **2**, pp. 5–37.

Garegnani, P. (1970). 'A Reply', *Review of Economic Studies*, **37**, p. 439.

Mainwaring, L. and Steedman, I. (1994). 'On the probability of reswitching and capital reversing in a two-sector Sraffian model', Mimeo, 37 pp.

Schefold, B. (1976a). 'Different forms of technical progress', *The Economic Journal*, **86**, pp. 806–19.

Schefold, B. (1976b). 'Relative Prices as a Function of the Rate of Profit', *Zeitschrift für Nationalökonomie*, **36**, pp. 21–48.

Schefold, B. (1978). 'Multiple Product Techniques with Properties of Single Product Systems', *Zeitschrift für Nationalökonomie*, **38**, pp. 29–43.

Schefold, B. (1990). 'Joint Production, Intertemporal Preferences and Long Period Equilibrium. A Comment on Bidard', *Political Economy. Studies in the Surplus Approach*, **6**, pp. 139–63.

Schefold, B. (1997). *Normal Prices, Technical Change and Accumulation*, London: Macmillan.

Sraffa, P. (1960). *Production of Commodities by Means of Commodities*, Cambridge: Cambridge University Press.

Appendix: Numerical example

I have calculated a number of examples in order to demonstrate that lagging behind takes place especially if a transition to a technique with re-switching is involved. A typical exmaple is given below.

The input–output matrix and the labour vector are given by

$$A = \begin{bmatrix} 0.11 & 0.36 \\ 0.34 & 0.09 \end{bmatrix}, \quad l = \begin{pmatrix} 1 \\ 10 \end{pmatrix}$$

This system defines a wage curve w^1. An alternative technique for the production of the first good is available; it uses inputs $a_0 = (0.22396, 0.26750)$ and $l_0 = 1.5$. If this alternative method is used in the first industry, one obtains a wage curve w^2, with switch points with respect to the former wage curve at $r_1 = 0.05$ and $r_3 = 0.15$. Note that this technique employs more labour, since $l_0 > l_1$. We construct a third wage curve, w^3, generated by a method $a_3 = (0.10343, 0.33852)$ which can also be employed to produce the *first* good, and it also employs more labour, $l_3 = 1.5$, as in the case of the first alternative technique. We then have $a_3 < a_1$; therefore, this is a case of demechanization with respect to the first technique. The new wage curve is lower than w^1 for low rates of profit, including the second switch point at $r_3 = 0.15$, and becomes dominant after the switch point $r_5 = 0.25$. The three wage curves are shown in Table A1.

The initial endowments are given by vector $q = (1, 1)$; this is also the vector of activity levels, which we shall keep constant. If the first technique

Table A1. *Three wage curves*

$1 + r$	w^1	w^2	w^3
1	0.09090	0.09086	0.08956
1.05	0.08719	0.08719	0.08611
1.1	0.08347	0.08348	0.08266
1.15	0.07975	0.07975	0.07921
1.2	0.07603	0.07599	0.07576
1.25	0.07231	0.07220	0.07231
1.3	0.06859	0.06839	0.06885
1.35	0.06487	0.06454	0.06540
1.4	0.06115	0.06068	0.06194
1.45	0.05743	0.05679	0.05848
1.5	0.05371	0.05287	0.05502
1.55	0.05	0.04892	0.05156
1.6	0.04628	0.04495	0.04810

is utilized, there results a net output for consumption of $d_1 = [1 - (0.11 + 0.34), 1 - (0.36 + 0.09)]$. We assume that we are first in a stationary state for a certain number of periods up to t^*. After t^*, a switch to the first alternative technique (a_0, l_0) takes place so that net output afterwards is $d_2 = [1 - (0.22396 + 0.34), 1 - (0.26750 + 0.09)]$. We thus start in the stationary state at $r_4 = 0.2$, where wage curve w^1 is dominant. After t^* periods, we move to $r_2 = 0.1$ and stay there, and approximate the corresponding stationary state.

We now calculate the long-run prices. They are expressed in terms of the wage rate. Writing price vectors as row vectors, we obtain $\hat{p}(r_4) = \hat{p}(0.2) = (8.71571, 15.19732)$ for the system pertaining to wage curve w^1. On the other hand, we have long-run prices $\hat{p}(r_2) = \hat{p}(0.1) = (7.54705, 14.23151)$ for the system pertaining to wage curve w^2; we are here in between the two switch points r_1 and r_3.

However, with intertemporal prices, a change in distribution from r_4 to r_2 does not necessarily imply a sudden transition of technique. Since we are at first in a stationary state, the long-run prices are equal to undiscounted prices in terms of the wage rate for the first t^* periods at r_4. We then have a change to an own rate of interest in terms of the wage rate which is equal to r_2. Undiscounted input prices in terms of the wage rate are equal to the long-run prices of the stationary state at the beginning of period $t^* + 1$, when interest has changed from 0.2 to 0.1. Prices then start to adapt. Table A2 shows this process of adaptation.

Table A2. *Adaptation of prices at r_2 to long-run prices, starting from long-run prices at r_4, all in terms of the wage rate*

$\hat{p}^{t^*+0}(0.1)$	(8.71571, 15.19732)
$\hat{p}^{t^*+1}(0.1)$	(8.07274, 14.76421)
$\hat{p}^{t^*+2}(0.1)$	(7.82343, 14.48086)
$\hat{p}^{t^*+3}(0.1)$	(7.68105, 14.35956)
$\hat{p}^{t^*+4}(0.1)$	(7.61579, 14.29431)
$\hat{p}^{t^*+5}(0.1)$	(7.58205, 14.26344)

It now turns out that the alternative method (a_0, l_0) is adopted only after five iterations, i.e. after prices $\hat{p}^{t^*+5}$ have been reached; only then is (a_1, l_1) replaced by (a_3, l_0) and $\hat{p}^{t^*+5}$ becomes the vector of input prices. Undiscounted intertemporal prices have by then adapted to the new long-run prices with a given accuracy: the sum of the absolute values of the deviations of undiscounted intertemporal prices from long-run prices is smaller than 0.1, and our calculation stops.

This may be compared to demechanization. Demechanization involves the use of technique (a_3, l_0) in place of (a_1, l_1). We again start from the long-period position at $r = 0.2$ on wage curve w^1. We now move to $r_6 = 0.3$, where wage curve w^3 is dominant. This is a case of demechanization with $a_3 < a_1$, $l_0 > l_1$. We again keep gross outputs equal to unity throughout, and net outputs are equal to $d_3 = (1.1) - a_3 - a_2$.

This transiton also starts from the same long-run prices $\hat{p}(r_4)$ as above: $\hat{p}^{t^*+0}(r_6) = \hat{p}(r_4)$. The new long-run prices to be reached will be $\hat{p}(r_6) = \hat{p}(0.3) = (10.04894, 16.35518)$. Table A3 shows the adaptation of undiscounted intertemporal prices in terms of the wage rate:

Table A3. *Adaptation of prices at r_6 to long-run prices, starting from long-run prices at r_4*

$\hat{p}^{t^*+0}(0.3)$	(8.71571, 15.19732)
$\hat{p}^{t^*+1}(0.3)$	(9.35869, 15.63043)
$\hat{p}^{t^*+2}(0.3)$	(9.63717, 15.96530)
$\hat{p}^{t^*+3}(0.3)$	(9.82198, 16.12756)
$\hat{p}^{t^*+4}(0.3)$	(9.91825, 16.22824)
$\hat{p}^{t^*+5}(0.3)$	(9.97550, 16.28257)

Here, it so happens that the demechanized technique (a_3, l_3) is adopted in the first period after the change in the rate of interest, since the adoption of this technique depends primarily on the change of distribution; the contrast between this transition and the previous case indicates that 'lagging behind' is a characteristic of re-switching. We then have five iterations, using the demechanized method, until undiscounted intertemporal prices approximate to long-run prices to the same degree as above: the sum of the absolute values of the deviations of short-run from long-run prices is smaller than 0.1.

Finally, we may construct a utility function, U^*, such that either transition is an intertemporal equilibrium. We only do it for the first case, involving re-switching, and therefore for the transition from r_4 to r_2, and we take $t^* = 2$ for simplicity. We only calculate the first and last factor in U^*, and write U^* as (since prices are here normalized as prices in terms of the wage rate, the utility function turns out to be only quasi-concave)

$$U^* = (1 + c_1^0 - \bar{c}_1^0)^{p_1^0} \ldots (1 + c_2^7 - \bar{c}_2^7)^{p_2^7}$$

When the equilibrium values for consumption are entered as parameters in the utility function, we have

$$\bar{c}_1^0 = 1 - 0.11 - 0.34 = 0.55 \text{ and } \bar{c}_2^7 = 1 - 0.26750 - 0.09 = 0.6425$$

The initial price needs no discounting, and therefore $p_1^0 = 8.71571$. The discounted price for the second good after $2 + 5 = 7$ periods is (cf. Table A2)

$$p_2^7 = \frac{[p_2^{2+5}(r_2)]}{(1 + r_4)^2 (1 + r_2)^5} = \frac{14.26344}{(1.2)^2 (1.1)^5} = 6.15032$$

From a didactic point of view, it would have been better to start from this utility function, from given endowments and from a given technology, including the appropriate assumptions about the availability of labour, and to demonstrate that the path which we have described is the equilibrium outcome. I might even have used a monotonic transfomation of the utility function in order to conceal the fact that the equilibrium values of consumption and the discounted prices can so easily be read off from the utlity function, as in the case of U^*, where they show up as parameters, but the procedure and the calculations would have been too lengthy for this article.

CHAPTER 11

Savings, investment and capital in a system of general intertemporal equilibrium

Pierangelo Garegnani

1 Introduction

1. The criticism of neoclassical theory based on the inconsistency of the concept of a 'quantity of capital' has been met from the orthodox side essentially with the claim that the contemporary reformulations of the theory do not rely on any such concept.[1] The present chapter is intended as part of a larger work concerned with showing that the deficiencies of that concept do in fact undermine those reformulations no less than they do for the traditional versions.[2] The limited aim of the

I wish to thank for useful comments the participants at several seminars held in Italy and elsewhere, where the ideas contained in this paper have been discussed since 1992. Thanks are due in particular to Professors R. Ciccone, G. Impicciatore, H. Kurz, F. Petri, B. Schefold, F. Serrano, D. Tosato, and Dr F. Ravagnani. Special thanks are owed to Dr M. Tucci and Professor M. Angrisani for help on the mathematical parts of the paper (see Dr Tucci's Mathematical Note at the end of the chapter).

[1] For example, that is the basic contention in Professor Hahn's article on the 'neo-Ricardians' (1982). Similarly, Professor Samuelson had written earlier:

> Repeatedly in writings and lectures I have insisted that capital theory can be rigorously developed without using any Clark-like concept of aggregate 'capital', instead relying upon a complete analysis of a great variety of heterogeneous physical capital goods and processes through time. (1962, p. 193)

The point also seems to have been widely accepted from the critically inclined side of the controversy. As we shall see, the contention essentially overlooks the role which savings – the *flow* expression of the *fund* 'capital' – have in any case to play as the single quantity on which individual decisions are taken about the acquisition of heterogeneous capital goods as *perfectly substitutable* providers of future income (cf. Paragraphs 34–5 below).

[2] By the qualification of 'traditional', we refer here to the versions of the neoclassical theory which are based on the notion of the traditional long-period equilibrium characterized by

continued

392

present chapter is that of providing a basis for the wider argument by bringing to light the form which the concept of capital takes in an intertemporal general equilibrium system.[3]

In Section 2 we shall introduce for the purpose the very simple model which Professor Hahn put forward in 1982 to counter what he took to be the 'neo-Ricardian' critique. That model will allow us to bring out the decisions to save and to invest of any 'year' which are implied in the

a uniform *effective* rate of return on the supply prices of the capital goods, which has been dominant in neoclassical pure theory until the last three or four decades (cf. however, p. 395, n. 5 below on today's frequent confusion between that kind of equilibrium and the quite different, more restrictive notion of a 'stationary' or 'steady growth' position). As has frequently been pointed out, the traditional equilibrium was inconsistent with a treatment of the capital endowment as a vector of distinct capital goods, and was in fact generally accompanied by a treatment of that endowment as a single 'quantity of capital' which could change its 'form', so as to allow for the *rentals* of the several capital goods to come into line with the uniform rate of return on their supply prices (e.g. Hicks, 1932, p. 20; for the past general use of a 'quantity of capital' in pure theory cf., e.g., Wicksell, 1936, quoted in Paragraph 2 below; Jevons, 1871, pp. 242, 244; Böhm-Bawerk, 1891, p. 391; Marshall, 1920, Vol. VI, pp. ii, 4; Pigou, 1932, pp. 114–15). Walras had been the outstanding exception in that respect but, sharing as he did in his *Eléments* that traditional notion of equilibrium, his treatment of capital was simply inconsistent (as he came close to admitting by the time of the 4th edition of the *Eléments* in 1900) and it deprived his equations of general equilibrium of economically significant solutions (cf., e.g., Garegnani, 1960, pp. 123–62, also 1990, Paragraphs 9–18; Robinson, 1970; Harcourt, 1972, pp. 170–1; Eatwell, 1987, Vol. IV, pp. 868–72).

A question which contributed considerably to the opacity of the capital controversies of recent decades may be pointed out in this connection. The italicized word 'effective' (above) by which we qualified the long-period notion of a uniform rate of return is meant to take care of the fact that the *definition* of such a uniform rate will entail a non-uniformity of the *own rates of return* of the several capital goods, when changes in their relative prices over time are considered (cf. Paragraph 6, below). In the capital controversies, that *inequality of own rates* has often been confused with the *inequality of effective rates on the supply prices of the capital goods*, which is instead due to the arbitrary initial physical composition of the capital endowment of Walrasian theory. This has had the result of obscuring both the mentioned necessity of the concept of a 'quantity of capital' for the traditional equilibrium, and the causes of the abandonment of the latter. Price changes in the *definition* of equilibrium came in as a consequence rather than as the cause of that complex evolution of the notion of equilibrium (cf. Garegnani, 1976, in particular pp. 36–9). For this *quid pro quo* between the two kinds of non-uniformities of rates of return, cf. e.g. Bliss's *New Palgrave* article on the 'equality of profits rates' which fails to draw the above basic distinction (1987, pp. 173–74) and Hahn (1982), where the condition of a variable physical composition of the initial capital stock, which would avoid the inequality of effective rates on supply prices, is incorrectly thought to take care of an inequality of own rates.

[3] We shall not be concerned here with 'temporary equilibria'. It should, however, be evident that if the 'quantity of capital' underlies the savings–investment decisions of an intertemporal equilibrium, that quantity will not be any less entailed in those of a 'temporary equilibrium'.

intertemporal equations. In Section 3 we shall then define what can be described as the 'general-equilibrium saving–supply schedule' and the 'general-equilibrium investment–demand schedule' for such a 'year'. In Section 4 we shall consider the determination of those schedules and then, in Section 5, the information they can provide on the behaviour of the system. Section 6 deals with alternative techniques and the effect of them on investment demand.

Finally, in Section 7, we shall consider the presence and significance of the concept of a 'quantity of capital' in intertemporal general equilibrium. Although we shall leave for the intended fuller essay the working out of the negative implications of that concept for the properties of the equilibria, some of these negative implications will, we trust, begin to emerge in that section.

Our analysis of general equilibrium will be conducted by means of analytical instruments different from those which appear to have become established since Hicks (1939). As already indicated, we shall use 'general-equilibrium demand and supplies' of particular commodities or factors, meaning by that the demands and supply functions of those commodities or factors when all markets other than the particular ones on which we focus our attention are in equilibrium. An equilibrium in the particular market considered will then imply an equilibrium of the whole system. The advantage of this is the possibility these instruments offer to trace the effects which the peculiarities of the market on which we shall thus focus our attention may have on the general equilibrium and its properties. Thus we shall here centre on those commodity markets which constitute the savings–investment market, so as to trace the effect of the phenomenon of 'reverse capital deepening' which affects those markets. The readers are therefore asked for some effort in entering a less familiar way of analysis, which however, we hope, may turn out to allow for some new results and for a better economic grasp of key phenomena affecting a general intertemporal equilibrium. In particular, they should try to take these unfamiliar instruments on their logic, and resist, if possible, the temptation to translate them too quickly into the language with which they are more familiar.

2   Decisions to save and invest in a system of intertemporal general equilibrium

2. To have a first, bird's eye view of the ground we shall travel, it might be useful briefly to focus our attention back on the traditional versions of the theory and consider the seeming contradiction between the assumptions underlying the (general-equilibrium) *demand*, and those underlying

the (general-equilibrium) *supply* functions for 'capital',[4] the single factor which characterizes those versions of the theory.[5] For the sake of a definite example we might refer to Wicksell's 'capitalistic production', where a quantity of 'capital' demanded, expressed as value in terms of consumption goods, is equalized to the economy's endowment of it (1934, pp. 204–5). The seeming contradiction lies in the fact that, whereas in the demand schedule the physical composition of the quantity K *demanded* at each interest rate is that corresponding to the techniques and productions most profitable at such a rate and changes with it, the composition of the *supply*, or endowment, of K cannot but be the given one of the stock in existence in the economy, which will generally be incompatible with that of the unknown equilibrium we aim to determine.

However, clearly, the contradiction is only apparent, because what is in fact implied in the supply schedule of 'capital' is that the physical composition of the stock required in any equilibrium position will be assumed by the existing capital stock *over a period of time* as, each 'year', a part of the capital goods in existence is replaced and a corresponding proportion of the labour force becomes, so to speak, 'free' to be re-equipped by appropriately investing the gross savings of the year.[6]

[4] For the concept of general-equilibrium demand and supply functions of 'capital' in the traditional versions of neoclassical theory, cf. Garegnani, 1970, p. 425. To develop analogous concepts applicable to intertemporal equilibria will, as we said, be a main aim of the present chapter.

[5] It should perhaps be noted here how in the course of the capital controversies, the traditional concept of equilibrium – in which the capital endowment is a *given* (cf. n. 2 above) – has often been confused with that of a steady state where that endowment is instead an *unknown*. This confusion, like the one concerning the two different kinds of inequality of rates of return we saw in n. 2 above, has considerably helped to hide the role of the 'quantity of capital' in traditional theory. The confusion has been favoured by the fact that the assumption of a steady state was alleged to be at the basis of the *constancy of equilibrium prices* assumed in the equations of those traditional equilibria. However, such a constancy was there a *direct assumption* founded only on the *persistence* attributable to those equilibria – a result, largely, of the assumption of an adjusted physical composition of the capital endowment dictated by the condition of a uniform effective rate of return on the supply prices of the capital goods. That 'persistence', for which changes in equilibrium prices could be ignored in the equations, had the clear advantage of cutting through the maze of difficulties which the 'dating' of equilibrium variables entails, from the arbitrariness of the 'initial moment', to that of the final horizon, or to the meaning of a stability for such 'dated' equilibria (see below, Paragraph 13). The assumption had, however, the decisive disadvantage that the adjusted physical composition of the capital stock and associated uniform effective rate had to rest on conceiving the capital endowment as a single magnitude (on this question, cf. Garegnani, 1976, pp. 33–6).

[6] Cf. the frequent use among those authors of expressions like 'free' or 'fluid' or 'floating'

continued

The implications of this are important. The demand and supply schedules for 'capital' (the fund) envisaged in Wicksell and the other traditional writers in their equilibria, were in fact intended to analyse forces supposed to operate through the demand for gross investment, and the supply for gross savings (the flows). The attention was concentrated on the *fund* (capital) rather than the *flow* concept (savings–investment) in order to analyse the basic mechanism of factors substitution in a purer form, undisturbed by monetary and other phenomena, which would have had to be considered when dealing with a savings–investment market. Once that is made clear, it should also be clear that the 'quantity of capital' cannot be absent in the new intertemporal versions of the theory where each 'year' will of course entail investment and savings.[7]

Our task now will therefore be, first of all, to render explicit the savings supply and investment demand which pertain to each 'date' in the equations of general intertemporal equilibrium.

3. A very simple model will suffice for that purpose. Assume an economy with two goods only, a and b, each being both a consumption and a (circulating) capital good. The economy lasts two 'years' in all, $t = 0$ and $t = 1$, which are indicated by their initial moments 0 and 1, respectively. Production therefore occurs in a single cycle for $t = 0$, with all output becoming available at the end of that 'year' (a second production cycle in $t = 1$ would make no sense, because it would be completed when the economy has ceased to exist). As usual, all markets occur at 'moment' zero, so that the prices P_{a1} and P_{b1} of commodities a_1 and b_1 available for

---

capital, as opposed to 'invested' or 'fixed' or 'sunk' capital (e.g. Jevons, 1957, pp. 242–44; Marshall, 1920, pp. 62, 341; Wicksell, 1893, p. 156; 1934, pp. 145, 234; 1935, p. 192). On the widespread idea that intertemporal general equilibrium analysis can usefully do without the aggregate notions of savings and investment, cf. Paragraph 12 below.

[7] Indeed, under our present assumptions of circulating capital only, and of yearly production cycles, the demand for gross investment and the supply of gross savings for the year would coincide with the demand and supply of 'capital' of the traditional theories. (For a more detailed examination of the connection between the two notions, see Garegnani, 1978, p. 352.) We may take this occasion to note how the connection between demand for investment and demand for 'capital' has often been obtained by referring to the demand for capital at a lower rate of interest, and by then 'spreading' the 'net investment' required in order to bring the capital stock to that level, over some given time period of adjustment (e.g. Patinkin, 1987; Robertson, 1958, Vol. II; Lerner, 1948). However, such a procedure either reflects a turnover period of aggregate capital, in which case our argument provides a foundation for it, or would be arbitrary, as it would overlook the fact that even under constant technical conditions, capital accumulation would generally entail changing most kinds of capital goods and not adding new capital goods to those already in existence. Capital accumulation can, in fact, only be generally conceived as parallel to the replacement of the existing physical capital.

'year' $t = 1$ are discounted to that moment, when they are quoted together with the prices P_{a0} and P_{b0} of the spot commodities a_0 and b_0, and with the wage W. We may at first suppose that one method only is known for producing each of the two commodities (this assumption will be abandoned in Section 6 below; l_a, a_a, b_a and l_b, a_b, b_b are the corresponding coefficients, which for simplicity we shall assume to be all strictly positive while the methods are of course assumed to be 'viable', i.e. capable of producing a surplus over the mere replacement of the means of production.

We shall then have the following equilibrium relations:

$$\begin{cases} P_{a1} = l_a W + a_a P_{a0} + b_a P_{b0} \\ P_{b1} = l_b W + a_b P_{a0} + b_b P_{b0} \end{cases} \tag{1e}$$

$$P_{b1} = 1 \tag{2e}$$

$$\text{(E)}$$

$$\begin{cases} A_0 \geq D_{a0} + (a_a A_1 + a_b B_1), & \text{if sign} > \text{applies, } P_{a0} = 0 \\ B_0 \geq D_{b0} + (b_a A_1 + b_b B_1), & \text{if sign} > \text{applies, } P_{b0} = 0 \\ L \geq l_a A_1 + l_b B_1, & \text{if sign} > \text{applies, } W = 0 \\ A_1 = D_{a1} \\ B_1 = D_{b1} \end{cases} \tag{3e}$$

In system (E), Equations (1e) are the usual competitive price relations for the products a_1 and b_1, while Equation (2e) chooses b_1 as the numéraire. Relations (3e), on the other hand, regard the demands for the initial endowments A_0, B_0, L of commodities and labour, and the utilization of the two outputs A_1 and B_1. System (E) thus has eight relations, only seven of which are independent, and seven unknowns: i.e. the four prices, the wage and the two outputs A_1 and B_1. Beyond the test of consistency given by these numbers, the enquiry into the existence and character of the solutions of (E) will be part of that analysis of the properties of a general intertemporal equilibrium which we intend to conduct by means of the mentioned general-equilibrium savings–supply and investment–demand schedules, and which will mostly be carried out in the fuller paper mentioned in Paragraph 1.

However, it is important to note that we have simplified the system by ignoring, in the present paper, the possibility of storing the two goods between $t = 0$ and $t = 1$, thus 'transforming' a_0 into a_1, and b_0 into b_1 – a simplification which does not affect the limited conclusions aimed at here, but the implications of which will be recalled below when necessary. It may thus be interesting to note that, had we considered that possibility,

(E) would have needed to be modified by replacing the last two equations in (3e) with the following relations:

$$\begin{cases} D_{a1} = A_1 + T_a(1 - \alpha_a) \\ D_{b1} = B_1 + T_b(1 - \alpha_b), \end{cases} \tag{3e'}$$

where, if T_i, the quantity of commodity i stored ($i = a_0, b_0$) is not zero, then for that i,

$$P_{i1} \leq l_i W + a_i P_{i0} + b_i P_{i0}, \tag{1e'}$$

with zero output of i when the inequality holds, and

$$P_{i0} = P_{i1}(1 - \alpha_i) \tag{1e''}$$

Equation (1e″) indicates a price P_{i0} low enough to make it convenient to provide, in part or in all, for consumption D_{i1} by the storage of a quantity T_i of the commodity at the cost here assumed, of a given wastage of α_i per unit due to the storage. Equations (1e) may then have to be replaced by relation (1e′), allowing for the inequality when D_{a1} is satisfied by storage only.[8] Thus, when $T_i > 0$, to that new unknown there will correspond the respective Equation (1e″).

A second observation may be in order in considering system (E). The choice of b_1 as numéraire in Equation (2e) entails that the variables P_{a0} and P_{b0} as emerging from (E) are relative prices P_{a0}/P_{bi} and P_{b0}/P_{b1} which involve commodities of the two different dates and which we shall here indicate as 'intertemporal' relative prices. We shall distinguish such relative prices from those which we shall call instead 'contemporary' relative prices, e.g. P_{a0}/P_{b0}. The distinction will be useful because we shall find that the properties of the two kinds of relative prices differ in important respects.[9]

---

[8] The form (1e′) of price relations (1e) with its inequality signs might be held to be necessary independently of storage. However if, as we may assume here, *some* consumption of perishable goods a and b has to occur in $t = 1$, then the goods have to be produced and the price relations have to hold in the form of Equations (1e), whenever storage is not possible.

[9] An example of this is provided already by Equations (1e″), which establish a link between 'intertemporal' prices which has no substantive correspondent for 'contemporary' prices. We shall also see below (Paragraphs 17 and 20) that the principle for which the zero price of one commodity in terms of a scarce commodity entails a zero price in terms of *any other* *scarce commodity* does not apply to intertemporal prices.

4. We can now come to the decisions to save and invest implied in system (E) for each year's life of the economy. Indeed, some readers might have been surprised by our reference in Paragraph 3 to savings *distinguished by year* in a context of intertemporal equilibrium – where all contracts are made in an initial 'moment', and therefore all income is received and disposed of in that single 'moment'. However, reflection shows that *outputs*, including of course those of capital goods, have to flow out year by year, and accordingly the *incomes* making up the prices of those outputs must also be distinguishable by year, together with their savings component.

The fact that, given the two years' life of the economy, production only makes sense in $t = 0$ entails that investment and savings will also only make sense for year $t = 0$. The aggregate decisions to invest I_0 of that period, distinguished in their two physical components I_{a0} and I_{b0}, will then consist of the parts of the two initial stocks A_0 and B_0 which are used as means for the production of a_1 and b_1 and will be given by

$$I_0 = (a_a A_1 + a_b B_1)P_{a0} + (b_a A_1 + b_b B_1)P_{b0} = I_{a0}P_{a0} + I_{b0}P_{b0} \qquad (4)$$

On the other hand, gross savings will be part of a social gross income $Y_0{}^{10}$ of $t = 0$ which, unlike Y_1 of $t = 1$, will not be the counterpart of a social gross product but only of the initial stocks A_0 and B_0. Thus, the aggregate gross decisions to save S_0 can be expressed as the following difference between the gross income Y_0 and the aggregate consumption G_0 in year $t = 0$:

$$\begin{aligned} S_0 = Y_0 - G_0 &= (A_0 P_{a0} + B_0 P_{b0}) - (D_{a0}P_{a0} + D_{b0}P_{b0}) \\ &= (A_0 - D_{a0})P_{a0} + (B_0 - D_{b0})P_{b0} = S_{a0}P_{a0} + S_{b0}P_{b0} \end{aligned} \qquad (5)$$

where the physical components of the aggregate saving decisions S_0 are distinguished by S_{a0} and S_{b0} and where the equilibrium magnitudes of system (E) of course imply $I_0 = S_0$.[11]

Similarly for the year $t = 1$, we have

---

[10] It should be noted that, contrary to general usage, we need here to include in the 'gross' investment, and hence in both 'gross' social product and 'gross' savings, the replacement of circulating means of production (the only means of production of our model).

[11] From the first two equations (3e) we obtain $D_{a0} = A_0 - I_{a0}$, $D_{b0} = B_0 - I_{b0}$, which, when substituted into equation (5) will give

$$S_0 = I_{a0}P_{a0} + I_{b0}P_{b0} = I_0$$

We have assumed the relevant relations (3e) to be equations. Should the inequality sign apply in any of the two, the corresponding price would be zero and the 'excess savings' in that commodity would not affect the value equality $I_0 = S_0$

$$S_1 = Y_1 - G_1 = (L_0 W_0 + S_0) - (D_{a1} P_{a1} + D_{b1} P_{b1})$$

where, however, the last two equations (3e) stating that the entire output of $t = 1$ is consumed, entail $I_1 = 0$[12] and therefore $S_1 = 0$.[13]

5. It may now be of interest to note how, in what is often called the 'wealth equation', relating to the entire lifetime of the economy, the savings of each year are bound to disappear. That equation is in fact only the sum of the *yearly* individual budget equations of the kind seen before, and in that sum the savings on the 'expenditure side' of the budget equation for any year t, reappears on the 'income side' for $(t + 1)$, and must therefore cancel out with the latter (the exception being the savings of the final year of the economy which are, however, generally assumed to be zero).

Thus, e.g., the two yearly budget equations of an individual in our two-years' economy can be written as follows, where the small letters y_0, s_0, l_0, a_0, b_0 stand for the individual's yearly consumption, gross savings and initial endowment, respectively:

$$\begin{cases} y_0 = a_0 P_{a_0} + b_0 P_{b0} = g_0 + s_0 \\ y_1 = l_0 W + s_0 = g_1 \end{cases} \tag{5a}$$

In summing the two equations (5a), the s_0's cancel out and we are left with

$$y_0 + y_1 = a_0 P_{a0} + b_0 P_{b0} + l_0 W = g_0 + g_1$$

where the terms after the first equality sign constitute the 'wealth equation'.

---

[12] It may be asked why the income $L_0 W$ is being excluded from Y_0 in Equation (5) and is included instead in y. However, 'yearly' production cycles, as distinct from continuous production, force us to distinguish between the period in which the participation of resources to production has occurred (in the present case $t = 0$) and the period in which the corresponding income must be supposed to accrue, *if* the equality between the *social income* and value of the *social product* is to be maintained. This does not preclude wages being 'advanced' in $t = 0$, but that would be out of the savings of capitalists in $t = 0$, unlike what we have assumed here.

[13] The relations we are describing are in the nature of accounting identities and would hold whether the economy is in equilibrium or out of it – whether, more generally, they refer to *realized* savings and investment or, instead, to *decisions* to save and invest under some *a-priori* specified, hypothetical circumstances. The latter is the case in Equations (4) and (5), where we have applied those relations to the equilibrium quantities of system (E), just as it will be the case when we apply them to the partly different hypothetical circumstances of system (F) of Paragraph 5 below, which imply equilibrium in some markets only.

Non-zero gross savings and investment being possible in our model only for $t = 0$, we shall henceforth simplify our notation by dropping the zero deponent from our savings and investment variables.

3 The general-equilibrium schedules of savings–supply and investment–demand

6. Our task will now be to bring out the role which the savings and investment decisions of Equations (4) and (5) can play in system (E) a task which will require examining how those savings and investment *vary* with prices. This is what will be done here by means of the two logical constructs which, as we said, constitute a central object of this paper: 'the general-equilibrium investment–demand schedule' and 'the general-equilibrium savings–supply schedule'. Basically, the two schedules will be obtained from the relations of system (E) by (a) treating one of the two own rates of interest of period $t = 0$, say r_b, as the independent variable,[14] while (b) releasing the equality between I and S implied in (E):[15] that is what is done in system (F) below. It first requires the introduction of the definitory equation

$$r_b = (P_{b0}/P_{b1}) - 1 \tag{6b}$$

[14] We have referred to 'one of the two own rates of interest' for period $t = 0$. In fact, since the relative prices of the two goods a and b will generally be changing from $t = 0$ to $t = 1$, arbitrage will impose different rates of interest according to whether the loan is in terms of a or b; it will have to be *lower* for the good, say a, whose relative value *rises* from $t = 0$ to $t = 1$, so as to compensate the advantage of the lender (and disadvantage of the borrower) with respect to a loan made in terms of b (cf. p. 392, n. 2 above). It should be noted that by taking as an *independent* variable the interest rate r_b we shall instead let

$$r_a = (P_{a0}/P_{a1}) - 1$$

be a *dependent* variable, determined by the unknown prices P_{a0}, P_{a1}.

[15] Cf. n. 11 above. The nature of these two constructs can perhaps be more easily grasped when we realize that they follow the simple logical procedure which underlies, in an elementary textbook, the representation of, say, the demand for labour, when the quantity demanded L^D is directly derived from the marginal product of that labour when employed with the given supply λ of land, the only other productive factor. At any point along that demand schedule, the following equations will hold:

$$Q = f(L^D, \lambda); \quad w = f_L{}^D(L^D, \lambda); \quad \rho = f_\lambda(L^D, \lambda); \quad L^S = \text{constant}$$

The wage w is the independent variable, leaving four unknowns in the four equations: the corn output Q, the rent rate ρ and the quantities demanded and supplied L^D, L^S of labour where, for simplicity, we have supposed the factor supplies L^S to be rigid. At any

continued

The release of condition $I = S$, on the other hand, generally will entail either $S_a \neq I_a$ or $S_b \neq I_b$ or both, and therefore a difference between what we may now call the total demand of a_0 given by $A_0^D = D_{a0} + I_a$ (cf. the R.H.S. of the first relation (3e), p. 397 above) and its total supply $A_0^S = A_0$, which can also be expressed as $A_0^S = D_{a0} + S_a$ (cf. Equation (5), p. 399 above) – and similarly for the total demand and supply of b_0. The result is system (F) below where

(i)   the two unknowns A_0^D, B_0^D replace the data A_0 and B_0 in the corresponding relations (3e) which now, in their form (3f), *define* the two total demands;

(ii) the data A_0, B_0, relabelled as A_0^S, B_0^S, appear instead in the relation (5f) defining savings.

7. We thus arrive at system (F) whose unknowns I and S constitute the points of the two schedules corresponding to each given level of the independent variable r_b.

$$\begin{cases} P_{a1} = l_a W + a_a P_{a0} + b_a P_{b0} \\ P_{b1} = l_b W + a_b P_{a0} + b_b P_{b0} \end{cases} \tag{1f}$$

$$P_{b1} = 1 \tag{2f}$$

(F)

$$\begin{cases} A_0^D = D_{a0} + (a_a A_1 + a_b B_1) \\ B_0^D = D_{b0} + (b_a A_1 + b_b B_1) \\ L \geq l_a A_1 + l_b B_1 \qquad \text{if inequality, then } W = 0 \\ D_{a1} = A_1 \\ D_{b1} = B_1 \end{cases} \tag{3f}$$

relevant level of w, equilibrium will hold in the remaining two markets: for corn, where Q is equal to the corn expenditure $(L_w^D + \lambda\rho)$ from the owners of the two factors, and for land, where the supply λ is fully employed. The two schedules $L^D(w)$ and $L^S = \text{constant}$, resulting as w varies, will therefore be 'general equilibrium schedules' in the sense meant in the text, and equilibrium in the labour market, i.e.

$$L^D \lesseqgtr L^S \quad \text{where if } < \text{ applies} \quad W = 0$$
$$\text{and if } > \text{ applies} \quad \rho = 0,$$

will be a general equilibrium of such a simple system. (We may note for future reference that disequilibrium in a single market – that for labour – is here evidently compatible with 'Walras's law' because labour income in the economy is taken to be $L^D w$, i.e. that corresponding to the quantity L^D of labour *demanded*, and not that corresponding to the endowments L^S: cf. Paragraph 9 below for the similar problem in the savings–investment market.)

(F)

$$I = (a_a A_1 + a_b B_1)P_{a0} + (b_a A_1 + b_b B_1)P_{b0} \qquad (4f)$$

$$S = (A_0^S - D_{a0})P_{a0} + (B_0^S - D_{b0})P_b \qquad (5f)$$

$$r_b = (P_{b0}/P_{b1}) - 1 \qquad (6f)$$

$$A_0^D / B_0^D = A_0^S B_0^S \qquad (7f)$$

All markets are here assumed to be in equilibrium except those of savings and investments, i.e., as we saw, the markets where saved and investible quantities of a_0 and b_0 are traded.[16] System (F) in fact implies equilibrium:

   (i)   in the markets for labour (see the respective relation in (3f));
   (ii) in the market for commodities a_1 and b_1 (see the last two equations (3f));
  (iii) in the markets of a_0 and b_0 *for consumption* (see the inclusion of D_{a0} and D_{b0} in Equation (5f)).

However, if we exclude equation (7f), to be discussed below, system (F) has eleven relations, ten of which are independent, containing eleven unknowns (the five prices; the two outputs A_1, B_1, the two aggregate quantities demanded A_0^D, B_0^D and, finally, I and S).[17] Were it not for Equation (7f), system (F) would possess the degree of freedom which we could have expected, since essentially we replaced with the two new unknowns A_0^D and B_0^D, the single unknown P_{b0}, which becomes a given in (E), once r_b,

$$P_{b0} = 1 + r_b, \qquad (6a)$$

is taken as a given in (F).

Before discussing that degree of freedom, and its closure by means of Equation (7f), we may, however, re-write the Equations (3f), (4f) and (5f) in the following form, which is easier to grasp, and which we shall occasionally use in what follows.

---

[16] See Paragraph 9 below, also n. 15 above, for the 'adjustment in expenditures' which allows the disequilibrium to be confined to the single market of savings and investment. As for the relevance of the distinction drawn in the text for the commodities a_0 and b_0, between their markets as consumption goods, and as capital goods, cf. Paragraph 12 below.

[17] The changes in methods of production which we might expect to occur along the schedules will be introduced in Section 6, below. However, it should be noted that the schedules determined by (F) already allow for substitutability between factors through consumer choice.

$$\begin{cases} A_0^S = D_{a0} + S_a \\ B_0^S = D_{b0} + S_b \\ A_0^D = D_{a0} + I_a \\ B_0^D = D_{b0} + I_b \end{cases} \tag{3f'}$$

$$I = I_a P_{a0} + I_b P_{b0} \tag{4f'}$$

$$S = S_a P_{a0} + S_b P_{b0} \tag{5f'}$$

8. In fact, the economic meaning of the degree of freedom we would have in (F) but for Equation (7f) is quite simple. We have aggregated all decisions to invest into the single magnitude I, but nothing has been specified about the *physical composition* of the out-of-equilibrium investment flows of Schedule I.

That physical composition cannot, however, be specified arbitrarily. Our use of the I and S schedules in order to analyse the properties of system (E) imposes two requirements. The first and stricter requirement is that when $S = I$, the aggregate demands of a_0 and b_0 are also equal to the respective supplies. The same correspondence between the behaviour of the schedules and the behaviour of the two demands and supplies should of course hold for possible 'extreme' equilibria at the level $r_{b\,min}$ to be defined below (Paragraph 14), with $S > I$, or in the upper range of r_b, with $W = 0$ and $S < I$ (see below, Paragraph 16). As we shall see in detail in Paragraphs 23 and 24, this will in fact be the case when the proportion A_0^D / B_0^D in which the two commodities are there 'demanded' are the same as the proportion A_0^S / B_0^S in which they are supplied, as is imposed by Equation (7f).

The second, less strict, requirement is that the proportion A_0^D / B_0^D should reflect a non-unplausible out-of-equilibrium behaviour of the economy. And, as we shall see in Paragraphs 25 and 26 below, Equation (7f), seems to provide a description of an out-of-equilibrium behaviour as plausible as any equally general condition can.

9. There remains a rather technical point we need to consider in order to complete our definition of system (F). It concerns Walras's identity and the often-assumed impossibility of a disequilibrium confined to a single market, such as we have assumed in (F)[18] However, that impossibility would follow only if the individuals could spend for the commodities available in $t = 1$ according to the total income which they would derive

---

[18] The fact that the single market for I and S involves the two markets, for a_0 and b_0, is evidently irrelevant here.

from selling exactly the quantities of a_0 and b_0 they wish to sell at the going prices (i.e. A_0^S, B_0^S in the aggregate, if we include the consumption by owners in the supply), but that is just what *cannot* happen when $S \neq I$. When, on the other hand, the purchasing power for $t = 1$ originating from the savings S_0 is appropriately 'adjusted' to what the going level of I would in fact allow them to sell – and this is what we have assumed in (F) – the contradiction disappears and system (F) is consistent.[19]

The 'adjustment' in expenditure we assume here, when compared with the more usual procedure of admitting disequilibrium in at least one further market, has on the other hand the advantage of not throwing

---

[19] The question is essentially the same as the one concerning the power to purchase 'corn' we considered in the simple example of general-equilibrium demand for labour of p. 401, n. 15 above. In our present model, let us indicate by D'_{a1}, D'_{b1} the consumption demands in $t = 1$ resulting from the equations of consumer equilibrium on the usual hypothesis that they dispose of the income resulting at the given prices from all the resources they own. Summing the budget equations, and after some simple transformations, we get

$$(A_0^S - D_{a0})P_{a0} + (B_0^S - D_{b0})P_{b0} + LW = D'_{a1}P_{a1} + D'_{b1}P_{b1} \tag{8a}$$

Clearly the L.H.S. of Equation (8a) gives the social *income* Y'_1, and the value of the purchases the individuals would carry out at $t = 1$ under the stated assumptions of complete sales of A_0^S, B_0^S, besides L. Then using relation (5) of p. 399 above, we have

$$Y'_1 = D'_{a1}P_{a1} - D'_{b1}P_{b1} = S + LW \tag{8b}$$

On the other hand, the value Q_1 of the gross social *product* for $t = 1$, as it results from system (F) by substituting for prices in accordance with Equations (1f), is given by

$$Q_1 = A_1 P_{a1} + B_1 P_{b1} = A_1(l_a W + a_a P_{a0} + b_a P_{b0}) + B_1(l_b W + a_b P_{b0} + b_b P_{b0})$$

$$= (l_a A_1 + l_b B_1)W + (a_a A_1 + a_b B_1)P_{a0} + (b_a A_1 + b_b B_1)P_{b0}$$

and using Equation (5f),

$$Q_1 = LW + I \tag{8c}$$

Thus the purchasing power $(S + LW)$ in Equation (8b) would face commodities of the value $(I + LW)$ in Equation (8c), and if we had used D'_{a1}, D'_{b1} in system (F), the system would have been inconsistent. The 'adjustment' of purchases mentioned in the text can, on the other hand, be represented by the following equations, in which we indicate by D_{i1}, as distinct from D'_{i1}, the 'adjusted' purchases in $t = 1$ appearing in our system (F):

$$D_{i1} = D'_{i1} \frac{LW + I}{LW + S}, \qquad (i = a, b).$$

It follows that the 'adjusted' aggregate expenditure and income in $t = 1$ is now given by

$$Y_1 = \sum_i D_{i1} P_{i1} = \frac{LW + I}{LW + S} \sum_i D'_{i1} P_{i1} = \frac{LW + I}{LW + S}(LW + S) = LW + I = Q_1$$

and consistency has been brought back into system (F). By definition, consumption purchases for $t = 0$ remain unchanged, i.e. $D_{a0} = D'_{a0}$, $D_{b0} = D'_{b0}$.

into question the constancy in the employment of labour as r_b varies, thus providing a more transparent basis for deducing the shapes of the S and I schedules. It also allows, it seems, for a simpler and somewhat better representation of the out-of-equilibrium behaviour of the system, in the sense mentioned that it is difficult to see how households failing to sell part of their A_0^S and B_0^S resources, because of excess savings in $t = 0$, could exert excess demand on the commodities of $t = 1$.[20]

10. Although, as we said, the object of the present chapter is not primarily an analysis of the properties of an intertemporal equilibrium, the use of the two schedules to discuss the form and role of the concept of a 'quantity of capital' in an intertemporal equilibrium will already render apparent how the schedules may be used for analysing such properties. Some preliminary observations concerning this method of analysis may therefore be in order, in addition to those of Paragraph 1 above.

As noted above, the general equilibrium nature of the two schedules means that to any equilibrium shown by them in the corresponding figure (see, e.g., points E^{II} or E^{III} in Figure 1 below) there will correspond an equilibrium of the whole system. Basic properties of that general equilibrium may then become visible in the diagram, in a form not unlike that in which analogous properties do in the case of partial equilibrium. It is in this way that in Sections 6 and 7 the two schedules will let a source of multiple and unstable equilibria emerge which does not yet seem to have been sufficiently noted in the literature. As illustrated in Fig. 1, the source in question lies in the way in which investment changes as intertemporal prices change.

Possibilities of non-uniqueness and instability have in fact been in the foreground of current general equilibrium literature. However, to date those possibilities seem to have been investigated in a mainly *negative* and unspecific way. The attention, that is, has been focused on the impossibility of obtaining uniqueness and stability under the general premises of the theory, rather than on the economic causes of those negative results. Sufficient, rather than necessary, conditions for uniqueness and stability have then been looked into.[21] Thus, apart from the demonstration of the

---

[20] Apparently less plausible is the behaviour assumed in the opposite case of $I > S$, when the purchases for $t = 1$ would have to *exceed* what is possible with the purchasing power obtained from the full sale of the A_0^S and B_0^S endowments. However, the extra purchasing power implied in our adjustment of expenditures may be taken to express the tendential rise of purchasing power available in $t = 1$ because of the excess demand in $t = 0$ and a resulting tendential rise in the prices of commodities a_0 and b_0 (in terms of which savings are effected) relative to those of a_1 and b_1.

[21] See, e.g., Marshall, 1949; Walras, 1954; Wicksell, 1934, pp. 56–61.

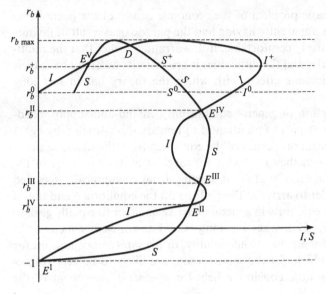

Figure 1

existence of solutions to the equations of general equilibrium, with respect to the specific questions of multiplicity and instability of the equilibria, current literature does not seem to have added substantially to what, owing to a more specific, though more simplified analysis, had been known since Walras, Marshall or Wicksell[22] about income effects being possible causes of the phenomena. In particular, contemporary studies seem to have left in some obscurity what should perhaps have been a primary purpose of the enquiry: whether, that is, 'income effects' in their several forms are or are not the only possible causes of (discrete) non-uniqueness.[23] Indeed, the lack of specificity in the analysis seems to

[22] Cf. 'Unfortunately, necessary conditions are unlikely to be available', Arrow and Hahn, 1971, pp. 207–44.

[23] 'Local' non-uniqueness, to which much work seems to have been devoted, seems much less worrying for the theory as it appears to be due to non-'smoothness' of the functions, or else to flukes. Thus, take a simple economy where corn is the only product obtained by labour and land according to a finite number of alternative methods. 'Local' non-unique-ness will exist whenever the proportion between the supplies of labour and land happened to coincide with those of one of those methods: the wage (and rent) will then be unde-terminate between the two 'marginal products' the method forms with the two 'adjacent' methods. This will not alter the stability or instability of that continuum of equilibria

continued

have made the basic problem of the economic causes of the phenomena less visible – thus apparently having had the paradoxical result of favouring the comparatively comfortable, if unwarranted, belief that the multiplicity of equilibria, and the difficulties it brings in its wake, all have their origin in those income effects with which the theory has in fact long managed to co-exist.[24]

11. The construction of general equilibrium demand-and-supply schedules may be seen as part of an attempt to remedy this situation by again tackling such central properties of the equilibria from the opposite side – the side from which they had been approached by the initiators of the theory. It is a question, that is, of starting from economically specified conditions in order to arrive at their effects on the equilibria – and not of starting from the equilibria in general to arrive at either (i) equally *general* properties which, given what has long been known, *cannot* include the key properties of uniqueness and stability, or (ii) *sufficient* conditions for such properties which, for the same reason, are likely to be very restrictive, while giving little conclusive help for a general assessment of the theory.

Thus the method of enquiry here adopted allows us to start from the savings–investment market – on which the changes in investment requirements as intertemporal prices (interest rates) vary obviously impinge *directly* – in order to arrive at whether and how those changes can affect the properties of the equilibrium. More generally, demand-and-supply schedules based on general equilibrium – a flexible tool capable of extension[25] – allow a searchlight to be aimed at the particular markets the

---

taken as a single set, nor cause any of the difficulties raised by multiple discrete equilibria. As for fluke cases, it may be interesting to recall Wicksell's wheat and rye example (1934, pp. 60–3) where Wicksell's preoccupation of course related to the rising shape of the demand curve for rye, rather than to its curious overlap with the supply curve over a certain price interval.

[24] Thus Hicks had written about stability in exchange and with reference to income effects:

It cannot indeed be proved a priori that a system of multiple exchange will be necessarily stable. But the conditions of stability are quite easy conditions, so that it is quite reasonable to assume that they will be satisfied in almost any system with which we are likely to be concerned. (Hicks, 1939, p. 72)

and he even thought that such a conclusion could be strengthened when introducing production (1939, p. 104).

[25] The method of the general-equilibrium demand and supply schedule is of course applicable beyond the case of investment demand and saving supply (cf., e.g., n. 15 above and n. 41 below).

implications of which, for the properties of the general equilibrium, we have reason to enquire into. From what we know about specific circumstances affecting those markets we can attempt to deduce the shapes which the schedules must have under alternative hypotheses, and then proceed to the corresponding alternative possibilities regarding the general equilibria.

An analysis so conducted will, of course, especially clarify the consequences of the forces acting in the particular market we set our searchlight on, but we may, where useful, help disentangle the reciprocal influences of the several markets by setting the same kind of searchlight on any further market we may deem relevant for our enquiry.

A word of caution must be added concerning our application of the method of general-equilibrium demand-and-supply schedules to the savings–investment market. Just because of their greater specificity, these tools of analysis bring to light questions which seem to have lain buried in the generality of the mathematical procedures more frequently used;[26] and because of its very specificity, the method requires that definite answers be given to such questions. Where possible, those answers have been attempted here, however provisionally. At other times the questions have been dealt with by means of restrictive assumptions – a procedure that appears to be legitimate given the critical intent of our argument.

12. Passing now from the method to the content of our argument, the reader may ask: why should we introduce in system (F) the *aggregate* savings and *aggregate* investment of Equations (4) and (5), in order to discuss a system (E) which, as we have shown, can be formulated independently of any such aggregates?

The answer will of course have to come from what follows in this chapter and in the intended larger work. However, we have indicated already how the total demands of a_0 and b_0, which we find on the right-hand side of the first two relations (3e). or (3f), are in fact made up of two heterogeneous elements each: the consumption demands D_{a0}, D_{b0} (which we assumed to be always satisfied along the I and S schedules) and the investment demands I_a and I_b. And the investment demands are ruled by principles that are totally different from those which govern consumption demands: hunger can be satisfied by corn, and not by

---

[26] See, e.g., the distinction between 'intertemporal' and 'contemporary' relative prices, shown also by the lower limits which equations ($1e''$) of p. 398 above set to relative intertemporal prices in cases of storage (for further examples, cf. Paragraphs 17 and 20).

coal; but desire for future income, the motive of the demand for capital goods coming from savers, can surely be satisfied by tractors, as well as by looms or any of the thousands of other capital goods, whichever of them offers a higher rate of return. In fact, as we shall see in Paragraph 34 below, different capital goods are perfect substitutes for the savers – although, of course, not for the entrepreneurs as the technical organizers of production.

Now, in view of the different principles thus regulating investment demands as distinct from consumption demands, and in view of the cause of those different principles – the perfect substitutability, that is, of heterogeneous capital goods for the saver, but not of course of the heterogeneous consumption goods for the consumer – it does *prima facie* stand to reason that the separation of the two kinds of demand, and then the aggregation of the capital goods demanded for investment, might help to lend transparency to the workings of the system.

13. In Paragraph 8 we mentioned 'stability' among the properties of the equilibrium which might be inquired into by means of our two schedules. That implies that the schedules should be applied to discuss adjustments to equilibrium. Although only hints of that analysis will be contained in the present chapter (Paragraphs 25 and 26, below), it should perhaps be made clear now what *can* be meant by 'adjustments' and 'stability' here, in a context of *dated* equilibria.

In fact, as I have argued elsewhere (1976, p. 38), an analysis of stability, capable of fulfilling its traditional role of ensuring 'correspondence' between theoretical and observable magnitudes, would seem to require a sufficient repetition of markets on the basis of approximately unchanged data. If a tendency to equilibrium could be established on that basis, it could also be generally supposed that disequilibrium deviations would tend to compensate each other, letting the equilibrium levels emerge as some average of observable levels, capable, therefore, of providing some guidance to reality. Essentially, the question in this respect would be to allow for a *time setting* in which

fitful and irregular causes in large measure efface one another's influence so that ... persistent causes dominate value completely. (Marshall, 1949, p. 291)

That meaning of the positions of the economy to which theory refers its variables, and the corresponding notion of its stability, appear in fact to have been the unanimously accepted basis of economic analysis until comparatively recent decades. At those earlier times, however, such a necessary repetition of markets on approximately unchanged data could be grounded on the traditional notion of long-period equilibrium referred to above, whose consistent definition depended in turn on the conception of the capital endowment as a single magnitude.[27] If the abandonment of that notion of the equilibrium (which had nothing to do, recall, with that of 'steady states'[28]) was by itself sufficient to undercut *in fact* the previous meaning of an analysis of stability by imposing data too impermanent to allow for a sufficient repetition of markets, the 'dating' of the equilibria appears to have jettisoned it even in principle by excluding repetition as such.[29] This appears to leave in some obscurity the precise significance of present-day analyses of stability, quite independently of their negative results.

Our present critical purpose seems, however, to exempt us from entering further into the question and to allow us to take the formal way out that is generally taken (at least when concern is still with the variables determinable by the equations of general equilibrium, and not with the indeterminable variables of a path-dependent equilibrium). This formal way out is, of course, that of 'recontracting', or of the 'tâtonnenment' as it has come to be named with a misleading reference to Walras.[30] In the modern fictitious theoretical world into which we shall enter by means of

---

[27] See above, p. 392, n. 2.

[28] See above, p. 395, n. 5.

[29] Thus in Hicks's *Value and Capital*, 1939, where the new notions of equilibrium and the associated 'dating' of equilibrium variables were used for perhaps the first time in influential Anglo-American work, Hicks felt forced to assume that transactions carried out at non-equilibrium prices would have very little effect on the amounts transacted, so that equilibrium prices could be assumed to be realized in the contracting done on his 'Mondays' (1939, pp. 127–8: the stability of those equilibria was evidently assumed). However, both in that book and in most subsequent works in pure theory (see, e.g., Bliss, 1975), it is not mentioned that the question in the preceding literature had been that of the compensation of deviations through repetition, and not that of the price actually hitting its equilibrium level and staying there. The same repetition of trading, and resulting compensation of deviations, was, incidentally, what dispensed those authors from having to use that assumption about perfect contemporaneous knowledge which Hicks had to introduce (1939, p. 123).

[30] Walras introduced re-contracting only in the 4th edition of the *Elements* (1900). In the previous editions, the word *tâtonnement* had covered only the process of repetition of actual transactions, which in his view (confirmed up to the posthumous 4th 'definitive' edition of 1926):

is perpetually tending towards equilibrium without every actually attaining it (...) like a lake agitated by the wind where the water is incessantly seeking its level without ever reaching it. (1954, p. 380)

In fact re-contracting with 'bons' (tickets) was introduced by Walras in the 4th edition of 1900 merely in order to avoid the effects of the changes of capital stocks due to the production occurring in the course of the adjustments – changes whose inconsistency

continued

that assumption, the repetition of transactions – admitted to be essential for an analysis of stability – is supposed to take place in some initial 'moment', or period, before the actual time, measured out by 'dated' equilibria, has rendered such repetition impossible.

4   The determination of the schedules

14. In Paragraph 7 we had a first check of the consistency of systems (F) by counting independent relations and unknowns. The existence of non-negative solutions of (F) in the economically relevant interval of r_b, $r_{b\min} \leq r_b \leq r_{b\max}$ (which will include negative values of r_b), is demonstrated in the Mathematical Note at the end of this chapter. However, an intuitive account of that demonstration is necessary here for a better understanding of the argument and of some assumptions we shall find it convenient to introduce.

We start by noting the lower limit of the relevant interval of values of r_b. Due to our assumption that no storage is possible for either commodity,[31] the 'intertemporal price' P_{b0}/P_{b1} can fall to zero and Equation (6f) of Paragraph 7 will therefore give

$$r_{b\min} = -1 \tag{6b}$$

The specification of the upper limit of the significant interval of values of r_b (for which $W \geq 0$) will, however, require a better acquaintance with the properties of system (F) and will depend on some additional assumptions: we shall therefore come to it later (Paragraph 16).

15. Using Equations (2f) and (6f), the second of the price equations (1f) can be written as follows:

with the equilibria to be tended to, he had apparently not realized before (cf. Garegnani 1960). It thus seems that the 'bons' procedure was adopted by him in order to approximate a *real* repetition of transaction, while abstracting from the changes in capital stocks it involved (which he evidently thought to be of subordinate importance) – and not in order to have *a notional* repetition of transactions in conditions in which a real one was prevented by the dating of the of equilibria or, in any case, by their impermanence.

[31] Should b_0 be storable, its intertemporal price P_{b0}/P_{b1} could not fall below unity, or below $(1 - \alpha_b)$, when there are storage costs α_b per unit of b_0 (cf. Equations (1e''), p. 398 above): i.e. r_b could not fall below zero or below $(1 - \alpha_b)$ respectively. It might seem that $r_b = (-1)$ when, contrary to our assumption (ii) of p. 414 below, b_0 were to be a free commodity. However, b_0 as a free commodity would then entail b_1 also as a free commodity, and their relative price would 'vanish' (cf. p. 421, n. 41 below). Our model would then turn into one where a single commodity a is produced by itself and labour, and a single interest rate r_a accordingly exists.

$$1 = l_b W + a_b P_{a0} + b_b(1 + r_b) \tag{1a}$$

where, having used (2f), P_{a0} is now in effect the intertemporal price P_{a0}/P_{b1}.

Two implications of Equation (1a) are of interest here.

(a) it is only for $b_b(1 + r_b) \leq 1$, i.e. for $r_b \leq (1 - b_b)/b_b$ that we *may* have non-negative values of *both* W and P_{a0}. Also considering Equation (6b) above, this means we may restrict our attention to the interval

$$-1 \leq r_b \leq (1 - b_b)/b_b \tag{6c}$$

where $(1 - b_b)$, and hence $(1 - b_b)/b_b$, must be strictly positive when the method of production of b is viable

(b) for any r_b in interval (6c), non-negative levels of both W and P_{a0} will further entail

$$0 \leq P_{a0} \leq \{1 - b_b(1 + r_b)\}/a_b \tag{1b}$$

It follows that given, as well as the level of our independent variable r_b, a level of P_{a0} in the interval (1b), Equation (1a) will determine a corresponding non-negative level of W. The first of Equations (1f) will then determine P_{a1}. Given r_b, the entire series of the four prices and the wage will thus be uniquely determined by Equations (1f), (2f) and (6f), *once P_{a0} is also given* in the interval (1b).

To that unique series of prices and the wage, there will then correspond the quantities demanded expressed by the functions $D_{a0}, D_{b0}, D_{a1}, D_{b1}$. The amount of total savings S in Equation (5f) with its components S_a, S_b will be determined as well. And, the two methods of production being given, that will be the case for the amounts of investments I, I_a, I_b. Such series of quantities need be neither a single-valued, nor a continuous function of P_{a0}. It will, however, follow common practice and not be unduly restrictive to make the following assumption:

Assumption (i): *Given r_b in the interval (6c), the quantities demanded $D_{a0}, D_{b0}, D_{a1}, D_{b1}$, and hence the aggregate quantities demanded A_0^D and B_0^D, are single-valued, continuous functions of P_{a0} in the interval (1b).*

Thus, then, at the given level of r_b in the interval (6c), any level of P_{a0} in the interval (1b) will entail a ratio $\delta = A_0^D/B_0^D$, which will generally differ from the ratio $\gamma = A_0^S/B_0^S$, equality with which is instead imposed by Equation (7f). As we then change P_{a0} in the interval (1b), there are three possibilities (cf. Figure 4 in the Mathematical Note at the end of the chapter):

(a)   At one or more levels of P_{a0}, $\delta = \gamma$. Equation (7f) will be satisfied and we shall have a solution of (F) for each of those values of P_{a0}.

(b)   Over the entire interval of Equation (1b) of P_{a0}, $\delta < \gamma$. That will mean that at the given level of r_b it will be impossible *to use a_0* (as a sum of both consumption and investment) in as high a proportion to b_0, as that in which we find the two commodities in the endowment.

(c)   Finally, over the entire relevant interval of P_{a0}, we shall have $\delta > \gamma$. This is, of course, symmetrical to case (b), namely, it is the case in which b_0 cannot be *used* in as high a proportion to a_0 as B_0^S/A_0^S (i.e. in as low a proportion as the reciprocal A^S/B^S of that ratio).

Cases (b) and (c) would exclude an economic solution of system (F) as we have formulated it above, i.e. with *equalities* in the first two relations (3f), but the simple economic rationale of the cases (a potential excess supply of either a_0 or b_0 when equality between demand and supply is achieved for the other commodity) indicates how a solution could be ensured by a slight formal modification of (F).[32] However, these two cases would complicate the exposition and risk obscuring the main points we wish to bring out, which are independent of them. We shall therefore leave those two cases aside in the present chapter by excluding any such excess proportions and instead making the following assumption:

Assumption (ii):   *At all levels of r_b included between $r_{bmin} = -1$ and the level r_{bmax} to be defined below (i.e. for $r_{bmin} \leq r_b \leq r_{bmax}$), the commodities a_0 and b_0 can be used in the proportion A_0^S/B_0^S in which they appear in the endowment.*

[32] The modification in question would consist of somewhat counterintuitively dissociating the aggregate quantities A_0^U, B_0^U of the two commodities 'used' (whether for consumption or investment) from the respective quantities 'demanded' $A_0^D B_0^D$ appearing in Equation (7f). We could then let the latter exceed the former, allowing for the corresponding inequality and associated zero price condition in the first two relations (3f), where the right-hand sides express A_0^U and B_0^U, respectively. This would allow the quantity demanded A_0^D or B_0^D of the commodity appearing in excess proportion in the endowment to exceed at zero price the quantity used, and be then *defined* by Equation (7f), so that it bears the proportion A_0^S/B_0^S to the quantity used of the other commodity (cf. Equations (3f) in the Mathematical Note below where those cases are admitted). This would allow for the existence of '(F) positions' of the economy in which solutions of (E) (the discussion of which is the ultimate purpose of system (F)) are in fact possible, as cases of excess supply of either a_0 or b_0.

We can then conclude that, for any level of r_b included between $r_{b\min}$ and $r_{b\max}$, at least one level of P_{a0} will exist satisfying Equation (7f), and thus solving system (F).

16. We said that under assumptions (i) and (ii) there will exist *at least* one solution of (F) in the relevant interval of r_b. There is, in fact no reason why, given r_b the value of P_{a0} satisfying Equation (7f), and hence (F), should be unique. However, the negative conclusions to which the present work will arrive would only be strengthened by any multiplicity of solutions of (F). For the sake of greater definiteness and simplicity of the argument, we can therefore grant the theory the following third assumption, whose significance will be shown in some detail below (Paragraph 17):

> **Assumption (iii):** P_{a0} *will increase as a continuous function of* r_b, *and therefore of* $P_{b0} = 1 + r_b$, *in the interval* $r_{b\min} < r_b < r_b^+$, *where* r_b^+ *is the level of the interest rate at which that joint rise will have to stop having resulted in* $W = 0$ *in Equation (1a)* *(Paragraph 15, above).*

As a result of assumption (iii), P_{a0} and the associated series of prices and quantities solving (F) will be single-valued functions of r_b in an interval $r_{b\min} < r_b \leqslant r_b^0$. The value r_b^0 will be no greater than r_b^+ for the following reason. The level zero of the wage reached at r_b^+ will permit labour unemployment in (F), and therefore levels of labour employment $L^D \leqslant L$, where $L^D = l_a A_1 + l_b B_1$ (cf. the third of equations (3f)). This will in turn allow for a continuum of solutions of (F) for L^D in the interval $0 \leqslant L^D \leqslant L$: in those solutions, r_b can fall from r_b^+ down to a minimum level r_b^0, and/or rise up to a level $r_{b\max}$: it follows that $r_b^0 \leqslant r_b^+$. It also follows that for the sub-interval $r_b^0 \leqslant r_b \leqslant r_{b\max}$ and, in particular, for $r_b^0 \leqslant r_b \leqslant r_b^+$, P_{a0} will no longer be a single-valued function of r_b. Since, on the other hand, for $W = 0$, Equation (1a) of p. 413 above becomes

$$1 = a_b P_{a0} + b_b(1 + r_b) \tag{1c}$$

along that continuum of (F) positions P_{a0} will have to change in a direction opposite to that in which r_b and P_{b0} vary.[33] It follows that the direct relation of assumption (iii) between P_{a0} and r_b, or P_{b0}, will hold for

---

[33] It may be useful to note that r_b^0, although no greater than r_b^+, must be larger than $r_{b\min}$. In fact, since as we shall see $P_{b0} = 0$ would entail $P_{a0} = 0$ (Paragraph 20 below), Equation (1c) above for $W = 0$ is only compatible with $P_{b0} > 0$, and $r_b^0 > r_{b\min}$.

$r_b^0 \lessgtr r_b < r_b^+$, only along what we shall here call the 'main branch' of the function $P_{a0}(P_{a0}, r_b) = 0$, the only branch, that is, for which $W > 0$ in that interval.

Thus, if assumptions (i) and (ii) ensure the existence of at least one solution of (F) for each level of r_b in the interval $r_{b\min} \leqslant r_b \leqslant r_{b\max}$, assumption (iii) ensures its *uniqueness*, but it does so only for the sub-interval $r_{b\min} \leqslant r_b < r_b^0$ (see Fig. 1, p. 407).

Two further important implications of assumption (iii) should now be mentioned. The first is that in the interval $r_{b\min} < r_b < r_b^0$, and also for $r_b^0 \leqslant r_b \leqslant r_b^+$, but only along the 'main branch' of $P_{a0}(P_{a0}, r_b) = 0$, r_a will rise monotonically as r_b rises.[34]

The third and last implication we need to mention here is that the assumption (iii) ensures an *inverse* relation between W and r_b for all positive levels of W, i.e. for $r_{b\min} < r_b < r_b^+$, though, again, for the sub-interval $r_b^0 \leqslant r_b \leqslant r_b^+$ that will be true only along the 'main branch' of the corresponding function $W(W, r_b) = 0$. In fact, Equation (1a) of Paragraph 15 makes clear that the rise of P_{a0} with r_b up to r_b^+ entails the fall of W over the same interval.

---

[34] Suppose that not to be so and thus r_a to fall as r_b rises in a sub-interval $r_b' < r_b < r_b''$ included in the overall interval $r_{b\min} < r_b < r_b^0$ (see Fig. a). At least two distinct levels, r_a^1 and r_a^2, would have to correspond to any level $\bar{r}_b$ in that sub-interval, since r_a must have initially risen from $r_{a\min} = -1$ together with P_{a0} (p. 421 below), as P_{a0} rose monotonically from zero together with P_{b0} (assumption (iii) above). However, that same monotonic relation between P_{a0} and P_{b0} entails that the two levels P_{b0}^1 and P_{b0}^2, corresponding to r_a^1 and r_a^2 respectively, must be equal because they correspond to a single value $\bar{P}_{b0} = \bar{r}_b + 1$. But then, for the reasons we saw at p. 413 above, P_{a0}^1 and P_{a0}^2 will have in common the same unique series of prices and therefore $r_a^1 = r_a^2$, contrary to our premise. We can therefore conclude that, given assumption (iii), r_a cannot fall as r_b rises in the interval $r_b^0 > r_b > r_{b\min}$. A similar reasoning, taking r_a as the independent variable, shows that r_a cannot remain constant as r_b increases.

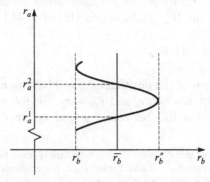

Fig. a

What remains to be done with respect to the determinacy of the I and S schedules is to explore the solutions of (F) at the two 'extremes', i.e. for $r_{b\min}$ and for r_b in the upper interval $r_b^0 \leq r_b \leq r_{b\max}$ Before coming to that, however, we shall have to deal with two general questions which are raised by the zero wage, or the zero intertemporal prices (P_{b0}/P_{b1}), (P_{a0}/P_{b1}) we find at such 'extreme' values of r_b. The two questions concern (a) the *supply* of a productive factor when the price of its service happens to be zero, and (b) the *meaning* of the zero intertemporal price of b_0 assumed for $r_{b\min}$. For that purpose it will be useful to start in the next paragraph from a closer consideration of a key relation in system (F): that between P_{b0} and P_{a0}, on which assumption (iii) above impinges. It will then be easier to proceed to the two questions, in Paragraphs 18–19 and 20, respectively.

17. Let us first drop Equation (7f) from system (F), and see instead the likely effect on A_0^D/B_0^D of a fall of P_{a0}, which were to be in strict proportion to that of P_{b0}. By thus keeping constant the relative 'contemporary' price of a_0 and b_0 while the 'intertemporal' prices P_{b0}/P_{b1} and P_{a0}/P_{b1} change in the same proportion, we can distinguish between, on the one hand, the pure 'intertemporal' effects of the fall of r_b and on the other, the side-effects which the fall of that single intertemporal price may have in changing the relative contemporary quantities demanded of a_0 and b_0 and hence, because of Equation (7f), the contemporary relative price of the two goods.

Now, the fall of r_b, which, as we saw, would also lower r_a, besides P_{a0}/P_{b1}, might perhaps be thought to affect in some definite direction the decisions to save and invest, but no general reason appears to exist why the ratios D_{a0}/D_{b0} or I_a/I_b, and therefore the ratio $A_0^D/B_0^D = (D_{a0} + I_a)/(D_{b0} + I_b)$, should be affected in one direction rather than the other. It follows that we could not expect any definite sign in the change of P_{a0}/P_{b0} necessary to keep A_0^D/B_0^D at its A_0^S/B_0^S level of Equation (7f): the 'contemporary' price P_{a0}/P_{b0} in system (F), that is, may move either way or even alternate the signs of its change as r_b falls. A tendency can therefore reasonably be supposed to exist for the intertemporal price P_{a0}/P_{b1} to follow the other intertemporal price P_{b0}/P_{b1} in its falls and hence for r_a to follow r_b, unless a very pronounced dislocation of the relative quantities demanded in $t = 0$ were to be involved, imposing a strong rise of P_{a0}/P_{b0} as r_b falls. This tendency of the two 'intertemporal' prices to fall together, though of course not necessarily in the same proportion, is what we postulated in our assumption (iii).

An important and perhaps surprising implication of what we have just said should now be noted. We saw that no reason exists why as r_b falls towards $r_{b\min}$, the relative 'contemporary' price P_{b0}/P_{a0} of b_0 should move in one direction rather than the other. However, the own interest

r_b falling towards $r_{b\,\min} = -1$ is in fact the intertemporal price P_{b0}/P_{b1} of b_0 falling towards zero. It therefore seems that in system (F) the tendency to a zero level of the *intertemporal* price P_{b0}/P_{b1} of b_0 does *not* entail the tendency to a zero level of its *contemporary* price P_{b0}/P_{a0}, contrary to what we would expect from a commodity which is becoming 'free' in the generally accepted sense: where, that is, a tendency to zero of the price of the commodity in terms of one scarce commodity (b_1 in this case) would entail a tendency to zero of its price in terms of *all* other scarce commodities (like a_0 in this case), whether of the same or of another date. We return to this important point in Paragraph 20 below.

18. We can now turn to the first of the two questions, which we said to be preliminary to discussing the solutions of (F) at the 'extreme' values of r_b: namely, the behaviour of the supply of a productive factor when the price of its service is zero, a situation verified at both $r_{b\,\min}$, with respect to P_{a0} and P_{b0}, and at the upper levels of r_b, with respect to W. The problem is perhaps best dealt with in two separate steps, i.e. the supply of labour first, and then the supplies of a_0 and b_0 as capital goods.

With respect to labour, it has often been noted that there is no reason why, as the wage *tends* to zero, the supply of labour should also tend to zero. If wages are the only income available to the worker for survival, the supply of labour can easily be imagined to *increase*, rather than decrease, as the wage gets indefinitely close to zero (a quarter of a pound of daily bread is better than nothing).[35] The situation only changes when the wage actually *reaches* zero and supplying labour no longer make any sense for the worker. It would thus seem reasonable to envisage a *discontinuity* in the supply of labour at a zero wage, where a jump to zero would presumably occur from the high level to which that supply would tend as the wage tends to zero.

That *discontinuity* would, however, have undesirable consequences for the theory in that it would eliminate the certainty of the existence of at

---

[35] A position we find exemplified in Morishima, 1964, p. 87 is to assume, at a zero wage, both zero supply *and* the continuity of the supply schedule for labour. It might seem possible to reconcile this position with the question of 'survival' discussed in the text only by assuming a nearly horizontal segment joining the origin of the axes with a sufficiently high level of supply for a wage close to zero (of course a strictly horizontal segment is instead the graphic representation of our assumption of continuity). However, it is not easy to see why a worker who has been progressively increasing his labour supply to try to survive should abandon that purpose by *decreasing* it when the wage is still positive. Even more arbitrary seems to be other assumptions ensuring continuity such as, e.g., that of each individual being endowed with some quantity of each resource (Debreu, 1959, p. 19), i.e. of a quantity of some other resource whose price must rise when that of the resource considered tends to zero.

least one economically significant solution to a system of general equilibrium. Thus, e.g., in our model the system would no longer admit the usual zero wage solutions when the supply of labour happened to exceed demand at all strictly positive wages. In order to preserve the certainty of the existence of at least one solution, we must assume continuity in the supply schedule also at zero wages and, hence, that the quantity of labour there made available is equal to the limit to which that quantity tends as the wage tends to zero.[36] In the case of our system (F), that limit is given by the assumed constant supply L.

19. Let us now proceed to the analogous question concerning savings, i.e. the supply of a_0 and b_0 as capital goods when ,as we shall have to see below (Paragraph 20), with $r_b = r_{b\min} = -1$, both the intertemporal prices P_{a0}/P_{b1} and P_{b0}/P_{b1} will generally have to be zero.[37] Also here we may envisage a state of scarcity for individuals whose only way to survive in $t = 1$ is through stocks of (non-storable) a_0 and b_0.[38] Their savings may then well increase as the intertemporal prices P_{a0}/P_{b1} and P_{b0}/P_{b1} of the two goods tend to zero (with both r_a and r_b tending to $r_{b\min} = -1$). However, as those prices actually *reach* zero, we face the need to choose between the same two alternative assumptions we saw for the case of labour.

We may assume *continuity* in the supply functions S_a and S_b of the two productive resources so that at zero intertemporal prices, we find the amount of physical savings to which the quantities S_a and S_b tend to, as the intertemporal prices tend to zero. Alternatively, we may envisage the savers to face the fact that *at* $r_b = -1$ they are unable to transfer *any* of their purchasing power from $t = 0$ to $t = 1$, and thus proceed to annul their useless savings, with a discontinuity in the supply of these productive resources whose negative implications for the existence of at least one solution to the general equilibrium system are the same as we saw in the case of the supply of labour.[39]

---

[36] We are here, in fact, implicitly using the general-equilibrium demand and supply schedules for labour, obtained from (E), by treating W as an independent variable and using the third of the relations (3e) to define a new unknown: labour demanded L^D.

[37] As we shall see in Paragraph 20 below, a zero intertemporal price of b_0 implies, under our assumptions, a zero intertemporal price of a_0 also.

[38] As already noted (n. 31 above), the question does not arise when at least one of the commodities is storable, in which case purchasing power can always be transferred from $t = 0$ to $t = 1$.

[39] The discontinuity would result from savings suddenly disappearing with a_a and b_0 being used entirely for consumption at a 'contemporary' price P_{a0}/P_{b0}, ensuring that relative

continued

As in the case of labour, we shall follow here what seems to be generally assumed about the continuity and positivity of a supply of productive resources at zero prices. This assumption, and the irrational behaviour it would entail under the circumstances considered above, should, however, be kept in mind when, in what follows,[40] the possibility of equilibria at $r_{b\min}$ or in the interval $r_b^0 \leq r_b \leq r_{b\max}$ (i.e. of zero intertemporal prices P_{b0}, P_{a0}, or of zero wage W) will emerge from the possible shapes of the two schedules.

20. The second preliminary to considering the extreme values of the functions I and S (Paragraph 16, above) concerns the meaning of the zero intertemporal price P_{b0}/P_{b1} we find at $r_{b\min}$. Contrary to what might perhaps have been expected, the zero *intertemporal* price P_{b0}/P_{b1} we assume in (F) when setting $r_b = -1$, does *not* entail that b_0 is a free commodity having, as such, a zero price in terms of *any* scarce commodity. As we saw in Paragraph 17, there is in fact no reason why b_0's contemporary price P_{b0}/P_{a0} should tend to zero when P_{b0}/P_{b1} does. Indeed, under our assumptions, the *contemporary* relative price of the two commodities will tend to a finite, strictly positive limit while then, as we shall presently see, arbitrage will make the two intertemporal prices go to zero together.

The two kinds of prices, contemporary and intertemporal, appear in fact to have an entirely different nature. The intertemporal price P_{b0}/P_{b1} expresses the conditions at which the commodity can be transferred over time – how much b_1 can be obtained by selling one unit of b_0. The contemporary price of P_{b0}/P_{a0} reflects instead the relative scarcity of b_0 and a_0 in $t = 0$. Now by setting $r_b = -1$ we did not assume anything about that relative scarcity, which is of course largely determined by the given endowments A_0^S, B_0^S and which remain exactly the same we have for all the other values of r_b, i.e. of P_{b0}/P_{b1} which we find along the I and S schedules, up to $r_{b\max}$. Indeed our assumption (ii) in Paragraph 15 above, that a_0 and b_0 can always be used in the given proportion A_0^S/B_0^S, has evidently excluded the possibility of either b_0 or

consumption demands $D_{a0}/D_{b0} = A_0^D/B_0^D$ should satisfy (7f). It is also possible to envisage that, through borrowing, wage income (reaching its maximum as r_b and r_a fall towards their minimum) be spent in increasing the consumption of both a_0 and b_0, (intertemporal) prices fall towards zero, thus engendering negative gross savings in the lower range of the S curve, in which case savings would become zero for some level $r_b > r_{b\min}$. This would render less consequential the discontinuity of the S curve at $r_b = -1$.

[40] Cf. Paragraphs 24 and 31 in the text below.

a_0 being free commodities in (F), whether $r_{b\min}$ or at any other level of r_b. And what we saw in Paragraph 19 about a plausible behaviour of the supply of savings entails in fact that both b_0 and a_0 might become *increasingly* scarce for consumption in $t = 0$ as r_b approaches its minimum level with, of course, the corresponding definite scarcity of b_0 *relative* to a_0 which is expressed by the contemporary price to which P_{b0}/P_{a0} tends as r_b tends to -1.

This non-zero, finite, contemporary price P_{b0}/P_{a0} leads us to another result which further reveals the different nature of 'intertemporal' as compared with 'contemporary' relative prices and which should now be looked at more closely. The impossibility of transferring b from $t = 0$ to $t = 1$, assumed by setting our independent variable at $r_b = -1$ means that the price of *any* commodity dated $t = 0$ relative to any commodity dated $t = 1$ should also be zero. Thus, $r_b = -1$ entails not only $P_{b0}/P_{b1} = 0$, but also that (P_{a0}/P_{b1}), (P_{b0}/P_{a1}), (P_{a0}/P_{a1}) should all be zero. This 'collective' zero *intertemporal* price for $r_b = -1$ is imposed by arbitrage.[41] Otherwise, b_0 could be transferred to $t = 1$, and thus contradict $P_{b0}/P_{b1} = 0$, by passing through a_0, or, alternatively, through a_0 and then a_1.[42] Now this 'collective' zero intertemporal price, accompanied by non-zero contemporary prices, appears to have no correspondent in the case of free commodities as commonly understood, where arbitrage would entail instead that zero price in terms of one (scarce) commodity be accompanied by zero price in terms of all other (scarce) commodities, without distinction of dates.

21. We are now finally ready to discuss the solutions of (F) at the lower and upper extremes of the values of r_b. With respect to $r_{b\min} = -1$, we know that, given the continuity assumed in Paragraph 19 for the supply of savings at $r_a = r_b = -1$ and, also, given assumptions (i) and (ii) of Paragraph 15 above, solutions of (F) would exist for $r_b = r_{b\min}$, no less than for the remaining levels of r_b in the interval $r_{b\min} < r_b \leq r_{b\max}$.[43] There is, then, no difficulty in

---

[41] This arbitrage condition, like any other arbitrage conditions, is in fact included in the definition of the price system in terms of $(n-1)$ prices. In our case, the assumed $P_{a0}/P_{b0} > 0$ with $P_{b0}/P_{b1} = 0$, entails $P_{a0}/P_{b1} = (P_{a0}/P_{b0})(P_{b0}/P_{b1}) = 0$.

[42] The reader may wonder how a coexistence of zero intertemporal prices between $t = 0$ and $t = 1$ and positive contemporary prices at $t = 0$, might be effected *in practice*: how, that is, it will be possible to discriminate between, on the one hand, producers of b_1 or a_1, who would get b_0 and a_0 for free, and owners of a_0 and b_0 who should instead give *some* of their commodity in order to get the other.

[43] Our reasoning in Paragraph 15 about the role of P_{a0} in adjusting A_0^D/B_0^D to A_0^S/B_0^S in Equation (7f) remains effective at $r_b = r_{b\min}$, despite the zero level of the *intertemporal* price P_{a0}/P_{b1} entailed here. The price of a_0 relevant for that adjustment is in fact the

extending to $r_{b\,\text{min}}$ our assumption (iii) about the single-valued character of the function relating P_{a0} to r_b, and conclude the uniqueness of the solution of (F).[44]

A peculiarity of the diagrammatic representation of that solution descends, however, from what we saw in Paragraph 20. Since, as we saw there, P_{a0}/P_{b1} must reach zero simultaneously with P_{b0}/P_{b1}, the diagram of the two schedules will show them converging to zero as r_b reaches (-1) (see Figure 1, Paragraph 10 above). The positive, finite contemporary relative price of the two commodities available in $t = 0$ entails, however, that should we choose to measure S and I by taking either a_0 or b_0 as the numéraire, we would find, under our assumptions of p. 419 above, two non-zero separate points S and I.

As we proceed to the determination of the I and S points of the schedules at the opposite extreme, we find the continuum of (F) positions we outlined in Paragraph 16 above. That continuum, we said, will correspond to levels of labour employment L^D between zero and L, with the corresponding changes of the investment required to equip that variable amount of labour.[45] Thus the continuum will start at $r_b = r_b^+$, where W reaches zero after falling monotonically as P_{a0} and r_b rise from $r_{b\,\text{min}}$ up to r_b^0, and then rises further along the 'main branch' of the function $I(P_{a0}, r_b) = 0$. The continuum will be such that beyond the amount of investment I^+, which we find for r_b^+, at the end of the 'main branch' of the function $I(I, r_b) = 0$, the schedule I will sooner or later have to turn left and it will extend to join the vertical axis as the investment demand falls to zero together with amount of labour L^D to be equipped by means of that investment (see Figure 1). Thus, starting from the value r_b^+, the

---

contemporary relative price P_{a0}/P_{b0}, which, as we saw, is not zero at $r_{b\,\text{min}}$ (cf. Paragraph 17).

[44] This uniqueness is not in contrast with the fact that, at $r_{b\,\text{min}}$, unlike at other levels of r_b, the position (F) may originate equilibria (E) with different levels of utilization of the physical savings supply (p. 419 above) depending on the amount of investment in that position (F), as shown by the inequality signs which will then apply in the first two relations (3e).

[45] Given the possible multiplicity of solutions of (F) in the interval $r_b^0 \leq r_b \leq r_{b\,\text{max}}$, the determination of the (F) positions for $W = 0$ is most easily envisaged by the artifice of letting L^D take there the role of the independent variable so as to obtain r_b (a single-valued function of L^D), and to obtain with it the unknowns of the (F) system. This will in fact allow tracing the levels of L^D and hence the (F) positions corresponding to the several levels of r_b, our true independent variable. Despite the constancy of W at its zero level, the four prices will in fact be generally changing with L^D because, as I changes with L^D, the proportion A_0^D/B_0^D would tend to change at constant P_{a0}/P_{b0}, and the latter will therefore have to change to keep the equality between A_0^D/B_0^D and A_0^S/B_0^S imposed by Equation (7f).

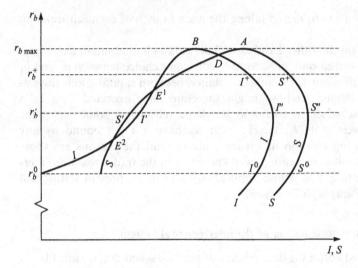

Figure 2

schedule I may either rise or fall as it moves right or left, to finally reach the vertical axis on the left having its highest and lowest points at, respectively, $r_{b\,max}$ and r_b^0.[46] The levels of S will similarly change as r_b varies in that interval, and that schedule may also extend either right or left as it rises or falls together with the I schedule, starting from point S^+ corresponding to the position F^+ defined above, although no reason exists why it should tend to zero as L^D tends to zero[47] (see Figure 2).

22. A few considerations regarding the general shape of the schedule emerging from system (F) may be useful at this point. No particular observation is required here for the S schedule where, for the well-known reasons, we can expect 'physical' savings S_a, S_b to decrease as well as increase as r_b rises. A bias towards increasing S and I schedules results from our choice of a commodity available in $t = 1$ as numéraire: assumption(iii) entails in fact that the prices of b_0 and a_0, the two physical constituents of savings and investment, rise monotonically from zero as

---

[46] Our assumption (iii) on the joint rise of P_{a0} and P_{b0} so long as $W > 0$ excludes that the possible multiple solutions for $r_b^0 \leq r_b \leq r_{b\,max}$ may include any for $W > 0$, other than those for the 'main branch' of $P_{a0}(P_{a0}, r_b)$.

[47] In fact, the income from which those savings come, is likely to change little as L^D changes since, with $W = 0$, only the owners of the initial stocks A_0^S and B_0^S will have an income which, by the first two of Equations (3fi), will correspond with the full utilization of those stocks.

r_b rises from (-1) to r_b^0 and (along the main branch of each schedule) up to r_b^+.

We may on the other hand note that, although alternative techniques will be introduced only in Section 6, consumer choice between a_1 and b_1 would already allow for a 'substitutability' between capital goods (investment) and labour, and we might therefore have expected I to be a decreasing schedule in so far as its shape reflects, in some sense, the physical investments I_a, I_b. However we have not felt bound by any such decreasing relation in Figure 1 above, and the reasons are those of 'reverse capital deepening', well known from the traditional non-intertemporal setting, and whose applicability also in the present setting will be seen in Paragraph 29 below.

5   The representation of the intertemporal system

23. Reassured about the determinacy of our two schedules, we must begin to see how they can aid our understanding of the behaviour of the system described by (E). In particular, in this and the next paragraph we shall see how the schedules can represent the equilibria of the system and then in the following two paragraphs consider the information they can provide on out-of-equilibrium behaviour.

A 'position' (F) of the system (i.e. the solution of (F) for a particular value of r_b) will also be an equilibrium (i.e. a solution of (E)) when the first two relations in (3e) concerning the aggregate demand and supplies of a_0 and b_0 happen to be satisfied: all other relations of (E) are in fact present also in (F). Leaving aside at first the case of 'extreme' equilibria occurring, that is, for $r_{b\,min}$ or for $r_b^0 \le r_b \le r_{b\,max}$, it can be asserted that when the system is in equilibrium the two schedules S and I intersect, and that the converse is also true. As for the first proposition, when $r_b > r_{b\,min}$, and P_{a0}, P_{b0} are accordingly positive, any solution of (E) will entail that the first two relations in Equation (3e) will be satisfied with an equality sign, i.e.

$$A^S = A^D \quad \text{and} \quad B^S = B^{D\ 48} \tag{3a}$$

and hence (see Relations (3f) in Paragraph 7)

$$I_a = S_a, \qquad I_b = S_b \tag{3a}$$

and

---

[48] Inequality signs in relations (3a) can be ruled out under our present assumption that $r_b > r_{b\,min}$, entailing $P_{b0} > 0$ and hence, given assumption (iii) of Paragraph 16, $P_{a0} > 0$.

$$I_a P_{a0} + I_b P_{b0} = S_b P_{b0} + S_a P_{a0}, \qquad \text{i.e.} \qquad S = I \qquad (3b)$$

The general equilibrium of the system thus entails an intersection of the two schedules.

As for the converse proposition, when we have an intersection E of the schedules in that same interval (see Figure 1), we must have Equation (3b) and therefore, adding $D_{a0} P_{a0} + D_{b0} P_{b0}$ to both sides,

$$A_0^D P_{a0} + B_0^D P_{a0} = A_0^S P_{a0} + B_0^S P_{b0} \qquad (3c)$$

Indicating the common value of the ratios appearing on the two sides of Equation (7f) by the constant γ, we may write Equation (3c) as follows:

$$A_0^S P_{a0} + \gamma A_0^S P_{b0} = A_0^D P_{a0} + \gamma A_0^D P_{a0} \qquad (3d)$$

from which $A_0^S = A_0^D$ and hence, from Equation (3c), $B_0^S = B_0^D$, thus fulfilling all relations (3e) in system (E), and ensuring that we are in a general equilibrium position.

24. Now turning our attention to the representation of possible 'extreme' equilibria of the system, we may note that equilibria in the upper interval $r_b^0 \leq r_b \leq r_{b\,\text{max}}$ will also be shown by intersections of the two schedules – but the converse proposition will not be true. Since different (F) positions may correspond to the same level of r_b, for $r_b^0 \leq r_b \leq r_{b\,\text{max}}$, an intersection between I and S may occur for a point representing an (F) position on the I schedule, which is *different* from the one which the same point represents on the S schedule. The intersections representing equilibria have then to be traced by checking whether the I and S points of intersection pertain to the same (F) position. That will be possible in the diagram because, e.g., starting from points like I^+ and S^+ (see Fig. 2), the two schedules will go through exactly the same values of r_b in exactly the same sequence: 'couples' of I and S points corresponding to same (F) position can therefore easily be singled out.[49] The reasoning conducted in Paragraph 23 will then apply to those intersections which, pertaining to the same F position, do in fact indicate an equilibrium.

---

[49] Thus, should the schedules be representable as in Figure 2, intersection D would *not* represent an equilibrium because, of the two (F) positions, (F') and (F''), that we meet in that sequence at r_b, as L^D falls from the full employment level of I^+ and S^+, point D corresponds to (F') on the I schedule, but to (F'') on the S schedule (as shown by the fact that it comes before B on I, but after A in S, where A and B correspond to the same unique (F) position corresponding to $r_{b\,\text{max}}$). Intersections E^1 and E^2, however, would each correspond to the same (F) position and would therefore indicate equilibria (like E^V, but not D, in Figure 1 of Paragraph 10 above).

As we proceed to $r_{b\min}$, at the opposite extreme, although the zero intertemporal prices P_{a0}, P_{b0} yield $S = I = 0$, we shall there generally have definite non-zero quantities I_a, I_b, S_a, S_b (p. 419 above). We need here first of all to recall how assumption (ii) of Paragraph 15 eliminates the possibility that either a_0 or b_0 should be a non-scarce commodity in consumption in $t = 0$, so that position (F) for $r = -1$ can only be of the kind characterized by that 'collective' zero intertemporal price of all commodities available in $t = 0$, which we discussed in Paragraph 20 above. Now, that (F) position will be an equilibrium when $S_b > I_b$, and hence, by (7f), $S_a > I_a$ (cf. the inequality signs in the first two relations (3e), p. 397). In that case we shall evidently have $S > I$ when r_b approaches $r_{b\min}$ and P_{b0} and P_{a0} are still strictly positive. Conversely, when $S > I$ for $r_b \to r_{b\min}$, then an equilibrium will exist at $r_{b\min}$.[50]

25. While thus representing the equilibria of the system, the two schedules can, as we said, provide elements for a discussion of its out-of-equilibrium behaviour.

Suppose first an (F) position for $r = r_b$ in the intermediate interval $r_{b\min} < r_b < r_b^0$, such that $S > I$. (See, e.g., Fig. 1, Paragraph 10 above.) Because of Equation (7f), the inequality $S > I$ means that $S_a > I_a$ and $S_b > I_b$. Given the assumption in (F) that the consumption demands of $t = 0$ are always fully satisfied, those excess savings in turn mean that $A_0^S > A_0^D$ and $B_0^S > B_0^D$. It would then seem possible to suppose an 'initial' reaction in the markets for a_0 and b_0, more directly affected by the disequilibrium – occurring, that is, *before* adjustments can take place in connected markets. In our case, the natural 'initial' reaction would be a fall of intertemporal prices P_{a0}/P_{b1} and P_{b0}/P_{b1}. It would, however, seem also natural to suppose that then the connected markets will broadly adjust, so that we may envisage an out-of-equilibrium behaviour in the recontracting dominated by movement along the two general-equilibrium

---

[50] Assumption (ii) of Paragraph 15 is not sufficient to exclude the case in which $r_b = -1$ were to result from the endowments A_0^S and B_0^B, being each so abundant as to make *both* a_0 and b_0 free commodities. In that case, the 'vanishing' of their price relative to one another (p. 412, n. 31) will accompany their zero price in terms of a_1 or b_1. However, it would then be generally impossible to envisage any level of r_b other than (-1). The two schedules would collapse into the single (F) position for $r_b = -1$, with physical savings S_a and S_b which, by assumption, will exceed the physical investment I_a, I_b. With no commodity storable, scarcity will, however, re-emerge in $t = 1$, when P_{a1}/P_{b1} would be determined by the direct labour content of the two commodities, while the only income in $t = 1$ will be that constituted by wages.

We may also note here the case not considered in the text, when equalities $S_a = I_a$ and $S_b = I_b$ were to hold at $r_{b\min}$. This case would only alter what we stated in the text in that such an equilibrium will not necessarily entail $S > I$ as r_b approaches (-1).

schedules. In this respect the key condition of Equation (7f) imposing a uniformity of sign and a proportionate change of the algebraic excess demands of a_0 and b_0 seems to be as reasonable an assumption as can be made at a general level: it may indeed be taken to represent a condition of 'even flexibility' of the price system in response to the excess demand of the two commodities, in the sense of allowing their excess demands to change in the same proportion. Our critical aim strengthens the legitimacy of assuming that the dominant out-of-equilibrium movement will be along the schedules: if instability were to result under that assumption, it would then be all the more plausible when obstacles to the adjustments to equilibrium are also considered in the connected markets which the schedules assume to be kept in equilibrium.

Then, as we start moving along the schedules, our assumption (iii) of Paragraph 16 ensures that the 'initial' fall of both P_{a0}/P_{b1} and P_{a0}/P_{b0} in response to the assumed excess savings will be confirmed and will result in a fall of *both* own rates r_a and r_b (Paragraph 16 above), thus causing a movement downwards along the schedules. This result can indeed be taken to be quite general – to be independent, that is, of our assumption (iii). It would in fact appear inevitable that, after adjustments in the other markets, the excess savings should result in the fall of at least one of the two own interest rates: this rate we may then identify with our independent variable r_b, justifying the assumption of a movement downwards along the schedules.[51]

---

[51] In fact, if we leave aside assumption (iii) we cannot be sure that r_a, i.e. P_{a0}/P_{a1}, which is a *dependent* variable in (F), will fall with r_b. As we saw in Paragraph 17, no necessity rules the sign of the change of the contemporary relative price P_{a0}/P_{b0} as r_b falls and, we may now add, the same is true for the other contemporary relative price P_{a1}/P_{b1}, which is regulated by the production conditions appearing in Equations (1f). This seems sufficient to conclude that as r_b changes no necessity rules the sign of the corresponding change of r_a given by

$$r_a = (P_{a0}/P_{a1}) - 1 = [(P_{a0}/P_{b0})(P_{b0}/P_{b1})(P_{b1}/P_{a1})] - 1 = r_b \frac{P_{a0}}{P_{b0}} \frac{P_{b1}}{P_{a1}} - 1 \qquad (6d)$$

However, the causes of a possible contrasting movement of r_a as, e.g., r_b falls because of excess savings, are quite different from those acting for a fall of *both* rates. The latter causes are the excess savings, i.e. that excess supply of commodities in general in $t = 0$, and that excess demand for them in $t = 1$, which is the meaning of excess savings in our model. Those excess savings would indeed tend to lower r_a together with r_b in (F) *if* the fall of r_b were to leave the contemporary relative demands A_0^D/B_0^D broadly unaffected, and hence, presumably, leave the relative contemporary price P_{a0}/P_{b0} broadly unaffected too (cf. Paragraph 17, above) – while, on the other hand, the coefficients of production were to allow for only small changes of the other contemporary relative price P_{a1}/P_{b1}.

continued

In conclusion, within the interval of values of our independent variable specified at the beginning of this paragraph, there appears to be no obstacle for supposing a fall of r_b in the presence of excess savings and a rise of it in the opposite case of excess investment. The consequences we may draw from that proposition are straightforward. Similarly to what can be argued on the basis of partial equilibrium schedules, given e.g. the equilibrium E^{III} shown in Figure 1 above – i.e. an intersection of the schedules such that, proceeding from left to right, the I schedule cuts the S schedule from above – we have elements for arguing a tendency toward that equilibrium, given any initial position in the interval $r_b^{II} < \hat{r^b} < r_b^{IV}$. In fact, as we have just seen, r_b can be expected to fall if $r_b^{IV} > r_b > r_b^{III}$ and to rise in the opposite case. A tendency away from equilibrium can instead be tentatively argued when, as we move from left to right, the I schedule cuts the S schedule from below (see, e.g., E^{IV} in Figure 1).

26. We may now proceed to the out-of-equilibrium behaviour of the system for the 'extreme' values of r_b. With respect to $r_{b\,min}$, we may note that if we happened to have $S > I$ in the proximity of $r_b = -1$, the fall of r_b, which we can assume in the presence of $S > I$, would imply the competitive recontracting to tend to the equilibrium with the zero intertemporal prices of both a_0 and b_0 we saw in Paragraph 24.[52]

Some novel problems are met when we shift our attention to the behaviour at the upper extreme for $r_b^0 \le r_b \le r_{b\,max}$. We may leave aside the 'main branch' of the S and I schedules (where with $L = L^D$ and $W > 0$ we have the conditions considered in Paragraph 25). In all other (F) positions of that interval, we shall have excess supply of labour and a zero wage. As we saw in Paragraph 24 the I schedule will there extend leftward to finally reach the vertical axis for the (F) position corresponding to $L^D = 0$ and any equilibrium possible there will then be shown by an intersection of the two schedules (although the converse will not be true).

Outside any such equilibria there will be the two possibilities according to whether in the given position (F) we have $I < S$, or the opposite condition.

Excess savings as such would thus make for a uniform movement of both r_a and r_b. The causes of contrasting movements of r_a are instead those changes of the relative contemporary demands which, as r_b changes, may cause changes of the relative *contemporary* price of the two goods in passing from $t = 0$ to $t = 1$. As Equation (6d) shows, r_a can rise as r_b falls only if P_{a0}/P_{b0} rises and/or P_{a1}/P_{b1} falls sufficiently, i.e. if, as r_b falls, the fall of the contemporary relative price of a in passing from $t = 0$ to $t = 1$ becomes large enough to impose a compensating rise of r_a.

[52] No tendency would be there to equilibrium of the 'fluke' case mentioned in n. 50, when $S_a = I_a$, $S_b = I_b$ at $r_{b\,min}$, but $S < I$ as $r_b \to r_{b\,min}$.

In the first case – exemplified by points I'' and S'' in Fig. 2 above – we can suppose that the excess savings, i.e. the excess supply of a_0 and b_0, will cause the 'initial' fall of both P_{a0}/P_{b1} and P_{b0}/P_{b1} we assumed in Paragraph 25, above. Since W will remain zero because of labour unemployment, that 'initial' fall of P_{a0}/P_{b1}, P_{b0}/P_{b1} will make it profitable for entrepreneurs to increase production and thus L^D. Unless an equilibrium were to be met in the process, that increase of L^D will continue until full labour employment is reached in position (F^+) for $r_b = r_b^+$. Excess savings and the consequent persisting 'initial' fall of P_{a0}/P_{b1}, P_{b0}/P_{b1} would then plausibly result in a positive wage W, together with a fall of r_b: the (F) positions would then enter the range of the already discussed (F) positions characterized by $W > 0$.

In the case in which, in that same interval of r_b, we instead had $I > S$ for the given (F) position – as exemplified by points I' and S' in Fig. 2 – then an opposite process of decreases of output and of L^D would become plausible, and lead towards an equilibrium which would then have to exist within the interval $r_b^0 \leq r_b, \leq r_{b\min}$. The excess investment would in fact mean excess demand of both a_0 and b_0, and hence an 'initial' rise of the prices P_{a0}/P_{b1} and P_{b0}/P_{b1} which, the wage being already zero, would make production of a_1 and b_1 unprofitable (cf. Equation (1c) of Paragraph 15) and would therefore plausibly result in a fall of output and of labour employment L^D. On the other hand, the existence in that case of at least one equilibrium to the left of that (F) position follows from the fact that investment I has to change continuously down to zero, while S also changes continuously, though presumably without reaching zero: a level of L^D must therefore exist with a common value of S and I, which will constitute an equilibrium – as exemplified by E^2 to the left of points I' and S'.

6   Alternative techniques and the investment demand

27. System (F), like system (E) which has generated it, still rests on the assumption that only one method of production is available for each commodity. It is time to drop that assumption and consider the existence of several alternative methods for each commodity, all sharing the properties we mentioned in Paragraph 3 above. We may call 'system of production' or 'technique of production' of the commodity a set of 'methods of production', one for the commodity and one for each of its (direct and indirect) means of production. Here, the 'technique' or 'system' of production of the commodity will accordingly include two 'methods of production', one for the commodity and one for the other commodity as means of production of the former. Thus one 'technique' for producing a,

will also be a 'technique' for producing b, and we may therefore refer to techniques $i = 1, \ldots, n$ without mentioning the commodity they refer to, since each refers to both commodities. Available 'techniques' will be formed by all possible combinations of the methods available, one for each commodity.

Despite our assumption that all alternative methods of production require the same three factors, there is no guarantee that marginal products, even of the discontinuous variety, will exist.[53] For the choice of the profit-maximizing technique, we can therefore resort to the more general method we find in Sraffa's *Production of Commodities*: namely, comparing the expenses of production of the commodities. However, at each level of r_b the comparison can only be done in terms of prices P^i_{a0}, P^i_{b0} and the wage W^i holding for the particular technique i 'in use' – meaning by it the technique i whose adoption we assume to be generally planned at the stage reached by the recontracting.[54] Maximization of entrepreneurial profits will then entail the recontracting to proceed to any method for each commodity which happens to be cheaper at those prices.

A question which is well known from the 'traditional', non-intertemporal assumptions then arises, about whether the *order* of the alternative methods of production of the commodity as to cheapness, might not itself change with the technique 'in use': with the possibility of either endless switching between techniques, or of the technique finally adopted depending on the one initially 'in use'.[55] Our critical intent, however, will again allow us to grant the theory the most favourable assumptions, and therefore to suppose what has been demonstrated under the traditional assumptions: that the order of cheapness of an alternative method is the same whichever the technique in (planned) use.[56] We can thus suppose that the choice of entrepreneurs will always arrive at one and the same technique, so that at

---

[53] Marginal products, whether of the discontinuous or the continuous variety, require that the available techniques be susceptible of being ordered so that they can be made to differ by the quantity of only one factor at a time. That, it seems, cannot generally be done when the factors are more than two: weighted averages of the different methods available which could give the above result will not generally make economic sense, since the methods entering such averages could not generally coexist.

[54] A sufficient unanimity concerning the technique i to be adopted has evidently to be assumed in order to let the corresponding prices emerge from the contracting. That unanimity has then to be replaced by a similar one concerning a second technique which had been found to be cheaper at those earlier prices, and so on and so forth.

[55] Cf., e.g., Garegnani, 1970, pp. 410–11.

[56] For the question in its traditional context, cf. Sraffa, 1960, Chap. xii, and the subsequent literature referred to in Kurz and Salvadori, 1995, p. 151.

any given r_b the cheapest technique or 'system of production' can be uniquely determined together with the corresponding series of the prices, the outputs, and the I and S quantities.

28. We shall here confine ourselves to reporting below the family (Fi) of systems of equations defining the two schedules under the assumption of a multiplicity of systems of production. Each member of that family is a system (F) like the one we defined in Paragraph 6 above, but applied now to the technique i which happens to be the one no less cheap than any other at the given level of r_b. Thus, to any level r_b in its relevant interval there will correspond a system (Fi) containing as well as the relations (F) pertaining to the technique i adopted, as many quadruplets of relations (8fi) and (9fi) as there are alternative 'techniques' or 'systems of production' $j \neq i$. The first two equations (8fi) reckon the production expenses of a_1 and b_1 with the respective methods j. The second couple of relations, namely (9fi), states that no method for producing each of the two commodities is cheaper than method i 'in use'.

$$\begin{cases} P_{a1}^i = l_{ai} W^i + a_{ai} P_{a0}^i + b_{ai} P_{b0}^i \\ \\ P_{bi}^i = l_{bi} W^i + a_{bi} P_{a0}^i + b_{bi} P_{b0}^i \end{cases} \tag{1fi}$$

$$P_{bi}^i = 1 \tag{2fi}$$

$$\begin{cases} A_0^{Di} = D_{a0}^i + (a_{ai} A_1^i + a_{bi} B_1^i) \\ B_0^{Di} = D_{b0}^i + (b_{ai} A_1^i + b_{bi} B_1^i) \\ L \geq l_a A_1^i + l_b B_1^i \\ A_1^i = D_{a1}^i \\ B_1^i = D_{b1}^i \end{cases} \tag{3fi}$$

$$\tag{Fi}$$

$$I^i = (a_{ai} A_1^i + b_{bi} B_1^i) P_{a0} + (b_{ai} A_1^i + b_{bi} B_1^i) P_{b0} \tag{4fi}$$

$$S^i = (A_0^{Si} - D_{a0}^i) P_{a0}^i + (B_0^{Si} - D_{b0}^i) P_{b0}^i \tag{5fi}$$

$$r_b = (P_{b0}^i / P_{b1}^i) - 1 \tag{6fi}$$

$$A_0^{Di} / B_0^{Di} = A_0^{Si} / B_0^{Si} \tag{7fi}$$

$$\begin{cases} P^i_{aj1} = l_{aj} W^i + a_{aj} P^i_{a0} + b_{aj} P^i_{b0} \\ P^i_{bj1} = l_{bj} W^i + a_{bj} P^i_{a0} + b_{bj} P^i_{b0} \end{cases} \quad \text{any } j \neq i \qquad (8\text{fi})$$

$$P^i_{a1} \leq P^i_{aj1}, \qquad P^i_{b1} \leq P^i_{bj1} \qquad \text{any } j \neq i \qquad (9\text{fi})$$

where i at the exponent indicates that the variable in question is calculated under the assumption that technique i is being planned for use at the given r_b, whereas i or j at the deponent indicates the method to which the variable in question (coefficient of production or price) pertains.

Correspondingly, system (E), determining the equilibrium of the system, should now be written in the form of the following family of systems (Ei) allowing for alternative techniques:

$$\begin{cases} P^i_{a1} = l_{ai} W^i + a_{ai} P^i_{a0} + b_{ai} P^i_{b0} \\ P^i_{b1} = l_{bi} W^i + a_{bi} P^i_{a0} + b_{bi} P^i_{b0} \end{cases} \qquad (1\text{ei})$$

$$P^i_{b1} = 1 \qquad (2\text{ei})$$

$$\begin{cases} A_0 \geq D^i_{a0} + [(a_{ai} A_1 + a_{bi} B_1)] & \text{if } >, \text{ then } P_{a0} = 0 \\[2mm] B_0 \geq D^i_{b0} + [(b_{ai} A_1 + B_{bi} B_1)] & \text{if } >, \text{ then } P_{b0} = 0 \\[2mm] L \geq l_{ai} A_1 + l_{bi} B_1 & \text{if } >, \text{ then } W = 0 \qquad (3\text{ei}) \\[2mm] D_{a1} = A_1 \\[2mm] D_{b1} = B_1 \end{cases}$$

$$\text{(Ei)}$$

$$\begin{cases} P^i_{aj1} = I_{aj} W^i + a_{aj} P^i_{a0} + b_{aj} P^i_{b0} \\ P^i_{bj1} = I_{bj} W^i + a_{bj} P^i_{a0} + b_{bj} P^i_{b0} \end{cases} \quad \text{any } j \neq i \qquad (8\text{ei})$$

$$P^i_{a1} \leq P^i_{aj1}, \quad P^i_{b1} \leq P^i_{bj1}, \qquad \text{any } j \neq i \qquad (9\text{ei})$$

where, as in the formulation of (E) in Paragraph 3 above, the relations corresponding to (4fi), (5fi), (6fi), (7fi) do not need to appear, $S = I$ being implied in (Ei).

29. The main question which the existence of alternative methods of production raises for us here are the changes in the investment requirements I due to the changes in the cheapest technique as r_b varies. We

might perhaps expect that owing to those changes, as well as to the needs of the changing relative outputs of a_1 and b_1, the schedule I would generally show a negative slope (cf. p. 423 above). However, such an expectation will have no better foundation for the present investment demand schedule than it had for the capital demand schedule of the 'traditional' setting.

A simple reasoning seems sufficient to show this. As has been pointed out,[57] the roots of reverse capital deepening, as well as of the re-switching of techniques, lie in the effect of changes in distribution (rate of profits) upon the *relative prices* of the alternative sets of capital goods required by the processes of production which are being compared – whether such processes are alternative methods of production for the *same* consumption good, or the methods of two alternative consumption goods. In the traditional, non-intertemporal setting, it is the changing relative price of two such sets of capital goods that can make a more 'capital-intensive' technique become more profitable – or a more capital-intensive consumption good fall in price – as the interest rate rises. And it is that same change in the relative value of the alternative sets of capital goods that can bring about 're-switching' among alternative techniques. Now, the same variability of the relative price of alternative sets of capital goods is clearly also present in an intertemporal setting.

To see the thing in more definite terms, let us consider first the case of alternative techniques as distinct from alternative consumption goods. From Equations (8fi) and (9fi) we may see how, at the given level of r_b, the choice between the cheapest technique i and any other alternative technique j, differing, say, by the method of production of a, alone hinges on the following relative costs of the two methods:

$$\frac{P_{ai1}^i}{P_{aj1}^i} = \frac{l_{ai}W^i + (a_{ai}P_{a0}^i + b_{ai}P_{b0}^i)}{l_{aj}W^i + (a_{aj}P_{a0}^i + b_{aj}P_{b0}^i)}, \tag{10}$$

technique i being more profitable than j at the given r_b when $P_{ai1}^i / P_{aj1}^i < 1$. Defining now

$$C_{ai}^i = a_{ai}P_{a0}^i + b_{ai}P_{b0}^i$$

$$C_{aj}^i = a_{aji}P_{a0}^i + b_{aji}P_{b0}^i$$

where the C_a's are the respective capital expenses estimated at the given level of r_b, we have the following relative production expenses of the two methods:

[57] Cf., e.g., Garegnani, 1970.

$$\frac{P^i_{ai1}}{P^i_{aji1}} = \frac{l_{ai} W^i + C_{ai}}{l_{aj} W^i + C^i_{aj}} \tag{10a}$$

With (C^i_{ai}/l_{ai}) and (C^i_{aj}/l_{aj}) as the respective values of capital per worker in the (direct) production of a_1, we have

$$\frac{P^i_{ai1}}{P^i_{aj1}} = \frac{W^i + (C^i_{ai}/l_{ai})}{W^i + (C^i_{aj}/l_{aj})} \cdot \frac{l_{ai}}{l_{aj}} \tag{10b}$$

Assume now, without loss of generality, that $C^i_{ai}/l_{ai} > C^i_{aj}/l_{aj}$. A rise of W, i.e. a fall of r_b (Paragraph 16 above), need *not* entail the fall of P^i_{ai1}/P^i_{aj1} we might have expected: a sufficient rise of C^i_{ai}/C^i_{aj} may well make P^i_{ai1}/P^i_{aj1} rise, and not fall as W^i rises. This means that the rise of W may well result in *the less capital-intensive method j* becoming the more profitable one of the two, and therefore being adopted.

The same change of C^i_{ai}/C^i_{aj} may entail, as can be shown by replacing P^i_{aj1} with P^i_{bi1}, that the less 'capital-intensive' consumption good b_1 may become cheaper relative to a_1 as W rises (r_b falls). Hence the freedom with which we were able to draw the shape of the I schedule in our Figure 1 (Paragraph 10 above).[58]

---

[58] To make r_b appear explicitly in Equation (11b) we should turn to the undiscounted prices, here indicated by the small letter p. By itself, this change in the equations does not, of course, entail any change in the assumptions of the model (e.g. in those of complete future markets or of an 'initial' contracting period): it only requires that each price be notionally referred to the date of delivery of the commodity by taking as numéraire for it, the good b of the same date. Then for the undiscounted prices of a_1 and b_1,

$$p_{b1} = 1 = P_{b1}, \qquad p_{a1} = P_{a1}/P_{b1} = P_{a1}$$

As for the undiscounted prices of a_0 and b_0, using Equation (6f) we have:

$$p_{b0} = 1 = P_{b1} = P_{b0}/(1 + r_b),$$

and since $P_{b0} = 1 + r_b$, we also have

$$p_{a0} = P_{a0}/P_{b0} = P_{a0}/(1 + r_b).$$

The first two relations (3fi) can then be written as follows:

$$p^i_{a1} = l_{ai} W^i + (a_{ai} p^i_{a0} + b_{ai} p^i_{b0})(1 + r_b)$$
$$p^i_{b1} = l_{bi} W^i + (a_{bi} p^i_{a0} + b_{bi} p^i_{b0})(1 + r_b) \tag{3fi$'$}$$

and the first equation of each couple (8fi) is

$$p^i_{aj1} = l_{aj} W^i + (a_{aj} p^i_{a0} + b_{aj} p^i_{b0})(1 + r_b) \tag{9fi$'$}$$

continued

7   Some conclusions

30. As was said in Paragraph 10, the two schedules will not be used here for a detailed examination of the properties of the equilibria (solutions of system (E)): their primary use here is to show how the notion of capital as a single 'quantity' enters the intertemporal equilibria, no less than it entered the traditional ones. That may usefully be done, while at the same time showing how misleading is the widespread idea that the adjustment between savings and investment in an intertemporal equilibrium raises no more problems than do adjustments to relative demands for contemporary commodities.[59]

It is of course true that if we assume no capital to be left at the final date, the savings at t must consist of demand for consumer goods at future dates $t + \tau$, at the expense of demand for the same or other consumer goods at t. It is then equally true that any excess of saving decisions over investment decisions must necessarily take the form of an excess supply of consumer goods at t, and of an excess demand of the same or other consumer goods at future dates. Thus, imagine that initial recontracting had brought us to the position $(\hat{F})$ of quantities and prices which system (Fi) associates with the interest rate $\hat{r}_b$, and suppose that $(\hat{F})$ would coincide with an equilibrium $\hat{E}$ (i.e. it would solve system (Ei) as well as system (Fi)) except for a positive small excess $\Delta S = (\hat{S} - \hat{I})$ of savings $\hat{S}$ over investment, $\hat{I}$, $\hat{S}$ and $\hat{I}$ being estimated at the price of $(\hat{F})$, as shown in Fig. 2.

From the households budget equations in (Fi) for $\hat{r}_b$ we obtain

Expressing now the undiscounted capital expenses as

$$c_{ai}^{i} = a_{ai}p_{a0}^{i} + b_{ai}p_{b0}^{i}$$
$$c_{aj}^{i} = a_{aj}p_{a0}^{i} + b_{aj}p_{b0}^{i}. \tag{10'}$$

By transformations analogous to those operated in passing from Equation (10) to Equation (10b) in the text, we obtain

$$\frac{p_{ai0}}{p_{aj0}} = \frac{1 + \dfrac{c_{ai}^{i}}{l_{ai}} \cdot \dfrac{1 + r_b}{W^i}}{1 + \dfrac{c_{aj}^{i}}{l_{aj}} \cdot \dfrac{1 + r_b}{W^i}} \frac{l_{ai}}{l_{aj}} \tag{10b'}$$

where the change in the p_{ai0}/p_{aj0} can now be seen to depend on the ratio $(1 + r_b)/W$.

[59] That idea seems, e.g., to be what Professor Arrow refers to when he argues that in any discussion of 'intertemporal allocation', the variables are 'today's prices for future goods'. There is then, he continues, 'a perfectly consistent story *that does not look any different from the story about choosing commodities today*' (Arrow, 1989, p. 155, our italics).

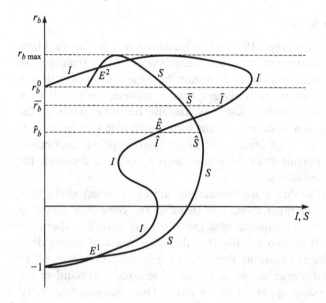

Figure 3

$$\Delta\hat{S} = -(\hat{P}_{a0}\Delta D_{a0} + \hat{P}_{b0}\Delta D_{b0}) = \hat{P}_{a1}\Delta D_{a1} + \hat{P}_{b1}\Delta D_{b1} \qquad (5b)$$

where the ΔD's indicate the differences in the respective quantities demanded between $\hat{F}$ and $\hat{E}$ which, for simplicity, we have supposed to be *both* negative in $t = 0$ and positive in $t = 1$.[60] Now, Equation (5b) looks similar to that holding in the case of contemporary commodities should ($\hat{F}$) have failed to be an equilibrium simply because of an excess demand of, say, b_0 relative to a_0, giving

$$-\hat{P}_{a0}\Delta_{a0} = \hat{P}_{b0}\Delta D_{b0} \qquad (5c)$$

However, the analogy between Equations (5b) and (5c) remains at the surface of the two phenomena and hides a basic difference between them which emerges when we consider the kind of adjustment which should lead to a new equilibrium in the two cases. That difference can perhaps be best brought out if, for a moment, we imagine an extension of our two-

---

[60] Equation (5b) holds before the adjustments of purchasing power mentioned in Paragraph 9 above.

years model to three years, which we shall call (-1), (0), (1), with the commodities a_0, b_0 now coming from production occurring in $t = -1$ with L_{-1} labour and A_{-1}^S, B_{-1}^S initial stocks, and not directly from initial stocks A_0^S, B_0^S.

31. For the contemporary commodities of Equation (5c), the question of achieving a neighbouring equilibrium will be the comparatively simple one of redistributing the labour and means of production of $(t-1)$ between the two industries, and no obvious obstacle stands in the way of achieving that as a consequence of the competitive rise of P_{b0}/P_{a0}, which will plausibly follow from initial competitive bidding.

The position is entirely different in the savings case of Equation (5b). Obviously, it will *not* be possible to shift the labour and means of production of $t = -1$, freed by the reduced consumption of $t = 0$, to *directly* producing the increments ΔD_{a1}, ΔD_{b1} of Equation (5b): the labour and means of production of $t = -1$ are not the labour and means of production of $t = 0$, which *can* directly produce ΔD_{a1} and ΔD_{b1}. Even less will it be possible to devote to the direct production of ΔD_{a1} and ΔD_{b1} the already *fully employed labour* and means of production of $t = 0$ which could directly produce them. No competitive rise of P_{b1}/P_{b0} plausibly following from the relative rise of consumption demands in $t = 1$ can achieve either of those two feats. How, then, can we raise the $t = 1$ outputs and consumptions and, moreover, do so at the expense of the $t = 0$ consumptions, as required by the excess savings of Equation (5b)?

The answer clearly remains that of traditional, non-intertemporal theory. That change of relative outputs over time can only be achieved by raising the (gross) *productivity* of the already fully employed labour L_0, by means of 'an increase', in some sense, of the quantity of means of production cooperating with it. It is a question, that is, of increasing, in some sense, the production in $t = -1$ by the quantities ΔI_a and ΔI_b in parallel with decreases in production ΔD_{a0}, ΔD_{b0}, and then using those increments of investment with the constant quantity of labour L_0 to produce increments ΔD_{a1}, ΔD_{b1} of consumption. And, what is more, those increments of investment can only be motivated by the rise of the intertemporal prices, i.e. the fall of the interest rates. No question of the increments of investment being caused directly by the consumption increments ΔD_{a1}, ΔD_{b1} entailed in the savings of Equation (5b) – contrary to what might at first seem to be the case in an intertemporal system.[61]

---

[61] See, e.g., the quotation to that effect from Keynes in n. 63 below.

Now, as we said, an assumed small redistribution of labour and means of production of $t = -1$ between the two contemporary industries a and b of Equation (5c) can reasonably be supposed to be motivated by a proportionately small change in P_{a0}/P_{b0}. However, what we learnt from the capital controversies about 'capital reversing' and 're-switching' in the traditional context will lead us to suspect (quite reasonably, as has already emerged from Paragraph 29) that the rise of the intertemporal prices $P_{i,t+1}/P_{i,t}$, $(i = a, b)$, i.e. a fall of the own rates of interest r_i, might fail to provide a motive for that increase, in some sense, of I_a and I_b which is instead required for the *intertemporal* adjustments in consumption. The result might then be the striking one that, however small the initial excess savings, the theory could force us to admit movement to an equilibrium with drastic changes in wages and prices (cf. in Fig. 3 above the equilibrium E^1 to which there would be a tendency starting from the position $(\hat{F})$ of our two-period model). The theory could even force us to admit a tendency to a zero wage $W_{(-1)}$ and zero intertemporal prices $P_{a(-1)}$, $P_{b(-1)}$ and, hence, also zero intertemporal prices P_{a0}, P_{b0}, in the case of excess savings with non-storable goods a and b.[62] As we also saw above (Paragraph 20), such zero commodity prices for a_{-1}, b_{-1} and a_0, b_0, far from being a sign of satiety, would mean that the attempt of some individuals to take care of even more acute scarcities in $t = 1$ runs counter to the inability of the market forces, as envisaged in the theory, to transfer consumption from $t = 0$ to $t = 1$.[63] Alternatively we might find

---

[62] The question will be dealt with in the fuller paper mentioned in Paragraph 1, above. However, we may note already how it may be incorrect to hold, with evident reference to reverse capital deepening and the reswitching of techniques, that

> it is only because we want to have some kind of geometric average, called the rate of interest, that we get some of these paradoxes. (Arrow, 1989, p. 155)

The paradoxes are present, whether we refer to the intertemporal prices which, as Arrow states there, are 'what we are really interested in', or to *the* rate of interest of the traditional equilibrium (see also n. 59 above).

[63] It perhaps ironical that Keynes should have been incorrect when he wrote:

> If savings consisted not merely in abstaining from present consumption but in placing simultaneously a specific order for future consumption, the effect *might* indeed be different. For in that case the resources released from preparing for present consumption could be turned over to preparing for the future consumption. (Keynes, 1936, pp. 210–11)

However, the 'might' we have italicized indicates, perhaps, Keynes' suspicion that his 'struggle of escape from habitual modes of thought' (1936, p. viii) could have gone further.

an equilibrium in which it is W_0 which has to become zero, with the attending labour unemployment, when the initial contracting had brought to a level $\bar{r}_b$ for which $\bar{I} > \bar{S}$ (see in Fig. 3 above the equilibrium E^2 to which there would be a tendency when starting from an initial position $(\bar{F})$ for $\bar{r}_b$: cf. Paragraph 26 above).

Thus, 'choosing commodities today' and choosing commodities of different dates are two essentially different processes[64] whose resemblance is only formal. An entirely different kind of adjustment is involved in the latter process, based on changes in the proportion of means of production to labour (or, more generally, to primary factors). Whether the signals which should cause such changes are expressed in terms of today's prices for future commodities, or of own rates of interest, or of the single interest rate of the traditional equilibrium, the essence of the matter is not really affected.

32. The above discussion of the conditions under which a neighbouring equilibrium position might be found starting from a position $(\hat{F})$ showing a small excess savings $(\hat{S} - \hat{I})$, allows us to begin to see how the concept of a quantity of 'capital' enters intertemporal general equilibrium.

Indeed, what have we been saying in Paragraphs 30 and 31 if not that in order to ensure the existence of a neighbouring equilibrium position, we should have the condition that at some r_b, just lower than $\hat{r}_b$, the most profitable technique, and/or the relative consumption outputs should require more or better means of production relative to labour? These 'more or better means of production' should fulfil a double role: first, to increase the (gross) labour productivity enough to satisfy the consumption increments ΔD_{a1}, ΔD_{b1} and, second, to absorb for their own production the resources freed by the consumptions decrements ΔD_{a0}, ΔD_{b0}. Now in that tentative adjustment process, what is relevant are not the specific kinds of capital goods which enter S and I. What is relevant are their *aggregates* S and I: and, in particular, the role which the increase in the proportion of I to labour should have in raising the productivity of labour, as a consequence, and at the same time as a cause, of a change in the distribution between wages and profits. In all this we have in fact had to treat savings $\hat{S}$ and investment $\hat{I}$ as a 'fluid' which increases the productivity of labour while taking the 'form' of *any* capital goods, depending on which gives the highest rate of return on its supply price. That, it seems, is what the 'quantity of capital' of Wicksell, Marshall or

---

[64] Cf., for the contrary view, the quotation in n. 59 above.

Hicks (1932) and the other traditional authors was always supposed to be — as they often recognized by referring to gross savings as 'free capital'.[65] It was, that is, the concept hopefully allowing to extend to the division between profits and wages the classical theory of rent, with its variable proportions of labour and land.

With the 'quantity of capital', of course, have also appeared its deficiencies.[66] We have just seen how, because of 'reverse capital deepening', we could not assume that a neighbouring equilibrium would generally be found. And as we know, 'reverse capital deepening' would not be possible if a consistent meaning and corresponding 'technical units' of measurement[67] could be found for a 'quantity of capital', setting it on the same footing as the classical quantities of labour and land. So in fact what we have said above has been that the 'quantity of capital' and its consistent measurement, are essential for acceptable results from the theory – zero wages or negative interest rate being, e.g., unacceptable results in the circumstances described by the model.[68]

---

[65] Cf. n.6 above.

[66] To this it might be objected that the 'quantity of capital' of traditional theory is in the nature of a fund, and not of a flow as 'savings' are. However, as we saw in Paragraph 2, the 'fund' of traditional theory was in fact meant for an analysis of the basic determinants of the investment flow: no surprise that we find the *flow*, 'savings', playing in the intertemporal equilibria the very same role which the *fund*, 'quantity of capital', played in the traditional formulations.

   Also, the fact that investment and savings are unknowns in system (E), whereas the capital endowment of the traditional versions was a given (cf. Wicksell, 1934, pp. 204–5, already referred to in Paragraph 2 above), might perhaps seem susceptible of taking care of the inconsistency connected with the notion of a given 'quantity of capital'. However, savings are an unknown only in the sense in which, say, the supply of labour is such when the hours worked depend on wages. Therefore, it cannot in any way take care of the inconsistencies of the concept of a 'quantity of capital' which, as we saw in Equation (10) of Paragraph 29, have to do with the dependence on distribution of the relative value of the sets of capital goods required by alternative production processes. As we saw in Paragraph 30, that dependence on distribution, and the connected phenomena of re-switching and reverse capital deepening, affect the allocation of an *unknown* amount of savings among capital goods, no less than they do the allocation of a *given* amount of capital among the same goods.

[67] Wicksell, 1934, p. 149; cf. also Paragraph 29 above, and the dependence of both re-switching and reverse capital deepening on the changes in the relative value of the sets of capital goods required by the alternative processes – changes which would, of course, not be possible if the 'quantity of capital' required by the two processes could be measured independently of distribution.

[68] Cf. e.g. 'Certainly ... we should not be much interested in an equilibrium with a zero real wage' (Arrow and Hahn, 1971, pp. 354–55)

33. This emergence of the quantity of capital in the intertemporal version of marginal theory should not come as a surprise. We have already stressed in Paragraph 12 how the demand for capital goods obeys principles which are altogether different from those governing the demand for consumption goods. Whereas the demand for a consumption good expresses individual preferences that are specific to the good, the demand of the capital goods from the savers results from individual preferences that are *non-specific* as regards the individual capital goods and are only specific with respect to the *aggregate* of the capital goods. It is on that aggregate quantity that the individual decides with respect to savings and capital, just as it is on the disaggregated quantities of the distinct consumer goods that he decides with respect to consumption. And it is because of this that we should have expected the 'quantity of capital' to emerge in an intertemporal equilibrium, no less than in the traditional equilibrium, just as the quantities of the individual consumption goods have to appear in an intertemporal equilibrium, no less than in the traditional equilibrium.

As is often rightly stressed, without perhaps fully realizing its implications, those preferences of the savers concern the choice between present and future consumption: as Walras put it with admirable lucidity, the demand for capital goods is the demand for the *single commodity* which he called 'perpetual net income'.[69] This means that for the saver the physically heterogeneous capital goods are *perfect substitutes* for each other, in proportion to their prices, as alternative equivalent sources of that single commodity 'perpetual net income', whose single price Walras described as the reciprocal of the rate of return on the supply prices of the capital goods.[70]

34. In fact the question of the 'quantity of capital' and its role in marginal theory seems ultimately to be no more than that of an application of Jevons's 'law of indifference'. Just as one chooses between alternative sources of, e.g., homogeneous corn, i.e. between different farmers,

---

[69] Walras, 1954, pp. 274 ff. It is of course irrelevant here that the two-years horizon of our model renders a 'perpetual income' impossible. Savings are then, in fact, the demand of the *single commodity* 'next year's income'. We may note here how that perfect substitutability between capital goods for the saver is confirmed in our model by the fact that the intertemporal prices of a_0 and b_0 must reach zero simultaneously (Paragraph 20 above).

[70] This single price (rate of return) would first be achieved by arbitrage on the *demand* prices of the capital goods, but as such prices, like the prices of other products, have to be equalized to the corresponding supply prices, that single price will turn out to obtain on the *supply* prices of the capital goods. (For this distinction between 'demand price' and 'supply price' of a capital good, cf. Walras's distinction, 1954, pp. 271 ff., between 'selling price' or 'prix de vente', and 'cost of production' or 'prix de revient' of any product.

according to the principle of the minimum price – so one chooses between alternative sources of 'perpetual net income', i.e. different capital goods, according to the minimum price of such 'future income': according, that is, to the maximum effective net rate of return.[71]

This fact is obscured by the other fact – quite irrelevant for the question we are dealing with here – that, unlike for homogeneous corn, the allocation of the demand for 'future perpetual net income' among potential sources of supply involves nothing less than the entire theory of production. In fact, whereas the allocation of the demand for corn among the potential sources of its supply is theoretically uninteresting beyond the elementary application of Jevons' indifference law of the minimum price, and the corresponding tendency to a *single* price – the allocation of the demand of the saver for 'future perpetual income' among its potential sources of supply, namely the several capital goods, is bound up with the determination of all that will be produced in the economy and how. The determination of the rentals of the several capital goods *relative* to their supply prices will depend on that.[72]

It is, in fact, this dependence on the theory of production which has created the misleading appearance of a demand for capital goods which is specific to each of them in a way not unlike that of a consumption good. This, let us stress, is only the result of a confusion between two different processes. The first, in which the *specificity* to the several capital goods is present, is the *allocation* of whichever demand for future income exists among the various sources of its supply – and it is there that production has to be analysed in order to compare the rates of return on the supply prices of the several capital goods, just as one compares the prices of homogeneous corn from different farmers as potential sources of its supply. The first *allocative* process, however, is no more relevant for an explanation of the rate of interest – or system of own rates of interest (of intertemporal prices) – than the allocation of the aggregate demand for corn among the several farmers or corn merchants is for the explanation of the competitive price of corn. Only the aggregate demand and supply of corn, or of 'perpetual net income' as the case may be, are in fact relevant for that, and this second, *price-determining* process is the one relating to just non-specific, aggregate demand for, and aggregate supply of, 'perpetual net income' itself.

---

[71] For the notion of 'effective' rate of return cf. n. 2 above.

[72] As the organizer of production, the entrepreneur estimates the returns obtainable from different capital goods, i.e. the relative cheapness of the various sources of 'perpetual net income' to be delivered to the saver, just as corn merchants do for the relative cheapness of the corn to be delivered to their customers.

35. Now, the nature of the demand for 'perpetual net income', and the consequent perfect substitutability of the different capital goods for the savers, entail that at some stage of the analysis, the quantity demanded of that single commodity – and hence of its bearer 'homogeneous capital' – has to emerge, because as we said it is on that quantity only that consumer preferences can operate.

Thus the traditional versions of the theory, with their equilibrium condition of a uniform effective net rate of return on the supply prices of the capital goods, entailed having to take care of that single commodity already at the level of the endowment of factors,[73] and those authors did so by expressing the capital endowment *directly* as a single 'quantity of capital', its constituent capital-goods vector then being an unknown of the system. The abandonment of that traditional long-period notion of the equilibrium – not to be confused, recall, with a stationary or steady state[74] – and of its specific uniform rate condition, has meant getting rid of the single commodity 'perpetual net income' and of its bearer, 'homogeneous capital', but only at the cost of assuming away, at the level of the factor endowment, the perfect substitutability of capital goods for the saver, and of Jevons' indifference law with it: no surprise then, for the methodological problems raised by today's pure theory.[75]

However, those high methodological costs may in fact have been borne in vain. They have been borne, that is, for what may turn out to have been essentially a cosmetic operation: getting rid of the obviously inconsistent notion of a 'quantity of capital' at the *immediately visible* level of the demands and supplies of the factors of production (at the level, that is, of the endowments) – in order to have it re-enter the theory at the *less immediately visible*, but theoretically equivalent,[76] level of investment–demand and savings–supply.

---

[73] See n. 2 above.

[74] Cf. n. 5 above.

[75] Cf. e.g. Paragraph 13 above.

[76] Cf. Paragraph 2 above. We may note how the need to introduce that 'quantity' to take care of the perfect substitutability among capital goods is strictly connected with the neoclassical demand-and-supply theory of distribution. That perfect substitutability does not appear to impose the notion of an independently measurable 'quantity of capital' in the classical theories, where the rate of interest (profits) is not explained by any demand and supply for quantities of 'factors of production', but is instead obtained, fundamentally, as a difference between an independently determined product and independently determined wages.

References

Arrow, K. J. (1989). 'Joan Robinson and Modern Economic Theory: an Interview', in G. R. Feiwel (ed.), *Joan Robinson and Modern Economic Theory*, London: Macmillan.

Arrow, K. J. and Hahn, F. H. (1971). *General Competitive Analysis*, San Francisco: Holden-Day; Edinburgh: Oliver & Boyd.

Bliss, C. J. (1975). *Capital Theory and the Distribution of Income*, Amsterdam: North-Holland.

Bliss, C. J. (1987). 'Equal Rates and Profits', in J. Eatwell, M. Milgate and P. Newman (eds), *New Palgrave Dictionary of Economics*, London: Macmillan.

Böhm-Bawerk, E. v. (1891). *The Positive Theory of Capital*, London: Macmillan. Translation of the 1st edn of Böhm-Bawerk (1889).

Currie, M. and Steedman, I. (1990). *Wrestling with Time. Problems in Economic Theory*, Manchester: Manchester University Press.

Debreu, G. (1959). *The Theory of Value*, New York: John Wiley.

Eatwell, J. L. (1987). 'Walras's Theory of Capital', in J. Eatwell, M. Milgate and P. Newman (eds), *New Palgrave Dictionary of Economics*, Vol. 4, London: Macmillan.

Garegnani, P. (1960). *Il capitale nelle teorie della distribuzione*, Milano: Giuffrè.

Garegnani, P. (1970). 'Heterogeneous Capital, the Production Function and the Theory of Distribution', *Review of Economic Studies*, **37**, pp. 407-36.

Garegnani, P. (1976). 'On a Change in the Notion of Equilibrium in Recent Work on Value and Distribution', in M. Brown, K. Sato and P. Zarembka (eds), *Essays on Modern Capital Theory*, Amsterdam: North Holland, pp. 25-45.

Garegnani, P. ([1978] 1979). 'Notes on Consumption, Investment and Effective Demand', Part I and Part II, in *Cambridge Journal of Economics*, **2**, pp. 335-53, and **3**, pp. 63-82, respectively.

Garegnani, P. (1989). 'Some Notes on Capital, Expectation and the Analysis of Change', in G. R. Feiwel (ed.), *Joan Robinson and Modern Economics*, London: Macmillan.

Garegnani, P. (1990). 'Quantity of Capital', in J. Eatwell, M. Milgate and P. Newman (eds), *Capital Theory*, London: Macmillan.

Hahn, F. H. (1982). 'The Neo-Ricardians', *Cambridge Journal of Economics*, **6**, pp. 353-74.

Harcourt, G. C. (1972). *Some Cambridge Controversies in the Theory of Capital*, Cambridge: Cambridge University Press.

Hicks, J. R. (1932). *The Theory of Wages*, London: Macmillan.

Hicks, J. R. (1939). *Value and Capital*, 2nd edn, London: Oxford University Press.

Hicks, J. R. (1965). *Capital and Growth*, Oxford: Oxford University Press.

Jevons, W. S. ([1871] 1957). *The Theory of Political Economy*, New York: Kelley.

Keynes, J. M. (1936). *The General Theory of Employment, Interest and Money*, London: Macmillan.

Kurz, H. D. and Salvadori, N. (1995). *Theory of Production: A Long Period Analysis*, Cambridge: Cambridge University Press.

Lerner, A. (1948). 'Alternative Formulations of Interest Theory', in *The New Economics*, New York.

Marshall, A. ([1920] 1949). *Principles of Economics*, London: Macmillan.

Morishima, M. (1964). *Equilibrium, Stability and Growth*, Oxford: Clarendon.

Patinkin, D. ([1972] 1987). 'Real Balance Effect', in J. Eatwell, M. Milgate and P. Newman (eds), *New Palgrave Dictionary of Economics*, London: Macmillan.

Pigou, A. C. (1932). *The Economics of Welfare*, 4th edn, London: Macmillan.

Robertson, D. H. (1957–1959). *Lectures on Economic Principles*, Vols. 1–3, London: Staple Press.

Robinson, J. V. (1970). Review of C. E. Ferguson, 'The Neoclassical Theory of Production and Distribution', *Economic Journal*, **80**, pp. 336–9.

Samuelson, P. A. (1962). 'Parable and Realism in Capital Theory: The Surrogate Production Function', *Review of Economic Studies*, **29**, pp. 193–206.

Sraffa, P. (1960). *Production of Commodities by Means of Commodities. Prelude to a Critique of Economic Theory*, Cambridge: Cambridge University Press.

Walras, L. (1926). *Eléments d'Economie Politique Pure*, 4th and definitive edn, Paris: F. Richon.

Walras, L. (1954). *Elements of Pure Economics*, London: Allen and Unwin. English translation of the 4th definitive edition of Walras (1874) by W. Jaffé.

Wicksell, K. (1893). *Über Wert, Kapital und Rente nach den neueren nationalökonomischen Theorien*, Jena: Gustave Fischer. English translation as Wicksell (1954).

Wicksell, K. ([1901] 1934). *Lectures on Political Economy*, Vol. 1, London: Routledge & Kegan.

Wicksell, K. (1935). *Lectures on Political Economy*, Vol. 2, London: Routledge & Kegan.

Mathematical Note

Michele Tucci

ROME

1   The model

Let us take into consideration the following model (F):

$$\begin{cases} P_{a1} = l_a W + a_a P_{a0} + b_a P_{b0} \\ P_{b1} = l_b W + a_b P_{a0} + b_b P_{b0} \end{cases} \tag{1f}$$

$$P_{b1} = 1 \tag{2f}$$

$$\begin{cases} A_0^{D'} \geq D_{a0} + a_a A_1 + a_b B_1 \\ B_0^{D'} \geq D_{b0} + b_a A_1 + b_b B_1 \\ L \quad \geq l_a A_1 + l_0 B_1 \\ D_{a1} = A_1 \\ D_{b1} = B_1 \end{cases} \tag{3f}$$

If in the first relation of (3f) the inequality sign holds, then $P_{a0} = 0$; if it holds in the second one, then $P_{b0} = 0$. However, as is specified in Paragraph 15 of the text, assumption (ii), it should be noted that such cases will not be taken into consideration in the economic discussion in the text. The inclusion in the present demonstration is due to the need for clarifying the mathematical passages.

If the inequality sign holds in the third relation of (3f), then $W = 0$.

$$I = (a_a A_1 + a_b B_1)P_{a0} + (b_a A_1 + b_b B_1)P_{b0} \tag{4f}$$

$$S = (A_0^S - D_{a0})P_{a0} + (B_0^S - D_{b0})P_{b0} \tag{5f}$$

$$P_{b1}(r_b + 1) = P_{b0} \tag{6f}$$

$$\frac{A_0^D}{B_0^D} = \frac{A_0^S}{B_0^S} \tag{7f}$$

446

where P_{a0}, P_{b0}, P_{a1} and P_{b1} refer to prices, W indicates wages, S and I represent savings and investments, respectively, A_1 and B_1 correspond to quantities of produced commodities, A_0^D and B_0^D specify demands, and A_0^S, B_0^S and L refer to endowments. The single-valued mappings D_{a0}, D_{b0}, D_{a1} and D_{b1} designate standard Walrasian demand functions, which are characterized by the following assumptions:

1. the set of independent variables in the functions are those indicated by the first five among the symbols specified above;
2. in the non-negative orthant of the independent variables, each demand function is positive and continuous.

For the sake of simplicity, we suppose that the technical coefficients are all strictly positive. Moreover, the usual vitality conditions will hold. Finally, r_b specifies the own interest rate of commodity b over period $t = 0$. The first eleven among the symbols listed above constitute the unknowns of the model, while r_b is exogenously defined.

Let us substitute Equations (6f) and (2f) into the second equation of (1f), thus obtaining:

$$1 = l_b W + a_b P_{a0} + b_b(r_b + 1) \tag{8}$$

i.e. Equation (1a) of Paragraph 15 in the text.

Easy passages allow the following propositions to be derived from Equations (1f), (2f), (6f) and (8):

(a) The quantities W and P_{a1} can be defined as functions of the single variable P_{a0}.

(b) Consider the interval $H_{r_b} = \{-1 \leq r_b \leq \max_{r_b}\}$, with $\max_{r_b} = (1 - b_b)/b_b$. Define $\beta_{r_b} = [1 - b_b(r_b + 1)]/a_b$. For every $r_b \in H_{r_b}$, we can determine an interval $H_{P_{a0}} = \{0 \leq P_{a0} \leq \beta_{r_b}\}$ such that, for every $P_{a0} \in H_{P_{a0}}$, $W \geq 0$, $P_{a1} > 0$.

(c) In the interval $H_{P_{a0}}$, the functions $W(P_{a0})$ and $P_{a1}(P_{a0})$ are continuous.

(d) If $-1 < r_b \leq \max_{r_b}$, then $P_{b0} > 0$; if $r = -1$, then $P_{b0} = 0$.

Due to the income correction, which is specified in Paragraph 9 of the text, the third of (3f) is always satisfied with the equality sign, except in border solutions, which are examined in connection with assumption (iii), Paragraph 16, and in Paragraphs 21, 24 and 26, where there will be a continuous set of solutions characterized by $W = 0$.

Let us assume that the equality sign holds in the first two relations of (3f). Substituting the last two equations of (3f) into the expressions on the right-hand side of the equality sign in the first two relations of (3f) and in Equation (4f), we are able to define the variables A_0^D, B_0^D and I.

Moreover, Equation (5f) defines the variable S. In the interval $H_{P_{a0}}$, the four above-quoted expressions are continuous functions of the unique variable P_{a0}.

Define

$$\delta(P_{a0}) = \frac{D_{a0} + a_a D_{a1} + a_b D_{b1}}{D_{b0} + b_a D_{a1} + b_b D_{b1}} \tag{9}$$

$$\gamma = \frac{A_0^S}{B_0^S} = \text{constant} \tag{10}$$

In the interval $H_{P_{a0}}$, the function $\delta(P_{a0})$ is continuous.

Taking into consideration Equation (7f), for every $r_b \in H_{r_b}$ one, and only one, of the following three sentences is necessarily true:

(I)   There exists $P_{a0}^* \in H_{P_{a0}}$ such that $\delta(P_{a0}^*) = \gamma$.
(II)   For every $P_{a0} \in H_{P_{a0}}$, $\delta(P_{a0}) < \gamma$.
(III)   For every $P_{a0} \in H_{P_{a0}}$, $\delta(P_{a0}) > \gamma$.

Figure 4 below shows an example of case (I). Here, $P_{a0} \geq 0$ and the first two relations of (3f) are satisfied with the equality sign. Assumption (ii) in Paragraph 15 of the text confines the main argument there to case (I) above. Therefore, the remaining two cases will be examined only for the sake of completeness.

In case (II), at the given level of r_b, commodity a_0, taken in the sum of both its consumption and investment uses, cannot be employed in as high a proportion to b_0 as the ratio γ in which it is found in the endowment.

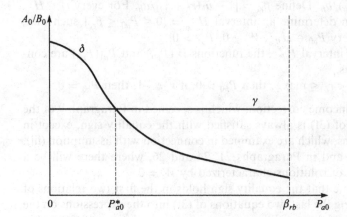

Figure 4

As a result, (F) can only admit solution if we allow the quantity A_0^D 'demanded' of Equation (7f), to exceed the quantity used expressed by the R.H.S. of the first of Equations (3f), provided $P_{a0} = 0$ (cf. Paragraph 15, n. 32 in the text).

In case III we have the case symmetrical to II, where b_0 cannot be used in as high a proportion to a_0 (i.e. a_0 in as low a proportion to b_0), as the ratio in which the two commodities are found in the endowment. The inequality sign of the second relation in (3f) will allow for a solution of (F) provided $P_{b0} = 0$, i.e. if r_b is set at $r_{b\,min} = -1$. But no solution would exist if we set r_b, our independent variable, at a level $r_b > -1$ – a case, however, which is of no economic importance since (F) could never, then, provide a solution of (E), where $r_b > -1$ implies $P_{b0} > 0$, and is therefore incompatible with an inequality sign in the second of relations (3e).

Author index

450

Subject index